The Baby Chicks

Julia Metzler

For permission requests, write to the publisher through Aurora Borealis Publishing's website.

Hardcover ISBN: 978-1-7781373-3-4

Any references to historical events, real people, or real places are used fictitiously. Names, characters, and places are products of the author's imagination.

Cover images by Julia Metzler

First edition 2022

Aurora Borealis Publishing

www.auroraborealispub.wixsite.com/website

Dedicated to my four baby chicks,

Kalea, Jayce, Laila and Nash

who make everyday a wonderful adventure

It was a snowy and cold February afternoon, and Mom had picked us up from school. She told us, "Get in the car. We are going on an adventure!"

We drove down the hill from school
and headed onto the highway.
"Where are we going?" we asked.
"You'll see..." Mom said with a smile.

We turned off the highway and drove some more. Soon we saw a sign that said Fort McMurray 468 First Nation. We saw dogs sitting in the middle of the road, and they started to follow us! We laughed and waved at them through the window.

Mom stopped at a house
at the end of the road.
A sign on a tree said
"FRESH EGGS $5".

A lady came out the front door of the house with a carton of colorful eggs! She handed them to Mom and said, "I hope these eggs hatch for you! They are a wonderful mix of eggs!"

Mom said thank you, and we drove away, the dogs running alongside us happily.

"What are those eggs for Mom?" we asked.

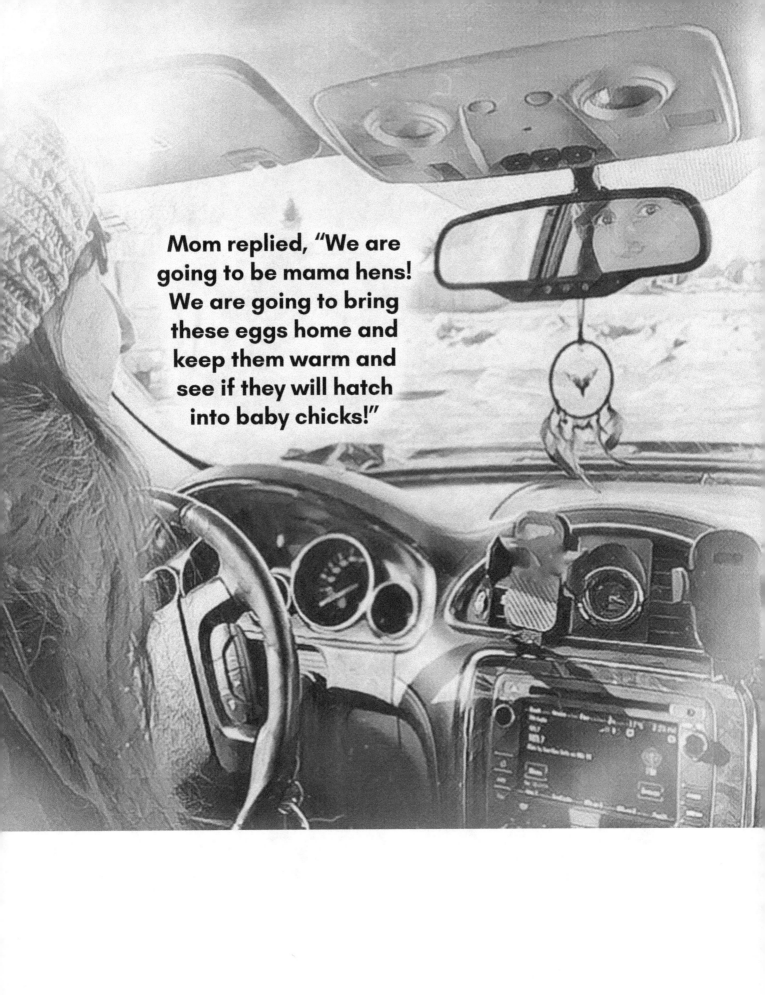

We all squealed in delight and chattered happily the rest of the drive home. We made plans for the new babies we would be bringing home.

When we got home, Mom pulled out a box with a plastic container inside. "This is an incubator," Mom said. "It will keep the eggs warm like a Mama hen would." She carefully put the eggs into the incubator, added a little bit of water to the bottom of the container and closed the lid.

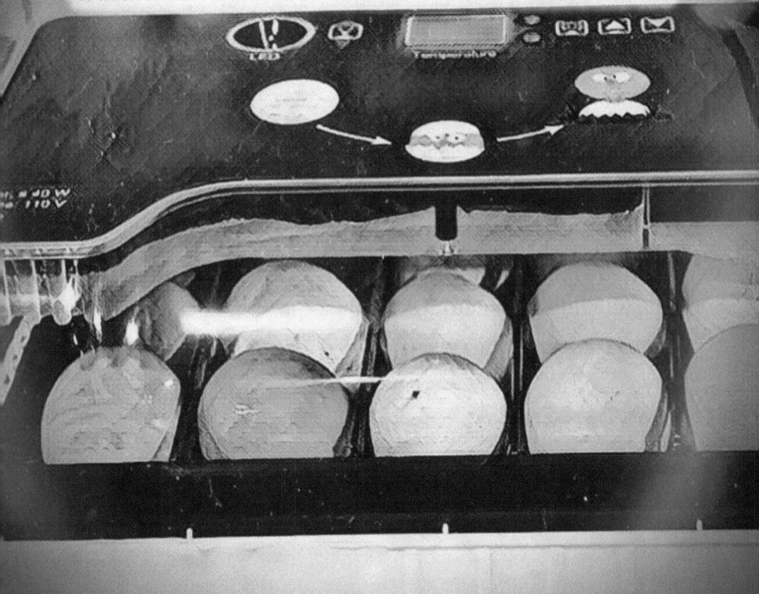

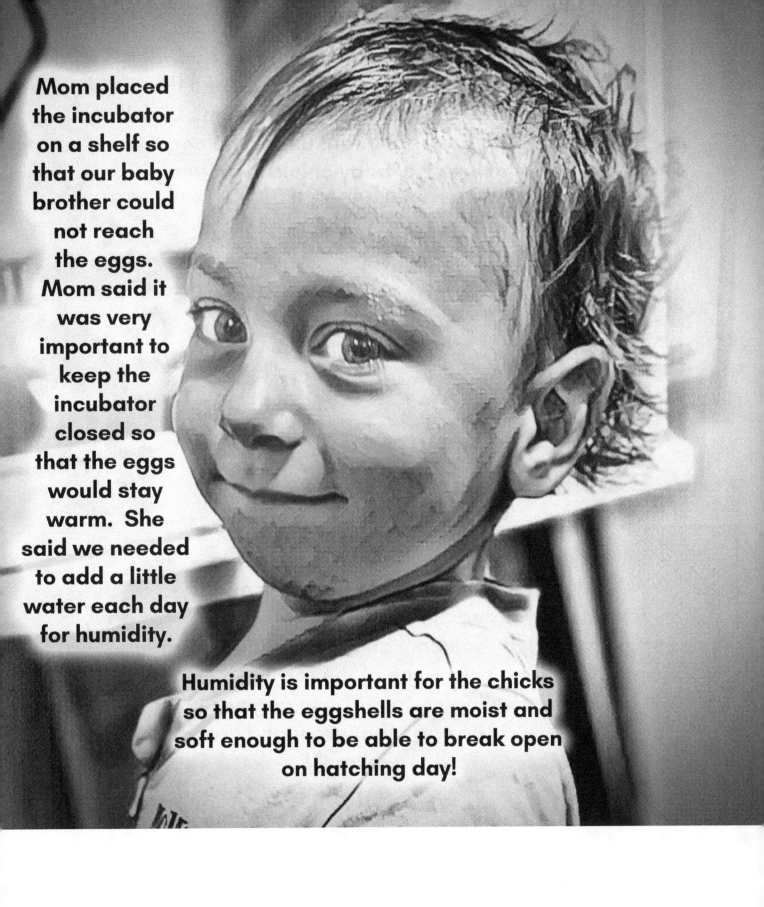

Mom placed the incubator on a shelf so that our baby brother could not reach the eggs. Mom said it was very important to keep the incubator closed so that the eggs would stay warm. She said we needed to add a little water each day for humidity.

Humidity is important for the chicks so that the eggshells are moist and soft enough to be able to break open on hatching day!

We waited and waited and waited some more! Mom would let us take the eggs out of the incubator to candle them. Candling is when you put a bright light under the egg to see how the embryo, baby chick, is growing.

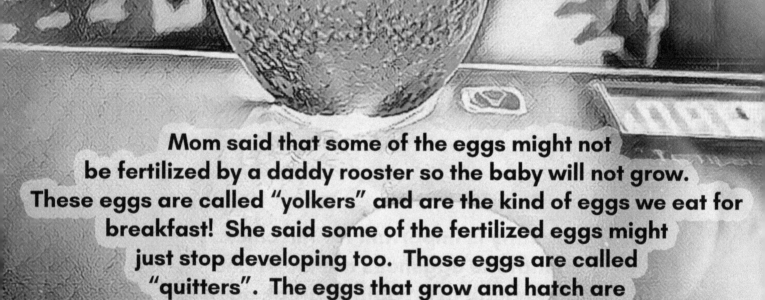

Mom said that some of the eggs might not be fertilized by a daddy rooster so the baby will not grow. These eggs are called "yolkers" and are the kind of eggs we eat for breakfast! She said some of the fertilized eggs might just stop developing too. Those eggs are called "quitters". The eggs that grow and hatch are the "winners"!

Finally, day twenty-one came...and there was no sign of hatching. "Be patient my children," Mom said. "The babies will hatch when they are ready." So, we waited some more.

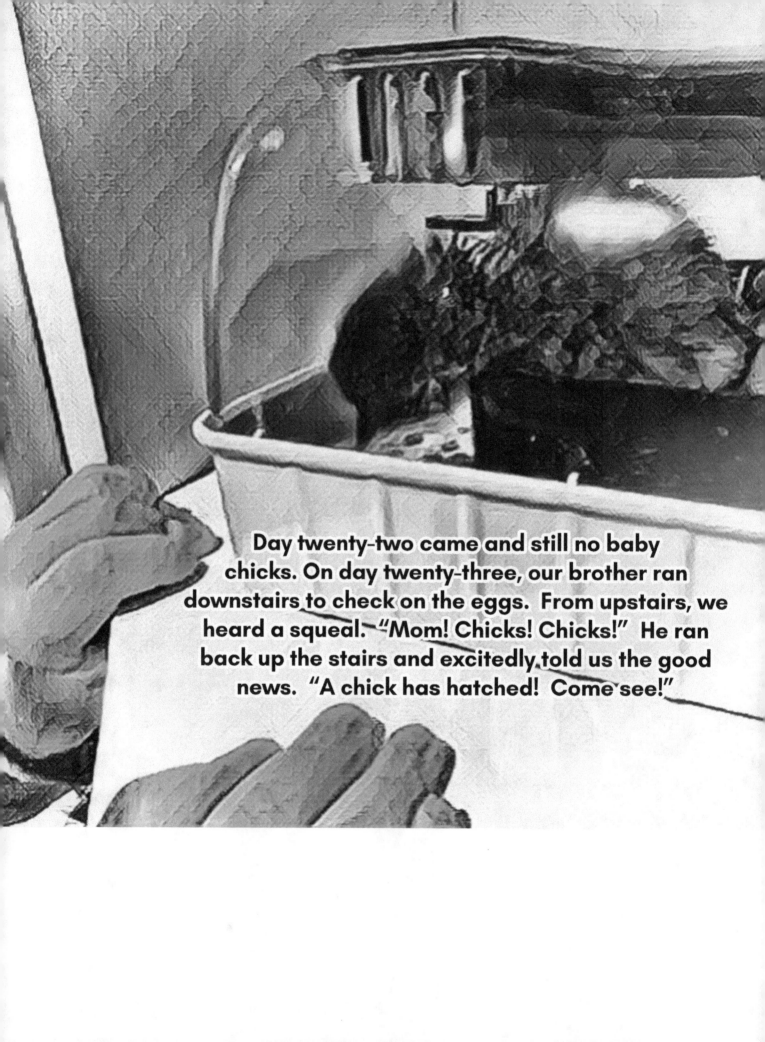

Day twenty-two came and still no baby chicks. On day twenty-three, our brother ran downstairs to check on the eggs. From upstairs, we heard a squeal. "Mom! Chicks! Chicks!" He ran back up the stairs and excitedly told us the good news. "A chick has hatched! Come see!"

The four of us peered into the incubator. In the corner was a black baby chick, sitting sleepily.

"The baby looks very tired, and she is very wet from the fluid in her egg. We must wait until her feathers dry off in the warm incubator. If we take her out too soon while her feathers are wet, she may get a chill and not survive."

We smiled at the baby chick from outside of the incubator. She would sleep and then wake up and walk on top of the other eggs.

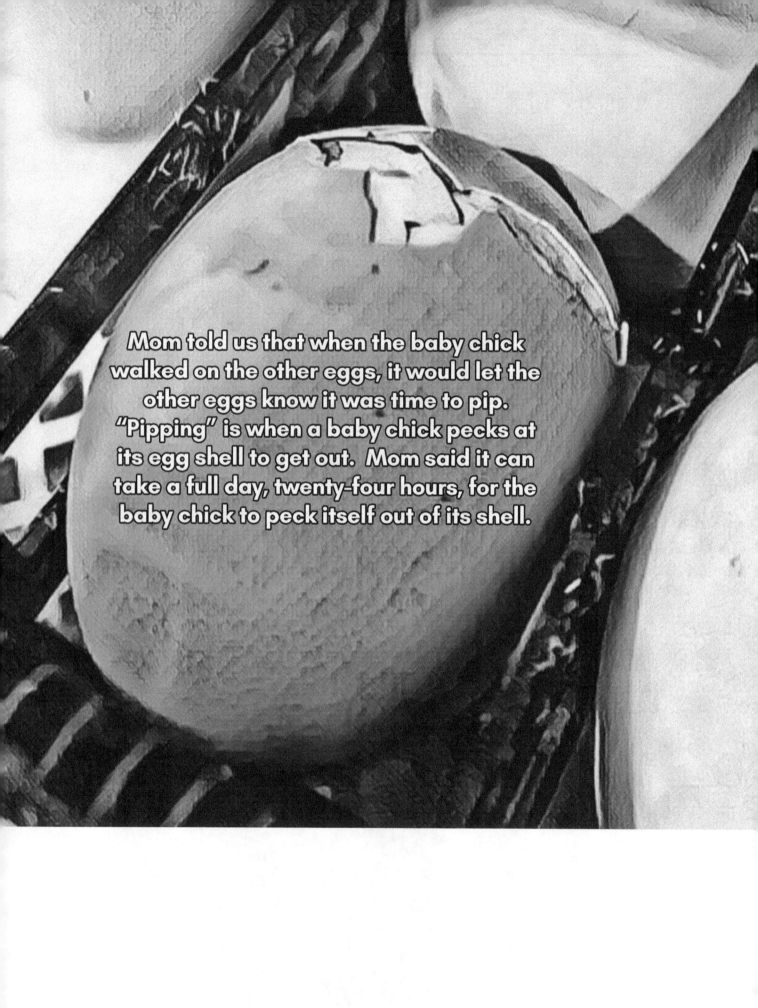

Mom told us that when the baby chick walked on the other eggs, it would let the other eggs know it was time to pip. "Pipping" is when a baby chick pecks at its egg shell to get out. Mom said it can take a full day, twenty-four hours, for the baby chick to peck itself out of its shell.

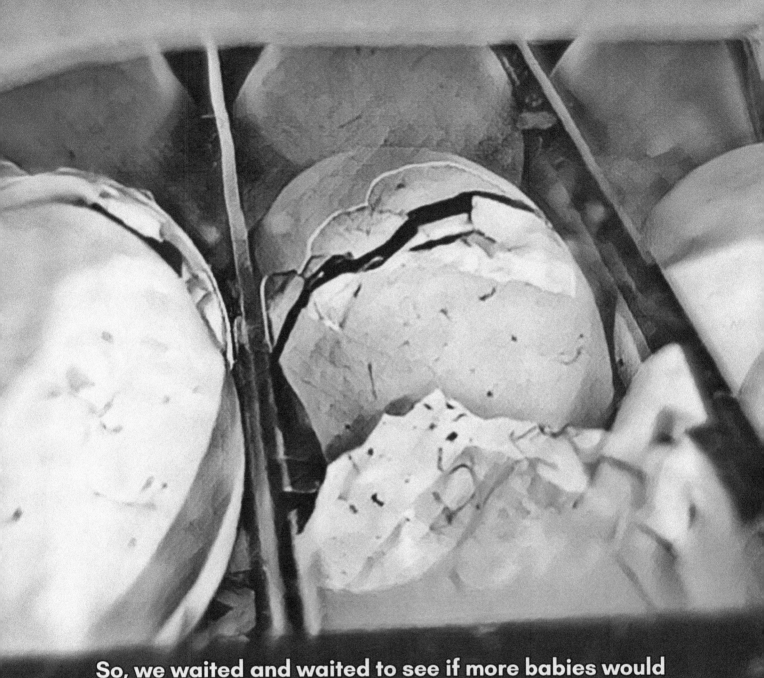

So, we waited and waited to see if more babies would hatch. Hours later, we noticed an egg was starting to crack!

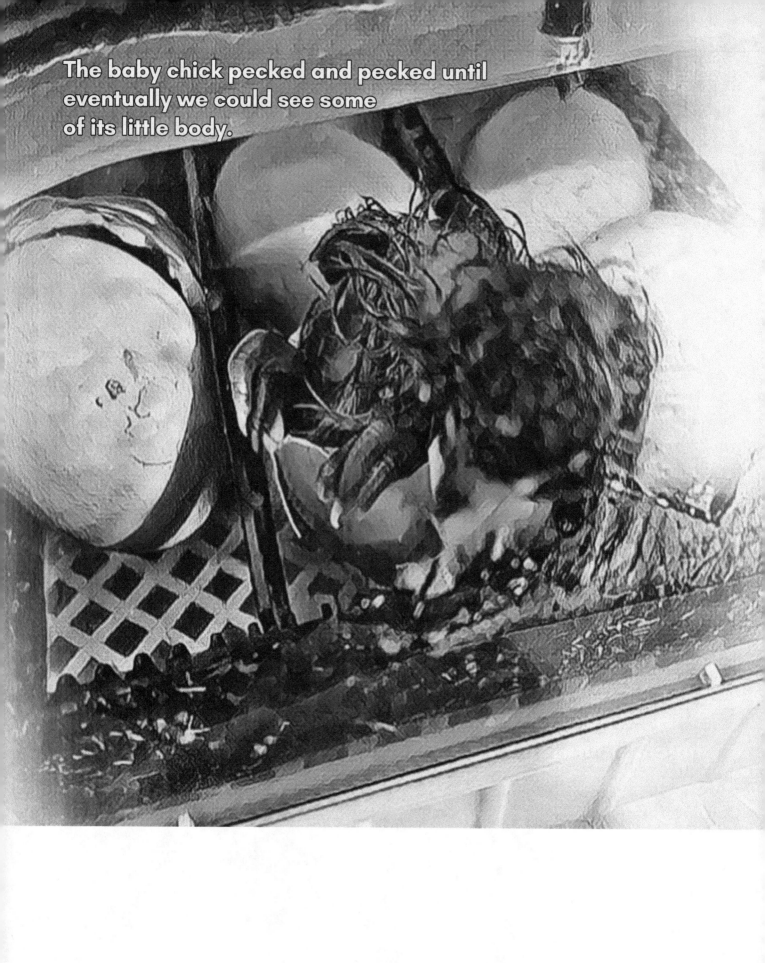

The baby chick pecked and pecked until eventually we could see some of its little body.

The second baby chick finally sat outside of her eggshell and looked at the world around her. The two chicks wandered around the incubator together, and we waited patiently for them to dry off and fluff up.

The next day, three more babies were born! All together there were now five baby chicks - four black and grey chicks and one yellow chick with black speckles. Mom told us the dark chicks were Austrolorp chickens and the yellow one with black spots was a Crele Orpington chicken. They were all so cute!

Dad said we needed to make a home for the chicks to live in! He said a chicken house is called a brooder. We helped him get the brooder ready. We used a rabbit cage and put a layer of wood shavings on the bottom of the cage.

We then put a thermo-poultry brooder in the cage. This looks like a little orange table, and it emits heat. The chicks can huddle underneath it in the same way they would hide under their mama! Dad hung a heat lamp from the top of the cage too, just in case the chicks needed extra warmth.

We moved the brooder to our sister's room, and we visited the chicks many times a day! The chicks started to eat seeds and drink water. Mom said chickens are omnivores, meaning they will try to eat just about anything they can get their beaks on! They like to eat fruits, vegetables and grains.

We introduced the baby chicks to our little brother...

And our cats...

...and even our dogs!

We learned that Austrolorp chickens are from Australia and they lay light-brown eggs.

We also learned that Crele Orpington chickens are from Britain. They are a sweet and docile chicken, and they lay light-brown eggs too!

We learned to take care of the baby chicks and to hold them gently...

...and we became best friends!

And became a special part of our family.

And just like our best friends and family, we made sure the baby chicks knew we would always be there for them. We would always stay close by, even when we were drifting away to slumber land.

"Sweet dreams,

baby chicks,

sweet dreams..."

The Encyclopaedia of Equestrian Exploration

Unabridged

Volume One

A Study of the Geographic and Spiritual Equestrian Journey, based upon the Philosophy of Harmonious Horsemanship

by

CuChullaine O'Reilly F.R.G.S.
Founder of The Long Riders' Guild

Cover Design was conceived and created by Brian Rooney of R7 Media.

Cover Image – The cover image of Jamie Maddison appears courtesy of Matt Traver. In 2013 these exemplary British Long Riders prematurely concluded their journey across northern Kazakhstan rather than imperil the welfare of their horses.

Copy-editing by Lucy Leaf, American Long Rider.

Dedicated to
my beloved,
Basha Gypsy Moon

Do what thy manhood bids thee do,

from none but self expect applause.

He noblest lives and noblest dies,

who makes and keeps his self-made laws.

Sir Richard Francis Burton
Historical Long Rider

Table of Contents

Table of Contents

Preface

CuChullaine O'Reilly is a phenomenon. He and his equally amazing wife, Basha, single-handedly transformed the world of long distance riding by publishing a comprehensive and unique collection of books by and about those who have ridden bravely and adventurously throughout the world, and they brought us all together through the Long Riders' Guild, which they created.

Now CuChullaine has assembled a vast compendium of information on the subject in a three volume encyclopaedia. This is not just the complete history of the finest way our species has devised of travelling, but it reveals all the physical, emotional and, yes, spiritual experiences that arise when humans and horses interact on a long journey. All mortal/equine communion is here as well as countless stories of hardship and joy, experienced in every corner of the world by people roaming intimately with one or more horses.

In these magnificent volumes all the great equestrian experiences throughout history are recorded and, above all, the love that can exist between humans and horses is revealed.

Robin Hanbury-Tenison
Founder Member of The Long Riders' Guild
President of Survival International

In 1957 Robin Hanbury-Tenison OBE was the first person to travel overland by jeep from London to Sri Lanka (Ceylon). He was also the first person to cross South America overland at its widest point and was awarded the Royal Geographical Society's Patron's Gold Medal. He has led many expeditions since then, including the Royal Geographical Society's Gunung Mulu expedition to Sarawak, taking 115 scientists into the rainforest for 15 months. This was the start of a global effort to preserve the rainforest.
Robin and his wife Louella have made Long Rides in France, Spain, New Zealand, China and Albania. Robin is the author of numerous books, including The Oxford Book of Exploration *and* The Seventy Great Journeys in History.

Foreword

What a surprise! If the *Encyclopaedia of Equestrian Exploration* isn't a Magnum Opus, then nothing counts. I believe CuChullaine O'Reilly has written the most astounding book in equestrian historical literature.

What dedication - and most accessible. Punctuated by photography, proof evident, bibliography, first-hand accounts, nothing is omitted. The references are so thick the mind staggers. The academics will reel. O'Reilly has put them to shame. It's nuts and bolts, philosophical, thoughtful, heart breaking, heart warming - and advisory. It lies before you - a real treasure.

What a solid, indivisible, scholastic, sensitive examination and revelation of man and his travelling horse it is. It is not describable in a few mere sentences because it's huge - the fruit of CuChullaine's many long years of effort - and if you wonder if it's paid off, then you might have to wait for eternity because that's how long it will last.

It's a staggering achievement.

To have sat down to compose a cyclopaedia is one thing but to deliver an encyclopaedia is quite another. Ben Jonson, one of the most learned men in the 17th century, composed an encyclopaedic work of the English Renaissance literary and social scene. Pierre Larousse was a French encyclopaedist who created an outstanding educational work in 19th-century France. O'Reilly ranks alongside Jonson and Larousse for his thoroughness and industry.

What an accumulation of detail, what a mind! I cannot imagine how exhausting it must have been because of the extensive nature of its composition.

And to have created *The Horse Travel Handbook* too. What a pair of masterpieces!

CuChullaine has fulfilled his purpose in life a few times over with these two diadems.

The *Encyclopaedia of Equestrian Exploration* will fall instantly into the collectible, a must for any horseman's library.

I'm deeply honoured to find my name and photographs in it, deeply honoured.

What a staggering achievement!

CuChullaine, you've joined the Immortals.

Jeremy James FRGS
Founder Member of The Long Riders' Guild

Jeremy James is the English equestrian author who undertook pioneering research into the role of the horse in the Ottoman Empire before writing the historically accurate book, The Byerley Turk. *He is also the author of the equestrian travel books* Saddletramp *and* Vagabond, *as well as* Debt of Honour: The story of the International League for the Protection of Horses.

Section One
Chapter 1
Overcoming Resistance

Why you chose this book

If you have made the decision to read this book then you are about to depart on an exciting literary journey, prior to setting off in search of the fulfilment of your equestrian dream.

Though I do not know you, I can guess what has happened. Some mental burr, which took its inspiration from a book, a film, a news story, an internet article or perhaps a chance conversation with a passing mounted stranger, has made its way under the previously smooth saddle blanket of your mind. That tiny concept is now quietly bothering you with the sharp relentless prick of an unrealised idea – namely to tack up a horse, take a deep breath, swing into the saddle, gather up your reins, and then point your mount in the direction of a distant horizon, a faraway land or a mythical point on the map.

What it is that lures you

Even in this age of anonymous air travel, which forces one to travel within the confining steel cocoon of a plane or car, riding a horse links one to the incredible world around us. You don't watch the world flying by. You interact with it. You don't travel at the speed of sound. You sashay along at the pace of the wind. You don't suffer through security checks. You slow down your heartbeat to join the rhythm of the horse's hoof beats.

When you ride your horse in search of adventure you find yourself gliding along. You greet what you didn't know you missed, aboard an animal who draws you into the natural world. You're no longer encased like a nameless cog in a corporate flying machine. You've broken free from the confines of today's increasingly restrictive world and joined a mounted fraternity of men and women who have explored every corner of the planet, including Antarctica, with their horses.

John Egenes was one such traveller. In 1974 the twenty-four year-old North American Long Rider set off to ride "ocean to ocean." Though he had expected unforeseen perils and hardships, he had not counted on discovering that the long grey road was also full of wonders.

"My horse and I rode along old Route 66. No one uses this road any more. But people don't know what they're missing. We came across antelopes, then saw a bunch of wild mares and colts running free across the countryside. Gizmo and I were lucky. We had time to stop and take it all in. You can't do that with a car. That night I stood by my horse, stroking his neck and watching the full moon come up over a butte in the distance. I listened to the quiet. No man-made noise out here, only the soft sounds of the Painted Desert night."

Why the dream lingers

One of the treasures which John had found was *amadrinado*, a term used by South American gauchos to describe the special friendship, and nearly telepathic bond, which develops between a Long Rider and his Road Horse. Such an animal liberates us from two of life's restrictions – gravity and the village – those twin restraints designed to hold us down and keep us back.

The ancient allure of these dual liberties explains why so long as humanity has fostered a desire to explore this globe, he or she has swung onto the back of a trusted steed and departed into the unknown, the void, the danger, the bleak, the frightening, the exhilarating, the glorious unexplored reaches of our world.

Yet while many people treasure a dream, even more feel they're unworthy, or incapable, of realizing it.

This explains why people allow life to intrude into their dream of making an extended equestrian journey. They devote themselves instead to attending school, going to work, or raising a family. In an effort to deny this equestrian dream they attempt to replace it with a variety of jobs, spouses, or the accumulation of belongings. Yet, as is often the case with our unpredictable lives, years pass during which time these same people may end up losing their marriage, wealth and even their health.

And patiently waiting is a private concept that never deserted them.

For regardless of their up and down bank account, despite the university degree on the wall, or the lack of one, notwithstanding their marital status, in sharp opposition to the years, and in contrast to how much equestrian knowledge they possess, the dream of making an equestrian journey never goes away.

How sad then, that so many people will never attain any of their life's dreams, simply because they honestly believe their dreams are unobtainable. Yet you must have cherished such a secret equestrian desire, otherwise why would you have chosen this book?

The dream doesn't die

If you are now wondering if you can make an equestrian journey, and just as importantly, should you, then take heart. Sir Francis Bond Head was like you. Even though he lived and rode in the early part of the 19th century he wrestled with balancing the same dream versus his everyday reality. A wealthy English officer with every reason in the world to stay close to home, he found himself instead riding alone across the Andes Mountains in 1825. During that time he wondered why some human beings, like him, were motivated instead to trade security for hardship.

"In almost every instance the home one has deserted is replete with luxury and comfort; and yet, from stuffed sofas, easy chairs, feather beds, soft mattresses, warm fires, good carpets, a well stocked library, cellar, larder and dairy, gardens, faithful servants and friendly neighbours we eagerly flee."

Why would you give up such luxury, he asked nearly two centuries ago? Head concluded the reason was, because "instead of being homesick, one had become almost sick unto death of home."

Where the dream comes from

If you are contemplating giving up the plush security of a hearth in favour of making an equestrian journey, then you have already unknowingly become part of a phenomenon which predates us both. It is something which doesn't recognize money, or religion, or sex, or nationality. It is something which is lodged deep within the DNA of a few of us. It is what sets us apart. It is what burns in us. It is what never gives us peace. It is what makes us Long Riders.

No matter where you live. Regardless of what language you were born speaking. Never mind the fact that you may not even currently know how to ride a horse, you have fallen prey to one of the most ancient, and alluring, equestrian concepts known to humanity, the dream of becoming an equestrian traveller.

Nor are you the first to harbour such a burning equestrian ambition.

Darwin and DNA

Though he is known today as the "father of evolution," famous English biologist Charles Darwin was also an avid equestrian explorer. During the five years in which he made his famous scientific journey around the world, the historical Long Rider took every opportunity to investigate the continents of South America, Australia and Africa on horseback.

Whether you agree with his famous *Theory of Evolution* or not, Darwin's impact on the course of modern events cannot be denied. His was a life whose resonance is still being felt around the globe. Yet it goes against the grain of common perception to think of this intellectual titan galloping over the pampas of Argentina, exploring volcanic islands on horseback, and lying down to rest on the bosom of the earth with his Road Horse nearby.

Darwin's diaries reveal more than just a meek naturalist searching the world for answers. They also disclose the inner man, the Long Rider who delighted in the liberty found riding on three continents. For as his varied diary entries explain, Charles Darwin the scientist, soon discovered, "the pleasure of living in the open air with the sky for a roof and the ground for a table."

One other thing Darwin did was to argue that the migratory urge is one of the strongest of instincts. Like you, his was a soul nourished by wanderlust. The articulate Welsh describe this vague uneasiness as *hiraeth*, a yearning for we know not what, a desire to go for reasons we cannot fathom.

What, you may be asking, is a Long Rider? And why should it matter to you?

Because Long Riders are the masters of equestrian travel and this book, which contains 6,000 years of their accumulated equestrian travel knowledge, is the first work of its kind in history.

As I said, Long Riders are different from the majority of human beings. First of all, they are not nomads. Traditional nomads were compelled to travel in a yearly search for fresh pasture. Long Riders are instead answering an urgent need which has been awakened in their soul and compels them to ride towards the unknown. The former represents a tribal migration, while the latter is an act of individual equestrian courage.

Yet when did such courage take root?

Horse Humans

Johannes V. Jensen visualized in his story, *Wolf the Horse Breaker*, how mankind might have first cautiously approached, and then mounted, a wild horse. The world was a new place then. Humanity was obsessed with the dual daily efforts of survival and food. The horse was seen as nothing but another source of protein, a tasty, fleet-footed, chunk of meat not easily delivered to the stone-age dinner table. Thus we will never know who made the first decision not to view the horse through the eyes of a predator.

The Celts have long cherished the oral tradition of Epona, a legendary female who could communicate with and ride horses. Regardless, some skin-clad man or woman, whose name is now lost in the abyss of time, listened to an inner voice and changed our collective history. Humanity reached out the hand of friendship to the wary equine and a new interspecies relationship was born.

Since then there has never been a more productive bonding of man and animal. The horse was soon ploughing the ground that nurtured our first hard-won seeds. He helped us round up our scattered flocks. He aided our scouts to warn us of advancing danger. He even put aside his peaceful nature and agreed to pull our war chariots to the walls of Troy. But more importantly, the horse set us free!

For what that first Stone Age horseman, or woman, discovered still holds true.

Pedestrians stay in their villages.

Horse Humans roam the world.

If you are seeking evidence demonstrating confirmation, then you need look no further than the Ukraine, where equine teeth showing the signs of bit wear indicate that our mounted ancestors were exploring Central Asia 6,000 years ago. Two thousand years later King Sulge of Ur was busy writing poems in praise of his mighty "horse of the highway." And when 1350 B.C. dawned, it saw Kikkuli, riding eagerly towards the land of Mitanni.

What drove those "prehistoric" humans to desert their huts and hearths?

Ask any Long Rider, then or now, and they will tell you that the world looks different from atop a horse. No distance is too grand. No desert cannot be crossed. No mountain cannot be conquered. No river cannot be swum. No geographic obstacle has ever succeeded in defying the combined bravery of horse and human. For thousands of years this four-legged friend has been taking horsemen to places beyond the daily definitions of dogmatic pedestrians.

Take Henry "Birdie" Bowers for example. He was the Englishman who used a horse to explore Antarctica in 1912. He wrote, "What if our heart aches for a kind of journey that defies description? The time has come to set out for the sacred ground, the mountain, the temple, the ancestral home.....swayed by an overwhelming impulse within me...a tidal pull....to abandon my home as a bird abandons a nest....impossible to satisfy but equally impossible to ignore."

Nor was he alone, for though Bowers died trying to reach the South Pole, Lady Florence Dixie, an elegant English aristocrat, articulated an answer to the same vague desire which has intrigued humanity for ages. When asked in 1879 why she wanted to journey to such an outlandish place as Patagonia, the author replied without hesitation that she was taking to the saddle in order to flee from the strict confines of polite Victorian society.

"Palled for the moment with civilization and its surroundings, I wanted to escape somewhere, where I might be as far removed from them as possible. Many of my readers have doubtless felt the dissatisfaction with oneself, and everybody else, that comes over one at times in the midst of the pleasures of life; when one wearies of the shallow artificiality of modern existence; when what was once excitement has become so no longer, and a longing grows up within one to taste a more vigorous emotion than that afforded by the monotonous round of society's so called pleasures."

Thus one of the primary reasons why Long Riders travel is because they are seeking to unravel the mystery of the oldest form of Equine-Human achievement, that ancient equitation known as Equestrian Travel.

Yet Long Riders have traditionally been opposed

You might be tempted to think that no one would object to someone else setting off in search of inner, and outer, knowledge. Yet regardless of the date on the calendar, whatever pedestrian culture is in power at the time will attempt to coerce the population into believing that it is better for them to remain where they are. For political power is undermined when bold individuals escape on horseback to where the grass looks greener, then return with tales of faraway lands gained via a mounted adventure.

There are a wide variety of reasons for this discouragement, all of which are a variation on the same theme. It's dangerous or deserted, cold or hot, infested with beasts or crawling with bandits. One of my favourite excuses was the one told to the young woman who wished to ride across England in 1939. Her outraged critics reminded her that she couldn't possibly do such a thing "in this modern age."

Regardless of the reason, the first thing you must learn is that settled people will do what they can to undermine your dream of setting off on an equestrian journey.

Why discourage us?

Sadly, the majority of humanity spend their lives like worms, content to die in the same clod of clay in which they were born. That explains why as long as some humans have been attempting to ride towards the sun, sedentary people have been busy urging them instead not to leave. These are the pedestrians who divided the landscape into "wild" and "domestic." They saw their "inside" life as representing security, all the while denouncing mounted life as uncouth. Such people betray their own dreams and become ghosts not to be remembered.

It was the Welsh Long Rider, Jeremy James, who wrote, "Men without horses are nothing! They huddle in squalor in their reeking towns and fear for their miserable lives. They hoard their precious belongings. They clutch their ill-gotten coins in their pale, soft hands. They carry their papers from here to there. They hide their faces from the sun and the wind and they stare into pavements. They stink of streets and of the filth of each other. They crawl into their linen sheets beneath their roofs and do not know the glory of the night."

Nor is he alone in his contempt, for the young Israeli Long Rider, Kareen Kohn, has also given voice to long suppressed equestrian discontent.

"After generations we have created the social and political conditions that control and determine our lives. We awake and automatically follow the common pattern for modern survival. We feed the system, so it can feed us in return. We work ambitiously so that we can briefly escape and be surrounded by nature, splurging for a few days so as to justify our personal sacrifice. For a brief lapse we surrender to tourism, an industry that sends tourists to saturated vortexes that peddle nature as a product. Thus, we pretend to be living freely, but when the clock ticks, enforced by custom and against our desire, we return to take up our part in a monstrous system. We have sacrificed our freedom for what? A roof, a meal, a colourful garment? We have become modern ants, deprived of will, subdued by conformity, postponing our happiness. The rigid walls we have built cover the stars that once guided us. Confined in our loneliness behind these walls, we dwell on filling our small spaces with more and more possessions, until we forget ourselves and become another object with a function. Mounting a horse and travelling is not a question of giving up technology, and the comforting of the senses, but uncontaminating our lives and minimizing our impact on nature, or removing the material possessions which block the door that leads to our freedom. We have fought for generations to be free of tyrants. Yet what dictator is holding us back from freeing ourselves? Thus, the new nomad is born, with the passion of the Gypsy, the tolerance of the Bedouin, the flare of the Artist, the courage of the Warrior, the instinct of the Indian, the madness of the Prophet, the hope of a Dreamer, the wisdom of the Long Rider and a thirst that can only be quenched when a distant personal ocean is finally found."

As this warning demonstrates, there are any number of people who are going to present you with a plethora of what they believe are perfectly logical, legal, emotional and spiritual reasons for why you should not make your ride. If it isn't the unsuitability of your horse, it will be some vague danger just waiting around the corner to get you, or the unstable political climate, or some other ghost. It all boils down to one thing. They're afraid of doing what you're planning to attempt. Therefore, feeling inadequate, they try to stop you from leaving.

Three who went anyway

Yet we are not discussing ancient history, for equestrian travel is as relevant today, and resonates as deeply in your soul, as it did to those who rode before.

For example, on the night in 1925 before his departure to ride 16,000 kilometres (10,000 miles) from Buenos Aires, Argentina, to New York City in the USA, the young Swiss Long Rider, Aimé Tschiffely, recalled that the carping of his critics caused him "to be assailed by a sickly feeling, as if my stomach were a vacuum."

Like many before him, Aimé's longing for adventure had brought him to the point of no return. The historic horseback ride which had previously sounded so thrilling was now looming with all its dangers, real and imagined, only a few hours away.

Perhaps it was in fact because he had no prior equestrian travel experience to fall back on that 29-year-old Tschiffely ignored the legion of critics who told him his quest was "impossible" and "absurd." The morning he was scheduled to leave rain was falling and the roads leading out of Buenos Aires were already hock-deep in thick, sticky mud. The reporters regarded the whole thing as a huge joke: "A lunatic proposing to travel overland to New York," ran one story.

The solitary horseman later wrote, "Eventually there was only one thing to do: screw up my courage, burn all the bridges behind me, and start a new life, no matter whither it might lead. Convinced that he who has not lived dangerously has never tasted the salt of life, that day I decided to take the plunge."

The brave Swiss Long Rider went on to survive a host of dangers, then wrote a best-selling book, *Tschiffely's Ride*, which exerted the strongest influence ever seen across every subsequent generation of Long Riders.

Yet less than ten years later, when Margaret Leigh was inspired by his example to announce that she was going to ride from Cornwall to Scotland, she too had to face the critics before she ever saw the road. In her own book, Leigh cautioned future Long Riders not to be discouraged before they ever set out. "I would warn you not to listen to the pessimistic comments coming from the host of clever people (in their own opinion) by whom you are sure to be beset when you announce your travel plans."

Nor had the carping critics ceased their work as the twentieth century came to a close. That's when an adventurous young Australian named Steve Nott announced that Tschiffely had inspired him to ride around the perimeter of that continent. Though the times, and continents had changed, the ridicule remained.

"You're mad. You'll perish in the desert. It can't be done," were some of the comments aimed at the would-be Long Rider before he set off in 1986. Nott didn't listen either and went on to successfully complete his 16,000 kilometre (10,000 miles) journey around the Australian continent.

Yet all three of these singular people were urged not to risk their lives, were told they would die, were reminded that their journey was irresponsible, dangerous, immature and ill advised. All three went anyway and no one now remembers the names of their cowardly critics. Yet we revere these heroes of the saddle.

Thus the decision to protect your personal resolve always marks a solitary movement of individual bravery in a person's life. For intertwined in your journey is a denial of death and a rejection of frailty.

All Long Riders make a lonely decision

How can those on the ground denounce us? Can a blind man tell you colours? Can those earth-bound lecture to those of us with equine wings?

That is why every person who became a Long Rider first had to make an initial lonely decision before they could swing into the saddle and begin their journey. For as any Long Rider will tell you, the initial challenge you have to overcome is the often-vocal and vehement opposition aimed at you by the current generation of well-meaning nay-sayers.

Don't think for a moment that anyone handed your predecessors the courage to easily change their existence or granted them the valour to quickly redefine the perimeter of their long-ago lives. They struggled then, like you will be called on to struggle now, with balancing a personal equestrian desire against a host of people who are urging you to listen to common-sense and remain at home.

That is why the English Long Rider, Mary Pagnamenta, ignored the critics. Realizing that not everyone who dies has lived, she rode across both the islands of New Zealand in search of "a freedom from ambition, freedom from the expectations of others, freedom from the need to conform and from the urge to rebel. The freedom to be."

So before you go any further with your planning, before you buy a map, dust off your saddle, look at horses and think about the onset of warm weather, you have another initial challenge to overcome. You must resolve the conflict between family values and Long Rider urges. You can't serve the saddle, and the hearth, and attempt to be successful.

Nor in today's accelerated society, with its disdain and impatience for activities that require patience and a commitment of time, should you be surprised at your lack of emotional support. Regardless of the fact that the sedentary life of your critics often times results in them dwelling in front of the television, or role playing a fantasy life via their computer screens, despite their pale cheeks, and ignoring the fact that life in the city results in more hospital visits and coffins than an equestrian journey, nevertheless these same people will beg you not to leave.

Beware of listening, and remember.

Change frightens the majority of people.

That is why the forefathers of these people told Columbus to stay at home. Not all souls are about "life." The majority of them are focused on "don't." That is why our real enemies are amongst us, born without imagination, said the famous Long Rider author, Don Roberto Cunninghame Graham. This is also why you must first of all guard the dream before you mount the saddle.

Who will greet you?

Let us say that you manage to elude your emotional pursuers. What will be your reward?

Right away you will discover that Long Riders are equestrian exiles from their own times, bred to wide horizons, who share a sense of inherited defiance. They are not a part of the caste-ridden, mainstream equestrian world. They are people from everywhere, who form a mounted diaspora of their own. They come in all colours and religions, are men and women, are rich and poor, and will not draw attention to your nationality, race, faith or sex.

They will instead surprise you, because they speak the same mother tongue you do – "horse."

Thus though they come from every corner of the globe, what will strike you will be the comradeship of these horse-humans who have been forged and tempered in a school of energy, courage and humanity.

Once you belong to such a group, no matter where the trail of life takes you, you will always carry with you that virtuous mounted magic.

What you will discover?

Where will such an inner, and outer, journey lead, you may well ask?

Long before this book was ever written, Captain Charles Colville Frankland had grown weary of the painful sameness of his life. That is why he decided to depart from the English navy and set off in 1827 to explore the Ottoman Empire and Egypt. During the course of his two-year journey Frankland made an extended equestrian exploration of Syria, at which time he adopted Turkish riding clothes and met Lady Hester Stanhope, the celebrated English aristocrat who had turned her back on life in London, preferring instead to raise pure-bred Arab horses in the mountains close to Damascus. The many colourful events combined to impress the young Long Rider with the beauty of the life he had stumbled into.

In his 1829 book, *Travels to and from Constantinople*, he wrote, "The charm of this vagrant kind of life which I led in Syria is inconceivable; its constant variety, its perfect independence, the excitement of difficulty, the apprehension of danger, were so many powerful but agreeable stimulants. My wants were few and easily supplied; my bed was the ground, my covering a cloak and my canopy the heavens; in such a climate I could desire no better. I halted when and where I chose and set out again as my fancy dictated. I could dine upon a morsel of Arab bread, content myself with a draught of water and sit upon the back of my horse from an hour before sunrise until nightfall without feeling fatigued. Thus I gained perfect liberty and independence."

Yet you can't go without wisdom

Peek into the footnotes of the history books and you will often find passing references to those second-sons, and footloose daughters, who once roamed the world on horseback. These Long Riders sprang from all parts, for their need was an individualistic expression, not a national trend.

This brings me back to why you sought this book.

By your act of reading this tome you have admitted, if only to yourself, that you are at a crossroads in life.

But there is more to being a Long Rider than just the geographic adventure because, as I shall explain, to depart without wisdom is to doom your journey to almost certain hardship and possible calamity. Mounted liberty demands that you adhere to a philosophy of equestrian responsibility.

My own struggle

In an odd way I am the perfect messenger to bring you the equestrian knowledge you now seek, as my life reads like a mix of "Genghis Khan meets The Matrix." That is because I was born on the cusp of two centuries, midway between the giants of Victorian exploration and the astonishing scientific advances of the internet age. I spent my youth gazing back nostalgically and now devote my time looking eagerly forward. Thus, though my present existence is monopolized by emails, websites and print-on-demand publishing, my impressionable youth was spent in the literary company of Long Rider authors like Gabriel Bonvalot.

In 1889 he set out to make an unparalleled journey from France to faraway French Indochina. After crossing Russia, the Frenchman mounted up in Siberia and then headed south towards Tibet. The resultant equestrian winter journey across the Tibetan plain and the Himalayan mountains is nearly too arduous to believe. Bonvalot routinely rode in weather so cold that his Siberian companions begged him to turn back when the mercury in the thermometer froze.

Inspired by this audacious Frenchmen, and others of his ilk, I set off in the 1970s to explore the world on horseback. I left behind an English riding school, and a classical dressage background, in favour of riding across the wilds of Afghanistan. In those days, before the Soviet Union invaded that still pristine country, I learned to wrap a good turban, subsist on a variety of unusual dishes, feel at ease among an assortment of jovial brigands and ride like my life depended on it among the remnants of the original great Central Asian equestrian culture.

What the Afghans couldn't teach me though was how to be an equestrian traveller. Thus through a series of unforeseeable mistakes, I made four separate attempts to ride across that part of the world, with every journey prematurely concluding due to a previously undetected obstacle. Regardless of the setbacks, which included being tortured and illegally imprisoned, I learned from my mistakes, refused to give up and always went back.

My equestrian Waterloo arrived in Kafiristan, the land of the pagans, which occupies a tiny corner of north-western Pakistan. It was there, during the course of my last journey, that I found myself one night holding the head of my dying pack horse. I was halfway through making the longest horse trip in the history of Pakistan, when this cheerful and mischievous animal fell ill. An injection of outdated medication by a well-meaning government veterinarian earlier in the day may have been what brought my horse and me to this tragic crossroads.

Regardless, he died like the cliché, in my arms, and not quietly either but with a great, painful sigh and a last rattle rushing up from deep down in his throat. The moon beams burned down like a spot light on my guilt. It was 12:17 a.m. and I had let a horse die on my fifth equestrian journey in South West Asia. A cloud of shock descended over my rational western mind. Sven Hedin, the famous Swedish Long Rider and Central Asian explorer, had gone on an expedition in the late 19th century and lost nearly a hundred horses. He had considered their deaths so insignificant that he mentioned it only in passing at the end of his book.

Yet this was no book. This was no armchair fantasy. This was the brutal reality of equestrian exploration and I was suddenly sick of it.

The next day, preoccupied as I was with saving my other horses, my life was forever changed. I had forgotten that this was brutal Pakistan, not home in the west where animals, especially horses, occupy a special niche in our collective hearts. While I was lost in thought the Kafirs skinned my dead pack horse, chopped him up into so much cold dead meat, ate him and robbed me forever of many of the romantic notions I had long cherished about the beauties of equestrian travel.

Thus I've spent thirty plus years trying to correct the injustice of being denied the basic knowledge I so deeply needed and longed for on that long-ago night.

Upon my return to more civilized realms, I swore that I would undertake a systematic study of equestrian travel. I would find all the great books, talk to all the wise horse travellers, and learn everything the Earth had to offer about my appointed subject. What I found instead was that there were neither masters nor answers awaiting me.

Lost Secrets of the Long Riders

While the idea of saddling up and exploring the world will excite you, it may surprise and depress you to learn that our equestrian forefathers never foresaw the day when their collective wisdom and daily practices would stand on the brink of extinction. For unlike sailors, Long Riders have not recorded the means and ways by which they set off to explore the world.

From the days of the ancient Phoenicians, sailors and sailing masters have contrived to create one of mankind's greatest logistical and exploratory treasures.

They did this by carefully recording "how" you sail a ship. No matter if it is a sleek Viking raider setting off to plunder Ireland or a dinghy departing on a Sunday sail across a local lake, there are a wealth of "how to" books which can, and do, teach people how to set out upon the water and safely reach their faraway destination.

For example, Ahmad ibn Majid of Oman was the premier Arabic sailing master during the fifteenth century. His book, *Kitab al-Faw'id fi Usul 'Ilm al-Bahr wa l-Qawa'id* (Book of Useful Information on the Principles and Rules of Navigation), which was published in 1490, contains an encyclopaedia of nautical wisdom, including the history and basic principles of navigation, an explanation of lunar monsoons, the difference between coastal and open-sea sailing, the locations of ports from Africa to Indonesia, a treatise on star positions, a warning about typhoons and other topics of immense interest to professional sailors. All this wisdom was drawn not only from the author's own experience, but the lore of generations of other sailors as well.

Yet though six hundred years have passed since Ahmad ibn Majid last dropped anchor and wrote his book, no such global study has ever been penned for equestrian explorers.

Thus, while the wisdom of the world's sailors has been carefully collected, maintained, treasured, protected, discussed, and passed on from one generation of nautical humanity to the next, sadly, equestrian travellers did not adhere to these lettered principles.

That is why historically there has been no equestrian literary point of reference for men and women such as you. The earliest mounted Argonauts of the past scoffed at book learning and pyramid building. They slashed away the chains of predictability and rode out into the world in search of the unknown, aboard horses fair and tall, freed from the restraints of gravity and the village.

Yet because many of these same early equestrian travellers were unlettered, they saw no need to retain for unforeseen generations practices which they took for granted. Plus, what few great early accounts were created have now vanished. For example, though they created the mightiest equestrian empire in the history of humanity, the horse knowledge of the Mongols, including the legendary horse book created by their ruler, Kublai Khan, is now lost to mankind.

Consequently that staple of world knowledge, the accumulated equestrian travel experience of countless generations, was teetering on the edge of oblivion when I began my search. In fact, during the darkest days of the

1950s fewer than a dozen people undertook a significant equestrian journey anywhere in the world. Even Aimé Tschiffely's book, the most inspirational equestrian travel title ever penned, had become largely unobtainable even in second-hand bookshops.

The search for knowledge

This isn't to say that there weren't a handful of other men and women, like myself, who were eager to learn from their mistakes. As my own failures had clearly demonstrated, there was a rudimentary science to riding great distances. Only where to learn it? And from whom?

At that point in my search, given the few historical accounts available, all I knew for sure was that the critical defining qualities of a Long Rider were courage and resolve. Equally obvious was the fact that these rare humans clearly came from every corner of the globe and that all of them acknowledged the saddle as their preferred residence. Yet there was no trace of their collective knowledge, the equestrian wisdom gathered by historical Long Riders and formulated into a mounted code of practice.

The world was, in fact, suffering from an abysmal case of equestrian amnesia. For example, one famous 19th century equestrian explorer set off with 94 horses in his expedition. Six months later only seven of these equines had survived. That meant that during the course of 182 days the explorer had lost an average of 2.09 horses per day. Yet the explorer didn't bother to discuss, or justify, his actions. He didn't devote any part of his book to discussing how he fed the horses, whether he shod them, what type of saddle he rode, etc. Why?

That's when it dawned on me. He took no more note of what was to him an everyday act of easily-accessible communal wisdom than you do. Have you, for example, taken the time to leave a carefully-worded treatise for your grandchildren wherein you explain how to dial a rotary telephone, parallel park, toast a pop-tart or boot up a floppy disc?

In desperation, I began my search by contacting Joseph Allen in London. He was the owner of the world's most famous equestrian bookshop, a nearly sacred spot for horsemen, which I had visited while attending school in England. Additionally, because he was also an equally famous publisher of equine books, I concluded that this was the one man in the world who could help me.

So it came as a great surprise when this equine lore master informed me that there was no such equestrian travel book, that the knowledge was long lost and it was up to me to rediscover it. I can recall my astonishment when I received this discouraging news. But with Mr. Allen's help, I began to search the world for every previously written equestrian travel book. As my collection of out-of-print equestrian travel titles grew, I began to discover tiny treasures left among the pages by an occasional Long Rider author. Lost among their journey might be a single hard lesson, perhaps gained at great personal expense. The knowledge was there, I learned, but it had to be sought patiently if it were to be rediscovered.

Unexpected Antagonism from the Traditional Horse World

While I was searching the world for books, I made another critical discovery.

The traditional 20th century horse world wasn't interested in aiding my search, acknowledging the equestrian travellers of the past, or in possession of the wisdom I sought.

It didn't take long to confirm that there were enough law-laden equestrian clubs, organizations, societies, associations, federations, leagues, and unions to fill a large phone book. If it was rules you sought, then one could easily join the Japanese Cowboy Federation, The Amalgamated Pinto Breeders of Lithuania or The Lords of Dressage Unlimited. But there was no place for Long Riders.

Nor could I hope to find answers to my equestrian travel questions among contemporary horse people.

My first inkling of this came when I drove across a portion of the United States to attend a public event where the guest of honour was a renowned mule packer. Thinking that I was about to interview a fellow equine traveller, I had a host of questions prepared. When I found this grizzled veteran of the Rocky Mountains, he was adorned in picturesque cowboy costume, spitting tobacco and weaving tales of his many mounted manly adventures. Hanging on to his every word was a sizeable crowd of tourists who had paid to listen to this fellow's tales of elk hunting and mule transport.

Meanwhile, standing beyond the crowd, tied up and waiting patiently in the hot sun, were half a dozen matched red mules. Unlike the lightly clad summer tourists, the mules were sweating under old fashioned sawbuck pack saddles. Each of the unfortunate animals was burdened by an immense canvas-covered load, both sides of which were festooned with enough complicated knots to puzzle a master mariner.

Burning with curiosity, but equally embarrassed at my lack of cowboy couture credentials, I hesitantly asked the great man what was the longest journey he had made with his mules. Adjusting his immense hat with impatience, he proceeded to inform me that he had been packing mules in the mountains for thirty years, had survived all sorts of wrecks and runaways and how dare I question his obvious visual credentials.

I don't know when it dawned on me that he was bluffing, or that he might be a logistical fraud. Taking a deep breath, I briefly explained to him, and the suddenly-antagonistic crowd, about my own equestrian journeys, how I had nearly lost my life on several occasions and had made a long auto journey to meet the great man so to further my search for knowledge. I concluded by politely, but firmly, asking him again to tell me how far he had actually travelled. Less than a hundred miles in any one direction was his angry answer.

There was a stunned silence from the crowd, but I was too busy taking on board the important realization that the mule packer was void of the type of wisdom and guidance I was seeking.

Mary Bosanquet also attempted to obtain information prior to making her solo ride across Canada in 1939. She too was disappointed.

"I did try to secure advice, but as my advisors almost all confined themselves to attempts at dissuading me from my foolhardy escapade, I soon gave up even this. Eminent authorities for the world of horsemanship told me why I could not possibly succeed in what I was undertaking. Instead people have all been asking me why? Why do I want to ride across Canada? Why am I not afraid of danger? Why on horseback? Why alone? Why, why, why?"

She was going, Mary explained because, "I was seeking an adventure such as had been experienced by heroic voyagers. I was determined to ride life bareback with my hands in the tangled mane."

Thus, my first rule, and yours, should be to never accept equestrian travel advice from anyone who hasn't ridden at least five hundred miles in a straight line.

Don't let their costume fool you, because the vast majority of people who are dressed like cowboys, Cossacks, Gauchos, Mounties and Mongols are little more than well-meaning opinionated descendants of once-great equestrian cultures. Whereas their forefathers might have been able to guide you, chances are that the man wearing the big belt buckle of today knows more about Chevrolets than he does about Criollos.

This isn't to say that you are not going to meet a host of horseback people who are eager to offer you their opinions on everything from your route to your horse and gear. But burdening mules, chasing cows, performing dressage or riding a trail on Sunday, isn't the same thing as leaving behind everything you know in the world and risking your life to become an equestrian explorer.

It takes another Long Rider to tell you instead about the reality of aching bones encountered after a week of riding 30-mile days, or the bitter taste of disappointment that fills your mouth when you come to a village only to discover nothing for you or your horse to eat. Long Riders know the way the rain always finds a way to run down your neck no matter how many times you pull up your raincoat with your cold, stiff fingers, or the fear that grips your stomach when your horse snorts and shies away from an unexpected stranger on a dark and lonely road.

For this reason too, don't look for answers among the deadening formalism and vindictive competitive world of the ring riders.

Ring riders are obedient to their customs, be it dressage, jumping or western pleasure. They travel in endless repetition in an attempt to strengthen what are basically emotional security patterns established with their horse. Their riding is not being used to meet any real risk, but rather to outrun it. They're not exploring. They're searching for competitive perfection. Thus they ride in the show ring like a man swimming in a goldfish bowl while pretending to be in the ocean.

In contrast, hidden in equestrian travel are the secrets you will never find in the ring. It's the magic of riding to the crest of the mighty Shandur Pass as the sun is setting over the Karakoram Mountains. Sitting up there on your horse on top of the world you suddenly see the sky splashed with purple, pink, and gold. Behind you lies a tortured insult called a trail, but down below in the valley you see a village glowing warm with the welcome of twinkling lanterns. So you pat your horse's neck and wish him a long life, a fair exchange for bringing you safely through yet again. Then you urge him to make his weary way down the darkening row of stony tiger's teeth to the end of another day, one of many you will never be able to adequately describe to those not of your own special breed.

Without doubt I did not find what I sought among trail riders either, for you cannot pigeon hole the activities and achievements of equestrian explorers under the placid title of "trail riding."

Unfortunately one of the corrosive effects of trail riding is the demise of any sudden surprise and the eradication of true adventure. Trail riders are always sure of reaching their destination and finding therein a warm meal, a soft bed, and a safe roof. Ask any of the world's equestrian explorers and they will laughingly tell you that no such safety net exists out on the high road to adventure. In a word these Long Riders are the astronauts of the equestrian world, the few who have made giant personal, professional, emotional and financial sacrifices in order to travel where few have ever ridden before.

No, equestrian exploration is dangerous, life threatening, and exhilarating but it is never the placebo known as trail riding.

Nor are Long Riders akin to tourists, who come back with souvenirs of physical locations but remain inoculated from experiencing inner wisdom. Such people expend their energy coveting vast mileage yet see nothing more meaningful on their journeys than post cards and casual impressions. Long Riders know better than to become obsessed with finding their destination on a map. They inherit from their horse-borne ancestors the knowledge that maps are flat-faced liars save that sacred document called your heart.

Thus, as the years passed, and my search for answers went on, I confirmed that Long Riders are not tourists, trail riders or ring riders. They are instead a tiny, hardy band of risk-takers and wisdom-seekers.

Equally, I was shocked to learn that the traditional corporate-owned equestrian magazines were either antagonistic, or too preoccupied with commercial concerns, to be of any assistance in my search. During the course of the last fifty years none of them had investigated, documented or encouraged equestrian travel.

Plus, the discovery of one startling episode highlighted the unspoken "gentleman's agreement" that Long Riders weren't welcome in these glossy magazines dripping instead with equestrian fashion and competitive events. One of North America's most well-travelled Long Riders, I learned, had ridden right up to the door of the leading American horse magazine. Not a soul on the staff emerged to greet this man who had already ridden nearly ten thousand continuous miles. Not only was he not invited in to share his incredible story, despite the blazing summer heat, neither he nor his horse was offered so much as a cup of water.

Why? What could have been so upsetting and frightening about this weary traveller that these so-called "horsemen" didn't have the decency to even acknowledge his existence?

If they had possessed the bravery to open their office door, this wise man could have unfolded a tale about the power of the equestrian journey to open something innate and hidden in all of us; the almost genetic need to travel by horse. He could have explained how rare riders who undertake such a journey become saddle-borne pilgrims leading a life based on physical freedom. He could have clarified how his horse had taken him on a journey away from the never-ending search for consumer products and shown him instead the way back to the ancient principles of our collective equestrian past; i.e. grass, water, fire and contemplation. Those were the keys to equestrian travel awaiting their discussion, if they had only opened that door.

Instead, they focused on publishing another forgettable issue of a magazine devoted to boutique riders, not equestrian mystics. This wise man, who rode right to their door, and the ancient wisdom he represented, were ignored by the journalists.

Thus, beware of seeking for help, advice or support from traditional equestrian participants or publications because chances are that you're not going to find answers, only antagonism. For what none of the equestrian magazines, the ring riders, endurance racers or horse-whisperers are ever going to tell you is that travel on horseback brings with it a special kind of wisdom, helps you see through the world's pretensions, and opens you up to the adventure of self-conquest.

Equestrian travel is not merely about covering vast amounts of mileage. It is the journey you and your horse take together to reach the borders of an otherwise invisible place. It is a journey you see from the top of that altar of freedom, your saddle. It is an antidote to the world's obsession with speed, because the three-mile-per-hour pace of your horse forces you to slow down your body, which in turn results in the opening of your spirit. Thus an equestrian journey does not merely transport you along the physical road stretching ahead, more importantly it allows you to ride on the secret trail traced deep inside your soul.

A Fateful Phone Call

After decades of searching and reading I had concluded that the Long Riders were a mounted tribe without a historian. Though they had accomplished the most amazing equestrian feats, their heroes had been exiled into the shadows. Though some of them had written great books in a variety of languages, their literature had been ignored. Though their traditions were centuries old, they were ridiculed by ring-riders and commercial equestrian interests. In the recent past they had been wrongly described as misfits and saddle tramps, instead of explorers and seekers. No one had ever thought to describe the virtues of being a Long Rider. No one had compared the rewards of equestrian travel against the foibles of a sedentary life style. Although settled people and pedestrians had expressed their disdain for equestrian travellers for centuries, the fact remained that throughout history there has always been a handful of independent spirits who chose the freedom of the saddle over the drudgery of the plough.

Ironically I also learned that we are suffering from a famine of equestrian freedom. The 21st century has placed horse owners in a paradox. They have access to pampered equine athletes, synthetic space-age tack, cell phones, Global Positioning Satellite technology, insurance on both horse and rider, and a host of time-saving gadgets. Yet when their souls become restless 99% of horse owners group like lemmings, never understanding that the traditional equestrian outlets favoured today are not going to answer the spiritual void eating away at their experience starved souls.

In 2000, I finished writing my book *Khyber Knights*, about my mounted adventures in Afghanistan and Pakistan. A few days later I chanced to see a front page newspaper article regarding a man who claimed to be riding from Tennessee to Alaska. Having just emerged from a nearly year long self-imposed literary cocoon, I was anxious to speak to another equestrian traveller.

The resulting telephone call changed the course of equestrian travel history.

Because his front page picture had seemed to portray a rugged frontier type, I took it for granted that I was telephoning another serious student of equestrian travel. Having obtained the traveller's phone number from the local reporter, I called the unknown rider at a nearby motel. When I explained over the phone who I was, the stranger became immensely excited. He began peppering me with questions, asking me how many miles he should ride every day, what should he feed his horse, had he purchased the proper saddle, etc., etc., etc. Though I barely had time to introduce myself, I could discern that the man was clearly close to panic.

"Wait a minute, "I said. "Let's start at the beginning. What type of horse are you riding?"

"A sorrel," he replied without hesitation.

There was a long pause as I groaned inwardly.

I took a deep breath and then said quietly, "That's a colour, not a breed." I then repeated my question.

"Well I've got a bill of sale with the details. Let me read it to you."

I waited a few moments, during which time I heard the stranger rustling around in the background. In an anxious voice he then read the results.

"Ok, here it is. He's a six year old sorrel. Is that a good horse to make a trip on?" he asked in all innocence.

"Stay right there," I said, "I'm driving over to see you."

What I found was a man pretending to be a Native American, wearing an Indian choker necklace, a fringed leather coat, a big cowboy hat – but despite the freezing November weather, no shirt. He had left home one step ahead of the law, managed to find a horse, then told a naïve local press that he was riding to Alaska so as to draw attention to the historical injustices done to Indians. He didn't have a map or a clue. What's worse, though he had been on the road for less than a fortnight, his horse was suffering from saddle sores.

Though I felt sorry for him, I felt even worse for his horse, which was clearly underfed, over laden and in trouble. With a mixed sense of guilt and anger, I informed the stranger that he was an equestrian travel disaster and that he should stop his journey. It didn't matter what I said, he set off again the next day. Only this time local vets stepped in so as to save his horse from any further harm. The last I heard the stranger had deserted his horse, abandoned his dream of riding to Alaska and disappeared so as to avoid any further legal entanglements.

Yet this horrific meeting convinced me of the need to call for the formation of an international association of equestrian explorers.

The Long Riders' Guild

In September, 2000 I hosted the first international meeting of equestrian explorers. Here were far-ranging roamers, men and women who had previously despaired of the everydayness of their lives. Though all of us had journeyed on horseback, none of us knew our tribe's history, or even the names of those champions who had ridden before our meek individual efforts. Names of legendary Long Riders like Dmitri Peshkov and Roger Pocock had been swept aside, while those of us left had ridden lost and alone in a wilderness of ignorance.

For three days and nights we spoke of nothing but horses and travel. Though our group was a confluence of countries and equestrian styles, one of the first things we agreed upon was that the definition of a Long Rider should be courage in the face of danger, resolve in the presence of hardship, and continual compassion for our mounts. It was agreed that the purpose of The Long Rider's Guild was to shed light in a time of darkness, to recapture the echoes of ancient nomadic equestrian cultures, and to seek out those equestrian elders who had already sought for the answers that tuned our own souls

Common to us all was the sense of awakened wonder we had each discovered with our horse.

It was during this meeting that we agreed that at some time in each of our journeys our horses were revealed in a different light. Though our individual mounts had stood close by for years, after travelling they were no longer merely objects to be possessed.

Geldings, mares, or stallions, it made no difference. We had ridden them over the desolate portions of the world's rough roads, while suffering disease, fighting off bandits, surviving deserts, swimming rivers, climbing mountains and outwitting corrupt politicians.

Our horses had shown us star patterns and mountain shapes, guided us through lands with no laws and few trails, and taught us that if we discovered fear on the road we could counter it with valour. The horse, we agreed, had showed us that the reason we journeyed was not to seek acclaim, but to discover happiness and the sacred source of life.

Thousands of hard miles and countless shared dangers had bonded us closer to our horses than to our mothers. The latter we loved. The former we entrusted with our lives on a daily basis. Travel had made human and horses part of a new herd dynamic. To us horses were no longer mute beasts. They were agents of change

That is how Long Riders from several countries came together to discuss the urgent need to educate people on how to make an equestrian journey properly. We also recognized the necessity of locating other equestrian explorers throughout the world. And we expressed the hope that some day we might rescue the world's valuable equestrian travel books from oblivion. Thus the Long Riders' Guild was formed to ensure that our lost global inheritance of equestrian travel knowledge would be available for future generations to claim and enjoy.

I am happy to report that fifteen years later, every major equestrian explorer alive today belongs to The Guild, including Hadji Shamsuddin of Afghanistan, who rode 1,600 kilometres (1,000 miles) through that war-zone; Jean-Louis Gouraud of France, who rode 5,000 kilometres (3,000 miles) from Paris to Moscow; Claudia Gottet of Switzerland, who rode 13,000 kilometres (8,000 miles) from Arabia to the Alps; Adnan Azzam of Syria, who rode 16,000 kilometres (10,000 miles) from Madrid to Mecca; and Vladimir Fissenko of Russia, who rode 30,500 kilometres (19,000 miles) from Patagonia to Alaska.

Additionally, nearly a hundred of these extraordinary Long Riders are also Fellows of the Royal Geographical Society, including:

Sir John Ure KCMG LVO, who rode across the Andes; Stephen McCutcheon of England, who set out to ride 16,000 kilometres (10,000 miles) solo from Delhi to Peking; Gordon Naysmith, of Scotland, who rode 20,000 kilometres (12,000 miles) from South Africa to Austria; Pedro Luiz de Aguiar, of Brazil, who at the age of seventy made a 29,000 kilometre (18,000 mile) journey across Latin America; and Robin Hanbury-Tenison OBE, who has made a number of equestrian expeditions in various parts of the world, including riding the length of China's Great Wall.

At three-thousand plus pages, and still growing, and having now been visited by more than millions of people world-wide, The Long Riders' Guild website is the repository of the largest collection of equestrian travel information in human history. (www.thelongridersguild.com)

Additionally The Guild's publishing arm, Horse Travel Books, currently publishes more than a hundred equestrian travel titles in five languages, making it the world's premier source of equestrian exploration wisdom. (www.horsetravelbooks.com)

When The Guild completed the initial work on its Long Rider Literary Collection, we launched a new project dedicated to preserving the vital equestrian travel heritage of that great Swiss Long Rider, Aimé Tschiffely. The purpose of this project is to make all of his terrific books available for the first time in history. (www.aimetschiffely.org)

The Guild has also launched a new project. Entitled The Long Riders' Guild Academic Foundation, its mission is to provide an academic forum for scientists to share their wisdom with equestrian experts. Every type of horse related knowledge is being investigated and published at this exciting new website, whose motto is "Science not Superstition." (www.lrgaf.org)

Yet despite these encouraging results, the primary purpose of The Long Riders' Guild remains to preserve, protect and promote the ancient art of equestrian travel in a mechanized world. I hasten to add that there are no dues or meetings involved in becoming a Member of The Guild. One is invited to join after having ridden a minimum of one thousand miles. Nor will you receive a silver trophy, a blue ribbon or a shiny big belt buckle from the Guild. All you will receive is the respect accorded to you by your fellow equestrian explorers, a respect earned by an elite group of men and women scattered around the globe, all of whom chose to saddle up their horse and then set out on a life-changing equestrian journey.

We adjourned our meeting with the promise to share whatever wisdom we had been blessed with to those about to set out on their own journeys. This book comes with their blessing. It is our gift to you.

The Final Piece of the Puzzle

Despite the passage of thousands of years, equestrian travel has changed very little. There have been improvements to the equipment but the basic laws still apply. Yet the few previous books which attempted to explain the topic of equestrian travel fail to educate a modern equestrian traveller for a variety of reasons.

Previous attempts fall into four classes. Books by cavalry soldier authors, like Lt. Jonathan Boniface, are more than a hundred years old and rely on the use of outdated equipment. Books by classic Long Riders like Gabriel Bonvalot never reveal the daily details necessary to make a modern equestrian journey. Books by North American mule packers focus on limited travel in one country. Books by late 20th century equestrian travellers are based on their personal travel experiences and regional equestrian practices.

Only the Swiss Long Rider, Captain Otto Schwarz, who travelled and rode on five continents, tried to organize a comprehensive global study. But his work was only available in German, though it serves as the basis for this, the world's first comprehensive international study.

Why this book differs and how it was written

At this point let me hasten to add that I am not boasting that I've solved the puzzle of equestrian travel, only that I've spent thirty-plus-years carefully studying it. Yet I've been on the equestrian pilgrim's road for a long, long time seeking answers to the technical and spiritual questions that originally eluded me and are now puzzling you.

Too many of the previous efforts provided little practical detail or offer the novice a useful regimen. Moreover, they were based upon a single person's views on the topic. This book is an attempt to break new ground, not just repeat past mistakes. It is an accumulation of pragmatic knowledge which combines traditional practices with the latest technological sophistication, everything from 13th century Mongol horse knots to 21st century solar powered Long Rider laptops. Most importantly it contains the most vital collection of equestrian travel information ever gathered, including the direct wisdom of hundreds of humanity's wisest Long Riders. Additionally it enlists the equestrian knowledge found in hundreds of horse books, stretching back for more than five hundred years.

In this book you will find varying bursts of equestrian travel information, with their size depending upon the amount of information known on that particular subject. This wisdom and these warnings were gathered from 400 Long Riders, both past and present. Some names appear more frequently, depending upon how much information each Long Rider contributed. Everything in the book is subject to change. Any topic can be added to. New discoveries will be listed.

Thus this book and The Long Riders' Guild are mutually designed to provide you with the intellectual answers and emotional assistance you need to ignore the critics, to listen to your heart, and to ride with confidence anywhere in the world, from Mongolia to Montana, so long as you possess the same two basic necessities required of all Long Riders down through the ages - Courage and a Horse.

Equally important, because *The Encyclopaedia of Equestrian Exploration* is an ongoing project designed to incorporate additional information as and when it becomes available or is discovered, you are welcome to contribute to this historically unique work after you complete your own equestrian journey.

The other essential principle is that this is not a mere "how to" book. It is more importantly a "why to" book.

In editing this vast body of knowledge I have attempted to air very few views of my own, trying instead to distinguish and publish what appeared to be the most reasonable point of view based on an international body of historic evidence. Yet it is inevitable that any editor must exercise his own judgement and may unconsciously express his personal point of view. Like any field of study, you will find controversies within equestrian travel. Such discussions and arguments may be necessary and valuable but they belong in a separate treatise. The purpose of this book therefore is to allow the reader to climb this mountain of knowledge and glimpse the wonders that await them when they set off to explore the world on horseback.

If you find anything in this volume to criticize, please let it not spoil your enjoyment of the rest. If you write to me, quoting your concerns, I shall be glad to consider your criticism; but let it not vex you if I exercise my own judgment in deciding for myself. On the other hand, if there is something that especially pleased you or helped you, please do not hesitate to write to me via The Long Riders' Guild. I have delayed my own nirvana, by not setting off on the World Ride, along with my beautiful wife, the Swiss Long Rider, Basha O'Reilly, so as to help you. Thus it will be a pleasure to know that my labour has not been in vain.

Summary

For more than a hundred years people have been predicting that mankind no longer needs the horse. We Long Riders know better.

We can look back now from the luxury of our computer-driven world and see how everything, and nothing, has changed since Aimé Tschiffely stepped up onto the back of his Criollo horse. For six thousand years each generation of mankind has been supremely confident, arrogant in the recurring belief that theirs is the ultimate expression of the human experience. Meanwhile the horsemen and women of history have watched from the sidelines while fires were first lit, wheels were invented, pyramids were built, railroad lines were laid, automobiles were driven, and computer screens were peered into. Throughout this vast never-ending stream of human experience and effort one thing has run through our collective unconsciousness, the need for terrestrial freedom.

Six thousand years after Epona first grabbed a handful of mane and swung on board that wild forest pony, we, her descendents, still dream of imitating her bold move. We long for the blood-stirring sound of horses' hooves pounding across the steppe. We long for the sweet smell of the leather saddle that takes us to adventure. We long for the feel of the gentle rain in our face, the hot sun on our back, and a happy horse between our legs. And most of all, like Aimé Tschiffely, and all those other equestrian heroes and heroines, we long for our eyes to be filled with the sight of a wide, free horizon. For 6000 years that altar of travel, the saddle, has been calling some of us to roam the world.

Sometimes our soul's song stirs. The ice that has confined us begins to crack. Lethargy burns off in the heat of a newly-discovered passion. Gypsy blood, long denied, sings to a moon, long ignored. And our life is suddenly taken galloping away from where we lived, from what we knew, from who we were.

Equestrian travel continues to thrill not because it has changed through the ages, but because it hasn't. It fulfils a craving for adventure, travel and excitement.

Thus, I leave you with this thought.

Truth seldom whispers to you and when it does the song is no louder than the beating of your heart. No one can travel this road for you. Only you can summon the courage to ride the sacred trail of which I speak.

So go on.

What's stopping you?

Read the book. Saddle your Horse. Explore the World.

Though his critics denounced him in 1925 as being "a lunatic," the young Swiss Long Rider Aimé Tschiffely successfully rode his Criollo horses 16,000 kilometres (10,000 miles) from Buenos Aires, Argentina to New York City. The intrepid equestrian explorer then wrote the most influential equestrian travel book of the twentieth-century, which in turn inspired generations of would-be Long Riders to follow his mounted example.

Overcoming opposition is the first challenge every would-be Long Rider faces. Prior to setting off to ride from Mexico to Panama in 2012, Orion Kraus struggled with various forms of opposition, including being publicly denounced on an internet travel forum. In the end he concluded, "Shall our perception of fear and risk overpower our desires and dreams? Anyone that has dealt with anxiety knows that this fear can be physically debilitating. Yet, it can be overcome. How do I know this? I am this! This is why I am riding. This is why this whole trip came about!" He later wrote, "Here I am, 3000 kilometres south from where I started and a changed man because of it."

Israeli Long Rider Kareen Kohn warned, "We pretend to be living freely, but when the clock ticks, enforced by custom and against our desire, we return to take up our part in a monstrous system. We have sacrificed our freedom for what: a roof, a meal, a colourful garment?"

In recognition of the dawning of a new age of equestrian exploration, Long Riders from five continents gathered in March, 2005 at the Royal Geographical Society in London. They were on hand to witness the presentation of the first set of equestrian travel classics known as the Long Rider Literary Collection. Published by the Long Riders' Guild Press, the Encyclopaedia of Equestrian Exploration represents the last major addition to this unique literary effort.

Chapter 2
Understanding the Journey

Why We Ride

All Long Riders have asked themselves, "Why set off on a difficult and often dangerous equestrian journey?" Likewise, it is a question that intrigues the pedestrians who meet us. "Why are you doing this?" they've asked us in a multitude of tongues in countries scattered around the globe. The answer to this ancient question is as complex as the wide variety of equestrian explorers represented by The Long Riders' Guild.

But before I discuss why we ride, let me comment on some related issues.

The Treasure of Travel Knowledge

During the last fifty years, the world has been reduced to mediocrity by travel machines. Great distances that would have defied our ancestors are now easily obtainable. Foreign lands have lost their mystery. Forbidden continents lie conquered in hours. Oceans are merely nuisances, overcome by a faceless pilot, as passengers struggle to stay awake during the second on-flight movie. The modern world defines travel in terms of jet lag instead of hardship. The dangers faced by countless early pioneers have been done away with. Modern adventurers fear a blow-out on the autobahn more than a robber in the woods.

Yet despite the changing calendar, the rigours faced by modern equestrian explorers closely resemble those known by their predecessors. Sadly, due to a variety of factors, including the onset of motorized transportation, there is a global lack of knowledge regarding equestrian travel. For 6,000 years brave men and women had been climbing onto horses and setting off in search of adventure and freedom. Yet despite being mankind's oldest link with the horse, this timeless equestrian legacy, and its attendant books full of accumulated knowledge, had nearly disappeared, not just from the market place, but from all human memory.

Just as that is an intellectual tragedy, in need of immediate repair, it brings with it a more immediate practical concern.

Whilst no one would attempt to fly a plane cross country without proper education, people think nothing of setting off across a continent on a horse without any training or preparation.

Thus, though you long to ride towards the horizon on your horse, you lack the basic information needed to do so. That is why you are attempting to learn before you go. As the story of the pretend Native American who tried to ride to Alaska mounted on his "sorrel" proves, 21st century people are all too apt to think they can simply purchase a horse and a hat and then muddle through.

Souls hardened

On the other hand, ask any Long Rider and he or she will tell you that equestrian journeys have a way of hardening your soul against adversity. You learn to dig down and push on when your road is a long one. This type of travel requires a special type of person, one who wishes to know the world intimately and to judge other people by first-hand experience.

It also brings you in direct contact with someone you should know more about – yourself.

It was the renowned modern camel and equestrian traveller, Arita Baaijens of Holland, who wrote, "The person I thought I was proved to be no more than the sum of what others thought of me. Having decided to quit my job, I felt a tremendous sense of relief. I was free as I had never been before, simply because I had nothing more to lose. Never again would I allow myself to be fenced in by convention and false certainties. From now on, I would rely on the voice of my heart."

Age is no Barrier

Just as there are no such things as national, religious, cultural, political or sexual restrictions against becoming a Long Rider, you will likewise find that there are no age limitations either.

Anyone familiar with the heroes of equestrian travel will have heard of the fabulous Abernathy Boys. Their names were Bud and Temple and they were once considered the most daring little Long Riders ever to set out on an adventure.

On their first equestrian journey in 1909 the tiny travellers, aged nine and five, encountered a host of Old West obstacles, including wolves and wild rivers, when they rode more than 1,000 miles from Oklahoma Territory to Santa Fe, New Mexico and back – ALONE!

The following year the brave brothers set their sights on New York City, which they reached after a month of hard riding. Along the way Orville Wright offered to take them up in his new-fangled airplane and President Taft gave them a warm welcome when they reached the White House. Kids envied them. Women adored them. Grown men pulled hair from their horses' tails to keep as souvenirs. This public frenzy culminated when Bud and Temple rode their Oklahoma ponies alongside Teddy Roosevelt and the Rough Riders in a victory parade witnessed by more than a million cheering New Yorkers.

Even though they were only six and ten years old, Temple and Bud Abernathy were a national sensation. In the summer of 1911, they did the impossible. They rode nearly 4,000 miles, from New York to San Francisco, in only sixty-two days. Once again, the Abernathy Boys had made a historic ride without any adult assistance and accomplished an equestrian feat which has never been equalled.

While such feats were to be admired, surely such astonishing children had long ago disappeared into history?

Yet soon after the Long Riders' Guild was formed, we received the startling news that the youngest person to qualify for entry was Hjoerdis Rickert. In 1986, with her parents walking alongside, this nine-year-old Swedish child had ridden 1200 miles from Le Puy, France, to Santiago de Compostella, Spain.

Next we learned about Fawn Fields, who rode bareback more than a thousand miles from Carlton, Texas to Prescott, Arizona. Fawn was five when she became a Long Rider.

Then we were informed about the ride Jessica Chitty made from Spain to Greece. Once again, the child had ridden while the parents walked beside. Nevertheless, Jessica was only three years old when she completed that three thousand mile journey.

Nor are the accomplishments of the valiant restricted to the young, as Long Riders have routinely set off on extraordinary journeys, even though others believe they should be confined to a rocking chair.

For example, Malcolm Darling was sixty-six years old in 1947 when he announced he was going to ride 2,500 kilometres (1,500 miles) across India. Because this former colony of the British Raj was due to become the separate countries of Pakistan and India in just a few months, the countryside was being torn apart by sectarian violence. However neither age nor religious intolerance kept this remarkable Long Rider at home.

Equestrian travel stories are full of adventures, adversities, dangers and drama. Yet the curious story of William Holt and his cart horse, Trigger, is one of the most inspiring equestrian travel tales ever told. After rescuing the gelding from slaughter, and then nursing him back to health, the 67-year-old Holt and his equally old horse set out in 1964 on an incredible 9,500 kilometre (6,000 mile), non-stop journey through Western Europe.

Holt never ranked himself above his mount. The resultant trip saw them sleeping out in the rough without a tent for more than 400 nights. Together they faced great hardships, suffering through storms, floods and whirlwinds. At one point in their travels the ageing pair were even marooned on a ledge and nearly drowned by the raging sea. Because of these shared dangers, Holt and Trigger maintained a legendary bond that touched people's hearts. An Italian princess had jewels set in one of Trigger's old shoes. When they rode into London the likeable duo were guests of the Queen of England.

Thus, regardless of their ages, Long Riders, both young and old, are by instinct those humans whom have summoned up the courage to take a life-changing journey on a horse that they love.

Ability – Not Disability

Not to take anything away from Neil Armstrong, the first human to walk on the moon, that was a lunar stroll in the park compared to the equestrian journey made by the Irish Long Rider Arthur Kavanagh, the man born with no limbs who rode to India.

Though descended from the ancient kings of Leinster, Arthur's birth in 1831 was initially thought by many to be a tragedy when it was discovered that the infant had been born with only tiny stumps instead of fully-formed arms and legs. Yet aided by a merciful doctor, and understanding parents, the child was reared to be so independent that it almost defies belief. Trained to have an indomitable sense of perseverance and an extraordinary amount of personal courage, Arthur, whose alert mental capacities far exceeded many so-called "normal" people, attended school where he studied art and the classics. Though he was sometimes carried across his father's vast estate on the back of a servant, Arthur also learned to move about the family mansion with the aid of a mechanical chair.

Yet it was his love of riding that unlocked the world to this adventurous young lad. Though he lacked limbs, Arthur's chest was muscular and his audacity was supreme. After long practice, he learned to use the stumps of his arms as if they were fingers. In this way, after having been strapped into a specially constructed chair saddle, Arthur could not only manage the reins, but could carry his whip as he rode to hounds and boldly jumped over the legendary and hazardous fences of his native Ireland.

While Arthur's life would be extraordinary by any reckoning, his status as an equestrian explorer is considered by The Long Riders' Guild to be the most astonishing account of the 19th century.

In 1846, at the age of fifteen, he accompanied his mother and older brother to Egypt, where they explored Cairo, ascended the Nile by boat and then journeyed on horseback overland across the deserts to Lebanon. It was during this journey that Arthur purchased, rode, and fell in love with his Arab horse.

"Poor beast, I cried the day I left him – he knew me so well. He used to lick my face when I came out of the tent in the morning to see him and at luncheon-time in the heat of the day, when I used to sit under him for shade, he would put his head between his front legs to take a bit of bread without moving for fear of hurting me," Arthur later wrote.

This desert sojourn was to prove to be of lasting importance, for in 1849 Arthur and older brother Tom set off for India. They went via Denmark, Norway and Sweden, before reaching Moscow, Russia. They then sailed down the Volga into Circassia. Here they mounted local horses and, carrying nothing but their guns, the daring brothers rode towards Persia.

In a remarkable entry in his diary, Arthur recalled, "The scenery is beautiful but the road villainous. In some places it is absolutely impassable to any but native beasts, as the path, about a foot broad and very slippery from the rain and mud, ran along the side of the mountain. Twice my horse slipped one of his hind feet over the side. If he had not recovered himself in a miraculous manner, he and I would have been dashed into a thousand pieces."

After avoiding bandits and surviving fevers, the courageous brothers reached India. In an amazing demonstration of his self-confidence, Arthur agreed with his brother Tom's decision to temporarily leave him in India. During the subsequent voyage, the elder Kavanagh died aboard ship, leaving Arthur stranded in India without funds. In what must count as the most remarkable act of equestrian confidence ever recorded, the unemployed and limbless Arthur Kavanagh obtained a job as an official government dispatch rider! In his spare time Arthur, always a keen hunter, bagged four tigers.

When notified of his financial situation, his family sent funds, allowing Arthur to sail home to Ireland. Upon his return, the now only surviving son became the heir to the ancient family estate. Soon afterwards, Arthur wed, went on to father four children, became a Member of Parliament and never lost his sense of humour.

"It's extraordinary," he once remarked to his hostess on arrival, "I haven't been here for five years but the station master recognized me!"

After spending a full life hunting, fishing, drawing, sailing his yacht and authoring a best-selling travel book, this inspiring man, and the most unique Long Rider in history, died of pneumonia in 1889.

Can't duplicate another trip

As Kavanagh demonstrates, though all of us face our personal physical challenges, courage and determination have helped humans to accomplish astonishing feats in the saddle. Now let me give you a quiet word of warning. Even though you can become inspired by another person's equestrian expedition, your journey must be your own.

That was the simple truth which Mary Bosanquet discovered when she set out in 1939 to ride from Vancouver, Canada, to New York. Along the way she was wooed by love-struck cowboys, chased by a grizzly bear and even suspected of being a Nazi spy, scouting out Canada in preparation for a German invasion. Despite her youth, Mary understood the singular nature of her ride.

"They did not seem to grasp the fact that you cannot copy a man's spirit. It is my own journey and no else's could be exactly like this. For no two people ever make the same journey. In a physical journey you know at what place you will eventually arrive. But in a journey of the mind you must not know where you are going; for if you do, all your travelling will only bring you back to where you started. You must follow humbly, letting the idea lead."

Riding through the Equestrian Brotherhood

On the other hand, give a thought to where your journey will take you, and by that I am not referring to the avoidance of dangers. Rather I am reminding you that one of the primary principles of safe horse travel is to always try and ride within the boundaries of an established equestrian culture.

When you are encased in the speeding steel tube called a car, you don't travel slowly enough to meet and speak to other people. There are no encounters at seventy miles per hour, only the isolation of man. Nor are mechanized societies prone to understand or tolerate you and your mount.

Academics are still trying to decide where and when man discovered the natural conditions which enabled him to become mounted. Why did that mounted event happen only after the end of the Ice Age, whereas the remains of recognizably human beings go back hundreds of thousands of years?

While we are still searching for those answers, we do know that the conditions needed to turn pedestrians into horse humans were to be found in the 'navel of the world' – the grasslands of Central Asia which became the cradle of the mounted way of life. It was after the post-glacial world, that offered mankind optimum climatic conditions for the life of the wandering stock-breeder, and permitted the herding of stock on the open range, and subsequently the riding of horses, which in turn eventually led to a mounted migration of mankind and ideas along that invisible line I call the Equestrian Equator.

Many ages have passed, yet equestrian traditions still run strong in numerous parts of the world, and it is those horse-friendly cultures which you should always seek. For example, when Australian Long Rider Tim Cope rode six thousand miles from Mongolia to Hungary, he discovered that ancient equestrian traditions still held sway.

"What steppe nomads lack in number, they make up for in hospitality. All along my route I was warmly welcomed by being presented with a bowl of kumis, or fermented mare's milk. This is a cultural legacy that dates back to the days when nomads first domesticated the horse, some time in the third millennium B.C. When I would resume my journey, my hosts would sprinkle kumis in my wake to wish me a safe journey."

Likewise, Long Riders have found that other traditional equestrian cultures are always more intrigued and hospitable than completely mechanized countries. When French Long Rider Jean Claude Cazade rode from France to Arabia, he and his Arab stallion stayed for a month at the Royal Horse Club in Amman, Jordan.

Thus, you will find that there is a sympathetic impression in the souls of other horse people, regardless of the obvious visual differences which separate you. Remember, even if they're not equestrian travellers, horse riders relish how their mounts make them feel like they are part of the world they are riding through. Thus, regardless of who first rode him, the horse has helped create a mounted celebration of mankind's diversity.

Understanding other Cultures

Yet let me warn you. Don't expect to encounter the same values regarding the treatment of horses or the issue of animal cruelty as can be found in Europe, North America or Australia. Despite the fact that all horsemen speak the same symbolic language, there is a strong chance they will not share your particular set of beliefs regarding a wide variety of cultural and culinary issues.

Such taboo topics might include never selling your saddle or eating your horse.

The South African Long Rider, Billy Brenchley, who set out to ride from the top to the bottom of the African continent, expressed this warning about the need to be polite and adaptable.

"We are not missionaries. Our goal is to be good ambassadors for our country and to come away having learnt as much as we can about the people that we meet. We are not there to tell them how to live their lives or to sit in judgment on them."

Thus, planning your trip through a horse-friendly environment is a positive first step. Yet while you must do everything within your power to protect your own horse during the course of the trip, you must leave any naive feelings of native cultural superiority at home. Instead, you should set out on this horse trip to seek knowledge, not to push your own cultural opinions on people who have the right to disagree with the personal views you hold based on your own limited understanding of a vast and culturally diverse planet.

Reasons to Ride

Equestrian travel is not merely about covering vast amounts of mileage. It is the journey you and your horse take together to reach borders of an otherwise invisible place. Though you are ostensibly aiming toward a spot on a physical map, you will find that you are seeking Elsewhere. Such a journey is about change as much as discovery. When you saddle your horse and set off you will be exposed to strange customs, sights and people. Curiosities that both attract and repel await you. Having told you these things, let us investigate some of the primary reasons people have set off, across the ages, in search of answers.

Reason One – The Personal Pilgrimage

Would you be surprised if I told you that the legendary star pilot, Luke Skywalker, would have been a perfect Long Rider?

I was twenty-three years old when the original *Star Wars* movie was released in 1977. Like Luke, I found myself being held prisoner on my own private Tattoine, that desolate and hopeless planet he was forced by circumstances to reside on. I have never forgotten the symbiotic pang of pain I felt when Luke stood looking up alone at the night sky. Like him, I too was longing to be somewhere else, wishing I were free of the claustrophobic confines of regulated society.

While George Lucas can't take credit for making me an equestrian explorer, we can congratulate him for having painted such a brilliant cinematic image of a soul, like mine was at the time, longing to be free. Nor is this film maker the first to understand and attempt to relate such a significant tale.

So long as humans have been hunkering around campfires, there have been inspiring legends of those few brave ones who ignored caution and made their own way. Disregard the numerical year and look instead at the theme. What do you find? Jason sailed away in search of the Golden Fleece. Bellerophon rode winged Pegasus. Moses walked up the holy mountain and came back with commandments. Aimé Tschiffely risked his life riding to New York.

These are all accounts depicting the plight of a "normal" person, like you, who left the safety of "home," and having overcome numerous trials and temptations, underwent a personal transformation. Such tales bring into play the eternal themes of self-reliance, loyalty, resolve and valour. Plus, unlike Moses and Jason, who walked and sailed to their goals, Long Riders have the added power of the semi-magical horse to carry them on their journey of self-discovery.

Sadly, the modern horse world has abandoned the mysterious for the banal and by doing so has failed to connect with people's longings and strangled the once vibrant spirit of the explorer. Yet regardless of how complex and civilized the world has become, the raw pain in some of our souls won't be assuaged until we have trusted our instincts and set off in pursuit of an often-dim personal goal. Such a traveller on horseback learns the trip is like a mountain, the higher and longer you go, the further you see.

Reason Two - Life is short

If Reason One is dominated by youth, Reason Two is the realm of maturity. There comes a time when we realize with a shock that our life isn't about time passing, it's about what little time remains. Close behind that discovery comes the conclusion that life is about time, not things.

Such a dual conclusion was reached by the fictional character, Shirley Valentine, who having reached mid-life, suddenly realized her most precious gift was about to be lost.

"I've lived such a little life and even that will be over pretty soon. I have allowed myself to lead this little life, while inside me there was so much more. And it's all gone unused. And now it never will be. Why do we get all this life if we never use it? Why do we get all these feelings, and dreams, and hopes that we never use? That's where I've disappeared to. I got lost in all this unused life," Shirley said sadly.

Often the legend of heroic quest involves a young person, who leaves home to embark on a spiritual, intellectual, emotional and physical journey. Yet as I have already demonstrated, age is never a hindrance to Long Riders. Sometimes people have been forced by circumstances to spend years attending to the needs of others before the moment arrives when they're free at last to pursue their dreams of terrestrial freedom. It is when we reach such a chronological crossroad that a person glimpses the eternal, realizes the frailty of their shell and decides to ignore the ancestral falsehoods which have kept them confined for years.

For example, it was the great French Long Rider Jean-Francois Ballereau who, having spent the majority of the last half of the twentieth century exploring the world on horseback, despaired of being trapped in a civilization "drowning in asphalt." Regardless of his age, and ignoring any danger, he preferred an adventure over the suburbs. "At least the adventure is real," he wrote.

There is, therefore never a point when you have to resign yourself to not participating in life.

Reason Three – The Horse

After completing her journey, North American Long Rider Andi Mills wrote a moving personal account which tried to explain what had motivated her to undertake a dangerous ride across the Mojave Desert and the American Southwest. In an article entitled *Why? Little Word, Complex Answer*, Andi began by saying, "Making the decision to do an equestrian journey is the first step down an unmarked path that will change your life forever."

Like many others, Andi was constantly questioned as to why she would want to undertake such a rigorous ride across such a harsh landscape.

Andi had valid reasons ready to hand.

"When I was asked why I wanted to walk out of my life for six months to ride my horse, I truthfully answered that I wanted to fulfil a childhood dream. And I told them that I was doing the ride for stroke awareness and to educate on the value of early detection of strokes."

Those were accurate answers; but they were uttered before she ever swung into the saddle. What Andi didn't understand until well into the journey was that she was undergoing an unexpected emotional renaissance.

"My vision changed dramatically. The first one thousand miles drove home the realization that the destination is not nearly as important as the journey to reach it. I learned the cavernous difference between "needs" and "wants." I learned, not only to endure and overcome difficulties, but to truly embrace them for the valuable lessons they teach me."

What she also discovered was that despite having spent her life with horses, the journey required her to spend all her time with her gelding, Jericho. The physical hardships they overcame together gave Andi a new perspective on the horse-human relationship.

"At some indefinable point, my trusty gelding, Jericho, and I ceased to be two separate entities. We were each an extension of the other, neither one complete alone. We learned to trust each other for our safety and comfort. It was a seamless melding of the two spirits so complete, you could no longer define us as individuals. We had become a Centaur."

A transformed woman bearing the same name returned from that journey and wrote, "By the time my journey came to an end, I no longer held any illusions about myself. I knew exactly who I was and exactly who I was not. How many people live and die, not knowing that simple truth?"

Reason Four - Charities, Campaigns and Crusades

Most Long Riders are individualists and while a few may welcome media attention, the majority of them shun publicity.

Long Riders have made journeys for a wide variety of reasons, including raising money for various types of medical research, educational efforts and others. While every one of these efforts was in itself worthwhile, you do not need to justify the journey. Riding for a cause complicates the journey. It detracts from the daily events. It intrudes upon your time. It forces you to be a book keeper, when your number one duty is to your horse. And the further you travel, the further away will seem the cause which you once held dear. By all means ride. And ride for a cause, if you hold it dear. Just don't think that you need to have a crusade in order to justify the journey.

The journey is the cause!

Yet if you do indeed have a strong cause, then your journey can make a difference for those around you.

However, you must also be very aware that people will donate and support a cause because of their personal interaction and belief in you. Rest assured that they have already heard of whatever charitable action you are supporting. And chances are they may not have previously supported it. Your arrival ignites a great deal of excitement, so in an effort to show their support, and maintain a bit of the magic which you brought into their lives, they will want to know how the campaign turned out. Their initial donation of trust, money and energy generates an intense sense of loyalty, concern and curiosity. Consequently at the conclusion of your journey you must make a clear public accounting of what funds were raised, how they were spent, etc. Not to do so not only imperils your own reputation, it also adds to the chances of other Long Riders being viewed with scepticism thanks to your post-journey indifference.

There are several cases of this type of behaviour. In the immediate wake of the 9-11 tragedy, an American rode from the Alamo to New York's "Ground Zero," all the while playing upon the people's feelings of patriotism. One small-town merchant, for example, provided several thousand dollars worth of celebratory tee-shirts, which were never paid for. Two other travellers made journeys connected to raising money for a college scholarship fund and a disabled riding centre. In both cases no public accounting was ever revealed, which in turn resulted in emails being sent to The Long Riders' Guild for years afterwards wherein donors expressed their dismay at not being told what had happened to the money. In the age of the internet, doubts about your personal integrity will not disappear into the sunset after you step down from the saddle. Emails will be circulated. Questions will be asked. Doubts will be raised. So do the right thing. Tell the public how the campaign ended.

Reasons Five and Six - Curiosity and Loss

As long as humans have ridden horses, people have been intrigued enough by a sense of geographic, cultural, spiritual or political curiosity to ride off in a sense of discovery. It may be no more than what is over the mountain. It might entail undertaking a ride like the one made by the young German Lieutenant, Erich von Salzmann, who rode 6,000 kilometres (3,700 miles) from Tientsin, China to Tashkent, Uzbekistan in 1903. He made this remarkable ride, including crossing the Gobi Desert, in only 173 days.

What drove him to do it? We don't know. But remember, von Salzmann chose to make his ride.

That is why I have not included military or commercial travellers, because they are not responding to motivations. They are following orders, or commercial requirements, handed down by a higher authority. That is not what you are reading about. You're studying to be a Long Rider, not a cavalryman.

Finally, there is loss.

The most touching recent example of this occurred to the North American Long Rider, Linda Losey, whose young son was lost in a tragic accident. In order to reconnect with her own soul, this young woman rode 5,000 kilometres (3,000 miles) "ocean to ocean." As Linda demonstrates, the motivation for your journey might be a tremendous tragedy. Yet as this brave mother proved, resolve leads to emotional resurrection.

Summary

Which of you has not longed for an existence free of the dull checks and balances of how life has defined you - a clerk of mediocrity, a cog in the wheel of some nameless corporate giant, the definition of your tribal soul mirrored by the brand name you wear, or drive, or strive for?

Historically Long Riders were not like that. They were Argonauts on horseback that would rather die than live like drones in the hive.

Mankind is still the same. Little has changed since Cheops tricked, cajoled and enslaved thousands of others into building his pyramid. Every man and woman still must realize, and then define, his or her own individual fear. Lest I am accused of preaching some obsolete picture of ancestral courage, let me ask each of you to deny the existence of that embryo of adventure that sleeps inside each of your stillborn hearts.

Our time will seem as romantic in 1,000 years to the effete descendents of this current generation. Yet still you linger, believing those cowards who say that all the mountains have been climbed, all the white spots on the map have been defined, all the courage ever needed was long ago spent by your grandparents. Such thoughts are not for Long Riders, they are for those who prefer to live life on motorized wheels full of emptiness. The world still belongs to those brave enough to venture out into its unknown dangers, and horses still stand eager and willing to take us there. The map of your life is yours alone to draw.

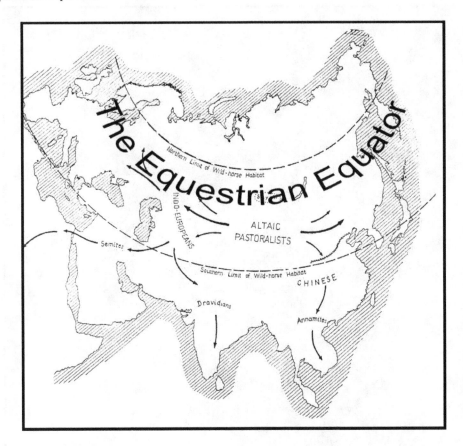

Academics are still trying to decide where and when man discovered the natural conditions which enabled him to become mounted. Why did that mounted event happen only after the end of the Ice Age, whereas the remains of recognizably human beings go back hundreds of thousands of years?

Becoming a Long Rider brings you in direct contact with someone you should know more about – yourself. Arita Baaijens of Holland, who rode through the Altai Mountains, wrote, "The person I thought I was proved to be no more than the sum of what others thought of me. From now on, I would rely on the voice of my heart."

Temple (left) and Bud Abernathy rode alongside Teddy Roosevelt and the Rough Riders in a victory parade witnessed by more than a million cheering New Yorkers. The following summer, even though they were only seven and eleven years old, they rode from New York to San Francisco, in only sixty-two days.

Little Long Rider Jessica Chitty was only three years old when she qualified to become the youngest person ever admitted into the Guild by making a 5000 kilometre (3000 mile) ride from Spain to Greece aboard her donkey, Hamilcar.

Being sixty-seven years old didn't stop Bill Holt from riding his aged cart horse, Trigger, 9500 kilometres (6000 miles) across Europe.

Despite being born with only tiny stumps instead of fully formed arms and legs, it was his love of riding that unlocked the world to Arthur Kavanagh. The adventurous young man rode from Circassia, across Persia and on to India, where he became a government dispatch rider and hunted tigers.

North American Long Rider Andi Mills made an important discovery during her journey. "At some indefinable point, my trusty gelding, Jericho, and I ceased to be two separate entities. We had become a Centaur."

Chapter 3
No Preparation, No Success

The Deceptive Lure

The idea of equestrian travel is always romantic, because one never realizes what lies ahead. There is instead a hazy notion of you and your horse riding peacefully across a nature-filled landscape. In such an equestrian reverie you never think about where you're going to sleep at night, because the sun is always shining. Nor do you give any thought to what you and your mount are going to eat, because in your daydream you're too busy being happy.

Yet time after time, decade after decade, and now century after century, history has demonstrated that those who fail to plan more often than not never reach their goal. Or, even worse, they kill or injure their horses because of their own arrogance, sloth and stupidity.

For example, at first glance one may wonder how qualified were the two young men who set off from a Texas border town bound for Mexico City in 1931. Joe Goodwin was a recent college graduate, who was hungry for a taste of peril. His companion, Robert Horiguichi, was the sophisticated son of an imperial Japanese diplomat. To say the two mismatched, would-be equestrian explorers were unprepared for the deserts, quicksand and brigands they encountered in the Mexican wilderness would be a mild understatement. Luckily before leaving the Lone Star state they had procured what they believed were the necessities, including a canteen, an old pistol and a typewriter to chronicle their adventures. They survived – barely.

Likewise when Mary Bosanquet tried to ride across Canada later that century, her only planning had consisted of reading Robert Louis Stevenson's *Travels with a Donkey*. Like her predecessors, Mary had trusted that things would work out. What she discovered instead was that she had started too late in the year, chosen the wrong route and bought the wrong horse.

Nor did this new century begin without its share of equestrian travel embarrassments.

A stark example was the young English woman who announced in 2007 that she was going to ride from London to Tokyo. After obtaining a number of donated pieces of equipment from leading suppliers, she set off full of hope and lack of experience.

It didn't take long for disaster to find her. First her would-be companion quit. So she struggled across southern England alone, with her saddle sliding out of place and gear tumbling to the ground. After taking the ferry to France, things became even harder.

Lacking the necessary linguistic and tactical skills, she managed to ride briefly into France but then abandoned the journey altogether and returned home.

What makes such people think they can just get on a horse and travel across immense distances?

In cases like this what we're dealing with is a trainload of fantasy and a thimbleful of reality.

Hollywood Doesn't Help

Horse travel isn't like science fiction. When you watch Godzilla attack Tokyo you understand that what you're seeing isn't reality. Yet while attempting to entertain us, film makers all too often provide poor equestrian travel examples. I could supply you with any number of famous movies which depict equestrian travellers who have ignored the basic physical laws of which we speak. Take the film *Lady Hawk*, during which Rutger Hauer rides his magnificent Friesian stallion across the landscape during a week of continuous travel. The horse is never fed or watered. Mind you, when Rutger isn't being turned into a wolf, he is busy trying to romance Michelle Pfeiffer and such things tend to distract one.

Yet the Long Rider Razzberry Award for the worst cinematic equestrian travel depicted in a modern movie undoubtedly belongs to *Gladiator*, starring Russell Crowe. Whereas hokey 1930s movies would often portray jolly cowboys sitting around late night campfires drinking coffee and eating beans, which had mysteriously appeared without the benefit of a pack horse, that fairy tale was a minor excursion into culinary fantasy compared to Crowe's gladiatorial romp across Europe. Early in the story the movie depicts a wounded Russell Crowe mounting a stolen horse, and grabbing a second mount to pull behind. He then sets off hell for leather across a winter's landscape in northern Germany, bound for his family farm in distant Spain. While ignoring the departure in logic which this action depicts, we can focus on the equestrian reality involved instead, as this hasty Roman general, who is supposedly a tough, seasoned campaigner, has departed with nothing but an attractive fur robe draped over his shoulders. He carries no food or shelter for himself and not a scrap for the two horses.

What we have instead are stirring scenes which depict Russell Crowe looking very determined as he gallops towards distant Spain. Magically, though there are no road signs, nor any indication of other Europeans, our hero never falters nor becomes lost. A series of scenes shows him instead mislaying the robe, looking tired and losing one horse as the German trees are mysteriously replaced by sandy-looking terrain. There is one obligatory scene where this pensive fellow is seen staring into a campfire. How he lit it, nor why he isn't dancing around in torment from hunger, is not explained.

Finally, his agony, and ours, is completed when he concludes his journey by managing to ride the second horse to death just as his family farm is seen on the horizon. In this Hopkinesque departure from the reality of equestrian travel, the Roman rider has crossed Europe in two days, with no equipment, and brutally ridden two horses to death in the process. That's the misleading and vile equestrian fantasy which Hollywood would have you believe is not only possible – but acceptable.

But equestrian travel isn't like Star Trek or the Gladiator. You don't just walk into the transporter beam or jump into the saddle, then magically reappear thousands of miles away. Which begs the question, what happens when real life fools set off on horses?

Cinematic Repercussions

During the 19th and early 20th century organizations such as the Royal Geographical Society held up renowned explorers such as Frederick George Jackson as examples of personal bravery, scientific endeavour, community spirit and careful expedition planning. Nor was it only men who were worthy of respect, for it was the fantastically brave English Long Rider, Isabella Bird, whose equestrian journeys in Hawaii, the Rocky Mountains, Japan, Persia and Tibet prompted the all-male RGS to elect the diminutive equestrian explorer to become the first female Fellow of that organisation.

But starting in the 1920s, there was a plague of young Americans who began racketing around the world, not only ignorantly but often arrogantly. In the footsteps of Marco Polo was one of their favourite themes. Poor Polo could have filed a hefty claim for extra travel expenses to some of the outlandish places he was alleged to have been. Upon their return, the tone of the traveller's recitals all too often emphasized discomfort, in other words, incompetence – "where I got bitten by lice, where I had to endure a cocktail without ice." In other words having a horrid time became their licence for giving lectures. Few of them brought back any information worth having and the public eventually lost interest in such exploits.

Sadly, with the recent appearance of so-called "reality television" we are observing the resurrection of this decrepit, and deliberately deceptive, cinematic formula. Nor are the Americans the only ones now guilty, for the once-sanctified halls of English exploration are now bustling with fame-seekers pretending to be explorers. One British national has made a career out of jumping out of hot air balloons wearing a tuxedo, wandering through the bush drinking his urine, or pretending he's been forced to survive on road kill and bugs. In fact, while supposedly living rough in the bush, an alert reporter found the lacklustre explorer actually downing a big blueberry pancake breakfast in the air-conditioned comfort of a local motel.

While I don't care what this gentleman eats, The Long Riders' Guild takes grave exception when cartoon explorers include horses into their money-making, fame-seeking schemes. A recent sordid example comes to mind; the Brit who set off to ride across Mongolia. Having apparently never bothered to study equestrian travel, he didn't realize it was a bad idea to tie up his horses and leave them while he wandered off to attend a party at a nearby town. During his ill-advised lengthy absence, the horses were eaten to death by insects.

This so-called "explorer" peddled his equestrian tragedy in print, thereby profiting from his foolishness, all the while he boldly violated and exploited the ethics of the animals whose lives he had wasted.

Because of a vacuum in global exploration leadership, glory-seeking individuals such as this will continue to enrich themselves and deceive the public into believing that they can follow Russell Crowe's example and just jump on a horse without any plan or preparation. The difference is that when a cartoon explorer includes a horse into his pretentious fantasy, the horse suffers, is maltreated or dies. As this book amply demonstrates, there is danger a plenty awaiting you. But not of the type you are expecting and it appears before you ever walk out of your door. What you have to do is forget Hollywood and focus instead on surviving the harsh equestrian realities which await you.

An Undisclosed Danger

Earlier in this book I told you about the pretend Indian I met who wanted to ride to Alaska. That was fine, I thought, until I discovered he had the wrong horse, wrong saddle, no previous experience, no equipment and no money. All he had was a dream, an inarticulate longing to travel that had forced him to leave his wife, children and job and set off towards the mythical north during the winter of 1999. Looking at him, wearing his beautiful fringed buckskin coat, his chest bare, and his eyes proud, I knew what he didn't know. The Long Grey Road, that sultry siren, had bewitched him with her alluring song of nomadic freedom. The would-be traveller had cast everything away to seek adventure and spiritual fulfilment with his horse.

A grand dream?

A worthy enterprise?

Another fool, just like I had been twenty years earlier when I stood on the dusty plains outside Bamiyan, Afghanistan with a horse, a saddle, a dream and not enough equestrian travel knowledge to fill a tinker's pocket.

So he and I both failed, as we were destined to do and for basically the same reason. Because though our two journeys lay separated by 20 years and 13,000 miles, our lives had intersected at the exact same moment.

We wanted the Road.

We longed for the Road.

We were neophytes ready to worship the Road.

And we were in turn rejected because of our ignorance and folly.

What neither that unprepared fellow nor I knew was that our desire to travel to the ends of the Earth was not enough. We could not see the fate of those who went before us. We had only an inkling of a spiritual and geographical longing. But we lacked the concrete knowledge of how to saddle and ride that treacherous wildcat called the Road. Thus, though we both had higher interests, the pretend Indian and I failed, because we had set out in haste and thereby innocently misused a special equestrian gift.

Instead our cherished dreams of reaching Alaska and Afghanistan were slain in the cradle by the harsh, unrelenting cruelties of equestrian travel. Yes, that long-ago fellow and I both rode through the fires of punishment but it was our horses that paid the penalty for our sins.

Thus the greatest initial danger is that you will set out unprepared. When you do, equestrian travel disasters happen – even to experts.

Even Experts Fail

In the midst of the 19th century, during what is known as the "Heroic Age of Exploration," master travellers, such as Francis Galton, published dire warnings about what awaited ill-prepared amateurs.

"An expedition is daily exposed to a succession of accidents, any one of which might be fatal to its further progress. The horses may at any time stray, die or be stolen; water may not be reached; one of the party may become ill, or the party may be attacked by natives. Hence the success of the expedition depends on a chain of eventualities, each link of which must be a success; for if one link fails, at that point, there must be an end to further advance," Galton cautioned.

But the perils of equestrian travel are so many, and the need to prepare in advance so great, that a failure to educate oneself in advance even caused some of the world's best equestrian travellers to suffer tremendous losses. This admonition is based not just on personal experience but on grave historical fact.

In the British military expedition of 1903 to Lhasa, 185 riding animals and 1,372 pack ponies were enlisted. Of those, 24 riding ponies and 899 pack ponies lost their lives. This equates to 65.5 percent of the pack ponies being lost, a fact that the British army did everything in their power to keep from happening as the soldiers' very lives depended on the survival of as many horses as possible.

With grazing on the Tibetan plateau always scarce, the normally equine-savvy English soldiers believed they were allowing their down-country horses to eat what appeared to be a harmless local plant. In fact many of the horses died during the Tibetan trip as a result of eating aconite, a poisonous plant better known in the British Isles as wolfsbane. Terrible conditions of the icy trail killed hundreds more. These pre-existing conditions decimated horses in an army that not only routinely included countless horses and pack mules, it also employed thousands of knowledgeable horsemen.

Yet horse deaths and accidents occurred then, despite their immense collective knowledge and the best intentions of the riders in charge.

The death of the horses in Tibet drives home this all-important point.

None of us know all the answers and when you venture away from home, you know even less. That is why no old time Rocky Mountain mule packer can tell you what to do in the wilds of Mongolia when you're sick with dysentery, the horses are going hungry and you're so weak you can barely stand, much less ride to the nearest village to try and communicate with the natives so as to arrange for fodder.

And I hasten to add to those old salts that "ain't never lost a hoss," that you've either been very lucky or never travelled in extremely dangerous foreign climes under harsh conditions. Remember, as conditions deteriorate in a foreign country, so does the benefit of any previous domestic equestrian experience.

None of the British horsemen stuck in the cold mountains of Tibet wanted to see their mounts die. And more importantly, their own chances of survival decreased with every equestrian death. Yet history tells us that they made the elementary mistake of allowing their mounts to graze on a poisonous plant they knew back in England by another name, yet failed to recognize in Tibet. And hundreds of other horses perished from nothing more preventable than slipping to their deaths from icy trails.

These fatal mistakes illustrate a critical point.

Don't think that you've got your equestrian act together because back home you ride your passive fat pony around the ring once a week, or every summer you lead a bunch of soft saddle butt hunters and a string of old pack horses for a 100 mile round trip jaunt through the nearby national forest. Equestrian exploration will surprise you. If it does you may be lucky and only your horse will die. If you're not lucky, you'll die too.

Thus, if one is preparing to set off on an equestrian exploration, then you must be inured in advance to the idea that penalties occur from inexperience, that nature is unforgiving, that the rider's lack of planning may have direct results on the horse's well-being, health and even life, that in short, horses may die or be injured before the outcome of the journey is achieved.

The cost of irresponsible dreaming

So if cavalrymen fail, what happens when amateurs attempt a journey without proper preparation? For example, what about the eager French woman who set off to ride round-trip from France to China, having never given a thought about how she was going to get the horses across the various antagonistic international borders en route? What happened? She never reached China.

The topic of preparation was a dilemma which the British Long Rider Mary Pagnamenta pondered when she made her ride across both islands of New Zealand. After having spent an immense amount of time carefully preparing for her 2001 journey, Mary had little patience with those who "followed their dream at the expense of the horses."

"One of the things that has upset me are the number of times I encountered tales of people trying to do something similar to my journey without having the basic knowledge needed to honour their commitment to their horses. At every stopping point I heard stories of people who had got into trouble; ill equipped, with unbalanced packs tied on with string, under prepared and unfit horses, and inadequate skills. I learned about horses suffering from gross saddle sores, in bad condition, with shoes hanging off. I heard of rude and inconsiderate riders who did nothing but waste the time and exhaust the patience of those who live and work in this exacting country," she wrote.

Mary issued this stern warning to would-be Long Riders.

"Too often, when horses are used, the journey ends up being at their expense. Instead I would say, if horses are involved leave your dream where it belongs, in the vacant hours, or follow it on a bicycle. Because more often than not the horses suffer as a consequence of the rider's failure to learn the necessary skills and make adequate preparations. Don't go following a dream unless you are prepared to put your back into learning what is needed first – and that does not mean a six month course of riding lessons. It means acquiring a far wider range of skills, including the time to find out your horses' needs, psychological as well as physical, before you start. It means being prepared to change your route and timetable as necessary to work within the horse's best interest. And it means putting your horses first at all time, however tired, wet and footsore you may be."

As these examples demonstrate, good intentions do not make for prudent and successful equestrian expeditions.

Equestrian Exploration Education

The best defence against the problem of equestrian disaster is EEE - Equestrian Exploration Education. The more background information you can soak up before your departure the better are your chances to succeed in a journey near home or a life-threatening ride across the wilds. More importantly, such education not only translates into a greater chance of expedition success, it greatly augments the very survival of the animals you cherish so highly to begin with.

The first thing you need to do therefore is match your dreams against your skills.

Equestrian travel has no room for false heroism. It is about preparation. To face the unknown perils of the road without knowledge or skill brings only hardship, suffering, injury and possible death to you and your horses.

Nor is this a new discovery.

In 1938 English Long Rider Edward Percy Stebbing completed work on a now-rare book entitled *Cross Country Riding*. In addition to sharing the wisdom gained from years of riding in India and England, the author recalled how his equestrian travel experiences had been of immense importance during his command of the previous year's "Long Distance Ride." This was a splendid, but now forgotten, event where hundreds of equestrians rode from all points of England so as to gather in a grand ceremony in southern Britain.

A host of British horse riders set out from eight starting points, bound for a central meeting place at Eastbourne. Not only were the editors of the sponsoring magazine, *Country Life,* surprised that more than twice as many people as expected decided to ride across Southern England, they also reported that one contestant came from as far away as Norway. Nor was age a factor, as the oldest rider was 76 and the youngest only 11 years old.

When reviewing that successful event, and his own equestrian travels on two widely diverse continents, Stebbing issued this caution.

"Despite its need for on-going simplicity, an equestrian expedition must be organised with precision. You need conviction in the merit of your objective and a great deal of persistence. But don't risk spoiling the journey by going off into the blue insufficiently equipped – by which is meant here with no knowledge of the country you propose to ride over, and with no practical knowledge of how to do for your horse. It is essential that you should possess this practical knowledge. The projected outcome cannot be compared with any other type you have undertaken, because in this case you have your horse to remember, and he must come first throughout the trip. On arrival at the night's resting-place, it is the horse and his well-being that has to be first attended to," Stebbing wrote.

Likewise, at the conclusion of her perilous journey across Persia in the late 19th century, the English Long Rider Ella Sykes recalled, "Advance preparation proved my salvation later on, and made me realize that the more trouble one takes beforehand, the more successful a journey is likely to be."

Unlike Ella, you will succeed by mastering a combination of the best of the so called "primitive" techniques which she and Stebbing knew, along with a dash of modern 21st century technology. Yet these basic laws of equestrian travel still hold true, then and now.

Adventures occur due to inexperience.

Recklessness will jeopardize your journey.

Determination is not enough.

Luck will not get you through

The goal must be clearly defined.

Preparation is all important.

Planning must be meticulous.
Time spent learning is never wasted.
And don't forget.
Be careful who you talk to.

The Danger of Advice

Let me say this again. The Guild cautions every would-be Long Rider to not take advice from anyone who has not ridden a minimum of 500 miles in a straight line on a non-stop equestrian journey. If they haven't ridden that far, they're not qualified to offer you or anyone else advice about equestrian travel. A lot of these well-meaning people attempt to give Long Riders "advice" based on what they honestly believe are the same equestrian circumstances under which they labour. Their advice is usually misplaced, albeit sincere. That is what the Anglo-Irish Long Rider Hugh MacDermott learned when he tried to ride across Chile and Argentina.

"At the moment I'm having a minor nightmare with my gaucho friends. They have a worldview that no one else in the world knows anything worth knowing about horses except themselves. I've tried explaining the reasons behind yours and the other Long Riders' advice and the fact that you have experience behind you but I might as well try and explain it to a pile of rocks. I now just say "Tienes razon" (you have a point) and ignore them every time they criticize me," Hugh wrote.

What Hugh discovered was the shocking truth that traditional equestrian cultures like the Gaucho, Cowboy and Cossacks are gone, replaced by descendants who wear the clothes but have lost most of their forefathers' knowledge regarding equestrian travel. English Long Rider Keith Clark found the same to be true when he also rode in the same part of Latin America.

"I've found in South America that the truck has killed off the network that used to be there even a short while ago for travelling by horse. Even a lot of the trails have fallen into disuse and it only takes a year or two for them to become overgrown and impassable, or as often happens here, fenced in. Plus, the gauchos of the Argentinean pampas have long ago succumbed to the internal combustion engine. They are now more of a romantic ideal," Keith wrote from the Argentine.

The need to be wary about listening to others is not geographically restricted. When North American Long Rider DC Vision was invited to step down from the saddle during the midst of his 22,500 kilometre (14,000 mile) ride, his audience of "back country horsemen" ended up lecturing the seasoned veteran on what he was doing wrong.

On a similar occasion, after having survived his ride across the African continent, Scottish Long Rider Gordon Naysmith recalled discovering some shocking reading on the subject of equestrian advice.

"Back to bed, where I read one of my host's many equitation books. The book informs me that I am doing many things incorrectly on this trip. All I can say is that the writers should go on a long ride themselves before venturing such an opinion," recalled the doughty Scotsman, who went on to ride 20,000 kilometres (12000 miles) from the tip of Africa to Austria.

Though more than thirty years separated Gordon in Africa from Hugh in Chile, they had both encountered the same entrenched equestrian point of view. While well meaning, most horse owners and riders are ignorant about the requirements of equestrian travel. They've never ridden more than 100 miles from home in any direction. Yet in their arrogance they will demean what they don't know.

Nor should you waste time arguing, as such people are rooted in extreme equestrian formalism. When you tell them about your needs and plans, they react like cattle who hear the sounds but cannot decipher the words. Though mounted, their allegiance is to the traditions of their ancestors, even if those were void of travel wisdom.

If you can't trust gauchos and cowboys, who can you trust?

As of the time this book is being written, only the extremely knowledgeable Canadian Long Rider, Stan Walchuk, offers a class in horse travel. Though limited to North America and the Rocky Mountains, not overseas situations, Stan's lessons are based on Long Rider principles which hold true in any clime.

But before you consider rushing off to Canada, there are fundamentals which you have to tackle yourself.

Concept and Pre-Planning

Let me warn you that the primary aim of your equestrian expedition should be perfectly clear and concise, both to you and anyone asking questions. You need to know where you are going and how you will get there. Consequently, these are some of the questions you should be considering.

Do you have the required equestrian skill needed to make a journey?

Where will you be riding from and to?

How many miles will you ride and walk?

How many horses will you employ?

Will you require a pack horse?

Will you employ a supply vehicle?

Who will ride with you?

Are they qualified to attend?

How will you keep the expedition fed and shod?

Do you have the proper riding and pack saddles?

What measures have you taken regarding governmental interference?

While you're still struggling to answer those questions, permit me to provide information regarding one of the living legends of expedition planning.

The Long Riders' Guild enjoys the friendship of one of the most talented expedition leaders of the last fifty-plus years. His name is Colonel John Blashford-Snell and over the course of the last forty years he has led expeditions all over the globe in conjunction with the organization he started, the Scientific Exploration Society. JBS, as he is commonly known in the exploration world, was still a serving British Army officer when he led an expedition from the top of Alaska to the bottom of Patagonia. Though he was ostensibly taking Land Rovers on this journey, when JBS came to the edge of the notorious Darien Gap jungle, he employed pack horses to help in the crossing of that deadly green hell.

The story of how JBS and his horses managed to survive will appear further on in the section devoted to equine jungle travel. Yet one of the primary reasons the seasoned Englishman's expedition eventually rolled their Land Rovers onto the Patagonian beach was because this master traveller understood the need to do his expedition home-work. Though his insights into "reconnaissance" were made before the development of GPS mapping technology, the explorer recognized the need to make every effort prior to your departure.

"Time spent on reconnaissance is seldom wasted," JBS wrote. "If you are unable to visit the region before your expedition I strongly suggest that you make a study of the best maps available. The paramount need for a good reconnaissance or if that is not possible the search for accurate and up-to-date information on such matters as local government, our embassy or consulate, a basic idea of the lines of communication involved, the likely base camp, availability and accessibility of local transport, knowledge of local food supplies, the nature of communications to be employed and whether they are permitted by the government, medical facilities. Secondly, a good appreciation of the fact that any expedition abroad is at the invitation of the country concerned and that we, the foreigners, are subject to their laws and dependent upon their hospitality. Thus a knowledge and understanding of languages, customs, religions, politics and the people is most important. Only by knowing what is involved can appropriate respect be paid."

He continued, "The successful expedition starts its planning early and allows for delays, inflation, frustration and bureaucracy. It takes into account things like the need for a balance between scientific fieldwork and the exploratory aim. It is also aware of the effect of attrition in the second half of a medium or long duration expedition. This factor alone is extremely important. It means in practice that after about six weeks of a really tough expedition most people start to run down. It is this phase where accidents can occur most easily."

So, have you given any thought to the logistics of your journey? Where will you obtain food for you and the horses? Who will shoe your mount? Does the country you plan on riding through even have a cultural practice of shoeing horses? What about equipment repairs? Can you adapt your plans to suit changes in weather and topography? If the situation demands it, can you be a flexible leader capable of keeping the expedition going?

Necessary Knowledge

While you're considering those expedition and equestrian issues, let me tell you one thing that you can not neglect; languages.

Don't think you can buy a Berlitz language course and learn how to say in Turkish "Can I please lodge my horse in your barn for the night"? Don't think that tourist language courses are going to provide you with words like stallion, gelding, saddle, oats, or even veterinarian. Foreign language courses are for tourists going to the opera, not equestrian explorers trying to stay alive in Africa.

For those of you who face severe linguistic challenges, the Long Riders' Guild developed a special Equestionary. Located in the Appendix section of the *Horse Travel Handbook*, it provides images of such standard equine items as you will need to ask for, locate, be warned of, etc. during the course of your journey. In this way, even if you cannot say horse, food, or even help, in Mongolian, at least you can point at the appropriate picture. But don't take any linguistic shortcuts. Even knowing but a few words goes a long way in creating goodwill and friendship.

The master equestrian traveller, Italian Long Rider Antonietta Spizzo, has made nearly a dozen rides across various portions of Russia and Europe. Even though she is an accomplished linguist, she always makes an effort to learn the vital equestrian words prior to her departure for a new country.

"Speaking the language, even if only a couple of sentences, is the most important thing," she said. "And I must recommend everybody to make this effort at home. It will be repaid ten times over when you are on the road."

Summary

Every successful equestrian expedition is based upon considerable investigation and preparation, which in turn serves as the foundation for your future success. For example, Jean Claude Cazade spent two years carefully laying the groundwork, before successfully riding his Arab stallion from France to Arabia and back.

As this former French Foreign Legionnaire, turned equestrian explorer, proves, the Long Rider must be a practical person, one for whom no difficulties are too hard to overcome, no people too hostile to divert the journey, in short a person who recognizes no obstacle. The Long Rider, once he sets out on a journey, carries it through in a thoroughly sound manner.

That is why before you leave you should be asking yourself a lot of basic questions. What sort of horse should I acquire? What must I do before I set off on that day's ride? What do I do once I'm on the road? How many miles should I travel every day? Do I walk, trot or canter? How do I handle the pack horse? How do I go uphill, downhill, through tunnels, across bridges, through rivers and past traffic? When do I water and feed? What about lunch for me and the horse? When do I start to think about stopping for the day? What kind of place should I look for? What do I feed the horse if I don't recognize any of the native food on offer? Do I picket, hobble, highline, blindfold, free range or stable my horse? What do I do if my horse gets away during the night? How do I handle horse thieves?

While it's not necessary for you to be an athlete, you should prepare yourself for the journey by honing your riding skills, increasing your knowledge of basic equestrian issues and becoming as strong and healthy as possible. Such a careful preparation ties in with the warning issued by the famous Norwegian polar explorer, Roald Amundsen. "Victory," he wrote, "awaits those who have everything in order - people call that luck. Defeat awaits those who don't. This they call bad luck."

No one proves this better than the Argentine Long Riders, Raul and Margarita Vasconcellos. On July 4th, 1984, they had the idea to ride from their home in Arizona back to their native country of Argentina. Despite their desire to mount up and take off, the Argentine travellers didn't leave until January 6th, 1987 after having learned horse shoeing, riding and mule packing. Yet thanks to their careful planning, they went on to complete one of the most successful and trouble-free equestrian journeys of the late twentieth-century.

In conclusion, we must remember what the great Swiss Long Rider, Captain Otto Schwarz said. "There is no complete or perfect plan for those travelling by horse. Even so, never go off without thorough preparation. "

Without a plan, Otto warned, your temper, journey and horse will all be in peril.

Preparedness is the key to success and victory.

Though Joe Goodwin (left) and Robert Horiguichi were emotionally excited about riding from Texas to Mexico City in 1931, in their innocence the would-be Long Riders packed along a typewriter so as to file news stories.

The journey made by Hugh MacDermott through the Andes Mountains of Chile and Argentina in 2005 was successful thanks to his careful preparations.

The best-planned equestrian expedition, either into or out of Latin America in recent years, was carried out by the Argentine Long Riders, Margarita and Raul Vasconcellos. They rode from Arizona to Argentina in 1987 on a near-perfect equestrian expedition.

In stark contrast was the young English woman who planned to ride from London to Tokyo. Her horse suffered and the journey was quickly ended.

Chapter 4
Finances and Insurance

While we're on the subject of preparation, let's not overlook another critical aspect of equestrian travel, namely finances. Regardless of how excited you are, in spite of all your noble intentions, ignoring for a moment your sincerity of purpose, you can't overlook this ancient law of travel.

Even Columbus needed money.

Therefore you're no exception to that non-negotiable rule. Plus unlike a bicyclist, you have the added responsibility of providing daily feed and care for your mount. So the ride proceeds only as and when you have the funding necessary to ensure the financial safety of you and your horse.

Budget

Before you proceed to purchase a horse, saddle, assorted tack, equipment, etc, you will need to determine two things: What kind of equestrian traveller are you and how much money do you need?

There are three types of equestrian travellers: a) independently wealthy b) corporate sponsored c) any combination of traveller/ pilgrim/explorer. Which one are you? Regardless, all three are valid because the problems encountered on the road are the great leveller of both Long Riders and Road Horses.

However, in order to help you arrive at some preliminary idea of the amount of funds needed, construct an approximate route for your proposed trip. Divide the total number of proposed miles by twenty miles per day to arrive at the minimum length of your trip. Figure on $15 a day for rider and one horse. Add an additional $5 per day for a pack horse. What's the total amount? Now factor in the cost of purchasing your Road Horse, Pack Horse, riding and pack saddles. Do you have the basic funds needed to even proceed on a horse trip? Can you raise it?

Before you get too depressed looking at numbers, it's good to remember the wise counsel of the elegant Swedish Long Rider, Countess Linde von Rosen.

During the 1920s and early 30s, when the ugliness of European political passions were boiling beneath the surface, the beautiful, photogenic, fun-loving, aristocratic Linde trotted into Paris on her equally famous horse, Castor. Next they took Rome by storm, when Linde rode there to meet the Pope. Thus, by ignoring the winds of war blowing in the background, Linde swayed politicians and enchanted half the men in Europe, turning her highly publicized journeys into mounted missions of equestrian tolerance.

"It is lovely this life," she wrote. "I feel it when I ride against the storm, and Castor rears up, his hooves dancing in the air. In that mad second, before my mount takes off in senseless fainting speed, I scream against the storm, I'm alive!"

Yet despite her poetic nature, Linde never lost sight of the financial practicalities of equestrian travel. In her autobiography, written in the late twentieth century, the now-elderly but still passionate pilgrim noted that even though money was essential for the well-being of the Long Rider and her horse, she had discovered that equestrian travel was a relatively inexpensive method of exploring the world.

"Finally a few words about the economic aspect. Most people believe that this is a tremendously expensive proposition. Of course, this will depend on how you live, but I want to stress the fact that the year has the same number of days, whether you keep a horse at home or on the road. The cost of basic maintenance for Castor and me was pretty much the same everywhere I travelled. Only if I stopped to spend time in a large city en route did it become much more expensive, what with entertainment, clothes, dinner and so on. However on a long ride you most often stay in small hostels and you are always moving."

You may not be planning on attending any grand balls, nor riding with European princes like Linde did, nevertheless you will still need money in your pocket. That fact wasn't lost on the English Long Rider Margaret Leigh, who completed a solo ride from Cornwall to Scotland in 1939. "A word about expense. If you are willing to camp, your ride will cost you very little. The chief expenditure will be on horses and saddlery, for both must be good. As for your daily outgoings, the cost of food is what you choose to make it. A night's grazing at farms was often free."

Castle bedrooms or a farmer's fields? These two cheerful European lady Long Riders enjoyed both. Yet like you, they too had to carefully consider the financial side of their journey before they departed.

Costs

Don't think that you are considering a topic which hasn't puzzled previous equestrian travellers. In his short booklet, *Twelve Days in the Saddle*, the North American Long Rider, Daniel Denison Slade recalled how in 1883 he and his daughters rode through primeval forests, alongside rushing rivers and ventured into the still unspoiled valleys of Connecticut, Vermont and Massachusetts. Yet in addition to this lovely story, Slade was wise enough to provide subsequent would-be equestrian travellers with a list of tips on how to make a successful journey. One of Slade's "Maxims" still holds true today.

"As some may be deterred from the thought of undertaking a horseback journey on the score of the greater expense attending it, I can assure you that the daily expenses are not so large as by the usual mode of travelling by train; at least, they need not be. Thus a month's journey in the saddle need not much exceed what is commonly spent in half that period when travelling by the usual modes of conveyance. To be sure, the amount of space passed over in a given time is not so great; but in the one case the traveller has seen the country through which he has passed, and in the other he has seen but little or nothing," Slade wrote.

Yet what sort of expenses go into making up an equestrian expedition?

Here is a list of potential expenses.

Horse and saddle. Pack horse and pack saddle. Bridle, halters, lead ropes, and saddle pads. Rider's personal equipment such as clothes, toilet gear, etc. Horse's equipment such as brushes, hoof picks, etc. Tent, camping and cooking gear. Food and lodging for Long Rider and horses. Diplomatic charges for visas, human and equine passports, and medical evaluations at border crossings. Insurance for health of horse and rider, kidnap of rider and death of horse. Transportation costs, ranging from local ferry across a river to international air fare across oceans. Local labour, be it a guide, veterinarian or farrier.

Before you can swing into the saddle, you must carefully consider all of these potential financial handicaps, because lacking the funds for any portion of your overall expedition will diminish your chances of successfully reaching your distant geographic goal. And regardless of where you're riding, the cost of the journey will always turn out to be higher than budgeted, so handle your financial preparations with extreme care.

That is why one Long Rider warned, "Plan to spend twice as much as you expect both in time and money."

Carrying Money

When it comes to money, let's talk about the dangers encountered when Long Riders carry it.

Before the tiny Abernathy brothers set out to make their first ride, their father laid down the law. The legendary U.S. Marshal, Jack "Catch'em Alive" Abernathy, earned his name by capturing wild wolves bare-handed. Thus in 1909, when Abernathy's nine and five-year-old sons, Bud and Temple, were preparing to ride more than a thousand miles from the family's Oklahoma ranch to Santa Fe and back alone, the tough lawman required his tiny Long Riders to promise to follow two rules.

First, the boy travellers were cautioned never to attempt to cross any river or stream on horseback unless they could see the bottom.

The second warning was a financial one.

"Don't carry large amounts of cash," he warned Bud and Temple, "because it attracts the worst sort of humanity."

What Jack knew, and most would-be Long Riders forget, is how isolated you are for long periods of time. Even though cell phones now allow an equestrian traveller to stay in more constant contact with the outside world, it is a thin electronic margin of safety whereupon a rider's life can hang in the balance, depending on local reception.

That is why, even though it's been a hundred years since his boys rode off towards Santa Fe, Catch'em Alive Abernathy's warning holds true today. When you swing into the saddle you're always a lonely, potential target. Add money into the equation and you heighten the risk factor.

Sadly that rule had been forgotten by the 1970s when two American brothers attempted to travel across Afghanistan with mules. Rumours swirled around the unlucky men as they made their way from Herat to Kabul. Trouble began when the foreigners revealed they were making the journey so as to collect donations for an international charity. Factor in the fact that the average yearly income for a backwoods Afghan was about thirty dollars a year, compound the problem by pitching English speaking Americans alongside Pushto-speaking Afghans and you've got a recipe for bloodshed.

Because they mistakenly believed the heavy saddle bags carried by the American's mules were loaded with vast amounts of silver coins collected en route, Afghan brigands ambushed and robbed the naïve travellers. One brother was murdered on the spot. The second was gravely wounded and left for dead. Neither the mules nor the fantasy "treasure" were ever recovered.

Thus, carrying cash, real or imaginary, can be beneficial but dangerous.

But cheer up, as things could be worse. You could be burdened with carrying your funds in a treasure chest.

Early equestrian travellers venturing into seldom-visited sections of Mongolia and Central Asia often had to travel more than a thousand miles between banking towns. These mounted explorers knew that paper money was scarcely appreciated and often refused by sceptical natives. For this reason nineteenth-century Long Riders were often required to carry the expedition's funds in hard currency.

One such British traveller to Central Asia noted this bit of financial trivia.

"The principal difficulty was to carry enough currency to pay for transport. A large expedition may carry its money in a treasure chest under guard; others may distribute it in the personal baggage and handle it only at night, one of the party carrying enough loose cash for daily small expenses. The supply of small cash upon expeditions is a matter normally neglected by writers and travellers in the field. In our case it presented an almost insurmountable obstacle. For days before we moved our quarters, messengers had to be sent to native courts, traders, chiefs and similar influential institutions to beg for pennies and shillings. Both are essential, as even natives used to European enterprise refer to paper notes as 'books' and refuse to accept them, believing them to have no more intrinsic value than an I.O.U. from a white man. Carriers are paid in shillings and food is bought with pennies."

As the twentieth-century progressed, things became easier. For example, Swiss Long Rider Aimé Tschiffely carried letters of credit on his journey from Buenos Aires to New York.

By 2001, when North American Long Rider Lisa Wood made her ocean to ocean ride across the United States, she only carried one hundred dollars at a time.

"I found it was helpful to carry my driver's license, the phone number of my vet, a phone card and an ATM card in my wallet. But I never carried more than a hundred dollars, which was more than enough to get my horse shod."

Likewise, when South African Long Rider Billy Brenchley set off in 2007 to ride from the top of African continent to distant South Africa, he too learned that plastic had its purposes.

"All bank cards work in Tunisia and Egypt. Libya only has ATM facilities in Tripoli and Ben Ghazi. Sudan has no ATM facilities at all. However, Byblos Bank in Khartoum can make an arrangement with Visa or Master Card for a U.S. twenty-five dollar charge." Billy recalled.

Regardless if you're riding to Tripoli or Tulsa, carry your paper money in small denominations, with enough money close to hand so as to handle expected daily expenses. Maintain the rest of your cash in a deeply secure wallet, hidden vest pocket, etc. Keep a reserve of traveller's cheques in case of an emergency, especially as border guards and immigration officials may demand that you verify you have enough funds to transit through their country. Use an ATM card with caution, regardless of what country you're riding in. If you must carry a large sum of cash, for example to buy several horses, disguise it, hide it and don't discuss it.

One final warning. Don't expect foreign banks to adhere to the same rules observed by your local banking institution. Money transfers can almost certainly take longer than expected and charges will often be exorbitant. Like many aspects of riding in foreign lands, you will need a tremendous amount of patience, tolerance and good humour.

Sponsors

Perhaps you are considering enlisting the aid of a financial sponsor. Is this a reasonable idea?

No one would realistically expect to contact one of the major American automobile companies, announce that they wanted to see the United States, and then ask a Detroit car maker to be so kind as to donate a new car and a tank of gas so they can make the trip. Yet all too often would-be equestrian travellers don't hesitate to ask for an assortment of free items including saddles, clothing and feed.

What many amateur travellers don't appreciate is how small the majority of equine-connected companies are. So making payroll and keeping the doors open is already tough before you show up asking them to sponsor your dream.

Also, don't forget that you're signing away a share of your independence in exchange for an assortment of "freebies," such as sleeping bags, tents, sunscreen and clothing. That's because you make a Faustian deal when you tie your expedition to a sponsor, as they expect media, demand reports and thrive on exposure. Anything you get comes with invisible strings attached. So if you can maintain your financial independence, by all means do so.

And while we're investigating the idea of enlisting a sponsor to help bankroll your expedition, let's not overlook this important fact.

One financial aspect of equestrian travel which has never been adequately explained is how the general rules of expedition planning can, and should, also be applied to equestrian travel. It's going to take more than an impressive letterhead to sway cynical corporate accountants. What's needed is an easy-to-read synopsis of your proposed journey. This document should include facts, images and maps which explain the significance of your journey. Your proposal should provide information regarding your equestrian qualifications and how those talents will help you overcome any difficulties you might encounter while travelling. The proposal should include intended departure dates and list the costs of the various aspects of the journey. It should also detail how the journey will benefit the corporate sponsor or individual donor.

And as the leaders of other major types of expeditions know, such a proposal for financial assistance needs to be submitted at least a year in advance, as most corporations set their budgets and allocate donations months, if not years, ahead. Consequently, any donation proposal should be professional and presented long before your actual departure, as a last-minute prospectus will not inspire either confidence or financial input.

Donations

Even if you ask for the moon a year in advance, what are your chances of getting it? Not very encouraging, I'm afraid.

In the early 1980s, when Jean Claude Cazade rode from France to Arabia, a company dispatched equine medicine and food supplements to some of the cities along the route. When the Russian Long Rider, Vladimir Fissenko, rode 30,500 kilometres (19,000 miles) from Patagonia to Alaska, the Easy Boot Company agreed to provide his mount with protective hoof boots. These two Long Riders were lucky.

John Egenes spent two fruitless years trying to entice corporate sponsorship for his 1972 ocean to ocean ride.

"After having been turned down by company presidents and advertisers, who I asked for sponsorships in the form of clothes, boots, saddle bags and horse feed, the only thing I got was four pairs of pants from Levi Strauss. They sent them to me in 1972 and I haven't heard from them since," the Long Rider recalled.

One final point about donations. If you receive it, use it, otherwise, return it.

There are several notorious examples of unethical horse travellers who exploited the generosity and trust of equine companies. The most flagrant example occurred when an American equestrian publisher managed to obtain everything short of the kitchen sink for her supposed ride across Arizona. After riding her horse into the ground, she ditched the trip but kept the equipment. In cases like these the donors are left wondering why they bothered contributing to a pony fantasy.

What these sorts of people do is poison the well of generosity for legitimate equestrian travellers. So if you receive a financial donation, acknowledge it. If you're given valuable equipment or services, repay the companies generosity by publicly endorsing their product on your website and to the equestrian press. If you don't depart, then have the ethical courage and courtesy to return the equipment.

Charities

It may shock you to learn that you are not required to make an equestrian journey so as to advocate anything. In fact, it often happens that hanging the cause of a charity on your saddle horn ends up denigrating the actual riding experience. This is especially true in Great Britain, where it too often appears that people feel they need an "excuse" in order to justify their longing to make a life-changing equestrian journey.

That's not the case. In fact you don't have to clutter up your journey by making public pleas for money to undertake penguin heart transplants, rescue obese orphans or counsel donkeys born on a Tuesday.

The Long Riders' Guild advocates instead that people make an extended equestrian journey for no other reason than to get in touch with themselves and to better understand their horses and the world that surrounds both of them.

Also, all too often, it's the people who tie their journeys onto a cause who come back with tales of how difficult it was and how they suffered in the cause of the charity. These self-appointed heroes invariably end up asking you to please buy their book because they've made you feel guilty. That's a hustler, not a Long Rider.

Work

One more thing about money. Don't plan on mixing working and riding. It may happen but you can't count on it.

North American Long Rider Stan Perdue was riding from Georgia to Arizona when a phoney saddle pad wounded his horses. Thanks to his ready store of talents, Stan was able to quickly obtain local work. In exchange Stan was promised room and board for him and his horses, as well as a small additional wage. Though the injured animals healed in a few weeks time, and Stan managed to resume his journey, it wasn't without delay and hardship, especially as his temporary employer took advantage of the equestrian traveller by keeping all the extra money he had been promised.

Another thing to be wary of are promises of income derived while you're on the road. This is especially prevalent among equestrian writers who count their journalistic chickens before they hatch.

When Norwegian Long Rider Howard Saether, and his Slovenian Long Rider companion, Janja Kovačič, set off to ride from Uruguay to Texas, they were counting on receiving money promised to them in advance by publications back in their native countries. That isn't what happened.

"We thought we would make money from articles while on the road, especially because a Norwegian magazine had promised Howard big money for his stories. Instead they only published one article in four months. Since then he hasn't heard anything from the magazine or even seen the money they owe him. The bastards! Luckily my own articles are more or less regularly published in a Slovenian Sunday newspaper. They only pay me a hundred and fifty dollars per article. But as long as they continue, I won't complain," Janja reported to the Guild.

Finally, one of the reasons Howard and Janja's journey ended prematurely in Bolivia was because of the loss of promised income. As they and Stan learned, no matter how hard it is to find a job at the best of times back home, your problems are going to be multiplied a thousand fold when you have the additional emotional burden of worrying about your horses in a strange place. So take this lesson to heart. Don't depart until you have enough money to guarantee the safety of you and your animals.

Insurance

Now, let me tell you one of the most valuable lessons you'll ever learn from this book.

The horseman's grave is always open.

That statement isn't intended to scare you. In fact compared to the accidents, broken bones, and even occasional deaths which routinely plague show jumpers, endurance racers, three day eventers and polo players, equestrian travel is one of the safest ways to enjoy a horse. In contrast to the dangers encountered in competitive equestrian events, though the Long Riders' Guild has fielded, mentored, sponsored or assisted equestrian expeditions on every continent except Antarctica in more than fifteen years, there has only been one major accident. It resulted in the death of my close friend and near-death of her companion.

This happened in 2013 when South African Long Rider Billy Brenchley and his fiancée, English Long Rider Christine (Christy) Henchie, were struck by a vehicle during their historic journey across Africa. They had crossed ten countries when an out-of-control bus struck the pair and the onlookers following them as they walked with their horses through a small village in Tanzania. The impact killed Henchie instantly and Brenchley suffered a broken leg. The accident killed two villagers and injured others.

A more common occurrence is what happened when an English Long Rider rode into a farm yard, where the unexpected sight of a peacock frightened that lady's horse. The rider was thrown and injured.

However, accidents can and do occur, even to the best of riders. Hence my warning, that anyone who works, mounts, rides or trains a horse is always moments away from a serious potential injury.

And no one proves that better than the English Long Rider John Labouchere.

The tall, dapper, polo playing equestrian traveller went to Argentina in 1990, determined to explore Latin America on horseback. While riding close to the border of Chile, John suffered an extraordinary accident. The trail he was riding on was cut into the side of a hill, which in turn overlooked the main road below. An on-coming lorry provided the noise needed to cause John's horse to lose his footing.

The English Long Rider fell off his horse backwards. Flying through the air, he sailed off the cliff and smashed into the ground eighteen feet below. Lying there on his back for a mere second, his upside down horse came crashing down directly on top of him. To make matters worse, the large camera which John was carrying in a belt around his waist was driven into his body by the weight of the horse.

Luckily a car was flagged down and the injured man was driven fifty miles to a hospital. There it was found he had three burst sections of intestines, a damaged spleen and internal poisoning caused by peritonitis. Though none of his other internal organs were damaged, nor any bones broken, the resultant surgery scar ran the length of John's body. During his subsequent recovery in hospital an incompetent nurse nearly let him bleed to death, his money was stolen and he lost forty-five pounds (20 kilograms).

Yet not only did he recover, he completed the journey and took his horses back to Great Britain.

As John's case proves, falling ill while travelling can be expensive, time consuming and potentially deadly for a variety of reasons. Because such an episode can be financially crippling, if not medically dangerous, you would be well advised to investigate the possibility of obtaining medical insurance which covers you while travelling. Though you may not have a horse land on top of you, chances are you might encounter dysentery, typhus, malaria, hepatitis or sunstroke.

If you fall ill while riding, ask the doctor to bill your insurance. If you pay cash, retain the receipts so you can be reimbursed upon your return.

You should also make insurance decisions regarding the theft of your property and horses. The loss of your tack and mount is both emotionally and financially devastating.

Pay attention to the issue of public liability insurance. In the back country of New Zealand, for example, property owners will be reluctant to let you camp or use huts unless you have fire suppression insurance. Landowners are thus more inclined to allow you to camp if they know that you're insured and reliable.

Don't overlook the problem of insuring your horse as well. If there is any kind of an accident caused by your horse, then you must accept responsibility. So consider taking out a third-person policy which would cover an accident caused by the horse.

Also, you should consider the option of insuring your mount in case of its injury or mortality. The cost of an annual premium to insure a horse against death and debilitating injuries is approximately five percent of the animal's value. While insuring horses against death, injury or theft will almost certainly not be available in places such as Mongolia or Central Africa, if you are riding in the Americas, Australia or Europe, then you may wish to speak to an equine insurance specialist about medical insurance in case of accidents, especially colic. Discuss theft and ask for details about mortality insurance. Remember, while your sentiment doesn't affect the value of the horse, taking these precautions before departure may ease the pain of loss and injury to you both.

Summary

Ask yourself this question. Is money a deciding factor in deciding whether you leave on an equestrian adventure? If so then you're not ready to depart. However, if you've secured the necessary funds, or at least remain optimistic about your economic chances, then prepare to discover more about yourself, your horse, the world and its people in the chapters to come.

The Swedish Long Rider Linde von Rosen, and her trusted mount, Castor, became Europe's most celebrated Long Rider during the "Jazz Age" of the 1920s. Yet even the elegant countess still had to watch her pennies while travelling.

During his journey from Georgia to Arizona, North American Long Rider Stan Perdue ran into trouble when a defective saddle pad injured one of his horses. Luckily Stan managed to obtain local work during the time needed for his horse to heal. But one shouldn't count on successfully mixing equestrian travel and employment.

The Horseman's Grave is always open, as Christy Henchie (left) and Billy Brenchley learned. The couple set off in 2005 with ambitious plans to complete the first ride from Cap Blanc in Tunisia – the most northern point in Africa – to its southernmost tip, Cape Agulhas in South Africa. Their dreams were halted in Tanzania when a speeding bus hit the Long Riders and their horses.

Though he set out to explore Latin America, British Long Rider John Labouchere instead lost forty-five pounds (20 kilograms) after surviving the most extraordinary riding accident in modern equestrian travel history.

Chapter 5
Choosing your Destination

Where we travel to is just as important as how we get there. That is why you need to spend time determining where you're going, personally and geographically.

Everyone has their own Mecca, that mythical spot on your emotional map that is calling to your soul.

The destination for some may be easily defined in geographic terms, such as those equestrian travellers who relish the challenge of riding three thousand miles "ocean to ocean" across the United States. That was the formidable task which Long Rider Captain Willard Glazier set for himself.

Known as the "soldier-author," Glazier had been a penniless schoolboy at the beginning of the American Civil War. He enlisted in a cavalry unit of the Union Army of the Potomac and was soon captured by Confederate troops. After a daring escape, he was recaptured, only to escape a second time, before finally reaching the Union lines again. At the conclusion of the conflict Glazier wrote a book describing his wartime experiences. When every New York publisher rejected him, the young cavalryman self-published his work, hoping to recoup his costs plus a hundred dollars profit. Instead, to his delight, the book took off like wildfire, selling 400,000 copies.

With the $75,000 profit realized from his efforts, Glazier decided to become the first person to ride from the Atlantic to the Pacific oceans. Leaving New York state in 1875 on his horse, Paul Revere, the former trooper set out for the distant Pacific. In his book, *Ocean to Ocean on Horseback*, Glazier describes his mounted adventures, including an account of how he was kidnapped by Arapahoe Indians en route to the "Battle of the Little Big Horn."

Yet equestrian travel isn't restricted to geographical goals, nor must it be overtly influenced by either current political or geographical events. Mighty empires come and go. Once-powerful Prime Ministers are relegated to the shadows. White spots on the map are filled in. Yet despite the passing of the ages, certain members of mankind still long to explore their planet for purely personal reasons.

If it is true that the age of national exploration is now past, the Long Riders' Guild believes we are witnessing the dawning of the age of the citizen-explorer, an enlightened era wherein individuals set out not to exploit the natural resources of their neighbours, nor to plant the flag of their country atop a mighty peak in another land, but rather to explore the frontiers of this planet and our own souls.

There are, for example, many equestrian travellers who elect to ride along the ancient pilgrim's path known as Saint James' Way, the legendary spiritual trail which leads across Europe to the historic cathedral of Santiago de Compostela. The English Long Rider sisters, Mefo Phillips and Susie Gray, undertook to ride this mediaeval Way from Canterbury cathedral to the Spanish terminus.

Mounted pilgrims may also consider exploring the new Abraham Path. Because more than half of the human race traces its history or faith back to that legendary patriarch, the Abraham Path was constructed to honour this shared cultural heritage by linking together into a single itinerary of outstanding interest and beauty the ancient sites associated with Abraham and his family.

Other Long Riders elect to follow more conventional paths.

For example the adventure-filled 5,000 kilometres (3,000 miles) long Bicentennial National Trail, which runs along the eastern coast of Australia, taxes the equestrian abilities of even the greatest and most skilled equestrian explorers. Likewise there is a new 7,000 kilometre long Iron Curtain Trail waiting to be explored. Described as being the longest heritage trail in the world, this horse-friendly path, which will stretch from the coast of the Arctic Ocean to the distant Black Sea, has yet to be explored by a Long Rider.

From investigating legendary houses of worship to riding "down under," the world is filled with potential equestrian quests that can only be determined by your own attitudes, beliefs, desires, skills and courage.

Obviously no matter what they have to offer, places are just places. What makes them special or not is the complex combination of you, the place and the moment.

Riding in the Wrong Direction

What you should fear, in terms of determining your destination, is the danger of making a predictable ride to a stagnant location.

As this new century dawns, we are collectively faced with the threat of living under the disapproving eye of governments who decry risk taking. We are told to wear helmets and stay off ladders. Our children are wrapped in suffocating layers of legal cotton wool designed to stifle their love of adventure. Even once great bastions of courage, such as the Royal Geographical Society, have abdicated their roles as exploration leaders, preferring instead to promote timidity rather than challenge seeking.

The majority of people are immersed in dull, boring, predictable existences which are designed to make them reliable citizens, routine tax payers, apathetic voters and avid television watchers. Their lives are about the avoidance of danger, the denial of the unknown, the rejection of mystery.

When these people temporarily escape, fleeing from their cages for a few weeks' holiday, they are apt to plod along a predetermined path to a safe location. Upon arriving, they discover hordes of similar travel robots; all seeking an authentic experience, in a place whose original mystery and spiritual energy was siphoned off and sold long ago. People who flock to such unfortunate places are tourists, not equestrian explorers. They are making do with second-hand experiences taught to them by guidebooks and peddled by carnival cruises. Such journeys are obsessed with schedules and flight times. They are about gathering post cards from locations that serve as spiritual souvenirs. Such journeys ultimately neither confront nor change the tourist.

Yet history proves that horses and humans equal a new energy and that a properly conceived equestrian journey injects a vitalizing force into a previously tedious life. Thus, while it is fine to set off on your horse, bound for a historic location, it is better to depart towards an inner unknown, some place that will challenge the emotional predictability of your life.

As the fabled travel master, Ed Byrne, once wrote, "you should approach travel as an adventure, not an advertisement."

So when you consider "where" you're going, you must recall that you are making two journeys, an inner and outer one. Your journey's destination should serve to unlock the complexity of your soul, instead of trying to control it. Your time in the saddle should be spent learning from the obstacles which you will undoubtedly encounter, not pretending that life is trouble free, as the colourful tourist brochures preach to the unwitting.

Organized travel is designed to turn you into a moveable conformist. Guidebooks tell you where to eat and what places to avoid. In contrast, when you explore the world on horseback you are stimulated, physically, geographically, intellectually, linguistically, emotionally and spiritually. When you become a Long Rider you saddle up and then slow down.

So your choice of destinations should reflect your desire to embrace personal change, as well as geographic achievement.

Equestrian Reality

If there is one fundamental difference between the safety of tourism and the stimulating uncertainty of equestrian travel it is the need never to lose sight of the imminent reality of your horseback existence.

Tourism is about the denial of reality. It is concerned with sipping pink cocktails on a sunny beach today, before returning home tomorrow to cope with a credit card topped out from tipping smarmy waiters. In contrast, horse travel demands that you pay your way every day as you interact with the local community, find shelter every night and avoid dangers all the time. The former is a temporary escape. The latter is a life-altering adventure.

Long Riders, therefore, who should always be grounded in historic, cultural and geographic reality, must pay close attention to where they're going, before they leave.

Two geographically diverse examples come to mind, as each demonstrates how easy, or difficult, things can be for an equestrian traveller.

Italian Long Riders Dario Masarotti and Antoinetta Spizzo spend as much time as possible in the saddle. Since 1993 they have ridden their horses every summer in a series of wide-ranging equestrian journeys. They always start from home (Premariacco, a small town in Northern Italy) and have already ridden through Germany, France, Slovenia, Hungary, Romania, Ukraine, Belarus, Poland, Russia and the Czech Republic.

Antoinetta wrote to the Long Riders' Guild about one such journey.

"In our experience, Austria and Germany revealed themselves not only as beautiful countries but also as a small paradise for riders and horses. People there are in general very fond of horses and know what they need. The persons which we had the chance to meet always accepted us in a very friendly way and helped us a lot. Riders and horses find everywhere everything they need and prices are generally honest. Some hostels on the horse-trails are really good models to follow. Anyway, horses are deeply rooted in the collective imagination and this fact opens up the doors and the hearts," the mounted traveller recalled.

In contrast, when the French Long Rider, Louis Meunier, and his Afghan Long Rider comrade, Hadji Shamsuddin, made a perilous journey from Maimana to Herat in 2005, they learned that the once-legendary equestrian culture of Afghanistan had become one of the unaccounted victims of decades of vicious warfare.

"One thing I noticed which might be of importance to other Long Riders is that except for Herat the entire area we have been through since Bamiyan has very little horse culture left intact. Indeed, horses have almost disappeared from the countryside as they were stolen during the fighting. Then, about four years ago at the end of the Taliban war, motorbikes were imported into the country. They have now largely replaced our equine friends. When we go back to Turkistan, the northern part of Afghanistan, we will again find people with great horse knowledge. But it is weird to be a horse traveller here in this new century and I always face the same questions. Why do you go by horse? Do you travel by horse to sell them? What do you have in your saddle bags? While many people have travelled across this country out of necessity because of the fighting and wars, it is still considered very strange to be a Long Rider in Afghanistan," Louis wrote.

Mythical Destinations versus Equestrian Reality

Louis' observations draw me to issue this special warning.

Leave the myths at home!

For example, while it is perfectly acceptable to be inspired by Long Riders like the legendary Swiss traveller, Aimé Tschiffely, don't bewitch yourself into thinking that you will discover what he did on his 1925 journey. Riding from Buenos Aires to New York, as Aimé did, is now full of immense geopolitical problems that didn't exist in his day.

Likewise, don't mount up and set off in search of the American West. If you're looking for cowboys and Indians, go to Hollywood and visit a cinema.

What you must do is base your destination decision on modern equestrian reality, not mythology. Don't set off thinking you are going to re-discover the Old West, the Old East, or any other 19th century legends. Roads now criss-cross continents. Barbed wire halts progress along historic pathways. Caravanserais are a dim memory in Central Asia. More Long Riders are injured in the United States by road-raged motorists than by wild animals.

If you want vast open spaces, without fences and political nonsense, then you should go to Russia, Canada, Alaska or Australia. If you're seeking unexplored mountains then ride in northern Pakistan. If you're anxious to see unexplored Europe, then go east.

Regardless of where you go, don't be tempted to mix myth with reality.

The most infamous example of this muddled and romantic thinking was the Russian equestrian criminal whose cruel journey to the Eiffel Tower in 2008 turned into an international diplomatic incident. Though lacking any equestrian travel experience this former convict turned would-be equestrian traveller treated his two horses so brutally that authorities in Russia, Poland and Germany attempted to stop him from riding them to death. The resulting journey became a travesty wherein the horses were seized and given emergency medical treatment, while the mounted criminal was eventually captured and imprisoned by the Russian authorities.

Nor should you piggy-back on to another's dream. By all means be inspired, but don't be afraid to be an equestrian pioneer. Follow instead the example of the legendary British Long Rider Robin Hanbury-Tenison. He made the first land crossing of South America at its widest point, led twenty-four expeditions and was awarded the Patron's Gold Medal by the Royal Geographical Society. More recently Robin and his Long Rider wife Louella made the first modern mounted exploration of Albania. Now they're setting off to explore Brazil on horseback. They're pioneers, not followers.

As the Hanbury-Tenisons prove, equestrian travel is exciting and rewarding, if you do it right. It can also be dangerous and discomforting if you make the mistake of starting in the wrong country

If at all possible, don't attempt an equestrian journey through a country which has no historical equestrian culture. The Arctic Circle is fine for huskies, not Haflingers. Research your route before you go! Look for modern traces of once-valid equestrian cultures. Read every book for equestrian clues. Study every map and speak to anyone who can give you valid travel information.

Anxieties and Antagonism

When planning where you will ride, remember that many anxieties are based upon a lack of local experience. Actual travel will prove the majority of concerns to be unfounded. For example, when the French Long Rider sisters, Evelyne and Corinne Coquet, made their celebrated ride from Paris to Jerusalem in the 1970s, they suffered terrible apprehension about the reception they might receive in Turkey. In fact they were pleasantly astounded at the nationwide sense of hospitality they encountered.

Yet in order to ensure the safety of you and your horse, it is your primary duty to anticipate the increasing danger of traffic, busy roads, lack of privacy, little grazing, pesticide sprayed alongside roadside vegetation to discourage mosquitoes, antagonism from officials, suspicion from locals, urban blight and towns that don't allow horses in the city limits.

Furthermore, if you plan on riding in the United States, you should anticipate encountering antagonism from anti-horse US park rangers. One such example occurred to John Egenes, during his 1970s ocean-to-ocean ride.

"I found a field full of tall, green grass that looked like a perfect place to camp, so upon arriving I unsaddled Gizmo and set up camp. The horse was grazing happily and I had settled back to relax, when the ranger drove up.

Sorry, but I'm afraid you can't have a horse in the park.

Is this part of the state park? I thought we were outside it?

Yes it is and I'm afraid I'm going to have to ask you to get your horse out of here.

Well, I've looked around and this is the only grass growing for miles, so I'd appreciate it if you'd let me spend the night for the sake of my horse.

If it was up to me I'd let you stay, but the other campers who stay here are city folk who don't like horses.

Well, I'm from the city and I like horses.

What I mean is that they don't like the horse manure and flies. You know how it is.

But there's nobody around here for miles.

Sorry son, but you better saddle your horse and leave immediately; otherwise you're going to be in a lot of trouble."

The ranger watched from his truck while the weary horse and Long Rider reluctantly broke camp and set off. The next grassy field turned out to be 75 miles away!

Nor is this an isolated incident. During the course of his 22,500 kilometres (14,000 miles) journey across the United States, DC Vision encountered the same official hostility. Only this time he was sound asleep in his tent when a ranger drove up and forced him to saddle up his mare, Louise, and set off in the dark.

Thirty years after John and DC were driven onto the road, this antagonism still exists. Here is an example of some antagonistic American national park rules.

"Horses are not allowed in the Paw Paw Tunnel Park, front-country campgrounds, or picnic areas. Feed for horses must be carried by the group. No grazing is permitted in the park. Trail rider groups are responsible for keeping the loading and unloading areas clean. Manure must be picked up and hauled away. Horses are restricted from crossing narrow wooden footbridges as they are not designed to carry the concentrated weight of the horses. Trail rider camping is allowed only in hiker/biker campsites and is limited to six persons, four horses, and one night per visit per site. Horses must be tethered at the furthermost portion of the campsite away from the tent and picnic table locations. Groups are responsible for removing from the park manure and leftover feed, etc. Horses/riders are not to exceed the speed of a slow trot. The watering, cleaning, or tethering of horses at park wells is prohibited. By use of a bucket or other container, water may be taken from park wells located at hiker/biker campsites and used for watering horses.

Horses must be loaded/unloaded and must enter and exit the towpath at public access points only. Access from private property is prohibited. Horseback riding is prohibited after dark. Horse riders must pick up after their animals, all manure must be removed."

It isn't the role of the Long Riders' Guild to comment on such bureaucratic brutality, only to warn you that it exists and that if you set off unprepared, then you and your horse shall certainly encounter it at the end of some weary day when, after having found what looks like a corner of paradise, you're driven back onto the long grey road.

Lack of Planning

As the example of the national park illustrates, you should be doing everything possible before you leave to determine what sort of obstacles you may encounter on the road.

Don't think you can make up for your lack of planning by imposing your pony fantasy on others after you start your journey. No one can undertake to plan another's journey, study the maps, negotiate for passage, talk to officials, cache fodder, schedule farriers or plan vet checks.

If you abdicate these formalities and duties to others, you're not a Long Rider; you're an emotional and logistical grifter.

Summary

There is one final thought you should bear in mind about your travel plans. After you've invented them, don't enshrine them. You're travelling by horse, not bus. Your schedule is largely dependant on his stomach and the weather. If something or someone exciting comes along, don't be afraid to linger or explore.

Upon your return you will discover that the majority of the people you previously knew have done nothing during your absence. Invariably, their first question will be, "why did you hurry back"? Thus, when you look back at your life, your equestrian adventure will resemble a brief flash of freedom, so don't hasten your journey in order to hurry back to an emotional mortgage.

Tell yourself before departing, "I'm going to head off towards (fill in destination). If I get there, fine. However if any one of a dozen different unforeseen problems keep me from reaching that physical goal I won't blame myself, my horse or life in general. I will instead be happy for every moment I spent in the saddle with (fill in horse's name).

Despite having survived the American Civil War and two escapes from a prisoner of war camp Long Rider Captain Willard Glazier encountered more dangers than he bargained for during the first "ocean to ocean" journey.

During their many journeys across various parts of Europe and Russia, the Italian Long Riders Antoinetta Spizzo (left) and Dario Masarotti noted, "People never try to disguise their surprise and curiosity when they meet us. They smile, greet us, and ask a lot of questions."

Though the French Long Rider Louis Meunier (left) and the Afghan Long Rider Hadji Shamsuddin undertook a perilous journey across the interior of Afghanistan in 2005 to investigate the legendary minaret of Jam, they did not let any romantic illusions overrule either their common sense or their need to survive possible attack by armed members of the Taliban.

When planning where you will ride, remember that many anxieties are based upon a lack of local experience. Actual travel will prove the majority of concerns to be unfounded. For example, when the French Long Rider sisters, Evelyne (left) and Corinne Coquet, made their celebrated ride from Paris to Jerusalem in the 1970s, they suffered terrible apprehension about the reception they might receive in Turkey. In fact they were pleasantly astounded at the nationwide sense of hospitality they encountered.

Chapter 6
Planning Your Route

If the last chapter was devoted to answering the question of "where" you should travel, it follows that this chapter investigates "how" you should plan to reach your geographic goal.

Once you've decided on a physical location, you must ask yourself what is the safest way you can go about arriving at your destination. Your immediate task is to construct a route that will take you and your Road Horse along a line of travel designed to eliminate as many busy roads and topographical challenges as is possible.

In order to accomplish this seemingly-easy task, you should first make a giant mental leap away from your current existence as a motorized citizen. You must develop a new visual and mental philosophy, that of a slower-moving Long Rider who is always on the lookout for unforeseen dangers.

If you encounter a problem while driving a rental car from Belgium to Budapest chances are that you will be able to call quickly upon expert mechanical advice to repair a flat tyre alongside the motorway. Likewise, if you encounter an unexpected mountain range during your climate-controlled cruise, you'll be so busy listening to your car's stereo that you will pay scant attention to the topographical obstacles whizzing by your window.

Equestrian travellers are not motorists. An impatient driver is forced to slow down slightly so as to negotiate a wiggly drive through the Italian Alps. The same road translates into a gruelling day in hell for a Long Rider and his mount. Likewise, a mile-long bridge across the vast Mississippi river causes a motorist to glance idly at the muddy water swirling below, while a Long Rider takes his life in his hands to make the same crossing.

Thus when planning your route, never think in terms of motorized distances, as the geographic challenges routinely ignored by drivers will imperil the lives of you and your horses.

And remember the old Long Rider joke.

"How was the shorter route?"

"Longer."

Armed with that word of caution, let us consider the conventional role maps play in equestrian travel.

Maps and Horses

Traditionally most people believe that having a good map is a great place to begin an equestrian exploration. There is a tactile charm to a map. It holds the promise of a distant place where anything might be possible. Spread out on its smooth surface is the joy of anticipation, minus the danger and disappointment. A map grants you magic, alongside trails and rivers. It whispers about the possibilities of travel, holding up the mirage of excitement, all the while not actually revealing the myriad tiny daily obstacles awaiting an unwary traveller.

What most people see when they first lay eyes on a map is a charming but deceptive romance. The thing they never realize is that many maps are deceptive. Allow me to explain.

Long Rider history proves that any time you place too much confidence in your map; you're riding straight into trouble.

One of the best summaries of this hazard was expressed by a remarkable Long Rider who rode across Siberia.

Kate Marsden was a nurse in Bulgaria during 1878, caring for the wounded of the war between Russia and Turkey. While there, she saw for herself the plight of lepers, and decided to make a 2000-mile journey to the leper colonies of Yakutsk in the depths of Siberia. She hoped to find a herb which was said to grow there and which was allegedly a cure for leprosy. Although originally she set out to improve the lot of the lepers of India, she ended up trying to help the Yakutsk lepers, and attempted to raise funds to build a hospital for them. Even though she had the support of Queen Victoria, the Empress of Russia and her Lady in Waiting, the Countess Tolstoy, not to mention a pastoral letter from Bishop Meletie of Yakutsk, nobody believed that anyone could make such a journey, least of all a woman! Yet after having completed this gruelling ride, Marsden became one of the first women to be elected a Fellow of the Royal Geographical Society in 1892.

Her immensely readable book, *Riding through Siberia*, is a mixture of adventure, extreme hardship and compassion where the author recounted her journey along the Great Siberian Post Road. One point Kate made sure to share was the danger of placing too much confidence in maps.

"On the official maps there is a road traced leading from Yakutsk to Viluisk, but in reality there is no such road—so do not be misled by official maps if you should go there. You will have to pass through unnamed marshes and never find any such road," Marsden warned.

Nor should you be lulled into thinking that such cartographic horrors have ceased to exist in this computer-dominated age. That's the painful lesson which British Long Rider Keith Clark discovered when he set out in 2002 to ride across the Andes Mountains separating Chile from Argentina.

"While I'm in Santiago I am trying to find better maps. The ones I have are 1:500,000, which are fine for the north where I could see the mountains and so work out where I was. Plus it helped that there were plenty of people to ask for directions. But as I ride further south I'm finding the maps less and less useful and people less and less numerous. Often I'm in thick forest and I'm sure that the guy who drew the map had a vivid imagination because I've ended up riding on roads that weren't marked and got lost looking for roads that don't exist. I've also been disappointed at the end of the day to reach what looked on the map to be a large village. Upon arriving I've often discovered that the village is just one house. Likewise I've found myself riding in bewilderment through large towns that weren't marked on the map. All I can say is that better maps are definitely needed if anyone plans on riding south past Puerto Mont," Keith told the Long Riders' Guild.

Despite being on opposite sides of a century and the planet, what Kate and Keith both learned is that maps are only good to a Long Rider if they're up to date and accurate. Thus when you're planning your route you must never forget that unlike motor travel, which can tolerate operator error, topographical accuracy can make or break an equestrian expedition.

Distances and Horses

One of the most common failings of would-be equestrian travellers is to over estimate their daily and overall mileage. With their map spread out before them, they cheerfully decide in advance that they're going to ride from Point A to Point B in so many months, weeks, days and hours because they have divided their proposed route into a number of intellectually digestible portions.

That's the material which pony picnic fantasies are made of, as these people are making the fundamental error of mistaking mathematical progress for equestrian reality.

Equestrian travel is never about a preconceived set of miles. If you haven't already ridden the road, you don't have any idea what challenges and delays are waiting around the corner. When you're in the saddle you will learn that the best you can do is calculate where you hope to be by nightfall, knowing that if you encounter an unforeseen trial then you must immediately reassess that day's progress.

Thus even before you swing into the saddle and set off, you must begin by altering your motorized mind to a new set of equestrian certainties. Geography is no longer to be ignored. It is to be carefully studied and hopefully overcome one hard step, one long mile, one punishing day at a time.

Jeremy James best explained this equestrian reality in his brilliant book, *The Byerley Turk*. In this historical study, Jeremy explained the immense difficulty encountered by an army of Turkish horsemen.

"One hundred miles to Edirne.

As a journey on horseback, what does this mean?

Until you have done it, a hundred miles is meaningless. Fifty miles is meaningless. A hundred miles has no significance. Is this fifty miles of rock? Is this a hundred miles of swamp? Is it fifty miles of rivers to ford, scree to scramble across and cliffs to confound you? A hundred miles of forests so dense that pioneers must be sent first to clear them? Fifty miles of mud, of clay so thick it is impossible to walk in a straight line for more than the length of the body of a horse? A hundred, two hundred miles of hail and wind and rain, sleet and snow?

The elements complicate distance: heat complicates it, cold complicates it and water complicates it. The effort trebles. The sweat runs, the wind chills, the soul cries out.

Gender complicates travel. A mare is easy, but not when there are stallions. Stallions scream and shout and lunge and pull; they are aggressive and lash their tails, kick and squeal and roar. They pull towards the mares, they threaten each other. The mares buck the stallions. They exhaust their riders. The stallions are so obsessed with the mares, they do not care where they put their feet. They flounder, reins cannot be held, shoes are ripped off, horses stumble, knees are cut, fractured, broken.

No. Distance on horseback is not measured in miles.

A pioneer corps of thirty thousand had set out two months earlier to clear and widen roads, repair bridges and build pontoons to span the shifting marshes but does this make the hundred miles shorter? It might make it easier, but the hills remain; the mountains do not move. The rivers still flow: the stallions remain stallions and mares remain mares.

Distance by horse is measured by time!

Distance on horseback is measured in miles only in hindsight," Jeremy wrote.

I might add that distance is still there waiting to challenge you on your journey too. So do not make the mistake of being too optimistic about your proposed mileage. Don't, for example, be naïve enough to think that you're going to ride ocean to ocean and average thirty miles a day. Such dreams are meant to be broken by the waves of reality on the rocks of disappointment. Plan instead on averaging between fifteen and twenty miles a day for five days, allowing two days for rest and repair. When planning your route, and estimating your progress, don't forget to consider obstacles, anticipate delays and be ready for logistical disappointment.

Preplanning Saves Horses

By assuming a position of equestrian reality before you leave, you are less likely to fail on the trail, for waiting up ahead is an assortment of obstacles, including laws, roads and traffic, which may well differ from those which you are used to.

For example, don't make the mistake of the young North American Long Rider who naively set out to ride from the Pacific to the Atlantic without first considering the topography he was up against. Predictably, he nearly died of thirst in the Southwest deserts and the horse often went for days without food. Why? Because the man's spirit of romance outweighed his equestrian common sense, which in turn saw him attempting to journey across country without any solid information about food, water, shelter. What's worse, while the Long Rider certainly suffered, his Road Horse suffered more.

Likewise, don't underestimate the weather when you plan your route. That's what happened when a young American couple set off in April to ride north from New Mexico to Colorado. Flush with excitement, but having failed to do any advance reconnaissance, they discovered their route was blocked by snow until at least July. "Funny how reality can ruin a year and a half of planning in the first two weeks," one of the disappointed travellers reported to the Guild. Even a phone call to accessible ranger stations would have saved them riding into distress.

In contrast, when you do your topographical homework it often translates into an equestrian travel accomplishment.

One example of this successful strategy was achieved by the mother-daughter team of Scottish Long Riders, Vyv and Elsa Wood Gee, who made a trouble-free ride from Land's End in Cornwall to John O'Groats in Scotland.

"We'd meticulously planned most of our route in advance," Vyv recalled, "with endless winter evenings spent pouring over maps, writing letters and ringing people. The Land Reform Act confirms a legal right of responsible access for walkers, cyclists and riders through most of Scotland, but that's little consolation if you've ridden 35 miles and find your way blocked by a padlocked gate or a five foot high deer fence. All but one of the estates, landowners and organisations we so painstakingly contacted in advance to identify and confirm our route through Scotland were helpful and supportive."

As Vyv points out, your progress may depend on access to bridle ways, trails, alongside unused railroad tracks or across private property.

When making her ride across both islands of New Zealand, Mary Pagnamenta issued this stern warning.

"Consider your responsibility to the land owners over whose land you hope to ride. Write well in advance to seek permission, and if it is granted, consider it to be a privilege and not a right to have access to wonderful tracts of private property. The landowner is the custodian of the land, and if you have permission to use it, you also have a responsibility to look after it. Don't cut fences. Shut all gates. Leave any hut that you stay in cleaner that when you found it and avoid leaving horse droppings around any campsites that you use."

Another bit of sound route-related advice was sent to the Guild by Billy Brenchley. He encountered several intrusive urban centres along his route.

"You should always avoid riding through major towns," Billy warned would-be Long Riders. "Before you come to a city ask people to give you the safest route around it. Then ride through the outskirts or completely around the town. One thing to remember is that it's often in major towns where you'll find yourself facing problems caused by bored people. When you're making your plans, a good GPS is essential."

Google Earth and Horses

We often tell reporters that the Long Riders' Guild is a unique combination of Genghis Khan meets the Matrix, in that equestrian explorers are fond of adapting cutting-edge technology so as to augment their Bronze Age activity.

This adaptation of ideas and technology has seen Long Riders incorporating an assortment of 21st century developments, including email, websites, blogs, Facebook, satellite phones, digital photography, solar panels and print on demand publishing into our global efforts to advance equestrian exploration.

One such important development was the merger of the Google Earth mapping technology into the field of equestrian exploration. The first person to enlist this new topographical tool was Andi Mills. She used that state-of-the-art technique in 2007 to augment a portion of her ride across the United States.

This was a landmark in equestrian exploration, as it confirmed that Long Riders could use Google Earth to accurately scout their trail in advance.

As anyone familiar with Google Earth knows, the technology allows you to study the terrain in varying degrees of detail. You can take a bird's eye view of your intended route, then zoom in and see close ups of the terrain, obstacles and challenges which might otherwise surprise you en route.

To make use of this method, first use the free Google Maps facility to plot a direct line between your two destinations. As previously noted, your first goal is to avoid large cities and obvious geographic dangers. Next use the Google Earth software to enlist the satellite imagery available to study the details of your route. By tilting the horizon, you can hover along your intended route, following it on the wing so to speak. This tool not only enables you to investigate the roads, rivers, mountains, deserts and towns which await you, it also enables you to estimate your mileage, which in turn allows you to determine each day's destination.

If you plan to use Google Earth to plot your route, break your journey down into five-day lots of 15 to 25 miles a day. Don't ever plan on trying to do more than 30 miles a day. You may make it but your horse will suffer from your ego. Remember this isn't an endurance race. So take your time and enjoy yourself. Thus stagger the miles so that you push yourself for a while and then reward yourself with easier days. Ride five days and then rest two. You may not think you need the rest, but your horse does. While you use the first day to do chores, repair equipment and send mail etc., your horse will be busy eating. The second day he will eat as well. But it is the rest gained during the second day that will allow him to restore his energy.

Using this new method, you can break your journey up into manageable sections and have an accurate idea before departure of how long your journey will actually take.

Social Networks and Horses

The other advantage of using this method is that it allows you to construct a social network of equestrian allies prior to your departure.

Imagine this. You've been in the saddle for months. You've lost weight. You're tired. Your horse is weary. The two of you are longing for a roof, a meal and a bed. According to your soggy map, there's a village up ahead. Thus, at the end of a long, hard day on the road, you have to arrive, tie up your horse and begin a series of delicate social negotiations designed to obtain food and shelter for you and your tired mount. Regardless of whether you're riding in Africa or Arkansas, this is a time-consuming and sometimes futile process.

By using Google Earth, you can determine in advance where you hope to spend the night. Once you've got the towns along your route figured out, you can make advance contact with them. For example, call the local Chamber of Commerce, mayor or sheriff's office. Explain your equestrian mission and then ask if their town has any feed stores, farriers, equine vets, camp grounds or horse show facilities which might help you arrange for a safe night's room and board. Chances are they will put you in touch with a local horse person. In this way you can construct a chain of prearranged places and people who will be able to provide you and your horse with shelter and food.

The other positive point about this system is that such a social network of local horsemen will usually be happy to alert someone they know and trust a little further down the road on your next day's ride. This in turns brings you into close contact with sympathetic local horse owners, all of whom will help ease your passage through their portion of the equestrian world.

Yet remember, the horse is the key to the village. It's not you, but your mount that has opened a door into people's lives and homes. It's thanks to your horse that you are treated with respect and courtesy by complete strangers. You are, therefore, placed in a position of extreme honour wherein your words and actions are constantly on trial.

Always offer to pay. Never use your horse to take advantage of people's trust. Be courteous, polite and clean up after yourself and your horse. Otherwise you leave a wake of ill-will behind you, spoiling the landscape for the next Long Rider unfortunate enough to be riding in your hoofprints.

That's what happened when a Long Rider arrived late one night in Nashville, Tennessee. Tired and hungry, he had been told that the mounted police department would be likely to give him and his horse a night's lodging. Sadly, upon arriving, he was turned away by the disgruntled mounted officers.

Why?

Because the last horse traveller, a mounted con man, had not only plundered the policemen's hospitality, he had even stolen equipment from their facility.

As you can see, Google Earth will not only arm you with the ability to investigate your route in advance, it will also enable you to prepare a social network of sympathetic horse people prior to your departure.

It is plain to see that Long Riders in the immediate future are going to be able to pioneer new trails across the globe using these technological and social networking techniques.

But there are drawbacks to relying on a system based upon computer logistics and telephone exchanges with strangers.

A Warning about Technical Addiction

Be warned.

Google Earth doesn't work in all parts of the globe. It's not always accurate or up to date. You eliminate the element of surprise by knowing in advance what's awaiting you. You are often confined to riding alongside roadways. Social equestrian networks have been constructed in the United States but not in Europe, Asia, Africa or Australia.

Yet the biggest disadvantage is that a person may have a tendency to place his strictly arranged schedule before the interest of the horse. This new type of peril occurred when a Welsh equestrian traveller riding from Canada to Mexico planned out his route in advance and then rode his horses raw in order to keep up with his prearranged social appointments.

The lesson here is that no map, technological marvel or social network ever takes precedence over your horse's welfare. While man has been given dominion over the horse, he has an obligation to practise justice and mercy. Placing the animal in jeopardy because of a misplaced technical allegiance negates the purpose of the journey.

Summary

Regardless of whether you use a traditional map or rely on computer-based technology, it is advisable to know where you will spend your first two nights on the road.

And remember that a good Long Rider is always flexible, changing his daily goals so as to accommodate the weather, topography, people, history, politics and team health. Nor can you avoid the cold, rain, hail and wind that a motorist sails through. So realize in advance that delays caused by outside factors are a part of your new world.

If you lose a day, it's lost. Period. If you instead push your horse harder the next day to try and make up for "lost time," you risk ruining your animal and your trip.

You must never forget to balance the urge of our restless and enterprising nature with a ruthless pragmatism. What you long to achieve will only come about thanks to careful planning.

Have courage in yourself, faith in your mount and never allow loyalty to the route to come before the welfare of your horse.

Any would-be Long Rider must begin by altering their motorized mind to a new set of equestrian realities. Geography is no longer to be ignored. It is to be carefully studied and hopefully overcome one hard step, one long mile, one punishing day at a time. It was Welsh Long Rider Jeremy James who wisely cautioned, "Distance by horse is measured by time! Distance on horseback is measured in miles only in hindsight."

During her ride across New Zealand, British Long Rider Mary Pagnamenta learned that what looks easy on a map takes on a different reality in the saddle. She was forced to cross the Mangawhai estuary two hours before high tide, so at its deepest it was just above the bottom of the saddle flaps. "Had we been ten minutes later it would have been a swimming job because the tide comes across those flats incredibly quickly."

Despite the size of the map behind her, British Long Rider Kate Marsden discovered that the so-called road leading across Siberia did not even exist.

It was thanks to the impeccable logistical planning made by the Scottish Long Rider Vyv Wood-Gee, and her daughter, Elsa, that enabled them to successfully ride across Great Britain.

Chapter 7
The Paperwork

Never forget what Long Rider Marco Polo once said.

"A stranger cannot have too many friends."

When you are on your horse, away from home, you are in danger from more subtle hazards than brigands, wolves and tornadoes. Chances are your journey won't be stopped by obvious dangers. You run a greater risk of being delayed by a small-minded official eager to exercise his authority or a petty sheriff trying to jail you unjustly.

This antagonism to travellers is an ancient evil, one which earlier equestrian explorers foresaw and took precautions to protect themselves against. They did so by use of the firman. Though this idea has been expressed through the ages by various cultures in a variety of manners, its most celebrated example was the pass issued by the powerful Genghis Khan to his ambassadors, friends and couriers. The mere sight of this potent travel icon instantly procured polite behaviour from obstructionist officials, inspired efficiency instead of arrogance, provided support in government guest houses and even opened jail cells. The great Khan's power would also produce horses for the next stage of a traveller's journey.

Thanks to the Mongol empire's lingering influence in Tibet, the latter benefit was still in effect when the Scottish Long Rider George Patterson set out to ride across the Himalayas in the winter of 1949. With the Chinese communists invading Tibet, where George lived and worked, local resistance leaders desperately needed a message pleading for international help to be delivered to the outside world. Accompanied by a trusted Tibetan friend, Loshay, the Scottish Long Rider mounted up and began an astonishing ride across a pass deemed so dangerous even the Tibetans wouldn't attempt it. During their ride from Tibet to India, George and Loshay used a firman, issued by the Khampa tribal leader, which authorized villagers to provide them with fresh mounts, skilled guides and every available assistance.

Another important aspect is the fact that the firman's latent authority was so great that the mere sight of it reduced previously proud officials into quivering wrecks.

That is what occurred when the Swiss traveller, Johann Burckhardt, was detained by corrupt petty officials during his journey across the Sahara desert.

Upon arriving at Souakin in the Sahara, Burckhardt's journey was nearly halted when a local emir attempted to steal the Swiss traveller's camel by pretending it was a tax. The outraged Burckhardt complained to the local Turkish official who was standing near by. Yet instead of adhering to the sacred concepts of hospitality and assistance towards travellers which Muslims are required by Islam to extend, the Turk sided with the corrupt emir and shouted, "You shall be thankful if we do not cut off your head."

That's when Burckhardt played his trump card. Reaching into a secret pocket, he brought forth an imperial firman presented to him by the Caliph of the Turkish Empire. Though this document was written in Turkish, not Mongol, and regardless of the centuries that had passed since Genghis Khan's riders originally made use of the firman, this powerful idea had migrated west and taken root within the kingdom of the Turks. Whereas a moment before he was being threatened with being beheaded, it was Burckhardt who now held the power of life and death.

"When they saw the Sultan's firman the villains became completely stupefied and looked at me with amazement. They kissed the document, protested in the most submissive terms and begged me a thousand pardons."

As we shall see, Long Riders still need a firman.

Wolves in uniforms

It was Long Rider Don Roberto Cunninghame Graham who warned, "Our real enemies are amongst us, born without imagination."

As the Burckhardt story demonstrates, regardless if you are a 19th century traveller in the Sahara, or a 21st century Long Rider preparing to depart, petty officials are apt to delay, antagonize, rob or harm you. This arises wherever you ride, because officials around the world are eager to enforce laws, even if they only exist in their own minds. Thus, no equestrian traveller, regardless of his importance, can hope to escape from this bureaucratic threat because a complete stranger riding through a district is an obvious nuisance to busy officials.

For example, during the five years in which he made his famous scientific journey around the world, Charles Darwin took every opportunity to explore the continents of South America, Australia and Africa on horseback. It was during the course of those mounted explorations that the young naturalist recalled, "the pleasure of living in the open air with the sky for a roof and the ground for a table."

Ironically, this scientific titan was forced to cool his heels by waiting to see a Latin American bureaucrat. On April 6th, 1832, Darwin complained, "The day has been frittered away in obtaining the passports for my expedition into the interior. It is never very pleasant to submit to the insolence of men in office. But the prospect of visiting wild forests tenanted by beautiful birds, monkeys, sloths, and alligators will make any naturalist lick the dust even from the foot of a Brazilian."

Passport and visas

Let's start with the obvious and what goes wrong when you don't have it.

It is critical that you document the legal, diplomatic and medical progress of your trip. Because every one of these steps is time consuming, and frequently takes longer than one might think, your documentation needs to be started early. We shall be discussing equine paperwork in a later section. What needs to be realized first is that unless your own papers are in order, there's no point in worrying about those of your horses.

There is a Long Rider saying that a unique occasion will produce a special man. When such a rare occasion arose in 1905 for a courageous horseman to ride from Kashmir to Peking, Major Clarence Dalrymple Bruce stepped into the saddle and cantered into Long Rider history. One reason he succeeded was due to the fact that he was armed with the official paperwork from authorities in both China and the British Raj.

Yet gone are the days of sahibs armed with imperial firmans, as when the next daring Long Rider attempted to reopen this historic route, he did not meet with the same level of success.

A tragic example of a paperwork nightmare ambushed one of the most important equestrian journeys undertaken in the early part of the 21st century. This occurred when the young British Long Rider Steve McCutcheon, who had optimistically set out to ride from Delhi, India to Peking, China, was stopped by bureaucrats, not bandits. Steve had already made modern equestrian travel history by becoming the first person to ride across India and into Pakistan. Next he survived a horrendous earthquake that devastated Pakistan and then made his way along the brigand-infested Karakorum Highway into China, where his diplomatic luck ran out.

After having obtained a new horse, baggage camels and trusted locals to guide him across China, Steve set off for Peking. His once-impossible goal was, it seemed, only a few hard months down the road. With his caravan barely in progress, Steve made a brief return to the nearest large town to consult with a farrier. That's when the storm broke.

"I'd been back from the farrier's shop no more than an hour when the phone rang," McCutcheon wrote to the Guild.

"Police here, come quick," my friend Korban breathlessly announced. I rushed back, anticipating more trouble with the Chinese officials.

"Where is your permit?" the officer demanded. "You should have a permit from Urumchi. Where is it?"

I had no permit, nor never had. I'd been plainly told before I left that none was needed. My route passed through areas freely open to independent travel and there shouldn't have been a problem. I did have paperwork stating my itinerary and purpose as well as my own information leaflets, yet neither was good enough for this weasel-like man.

'Out of the frying pan…' I thought. "Would I ever make it to Beijing?"

Though I'd been previously informed by local big wigs that I would be allowed to continue my journey towards Beijing, in fact no police officer at their station was now willing to back up those events. The reality, it seemed, was that they probably shouldn't have let me continue in the first place and now nobody was willing to take responsibility for their original actions.

Nor did it help matters that Karchung, where I was, lay in a different county to Kosrap, where I had started. That allowed them to tell me, "different county, different rules."

To add to my troubles, the government weasel's superior officer then tried intimidating me. He growled over the phone line, "sell your camels or you will be punished."

I was obviously dealing with unreasonable men.

As the afternoon wore thin, I suggested meeting in Yarkand the following morning, where I hoped to recover the mobile numbers of the officers who had previously authorized me to come to Karchung. In the meantime, I was forced to hand over my passport. I wasn't riding anywhere.

Ignoring my urgency, the local police officers spent all of the next day prospecting for minerals. They didn't return all day. To make matters worse, a friend called to inform me that every major police station from Karchung to Urumchi now knew about my case.

Now it turned out that despite my route lying through areas open for travel, it appeared that I actually did require a permit to cross Xinjiang with camels.

Then things got worse.

The police informed me that if I wanted to continue my ride to Beijing "you must first send your camel drivers home, then arrange the permits you need in Kashgar."

Thankfully the local authorities eventually allowed me to keep my horse and the camels in Karchung whilst I left to organise the relevant documents. My friends, Rosa and Korban, were forced to return to their respective homes, while I, after being weighted down with three camel loads of gear, was soon on the bus headed back to Kashgar.

In retrospect, given the inadequacy of my previous paperwork, my run-in with the police in Karchung was bound to happen sooner or later. China isn't Pakistan or India and now that I understand the country a little better I'm presently applying for permits for every province from Xinjiang to Beijing. I hate being separated from my team and my caravan. The only bright side is that my animals are entrusted to a great family whom I know well.

Yet sadly, at the end of the day Marco Polo needed permits and it turns out so do I."

Not only did the Chinese government deny Steve the authority to resume his journey, they also presented him with a hefty fine and required him to leave the country without delay.

There are few greater living equestrian explorers than the British Long Rider Christina Dodwell, who has ridden through enough adventures to fill a dozen books. This savvy rider always takes precautions with her passport and visas.

"Keep your passport with you at all times," she warns. "But be sure to also make a photocopy of it and keep it somewhere separate."

Christina also advises making copies of your driving licence and birth certificate. And because many countries require a traveller to provide several photos per visa application, she suggests you always carry extra passport photos so as to stave off problems en route. If possible, she warned, obtain your visas in advance and always be aware of their expiration date.

Another great idea was sent in by Billy Brenchley, who said, "When it comes to paperwork and documents, be practical not paranoid. I carry several colour copies of my original documents. This way, if a corrupt official threatens to confiscate it unless you pay a bribe, say go ahead, keep it."

One final word regarding visas. When Tim Cope made his journey from Mongolia to Hungary, he had the great idea of not applying for a tourist visa. Instead, by applying to the media minister, Tim secured a four month visa as a 'Foreign Correspondent.' Given the extra length of time needed to make his equestrian journey, the additional months were a decided benefit.

Ownership papers, equine passports, brand inspections, inoculation certificates and the firman. There is a great deal more paperwork involved in equestrian travel than most would-be Long Riders realize.

And never keep your passport and other vital papers in your saddle bag. One unlucky Long Rider's horse ran away, leaving her stranded on the steppes of Mongolia.

"To my horror my horse galloped off over a hill out of my sight. Shit! I had not only just lost my horse but my money, passport and bank card."

Always carry your passport and papers on your person.

Health Certificates

Regardless of where you're planning on riding, it is imperative that you confirm what medical tests, inoculations and health certificates you and your horse will require before setting out. Germ-borne threats await the unwary in a wide variety of forms. For example, tick-borne encephalitis can be found along the Equestrian Equator which stretches from the Atlantic coast of Europe, across Central Asia and through southern Siberia to the Pacific Ocean. In Austria, the entire population is routinely vaccinated against this prevalent disease every year and international health experts strongly recommend visitors to be vaccinated against this disease.

Failing to investigate these medical frontiers prior to departure has even caught some of the world's most talented equestrian explorers off guard. So be forewarned.

The Firman

The firman invokes a sense of power. Among the uneducated it is held in awe. To officials in distant locations far removed from the national capital, it is a reminder that the printed word is sacred.

The concept of the firman has been used in a variety of countries and is known by various names.

When George Ruxton made a perilous ride across Mexico in 1847 he carried a *carta de seguridad*, letter of security, "which is indispensable and by which the traveller's transit through the territory of the republic is sanctioned."

Before setting off to ride across Persia in 1873, the British Long Rider Hippisley Cunliffe Marsh obtained a *tushkereh* from the Shah. It urged local authorities, "The lofty one mentioned should be treated with great respect. For our sake, conduct him without delay and foster our guest with care."

Captain John Cochrane relied on a national ruler to issue commands designed to enlist the aid of officials, police and subjects encountered en route. In addition to his British passport and Russian visa, Cochrane was armed with a letter that bore explicit instructions from the Czar.

"An Open Order of his Imperial Majesty: The bearer hereof, Captain John Cochrane, of his Britannic Majesty's Royal Navy, having undertaken to travel through the Russian Empire, is now on his way to Kamchatka, intending from thence to pass over to America. The police of the towns and provinces lying in his track from St. Petersburg to Kamchatka, are, in consequence hereof, not only forbidden to obstruct Captain Cochrane in his journey, but are moreover commanded, in case of necessity, to afford him every possible assistance."

Though the years change, the concept still holds true. When Sir John Ure set off in 1972 to ride across the Andes Mountains from Chile into Argentina, he realized his route would require him to cross the border via a remote pass frequented by smugglers. Fearing that his intentions might be viewed with suspicion if he were intercepted by mounted gendarmerie patrols, he carried a special document explaining his equestrian mission.

"I had left nothing to chance and kept in my saddle bag an ever more grubby envelope, sealed and heavily embossed with a coat of arms. Inside this was a copy of a letter in exquisitely ornate and diplomatic Spanish from the Argentine Ambassador in Santiago to his Foreign Minister in Buenos Aires explaining that I was a diplomatic colleague bent on an eccentric but innocent expedition and requesting any help and assistance of which my companions and I might stand in need."

Jonathan Danos set off in 1979 to ride his Criollo mare through the Andes Mountains from Chile to Argentina.

"Before entering Argentina, the Chileans very generously gave me a *salvo conducto* – a safe travel pass guaranteeing my behaviour in Argentina," Jonathan wrote.

Likewise, when I made my last equestrian journey through Pakistan, I carried a firman issued by the national government which confirmed my identity to the police, authorized me to use any of the government bungalows found along the way and verified the importance of my horses to local medical authorities.

Even if you can't enlist the aid of Tibetan rebels like George Patterson did, you should make every effort to obtain some sort of firman from the authorities prior to your departure. If your journey is to be a domestic one which keeps you within the borders of your own country, have your governor, state senator, local congressman, mayor or even police chief, issue you a document urging other officials to respect and expedite your journey through their areas of influence.

If your journey will take you through foreign countries, then arrange a courtesy call to the embassies of each of the lands you wish to ride in. Request a brief meeting with the ambassador. During that meeting ask the ambassador if he would be kind enough to sign a letter you have prepared in advance which describes your intentions, route and the fact that you have discussed your journey with this high-ranking government official. If possible, have the letter stamped with an official seal. And in this age of instant digital photography, ask if someone can take your photo as the ambassador hands you the firman. Such diplomatic precautions may save you countless delays, or rescue you and your horses from unforeseen bureaucratic entanglements.

But remember, these elementary precautions don't come easy.

The French Long Rider Jean-Louis Gouraud made one of the most important equestrian journeys of the late twentieth century, when he rode his French Trotter from Paris to Moscow. Yet that journey only came about thanks to the incredible tenacity and long term planning of the Parisian.

"After five years of trying, Moscow has finally given me the green light. I am to be allowed to ride into the USSR! This is the first time that permission to do such a thing has been given to an Occidental since the 1917 October Revolution! The Soviet Federation of Equestrian Sport has written to me: 'Be at the border of Brest (Litovsk) on 23rd June before noon!'"

Thanks to his careful diplomatic planning, Jean-Louis not only completed his historic ride, at the end of his journey he gave his horses as gifts to Raisa Gorbechev, the wife of the Soviet ruler, Mikael Gorbechev.

Letters of Introduction

If you can't manage to obtain an official recognition from the federal government, then aim lower, but keep trying.

The famous nineteenth-century English travel writer, Francis Galton, wrote a "how to" book wherein he warned travellers to foreign countries on a number of vital topics, including how to avoid being attacked by natives in Africa, where to procure camels in Arabia and how to open minor diplomatic doors.

"A letter of introduction from a person of authority to other officials will smooth away many small difficulties and give you a recognized position during your travels. If possible obtain letters of recommendation to ambassadors, bankers, merchants, doctors, lawyers, booksellers and respectable tradesmen. In addition to being helpful, such people are able to give you a great deal of interesting information," Galton warned his readers.

This concept has proved successful for a wide variety of Long Riders.

In 1966 the North American Long Rider, Verne Albright, eased his passage from Peru to California by obtaining a letter of introduction from a Secretary of Agriculture. Having met at a party in Costa Rica, the government official expressed his support of Albright's ride. Not only did he give the Long Rider a letter of introduction to local officials, he also urged the other secretaries of Agriculture between Costa Rica and the US to assist Verne.

Also, before the French Long Rider Evelyne Coquet set off in 1972 to ride 6,000 kilometres from Paris to Jerusalem, she too obtained, "a letter of explanation in advance from each country's embassy explaining in the local language what I was doing, where I was going and asking whomever they met to give me and my horses aid and assistance in finding shelter, lodging, a blacksmith or a vet."

Likewise when the Jean-Claude Cazade and his companion Pascale Franconie rode into Amman, the capital of Jordan, they managed to obtain the official support of Princess Alia, the eldest daughter of King Hassan.

"Though we still had no visa or permission to enter Saudi Arabia, a few days later our patience was rewarded when we were assured that this government now wished to help us. First the Saudi Arabian Consulate telephoned to say we could come and collect our visas. When we got there we were also given a letter of introduction to the Amir of Tabuk. Plus, as we proceed through Jordan we found a miracle in the desert. Hay and alfalfa had been placed in advance for our horses," Pascale recalled.

And it was thanks to a letter of introduction that New Zealand Long Rider Ian Robinson was able to make his solo ride into Afghanistan's isolated Wakhan Corridor in 2008. Prior to leaving Kabul, Ian had obtained a letter from a high-ranking federal official.

"As it turned out," Ian wrote, "Mr. Afshar's letter was like a golden key to open every door from Kabul to the end of the Wakhan Corridor. Along the way I would have to present it at local police stations. No one dared try to overrule the Deputy Minister's authority."

What happens when you don't make an equestrian journey without carrying such beneficial papers?

One such example struck John Egenes. Despite having neared the trouble-free half-way mark on his ocean to ocean ride across the United States, John then lost a Letter of Introduction issued by the American Quarter Horse Association, along with his other forms of ID. To his dismay, John was arrested on an imaginary charge and jailed in

Arkansas, at which time the authorities quickly exploited what they believed was a friendless traveller. Luckily, local citizens demanded that the corrupt sheriff release the young Long Rider.

Thus John learned that without the proper papers a Long Rider can be easily incarcerated without cause.

Explanatory Flyers

There is one other powerful piece of paper you should arm yourself with, namely the explanatory flyer.

Regardless of where you ride, you are going to be peppered, day after day, by curious people asking you the same questions. Where are you coming from? Where are going? What kind of horse are you riding? How much did you pay for him? Why are you making this ride? Aren't you afraid you're going to be a) killed, b) kidnapped c) robbed d) all of the above? Are you married? Do you want to be? How much money do you make? What religion are you? And on and on and on, every day.

Two modern pioneers who are adept at handling this problem are Robin and Louella Hanbury-Tenison. Though they made equestrian journeys in Spain, New Zealand, Albania and China, all of those subsequent journeys followed the successful experiment they conceived when they made their first ride across France.

Having foreseen the avalanche of questions awaiting them, Robin composed a simple one-page flyer. Thanks to this French-language explanation, copies of which were always kept close at hand or in a saddle bag, Robin and Louella managed to remain friendly, provide accurate information and still make good daily time in the saddle.

Thus, Explanatory Flyers work anywhere, in any language, and save you the trouble of having to deal with an annoying daily barrage of repetitive questions.

Religious Passports

The Way of St. James, which is one of Europe's most ancient pilgrim routes, terminates at the cathedral in Santiago, Spain where the apostle Saint James is said to have been laid to rest. Pilgrims, either on foot or in the saddle, are required to carry a special passport. The *credencial*, a distant successor to the safe-conducts issued to medieval pilgrims, is a document printed and issued by the cathedral authorities in Santiago, and made available to bona fide pilgrims at points along the route. Travellers are required to obtain signatures from authorities along the way so as to document their journey.

A number of notable Long Riders have obtained, and completed, the *credencial*. Robin and Louella Hanbury-Tenison rode to Santiago in 1989, and Robin's classic book, *Spanish Pilgrimage*, movingly documents their journey. In 1987 little Long Rider Hjoerdis Rickert, aged 9, made the journey with her parents and a horse called Oualipo. And the mounted pilgrimages made by British Long Rider Mefo Phillips and Irish Long Rider Stephen O'Connor inspired both travellers to write excellent books about their journeys. And the most travelled Long Rider in the twentieth century, Captain Otto Schwarz, rode to Santiago from his home in Switzerland several times.

Certificate of Call

There is one last type of documentation you may need to consider. This is known as the "Certificate of Call." This document serves as an official recognition of your arrival at, or departure from, a designated location.

The most famous exponent of the Certificate of Call was George Beck. In 1912 Beck set off, with three companions, to make a non-stop journey to all 48 state capitals in the continental United States. In order to document their arrival at each capital building, Beck requested that state's governor to issue a Certificate of Call, which confirmed the date of arrival.

When possible, the clever Long Rider always requested a photograph be taken with the travellers. Every meeting concluded with Beck asking the governor if he would be kind enough to provide the governor of the next state with a letter urging official support for the Long Riders. This procedure was faithfully duplicated during the entire 20,000 mile trip.

Even if you do not require such a legal confirmation of your arrival, it is also a good idea to carry a small Friendship Book which people along your route can sign. Thanks to this method you can retain names, comments and contact details from people you meet en route. The chapter on "Ethical Travel" also explains how the Friendship Book provides you with a layer of protection from suspicious police and validates the authenticity of your journey.

Summary

Bureaucracy is not a happy topic, but in this world of regulations it is unavoidable, so be absolutely certain that you have every possible document for yourself and your horse including a new passport, valid identification documents, veterinary documents, etc, as customs officers, state veterinarians, border guards and the police can always be counted on to inspect a Long Rider's documents very carefully.

Let me conclude by presenting you with this final warning.

Remember, you can never take anything for granted when it comes to paperwork, horses and Long Riders. This was demonstrated when Tim Cope arrived at the border between Kazakhstan and Russia. Though the Russian authorities had issued Tim with a document which apparently allowed the traveller to enter their country, the Long Rider was turned away at the border.

Why?

Because when the Russian officials in Moscow had issued the travel document, they had not specifically stated that Tim was allowed to enter their country "ON" horseback. In contrast, the document instead stated that Tim was allowed to enter Russia "WITH" horses. Thus, in this motorized age when border guards are used to seeing horses being transported via trucks but no longer being ridden, the mere absence of the correct wording resulted in Tim's progress being halted for weeks, while he pleaded with the bureaucrats on both sides of the border to permit him to proceed. Finally, with only a few hours left on his Kazakh visa, Tim was allowed to enter Russia.

This paiza, or passport, made of cast iron and silver, dates from late 13th century China under the rule of Kublai Khan. It was large enough to be hung from a traveller's belt to display his right to unfettered passage in the Mongol realms. The same concept was used by George Patterson when he made his historic ride over the Himalayan Mountains in the winter of 1949.

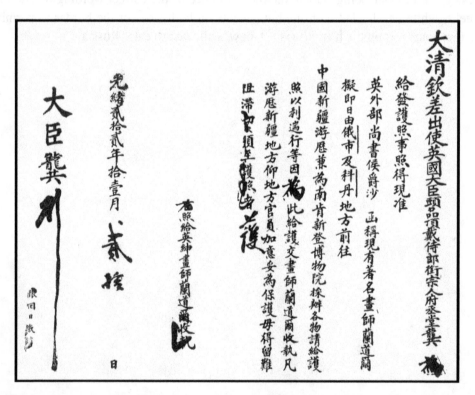

This Chinese firman directed government officials to assist Major Clarence Dalrymple Bruce during his 1905 ride from Kashmir to Peking.

The English Long Riders, Robin and Louella Hanbury-Tenison, presented this Explanatory Flyer to people they met during their first ride across France.

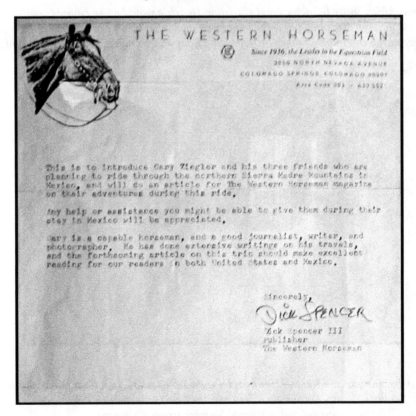

In an attempt to solicit local support before setting off to ride across Mexico, North American Long Rider Gary Ziegler procured this "To Whom it May Concern" letter from the publisher of America's leading equestrian magazine.

African Hoofprints CC
CC Registration No: 2004/095062/23

29 Ninth Avenue
Fish Hoek
7975
Cape Town

PostNet Suite #123
Private Bag X26
Tokai
7966
Cape Town

Email: info@africanhoofprints.com
Website: www.africanhoofprints.com
Tel: 0721342836

29th September 2005

To Whom It May Concern,

RE: Horseback Tour

Christine Henchie and William Brenchley are attempting to ride 15 196km across the Africa continent, traversing 13 countries through some of the harshest terrain and most extreme conditions.

We will use three Tunisian Berber horses which are renowned for their adaptability, toughness and sensibility. They will fulfil the veterinary requirements according to Tunisian law.

One horse will feature as a pack horse for food and water. 55km per day is accepted as a good average to travel, with one rest day per week. Thirteen months have been set aside to complete this venture.

The local population will be relied upon for water, food and accommodation. We have a pre-planned route with GPS navigation but will accept guidance through "hot spots" from the locals.

We have medical insurance but do not know if the horses require medical insurance. It is also not known which travel permits and import/export permits are required for the horses.

Christine will take photographs, sketch, paint and keep a diary of our adventures which will form the basis of a book to be written.

William has undertaken to do research and development of a hoof boot for the main sponsor African Hoofprints CC (RSA).

Christine is a riding instructor with experience in training disabled and traumatized children. She is also a young-horse trainer.

William is a farrier specializing in the treatment of pathology. He has crewed for two horseback expeditions: 1800km from Windhoek, Namibia to Cape Town, South Africa and 3500km from the East to West coast of Africa crossing through Mozambique, Zimbabwe, Botswana and Namibia.

For more information, please call 072 134 2836.

Yours faithfully,

Christine Henchie   William Brenchley

During their journey across Africa, Billy Brenchley and Christine Henchie would make courtesy calls to the embassy of the next country they planned to ride through. This two-page document was presented as an explanation of their journey. Sometimes they were greeted by junior Secretaries but in many other instances the Long Riders met the Ambassador and received his direct help.

The German Long Riders Albert Knaus and Kerstin Hüllmandel rode 1,500 miles from their home, along the Way of Saint James, to the ancient cathedral at Santiago, Spain. During their journey, they carefully obtained the signatures needed to complete their credential, a special Spanish travel document.

Irish Long Rider Stephen O'Connor carried this Pilgrim's Passport when he made his ride from Santiago, Spain.

Another way of establishing your local credentials is to carry local newspaper stories, which is what the French Long Rider Thierry Posty used during his ride across Japan.

North American Long Rider George Beck, (left) and his three companions The Overland Westerners, made a point of obtaining a "Certificate of Call" from the governor of the state of New Hampshire (centre), as well as the other forty-seven governors they met during their 20,352 mile journey.

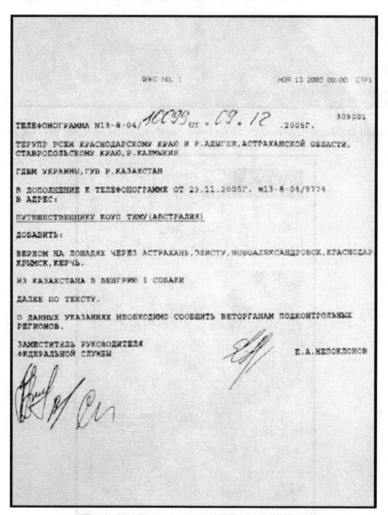

Tim Cope learned the hard way that modern officials, especially border guards, are not prepared to accommodate equestrian travellers who show up unexpectedly and are carrying documents which do not accurately authorize their continued progress. Tim's Russian document was considered invalid because it lacked the words "on horseback."

Stranded between Russia and Kazakhstan, Tim Cope (second from right) struggled to obtain permission from Moscow. After an international effort, including a letter from the Long Riders' Guild to President Putin, the Australian Long Rider was finally allowed into Russia.

Chapter 8
Your Choice of Companions

The longest day is made shorter by a good companion.

Yet even a good rule can be taken to extremes. For example, when the Ottoman ambassador, Evliya Çelebi jour-neyed to France in 1729, this Long Rider-turned-diplomat was accompanied by a physician, imam, interpreter, secretary, treasurer, steward, barber, perfumer, master of robes, tailor, pipe filler, two valets, laundryman, chief cook, coffee maker, six kitchen aides, candlestick maintainer, twenty footmen, four tent guards, water bearers, two grooms and five caterers.

I strongly suggest that you can make do with fewer companions. But the choice of a comrade is a preliminary test filled with unseen perils, many of which are not recognized by would-be Long Riders prior to their departure. Nor is this a modern dilemma.

The ancient Buddhist spiritual text, the Dhammapada, warned that if on the journey of life a person can find a wise and intelligent friend who is good and self-controlled, then let him go with that traveller; and in joy and recollection let them overcome the dangers of their trip together. But if on the journey of life a man cannot find a wise and intelligent friend who is good and self-controlled, let him then travel alone, like a king who has left his country, or like a great elephant alone in the forest.

As we shall see, what you need in a companion on the ride is a guide at the crossroads, strength when you are weak, defence against danger, solace in moments of discouragement and firmness of purpose, for an equestrian expedition is only as strong as its weakest link. If your journey is to succeed, everyone must come together to form a powerful team that shares the same vision.

The Wrong Message

Unfortunately many aspects of the modern tourism industry are designed to mislead you, as and when you attempt to make the proper choice of a critically important companion.

To begin with, it is often difficult to find anyone even to consider accompanying you. This is because most people are urged instead to stifle any desire to explore the vast world until such time as they reach physical maturity and have obtained a strong degree of financial security. Long Rider Verne Albright ridiculed that idea. In the mid-1960s, young Albright set off to ride his Peruvian Paso mare from Peru to California. Though he was admonished for having placed his successful banking career on hold, he rejected loyalty to money, choosing instead to live life to the fullest.

"When Americans are young they plunge into their careers, so most don't get around to travelling until they are older. That's backward. People should travel when they're young. That way the things they learn can be put to good use and for a long time. Furthermore, when most people travel, they stay in the best hotels, eat at the best restaurants, take guided tours and otherwise isolate themselves from the local culture. Even in their own country, these people travel in cocoons. They go into the wilds with campers, trailers and all the comforts of home," Verne warned.

The polar opposite of equestrian exploration is air travel, which offers no involvement with the outside world. The airplane is a symbol of everything your horse isn't. It is fast, sterile, boring and complex. It presents the traveller with passive attractions, forgettable food, and sterilized companionship. It is the antithesis of personal freedom, a servant of money and corporate interests. It is an indoor experience pretending to be a gateway to adventure.

Planes are populated by crowds of people, the majority of whom would be unsuitable to accompany you, as they are pawns of the tourism trade and not independent travellers such as you seek.

Though mostly well-intentioned, tourists are pseudo-travellers in economic servitude to the travel agents, plane companies, hotels and entertainment industries who lure them away from home with false promises. By granting access to their bank accounts, naïve tourists are taken to global vortexes where customs are flaunted and once-sacred places are eroded into caricatures. Mount Everest and Machu Picchu are prime examples of locations whose original integrity have been subverted by swarms of tourism locusts. Tourism is a blight that destroys what it pretends to enshrine, aided by tour guides at places like Petra who sell their own integrity, and that of their homeland, to the highest bidder. Tourists use their money to avoid personal involvement, preferring, as Verne said, to reside in safe hotels and stay on well-beaten paths. These people have spent a fortune and gone nowhere.

Long Riders are not about travelling in cocoons, either physically or mentally.

An equestrian traveller is someone who isn't entangled in tourist dogma. This person is striving to travel light, to unburden their soul of physical possessions in order to join a fraternity of free riders who are sound in mind and body. Fliers and drivers are lucky if they achieve a small proportion of the blazing first-hand experiences which await a Long Rider. When you are in the saddle, you find yourself, not a bland tourist trap.

Though you are contemplating looking for a companion, what you will quickly discover is that even a million air miles is no guarantee of courage. This is because the majority of tourists spend their time avoiding any confrontation with their fears. They are seeking to maintain their customs, albeit with bottled water and a waiter who speaks their native language. Freedom isn't granted without effort. Courage is a rare commodity. Finding someone who understands the former and possesses the latter is exceptionally difficult. Nor can you expect any sympathy from the inhabitants of the tourist world who have swapped their labour for a holiday in an insipid location. They are materially rich but spiritually poor.

In contrast, Long Riders are not attempting to disrupt the local culture. Their horse dictates that they live alongside the native people. Their journey is not about spending money or disrupting a culture. They are interested in learning the language, observing the customs and interacting with the people as they ride through a country. In return for friendship, they receive rich experiences, not fancy service. Their coin of the realm is honesty and respect, not arrogance.

To travel and ride in such a way brings you a happiness which cannot be obtained by money. By exploring the world in this manner you break down the geographical, emotional and cultural boundaries of your previous existence. Though filled with uncertainty, and occasional danger, the Long Rider discovers a world which tourists can only read and dream about finding. Such a place is a mirage to a tourist but a daily reality to a Long Rider.

There are few people capable of summoning the courage to set off on such a journey. The chances of finding a second such person, able and willing to accompany you are therefore slim. That is why this book is for the special few, the new nomads, the Long Rider.

Equestrian travel is complex and difficult in its challenges, but magnificent in its rewards. Which is why, while you are defining your own equestrian commitment at this early stage, you must first determine if you will ride alone or with a companion.

A Rude Awakening

Before she set off on her 1939 ride from Cornwall to Scotland, Margaret Leigh was filled with excitement and anticipation about her forthcoming journey. Unfortunately her dream trip soon became a nightmare thanks to her surly male companion. This disagreeable individual turned discourse and decision-making into a daily battle. Margaret was therefore relieved when he chose to go fight the Nazis and leave her to ride on alone.

"It takes some imagination to see that a long ride on horseback, which sounds so thrilling in prospect, may in actual fact be immensely wearisome and monotonous, especially with a companion who does not think or act as you do," she wrote in her book, *My Kingdom for a Horse.*

As Margaret learned, few people are born travellers who can rest anywhere and get along with anyone.

"As I lay in my tent, I pondered deeply on this problem. Two women left alone will often fight like cats over trifles, while a man and a woman travelling together will end either in love or hate."

What Margaret learned at great personal expense was that only a few people can become Long Riders. The majority of people, though initially intrigued with the idea, soon learn that they either suffer through or end up hating the experience. When that occurs, the would-be Long Rider is facing hell in the saddle.

Hell in the Saddle

Let me make this perfectly clear.
Your equestrian dream will turn into a nightmare if you set off with the wrong companion!

Nine times out of ten this is your dream and a potential companion often serves as a convenient emotional security blanket which you think you need at this early stage of the trip's development. As history has demonstrated time after time, the immense physical and emotional hardships of an equestrian journey place a tremendous strain on friendships, families and marriages, many of which will not survive unless everyone involved is equally passionate about completing the trip.

What you will discover is that as your mounted skills increase on the trail, your previous emotional need will diminish as your confidence grows. Moreover, the further you ride into your new world, the more interactions you will enjoy with an exciting assortment of newly-met friends. Thus, as your own courage and resolve increase, your original companion's value will often diminish. That is an issue which requires honesty on both your parts, as the journey will demand that you stay equally committed.

Yet what happens when you quickly realize that things are very wrong – right from the beginning? When this occurs you are facing a critical social disaster, one which can, and has, scuttled many an otherwise carefully planned equestrian journey.

That's what happened to the young American woman who attempted to ride ocean to ocean with the wrong companion. Though the planning had all gone well, the journey had barely commenced when the companion's antagonism came boiling to the surface. Not only did the other woman withdraw from the journey, she took the riding and pack horses with her, effectively stranding the first young traveller more than a thousand of miles from home.

Another terrible trap is discovered when you set out with someone whose commitment doesn't match your own.

This isn't a new problem. When Thomas Stevens set off to ride across Russia in 1890 he invited a young man to accompany him as an interpreter. Being a hardened traveller, Stevens knew what sort of adversity lay ahead. Not so his companion.

"His idea of a two months picnic on horseback had of course vanished like a shadow ere we had been on the road a week. His moral stamina was not equal to the prolonged hardships and discomforts of the ride. He wavered between the ambition to finish what he had set out to do and a hankering after the comforts of his home in Moscow."

The Russian fled for home, leaving Stevens to carry on alone.

Nor should you believe that the destructive effect of a fantasist is a thing of the past.

After more than a year of careful planning, the first modern equestrian journey across Indonesia was cancelled because of this reason. The Long Rider was left in a lurch when his companion suddenly announced he was going home after only ten days in the saddle.

This type of person is becoming more common in the equestrian travel world. They can be found frequenting chat rooms wherein they announce how they're going to undertake an important ride. Countless hours are wasted talking about saddles and horseshoes, though an actual route is often overlooked. Trusting people are recruited, who end up wasting their own time, money, and experience on these misguided dreamers.

One recent example occurred when an American woman announced that she was going to make the End to End ride, from the bottom of Cornwall to the top of Scotland. Her Scottish Long Rider host was recruited to help locate and purchase a suitable horse, organize the trip, plan the route, etc. Yet upon arriving in Scotland, the fantasist spent most of her time lounging in her mentor's kitchen and making long distance phone calls back home. When finally faced with the day of departure, she deserted the horse and flew home to the States, preferring to blame her astonished hosts instead of accepting any personal responsibility.

As one Long Rider warned, "It's seriously not funny travelling with someone who can't differentiate fact from the figments of their imagination. In the end, several days before we reached our destination, my companion rang her partner and got him to come and collect her, so I finished my trip alone, which is infinitely preferable to travelling with someone untrustworthy."

However, the very worst discovery is when you learn that your companion is a horse hater. This happened to the woman who rode with a man whose contempt for his mount turned into physical abuse. The insecure bully routinely turned his antagonism against his horse, treating it like a rental car. At one point, when the horse pulled back in fear, the bully shouted, "I'll give you something to be afraid of," and began hitting the horse. Thus what should have been a memorable adventure descended into a costly disaster, which in turn resulted in the woman departing for home with her original travel plans shattered.

As these examples demonstrate, you had better hope that you never find yourself riding alongside an angry companion, or sharing a tent with a person who hates you for having "talked" them into sharing your dream. Being stranded alone on a desert island is a far better than finding yourself trapped in such a plodding nightmare, riding at three miles an hour alongside a furious companion.

As these examples prove, some people can ride ten miles, or ten thousand, and never comprehend what equestrian travel is about. Thus, while it seems obvious that we do not wish to set off with fickle, boring, or disreputable companions who don't understand horses, who can we consider and depend upon? The answer is simple.

There are always two companions you can trust to understand your journey – you and your road horse.

Riding Alone

Having discovered what happens when you set off with the wrong person, it's no wonder that the majority of would-be Long Riders decide to travel alone.

J. Smeaton Chase was the English naturalist who rode from Mexico to Oregon, and then explored the Mojave Desert, during the early part of the twentieth century. Though he opted to ride with a partner on his first journey, Chase decided to undertake his perilous desert trip alone. Why?

"One of the compensations to be set against the lack of a companion was that I was free to stop or proceed, hurry or delay, camp here or there, entirely at my own choice, with my only regard being my horse's needs as to forage," he wrote.

Likewise a European Long Rider originally began her journey across Argentina with a companion, but then decided that solo travel suited her better.

"I am travelling alone and this time I am enjoying myself - making the most of being able to decide what I want to do without consulting anyone else," she recalled.

Another benefit is the reception offered by potential hosts.

Argentine Long Rider Benjamin Reynal recalled, "People who hosted me when I was alone were much nicer than the few times when I had a temporary companion. For example, if I arrived alone at a ranch and presented myself, they would invite me to stay at the house and sit at their table. But if there were two of us, they would give us food and send us to sleep in the barn. In their eyes I already had a companion, so they did not feel any need to take me in. Therefore the relationship with hosts is not the same or as rich."

What these travellers demonstrate is an ancient truth known to all Long Riders.

Don't be afraid, you already have the ideal companion.

Your Best Friend

Though it may seem obvious, most humans overlook this fundamental truth. A great portion of the journey is about the involved relationship which develops between two species, namely you and your mount.

Your horse is your primary companion. Part of your mission is to explore, expand and understand the journey alongside this majestic animal. Solo travelling certainly has its compensations. You have no one to consider but yourself. You can go where and when you like, stop when you want to, eat what and when you fancy, without reference to the curious and unpredictable tastes of a comrade. Yet even then you are not really alone, for you have your horse, and it is thanks to your mount that everyone is kind to a lone traveller. It is the horse who will spark more interest, talk, friendliness and hospitality than any human companion.

But say for the sake of argument if you're going to travel with someone, then whom should you choose?

Careful Considerations

Imagine this.

You've been on the road for six weeks, during which time you've lost weight and patience. The rain is lashing down, the sun is setting and you're a soaking, miserable, cold wreck. The so-called road is a boggy nightmare and the village you were hoping to find is nowhere in sight. Your road horse is dead tired and the pack horse has pulled back on your arm so often that your right shoulder is on fire. At such a moment are friendships lost over a misplaced word. Tempers snap, curses are exchanged and journeys are ruined.

Or, a smile, an encouraging glance, an attitude of "we can do it" from a treasured companion will change your dreary rainy day into something you know you'll both look back on and laugh at.

That's what's at stake here.

As previously noted, equestrian expeditions are often the original dream of one person. Yet while many dream about making such an expedition, few are willing to assume the responsibility of taking command. This is why many times, because of knowledge, enthusiasm and personality, the journey's originator accepts the role of leader. While many people are happy to daydream about reaching their faraway goal, they're less likely to discuss the mechanics of who does what and when once you're on the road. To avoid future conflict, it is vital that all members of the expedition agree in advance on what their various duties will be. If you experience any pre-trip antagonism, or sense any failure of resolve, then terminate the relationship prior to your departure, as it is better to be blunt now than suffer in the saddle later.

Recipe for Success

Unfortunately, you can't wish for a perfect Long Rider. But here's a recipe for emotional and tactical success.

When looking for a companion, remember personal qualities mean more than money. Find a person who is inclined to your own view and sympathetic to the things you enjoy. Always choose enthusiasm before academic knowledge. Courtesy is priceless. A sense of humour is a must. Tolerance of others, resilience in the face of adversity and adaptability in the face of emergencies are always required. Endurance and keen motivation are foundations for success. The ability to thrive in isolation is necessary. Courage can never be underestimated. A proficiency in equestrian skills is a delight, as are linguistic skills and cooking. Above all else, prize loyalty, as this gift will help overcome the stresses and strains found on any rigorous journey.

When considering a companion, you will be tempted to compromise. Listen to your instincts. Forsake any type of inflexible expert. Shun anyone whose political or religious convictions cannot be constrained. Leave drunkards and party animals behind, as their lack of discipline will translate into future trouble for your horses. Above all, avoid anyone who is selfish, immature and lazy. Equestrian travel will test the toughest and break the weak. So don't burden yourself in advance with the wrong companion.

Finally, ask yourself if you would be willing to spend long periods of time with this person, trapped in a small room, facing unexpected troubles, plans gone awry? If the answer is yes, then you're considering the proper sort of riding companion. And such mounted treasures come in a variety of forms, some of which may surprise you.

Friends

People with powerful personalities do not necessarily make the best travellers. A tedious journey is apt to make anyone irritable, which in turn often leads to harsh words. It is at such times when gentle and forgiving friends are a true treasure. Three companions who overcame tremendous adversity were the North American Long Riders Merian C. Cooper, Ernest Schoedsack and Marguerite Harrison.

Though he is most often remembered today as being the creator of the original film, *King Kong*, Merian C. Cooper led a life so filled with adventure that his story would have amazed anyone. In the early 1920s, Cooper volunteered to fly in the Polish air force against the invading Soviet army. Shot down, the young aviator was imprisoned and nearly starved to death, before escaping his tormentors and fleeing back to Poland, where he was awarded that country's most distinguished military medal. He next turned his attention to film making, joining up with camera man Ernest Schoedsack and American socialite turned military spy Marguerite Harrison. The trio journeyed to Persia, where they met the Bakhtiari nomads. During the course of making his first feature film, "Grass," Cooper swam raging rivers, climbed ice covered peaks and rode alongside the nomads from the Persian Gulf to the pastures on the far side of the Zagros Mountains. Though Cooper went on to enjoy a successful film career, he fondly recalled his time as a Long Rider and often lamented not being able to return to Persia.

Though their backgrounds varied, their journey proves that the difficulty lies not in taking up quarrels, but in avoiding them.

Couples

Too often people are told that upon reaching maturity they should decline with dignity. Rubbish.

John Codman was a sea captain by trade, but spent his leisure hours in old age on land riding his mare, Fanny. A self-confessed "septuagenarian," Codman was never shy about sharing his horse-based opinions. Walking, Codman said, was a "solitary entertainment" and the bicycle he dismissed as being "unnatural." Thus it was from the back of his horse that the old sea captain sailed over the land of his birth. His famous book, *Winter Sketches from the Saddle* was first published in 1888. It recommends riding for your health and describes Codman's equestrian journeys through New England during the winter of 1887. "There is no greater pleasure than to find myself on a horse," Codman wrote, and went on to praise the healthy benefits derived from "equestrianopathy."

A number of important Long Riders have consisted of husband and wife teams who followed Codman's advice and kicked over the rocking chair on the porch in favour of the saddle and a distant horizon.

Phillipe and Catherine de Bourboulon rode 19,500 kilometres (12,000 miles) through some of the most desolate and dangerous portions of China, Mongolia, Siberia and Russia in 1850. Quincy and Ella Scott spent their horseback honeymoon riding across the United States at the dawning of the twentieth century. Cora and Jan Gordon explored Albania in the 1920s and Arthur and Eleanor Hopkinson rode across Tibet in 1947.

More recently the Swiss Long Riders, Hans-Jürgen and Claudia Gottet rode 13000 kilometres (8,000 miles) from Arabia to the Alps, while Ken and Sharon Roberts were the first Long Riders to journey the length of Australia's difficult Bicentennial National Trail.

Families

Nor do you have to look beyond your family for possible companions.

Plenty of parents have sought adventure with their offspring. Barry and Bernice Murray took their three children, Colette, Bernadette and Barry Jr. on a journey from Mexico to Canada. And Fawn Fields was only five years old when she rode her pony from Texas to Arizona, alongside her parents' covered wagon.

The Coquet sisters, Evelyne and Corinne, rode from Paris to Jerusalem. The de Aguiar brothers, Pedroca and Jorge, racked up 18,000 kilometres in Latin America aboard their Manga Larga stallions. Mothers and daughters, like Pat and Linda Schamber, have ridden ocean to ocean, and fathers and sons, such as Colonel Charles Callahan and his four sons, explored Argentina in search of Butch Cassidy.

Sometimes family aspirations join together in mounted discoveries such as these.

Groups

The rarest type of equestrian journey is one undertaken by large groups. There are two major reasons for this. The first is logistical.

A practical rule is to never allow the party to exceed four in number, as there is less ability for villages or private home owners to host a large mounted party. This is especially true because unlike previous equestrian ages, when you could count on finding inns, stables or *chai khanas* which would admit a large number of horses, today's motorized world is hard pressed to accommodate the unexpected arrival of two or three horses.

The second handicap is emotional.

The difficulty lies not in taking up quarrels but in avoiding them.

The only modern major equestrian journey successfully undertaken by a large group has been the one organized by Kareen Kohn. This group, known as Nomads United, is a flexible collection of mounted young people. They come from all parts of the world, and join and ride with the Nomads during their adventures in India and Latin America. Yet, even though they share a philosophy of peace and personal tolerance, troubles still arise.

"We got to know each other quite closely. There was treason, apathy, jealousy and greed. Finally, in the thunder of the moment, there was nothing left to hide. Masks fell and you weren't who you wanted to be or thought you were," Kareen warned.

When deciding how many should ride, an even is better than an odd number and the smaller the group the greater your chances of success.

Travelling with Dogs

Long Riders are often tempted to take a dog as a travelling companion. There have been rare exceptions but this usually proves to be a fatal decision for the trusting canine.

Their presence provokes fights with other dogs. Homer Davenport adopted a local dog while riding across the Ottoman Empire in 1906. The friendship didn't last long because the American Long Rider's dog was killed by a pack of hostile canines hovering near an Arab encampment.

"Before I could dismount and come to the rescue, my puppy was torn and dead."

They are often seriously injured by kicks from irritated horses. That is what happened on Aime Tschiffely's historic journey.

"I had originally intended to take as a companion a dog which had been presented to me by a friend. This plan was upset by the fact that on the first day of the journey the dog came too near Mancha and received such a kick that I was obliged to leave him behind."

They attract predators and are often wounded by porcupines.

Many die from snake bite. That was the fate of Günter Wamser's dog Liesl in 2003, which was killed by a viper in Central America.

Unlike the horse's hard hooves, the softer pads of the dog often suffer injury. When Alexandra Kudasheva set off to ride across Siberia in 1913, she took a St. Bernard named Farab.

"The dog proved unable to keep up the pace and was soon left behind."

Dogs are susceptible to heat stroke. They have been kidnapped and nearly eaten by hungry natives. That was the fate of Tigon, Tim Cope's dog, who narrowly escaped death in Kazakhstan.

However the leading cause of death occurs when dogs wander in front of traffic. One such example was Keeter, who was travelling from Michigan to Alaska with Suellen Fintari when he was killed by a motorist in 1995.

There are other reasons not to take a dog. Some national parks will not permit them. Locating their food is an additional challenge. If the dog becomes injured or ill the pack horse is employed to carry the canine's additional weight. They represent an extra emotional and logistical burden at a time when your priority should be your horse.

Summary

As all of these examples demonstrate, be it husbands and wives, best friends, or brothers and sisters, your primary necessity is co-operation among all the members of your team. You must therefore exercise extreme caution in the choice of a companion for a long equestrian journey, for if the proposed person does not share your same turn of mind, or is not eager to pursue the same interests, if the companion be not good-natured, active, and tolerant, he will instead become an intolerable emotional burden.

Vyv Wood Gee said it best when she warned, "Moral of the tale: choose any human travelling companion even more carefully than you do your equine companion(s), and don't allow yourself to be deceived by someone all too plausible but whom instinct said from Day One was not quite who or what they make out to be (nor capable of what they claim)."

Many married couples undertake exciting equestrian adventures. Swiss Long Riders Hans-Jürgen (left) and Claudia Gottet rode 8,000 miles from Saudi Arabia to Switzerland.

Brazilian brothers, Pedro (left) and Jorge de Aguiar were in their seventies when they set out to explore South America on their Manga Larga stallions.

Fathers and sons become Long Riders. During his 16,000 kilometre (10,000 mile) ride from Canada to Brazil Filipe Leite (right) was joined in 2013 by his father, Luis Corsi Leite during a dangerous thousand mile portion of the journey in Mexico.

Likewise mothers and daughters set out in search of adventure together. When Dutch Long Rider Eva Hietkamp (right) decided to explore Spain on horseback, she invited her mother Ingrid Verdaasdonk to accompany her.

Having three school age children didn't stop Barry Murray (centre) from taking his family on an equestrian journey from Mexico to Canada.

The fun-loving Nomads United consist of 30 young people from around the world who gather to explore the world on horseback.

Chapter 9
Before You Saddle Up

As the previous chapters amply demonstrate, equestrian travel is uncompromising. It must, therefore, be considered through the disenchanting view of reality. Yet there are two things certain to be awaiting you – excitement and freedom.

The night before she set off on her 1939 ride from Cornwall to Scotland, Margaret Leigh couldn't sleep because of the anticipation of what she and her mare, Lady Bird, would encounter the next morning.

"That night I did not sleep very much. The mattress and sleeping bag were comfortable, not to say luxurious, but I was filled with that restless excitement and foreboding which makes a journey's eve it's most appalling moment. We long for change, for adventure, and when it is near would like to call it off. What madness led us here, we ask ourselves; could we not even now get out of it? Yet now I was as free as air, with nothing but my horse and the auctioneer's cheque in my pocket. I was rid of all the clogging household junk that makes so much labour and gives so little satisfaction," the about-to-be Long Rider wrote.

Likewise, Ella Sykes had no way of knowing what incredible adventures awaited her when she shifted her allegiance from the hearth to the saddle.

At a time when polite Victorian society severely curtailed a woman's activities, Ella Sykes risked her life on a daily basis. Her bachelor brother, an English officer turned diplomat, had been ordered out to Persia. Lacking a bride, and knowing he would face considerable domestic difficulties, he gave his younger sister an option. Round up her things, organize everything needed to run a foreign embassy and be ready to leave in a few days' time. The young Miss Sykes didn't hesitate.

On their first adventure, the hard-riding Sykes siblings made a 2,000 mile ride from the Caspian Sea to India. Religious fanatics failed to frighten Ella. Forsaken, hostile deserts never slowed her horse-bound progress. Instead Ella rode across parts of the world which few European women had ever visited. That journey was Ella's baptism of fire and resulted in her writing *Through Persia on a Side-Saddle,* a fantastic story, replete with rajas and rogues, camels and caravans, and illustrated with Ella's photographs.

Later she and her brother made another remarkable ride, this time exploring the fabled kingdoms of Central Asia. But by then she had learned what to anticipate.

"The shackles of civilization are left behind. There are no trains or steamboats to be caught, no crowded hotels to stop at. Camp after camp is pitched and then struck, inducing an eagerness to press on. And yet there is no hurry about it. The caravan stops at the pleasure of its master," this inspiring Long Rider wrote.

Thoughts on Travel

If you are about to set off on an equestrian journey then you will soon have more in common with Ella in long ago Persia than any of the pedestrian acquaintances currently occupying your world. For what challenged her is awaiting you.

Largely forgotten today by most would-be modern Long Riders are the critical historical factors considered by travellers from the first wandering Cro-Magnon to the last overland hippie. Weather conditions, political unrest, the outbreak of disease or the strength of the modern nomads are now seldom mentioned by departing jet setters. If it rains in Acapulco, settle for the Bahamas. The vital word now is 'rescheduling.' Distances are no longer important. Visas are easily obtainable. Credit can be extended. Travel agents are everywhere offering tickets to anywhere. The tourist's brain is staggered by the possibilities. The body has become the ultimate impediment, something to be fed, watered and rested until the brain can touch down.

Travel has been redefined by machines into a safe, if sterile, worldwide business. Thanks to jets and computers, ancient rules are being forgotten or rewritten. Most people no longer associate the physical transference of their bodies in relationship to the old formula which states that a journey used to equate pain, insanity and hell. Gone are the days when rovers bid their families tearful farewells before setting off for places whose very name resonated danger:

Mecca, Lhasa and the New World. Roaming was for the adventurers, lunatics and pioneers. Today, children cross continents unescorted. Travel, once as dangerous as war and pestilence, has been de-clawed.

If travel in earlier days had its downfalls, it offered its rewards. In the days of physical touring every step was an achievement, every sunrise a success. The strong and the lucky survived on a diet of hardship and adrenalin. Life for the journeyer was a brilliant exaggeration of experiences. As Ella Sykes learned, gone was the dull routine, the village mentality, the suffocating conformity. Travel seduced, offended and ultimately bewitched its acolytes. Apples lay forsaken for passion fruit. New animals, people and places, new flowers, mountains and food turned the smallest trip into a person's greatest lifetime experience. Mankind's incredible diversity lay exposed to those cultural conquistadors brave enough to seek it.

Yet the machines have changed all that. They are killing the travel god they serve. Millions stand meekly in line where yesterday only hundreds applied. Reservations are required. Travellers' cheques make good sense. For the first time in history, excursions are safe and cheap. As a result, the masses are demanding a vacation. With increasing frequency, they are getting it.

The world, once a miracle of variation, now caters to the conformist and the price being paid to ease the passage of these fops and carpet knights is excruciatingly high. Nepal lies deforested, a victim of cold tourists and money-hungry natives willing to sacrifice ancestral forests for a quick buck. Hawaii's native people have been pushed to the ends of their islands to make room for beach-bound landlubbers intent on finding a luau. Japanese craftsmen, forsaking generations of tradition, now mass produce ceramic pots to satiate swarms of souvenir-hungry tourists. In order to attract dollars, yens and deutschmarks, universal norms are being embraced. The hamburger rules triumphant.

Machines have granted the wish of easy touring, but unknowingly created an unforeseen dilemma – the breakdown of the cultural diversity that once heralded mankind's pride of race and nation, the exact things early travellers sought in the first place. It is possible to board in Munich and deplane in Pago Pago without slowing acclimatising yourself physically and culturally as earlier travellers did on such a trip. There is no steady acculturation possible for aeronauts confined in a sterilised compartment sailing at 30,000 feet. Instead, they are thrown into the air like a pizza, where they orbit the earth for an hour before landing with the same tastes and expectations they took off with. Sadly enough, they are usually not forced to change those tastes.

This ease of excursion has brought with it the danger of cultural genocide. Frequent flyers board a plane in Korea and are served roast beef and potatoes. Syrian stewardesses speak English. Greeks carry Japanese cameras. Cultural diversities are being worn away in an effort to make landings and take-offs easier. In order to service the maximum amount of customers, unsightly foreign customs are stored next to difficult languages. Travel is becoming homogenised. The world is being turned into an extended village of MacHumans.

The Western world is the hub of such commercial travel. The further one gets from Tokyo, New York or Paris, the greater one's chances of being delayed, sick or shot. Maybe that's why you are now planning on heading your horse into some remote part of the globe. Perhaps you long to be delayed a century or so. Conceivably you hope to find people in the lost reaches of the world who think of horseback riding as a local skill, not a refuge for the rich.

I believe in the outdated idea that travel should be a day-by-day awakening of body and soul, not a mindless transference of a blob of meat. When I set out on my equestrian explorations I longed to experience as much as I could, despite the hardships and the dangers the journey would entail.

But as the first few chapters of this book have demonstrated, you ride well, or you don't arrive.

Getting Ready for the Road

Your horse needs no favours. He only looks for a square deal. If you already have a suitable Road Horse, then now is the time to start training rides. Begin by doing ten miles a day. Then work your way up to a weekend away from home for you and the horse. Make a two- or three-day loop, ending up at your own barn. Riding in circles in a dressage ring is akin to a goldfish circling in a glass bowl. It is NOT the same as riding towards the horizon, which is physically tough on horse and rider. So start by breaking out of your normal routine. Get your horse used to traffic right now. Nothing in the ring will prepare you and your horse for a life on the road. It's a different universe once you leave the safety net of the stable.

And it is mounted fools who run horses to their death. When the goal becomes more important than the horse, you don't belong on the trip. Learn to slow down, while you're learning to ride ahead.

If you're going to make your journey overseas, then speak to the airline about the cost of transporting your tack and equipment. Saddles and Long Rider gear are heavy, bulky and valuable. Keith Clark forgot this part of his pre-planning. That oversight resulted in him having to pay a hefty surcharge in the British airport because his equipment was so heavy. To make matters worse, upon arriving in Chile, he nearly had to pay import duty on top of his original unwelcome travel tax.

Start work on your paper work immediately. Investigate your medical, legal and travel document needs. Find your firman or make one. Ask your lawyer, mayor, congressman, senator, Member of Parliament, and vet to provide you with this critically important paper protection.

Obtain a copy of the Horse Travel Journal which can act as a Friendship Book, and begin documenting your preparations. This becomes an international document of camaraderie which lists names, contact details and comments. Even the people helping you organize your trip will be pleased to be included in this time-honoured way.

Long Riders resemble live musicians in that their masterpiece can only be experienced in the moment. An equestrian journey is not like a painting. It is an ethereal personal experience that will disappear like the mist if you don't commit it to paper. Starting to write now will help you develop the discipline you'll need later to record important daily events, temperatures, etc.

In the days to come you should be thinking about horse shoes and saddlery, first-aid for rider and horse, navigation and map-reading, camping techniques, traffic rules and trail locations, insurance and finances.

That's quite a lot, you will think. Have no fear, you will make it. You do not have to have the complete knowledge of a horse shoer or a veterinarian. And because you are searching to learn the basics, people will be glad to help you.

There is, however, one thing that only another Long Rider can tell you.

Preparing for Failure

You must prepare yourself for failure.

As I write this page, an English woman is nursing several broken bones at her home in Wales. Her highly publicized ride from Peking to London came to a crashing halt when her horse threw her a few days after the journey began. Despite the best-laid plans, her desire did not translate into an equestrian reality.

Likewise another woman's recent journey in Chile failed when her horse was bitten by a snake.

The way equestrian travel works is like this. You do everything you can to plan, prepare, and forestall every foreseeable calamity. You train your horses, buy the best equipment, get fit and then set off full of hope. Yet sometimes, as both these examples illustrate, you gallop straight into a mountain of bad luck and your trip is cut short.

How can I speak with such authority?

Because I have wept in anger and frustration when my best careful planning came to naught. And it's much more personal than you might believe.

My own equestrian travel career began in the mid-1970s when I left an English riding school and journeyed overland to Afghanistan. I planned on riding from Bamiyan to Mazar-i-Sherif, a distance of many hundreds of miles over some of the country's most dangerous mountains. I had arranged for horses, and even managed to procure a guide who swore he could lead me to my faraway destination.

Then the local governor got wind of my plans. He let it be known that if I left on horseback, my guide would be arrested and I would be deported. But that unfair edict didn't matter because by the time it came through I was unconscious, having been stricken by a dire illness. I have since survived a plethora of exotic diseases that could slay a pub full of people. But I shall never forget the first time I was hit by amoebic dysentery. In no time at all I was too weak to ride, then I couldn't walk, then I was flat on my back, then I was running a temperature, passing in out of consciousness and too sick too move.

Realizing that I was about to die in their town, the locals bundled me onto a tiny bus heading back to Kabul. I was stretched out on the back seat and left to expire quietly. Luckily I made it back to the capital, regained my strength, and went on to have other equestrian adventures of an even more dangerous nature, which included other calamitous medical emergencies and delays.

The point is that equestrian travel isn't for wimps. When you put your foot into that stirrup, swing into that saddle, and set your horse's nose towards the horizon, you don't know what the hell is going to happen.

But - as these busted journeys attest - just because you set off to sail to the New World, doesn't guarantee that you'll reach that faraway beach like Columbus did. As history demonstrates, many of the so-called "pioneers" got lost, became ill, were attacked, and died from a wide variety of diseases. So like them, you and your horses can't be faulted because you bumped into snakes and sickness.

What you must realize, before you leave, is that regardless of the dangers, disappointments and even loss of your geographic goal, you will receive an immense emotional reward that you would never have found riding in a dressage ring, jumping horses over painted sticks, or exercising race horses. What you will find instead is what other Long Riders have discovered before you - the deepest possible emotional bond with your horse and an intense love of life that can't be adequately described to anyone who is not a fellow equestrian explorer.

Thus, there is no "failure" if you are a Long Rider. Every journey presents a brilliant opportunity for you to enshrine a lesson for years to come; namely, that despite the hardships, the setbacks, and perhaps even a premature ending, you wouldn't trade every hard-won mile for all your previous equestrian experiences.

The richness of life isn't dependent on the miles, but on the value of where you rode emotionally and what you learned spiritually along the way. If you come away with that lesson then you will make this journey a success that isn't dependent upon reaching a distant geographic goal.

If you learn that going is more important than arriving, then you'll have accomplished something of immense value before you ever leave.

Recognizing the Odds

One final word of warning, before you read on and press ahead with your plans.

Your horse is mortal. He could succumb in the pasture tomorrow from a variety of ailments. There are no guarantees that either of you will reach old age. Thus it behoves you to realize then that you and your trusted mount are departing upon an adventure which may result in the injury, or even death, of one or both of you.

There is only one Long Rider fatality to report. In fact, when you consider how many hundreds of thousands of miles Guild Members have under their collective saddles, it is amazing to consider how few accidents have befallen them.

Sadly, Road and Pack horses do occasionally meet with misadventure. Pack horses have placed a foot wrong and gone off cliffs. Beloved riding horses have been bitten by vipers. Treasured equine comrades have given their all, and asked nothing in return, except to be part of their Long Rider's adventure.

That was the heartbreaking lesson which the German Long Rider Esther Stein, and her Austrian Long Rider colleague, Horst Hausleitner, discovered on their ride across the African continent. The determined duo rode across South Africa, Botswana, Zimbabwe, Zambia, Malawi, Tanzania, Rwanda and finally into Kenya. They had survived deserts, been attacked by mobs, and suffered in more physical ways than they could have ever imagined.

That's when the true disaster struck. Only two days away from success, their lovely horse Misty died without warning. Though their trip was a geographical success, it came at the price of seeing Misty's name carved on a wooden branch above her grave.

Would Misty have led a longer life if she had remained in South Africa? Possibly. Would we be remembering her now? Absolutely not. Her name is enshrined along with those other brave road horses that were "lost on the trail." And that is an emotional factor which you need to accept right now, before you press ahead with your plans.

Neither you, nor your horse, may make it to where you wish to go. That's the rugged way of equestrian travel. There are no guarantees when you're a Long Rider. This is a timeless adventure and you stand a good chance of winning through. But it is not an airplane ride.

A Promise to Yourself

As these hard truths demonstrate, you have to travel the path of instinct alone, and on that journey it is necessary for you to accept the tremendously long odds of what you're about to do. Before you set out ask yourself if you are you willing to make the following promise to yourself and your horse before leaving?

I'm heading off towards (fill in destination). If I get there, fine. However if any one of a dozen different unforeseen problems keep me from reaching that physical goal I won't blame myself, my horse or life in general. I will instead be happy for every moment I spent in the saddle with (fill in horse's name).

Signed.

Summary

Now that I have issued my warning, allow me to remind you of this other vital fact. Stop for a minute and savour this truth. It is a delicious moment, knowing that your journey is about to begin. Your life is about to change.

Such anticipation leads to freedom.

There once was a brilliant Long Rider named George Borrow. A fabled adept at acquiring new languages, Borrow's knowledge of Spanish, Welsh and Russian, just to name a few of the many tongues he spoke fluently, allowed him to travel with ease through societies that normally kept outsiders at bay. His most famous cultural observations resulted from his lifelong fascination with the Gypsy nomads of Europe and North Africa. Having a command of their language allowed Borrow to become the first outsider to infiltrate and report on their closed society. In addition to being a noted author, Borrow was a devoted equestrian traveller. In 1835 he issued this admonition.

"O ye gifted ones, follow your calling, for, however various your talents may be, ye can have but one calling capable of leading ye to eminence and renown; follow resolutely the one straight path before you, it is that of your good angel, let neither obstacles nor temptations induce ye to leave it; bound along if ye can; if not, on hands and knees follow it, perish in it, if needful; but ye need not fear that; no one ever yet died in the true path of his calling before he had attained the pinnacle. Turn into other paths, and for a momentary advantage or gratification ye have sold your inheritance, your immortality. Ye will never be heard of after death," Borrow wrote.

Likewise Gabriel Bonvalot wrote, "The world is all delusion and man is always looking for the realization of desires which it would be as difficult for him to obtain as it would be to seize the moon, though he sees her every night. Yet this is no delusion, and with careful planning, can be achieved."

Borrow and Bonvalot. You and your horse. Then and now. Nothing changes. Everything remains the same. They would recognize and encourage your desire to follow in their hoofprints.

This is the fantasy. Green grass. Beautiful sunsets. Friendly natives. Happy horses. That's what the European Long Riders Esther Stein and Horst Hausleitner thought they would find in 2003 on their perilous ride across the African continent.

This is the reality; Esther on a rainy day in Tanzania. Wet. Cold. Demoralized. Wondering what in the world lured her into making such a journey?

Another example of the reality, not the fantasy, found in equestrian exploration. Horst and his horse both rest in the African sand.

Section Two
Chapter 10
A New Herd Ethic

Paddock Potatoes and Road Horses

Before you set out to find the perfect horse for your journey, let me first give you a word of warning. In this age of internet dating, discovering your ideal romantic mate would be far easier than locating a suitable road horse. Why, you ask, with millions of horses standing about idle and equine rescue missions groaning from overuse, will you have any trouble uncovering the horse of your dreams?

The answer is easy. The vast majority of the animals on offer are pasture pets, not the hardened type of equine warrior you require. Though the newspaper may be filled with "For Sale" horse ads, chances are that the animals listed will be found to be unsuitable. While there are a variety of reasons, including temperament and training, one of the most important factors is that you're in need of a horse from the past, not someone's personal pet of the present.

The Horse – Nature's Nomad

The genuine wild horse of the Central Asian steppes foraged northward in summer to a considerable distance and migrated southward early in autumn. The result was a migratory cycle of travel and grazing, one wherein the horse became a natural nomad.

Even in remote parts of western North America, where water was at a premium, wild horses would graze in enormous circles around the local water hole. While making his solo journey down the entire length of the hazardous Outlaw Trail, British Long Rider Roger Pocock noted this nomadic behaviour among wild Equids.

"These wild horses do not travel beyond their necessities of grass and water. Leaving the water they graze outwards, forming a trampled area which widens daily as they feed at the edges. I have come to a line where the pasturage ended abruptly and beyond were innumerable pony tracks leading from six to ten miles to a water hole. The wild horse looked upon that ring area as the tame horse does his stable, with water and feed conveniently arranged. That was his home and if a man or a storm or wolves drove him a couple of hundred miles away to better feed and water, he would always break back at the first chance, travelling steadily with little delay for grazing," Pocock observed.

Nor were horses, wild or otherwise, at a loss in terms of sensing directions while travelling.

The celebrated Scottish Long Rider, author and horse expert, Don Roberto Cunninghame Graham, spent years observing mounted life in late 19th century Argentina. Like Pocock, Don Roberto learned that horses had an uncanny sense of direction and distance.

"If a man came to a house with a tired horse and asked for the loan of a fresh mount, a service never denied upon the desolate pampas, the lender always requested, 'when you have arrived at home, (between 30 and 60 miles away), let loose my horse at night and he will soon be back'. Homing horses on the pampas could be distinguished readily by their travelling on a line, stopping to graze but rarely and when upon the move, carrying their heads high as if they sought to explore the horizon for the way," Don Roberto wrote.

This Argentine example not only demonstrates the horse's extraordinary sense of orientation, it also draws our attention to another critical element in his psychological make-up, namely his strong sense of community.

Gregarious by nature, the horse is passionately fond of company and often has a great aversion to being left alone. There are horses that refuse to proceed when their companions are withdrawn or become frantic when removed from their established environment. This companionable temper results in playful gambolling with other members of the herd and in the exchange of small kindnesses, such as mutual grooming and insect avoidance, with close equine friends. Like man, horses take up deep friendships and form intense emotional bonds.

This ability to form poignant relationships helps explain why horse and human have formed the most historically vital partnership since animals were domesticated. In addition to his other duties, the horse is traditionally the only animal whose role as comrade-in-arms has helped change the course of human events and development. For these reasons, the horse was traditionally granted immense personal honour and treated with respect on an individual basis.

Killing them with Kindness

Sadly, we have broken up the family life of our horses, and are apt to forget that they ever had private affairs of their own. Plus, as the horse's time-honoured roles of warrior, labourer and journeyer were dismissed, his original nomadic nature has been neglected or forgotten. Thus the majority of horses available for sale in developed countries fall into two categories.

Either they reside in pastures, where they receive occasional work via a short weekend trail ride, or they are lodged in confining stables, and are taken out into the open for a limited time so as to participate in a competitive event. In either case, the horse's natural desire for travel and freedom has either been denied or erased.

This system of stabling, and over-emotional compensation, is not without its drawbacks and critics. As Dr. Elaine Walker, author of *Horse*, wrote, "The presence of so many illnesses associated with domestication, such as laminitis, suggest that the cosseted lifestyles of many modern horses with rich grazing and high energy feeds can be at odds with their nature as survivors."

Likewise British equestrian journalist, Garry Ashton-Coulton, published his concerns about the fate of modern horses.

"In our western society the horse has been liberated from much of his work-a-day drudgery. He no longer pulls the plough, strains in the shafts of an overloaded cart, or faces the bullets of an enemy that was never his. The horse has become a means of relaxation, an object of pleasure. Yet we tie him down with ever increasing ingenuity, ever more sophisticated systems of training and hardware. He gives us so much and what do we give him in return? A new rug and a bag of carrots! The most precious thing we can give is the simplest yet the most finite. It is our time. Imagine spending 24 hours a day, seven days a week, month after month, even year after year, relying totally on your horse, and he on you, for mile after mile, for hundreds, thousands, even tens of thousands of miles," the concerned horseman wrote in one of England's leading equestrian publications.

And a Swiss study made in 2014 found 83.5 percent of horses from twelve different riding schools were housed individually and not allowed to be turned out together because the owners believed injuries were more likely to occur if the animals were permitted any degree of freedom.

The study also revealed that many horse owners believed that permitting a horse to run freely was unnecessary. The horse owners contended instead that their animals got all the exercise they needed from being ridden. A 30-year-old research paper found that the riding-school horses studied received on average 41 minutes of exercise, six days a week. This contrasted with the results of a 2010 study showing feral horses travelled an average of 18 kilometres (11 miles) a day.

As history demonstrates, Long Riders understand that horses are animals, not commodities, which should not have to stay locked in a stall until the owner can be bothered to exercise them.

The result of these modern methods is that while you will discover countless numbers of horses for sale, there are few if any of what the cavalry used to classify as "hard" horses available for your consideration. Such animals, which would have been in the peak of condition, could routinely travel long distances without fatigue. In contrast, what you will largely see on offer today will be horses that are fat, not fit.

Symbiosis of human and horse

A mystery still surrounds how horses determine leadership. It is not simply a matter of sex. While mares often demonstrate a capacity to take charge, there are Central Asian accounts of "sultan stallions" who banded together to fight off packs of wolves. Thus, certain observers contend that equine leadership is determined by individual spirit, not sex.

Regardless, it is astonishing what a lovable, intelligent animal a horse is when he finds he is understood.

Jeremy James noted this when he wrote, "A man's inner instincts are minutely recorded by horses. The voice the horse hears is not the outer but the inner one. It is the inner voice to which a horse first responds and then to the outer. If these voices are at odds then the horse obeys at a level which is robotic and will work only mechanically."

Jeremy believes that horses regard most humans as an "irrelevant curiosity." Yet during one of his journeys he learned that a road horse is different from his pampered domestic cousin.

"Long distance travelling alters a horse. He becomes more alert, his mind widens, becomes sharper, more acute. Yet his wisdom also deepens, he becomes more malleable, more accepting. On the move he will eat food that he would not even have looked at back home; he accepts other horses that he would batter into a corner in his stable. Yet though his mind becomes broader, so also he becomes more tightly fused to his companions (to the other horses and his Long Rider). He calls for his rider if he walks away. He recognizes him from afar."

This is a description of an inscrutable, but common, emotional partnership known to equestrian explorers, which occasional riders mounted on domesticated equine slaves rarely experience.

Trust between Species

As equestrian travellers like Jeremy James know, something emotionally immense often occurs to road horse and Long Rider during a lengthy journey.

One of the most remarkable examples of this mutual compatibility was demonstrated by the English Long Rider William Holt. Along with Trigger, a former peddler's cart horse, this congenial duo travelled thousands of miles together throughout Europe. During that journey, Holt forsook the opportunity to sleep in numerous comfortable beds, including a stay in the castle of an Italian countess, preferring instead to rest next to Trigger every night.

"There is no secret so close as that between a rider and his horse," Holt recalled in his thoughtful book, *Ride a White Horse*.

Thus Long Riders, who originate in numerous countries and have ridden on various continents, have all made a number of consistent emotional discoveries regarding their road horses.

After a certain number of days travelling, the road horse develops a new herd ethic. As ancient genetic impressions are aroused, the horse's memory of 'home' is replaced by a new cosmic order which centres on his rider and the sun.

Because his geographic world is now constantly changing, the road horse develops an intense emotional bond with his rider. The sun comes up – the road horse sets off and observes the world around him changing – again and again and again. Yet despite that day's emotional surprises, the Long Rider is there to reassure the road horse. The sun starts to set – and the road horse learns that his rider will provide food and security throughout the night.

This constant geographic alteration prompts an intense sentimental need among many road horses who long for a sense of stability. As the journey starts to take hold, the road horse learns that food and safety can be found close by the Long Rider's camp. Thus the emotional connection and sense of trust that exist between road horse and Long Rider is a hundred times deeper than that of a ring-ridden horse and his weekend rider.

This touching co-dependency is symbolized by the ancient, but still valid, factors which demonstrate that both species are experiencing an immense mutual emotional profit, despite the fact that their shared geographic world is presenting a host of daily dangers.

Riding towards the Horizon

Long Riders, past and present, have remarked on this intense relationship with their mounts.

For example, during her many equestrian expeditions in various parts of the world, Christina Dodwell learned the truth of an olden equestrian law, that no amount of ring riding will ever create the type of herd connection which exists when you live and travel with your road horse.

"Because you are the only constant in the ever-changing landscape, it tends to create a closeness and feeling of trust between the two of you," Dodwell recalled.

Regardless of the year, century or the country Long Riders have discovered this bond between horse and human to be true.

When Joseph Smeaton Chase rode across the Mojave Desert in 1910, he noted, "The relations between man and horse who are much alone for long periods takes on a touch of sentiment that to some might seem overdone. The loyalty of my horse, patiently doing his best, accepting my will without thought of dispute, and taking for granted that his service will be repaid by care for the needs which he is prevented from supplying for himself – the pathos of this becomes better recognized in the daily sharing of chances. And whenever my trusty companion has had to suffer, I don't mind saying that it nearly brought me to tears. When it comes to magnanimity, few of us can equal the average horse."

Nearly a century later, and another continent away, when Keith Clark rode through the Andes with his road and pack horse he discovered the same principles to still be true.

"Being with them twenty-four hours a day, day in day out, I knew what my horses were going to do before they did."

A Mutual Emotional Reward

Travel by any type of engine and your journey is firmly rooted in the industrial present. Travel by horse and you travel by time machine. The new world slows down and an old world opens up before you.

This is the world of the Long Rider and one of the first lessons is that the bond which occurs between you and your horse will come as a result of the two of you having survived the unknown elements of the trip together.

For when you make your journey, you will be no different than your 6,000 year old ancestor who first swung his or her tentative leg over the back of a wild Central Asian pony and galloped toward a distant and dangerous horizon.

That is why, during the first international Long Rider meeting, those of us in attendance all realized that at some time in each of our journeys all of our road horses had been revealed in a different light. Though our individual mounts had stood close by for years, after travelling they were no longer merely objects to be possessed.

The rare riders who undertake such a journey become saddle-bound pilgrims leading a life based on physical freedom. Their horses take them on a daily journey away from the never-ending search for consumer products and show them instead the way back to the nomadic principles of the past: grass, water, fire and contemplation. These are the keys to equestrian travel. Such a journey transforms current equestrian stereotypes into spiritual equestrianism and develops the boutique rider into an equestrian mystic.

Summary

The good news is that while a road horse will challenge you, once discovered, all these things will redefine the herd ethic and alter your view of an animal you believe you already know well. This begins to happen when you, not the stable, become the most primary object in your horse's life.

In a world that changes every day, where every night brings a new roof or no roof, where one day brings feast and the next famine, you will represent emotional consistency to your horse. No bond in your life will ever be stronger than the one you develop with the horse you sleep, travel and share the road with. There is no leaving such an animal emotionally, for the journey and the horse will have placed a lasting spiritual mark on your soul.

Now the question remains, what is a road horse and where do you find him?

It's a matter of trust. German Long Rider Barbara Kohmanns swimming with her horse during their ride across parts of South and Central America.

Good friends, Margaret Rumpl and her stallion, Galipolis, travelled 3,100 kilometres (1,900 miles) together from eastern Austria to Santiago de Compostela, in the north-west of Spain.

Chapter 11
One Horse or Two?

It may seem like an obvious question but one of the first decisions you have to make is - one horse or two? The answer depends upon a number of factors.

Where will you ride; in a country rich with easily obtained resources or across a terrain filled with geographic and climatic challenges?

Will you be travelling across a lonely landscape devoid of traffic or riding alongside busy roads inhabited with motorized threats?

Shall the countryside aid or hinder you: can you count on encountering a regular series of hospitable hosts or will friendly faces be few and far between?

Can you depend upon routinely obtaining food and grazing; or will a lack of supplies require the employment of a pack animal?

How much is needed to ensure your safety and comfort; are you one of those who can sleep comfortably in a roadside ditch or do you require amenities such as a hot meal every night?

Are you strong enough; can you carry supplies in a backpack and walk for miles alongside your horse?

If the decision is made to only use one horse, will you be able to locate an animal with the suitable strength and emotional loyalty?

A Fundamental Problem

Let us say for the sake of argument that you are thinking about making an equestrian journey and are debating the idea of employing a pack horse. Who better to ask than General William Harding Carter? He served with the United States Sixth Calvary and was considered one of that country's foremost experts on the horse and his equipment.

In his book, *Horses, Saddles and Bridles*, the wise cavalryman wrote, "All soldiers of experience know well the value of carefully preserving the strength of the horse. While the weight of the pack saddle does not appear to diminish the rate of speed upon the march, it necessarily increases the fatigue of the horse and ultimately tends to reduce his length of service."

Carter went on to explain that the more weight the horse carries, the higher the chance he will suffer a sore back. That is why, he wrote, "It is customary to reduce the weight of the pack saddle to its lowest limit."

Cavalrymen like Carter knew the hazards of placing a heavy weight on a horse. Thus deciding not to employ a pack horse means the road horse will be required to carry more weight, which increases the rate of risk.

This provokes an important strategic and ethical question before departure. Can you travel safely with one horse?

As some Long Riders have proved, given the right set of circumstances the answer can be 'yes.'

Size Matters

First, unlike the world of magazine models that are often dangerously underweight, a Long Rider needs to ideally employ a big horse, one with plenty of power.

Louise, DC Vision's Shire mare, was the ultimate example of this one-horse philosophy. Having been previously employed pulling logs out of the Maine forest, Louise loved the idea of making a journey. The lovable mare happily carried DC and all his possessions for 22,500 kilometres (14,000 miles), trying to consume every carrot in America along the way. After years of travelling, Louise was the picture of happiness and health when the journey finally stopped.

Another remarkable champion traveller was Igor, the tough gelding who carried Lucy Leaf through the United States for years.

Igor was 16.1, weighed about 1300 pounds, was big of bone and had size 3 hooves. Originally from Texas, according to Lucy Igor resembled a cavalry horse, perhaps the kind that might even pull a wagon. His thick skin, mane and tail provided him with protection from bugs in summer and cold in winter. Like Louise, Igor had a tremendous appetite and his strong stomach enabled him to eat nearly anything.

Undemonstrative by nature, Igor was stubborn enough to take care of himself. Lucy recalled that Igor was "not the most fun kind of horse to ride" but above all he was "practical."

Mounted Experience

Let's say that the idea of using one horse is appealing but you still harbour doubts. Then let us begin this investigation by seeking the opinion of a Long Rider who is uniquely qualified to comment on the differences between using a pack horse as opposed to travelling with one equine.

In 1982 Lisa Stewart made a 4,900 kilometre (3,000 mile) equestrian journey across the USA in the company of Len Brown and five horses. More recently the experienced Long Rider completed another journey; only this time she chose to only use her horse, Chief.

"I loved feeling so free with just one horse. I loved knowing I could control my horse. And I liked the idea of asking to stay on someone's property, knowing it was only one horse, not five like with Len's and my trip. This meant I didn't have to call ahead or plan in advance. I could just ride up to a house that felt right and knock."

Lisa felt so strongly about the subject of how many horses to employ, that she wrote, "As far as whether to take one horse or two, I would never again make a ride in which I had to lead a pack horse. I want both hands on my road horse at all times."

In her opinion, "The only reason to take a second horse is if you are riding through country that is so remote you literally cannot restock once a week."

Across Australia

Even though Lisa's experiences have been in the United States, she could have been talking about Kimberley Delavere when she mentioned "remote country."

In 2016 Kimberley set off with two horses on a 5,200 kilometre (3,200 mile) journey along Australia's Bicentennial National Trail.

Like many would-be travellers, Kimberley had debated how many horses to use.

"A lot of people recommended I take three horses but I knew my limitations as a novice horse rider and handler. Travelling with three horses would not only have been difficult, I would have been stressed and felt outnumbered."

Worried about making the right decision, Kimberley thought, "The idea of taking only one horse occurred to me a few weeks before I was due to depart, and although I experimented with having my horse Clem carrying all of the gear it still didn't seem possible."

And there was one other reason Kimberley decided to use two horses. She was worried about criticism.

"I was concerned that people would think I was taking a real risk travelling with one horse so I stayed loyal to my original plan of using a pack horse."

When Kimberley set off she rode Clem, while Pippin carried the pack saddle alongside. But a saddle-sore developed which required the pack horse to be rested. This forced Kimberley to make a decision; stop the journey or continue with Clem.

Kimberley decided to travel on with just one horse. The results surprised her.

"I've found there are plenty of unexpected benefits connected to travelling with one horse. Everything is easier. For example, walking alongside one horse was more comfortable."

And there was another unexpected advantage. Clem's emotional connection with Kimberley was strengthened when she became "the only other member of the herd."

"Me and Clem have gotten a great deal closer. He is a lot more docile, is less likely to wander off, behaves better and follows my lead when I'm riding. My respect and love for him has really increased."

Having departed with two horses, but switched over to one, Kimberley believes there are benefits to this option.

"I have enjoyed it so much more than travelling with two horses. Of course, this could be because Long Riding evidently gets easier after the first two or three weeks, after one settles in to a routine, becomes acclimatised to the trail, etc, but I really wish I had committed to doing the entire trail with one horse from the very beginning."

Crossing a Continent with Certainty

Lisa Stewart changed her mind. Kimberley Delavere found a solution by mistake. Lucy Leaf on the other hand never had any doubts.

"When dreaming up my cross-country trip on horseback in the early seventies, the idea of having a pack horse never entered my mind."

A recent graduate from the University of Maine, John Steinbeck's *Travels with Charley* provided Lucy with the inspiration to explore America on horseback.

The original trip was planned from Maine to Montana. At the time Lucy had no idea that she would end up circumnavigating the nation.

Prior to departure, Lucy sent out more than 200 letters requesting information about where she might camp, the availability of feed, veterinarians and blacksmiths. The letters not only invoked the arrival of helpful information, they also led to many invitations being extended by horse owners along Lucy's intended route.

"I had done a couple of short camping trips on horseback in Spain where I rode a horse and carried my gear in cloth saddlebags lashed to the saddle. So I knew it could be done."

Luckily, Lucy found Igor, a rich bay with black points and a long thick tail, who was calm, quiet and had superb feet.

"I realize that I am in the minority, having used just one horse in all my travels," Lucy said. "Personally, I loved riding just one horse because I love simplicity. "

Another reason Lucy preferred one horse was because of safety.

"Leading a pack horse on the roadside takes up more room, and you don't have the control of getting your horses off the road fast when you need to. I'm thinking of the logging country in the North West where I had to get Igor completely off the road fast, and even acquired spurs as a safety measure, for there was not time to dally. A pack horse balking for even a moment could have spelled disaster."

Upon reflection, Lucy recalled that using one horse "wasn't always perfect" but the cumulative effect of the journey she made with Igor left a lasting echo in her life.

"Thirty years have passed since Igor and I finished our journey together, a journey long enough that it became a way of life for both of us. Aspects of that trip still characterize my life: a nomadic tendency, a desire for simple living, and a continuous pursuit of dreams. The things that seemed daunting in the beginning of the trip - where to camp, how to feed the horse properly, how to keep shoes on him, how to protect him from bugs, snakes, lightning, tornados, and sand storms - all of those concerns just melted away under the steady rhythm of Igor's hoof steps, mile upon a few thousand miles, as we indeed lived and breathed the country we travelled."

What started out as a cross-country trip on horseback became a four-year journey with a horse that changed a woman's life.

Always a safe and steady ride as well as a best friend, Igor lived to the age of 27.

Careful Planning

Unlike Lucy, who had gained some limited equestrian travel experience before she set out, William Reddaway described himself as "an inexperienced 65 year old."

Yet that didn't stop him from riding his horse Strider to the four corners of England, during which time they visited thirty historic cathedrals and abbeys. The ride raised money for the Wormwood Scrubs Pony Centre, which brings the transforming power of horses and ponies to inner London children and young people who face physical, mental or social challenges.

Though he was motivated by the highest ideals, William recognized the need to take precautions regarding the largely urbanized environment in which he would be travelling.

"I chose to make my ride in England because I am neither much of a rider nor of a horseman and I wanted to be in an environment with easy access to advice and professional support."

He had reason to be concerned. England is a densely populated country, and because he was raising money for charity, eighty per cent of William's route lay along roads that took him through busy cities. The idea of leading a pack horse in traffic was unappealing. Plus there were other reasons why William decided to only use one horse.

"I planned the ride to be done with one horse because a) I could not afford to buy and keep more than one horse and b) I had little enough experience for managing one horse and none in working with two."

William realized additional benefits included, "lower ongoing costs (feed, farrier, vet, insurance etc); easier passage through the many gates off-road; a narrower and more agile profile on-road; easier to find people who could accommodate one horse."

Having made the decision to travel with one horse, William spent a great deal of time carefully planning his route. He then contacted people in advance so as to arrange for him and Strider to be fed and sheltered.

"I reckoned that the travelling would be tough enough for me as an inexperienced 65 year old and that a bed, shower and food each night would be a better bet than camping. I had 85% of our accommodation arranged before I started. For 99% of our nights Strider or both of us stayed with people who had horses."

In addition, William organized to have feed for Strider delivered along the way. He also scheduled appointments with the farrier in advance.

"These factors were important in reducing what we needed to carry."

One of the benefits of riding across a modern landscape was that William and Strider were seldom far from potential help via a quick call on the cell phone.

Having set off in spring, the team concluded their historic journey before the snow began falling in December.

"On my ride the team was 'We' and 'We' was definitely Strider and me."

Team Work

Even though he lacked equestrian travel experience, William had a load of common sense. He realized that there were two strong factors influencing his decision to use one horse or two; distance and the time needed to travel to the next place with resources.

Because food, shelter and help were in abundant supply, William's ride across England went smoothly. Alina Grace Dudding on the other hand knew that finding food would be difficult and that shelter would rarely be seen along the rugged Pacific Crest Trail.

The Pacific Crest Trail winds 4,200 kilometres (2,650 miles) from its southern terminus near Mexico to its northern terminus in Canada. It twists and turns through California, Oregon and Washington, forcing the traveller to ride atop the spine of the Sierra Nevada Mountains. Along the way travellers can expect to see the glories of Nature; but food, shelter and help are often far away.

Having grown up in Alaska, Alina was an experienced camper. That is why she understood that she and her horse Valentino would need additional support.

"I had to do all of my own research and planning, so I drove the entire trail in 2012 and took pictures of re-supply points to plan out my journey."

Alina then enlisted the aid of her brother Cameron. In 2013 he provided vital support by transporting supplies, including water, food and hay to pre-arranged spots along the trail.

Jon Dudding, father of the Long Rider, wrote to the Guild to say, "Many thru hikers think that one has it easy because you are riding a horse. They have no idea of what that really means in terms of meeting the needs of not only yourself but your horse for feed and water and everything else."

The preparation which Alina and Cameron made was very commendable and their system of keeping her re-supplied was excellent. Yet a tough trail like the PCT puts even the best laid plans to the test.

After having nearly completed the journey, Alina and Valentino's progress was blocked by a heavy snow fall. In a demonstration of incredible determination, Alina packed a snow shovel on her backpack and swung into the saddle. What occurred next is surely one of the most remarkable horse adventures in modern times.

It took Alina and Valentino a month to do the last sixty miles. Along the way they survived freezing weather, deep snow and travelled along a snowy cliff. After months of anticipation, the tired Long Rider finally reached the end of the trail in the pitch dark.

"This was definitely not the ending I'd been picturing for the previous six months! I had imagined how I would react when I saw the monument but it was surprisingly anticlimactic," Alina recalled.

But she had done it – and used one horse to do so.

As a result of this life-changing experience, Alina is the first woman to twice ride the length of the Pacific Crest Trail solo.

Drawbacks

As Alina's journey demonstrates, there are disadvantages to using one horse.

Travelling with one horse requires you to reduce what you can carry, including cooking gear and food.

Lisa Stewart remembered, "It was hot part of the time, so build a fire? No way. I personally couldn't conceive of cooking after riding all day and taking care of my horse."

William Reddaway found his meals at nearby pubs or with friendly hosts. But Kimberley Delaware's diet was affected by the decision to only use one horse on the Bicentennial National Trail.

"In order to cut down on weight, I don't carry cooking gear anymore. In my front saddlebags I carry oatmeal, cous cous, dried fruit and muesli bars. On my rest days I had noodles which I would cook over a fire. I was a bit hungry a lot of the time but I walked into town feeling like an Amazon."

Packing and unpacking takes a shorter amount of time; but balancing the weight being carried is of vital importance.

Long Riders routinely walk. Using one horse requires them to walk more often.

"Travelling with one horse means I must have walked a least half of each day," Kimberley explained. "I walk for about half an hour at the beginning of each day. I walk up and down hills. I walk at the end of the day when I know we're close to camp. Twice I walked the entire day. I have enjoyed the walking as much as the riding, and with a change in my diet, I am feeling amazing."

There is a great deal of difference between travelling across the Australian Outback and across the English countryside, but William Reddaway also spent a great deal of time out of the saddle.

"My travelling days were mostly between six and ten hours. I always walked and led for at least 30 minutes in each two hours travel. If there were steep hills I would walk them - up and down; if gates could only be opened by dismounting and there was nothing to mount off I would walk till I found something; if I had any concern about Strider's condition I would walk more".

There may be an emotional disadvantage in that most horses are gregarious by nature. A lonely horse may seek company during the night, leaving the Long Rider stranded.

"Strider was generally overnight in places with other horses around. He settled well when on his own but certainly liked to have another horse in sight," William wrote.

The Essentials

The issue of what a Long Rider wears, uses and carries is so complex that it is dealt with in several separate chapters.

Yet for the purposes of this specific study, let us consider what each of the Long Riders quoted in this chapter thought were essential items and equipment

Lucy Leaf said, "I liked clothes that were quick drying and lightweight. I quit wearing jeans, replacing them with lightweight hiking type pants. Chaps are unnecessary and very hot unless you are travelling in brushy country. A hat is very important. Myself, I went for a simple visor cap. I used light hiking boots, never riding attire, because I walked a lot. A small waist pack to hold essentials is a good idea because you may get separated from your horse."

William recommended wearing walking trousers and a traveller's vest, both of which come equipped with "lots of good pockets".

Lisa Stewart shared her thoughts about how to keep clean and healthy.

"I had no problem carrying everything I needed on one horse."

She carried a disposable razor, small scissors, a nail file and tweezers. Her medical kit included Advil, a small tube of antibiotic ointment and a tiny bag of vitamins. To keep clean, Lisa carried baby wipes and washed with peppermint biodegradable soap. She took no makeup or hair brush.

"I washed my hair when I got off every day with the peppermint soap and pulled it back in a ponytail holder wet, and it dried. I also rinsed my hair multiple times a day, when I watered Chief to try to cool down as it was in the 90s much of the time."

Kimberley reduced her kitchen and put her book to an unusual albeit practical end.

"I don't carry my stove anymore, just a bowl and spoon which I can cook with over a fire. My book burns as we travel, which was the hardest thing to do at the beginning. Rolled into a canvas attached to the back of the saddle is my lightweight tent and my sleeping bag."

Items for the horse included insect repellent, collapsible water bucket, a minimum size grooming kit and a hoof pick.

A headlamp, compass, first aid kit and a Swiss Army knife were all found to be useful and light weight.

Practicality

Each of the Long Riders mentioned was specifically interviewed for this chapter and provided valuable advice.

William Reddaway carried his possessions in separate dribags.

"During training preparation I weighed the different bags to get a good sense of what the weights were."

He then balanced the bags by weight, softness and volume, with the greater weight being placed in the pommel bags.

Hot summer weather proved difficult for Lisa Stewart and her horse.

"My routine at the end of the day was to get off and pile my stuff where I would pitch my tent. Then I would take Chief to a hydrant and spray him off (or collect water in the bucket and wash him down with a towel), then rub him down with insect repellent. Then I stripped, washed all my clothes in peppermint soap, rinsed them and threw them over something to dry. Next I bathed myself and put on shorts and a t-shirt. Then I pitched camp, or grazed Chief if we were staying where he couldn't freely graze throughout the night. I would graze him several hours on the lead rope if he would have to be tied up at night. Finally I pitched my tent and organized my belongings, usually using my rain poncho as a doormat in front of my door. I kept as much of my stuff in my tent as I could and used my extra clothes for a pillow."

Summary

Lucy Leaf recalled, "I got my gear down to rock bottom. It was so rock bottom, I later added to it."

One of the important lessons she learned right away was that protecting the welfare of her horse was of paramount importance. Another, more subtle, lesson took longer to detect.

Lucy has begun to wonder about Igor's story and how the journey affected him.

She wrote, "We have come into a new consciousness that horses have much to teach us, not only about them but about ourselves as well. As my explorations now take me into spiritual and mystical realms, I wonder what other kinds of help there were on this journey, most of all, from an extraordinary horse. It seems that the real journey is just beginning.

"So Igor, what do you have to say?"

"We horses don't speak, you remember."

"Yeah, but help me out here."

"That's where the learning is, your own knowing."

"So, I suppose you're telling me I already know."

"Yes, of course. You already have the knowing."

"All right, then, I must have known all along that you were the right horse, a good choice, after all, for me. But what about you, Igor? It couldn't have been your choice to pack me across the country and back again."

"Are you really sure about that?"

"Wait a minute. You mean, you chose…to make this journey… with me?"

"Do you not believe that we horses can also make choices?"

Lisa Stewart began her equestrian travels by using pack horses. She later opted to only use Chief and found she could carry everything she needed on one horse.

One reason William Reddaway chose to ride Strider was because the horse was big, strong and powerful.

Choosing to use one horse can present a Long Rider with unexpected restrictions. For example, after having ridden most of the Pacific Crest Trail, Alicia Grace Dudding thought her journey was nearly at an end. She packed a snow shovel "just in case" and spent a month riding the last sixty miles through deep snow.

Lucy Leaf learned that protecting the welfare of her horse Igor was of paramount importance. Their four-year journey changed her life and left Lucy wondering what Igor had felt about the journey. "Do you not believe that we horses can also make choices?"

Chapter 12
That rare thing, the Road Horse

The Need for Careful Preparation

During what is now known as the Heroic Age of Antarctic exploration, one man stood apart from his contemporaries. Numerous men from various nations had attempted to be the first human to reach the South Pole. Yet it was the Norwegian explorer, Roald Amundsen, who in 1911 led the first successful expedition to reach that dangerous geographic goal.

Unlike the German, Japanese and British expeditions which preceded him, the secret of Amundsen's success was that he acquired knowledge, then bought his ship, instead of doing what most explorers had done, bought the ship first and then acquired the requisite polar knowledge.

Amundsen's Rule, for lack of a better term, is simple. Regardless if it's dog sleds across Antarctica or horses in a more temperate climate, failing to plan means planning to fail. You must never allow a romantic vision to cloud your better judgement. Things will not "work themselves out" when you are on the road. Nor will a physically or emotionally unsuitable horse mysteriously transform itself into a wise road horse after you have set off.

Thus, even though we are discussing equestrian travel, not polar exploration, the laws linking preparation and success have been recognized by Long Riders through the ages, and one primary point always rings true. Regardless of the year and place, your chances of geographic success are directly linked to your choice of mount.

For example, in 1883 Long Rider Daniel Slade shared his concerns about the lack of preparation some people took before setting out on an equestrian journey across the United States.

"I have been astonished at the ignorance shown in the treatment of horses on a journey by individuals who are daily accustomed to using them at home under the saddle, but beyond this know nothing from experience," he wrote.

Jump forward to the dawning of the 21st century and you will find Allen Russell, one of the world's most respected Long Riders, passing on a warning that mirrors those of other like-minded tribal elders in the Long Riders' Guild.

"Without question, the choice of a mount for your Long Ride will be the most important decision you make in planning your journey. Not only will it greatly determine if you reach your goal but moreover it will affect every step of your trip. You may get where you are going on a horse that isn't right for you but it won't be much fun," this seasoned traveller warned.

Therefore Amundsen's Rule demands that you pay strict and careful attention to pre-trip planning, the first example of which is the need to realize that not just any horse will do.

If that's the case, then what do you ride?

It was Margaret Leigh who provided a hint about what sort of horse you need. In 1939 she wrote, "The best mount for a long journey is not a hunter or a riding school hack, but a solid, hardy farm cob or herdsman's pony, with plenty of grit and endurance, easy to catch and quiet in traffic. And remember, in long distance riding the walk is the pace that counts and a fast walker with a long smooth stride is always to be preferred."

Yet before we take Margaret's advice and look at today's horses, let us move back in time so as to inspect what previous equestrians accomplished on horses of a by-gone era.

Once Upon a Time

"On the 5th of July in Mongolia there was a horse-race on the banks of the Orkhon River which passed over a distance of twelve miles. There were eleven hundred and ten horses on the course at one time, of which one hundred were declared the best. Next day there was a race of sixteen hundred and twenty-seven horses, six years old. The goal was but ten miles distant. On the 7th a third race took place between nine hundred and ninety-five horses, four years old. They had to pass over a space of eight miles," wrote Egor Fedorvich Timkovski in 1820.

Later in that century, the legendary Cossack Long Rider, Lieutenant Dmitri Peshkov, rode his Yakut pony, Seriy, an average of thirty-eight miles a day during their 9,500 kilometre (6,000 mile) journey from Blagoveshchensk, Siberia to St. Petersburg, Russia.

Lest you make the mistake of thinking that only Central Asians rode tough horses, Kit Carson made a non-stop equestrian journey from Omaha, Nebraska to Los Angeles, California, then immediately rode to San Francisco in six days.

Long Rider Roger Pocock, who made his 6,000 kilometre (3,600 mile) journey along the length of the Outlaw Trail in 200 days in 1899, made this remarkable observation after meeting Butch Cassidy and his hard-riding criminal companions. "Among the Robbers' Roost gang of outlaws I found it was their custom to plant little bunches of ponies here and there in pasture. When they happened to be in a hurry they would travel from pasture to pasture, and at each of these take a fresh mount. Six hundred miles in six days was not unusual they told me."

Nor were impressive distances automatically eclipsed by the dawning of the automobile age.

The Los Angeles Times reported on August 17, 1927 that a legal affidavit had been delivered to the US Postmaster General stating that the 20-year-old horse owned by rural mail carrier Leroy Caldwell, of Craig County, Virginia had faithfully carried the mail for 55,896 miles, a distance of more than twice around the Earth.

Yet true horsemen were already worried.

Before making his ride from Kiev to Paris in 1889, Cossack Long Rider Mikael Asseyev issued this stern warning to his fellow Russian cavalry officers.

"We are in the process of transforming our horses into drawing-room creatures," he exclaimed. "Just because a racehorse is exhausted after a 200 metre gallop, it doesn't mean that no horse is capable of covering long distances at a reasonable speed. Just because an hour's schooling brings a dressage horse to his knees, it doesn't mean that the army horses have to be shut up in a loosebox for 23 out of 24 hours! We're turning our horses into weaklings!"

For much of the horse world, Asseyev's prophecy has come true.

Oil Horses

While there is a plethora of equestrian magazines, the majority of which are busy churning out one forgettable issue after another, none of them have sensed the need to investigate the connection between the overall physical decline in horses and any link to the growth of "Big Oil."

To put it plainly, the rise of the automobile has seen the decline of the horse, in terms of overall strength, perseverance and travel performance.

This is because 20th century America encouraged the development of a new equestrian way of life, one dependant upon a constant supply of cheap petroleum and pretty horses. The result gave rise to luxury equestrian events inhabited by "oil horses," a type of prestige possession which had been bred for looks, not results.

In his ground-breaking work, *Race, Ethnicity, Species, Breed Totemism and Horse Breed Classification in America*, Dr. John Borneman described how citizens of the United States adopted certain horse breeds to reflect their view of themselves in the 20th century. The Arabian was thought to be fiery and sensual, the Mustang apt to be described as tough and combative and the Thoroughbred believed to be a reflection of an owner who was rich and sophisticated. In any case, because the owners were not actually using the horses to travel great distances, the relative merits of each breed are largely a matter of coffee house chatter and internet banter.

Horses are thus not being used to achieve a sense of personal geographic liberty but to define an owner's definition of themselves to others, in the same manner as a Harley-Davidson motorcycle, a Hummer four-wheel-drive off-road vehicle or a luxurious Mercedes Benz sports car might be. For these people, it is not how far you ride, but what you own, that makes all the difference.

Another aspect of this social dilemma can be linked to the Baby Boomers, which contain nearly 80 million members, making it the largest generation in America's history. Having spent their childhood watching romanticized galloping cowboy programmes on television, as the Baby Boomers matured they changed from passive childhood horse-watchers into adult horse-owners and breeders. Yet with this transformation came serious social repercussions. Alongside the rise of the late 20th century neighbourhood horse show came a corresponding explosion in horse breeding, as amateur backyard owners bred millions more horses than were actually needed. For decades the equine slaughter industry served as a silent conduit for those animals which were unwanted, all the while the shows continued to award blue ribbons and encourage the breeding of disposable equines aimed at ego boosting.

With the Baby Boomers having now reached the average age of 45 to 60, they are entering their retirement years and are less likely to spend money on horses than they did in their thirties. With only half as many members, Generation X presents far fewer potential riders and horse owners. Additionally, a world-wide economic recession has further devastated the incomes of previously-rich horse owners who had formerly counted on access to cheap hay, horses and petroleum.

Despite the overwhelming evidence of a drastically-decreased domestic market, breed organizations such as the American Quarter Horse Association, for example, continue to encourage the production of more horses than are necessary.

Plus, due to the virtual extinction of the American equine slaughter industry, an already over-taxed horse market is now seeing horses being routinely abandoned, turned loose in national forests to fend for themselves or left to starve, as once-rich owners struggle to make mortgage payments instead of maintaining a country gentleman lifestyle. Increasingly, equine classified ads now offer horses for free to good homes.

These equine charity cases mirror a domestic market that is awash with an over abundance of horses who are usually too young, unbroken or otherwise unsuitable for the transition into a road horse.

In addition to aiding in the decline of equestrian travel, there have been other unforeseen problems. Luxury horses raised in comfort require constant care, as the more removed they are from their natural environment, the more dependent they have become. While often suffering from an impoverished equine emotional life, these animals are fed, groomed, cleaned and pampered like infants by doting owners who are content to ride in circles like goldfish circling inside a glass bowl, while pretending they're in the ocean.

Can there really be such a dramatic difference between a hard-working horse and one who is slightly ridden? Long Rider Roger Pocock proved it at the dawning of the First World War.

With the Kaiser's German cavalry obviously preparing for combat, this experienced equestrian traveller urged the British government to take equestrian action. For the purpose of isolating the most important factors in horsemanship, Pocock managed to organize a series of tests on English highways. In each test two groups of four horsemen apiece, working in rivalry, rode fifty miles on a Saturday, then back again on the Sunday. Afterwards a veterinary surgeon reported that all of the working horses, who normally spent their days drawing London's wagons and cabs, used by Pocock's riders finished fresh and on time but the pleasure horses broke down and had to come home by train.

"The pleasure horse and his equipment are so highly specialized for running and jumping that they have ceased to possess the slightest value for civil and military working horsemanship," Pocock concluded.

If things were bad then, they're worse now.

Pocock warned, "The civilized stable management with grooming and massage, clipping and trimming, and all the practice which involves the use of clothing, is excellent for the indoor horse, in the same way a hospital is good for the sick. The treatment makes the horse glossy and beautiful, but sensitive rather than robust. It does not make the horse an outdoor person able to face bad weather, rough feeding and long marches. For that we must consider outdoor management as applied to outdoor horses. By all means let the high-strung, highly-fed, massaged, hospital-bred, courageous, and powerful but exceedingly delicate blooded horse be used for pleasure and for pleasure only. One does not use a racing yacht for cargo because she has no stowage. Our pleasure horses are excellent for sport but are expensive, delicate, unsound and lacking in endurance when we put them to serious work."

Thus, when it comes to deciding what you will ride on an equestrian journey, the first thing to recall is that a horse which has spent its life living in a luxurious stall will be sensitive to the weather, less apt to endure hunger and prone to fatigue. Such a horse will require a lengthy time to transition to the rigours of a life on the road, with the chances of that success being dependent upon a great many unforeseen factors.

Because of these social and cultural reasons, finding a road horse in the early 21st century is apt to be an immense challenge, even before the wrong people try to fill you with misleading advice.

Difficulties

There is an additional challenge: misguided people.

All too often you'll find that everyone is an expert, even if they've never ridden out of town. Plus, depending on what part of the world you're riding in, you will encounter people who are eager to share local equestrian beliefs, traditions, taboos and superstitions.

Here are some examples.

Enthusiastic ignorance - "What breed is he? Why mister, that's a pure-blooded sorrel."

Cultural ignorance - "You can't ride a pinto because that breed of horse is the brother of the cow."

Sexual ignorance - "Geldings are weak. No, mares are weak. Well at least we agree that all stallions are crazy."

Age ignorance - "Only travel on a young horse."

Conformation ignorance - "This is a beautiful horse for your journey. Yes, but he's lame!"

Breed ignorance -"That (fill in the breed) of horse will never make it."

As Allen Russell warned, "Though advice from experienced horsemen can be invaluable, be careful that you aren't misled by those who are quick to hand out misinformation."

A good rule of thumb, Allen believes, is to look at the horses of those making suggestions, as the quality of their mount will speak louder than their words.

Therefore, if history proves we must exercise extreme care in selecting a mount for our journey, how do we use rational research to help define what a road horse is – and isn't?

What is a Road Horse?

The term "Road Horse" was once commonly used to describe an equine capable of successfully completing extended journeys under a variety of conditions, across any type of country, in any type of weather.

The Romans, for example, had different categories of horses: *venedi* for hunting, *cantherii* for pleasure riding and *itinerarii* for travel.

In 1847 author and equine travel expert, Rollo Springfield, defined what qualities were needed for such an animal.

"The Road Horse is a strong, vigorous, active kind, capable of enduring great hardship; its stature rather low, seldom exceeding fifteen hands; the body round and compact; its limbs strong," Springfield wrote, then went on to say, "sadly this breed has of late been neglected by those preferring fashion instead of utility."

Before setting off in 1925 on a journey to all 48 American states, Frank Heath declared, "What I wanted was a road horse. The problem is they are scarce."

Even the most famous equestrian traveller of all time had a hard time finding the right horse. After Aimé Tschiffely completed his ride from Buenos Aires to New York he took up residence in London. In 1936 the man who had ridden 10,000 miles across the Americas decided he would like to ride from the south of England to Scotland. The problem was that the Swiss Long Rider couldn't locate a road horse!

"I found that the horses on offer were too pampered, too nervous, too big or too small. One such heavenly pet had a habit of rearing up and falling over backwards. The problem of finding a suitable horse was so difficult, that had it not been for the distance, I would have had my old friend Mancha brought over from the Argentine. However since this was out of the question, I finally decided to put an advertisement in one of leading sporting magazines."

Luckily the owner of a suitable Cob mare contacted Tschiffely, who then rode the physically strong and emotionally reliable animal to Scotland in 1936.

The most knowledgeable equestrian traveller of the late 20th century, Swiss Long Rider Otto Schwarz, likewise reported the challenge of deciding on the "perfect" travelling horse.

"To choose a horse that will later become your companion and comrade is exciting but always delicate. If we want to travel, then we will need a horse that lends himself to the task. Maybe you have one already. Is it a hardy Icelander or a tough Camargue? Is it warm-blooded or cold blood? Is it from France, Patagonia or New Caledonia? Regardless, you will always need a horse with the capacity to work who is gentle and safe in traffic."

With Otto's admonition ringing in our ears, what general features did the man who rode 48,000 kilometres (30,000 miles) on five continents believe a road horse must possess?

"What then do we ask from the road horse?" he wondered. "Every road horse must be capable of carrying heavy loads, consisting of the saddle, the Long Rider and their mutual essentials. Therefore he must be a robust weight-carrier. He must be able to pull through without shying, even in difficult terrain. An older horse can be very good for a long trip. So as every man has a picture in the back of his mind of the ideal wife, so does every Long Rider carry a picture in his heart of the ideal road horse."

Even when we are armed with such general rules, in this mechanised age it has become increasingly difficult to obtain fundamental experiences with horses. Therefore any aspiring Long Rider who is embarking on his first venture may be worried where his lack of knowledge will land him. Let us then investigate some of the factors which will influence your choice of horses, starting with the ancient rule that the beautiful horse you already own doesn't always make the best road horse.

Your Own Horse

Perhaps you already own a horse. That doesn't automatically presuppose that this animal is capable of making a long, challenging, and perhaps dangerous journey.

After having ridden over the Andes mountains in 1823, Sir Francis Bond Head, cautioned other would-be travellers not to think that the horse they had at home was automatically capable of making a strenuous journey.

"When a man has ridden a horse for many years," Bond Head said, "he is fully persuaded that he knows what he is made of. But the truth is he only knows what he has done and what he can do under the maximum of excitement he hitherto has ever experienced; what he does not know, and indeed what without trial he can have no idea of, is the enormous test a journey will place upon him."

While it is correct to assume that it helps to be mounted on a horse you already trust and ride, you must not allow love to overrule logic. What is needed is a merciless evaluation of the animal's strengths and weaknesses.

Does the horse have the physical strength required? Does he have the temperament needed to face a vast array of emotional obstacles? Can he adapt to spending the night in a variety of strange places? Can he travel through traffic calmly? Is he a hearty eater?

If you already own such a horse, fine. However, if you have any doubts about the horse's suitability, look for another mount. Any journey requires a horse to tap into its deepest reserves of emotional courage and physical fortitude. Therefore do not be blinkered by misplaced loyalty into placing an animal you deeply love into a situation which he cannot withstand, overcome or even survive.

Two Historical Precedents

If you set out to find a road horse, you should keep in mind the fact that there were two dramatically different equestrian philosophies at work in the old world: Mongols versus Persians.

The harsh Mongolian environment played a strong part in developing small, sturdy horses which were as tough as the warriors who rode them across every sort of geographic obstacle. Mounted on such magnificent animals, Genghis Khan's cavalry crossed the steppes with ease, traversed the mighty mountains separating them from India, swam every river, rolled through Europe, invaded Korea and even jabbed their way south across the desert to the gateway of Egypt. These small horses routinely made journeys of astonishing distances, were largely self-sufficient, emotionally independent and hard as iron.

A totally different mindset arose in Persia, where the Shah's horses were bred for beauty. These were occasional riding horses, four-legged show pieces designed for looks and elegance. Like the Arabs further south, the Persians too were preoccupied with equine pedigrees and selective breeding. Splendour was more important than strength. Status conquered speed.

Yet Long Riders have always been aware of the dangers of placing beauty ahead of functionality.

In 1823 an American named Josiah Harlan survived an extraordinary series of mounted adventures in Afghanistan. After having ridden from India to Kabul, and then penetrated through the infamous Hindu Kush Mountains to the edge of the grasslands beyond, this determined rider made a succinct observation.

"Vastly different is the horse bred for display than that bred for hard work. The horses of the predatory Central Asian cavalry have firm muscles and nerves of steel. They will travel one hundred miles daily and pass over one thousand miles in ten consecutive days. The horse capable of performing such a service resembles a cast iron figure," Harlan wrote.

Another fallacy was expressed in the 1920s by Robert Cunninghame Graham, who warned about placing too much emphasis on the legendary origins of a particular type of horse.

"The Andalusian horse of the eighteenth century was certainly superior to the wild Criollo horse of the Argentine pampas in beauty and in size. In all the other qualities he must have been as he is today, vastly inferior. The Andalusian horse, today at least, is a long legged, rather showy animal, deficient both in bone and stamina and much more fitted for parade than for hard work."

Thus, when we set about to look for a road horse, we must be careful not to fall into that first fatal trap, namely setting our hearts in advance on riding a specific breed, rather than locating a suitable animal.

Breeds

Like ancient Persians, too many horse owners in the west are obsessed with breed standards which focus on appearance, conformation and exaggerated artificial gaits.

Long Riders want horses that are strong, brave and faithful. They're searching for courage, not fairy-tale origins. They're pragmatists, not preservationists.

That's not to say that Long Riders are not strong believers in the vigour and resilience of resident breeds. Many Long Riders have used native horses in all parts of the world.

In 1925 Aimé Tschiffely rode his Criollo, Mancha, 16,000 kilometres (10,000 miles) through South, Central and North America.

More recently, Tim Cope rode 6,000 miles solo from Mongolia to Hungary on hardy native horses. Tim, who was on his first equestrian journey, quickly learned how durable his road and pack horses were.

"It is well known that Mongolian horses are very tough - they are always left to their own devices. They always find grass themselves, often drink no more than once a day (especially in desert regions) and in winter do not drink at all and get by digging up grass under the snow with their hooves."

Hardy native horses are, by definition, perfectly adapted to the local geography and conditions, be they mountains, jungles, deserts or marshes. In North America, that means the fabled mustang. In South America, it's the legendary Criollo. France has the Camargue horse, and there are hundreds more examples of native breeds around the world that are tough, intelligent and resourceful - and affordable!

As these examples demonstrate, blood lines are not the ultimate deciding factor. It is individual ability that counts.

That is why there is no "chosen" breed for equestrian travel. One line of horses doesn't warrant greater praise than another. Long Riders give every breed and every individual horse a chance, and when the breed or individual horse fails to live up to the rigours of the road, he or it must give up its place to others. You steer the course but it is the strength and courage of the road horse that gets you both through.

Therefore, do not allow an illusion to set your heart in advance on a particular breed!

Nor should you begin your efforts by falling under the misconception that all locally-bred horses are either tremendously strong or error free. While it is true that too many horses in Europe and North America are large but soft-muscled, this isn't to say that overseas horses are not without their drawbacks too. Many countries such as Tahiti, Kyrgyzstan and Japan possessed small horses which were anything but perfect.

When the American Long Rider Raphael Plumpelly attempted to ride across Japan in 1865 he discovered this to his dismay.

"The next morning began our experience with the vicious brutes of the country, which, being unaccustomed to foreigners, did all they could to throw us. The Japanese horses are small and strong, but badly built, and are evidently the degenerate offspring of the Tartar stock. As they are always stallions, their worst qualities are generally the most apparent."

The discipline of travel requires more than breeding and myth, as an illegitimate nag with no papers, but deep wind and legs of steel, will out-travel a pampered, stable spoiled, finicky eating, blue-blooded equine.

The most important criterion is to pick the horse from a breed that has the correct model and a body weight in accordance with the Long Rider and his equipment. Such an ideal road horse is one who enjoys travelling, can eat and drink anything, has good, strong feet and is happy being in a new place every day.

This is a state of mind, not a breed.

A Word of Caution

While it is true that native breeds have many good qualities, you should be sceptical of being offered a potential mount whose main claim to fame is that it is descended from a feral fantasy. The problem in this scenario occurs when romance overrides reality.

Just as gauchos, cowboys, Cossacks and Mongols no longer travel great distances on horseback as their forefathers once routinely did, most modern "wild" horses do not automatically possess the range of skills you will need in a road horse.

The Brumby of Australia is one such free ranging wild horse. He is descended from a wide variety of ancestors, including Timor ponies from Indonesia, Cape Horn horses from South Africa, Arabians from Syria and Thoroughbreds from Europe. Legend has it that the term was first used to describe horses originally owned by Sergeant James Brumby. Upon leaving his property in New South Wales in 1804 to journey to Tasmania, Brumby supposedly freed the horses to roam across the countryside. The result is that Brumbies now number in the hundreds of thousands and Australia has the largest feral horse population in the world. Yet, despite the fact that this feral horse population increases at a rate of 20% a year, there is a low demand for adoption for these horses.

The United States is also home to an extensive wild horse population. Commonly known as mustangs, their bloodlines, like those of their Australian cousins, include a potpourri of equine influences. This is due to the fact that North American horse populations were much more fluid than is often assumed, with Europeans, Americans and Indians deliberately introducing or loosing horses into the gene pool at frequent intervals.

One such overlooked example occurred in the late 1920s when Philip Chappel, of Rockford, Illinois, intentionally introduced large draught stallions into the wild mustang herds of the far west. Having invented the process of canning horse meat for dog food, and thereby making his brand, Ken-L-Ration, a multi-million dollar business, Chappel captured and canned hundreds of thousands of mustangs to satisfy his hungry canine customers. Believing the mustang did not carry enough meat to satisfy his purposes, Chappel deliberately released Percheron and other massive draught stallions onto the range so as to create a larger, meatier mustang for his mercenary purposes.

The U.S. Bureau of Land Management is entrusted to oversee the welfare and protection of America's wild horses. Yet like Australia, this government agency faces the constant issue of how to cope with an ever-increasing equine population. As has been noted, certain Long Riders have successfully used BLM mustangs, but only after they have been extensively tamed and trained.

As Professor John Borneman notes in his ground-breaking study of American equine tribalism, "Such horses can be domesticated, but they are rarely profitable in any sense of the word. Most frequently, they are difficult to train and, not being bred selectively for riding, they do not make particularly good mounts. Most of the adoptive parents only take them by projecting qualities onto them (such as wildness and freedom), or simply out of the joy of caring, and they in fact have to sacrifice a great deal of time, money, and even status."

One of the greatest risks when scouting for a road horse occurs when people offer you a feral horse whose pedigree is laced with romance or spiced with fiction. This is especially true among wild horse idealists, who claim their horses are purebred descendants of horses lost by Spanish explorers. The majority of these vanity breed associations do not date any earlier than the 1950s. As previously mentioned, many people have focused on breeding horses whose primary purpose is to serve as an emotional object of desire. Whereas our ancestors invariably judged a horse on its individual qualities, all too often horses that fall into this modern category have been bred in an effort to promote a specific historical, political, geographic or cultural agenda.

Thus, whereas North American Arabian breeders focus on creating the perfect dished head, and Quarter Horse breeders fixate on a large hind quarter, "Spanish" mustang preservationists devote themselves to defending a fetish about their horse's origins. Though it is often claimed that these animals are capable of tremendous athletic abilities, they have been over-produced and under-trained. For example, one ranch in Wyoming is home to more than 300 of these "Spanish" mustangs, yet few of them appear to have been tamed or trained.

These sentimental practices have resulted in large herds of wild horses, most of whom will never know a saddle. When asked to defend this methodology, preservationists become passionate about their horses, choosing to disregard any historical or genetic facts which contravene their starry-eyed ideals.

This situation is illustrated by a "For Sale" advertisement for one such "Spanish" horse.

"I love this horse, but I am not the right home for him at this time in my life. Since purchasing him I have had two babies and do not have the time to train him myself or the money to afford to pay someone else to do it," the current owner explained.

After describing him as "a puppy dog with a big heart," she admitted that the horse did have a few minor problems.

"He has some training issues and will need someone who is either experienced at training these horses, or someone who can afford to send him to the right trainer. He also has some trust issues and some avoidance tactics that make me think he was abused by a previous trainer," she wrote, before adding that she hadn't actually been able to catch the horse for almost half a year.

"I made the mistake of turning him loose in the pasture when I first got him and it took me five months of working with him before he trusted me enough to let me walk up to him without him leaving."

As an afterthought, she remembered to say, "He has learned the rather nasty avoidance tactic of pulling away from you and bolting if he thinks you are going to do something nasty to him, like the farrier, getting his shots, etc."

She concluded, "He's a great horse and I want him to go to someone who knows and loves the breed."

Despite this type of widespread problem, a well known mustang preservationist proudly announced to the press, "If Columbus was here today, he'd say "This is the horse I want.""

Perhaps, being a sailor, Columbus might settle for a horse that is untamed, untrained, won't let you catch him for five months, doesn't trust humans and runs away when you attempt to provide him with basic medical or farrier care, but that's not the sort of mount needed by an equestrian traveller.

The horse is a living creature, not a collector's piece and as Long Riders we must concentrate on performance, not politics.

Unlike the Americans, the Australians do not seem anxious to prove that a certain percentage of their wild horses are direct descendants of any prior import. But in America you will be offered horses with pedigrees that include such colourful terms as "medicine hat" or purporting to be descended from that mythical Hollywood mustang, *Hidalgo*. Australians, on the other hand, are not prone to offer you a direct descendant of the Godolphin Arabian or to pretend their Brumby is a lost cousin of Pharlap.

While you can indeed find excellent, well-trained horses in any number of breeds who purport to be of Spanish descent, your decision making must rest on that animal's combined skills, and not according to any would-be links back to the stallion once ridden by the conquistador, Cortez.

Thus, you should be sceptical of any feral horse in North America who is offered to you primarily because he is supposedly a pure strain of anything. Don't let them unload their problem on to you. Don't purchase a fantasy. That is a quick fix that does not last. Like the horsemen of yore, you require a utilitarian, functioning horse, not an object of desire.

Climate and Terrain

Think climate, not papers.

It is imperative that the horse chosen for any journey must be suited to the local conditions as far as possible. For example, don't take a tropical horse into the mountains, as most horses do not adjust well to radical changes in climate and terrain.

Therefore, fear terrain, not a lack of social standing. Consider if you will be riding through rugged country or alongside more sedate roadways.

Where you are going will affect what you ride, so a local horse should always be considered a priority as acclimatised native animals are found to be more effective than imported mounts.

Remember, a modest exterior can contain the most dazzling of talents. For instance, during the Second World War the German army adapted the scrappy-looking little Russian panje horses for their winter campaign because these tough animals could be fed for weeks on end with straw taken from house roofs. It was also noted that these tiny horses had a highly developed sense of direction.

Strength & Conformation

It is no easier to draw up the specification of a universally-desired automobile than of a horse that will suit every equestrian traveller. Yet we can determine some critical and uncompromising elements upon which all can agree.

What is the road horse to be used for?

To carry a Long Rider and his supplies.

Because the road horse must perform hard physical duty and carry continuous loads, he can't have any weaknesses in his general conformation, as any faults in build or balance must be compensated by the use of extra energy. That is why in terms of the road horse, small physical defects that may not make big differences in jumping, dressage or the show ring can create larger problems for a travelling animal.

Beauty should be a secondary consideration.

Before setting off to ride across Russia, Thomas Stevens made the mistake of purchasing an unsuitable horse.

"Texas was as handsome a horse as ever wore a shoe. But he shied at houses, people, cattle, dogs, sheep, hillocks and his own shadow. He was terrified of even the smallest stream and feared bridges."

In striking contrast was the legendary Yakut horse, Seriy, which carried Dmitri Peshkov from Siberia to St. Petersburg.

Stevens met Peshkov as the Cossack Long Rider was nearing the end of his journey. The American made a note of how tough the Russian's horse was, even after enduring winter storms which ranged as low as minus fifty degrees Fahrenheit.

"Peshkov's horse was a big-barrelled, stocky, grey pony; about fourteen hands high, the exact counterpart of horses one sees by the score in the bronco herds of Wyoming. He was well chosen for his task. He was all barrel, hams, and shoulders. His neck and head seemed scarcely to be parts of the same horse. His pace was a fast, ambling walk that carried him over the ground at five miles an hour and left the big chargers of the Czars honour guard far to the rear. The escort had to trot occasionally to keep up. The gallant little grey was as sleek and well-conditioned as if he had just come out of a clover pasture."

In choosing a road horse you should first look for a sturdy type with sound limbs. One then looks keenly for a wide enough windpipe, supple neck, good teeth, a strong back with good connection to the pelvis, a wide deep chest, a free-moving shoulder, supple knees, flexible tendons, very hard hooves and high endurance.

Clear, bright eyes and active, alert ears are most desirable. Also, the road horse must always be well balanced.

Canadian Long Rider Stan Walchuk, who operates a packing service in the Rocky Mountains, has studied the requirements for road horses. He believes that the perfect mind in the perfect body are ideals we strive for but seldom achieve.

"Our favourite horses will likely have some quirks and body-parts that are less than ideal," Stan cautioned.

In his excellent book, *Trail Riding, Pack and Training Manual,* Walchuk has shared his years of wisdom about road horses and equestrian travel.

In addition to the above-named requirements, he urges would-be horse buyers not to overlook several other vitally important factors. One important fact is that a road horse needs to have heavier bone than the casual weekend riding mount.

"When assessing the bone on a horse, go beyond looking at how big the front foot, ankle and knee appear. Look at the circumference of the pastern (the narrow section between the ankle and foot) and also the size of the back foot. We could say that the pastern needs to be an 8" circumference, but you need to compare horses to each other to appreciate good-sized bone."

Walchuk also believes that the withers are probably the most important aspect of the back. They should be well defined but not too high or too narrow.

"The wither stabilizes the bars on the saddle and therefore secures the load. With no wither, the saddle rolls side to side, increasing the chance of sores and creating a horse that may require constant attention to re-pack a slipped load."

Allen Russell confirmed his fellow Long Rider's opinion, when he too warned, "A round backed horse will not hold the saddle well and is much more likely to sore up. Also you have to cinch them much tighter and that becomes a factor when using every day."

One final consideration, Russell warned, is to be very meticulous regarding your mount's legs. Even though a horse may look magnificent, its legs are often inadequate.

Locating an ideal road horse with these qualities will provide you with a mount which is strong enough to carry you through adverse conditions for months on end. But will it have the emotional courage to face the hardships of the road with you, and what sex is best?

Gender

Horses and sex?

Mares, geldings or stallions?

Can the gender of your mount influence the outcome of your trip?

A resounding "yes".

Rest assured, it's a tricky subject, as you can't make a decision based simply on biology. Are you riding with a companion? What they ride affects the equation. Are you riding in a country that denounces or prefers riding one gender more than another?

What do you ride and does it make a difference?

Depending on where you go, the gender of the road horse has a tremendous influence on daily events and will affect your long-term chances of success.

The first thing to realize is that all horses, regardless of their gender, have the potential to become good road horses. If you take the time to study the Equestrian Travel Timeline, published on the Long Riders' Guild website, you will not only discover that every breed of horse imaginable has been used to make successful equestrian journeys, additionally, so have mares, geldings and stallions. For instance, D.C. Vision rode his Shire mare, Louise, 22,500 kilometres (14,000 miles) across the United States, George Younghusband rode his gelding, Joe, across the jungles of Burma and Basha O'Reilly rode her Cossack stallion, Count Pompeii, from Volgograd to London.

So it's not merely a matter of sex, as any mare, gelding or stallion has the potential to be an excellent road horse. What you have to consider are the cultural implications of where you ride, before you decide what you mount. Let us then look at the ancient, and modern, prejudices which surround this thorny topic.

A stallion is a male horse used for breeding. An entire is a sexually intact male animal that is trained to ride or drive. In the past the primary purpose of a stallion was to propagate the breed. An entire, on the other hand, was a trained male animal whose social manners did not preclude it being introduced into polite equestrian society. It is because those horses known as entires are rarely used in the English speaking world that this prejudice has come about.

Sadly, as I write this book, I can think of a perfect example of this situation currently existing in North America. A Palomino Quarter Horse stallion I know of has been allowed to exist, without benefit of any human kindness or interaction, for the last ten years. During that time the horse has never been brushed or shod. He is allowed to exist solely so his female owner may once a year use him for her financial benefit so as to breed other Palominos. This horse has no social skills and largely stands in one spot in a large pasture, transfixed with anguish and boredom. Because he eagerly attacks any other horse naïve enough to venture near him, this stallion helps perpetrate the myth that intact male horses are too savage to be trusted.

Nothing could be further from the truth, as is amply proved by the entire who resides a close distance away on the same property.

The legendary Count Pompeii is a Cossack entire. Unlike his sad Palomino neighbour, Pompeii possesses excellent social manners and is constantly ridden by my diminutive wife, Basha, through every type of obstacle on a simple snaffle bit.

How can two sexually intact male horses standing a few hundred yards from each other on the same property be so radically different? It is because they symbolize two drastically varied ways of raising and training horses.

Unlike the emotionally abandoned Palomino stallion, whose violent interactions with other horses borders on the criminal, the Russian entire was born and raised in a natural equine environment.

The main reason Pompeii is so well behaved is because he ran wild on the steppes of Russia until he was caught and trained by the Cossacks. During his formative years, he belonged to a large herd of largely wild horses that roamed freely across the vast steppes. Growing up among this moving equine society, as a horse was designed to do, Pompeii was taught his manners by the senior stallions and the mares of the herd. Both sexes trained him to curtail his sexual desires, otherwise there were immediate, and often painful, lessons to be learned from their hard hooves or sharp teeth. As Pompeii proves, entires which live with mares often pay little or no attention to them.

What is seldom appreciated is that this active sexual nature tends to strengthen a stallion's nomadic character. He is always on the move in nature, be it to circle the herd in wary defence or to run miles on end so as to elude danger. Plus, he's stronger than either a gelding or mare. He's alert, sensitive and wakeful. This is a powerful, fast-moving, robust horse who likes to overcome obstacles and take the lead. Thus, in addition to learning how to behave himself, Count Pompeii grew into a magnificent road horse.

With those sorts of qualities, it is not surprising then to learn that Basha rode Pompeii 4,000 kilometres (2,500 miles) across Russia, Belarus and Europe, during which time he cheerfully travelled alongside the other entires, geldings and mares encountered along the way. Needless to say, he enjoyed every bit of the journey. In fact, Basha didn't have any trouble until she returned home to England, whereupon she was immediately told that such a "dangerous" animal couldn't be trusted around other horses.

What Basha and Pompeii encountered in England is a widespread prejudice which has taken root in the west. It states that sexually intact male horses are automatically deemed too dangerous to ride in society or around other horses. As Pompeii proves, if this is true it is largely the fault of the humans whose mismanagement allowed the situation to become a scandalous problem.

When considering the sex of a road horse, you should first consider the training of the male horse in question. If he is a sex-mad outlaw stallion, like the poor Palomino, then the horse is certainly ruled out. However, if he is a well-trained, sociable entire, like Count Pompeii, then you could consider using him for your journey.

The final deciding factor regarding stallions and entires is whether you will be crossing international borders. Whereas it is difficult to cross any border with a medically certified mare or gelding, it is ten times more complex to attempt this with a stallion.

All too often the question of riding an entire doesn't rest with you. It's a matter of geography.

You should carefully bear in mind where you are going to make your ride. If you're about to go across Kyrgyzstan, where everybody rides anything, then riding a stallion isn't going to impact your daily decision-making. However, if you're trying to find a suitable barn one late night in Kansas, you're bound to encounter suspicion, fear and hostility if you arrive on an entire.

But don't think that this cultural antagonism only extends to the male sex, as there are portions of the world where it is a grave insult to ride a mare.

This antagonism is strongest among the gauchos of Argentina and the huasos of Chile, as both these legendary equestrian cultures believe it is an affront to mount a man on a mare. In stark contrast to this Latin American philosophy is that of the Arabian world, where warriors, traditionally mounted on their beloved mares, would carry out extended raids across the desert.

Yet prejudice against the female sex wasn't restricted to the pampas.

The 19th century French dressage master, James Fillis, expressed a common complaint about mares, namely that they become emotional and high-strung when they come into season.

"I never buy mares because they often become peevish," Fillis complained.

While modern history is replete with instances of the lovable, steady, bell-mare that leads the herd of horses out of danger, what is overlooked is that many female horses are not always dependable, as the vagaries of mares at certain seasons can create and exaggerate problems. Thus, when they are in heat, mares can lead horses away when it is time to be caught. Plus, when a mare bickers and fights, it encourages foolish and distracting behaviour among other horses.

The worst problem of travelling with a mare though is that she runs the risk of becoming pregnant during the journey. This occurred to mares belonging to several equestrian travellers, including North American Long Rider Katherine Boone who journeyed through Spain.

While caution is essential in choosing any potential road horse, mares are generally viewed as an emotional advantage as they are often responsible for encouraging a strong sense of cohesion among any group of horses.

But if given a choice, what did history's most influential horseman prefer?

Genghis Khan controlled an estimated twenty million horses, yet preferred to mount his warriors on geldings during military operations.

Why?

Because history demonstrates that the gelding is nearly always the ideal travelling horse, as the operation generally renders him pleasant, but spirited, brave, but not uncontrollable, tractable, but confident. According to his individual personality, if the horse is operated on at an older age, he often retains the characteristics of the stallion but without its wildness. Overall, a strong, reliable, well-trained gelding will be found to maintain the majority of those characteristics needed by a Long Rider, making such a horse most welcome on a long journey.

Colour

The English are credited with having been the first to say, "A good horse can never have a bad colour." This is only partly true, as while no good horse is a bad colour, it's equally correct to point out that there are inefficient colours, especially if you're a Long Rider.

To begin with, too often an inexperienced person will obsess about the exterior of the horse, ignoring his interior. Beauty in horses is a relative term and must depend upon the particular purpose. As a result, the best-looking horses don't always make the best travelling horses.

When it comes to the perfect colour for a road horse, there isn't one. Every country which once hosted a thriving equestrian culture will still have some remnants of the ancient superstitions which were connected to each colour, even shade, of horse.

The Arabs considered the Palomino so unnatural that it was known as "Jew yellow" and restricted the breed to be ridden by those of that religious practice. American cowboys thought white horses attracted insects. There were preferential prejudices as well. The Swiss believed that a grey horse possessed the greatest power of recuperation. Mamelukes believed the black, though brave, wasn't as fleet as the bay and Canadians favoured duns because of their legendary endurance abilities. Overall, all these stories were based upon the long-ago experiences and observations of early riders, whose lives often depended upon the athletic ability of their mount. As in all legends, there may be a grain of truth in each episode.

However, in terms of modern equestrian travel, the primary consideration when choosing a horse is not what colour he is, as journeys have a way of hardening rider and horse almost beyond recognition.

What you need to consider is that a lack of pigment makes a horse more prone to sunburn. This is especially true about horses with pink noses and pale skins. The other drawback of having a light-coloured horse is that as and when he rolls in dung, you find your pretty pony is now adorned with a garish coat of green. Given the normal rigours encountered during any journey, you may trust me when I tell you that upon struggling out, still tired, into the early dawn, the last thing you wish to confront you is an impish horse, such as my dun was, who has successfully managed to stain himself a disgusting sort of dung green colour. Thus, the normal early morning duties are immediately increased, as you try fruitlessly to brush off your ignoble beast's attempts at self-decoration and your carefully-timed departure is delayed.

Thus, if there is a general rule of thumb regarding the appropriate colour for a road horse, always choose a darker rather than a lighter shade.

Age

Traditionally, the age of horses is always calculated from the first of May. Yet regardless of when he was born, the Long Riders' Guild always recommends that equestrian travellers not set out on a journey unless the horse is at least six years old. This is because it is essential that the horse be fully grown and the skeleton is solid and completely finished in its shaping. While most horses are fully grown by that age, some larger animals may mature more slowly.

Plus, the majority of horses conclude their physical growth before they reach a state of emotional maturity. Because of these various reasons, you should avoid choosing a young horse.

Do not harbour a grudge against an older animal. Aimé Tschiffely's famous Criollo geldings, Mancha and Gato, were eighteen and sixteen years old when he set off on his ride from Buenos Aires to New York. As long as the horse is in good health, there is no reason an older animal cannot take to the road with confidence.

Height and Weight

Just as you wouldn't purchase a pair of boots that were two sizes too big, you should not obtain a horse too large for your purposes. When considering a possible road horse, the first thing to note is its height and weight-carrying power. Does it match your logistical and physical needs? Larger riders require heavier horses. Smaller riders can make do with lighter limbed animals.

The ancient rule of equine measurement states that one "hand" equals four inches. Thus an "average" horse may be said to be sixteen hands high. When considering the height of your possible mount, what you must bear in mind first and foremost is the fact that the taller he is, the higher you must reach to put on the saddle. Saddles are heavy, and become even more so as they are taken on and off, day after day, by Long Riders. So avoid adding to your already considerable physical effort by the purchase of an extremely tall horse.

Nor should you fall prey to any prejudice against small, but hardy, horses.

The famous French Long Rider, Jean-Francois Ballereau, who rode in a wide variety of countries around the world, was fond of saying "for a long journey, leave the big and saddle the small." He knew from his travels that many of the smaller breeds are not only exceptionally strong; they also require less grazing than larger horses.

The most amusing example of this "ride the small" philosophy was entered into the Long Rider records by the British Long Rider George Younghusband.

In 1887 the young British subaltern was, "sick of the pomp and vanities of this civilized world of ours." Though stationed in colourful India, Younghusband decided to spend his army leave by exploring southern Burma.

The resultant book, *Eighteen Hundred Miles on a Burmese Pony*, is an equestrian surprise, as this is not another one of those tired 19th century tales about a heroic white man making his way through a tract of nameless jungle. In fact, there is no tale in all of equestrian travel literature which paints a picture of a more loveable scamp than Joe, the delightful four-footed rascal which the author rode.

Younghusband's Burmese mount, despite his diminutive size, gave the professional horseman more than he bargained for.

"I saddled up my little 12.2 (1.25 m) charger and casually sauntered on to his back. Now having been a cavalry soldier for some years, and rather fancying myself as a decent rider, I had never viewed this small atom of horse-flesh otherwise than in the light of a means of conveyance when I was tired. However, he very soon knocked all that nonsense out of me; for he went off like a streak of lightning, stampeded the two elephants, who immediately devastated the village, and shed my goods and chattels on the roofs of houses and up high trees; he then galloped as hard as he could straight at a twelve-foot palisade. I thought he was going to try and jump it, and said my prayers accordingly, but he was no such fool; he stopped as dead as a mummy about three feet off it, and shot me violently into the hardest palisade ever made by man. He then stood quite still and sniggered at me. No other pony have I ever seen even smile, but that little rat distinctly grinned. I was rather wrathful and very much bruised; but mounted again, thinking that, having had his little joke, he would go along in a decent and decorous frame of mind. Not a bit; he went off harder than ever, this time through almost impenetrable forest, where he very shortly left me hanging over a bough like a night-shirt on a clothes' line. After that I led him till I got on to a good open bit of road, intending to have my joke there; but he wouldn't play at all then, and neither whip nor spur would stir him out of an old gentleman's trot. A tremendous wag that pony – I say it without malice – but in spite of my earnest endeavours to rival him in that respect, he invariably, throughout our long partnership of 1800 miles, managed to turn the tables on me, and make me the butt of all his little pleasantries."

What Younghusband discovered is that a once-in-a-lifetime horse doesn't have to be tall to do the job or steal your heart.

What you are seeking is a sturdy combination of strength and a capacity to endure. As Joe the naughty pony proves, big hearts come in small packages. However, a general rule of thumb is that a strong horse, designed for road work, will, on the average, weigh from 900 to 1,200 pounds (about 500 kg.).

Emotional Stability

The safety and success of the Long Rider are dependent on the qualities of the road horse. Yet one of the major problems we face when trying an animal is the need to form a reliable estimate of the horse's temperament, by no means an easy task, in the fleeting time we have at our disposal.

Handsome is as handsome does, and though some of the best road horses ever known were as ugly as sin, their mental make up was a vital part of their success. We are not discussing a show horse, bred for looks, not performance. Nor is a young horse, which is still developing its experiences of the world, ready for the multitude of challenges that will face him on an extended journey. Experience comes with age.

An emotionally-sound horse is one that creates no trouble and does not have such a dominant personality that it is difficult to control. Nor are stubborn trouble-makers suitable.

Because of the rigours of the road, including heavy loads, long hours, rough terrain, unsavoury fodder and irregular shelter, what is needed is a calm temperament that can bear up under all challenges.

This sort of quiet disposition results in a horse that is able to maintain a constant pace all day, then eat what's on offer, before bedding down in a strange stable.

A perfect example of this type of road horse was the cob, Remus, ridden by British Long Rider Richard Barnes. In 1972 the two of them made a journey around the entire perimeter of Great Britain, during which time Remus not only showed immense loyalty to his rider, in addition, he was "patient, hardworking and loyal, a proper roadster."

In his lovely and touching book, *Eye on the Hill,* Barnes recounts their journey and explains why Remus was such an exceptional animal. Like all good road horses, Remus stood like a statue when being mounted.

Confidence

So long as everyone had been accustomed to travel on horseback, there was no lack of horses that had the potential for service on the road. But as soon as mankind took to travelling by car, traditional sources began to dry up. The result was that horses became soft, lethargic and unsuited to prolonged exertions. As fewer riders ventured out onto the road, the number of horses capable of being emotionally independent plunged as well.

North American Long Rider Lynn Lloyd learned this lesson the hard way, when she discovered that her borrowed mount lacked confidence and experience away from the barn and out of the ring.

"The first few times I had tied Sielem alone he had spent the night anxiously pacing back and forth. Like people, horses are born either dependent or independent, and Sielem definitely preferred the company of others. I was camped in a field and having a mental debate. Sielem was giving up and I knew would not make it much further. It was not his age holding him back, but his mental attitude. For twenty years he had been getting along just fine. He had served contentedly as an above average school horse and carried my friend, Kristin, in horse shows, fox hunting, gymkhanas and trail rides. All this topped off by a bit of dressage and point to point racing. Now suddenly his life had changed. There was a new person on his back who seemed to have definite ideas and long range goals that taxed his body and soul. He didn't feel the need to accomplish any great feat this late in life. As a result he was losing weight and becoming more sluggish. I didn't know how to tell Kristin that her beloved horse was suffering from depression. Even worse, I didn't have another horse so I really was in a pickle," Lynn recalled, before making the painful decision to send this horse back home.

In stark contrast is Countess Linde von Rosen, whose gelding, Castor, was celebrated in 1920s Europe for having carried his hard-riding mistress to a host of distant destinations, including the Vatican.

"A road horse should be fearless," Linde said. "His sense of independence is of far more importance than his good looks. It is better to dispense with a flowing mane, a bright colour – even that real charm, a pretty head. Such animals, good looking as their owners think them, are not worth keeping, if they can't make the miles"

As Linde and Castor prove, while a road horse must possess spirit and stamina, the most important traits he can have are a fast walk with a long smooth stride, plenty of courage and a constitution of iron.

While every horse will scare at something, a road horse should have an "I can do that" attitude when the two of you encounter something new, challenging or frightening. The important thing for you, his rider and partner, to remember is that confidence only comes if there is trust between you. Trust is earned, not given, so choose your horse wisely and hold up your end of the emotional bargain. The result is an increase in the Long Rider's self-assurance.

The happy horse is the tranquil one. The one that will go at any speed the rider asks without question and without excitement.

Gait

One of the most remarkable rides of the early 19th century was undertaken by Thomas Singleton, who rode Samson, a 13.2 Fell stallion pack horse, 1,000 miles in 1,000 hours. The English journey took the resilient duo nearly seven weeks. A journey such as this, which was essentially a race against time, relied on using all of the natural movements of the horse, which are the walk, trot and gallop.

While road horses and Long Riders need every gait, it is the walk that makes or breaks the journey, as the keener the horse is to go, the less tiring he will be to ride. Ella Sykes discovered how critically important it is to avoid setting off on a horse that has no gait between a slow walk and a trot.

"We reached our first night's lodgings about four o'clock and I was glad to dismount, as riding at a foot pace on an animal that is a slow walker is a tedious business," Sykes wrote about her journey in 1896 from Turkey to India.

This is why one of the most essential requirements in a potential mount is that he has a long, forward and ground-covering walk. This should be a fast, pleasant pace, so as to ensure that your daily miles become a pleasure instead of a constant struggle.

History proves that for a long journey an ambler, or pacing horse is invaluable, as the Mongols, Tibetans, Turks and Chinese all favoured the use of a horse with a fast, smooth walk. The horses of the Central Asian Turkomans were also famous for their fast walk, a remarkable pace which allowed the riders to make long journeys of eight days, about 120 miles a day, staying in the saddle for 20 hours out of the 24.

More recently the North American Long Riders Jim and Janine Wilder used two Paso Fino geldings, named Max and Smoke, to travel an astonishing number of miles during their twenty-years of constant trail riding in the United States.

There is, however, one strong drawback to having a pacing horse, namely that any horse not similarly gifted cannot be expected to keep up with these quicker animals during the course of the day. Thus, mixing pacing horses with non-pacers is not recommended.

Regardless if your road horse is a fast walker, or quick footed pacer, as the journey unfolds, and as the road horse and Long Rider begin to know each other, it is astonishing how much alike they will become in their movements.

Training

When you find yourself considering various horses, don't forget that there is a vast difference between a barely-tamed horse and a well-trained one. The definition of trained will vary enormously depending upon which part of the world you find yourself in. A trained horse in Tajikistan might be one who agrees to be saddled, while a trained horse in Texas will be required to possess another set of social and equestrian requirements.

To begin with, a lack of fundamental training will not only place the successful outcome of your journey in question, it may well place your life at risk, as no amount of post-sale tenderness can overcome a horse's flaws in basic courtesy and education. You are looking for a horse that not only has a minimum number of skills, but takes his work seriously.

A road horse should stand still when being brushed, saddled and mounted. Nor should he pull back when tied.

In addition to being quick to walk, trot and canter, he must move forward with a minimum of urging, turn easily and stop quickly.

It helps if he neck reins, but it is essential that he respond to the bit and reins, regardless of what local system you decide to use.

He must not evade being caught, as a runaway horse is a time-waster who will eventually leave you stranded and afoot. Depending on where you travel, he must quietly agree to be hobbled, picketed or placed in a barn other than his own.

While it is essential to encourage him to exercise his own personality and judgment when encountering obstacles on the trail, etc., because the final decision is the rider's, the horse must be obedient and trusting.

This is why a solid equestrian education is a fundamental requirement for a road horse and the further you stray from these principles of mutual respect, common courtesy and basic training the more likely you are to encounter trouble or be injured.

Because we are discussing the need for trained horses, you might be forgiven if you instantly thought of the dressage ring, etc., as it might be tempting to think that any number of horses trained to participate in a competitive event might automatically adapt themselves to the life of a road horse. In fact, their life in such a controlled, discipline-heavy, environment all too often renders them incapable of adjusting to the emotional challenges discovered on the road. Therefore, be sure that any horse you consider, regardless of his level of training, shows strong signs of being able to adapt to the emotional uncertainties encountered during a journey. You are searching for bravery, absolute trust and eagle-eyed attention, not the ability to perform an extended trot or levade.

If the pendulum swings too far in the other direction, you may find you are being offered someone's lovable pet. Paddock potatoes, while they may be adorable, are seldom capable of withstanding the hardships of equestrian travel.

Nor should you automatically believe that a trail horse is your answer, as all too often these horses are weekend warriors who may be spoiled or hard to handle.

While these cautionary words may sound as if they automatically rule out the majority of horses, in reality they are issued so as to arm you with the knowledge that you should not be lured, swayed or intimidated by labels. Remember the first rule of equestrian travel is to not accept advice from horsemen, regardless of how well meaning, if they have not performed an equestrian journey themselves. That is why, when it comes to trying to locate a horse that may in time become a good road horse, you do not want to be bullied by the label placed upon a horse by its current owner, nor should you allow the horse's impressive ring achievements to undercut your specific needs. What you are seeking is a physically strong, emotionally rock solid, dependable horse.

Thus, when you set about testing various possible mounts, in addition to the above-listed minimum requirements, take time to study the way the horse lifts and places his feet. When your goal is thousands of miles away, you don't want to find you're mounted on a clumsy horse.

Nor should you overlook the horse's manners around the barn, as if he acts up at home, he is bound to be worse in the field.

Plus, regardless of what system you decide to use, barefoot, boots or shoes, a horse who acts badly around the farrier will be a constant source of trouble. A road horse should stand quietly when he is trimmed or shod.

One final word about training: the journey represents a unique opportunity for you and your horse to learn together. As the horse's sense of trust grows, you will discover that the most imperceptible cues will bring instant results. Because of this intense bonding, many Long Riders have performed extraordinary journeys while their mounts wore only a halter and reins. DC Vision, for example, rode his Shire mare, Louise, for four years without using a bit. This isn't to encourage you to ever cut a corner when it comes to the topic of training, only to recognize that today's definition of that word has been compromised by people who spend 98% of their lives riding in circles.

Feeding

You might be tempted to think that a horse's appetite isn't a vital element of equestrian travel. In that case, you're wrong.

Because the road horse has been removed from his original home, he must be able to adapt an attitude of nutritional independence. That means he must be eager and willing to eat anything.

Starting in the early 1920s Welsh Long Rider Thurlow Craig spent many years exploring the infamous Chaco jungle of Paraguay on horseback. Mounted on his trusty grey Criollo, Bobby, this team survived enough dangers to fill several of Thurlow's exciting books. In one such study, Thurlow commented on the need for a road horse to have a hearty appetite.

"He can't just be a good feeder. He should be a glutton that will eat absolutely anything. This type of horse is a survivor. They're always looking for food, which shouldn't be discouraged, as this is a valuable characteristic in a travelling horse."

The most famous example of this philosophy was the two Criollo geldings, Mancha and Gato, whom Aimé Tschiffely rode from Buenos Aires to New York. According to the Swiss Long Rider, "These equine savages were physically unattractive, having none of the finer points of conformation that appealed to the haughty hidalgos of Buenos Aires. Their sturdy legs, short thick necks and Roman noses are as far removed from the points of a first-class English hunter as the North Pole from the South."

The two animals had recently been brought down from the wilds of the Argentine pampas to a local estancia after a road march of more than 1,750 kilometres (1,000 miles), in the course of which they had lived on what little they could find. Neither horse had ever seen a city, houses, automobiles or a stable. They ignored the luscious alfalfa and oats put before them, instead devouring with relish the straw put down for bedding.

As Aimé's horses prove, it is vital that you determine if your potential mount is an easy keeper, who can cover a great deal of ground, then be content with a strange or scanty dinner in yet another different stable.

One word of warning before we take leave of the equine kitchen; avoid setting out on a skinny horse, as he will never put on weight during a long journey.

Summary

While your efforts to locate a suitable road horse may be fraught with difficulties, and inevitable disappointments, there are several points which you should always keep in mind while undertaking your search.

Sore backs, youth and pregnancy are the chief things to avoid.

Don't begin your ride with an exhausted or under-weight horse.

Don't accept any dangerous stable vices, such as rearing or biting.

Don't underestimate the importance of a rapid, ground-covering walk.

Don't place beauty before wisdom and a large appetite.

Don't allow a romantic pedigree to take precedence over strength and emotional confidence.

Don't buy a horse which is too tall, seek instead for intelligence, bravery, maturity, hearty appetite, strong bones and rock-hard hooves.

Don't overlook the need for the horse to stand when mounted, lift his feet for the farrier and act sensibly in traffic.

The Polish Hussars said, "A man without a horse is like a body without a soul.'"

But remember, the road is no respecter of papers, blue ribbons or well bred paddock potatoes. While there is no such thing as a perfect road horse, choosing the wrong mount can lead to disappointment, delay, disaster or even death.

Function versus beauty. This Siberian horseman, who is seventy-five years old, routinely rides his Yakut horse in minus 64 degree Fahrenheit weather, as seen in this photo taken by the Swedish Long Rider Mikael Strandberg. This is the same type of horse used by Dmitri Peshkov to ride from Siberia to St. Petersburg.

In stark contrast to the Siberian is the Shah of Persia, who is an excellent example of the philosophy of prestige transport.

It's not the size that determines the miles. Fawn Fields was five years old, which makes her the second-youngest person to be inducted into the Long Riders' Guild, when she rode her pony, Peter, bareback alongside her parents' wagon from Carlton, Texas to Prescott, Arizona.

When Alpamis Dalaikhan set off to ride across his native Kazakhstan, he chose to ride these tough native horses.

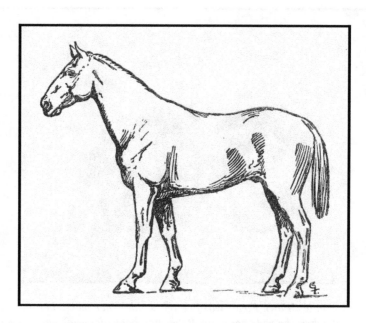

Basic requirements don't change. In 1847, English author, Rollo Springfield described the type of horse needed by today's Long Riders. "The Road Horse is a strong, vigorous, active kind, capable of enduring great hardship; its stature rather low, seldom exceeding fifteen hands; the body round and compact; its limbs strong." That explanation could have been written to accompany this illustration from the 1908 British cavalry manual.

The renowned African game ranger, Nick Steele, not only made many long distance journeys in South Africa aboard one such horse, his gelding, Nero, but the brave duo also tracked, sedated and captured rhinos in the bush together.

Finding a road horse can be a challenge, as Aimé Tschiffely discovered in 1936. Luckily he was able to ride a Cob mare named Violet across England and Scotland.

Chapter 13
Before You Buy Horses

To comprehend the present, we must understand the past.

In the 19th century, European armies were ordered to march thirteen miles a day but the cavalry was required to advance thirty miles per diem. To realize how many top quality horses this represented, let's consider these numbers.

A patrol required twelve mounted soldiers. A platoon consisted of sixty. A company had two hundred and fifty mounted warriors. A battalion counted on one thousand men and horses. A regiment of cavalry had three thousand cavalrymen and a brigade was five thousand horsemen strong.

Five thousand four-legged fighters; with each and every one of them being in tip-top shape? Imagine for a moment the immense amount of finely-honed equestrian expertise required to purchase five thousand strong, reliable, courageous horses.

Nor were the military men the only ones in the market for good horse flesh, as at the dawning of the 20th century Manhattan, Chicago and Philadelphia had an estimated 255,000 horses working in their three cities alone. The immensity of the 19th century horse world is largely lost on today's readers. In 1854 an estimated thirty-four million passengers rode the horse-drawn omnibuses in Paris. New York City had hundreds of urban stables which sheltered the equine work force. One four-storey stable independently housed 1,230 horses.

Because this book is aimed at readers living in today's 21st century mechanized world, let us compare today's motors with yesterday's mounts. In the year 2014 any amateur driver can stroll around a second-hand automobile and make some rapid, accurate observations. Bald tyres, cracked windscreen, torn seat covers, black smoke pouring out the exhaust, a knock in the engine, a transmission that slams into gear and an out-of-date licence are all indicators that an old car is on its last legs.

Yet such powers of observation and collective cultural wisdom were once a part of the horse world. Like today's amateur driver, any 19th century would-be horse buyer possessed the basic knowledge needed to quickly rule out a horse which had a bog spavin, was moon blind, knock kneed or cow hocked, cribbed and roared, suffered from thrush or had a ewe neck. Thus, whereas today the vast majority of mankind recognizes the words "Rolls Royce," only a few generations ago the term "Galvayne's groove" was of equal importance.

Sydney Galvayne was an Australian-born Irishman who became a noted horse trainer in the late 19th century. Utilizing humane methods, he became very successful in England. He also invented a new method of determining a horse's age by inspecting the animal's teeth. Galvayne claimed that the groove which appears on the upper corner of the incisors indicated the horse's age. The practice came to be known as "Galvayne's Groove."

Why does it matter?

Because when the horse is bad, the road is long.

Thus purchasing the proper road and pack horses is critically important. That timeless lesson was amply illustrated by Long Rider Robert Shaw, whose journey over the Karakoram Mountains in 1870 began with an equestrian purchase that quickly became a nightmare.

"I presented my order for ponies to the head-man of Ladakh. Though civil, the man is otherwise useless. Upon his orders, all of the town's lame and seedy ponies were brought for my inspection. I rejected all but four and then asked that others be sent in from nearby villages. That's when the headman became an awful obstructionist, until I threatened to return in the morning with a stick in my hand. The next day eight more ponies had been brought in but all of them were hardly bigger than rats. Having at last agreed on twelve ponies for my nine loads, we finally started at 1 p.m. To my annoyance, I found that the ponies were so small and weak that I was forced to stop the caravan after only seven miles. This is not a promising start for crossing Central Asia," the disgruntled Shaw wrote.

It is often said that too many of us spend our lives in thrall to the momentum of mediocrity. As Shaw learned, buying a horse is guaranteed to rattle your domestic tranquillity.

The History of Horse Buying

Regardless of what age mankind finds itself in, one rule remains the same.

When you buy horses, be on your guard against making any mistakes, as it is more difficult to judge horses than men.

That's what the Hittite king learned in 1,400 B.C. when he launched the exercise by agreeing to pay thirty shekels for a trained chariot horse. Three centuries later, King Solomon was outwitted by cunning Tyrian merchants who charged the Israelite monarch seventy-five shekels per chariot horse. According to the second Book of Chronicles, Solomon owned twelve thousand horses. Thus the horse dealers must have prayed for his long life.

Though history moved on, the crafty horse dealer survived and prospered.

By 1082 A.D. Persian gentlemen were not only able to read up on horsemanship in the *Qabus Nama* (A Mirror for Princes), they could also study the deceptive practices of cunning horse dealers. This manual for gentlemanly behaviour and savoir-faire had its counterpart in several European medieval works such as the Norwegian *Konungs Skuggsja* or the Latin *Speculum Regale*, both of which included rules for riding, as well as hints on buying horses.

With the dawning of the modern age, Nikita Khrushchev, the former ruler of the Soviet Union, had a magnificent sleigh team of five Arab mares presented to him by the vassal rulers of Hungary in 1964. But the majority of horse owners throughout history have had to sharpen their wits and protect their pocketbooks when they went in search of a mount. Thus, let us begin by remembering the original ancient law of horse-buying.

The opinion of the man in the street is usually valueless.

Most people compare a road horse to a thoroughbred racer, or some other equally exotic desirable-looking creature. They overlook the fact that there is a vast array of breeds, sizes and strengths available for our consideration. To begin with, you must know what definition of horse suits your needs, matches your personality and fits your budget; and because we're discussing equestrian travel, if you want use you must have a useful animal.

Hire or Buy?

Lest we forget, you don't have to own horses to make an equestrian journey. It is possible to lease them. Given the current global financial recession, many horse owners are facing economic hardships, which in turn might entice them to provide you with a riding or pack horse in exchange for guaranteed long term care of their animal. Likewise, breeders who are anxious to promote the strength and durability of their favorite horse might be another avenue.

Aimé Tschiffely's famous Criollo geldings, Mancha and Gato, were obtained in this manner from Dr. Emilio Solanet, an Argentine breeder who wanted to prove to the world how strong his nation's horses were.

Jean-Claude Cazade received an Arabian stallion on similar terms, which he then rode from France to Arabia and back.

Finally, there are on average more than 100,000 unwanted horses in the United States every year. Of these only 13,000 find homes via the 236 registered American rescue organizations. Many equine rescue operations might be prepared to provide you with horses, if you in turn not only help promote their efforts but give the horses suitable homes.

While leasing, borrowing or having a horse donated is possible, the vast majority of Long Riders, especially those preparing to travel in Asia, Africa and Latin America, must be prepared to begin bargaining.

So where do you begin to find good horses?

That depends on what part of the world you're in when you start your search.

Cautious Shopping

Before we think about "where," let's not forget "when." Many horse owners will be anxious to sell an animal before the onslaught of winter, so as to offset the high cost of feeding during the cold-weather months. Likewise, with the resumption of warmer riding weather, buyers are more frequent. Both these facts must enter into your original plan, as when you buy determines what you pay.

The world is vast and Long Riders journey everywhere, so we must consider specific locations, as well as remembering some general observations, when we look for suitable horses.

To begin with let us bear in mind buying horses in North America where a combination of social and economic events have worked together to drive prices to a record low. This occurred when hay prices sky rocketed, once-prosperous baby boomer back yard breeders produced millions of unneeded animals and equine meat packing plants provided a traditional financial outlet and incentive for unwanted horses.

The ugly result is that horses are being discarded in national forests or abandoned at auction yards. Equine welfare organizations were already hard pressed to deal with the growing problem, when the unstable situation was compounded by horse hoarders who collected animals as a hobby in more prosperous times. Law enforcement officials are increasingly being called to confiscate these animals and arrest the owners when herds of horses are found starving to death in grassless pastures.

Thus, impoverished or disenchanted horse owners are increasingly likely to want to sell their animal. In some cases the horses will be given away free to good homes. However, such under-weight and weakened animals would be unsuitable for equestrian travel.

Despite these bad times, and throughout history, most horses are procured thanks to personal relationships. This still works and we shall investigate that procedure at length.

Another traditional method is via newspaper or magazine advertisements. Such ads can work in your favour if the seller is in a hurry and is willing to negotiate on the price. Yet extreme caution should be used as all too often the current owner is attempting to unload his equine problem onto an unsuspecting buyer.

Buyer Beware

Plus, with the onslaught of the internet, it is now possible to shop on line for horses in any part of the world, as this free service will allow you to initially inspect thousands of horses from the comfort of your home. Yet if its true that a piece of paper will lie down and let you write anything on it, the same holds true for a deceptive internet horse advertisement.

When shopping for a horse on line, you should be extremely cautious as the factors of distance and anonymity create a peculiar mixture of vulnerability and trust between buyer and seller. This is especially true if you see a horse being sold on extraordinarily good terms, as throughout history cheapness has been the surest bait in the world for catching the majority of customers.

The Federal Bureau of Investigation and the United States Postal Inspection Service recently ran an undercover operation designed to capture one such disreputable computer criminal who was running an international internet horse fraud.

After her arrest, the California-based crook explained to the court how she posted images of quality horses, which she did not own, on various well known equestrian websites. Her ads also made false claims about the horse's breed, abilities and health. Promising a money-back guarantee, she encouraged interested buyers to place large deposits or to pay for horses in full by falsely representing that others were interested in buying the animal.

FBI agents proved that after receiving payment the internet swindler defrauded customers in a variety of ways including delivering horses which had been falsely coloured, were starved, covered in sores and cuts, had hooves so long the horses were unable to walk, or were suffering from the contagious respiratory disease, strangles. When victims complained or sought to exercise the promised guarantee, the phoney seller refused to return phone calls or emails, falsely claimed the victims had themselves breached sales contracts, and threatened to sue them for defaming her. Before her conviction, the woman admitted she had duped and defrauded more than sixty prospective horse buyers residing in 23 states and Canada.

Other Options

Another option is to purchase a horse at a livestock auction. However, again be warned. Unless you are extremely knowledgeable about horses, this is a method fraught with menace, as there is little time to adequately inspect a horse prior to sale. Many times auctioneers turn a profit on your lack of experience.

Further south, in Latin America, suitable horses may be located on estancias which still work cattle. These working horses are usually well trained and in sound condition.

In certain cultures, such as Ireland and Tibet, there are still many horse owners who will be willing to discuss selling their animals without delay. Yet buying horses from private individuals may restrict your options. When Long

Riders Billy Brenchley and Christine Henchie set off to ride from Tunisia to South Africa, they found that the Tunisian Ministry of Agriculture were willing to sell top quality Arabian, Barb and Thoroughbred horses at the government stud farms.

Yet in Eastern Europe you may find that politics has limited your options. Before 1990 millions of horses could be found in the Eastern Bloc countries including Semnigreu, Stara Planiona, Nonius, East Bulgarian, Romanian, Bosnian Blues, Serbian Silvers, Balkan Greys and Hutsuls. These breeds provided tough, malleable, good looking, easy to handle, easy to school, easy to feed horses. Sadly, this treasure trove of horses quietly disappeared in a largely unrecorded episode of modern equinocide.

What happened?

The horses were eaten by the French, Belgians, Germans, Serbs and mainly the Italians. With the collapse of communism the state studs closed and farmers were hard pressed for cash. Thus former political satellites of Moscow were swept clean by horse meat buyers eager to convert the Soviet Union's immense equestrian empire into sausage. As the communist world collapsed and as this huge pool of horses suddenly hit the market, one of the biggest trades in live animal transport also got under way. The result is that many of these countries are now largely depleted of available horses.

Likewise, the Central Asian nation of Kazakhstan will also present challenges for potential Long Riders. That's what Tim Cope discovered when he tried to find horses there.

"I found buying horses in Kazakhstan more challenging than in Mongolia. There are a few things to take into consideration in regards to horses in Kazakhstan. First of all, after perestroika about seventy percent of all horses, cattle and sheep were either sold, stolen, traded or slaughtered. The collective farms were left in a wreck and basically Kazakhstan was left with only remnants of its former agriculture. Nowadays the number of livestock is increasing but generally horses are not yet abundant. Secondly, koza – horse intestine stuffed with salted horse meat and fat – is the national meal and considered a delicacy. It retails at about seven dollars per kilogram. This means that the price of horses is remarkably high. What's more the price of a horse has little to do with its age, behaviour or breed, but how fat and big the horse is, as horse fat is considered extremely important for the Kazakh's winter diet. Because of these reasons, be prepared to fork out a minimum of $400 for a very average horse and $1000 for a good horse. The price varies from region to region. For example, the meat price for the average horse near cities like Almaty and Astana is about $1000 US. You would do better to find a horse where they are more abundant and that is far away from the cities with their horse sausage factories. Generally the north and north-east of Kazakhstan have more horses. I bought my horses in North Eastern Kazakhstan in the Altai Mountains. Here horses are used for work with carts and for herders. The remote villages are hard to access for trucks and therefore they have less opportunity to sell horses to abattoirs in the cities (that send out trucks on roaming horse-buying expeditions). The cheapest horse I could find was about $400 US, with well-behaved horses costing $800 in that region."

Cultural Traps

While buying horses is always fraught with economic peril, if you attempt to purchase them in certain foreign countries you must be prepared to encounter additional cultural challenges during an already complicated psychological procedure.

Jeremy James, for example, recalled, "It is bad luck, as every Muslim knows, to buy a horse on a Thursday, the 6th day of the week."

Likewise when English Long Rider Thomas Bartz rode from Kyrgyzstan to Afghanistan he too discovered unforeseen problems.

"There are awkward situations which can arise from misunderstandings. For instance, when we bought our horses we thought we could bargain but what happened is this: the nomads showed us a horse and asked us what we thought of it. Not wanting to offend them, we said it looked good, which it did at a glance. For them, you see, this was as if we were already agreeing to their price because after they told us how much they wanted, we could no longer say we wanted to pay less, because we'd already said we liked the horse. Get it? This sort of thing happened many times. It was most annoying and costly!"

Consequently you must not remain a prisoner to your upbringing but should instead take the practices and beliefs of the local equestrian culture into account. Bear in mind that there are some cultures where lying is considered a fine art and there is no shame in being found out. While they expect you, the rich foreigner, to be honest, they believe they are justified in lying through their teeth.

That was another tough lesson Tim Cope learned when he rode from Mongolia to Hungary.

"Generally," Tim said, "the whole village will support the lie of a horse owner, so it is hard to get the truth."

In such cases the entire village will conspire to see that you pay the most for the least and that the local seller triumphs over the rich foreigner.

Trial and Error

As any Long Rider will tell you, it takes time to find horses and strike a bargain.

That is why when you set out to purchase horses for your expedition, you must prepare yourself for a challenging quest. Unless you are carefully prepared, you are facing a long, frustrating, expensive and fruitless search.

For example, when Verne Albright set off to ride from Peru to California in 1966 his first difficulty was locating good horses.

"The Peruvian word for endurance is *resistencia*, meaning literally resistance. It is an excellent word to describe the physical and mental qualities a horse must have in order to stand up to the trials and tribulations of the trail. They may have to resist changes in altitude, changes from brackish water to alkaline, new feed every day, to work all day and then bed down in strange surroundings, have to resist the diseases they would come in contact with, suffer the bites of countless insects and attack by vampire bats, travel in every kind of truck, train and plane. In short, they would have to be tough to survive," Verne wrote in his book, *The Long Way to Los Gatos*.

Even though Verne knew what type of horse he needed, the would-be Long Rider was hard pressed to find such animals.

"I spent days visiting local breeders before the truth began to dawn on me. The haciendas could no longer afford to spare water for hay – so their horses went hungry. It was more expensive than ever before to hire trainers – so the horses went untrained. Machines were replacing the horse and most of the breeders could no longer use or sell horses – so they were simply allowing their herds to thin out. They did not want to sell their best horses. The others I did not want to buy," Verne wrote.

Thirty-seven years later the French Long Riders Marie-Emmanuelle Tugler and Marc Witz encountered similar problems when they set off on their ride from Brazil to Peru.

"Almost two months have gone by between our arrival in Brazil and the real start of our trip. One month was spent just looking for the right horses. This was not without some difficulty, as most of the horses offered to us were too expensive, too thin, too excitable, or had saddle sores and girth galls. Even when we located the proper animals, it took two more weeks to obtain the health certificates." Marc wrote.

A Word of Caution

Regardless of where you look for a horse, remember, everyone is an expert, even if they've never ridden down the road.

When you are buying a horse it is the faults you want to know about, not the virtues. Yet many buyers will seldom find what they have expected or they buy without forethought. In their disappointment some will call the horse-trader a fraud, though the responsibility is really with the buyer himself. This is because all too often the buyer was hasty, ignorant, greedy, naïve or ill prepared. Great vigilance and thorough knowledge is needed. The latter can only be obtained by practising, never from theory or a book.

With that said, let us proceed with caution into this ancient equestrian minefield.

The Seller

There is no object of trade that is harder to buy than the horse. This is because the buyer and seller base their estimates of value on very different grounds. Thus history proves that the buyer has all too often been on the losing end of this arrangement.

Who is the seller?

He is any person who tries to present his horse in the best possible condition, in order to reap the greatest profit from the sale.

Tradition demonstrates that trickery, fraud, and deception are in this situation inherent in the very nature of things. The difference between one seller and another will be merely a difference in degree, the result being that the most honest man in the world, whose word would pass in the bank for any amount, can not help lying when it comes to selling a horse.

Even the most scrupulous seller will acknowledge only certain defects in their horses; the discovery of others they will leave to the sagacity of the purchaser. Therefore a man's own mother cannot be trusted in a transaction of this kind without looking into the horse's mouth and examining its feet.

As to those who are less honest, they conceal everything except the qualities which they exaggerate. To declaim against these tendencies is a waste of time. Your only defence is to be able to judge the quality of the horse you are about to buy.

Tricks of the Horse Trade

Purchasing an animal from a professional horse dealer has always been fraught with hazard. It is a notorious truth that honesty and horse-selling seldom dwell together and no dealer keeps a horse unless he hopes to gain some financial advantage by doing so. Thus the time honoured-warning, "Caveat Emptor: let the buyer beware," still rules as there are scoundrels about who keep alive the ancient practice of deluding and plundering travellers and horsemen.

Though today the term jockey refers to a professional rider of race-horses, it did not acquire this meaning until the late eighteenth century. Prior to that the word described a low-class horse dealer. These cunning individuals would promise paragons of equine virtue and then produce nags, wind suckers, lunatics and cribbers. As a rule jockeys would show their worst animals first, hoping to obtain the maximum price for them. They were noted for the tricks of their trade, many of which were designed to make a poor animal appear in a positive light.

Experts at hiding sores, jockeys would often fill the animals with water prior to exhibiting them, so as to give the belly a plump appearance. Another vile practice was to pierce the flaccid skin above an aged horse's hollow eyes, insert a straw and then blow in air so as to make the animal appear younger. Even the colour of a horse couldn't be trusted as stolen animals were routinely disguised by false marks or paint. A common trick was to insert a thin sheet of lead under the skin between a horse's eyes. The metal would cause a white blaze to appear, thus transforming the legal description of the stolen horse.

There were many tricks of this nefarious trade and they often made use of aggressive negative reinforcement. For example by continually poking a horse with a sharp needle, it would prance at the slightest touch when displayed to potential buyers. Another shameful swindle was to repeatedly clank a metal bucket full of rocks near a horse until it was driven nearly insane. Later at the horse market the mere sight of the bucket, even glimpsed at a distance, would be enough to transform a normally-lazy horse into what appeared to be a fiery mount.

The list of these historical tricks is extremely long but one example from the early 19th century demonstrates the calculating slyness involved in the trade.

Upon arriving at a hostel, the jockey would single out the best horse in the barn and manage to have his animal stabled next to the traveller's horse. By casually ordering oats for his horse, the jockey would arrange for the ostler (stable hand) to be temporarily called away on duty. Being ignorant of any mischief, the stable hand would vacate the scene on this routine errand. During that absence the jockey would quickly insert a sizeable stone into the valuable animal's rectum. When he returned with the oats, the ostler would see the jockey involved in the innocent act of brushing down his own horse prior to giving it the requested evening feed.

In less than a quarter of an hour the affected horse would begin to sweat mightily, commence to tremble and stare as if his eyes were ready to jump out of his head. When the signs of distress were adequately pronounced the jockey would urge the naïve ostler to run and tell the horse's owner that the animal seemed to be dying. Upon arriving the distressed owner would be informed by the jockey in a casual manner that the animal might be the victim of an accidental poisoning. This immediately cast doubt on the safety of the stable and the integrity of the innocent ostler. The confused, upset and angry owner would then be urged by the sly jockey to either sell the "dying" horse at an immense loss or pay the charlatan for administering a curative potion to the animal. In either case, while the owner's eye was distracted, or after he had departed, the stone was removed and within half an hour the horse would have been perfectly well. By such clever deceptions were valuable horses obtained under false pretences from ignorant owners.

Not all horse dealers run a racket and things are, on the whole, better nowadays. However though the tricks may have changed, deception is still a time-honoured rule among horse dealers. With the emphasis today being on looks and breeding, a common trick is to falsify documents and accomplishments. By erroneously claiming the horse has won shows, or is descended from legendary parents, the price can be falsely adjusted in favour of the seller. Another tactic which is still in evidence is drugging and running. In this case excitable animals are doped on muscle relaxants, or run to the point of exhaustion, then bathed and groomed before being presented to the unsuspecting buyer. Regardless of which of these types of fraud is chosen, the result is an animal that is temporarily placid and artificially easier to control. Modern crooks have also been known to use a bait and switch method, where they advertise one horse on the internet, then replace it with a similarly-marked animal.

The good news is that most modern horse dealers have a reputation to maintain, therefore they are dutiful, have access to valuable knowledge and can show you a great many horses in a short period of time. The best advice that can be offered is to deal with a horse dealer to whom you have been recommended, one who is of fair character and established circumstances, as such a person has every reason not to forfeit his credibility.

Summary

Mere quantity strikes the eye at once and may be estimated by an uneducated person. But to discern the quality of horses requires experience and judgment. Because it takes time to acquire this rare wisdom, you may find it necessary to negotiate with a horse dealer. If so, be on your guard, as the tricks of this ancient trade are still flourishing.

For example, in 2008 a buyer purchased a horse from a dealer at a horse fair in Lelesti, Romania. After hitching the new animal to his wagon, the buyer realized that the horse couldn't be properly controlled. The chaotic episode came to a tragic end when the runaway horse smashed the wagon into an elderly man sitting on a bench. The 86-year-old victim died, the owner was arrested and the horse was found to have been drugged with an extremely high amount of alcohol so as to make it appear to be stronger and healthier.

Bearing these historical lessons in mind, let us see how a potential Long Rider can arm himself against deception when he sets out to find, inspect and purchase his road horse.

The date on the calendar has changed since these horses were sold in 1900 but many horse sellers still use treachery and trickery to defraud trusting buyers.

Though film star Tom Selleck is rightly celebrated for his roles as an outstanding horseman, the devoted rider was awarded more than $187,000 by an American court, which found that Selleck had been deliberately duped into purchasing an injured horse by a nefarious California horse dealer.

Chapter 14
Inspecting Horses

Early Selection Process

Having explained of whom to beware when trying to purchase a horse, let us consider how to make an early determination of what basic requirements a potential road or pack horse must have.

Many would-be Long Riders have found themselves in the same position as the inexperienced traveller who wrote, "Other than some advice about buying a horse with a leg on each corner, I didn't have a lot to go on."

The most elementary logic commands the buyer to purchase only a healthy horse. Moreover the buyer should have determined exactly what type of animal he is attempting to purchase; this includes knowing the size, sex, age and approximate price. Once you have made these basic decisions, you need to rule out unsuitable animals prior to physical inspection. To do this you must present sellers with as many preliminary questions as possible so as to confirm the horse's strengths and weaknesses. Either by phone, or before you ever walk out to the barn or over to the pasture, you should save yourself a lot of time by asking these sort of questions.

Why is the seller disposing of the horse? If it is because the horse is old, infirm or dangerous, terminate the interview.

Is the horse fitted by training and disposition to the task at hand? If it is too young or unbroken, terminate the interview.

Is its confirmation sound? If it is partially sighted, sway backed or suffering from any type of open wound, terminate the interview.

Is its temperament good? If it bites, bucks, strikes, kicks, rears or runs away, terminate the interview.

Can it be easily caught, groomed, saddled and bridled? If it doesn't stand quietly when mounted, terminate the interview.

Will the horse be able to use your saddle and bridle? If it requires special expensive gear, terminate the interview.

When was the last time the horse was ridden and how far did it go? If there is any hint that the animal is disobedient or dangerous, terminate the interview.

Has the horse ever travelled and was it road-worthy? If the horse runs away from dogs or spooks in front of traffic, terminate the interview.

Has the horse been ridden on trails and if so does it cross water and load into a trailer? If it bucks while being ridden on a trail ride, terminate the interview.

Is it a hearty eater? If it is severely underweight, requires a special diet or suffers from colic, terminate the interview.

Does the horse behave quietly while being shod? If it has bad feet or can't be shod, terminate the interview.

Can it be hobbled, tied to a picket pin or a high line? If it fights with or runs away from strange horses, terminate the interview.

Has it been wormed and vaccinated? If it has any sign of disease, terminate the interview.

Are the horse's medical papers up to date and is its Coggins test negative? If the owner can't provide medical certificates and a bill of sale proving he is the legal owner, terminate the interview.

There is nothing more frustrating than buying the wrong horse. That is why these types of basic questions will help you determine the horse's ability, performance, dispositions, habits, training and health.

When you phone the seller, listen to the answers carefully so as to get a sense of whether the person is telling the truth or withholding vital information. If you believe the seller is being evasive, deceitful, or if there are negative or dangerous aspects associated with the horse, then be prepared to conclude the discussion before you've ever seen the horse.

Remember, the more horses you inspect, the more comfortable you will become in the buyer-seller situation. This in turn will inspire your confidence, increase your knowledge and help you to make correct decisions.

Trial Period

If the horse in question sounds promising, then before you proceed to the physical inspection, ask if the seller will allow you to use the animal in a trial period of several days. Because you will be using the animal for an extended journey, it is imperative that it be physically sound and emotionally reliable.

In Central Asia it was sometimes allowed for the horse to be used for three days, during which time either side had the right to break the bargain.

Depending on what country and culture you find yourself in, obtaining a trial period will allow you to detect any critically negative factors while the animal is being ridden or packed.

Misleading Emotions

What you are seeking is a horse that is fit and guaranteed free from disease or defects. What you don't want is the "love at first sight horse." Remember, bad horses have as good an appetite as the best. You're in the market for a road horse, not an emotional commodity. Thus, you must be brutally candid with yourself.

To begin with, you cannot hope to buy perfection; not that publishers would have you think otherwise, as throughout history they have released books which provide a list of the real and imaginary details of a flawless horse. Yet no animal ever came up to the standard of excellence created by the authors of those works. These writers have brought together a collection of equine merits and made it appear to the general reader that a sound and good horse possesses them all. Such an argument is based on literary fantasy, not equine common sense. You're as apt to compare the average human form to the divinely beautiful Venus de Milo. No horse can be perfect if held up to such an artificial standard.

In fact to define a perfect horse is almost an impossibility for this useful and beautiful creature is an assemblage of individual distinctions and personal faults. Thus not only are appearances deceitful, it is a hard thing to say but a very true one that amongst today's horses a person can hardly hope to find one in fifty fit for a journey. Few things are more difficult to find than horses that are exactly what you wish, and compounding that problem is the fact that too many modern horses are merely fair-weather playthings.

So when we first look at a horse we must keep our emotions in check. While it's true that a beautiful horse not only strikes everyone's fancy, all too often we immediately take it for granted that such symmetry must be accompanied by other qualities such as strength or swiftness. Sadly, in the selection of a horse buyers rarely seek for latent good qualities, preferring to focus on a dramatic exterior instead.

True equine judgement is displayed when you select a horse possessing great powers, though they might be hidden under the cover of an ill-favoured outward appearance.

Public and Private Examinations

The examination of the horse cannot always be made at one's leisure, although enough time should always be taken so as to make the inspection a detailed one. Moreover, the location of the inspection is of tremendous initial importance. As a rule, inspections are made at a highly public horse market, a dealer's stable or a private owner's home.

If you plan to buy a horse in a foreign country, don't overlook the fact that despite your desire for privacy, you may well be surrounded by an audience of curious locals who are equally interested in observing you. Such circumstances tend to make an already-complicated investigation all the more cumbersome, as the locals may feel free to offer advice, tease the horse or attempt to assist the seller in cheating you. Add in the element of a foreign language and you can foresee the problems.

In contrast, the initial benefit of examining a potential horse at the stable of a private owner is that the purchaser can proceed in privacy. Yet regardless of where the inspection takes place, the best time to initially inspect the horse is when you are not expected, as in this manner you will find out more defects than any other way.

Age

Regardless of where you shop for the horse, his age plays a critical role in your potential geographic success. The age of a Thoroughbred horse is calculated from January 1st, all others from May 1st. The term rising; for example "rising six" means nearly six; "six off" means past six but not yet seven.

Various factors demonstrate that young horses are unsuitable for extended equestrian journeys.

To begin with, it is a mistake to suppose that young horses will last longer in work than old ones. A mature horse does not tire so soon. After a night's rest, he will come out of his stable settled and sober, then proceed to work a younger horse off his legs. Another consideration is that as your road horse travels cross country, he will be constantly exposed to various equine ailments. Here again, a well seasoned older horse is less liable to disease than a younger one.

For these reasons, I repeat my recommendation that a road horse should not be less than six years old, especially if he is to be ridden near traffic. Horses that have not been taught how to behave in such situations are extremely awkward, unmanageable and often cause accidents. A horse of six, if sound in wind, limb and sight, should last you eight or nine years. And whereas a young horse will be prone to youthful indiscretions and diseases, an older horse will never fail you.

The horses chosen by Aimé Tschiffely are a perfect example of this "older is better" equine philosophy.

Mancha was an eighteen-year-old Criollo gelding, who delighted in attacking and kicking anyone foolish enough to come near him. His Criollo companion, Gato, was a sixteen-year-old gelding only slightly less bad-tempered.

These wild equines were not physically attractive, having none of the finer points of conformation that appealed to the haughty hidalgos of Buenos Aires.

Yet handsome is as handsome does. The two "old" horses marched more than 16,000 kilometres (10,000 miles) from Buenos Aires to New York. Gato died at the age of thirty-two, while Mancha passed away in 1947 at the age of thirty-seven.

Colour and Pedigree

Don't be surprised if the seller attempts to entice you to pay more because the animal in question is an excellent representative of a special breed.

Horses are like angels. They have no nationality.

Today's modern breeds represent an attempt by humans to create horses which exhibit the same physical characteristics. Knowing what breed of horse is on offer may provide you with some idea of what you can generally expect from this type of horse. Yet you are searching for an individual mount, not purchasing a brand name. History proves that every type of equine can be successfully used as a road horse, if the circumstances fit the animal. Thus, don't let the seller confuse you with tales of a wonderful pedigree.

As the North American Long Rider Stan Walchuk once said, "This is an equestrian journey, not a beauty contest."

Another aspect which may affect the asking price is colour.

In various nations opinions can be found which pretend to explain how a particular colour may influence the constitution of the horse. In actuality a horse's colour does not affect either its performance or temperament.

Yet many will not buy a horse which has a white leg, though white legs are as likely to run as black legs. Chestnuts are associated with headstrong dispositions and are considered to be impetuous and excitable. Duns are considered strong but boring. Gray horses are unlucky and white horses are weak. A piebald is black and white, while a skewbald is any other combination of colours, yet both are derided as being unseemly.

Remember, a good horse is never a bad colour.

If you purchase a horse for useful purposes you must not be too preoccupied about either his colour or the condition of his coat. You should instead be contented with the useful qualities of the animal, for example its strength, speed and disposition. Thus if you find yourself in an equestrian culture which tolerates these superstitions regarding colour, you may be able to purchase a capital horse at half the cost.

Also, a word on brands, which are often found on horses in Australia, America, Argentina, Canada and Pakistan. Military brands are usually seen on the lower part of the shoulder, with a broad arrow being the most common. Private owners often brand their horses on the hip. Freeze branding can be located under the mane, along the crest of the horse's neck. An unsightly brand may affect the price in your favour. However any significant scars should lower the horse's price.

Vices

You must bear in mind that a vicious horse may also be a sound one. While there are a number of offences, the discovery of any dangerous vice should automatically rule out purchasing the animal. Beware, as sellers use tricks so cunning that the best judges of horse flesh may be deceived into believing the horse has none of these defects. When determining the price, any negative element works in your favour. Yet certain wicked crimes rule out an animal as a potential road horse.

You should never, if in your power to avoid it, ride a horse addicted to any vice, or one having a fault likely to endanger your safety. It is not only disagreeable but dangerous to ride an animal that is ready upon the least excitement to buck, shy violently, endeavour to run away or attempt to harm you.

Of all the defences which a horse makes, that of rearing is the most dangerous. Some horses will rear so high as to fall backward on top of the rider. When a horse rears, the rider must immediately cease bearing on the reins, and incline his body well forward, so as to throw his weight upon the horse's shoulders and oblige him to come down. Under no circumstance purchase such a horse.

Running away is a serious vice and horses addicted to bolting are decidedly dangerous, both for the rider and those they encounter. A runaway might be caused by fear or high spirits. But a true runaway does it when he becomes irritable and runs away to defend himself. The animal usually breaks into a gallop and rushes forward headlong with all the speed of which he is capable. The animal becomes unmanageable and in a short time is beyond control. Once started, he no longer knows what he is doing, no longer sees, hears or smells; he runs away, and this seems to be the only thing he has the desire or the ability to do. Nothing calms him. He is deaf to threats, insensible to traction on his bit, and no longer recognizes any danger. The efforts made to stop him serve but to increase his fright. He stops only when utterly worn out in strength and wind, or when his running is halted by collision with another horse or an immovable object. It is necessary to turn the horse's head strongly around to the left or to the right in such a way as to slacken his gait, hamper his movements, and produce a sharp pain upon the bars of his mouth. Even if such an animal is offered as a gift, the wisest thing to do is not to accept it, nor ever attempt to use it on a journey.

Never purchase a horse which threatens or frightens you, for such an animal keeps the rider in fear and anxiety.

Some horses have a trick of suddenly stopping when going at a fast pace. A horse of this kind is dangerous because of the likelihood of throwing the rider over his head.

Your road horse should be free from the slightest suspicion of stumbling, which leads to falls.

Avoid buying a fearful horse. Likewise a fretful horse is also to be avoided.

Never purchase a horse that sets his ears back or stamps his feet when you approach or try to groom him.

A horse which is difficult to saddle or mount has no place on a journey.

Horses which are difficult to shoe should also be avoided, as the neglect of this basic requirement will result in very serious consequences once the journey has begun.

Kicking at other horses, or at people, denotes an ill nature.

Likewise a biter should always be avoided.

A horse who has acquired the habit of backing up, so as to avoid the bit, is not only a danger to the rider but may injure anyone in close proximity.

Any horse which is indolent, timid, bad mouthed, balky, stubborn, cowardly, skittish or spiteful is to be rejected however perfect he may otherwise seem to be.

The majority of vices are consequences of a faulty education laid on by early instructors who have been both ignorant and brutal. The sad result is horses that have become obstinate and vicious. Nevertheless, your journey requires you to try and obtain a horse which is free from any life-threatening, harmful or disturbing vice. As prevention is better than cure, an animal addicted to a dangerous vice should never be selected. Thus the discovery of such defects does not lower the price, it kills the deal.

If you don't want trouble, don't mount it and never buy it.

Defects

The following are some of the most common forms of unsoundness in a horse, all of which should withdraw an animal from your consideration.

Lameness is the language of pain and its presence automatically rules the horse out. It tells the plain and honest truth, with the greatest simplicity. When horses are more tender in one foot than the other, they droop their head when they step upon the unsound hoof, then raise it again when stepping on the sound one.

Broken knees results when the horse has been wounded by falling. Where there is an obvious scar from a cut on the skin, it is evidence of a broken knee. Although it may indicate the horse tends to stumble, you can still consider him If the mark is now only a blemish and the injury is well healed.

Splints are hard bony lumps at the inside of the leg, towards the back of the cannon bone, anywhere below the knee and above the pastern joint. They frequently cause great lameness on account of inflammation.

Roaring is caused when the animal's breathing is impaired. The horse wheezes when ridden hard and may begin to cough. No animal that has breathing problems should be chosen for a journey.

Visually impaired horses shy frequently, stumble easily and should never be considered.

First Impressions in a Public Market

In order to buy the right horse, you must follow the proper steps. Yet many people get the first impression wrong.

When a horse which seems to answer the requirements has been found at a public horse market, he should be brought away from the other horses, and, if possible, led to a quiet place, where he can be easily observed.

Upon first seeing the animal, ask yourself if this horse is equipped by nature to handle your route. An untravelled person is apt to think that horses are more or less the same all over the world, though nowhere as good as in his native land. Horses however are as greatly modified by the effects of climate as men, with each country having its own particular type of horse just as it has its own particular type of human.

For example, if the horse has been bought in a warm land, chances are that when ridden up into a colder climate the animal will suffer. Therefore are you looking at a lowlands horse, before you set off over the Himalayan Mountains or perhaps a grassland horse who won't survive in the desert?

Only a general inspection of the whole animal need be made at this point, by a glance of the eye; so as to determine if he pleases or he displeases. As you first approach cast your eye over the animal to determine if by his size, weight and general development he fulfils the required purpose. Does he appear to be in good and healthy condition? Is he standing quietly on firm feet and does he seem well-mannered?

As you near, how does he react? There are five things to breed for and the first three are disposition; the other two are performance and conformation. Manners make the horse and never more so than in an equine travelling companion.

After you've had time to study the horse, ask the seller to provide the horse's age and breed.

Finally, his price should be asked.

If these first impressions are not favourable, or if the price is too high, it is useless to proceed further with the examination.

First Impressions in a Private Stable

Your initial inspection begins the moment you near the horse in his stall, as valuable information is on offer even though you're still several feet away.

Before you even glance at the horse, look around the stall for any evidence that the horse cribs or chews. This is a self-destructive habit that is often taught by other horses. If the animal cribs, conclude the inspection, as travelling horses are required to lodge in a different place every night. The last thing you need is for your road horse to spend the night eating part of your host's barn or stripping the bark off his trees.

As you near the stall, you should note the manner in which the animal is tied to the manger, how he stands in the stall, the way in which he holds his head, the expression of his countenance, the movements of his ears. As you draw near; this is the time also to observe the conformation. When the stall door is opened, does the horse stand easy or does he pace about the stall nervously? Does he move towards his visitors or back away?

Take heed to how the animal is handled while it is taken out of the stall. An old trick is to insert a small piece of ginger in the anus when the blanket is taken off or the horse is being brushed prior to being put on display. This sly trick causes the horse to act in an artificially animated manner.

While there are a variety of things to observe at this stage, the first is temperament. There is as much difference in the tempers, dispositions and intelligence of horses as in human beings.

While the animal is being groomed observe his general manners, study his disposition and watch his eye. The eye of a horse is a good index of a horse's temper. A horse never plays a vicious trick without showing his intention to do so by his eye. Therefore, if much of the white is seen, and that restless and cast backwards, it may be suspected that he is dangerous and is an indication of the kick which he is about to aim. If you are near, it would be advisable either to go boldly up to his head and seize it, with the right hand on the halter close to his muzzle, or else keep out of the range of his heels; for you may rest assured that the horse is slyly watching for an opportunity to do you a mischief.

The other indicators of temper are the ears. The hearing of the horse is much more acute than that of a human being and the ears are the interpreters of his passion, particularly of fear, anger or malice. They are always in motion, quivering and darting their sharp points towards every object that presents itself. This holds true for groups and individuals. Where four or five horses travel in a line, the first always points his ears forward, and the last points his backwards. An experienced observer can often tell by the motion of the ears most of what the horse means to do. This is especially important when the horse lays his ears back flat upon his neck and keeps them so, as he most assuredly means to harm the bystander with either heels or teeth.

A Closer Look

Upon taking the horse out into the yard, a closer examination must be made of the animal.

On the horse being led out of the stable, first walk up to the horse's withers to ascertain if he is of the required height. Too often buyers look at horses as butchers do at cattle, and value them in proportion to the amount of fat they carry. This of course is an error.

The horse having been led out, have the owner stand in front of him, placing the animal a step forward or backward until his fore-feet and hind feet are respectively on a line with each other; after which the horse's head is kept in a fixed position.

Then visually examine the animal in sections (feet, pasterns, fetlocks, canons, knees; forearms and thighs, shoulder and croup, neck and withers, back, chest, abdomen and flank). As to the head, it is to be reserved for the last, because the eyes, nostrils, mouth and ears should be particularly examined.

Take your time studying the horse in profile, on both sides, in front, behind, and obliquely from in front and from behind. This survey should be made at a distance of four or five steps, while walking around the animal slowly, stopping for an instant at each of the points we have just enumerated.

In judging on the whole, we should take into account the general harmony of the lines, the height, length, size, equilibrium and expression of the horse's face.

Perhaps this is as good a place as any other to remark upon the absurdity of buying an animal that had once in his life performed a particular feat well, instead of seeking to possess a horse with the capacity for general usefulness. Choose a horse based upon his current ability and willingness, never upon a former sporting victory.

This part of the examination should be made as much as possible without touching the horse. The purchaser should have sufficient experience to recognize at a glance if serious blemishes exist. If there be any doubt in his mind, he should remove it by examining the parts with the hand.

The Intensive Inspection

Having carefully studied the horse from both sides, as well as from the front and rear, you should move toward the animal and commence a careful hands-on evaluation.

To begin with, never consent to inspect an animal that is either saddled or wearing any type of blanket. One of the oldest tricks in the book is to distract an unwary seller with a lot of fast talk, all the while presenting the horse fully saddled and ready for a test ride. The purpose of this deception is to conceal saddle sores, or other injuries, under the saddle or blanket. No horse can be properly evaluated if its defects have been hidden in this manner.

Pay no attention to the seller's misleading chatter. Ensure instead that the animal's physical condition is not camouflaged in any way and then order the horse to be held quietly for your further inspection.

To begin with study the animal's overall weight. Because of the inherent rigours of equestrian travel, never purchase an animal which is under-weight. Unlike pampered animals kept in stalls, road and pack horses work in an environment where feeding is an open-ended daily challenge. While it is possible to keep your travelling horses in excellent shape during their journey, hard exercise and sporadic diet will almost certainly ensure that they never grow fat. Thus you need to purchase animals that are neither fussy feeders nor initially undernourished.

Regardless of how calmly the animal has acted around its owner, don't forget that when a horse is startled or suspicious, he can kick or bite with great speed. Thus, always use extreme caution when first approaching a strange horse, making sure his head is being held up and that the animal is paying attention to your approach. Remember, because horses have good and bad days, they experience strong emotions which can cause them to become impatient or turn angry. Furthermore, since the horse is remarkably perceptive, he will respond to any impatience or fear he may sense from you.

Move toward him in a confident, unhurried manner, initially approaching in the direction of his left shoulder. This is known as the safe zone and by standing slightly ahead of the shoulder and to the left, you reduce your risk of injury. Always maintain a point of contact with the horse. This permits the horse to know where you are at all times, while also allowing you to feel if the animal is about to shy away abruptly.

The Back and Withers

Begin by gently stroking his shoulder and withers, as these are his least threatened areas. Next, gently rub your hand along the horse's back. Then run your hands up his neck, across his chest and finally along the length of his stomach. An animal that has been properly groomed should show no displeasure at this attention.

Because equestrian journeys can be halted due to saddle sores, you must next pay close attention to the horse's withers and back.

The withers for a road horse should be of a moderate height, so as to provide a surface for the saddle. Low, thick withers are undesirable as they allow the saddle to slip. The back is an indefinite term which is used to denote the whole length of the trunk from the withers to the croup. On this comparatively small space the whole of the saddle rests. When it comes to bearing a load on a long journey, a long back is a weak one. Neither the withers nor the back can sustain undue pressure without injury.

It is not uncommon for such previous injuries to leave white hair where the saddle has pinched, galled or injured the animal. Yet saddle sores may not leave such obvious clues.

Though a previous injury might not influence a horse's current performance, begin this critical part of the inspection by asking the owner to provide an explanation for every visible discoloured mark or scar on the animal's back, as each and every one represents a potential weakness in the animal's future travel performance. White hair represents the location of where such an injury once occurred. However, while these parts of the body might be slightly weaker, they do not necessarily mean the horse is actually injured at the time of the inspection.

Next, carefully run the palm of your hand along the withers, top of the shoulder blades, along the spine, and the top of the rib cage, all the while looking for any signs of swelling or heat, as these are strong indicators of saddle-related injuries. As you carefully move your hand along this portion of the horse's body feel for lumps under the skin. Meanwhile, use your eyes to look for evidence of hard skin and search for any signs that the hair is coming off. These clues indicate the horse is carrying invisible injuries caused by a saddle.

Subsequently, use the tip of two fingers to apply an even amount of pressure along the horse's withers, his back and anywhere the saddle comes in contact with his body. Do not let your fingernails hurt the animal. What you are attempting to locate is any area which may be tender. As you press on his withers and spine, watch the horse's ears and eyes, as they are strong indicators of pain. Also, note any tension in the animal's skin. If, during this part of your investigation, you discover a place which appears to be tender, stop pressing, inspect the area visually for any confirmation of a saddle sore, then carry on your investigation.

Be sure that you carry out this portion of the examination with equal care on both sides of the horse's body. If the animal becomes distressed, attempts to shy away from the pressure of your fingers, or tries to bite or kick you, then regardless of the lack of any strongly overt visual evidence, you may be inspecting a horse which is carrying undisclosed saddle sores. These wounds can, in a very short time, become open sores, which in turn will immediately conclude your journey.

If you find any hint of damage to the horse's back, quiz the seller ruthlessly about the nature and date of the injury. If he protests that the animal is in fine condition, then reapply finger tip pressure to the affected area. If the horse reacts painfully, pulls away, or attempts to move his back so as to escape the pressure, ask the owner to explain the circumstances. If you have any hint that the seller is being evasive, terminate the investigation, as the physical evidence suggests that you are being lied to.

The Head and Mouth

During the time that you are inspecting the animal use a few reassuring words or comforting signs around the horse. Most people are injured by so-called "gentle" horses, so always keep a wary eye on the horse that is strange to you.

Following the pressure test, take time to carefully examine the horse's head, ears, eyes and mouth.

An old expression stated, "You don't ride his head," i.e. it doesn't matter if the horse's head is ugly or large. Yet the head should not be large in proportion to the animal's size, as big heads are heavy, and every pound tells when a horse is tired, which is a common condition on an equestrian journey. There should be a general look of leanness about the head, with the nostrils standing well open, so as to provide a capacity for easy breathing during exertion.

The neck differs according to breed and sex of the horse. The upper portion of the neck, from the poll to the wither, and from which the mane strings, is called the crest. It attains a much greater development in stallions than in geldings or mares, being in some cases so heavy and high that it flops over to one side. This is a very undesirable aspect of conformation, as it adds to the burden carried by the forelegs, which normally support more than half the animal's entire weight. The neck therefore should be strong but light and the line of the crest from poll to withers should be firm to the feel.

The ears should be carried upright and forward. Lop ears, which flop down sideways, usually denote a lack of energy. Bad-tempered horses frequently carry their ears flat against the side of their neck when they are approached or about to kick.

The lips should be closed firmly over the teeth. Most people forget that the lips of the horse take the place of our hands. They serve both as organs of touch and as instruments for grasping an object, however small. This may be seen when the animal is feeding. He can gather up the smallest morsel of grain with his sensitive lips, or pull the grass into a tuft before he bites it. The lips should be thin, but firm and regularly closed. Flabby, pendulous lips indicate weakness or old age, dullness and sluggishness.

It is imperative that a road or pack horse have good teeth. The horse's teeth, unlike those of either man or the dog, do not grow to a certain length and then remain so. On the contrary, they continue to grow until old age. As horses age their front teeth become longer and project forward, while the outer edges of the molars become sharp. This inhibits their feeding and causes trouble with the bit. Variations are considerable and it takes skill and practice to be able to ascertain the age of a horse by an inspection of the teeth. Ask the seller when the horse's teeth were cared for. If you lack experience, make this part of the subsequent veterinarian examination. Should the teeth need attention, have the vet carry out this quick and painless procedure prior to your departure.

The eyes of a road horse require a very careful examination. A horse with perfect eyes seldom shies, unless from mismanagement and savage cruelty. Hence, your life and safety depend upon their proper action.

The eyes should be set well out at the side of the head so as to command a wide range of vision. An animal with a wide field of vision is not so likely to be nervous as one with less ample range of sight.

Bad-tempered horses frequently show the white of the eye in looking backwards.

When undergoing this part of the examination, it is absolutely necessary that good light should be obtained, in order to inspect the eyes most carefully. Care should be taken that the animal is held quietly, so as to allow you sufficient time to observe these organs narrowly and collectively. The light best suited for this purpose comes from above. Having placed the horse under the light, you will be able to see the eye as though you were looking at a piece of crystal. Examine each eye carefully. Now stand opposite and examine both eyes. They should be clear and dry. Also inspect the eyelids and eyebrows. Any disease which results in rheumy eyes, even from the slightest cold, until it be completely cured, stamps the horse as unsound.

Likewise pass up any horse that has saliva dripping from its mouth, a discharge running from its nose and any evidence of a cough or chest infection.

The Bones and Muscles

Having inspected the upper portion of the horse, you should now divert your attention to the bones, muscles, hooves and lower part of his body.

The hind-quarters, providing as they do the propelling force for the horse's body, must be muscular and proportionate to the rest of the frame, with enough bulk being essential so as to provide strength.

The ribs, eighteen in number, springing from the backbone above and attached to the breast-bone below, should be well sprung and deep, so as to give plenty of room for heart, lungs, stomach and bowels. Shallow bodies wanting depth are to be avoided as they are not shaped to withstand hardship or long travel.

On the inner side of leg may be noted a horny prominence known as the chestnut or castor. This growth does not denote weakness or illness.

While history demonstrates that every type of horse and pony can be used as a road horse, you ideally wish to purchase an animal with a sufficient amount of bone to handle the rigours of the road. Sadly, as horses have become more used for display than function, many breeds have been bred to be elegant, all the while their bone structure has become more delicate - not only the bones in their legs but their whole skeleton. The argument that a good muscular system balances this out is not logical because if the bone structure isn't strong enough, the muscles are not able to carry the weight alone.

The knee should be, like all joints, big, to afford plenty of room for the attachment of strong muscles. It should be broad and flat, deep from front to back, with a slight bulge forward in front, and the bony knob at the back large and prominent.

Check the horse's legs by slowly running both hands down the length of each leg. Each limb should be cool and the horse should show no sign of pain while his legs are being handled.

The Feet and Shoes

The integrity and conformation of the hoof are of the utmost importance, for a horse with bad feet is like a house with a weak foundation. Therefore you must carry out a careful examination of each hoof.

In appearance, the feet should be smooth and tough, with dark-coloured hooves preferred to lighter ones. Avoid feet which are brittle, spongy or rotten. The heels should be firm, the frogs horny and dry. The sole, which is somewhat hollow, should resemble the inside of a bowl. In terms of size, large hooves are more difficult to shoe, especially if your journey takes you into countries which have no history of horse shoeing. Hard, dark, medium-sized hooves will be less likely to disappoint.

It is critically important that a road horse will allow you to work with his feet.

Before you begin this part of the inspection, ask the seller when the horse was last shod, and how the animal reacts to his feet being worked on or inspected? Once you have obtained that information, begin by comparing it to the evidence available for your inspection.

Starting with the left front leg, run your hands down to the fetlock, then see if the horse allows you to lift his hoof. Any well-trained horse will permit you to pick up any of his hooves, and while it is being inspected, be able to stand quietly on his other three legs. Tap on the bottom of the hoof, or shoe, to see if the horse objects or tries to drop his foot. If the animal refuses to allow you to work on his feet, then neither you, nor a farrier, will be able to keep him shod without difficulty during your trip. Such an animal is not ready for a journey.

After you've picked up the horse's foot, inspect the hoof to determine its overall condition. If the horse is shod, is the shoe nailed firmly in place? Has the frog been overly trimmed? Are the heels cracked? Is the foot cool to the touch? Is there any sign, or smell, of the hoof disease known as thrush?

If the horse stands calmly, lower the hoof, then work your way towards his haunch. Once again, brush him gently, this time attempting to lift his rear hoof. During this part of the inspection, your left shoulder should be in close contact with the animal's flank. If the horse shies, or attempts to kick while you are checking his hooves, then move away.

If any of the hooves are found to be injured, or the horse refuses to allow you to lift his feet, then terminate the inspection.

The Tail

Finally, don't forget to check the animal's tail. Making sure that you are still standing next to the animal, not behind him, gently move the tail in various directions. If the animal has been used as a pack animal, inspect under the root of his tail so as to make sure a crupper has not blistered him.

If at any time during the close inspection a horse attempts to bite or kick, then terminate the inspection. If the animal can't be handled by the seller during a quiet routine inspection, in its own stable and under the best of conditions, then you will be risking life and limb later on the road.

Remember, a good horse is one with many good, few indifferent, and no bad points. But what cannot be debated is the fact that any potential road horse must be sound in eyes, wind and limb, before you proceed to the next stage of the inspection.

Examining the horse in action

If the horse has passed the physical inspection, it is important, after this, to witness the animal being tested at the walk and trot. If possible, this trial should take place on a paved surface, as this assists in detecting any lameness.

In the first of these exercises the horse will be led by the halter. The buyer must ensure that the seller's hand does not furnish a point of support for the horse's head. With this in mind, the seller is to be instructed to allow considerable freedom to the horse's head while the animal is moving at the walk and trot. Moreover, the seller should be requested to abstain from any extraneous means of excitement, such as cracking a whip, shouting, gestures, etc.

Have the seller walk and trot the horse in a straight line as you stand behind. Observe well if the horse demonstrates any inequality in his motions, favours one leg or bobs his head in pain. Take notice to see if he steps firmly on the ground. Have him stopped often. Then order him to start again. Observe whether in setting off he has a partiality for either leg, beyond that which seems to be natural to horses in every part of the world, of taking off with the left.

It is vital that a road horse have easy gaits, be firm on his feet, and, above all, possess a fast walk. During this exercise, the horse should be examined in profile, from the left and right, in front and from behind, either by running him successively from one side of the yard to the other or making him turn around in a circle. This will give an opportunity of noticing how he turns and how he backs.

The Cold Ride

As a final test, there must be the trial under saddle, what is known as the cold ride. To begin this mounted trial, it is sensible to see a horse ridden by the owner before trying him oneself, as this gives the opportunity of judging whether the animal is quiet to mount and quiet to ride.

Does the animal stand calmly while he is being groomed and his feet picked out? Does he object to have the girth tightened or does the horse allow himself to be bridled and saddled peacefully? Does he stand still while being mounted? Does he perform the walk, trot and canter calmly, or does he buck, halt, resist and run away? By putting the horse through its paces in such a way, the observant buyer can judge the horse's action, wind, strength and training, with no risk to himself.

This portion of the test begins when the horse is saddled and bridled, so as to notice if he bears both calmly. While the seller rides, the horse should be seen in profile, right and left, in front and from behind during this test, all the while the buyer observes how the animal starts off, trots, turns, backs and canters. Also, have the seller walk and trot the horse in a straight line as you stand behind, as this affords you a better opportunity to detect any subtle signs of lameness. Have the horse stopped often, then ask for him to move on again, all the while you watch carefully for any signs of lameness.

By observing every detail the seller can determine how the animal allows himself to be ridden and if he enjoys the experience. Remember, if the animal acts disagreeable with his current rider, in this familiar environment, then chances are that the horse is unsuitable for travel. You should ascertain also that the horse is good in his wind, that he is gentle and tractable, that he steps firmly on the ground and that he does not become frightened at unfamiliar objects or noises.

At the conclusion of this test you should have a good idea if the horse suits you and matches your riding ability.

The Test Ride

If all has gone well during this preliminary mounted examination, the last test is the mounted trial by the buyer.

Begin by taking the reins and walking beside the animal for some distance by yourself. Does the horse follow quietly, stop when required, and walk on when asked? Does he invade your space, act pushy and aggressive or is he respectful and calm? Aggressive behaviour is a characteristic which will add to your worries while travelling.

Horses are measured by hands; a hand being four inches (about 10 cm). A pony is usually defined as not more than 14 hands. Cobs generally do not exceed 15 hands. The average height of horses is considered to be 15.2 hands but the variations range from about 9 hands in the Shetland pony to 17 hands in the Shire draft horse.

What you must concern yourself with is having a horse which is comfortable to mount and whose weight corresponds in proportion to your own.

A Long Rider's horse should be safe on its legs. Nothing destroys nerve more than a stumbling, falling animal. Likewise, a horse that shies badly is very trying to a rider with a weak seat. Thus, you are seeking a equine whose level of composure will reassure you about the task at hand.

Begin your test by noting how quietly the horse stands when you mount.

And let me interject a note of caution about mounting.

Different cultures practise different equestrian habits; the most noticeable is which side do you mount on.

This was a lesson Thomas Lambie learned while exploring Ethiopia on horseback.

"He was an excellent horse but always hard to mount. The reason for this is that the Abyssinian always mounts from the horse's right side, while almost all Europeans mount from the left. A nervous animal wonders why the rider approaches from the wrong side."

Once you are in the saddle, take up the reins and begin to judge how sensitive the animal's mouth is. The road horse should be a fast walker, as this is the quality most desirable though not often sufficiently considered, so begin by determining if he has a brisk walk.

As you proceed to trot, notice if his gait is smooth and if the horse carries his head up. Can you ask him to give you a collected canter without risk of a runaway? Is he observant and tranquil under saddle or does he shy and fret? Does he feel deliberate, calm, relaxed and fun to ride?

After a sufficient amount of exercise, listen attentively to the sound of the horse's respiration and observe the movements of his flanks, to be sure he is not short-winded.

If a safe opportunity presents itself, ride the horse near traffic so as to see how it reacts. Also test it, if possible, on an asphalt road, as this hard surface may reveal faults which a softer surface may conceal. If the horse is in pain, his head will bob up and down with each step.

A final test is whether the horse will allow you to quietly ride it away from the stable and/or his equine companions. If the animal is psychologically herd bound, he may become belligerent and fight if asked to depart from his home. Such an animal is obviously unsuitable for a journey. It is better to discover this damaging fact prior to purchase than to find out after the horse has been loaded onto a trailer and the obstinate animal is then deposited, upset, angry and fearful, at your home.

Remember, you are searching for a road horse that is ready to assist you with your journey. Travel is already filled with enough unforeseen hardships and dangers without taking on the additional burden of purchasing someone's training project. Therefore, if at any time during your test ride the horse acts nervous, becomes fearful, attempts to buck, or tries to run away, you should terminate the ride and the inspection immediately.

After the Ride

There are several things you should look for at the conclusion of the test ride.

To begin with, once the saddle has been removed, inspect the horse's back and withers again for any signs of swelling or soreness. Does the horse pull away from your two fingertips when you test his muscles for soreness?

If there is a pasture or pen nearby, ask the seller to turn out the horse. Watch how the animal reacts once he is released. Does he appear calm and relaxed? If there are other horses nearby, carefully observe how this horse reacts and is treated in turn. If he becomes aggressive with other horses, he may in turn present an emotional challenge once you are on the road. After he has had a few minutes of freedom, try and catch the horse yourself to see how he reacts.

Should the animal seem sound, and if it rides well, then it is time to ask the veterinarian for a final inspection.

Vet Check

Let us assume that the seller is a person of undoubted integrity and honesty, one who is under the impression that his horse is sound. Nevertheless, a little knowledge is a dangerous thing and even horsemen of great experience stipulate a veterinary examination, on the principle that two heads are better than one.

Regardless of what country you plan to ride in, if the option is available, you should not hesitate to call in the aid of a medical expert. Whatever the expense of consulting a professional, it is not to be compared with the loss which would result from a wrong selection. Veterinarians in every country will be found to be the safest guides in such matters. Their special studies and knowledge enable them to give the best advice and to judge the qualities, defects and blemishes of the animal presented and of his state of health or of disease.

Explain the nature of your journey to the veterinarian, making sure the medico understands that while the horse will not be involved in hard galloping or jumping, you need to be ensured that the horse's stamina is sound, that his feet are good, that his eyes and teeth are in working order and that he has no previously-undetected ailment.

The Horse's Decision

This chapter provides an extensive list of ways to try and determine the physical and mental abilities of the horse.

What must not be overlooked is the equine's emotional ability to express his or her opinion of you.

One Long Rider, who successfully rode his mare more than 10,000 miles, commented on the horse's capability of "choosing" the rider.

"The affinity between man and horse is largely a matter of instinct on both sides. The horse may read instinctively something in the man's expression, but he will invariably verify this impression by smelling the man over before he finally takes up with him. It is presumed that the man has the natural faculty of selecting the horse that is amenable to kind, understanding treatment. The horse selects the man, and the man selects the horse."

Summary

When it comes to the choice of a road horse, the truth is that not one horse in a thousand is dangerous if he is properly broken and has enough work to do. It is your idle horse, like your idle man, that often earns a bad reputation and has time enough to learn stable vices.

If a horse has good vision, turns normally in either direction, has a brisk walk, trots out gaily on hard ground, makes no unusual noises when cantered, has clean healthy feet, shows no heat or swelling about his legs and comes out sound when cooled down after work the traveller may buy him, knowing that he has done all that can be expected of him to secure himself from fraud.

Having now checked the animal thoroughly, let us attempt to purchase him.

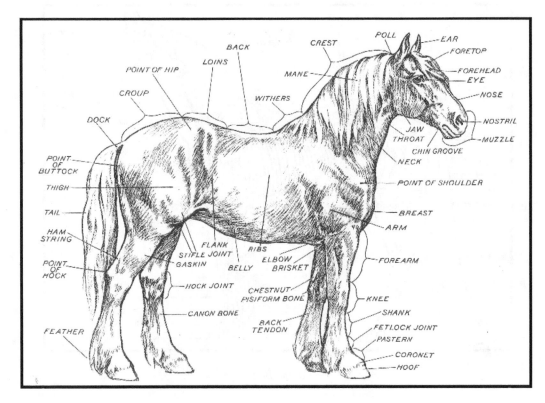

Points of the Horse

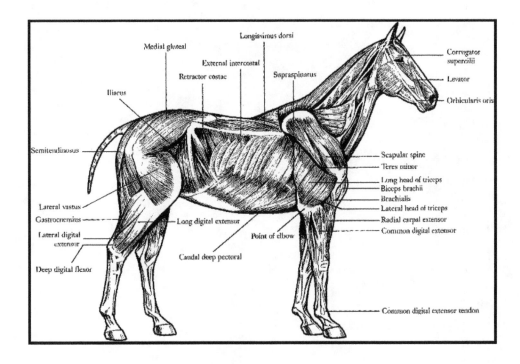

Equine Muscle

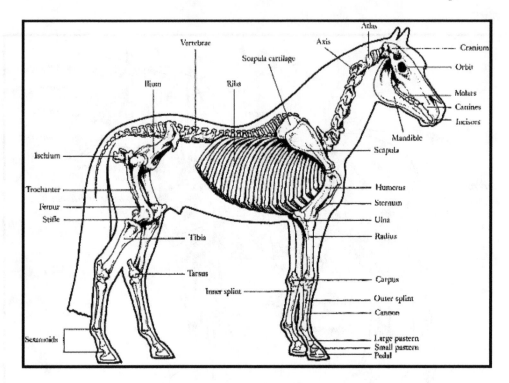

Equine Bone

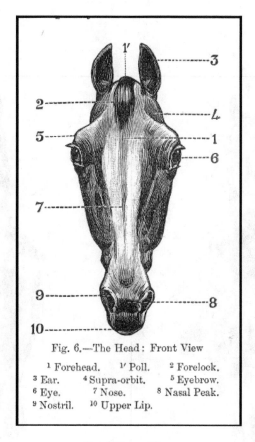

Fig. 6.—The Head : Front View

¹ Forehead.   ¹ʹ Poll.   ² Forelock.
³ Ear.   ⁴ Supra-orbit.   ⁵ Eyebrow.
⁶ Eye.   ⁷ Nose.   ⁸ Nasal Peak.
⁹ Nostril.   ¹⁰ Upper Lip.

Head Front View

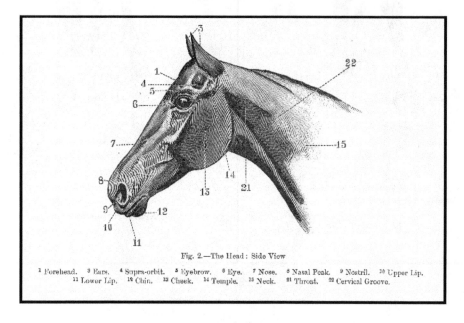

Fig. 2.—The Head : Side View

¹ Forehead.   ³ Ears.   ⁴ Supra-orbit.   ⁵ Eyebrow.   ⁶ Eye.   ⁷ Nose.   ⁸ Nasal Peak.   ⁹ Nostril.   ¹⁰ Upper Lip.
¹¹ Lower Lip.   ¹² Chin.   ¹³ Cheek.   ¹⁴ Temple.   ¹⁵ Neck.   ²¹ Throat.   ²² Cervical Groove.

Head Side View

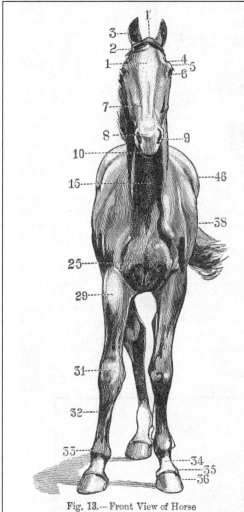

Fig. 13.—Front View of Horse

¹ Forehead.   ¹ʼ Poll.   ² Forelock.   ³ Ear.
⁴ Supra-orbit.   ⁵ Eyebrow.   ⁶ Eye.   ⁷ Nose.
⁸ Nasal Peak.   ⁹ Nostril.   ¹⁰ Upper Lip.
¹⁵ Neck.   ²⁵ Breast.   ²⁹ Forearm.   ³¹ Knee.
³² Canon.   ³³ Fetlock-joint.   ³⁴ Pastern.
³⁵ Coronet.   ³⁶ Foot.   ³⁸ Chest.   ⁴⁶ Haunch.

Front View of Horse

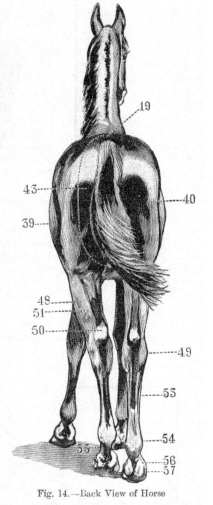

Fig. 14.—Back View of Horse

¹⁹ Croup.   ³⁹ Abdomen.   ⁴⁰ Flank.
⁴³ Buttock.   ⁴⁸ Leg or Gaskin.   ⁴⁹ Hock.
⁵⁰ Point of Hock.   ⁵¹ Tendo Achilles or
Ham-string.   ⁵³ Canon.   ⁵⁴ Fetlock-
joint.   ⁵⁵ Pastern.   ⁵⁶ Coronet.   ⁵⁷ Foot.

Rear View of Horse

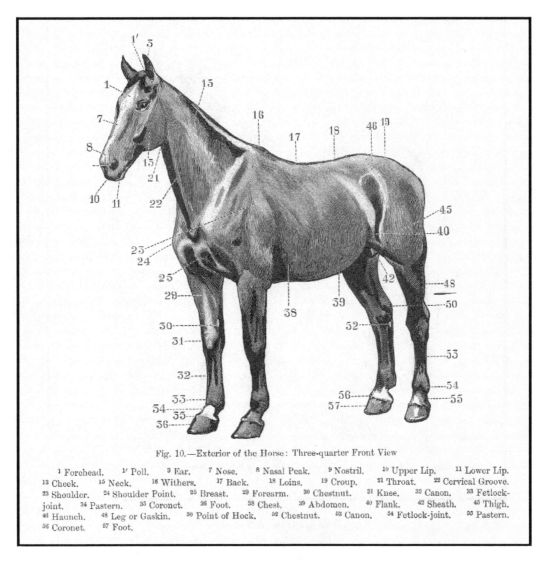

Fig. 10.—Exterior of the Horse: Three-quarter Front View

¹ Forehead.　¹ʹ Poll.　³ Ear.　⁷ Nose.　⁸ Nasal Peak.　⁹ Nostril.　¹⁰ Upper Lip.　¹¹ Lower Lip.
¹³ Cheek.　¹⁵ Neck.　¹⁶ Withers.　¹⁷ Back.　¹⁸ Loins.　¹⁹ Croup.　²¹ Throat.　²² Cervical Groove.
²³ Shoulder.　²⁴ Shoulder Point.　²⁵ Breast.　²⁹ Forearm.　³⁰ Chestnut.　³¹ Knee.　³² Canon.　³³ Fetlock-
joint.　³⁴ Pastern.　³⁵ Coronet.　³⁶ Foot.　³⁸ Chest.　³⁹ Abdomen.　⁴⁰ Flank.　⁴² Sheath.　⁴⁵ Thigh.
⁴⁶ Haunch.　⁴⁸ Leg or Gaskin.　⁵⁰ Point of Hock.　⁵² Chestnut.　⁵³ Canon.　⁵⁴ Fetlock-joint.　⁵⁵ Pastern.
⁵⁶ Coronet.　⁵⁷ Foot.

Three Quarters Front View

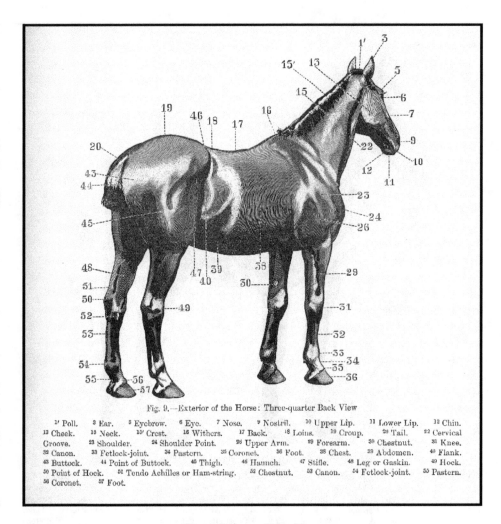

Fig. 9.—Exterior of the Horse: Three-quarter Back View

1' Poll.   3 Ear.   5 Eyebrow.   6 Eye.   7 Nose.   9 Nostril.   10 Upper Lip.   11 Lower Lip.   12 Chin.
13 Cheek.   15 Neck.   15' Crest.   16 Withers.   17 Back.   18 Loins.   19 Croup.   20 Tail.   22 Cervical
Groove.   23 Shoulder.   24 Shoulder Point.   26 Upper Arm.   29 Forearm.   30 Chestnut.   31 Knee.
32 Canon.   33 Fetlock-joint.   34 Pastern.   35 Coronet.   36 Foot.   38 Chest.   39 Abdomen.   40 Flank.
43 Buttock.   44 Point of Buttock.   45 Thigh.   46 Haunch.   47 Stifle.   48 Leg or Gaskin.   49 Hock.
50 Point of Hock.   51 Tendo Achilles or Ham-string.   52 Chestnut.   53 Canon.   54 Fetlock-joint.   55 Pastern.
56 Coronet.   57 Foot.

Three Quarters Rear View

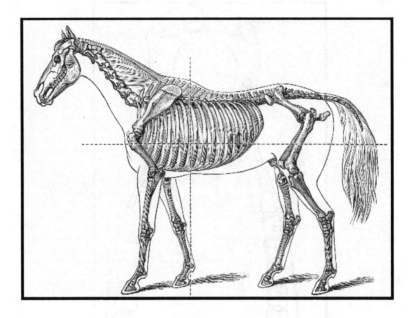

The Horse's Centre of Gravity is where the dotted lines cross

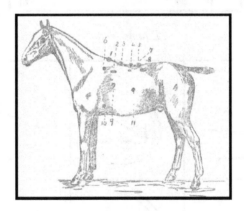

Common Points for Injuries

1.	*Injury from front arch*	*7.*	*Injury from side bar*
2.	*Injury from narrow arch*	*8.*	*Injury from "fans"*
3.	*Injury from roller or seat sinking*	*9.*	*Injury from sweat flap or girth attachment*
4.	*Injury from riding bare-backed*	*10.*	*Injury from girth gall*
5.	*Injury from rear pack*	*11.*	*Injury from sword or carbine bucket*
6.	*Injury from burrs*		

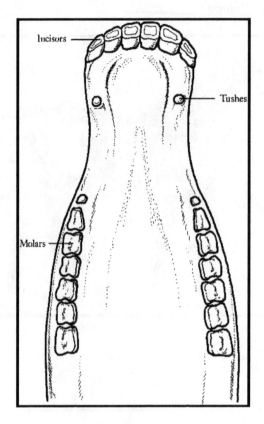

Equine teeth

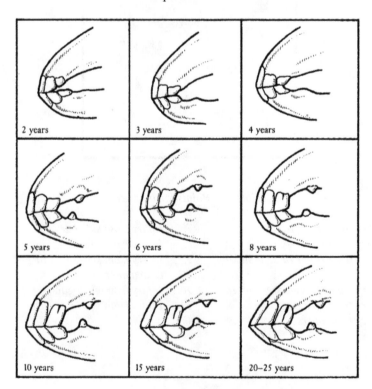

Judging the age of a horse by its teeth

Chapter 15
Buying Horses

Telling a person how to buy a horse is akin to advising another on how to carry on a romance. Because we are discussing two human beings, buyer and seller, the alternative endings are incalculable. If you factor in the possibility of attempting to make the purchase in a country other than your own, then sprinkle that experiment with a smattering of a foreign language, you are contemplating becoming a participant in one of mankind's most enduring business transactions. The trick is how do you ride away on a good horse without having your pockets turned out by the seller?

The Dealer's Excuses

In order to protect yourself from deception, you need to use your logic against the seller's emotional, misleading, and often times fraudulent, appeals. Remember, you are under no legal obligation to purchase the horse, so if at any time you feel threatened, or you sense the seller is deceiving you, then terminate the transaction. This is especially important if you are in a foreign country where you may have little or no recourse to legal action, if after the purchase you discover you have been swindled.

After having carefully examined the horse, your job is to keep your hand on your pocketbook, all the while you proceed cautiously through this minefield of a marketplace manoeuvring. To begin with, you should count on the seller having plenty of excuses at hand to explain anything suspicious or discouraging that may have been discovered during the various parts of the physical examination.

If the horse tried to bite you when you first approached, it was because he is so affectionate and will be such a close friend during your Majesty's trip.

If the horse is underweight, all the good grass encountered during the journey will soon rectify that, your Worship.

If the horse bucked, snorted, and reared when the seller first mounted, it was the first time the animal had ever behaved this way and is evidence of the strength he will have to bear you and your luggage, oh great Effendi.

No matter what went wrong, the seller will do everything possible to appeal to your vanity, all the while he works to convince you that black is white and that what you witnessed with your own eyes was not what you saw.

Don't let his honeyed words distract you. He will swear to anything except the truth.

What you must assume is that the horse has been produced for the trial in the best condition possible.

Thus, do not argue, as the facts speak for themselves. Nor should you allow yourself to be cajoled or bullied. You must begin this stage of the procedure by carefully considering the accumulated evidence.

Three Options

Having ended the inspection portion of the experiment, there are now three courses open to you.

First, you must refuse the horse outright. Second, you must make an offer on the horse, subject to a veterinary examination. Third, you must stipulate a further trial.

If you refuse the horse the decision should be conveyed to the owner firmly, ignoring any pleas about how his children will starve because of your stinginess and cruelty, etc.

Asking Price is no Guarantee of Value

Should you decide that you wish to buy the horse, then straight away you should realize that the asking price does not reflect the animal's true value. A seller can ask a million pounds, yet the horse will remain a jade. Likewise, a fabulous animal might be found disguised under a low price.

This is what happened to the North American Long Rider Lucy Leaf.

"I figured I travelled about 7,000 miles with Igor. He was a 16.1 hand bay horse who was five to eight years of age during the trip. I purchased him from a dealer in Connecticut for $150 because Igor was recovering from shipping fever. After the trip, he was retired in Maine and lived a healthy and active life until he died naturally at age 27," Lucy recalled.

Seven thousand miles on a horse valued at $150?

If the seller had known, the price would have been a great deal more, which in turn means that you should not trust the asking price.

Determining the Price

As these facts demonstrate, the purchase of a horse is a difficult and delicate matter and arriving at a proper price is one of the largest obstacles you must overcome.

Too many people set off to find a horse, equipped with large dreams and a small bank account.

To begin with, you must be inspecting a horse which fits within your budget. Not only do you place your journey in financial risk, you place yourself at a tremendous emotional disadvantage if you attempt to purchase a horse you cannot afford. There must be an absolute financial high point beyond which you will not yield, as to do so imperils your mission. Your task is to obtain a suitable horse for as low an amount as circumstances, and your sense of personal honour, allow. In order to determine what you offer you should consider these aspects of the horse in question.

Is the horse the proper size and weight for your journey?

You need a weight-carrying animal which is easy to mount.

Is the horse sound and free from any visible defect that affects its ability to travel?

You need a horse with sharp eyes, a strong back, feet like iron and legs of steel.

Is the horse emotionally dependable, obedient, courteous, kind and eager to befriend you?

Your life depends on riding an animal you can trust.

Is the horse the right gender for your journey and your equestrian experience?

Geldings generally make the best road horses, while stallions and mares both have drawbacks.

Is the horse responsive when ridden and does it have a fast walk?

A slow horse makes for a long journey.

Is the horse priced comparable to similar animals in that market or locality?

This last point can be of vital economic importance, because if you are purchasing a horse in a foreign country you must try not to allow your national origin to be used against you so as to inflate the asking price beyond what locals would be expected to pay. Prior to bargaining, you should have made a dedicated attempt to establish what locals normally pay for the type of horse you are attempting to purchase.

One way to uncover this vital information is by using the "hair cut and bananas" rule favoured by French Foreign Legionnaires. While obtaining a hair cut, ask the barber what bananas cost? While buying a bunch of bananas, ask the seller how much a hair cut costs? By appealing to various members of the local economy, none of whom have a vested interest in horses, you may be able to establish a rough idea of local horse prices prior to trying to buy the animal.

Another option is to enlist a sympathetic local to help you establish what local prices are. Before starting his journey, Tim Cope found a Mongolian who not only helped locate horses, but bargained for them, so as to ensure that the foreigner Long Rider wasn't overcharged.

"Generally speaking it's better to get a local to help you. Contacts seem to be everything in Mongolia, and foreigners are seen to be people who know nothing about horses and have lots of money," Tim said.

Making an Offer

Having concluded that the horse we wish to acquire isn't likely to try and murder us before breakfast or go lame by lunch, let us attempt to purchase the animal.

One thing which can be relied upon throughout the march of history is the fact that it is not possible to close a transaction for a horse without bargaining. Thus regardless of what age, or country, in which the transaction takes place, you can count on the seller asking as much as he dares.

Buying a horse is akin to a magic trick. You know the magician is deceiving you, yet regardless of being forearmed with this knowledge you can't uncover his secret. Like the magician, the seller is working in the open, all the while trying to mislead you by asking more than the two of you know will ultimately be accepted. He in turn expects you to proceed on the principle that you will attempt to start low enough in the hope that the two of you can meet somewhere in the middle.

By allowing the seller to set the asking price, you instantly surrender part of your power.

Remember, horses are not saddles. A saddle can be kept for years and then sold for a profit. Yet every day the seller retains possession of the horse, the animal eats a portion of his potential revenue. This psychological fact plays in your favour, especially if the seller is anxious to dispose of the animal. Plus, the seller knows that the world is full of potentially suitable horses, any one of which might better fit your needs than his horse. Thus, the most powerful tool at your disposal is your firm and obvious determination to walk away at a moment's notice, as your emotions are under control and your pocketbook shall remain resolutely closed unless there is movement from the other party.

For the sake of this experiment, ignore the asking price of $500.

Offer 25% or $125.

The seller will probably counter with $450.

Up your offer to 30%, or $150.

If the seller says no and offers his last price again, refuse his offer, thank him and walk away.

If he calls you back, re-offer $150.

Often, if you've done your homework, established the local price, and make an offer close to this amount, the seller will accept your lower offer.

If he insists on continuing the bargaining, you are now working upwards from $150, and not from his inflated asking price of $500.

Remember, only offer what you can afford and never pay more than your previously determined limit.

Another thing to anticipate is that the seller might accept your original offer without any hesitation. This is disconcerting as it indicates that your original offer was too high. On the other hand, while you can always offer more, you cannot reduce your bid; hence your need to cautiously begin at the low end of the possible sales price.

All the while you are attempting to protect your economic interests, you must not lose sight of the fact that you should not offend the seller. Driving a hard bargain is one thing, but haggling over a few dollars will only cause hard feelings and may lose you the horse. Make sure the seller knows you appreciate his horse; however you have restrictions which do not allow you to compromise beyond a certain financial point.

Keith Clark successfully bought several horses during his journey in Chile and Argentina. He offered these thoughts.

"I can't help much on the buying of the horses except to say take your time. I made the mistake of rushing into it, which in turn caused me to have to sell one horse as she wasn't suited to the mountains. When people hear that there is a foreigner interested in buying horses they will bring out every unsuitable nag there is. Try to get away from the towns and villages to where horses are used daily. That's where you'll find good ones. Remember in Argentine the dollar rules so don't be rushed. They'll want your money as much as you want their horses," Keith advised.

A Central Asian Alternative

While the scenario described above will certainly take in most of the horse world, be aware that in some parts of Central Asia horses are bought and sold without a word being spoken.

Kazakh horse trading follows a prescribed ritual which includes a buyer, seller and middle-man. After inspecting the horse for sale, buyer and seller sit down on the ground on either side of the middle-man. He holds the left hand of one and the right hand of the other hidden within the long sleeves of their coats.

By bending and moving his fingers, the seller can transmit his offer silently. The middle-man relays the message using his fingers to the buyer, who in turn uses his fingers to make a counter-offer. In this way the bargaining proceeds via a non-verbal manner.

The Kazakhs believe that this silent, cryptic bartering avoids arguments and dispenses with the usual exaggerated praise of horses being offered for sale.

Conditions of Sale

Even if all goes well, and the price is agreed upon to your satisfaction, your work is still far from done.

In common with any type of business arrangement, the details are as important as the price and it is critically important that seller and buyer agree on all points concerning payment, transfer of ownership, medical condition at the time of sale, and transport after the sale.

For example, how and where will the funds be paid? Will you be presented with papers proving that the seller is the recorded owner of the horse? Is the seller willing to guarantee the overall health of the animal for 48 hours after the sale? If the sale occurs in North America, did the seller provide you with medical evidence demonstrating that the horse has a negative Coggins test at the time of the sale? Will the seller provide you with all of the horse's registration papers and any relevant medical documentation at the close of sale? If the horse has to be moved, is it clear how much time you have to transport the animal? Does any equipment come with the horse?

The best way to protect yourself is by clearly defining all aspects of the sale. It isn't necessary to have a solicitor to draw up such a document, as both parties can compose a letter describing the responsibilities of both parties. After the seller and buyer have both signed and dated this paper, you will possess a legal document detailing everyone's intentions. This in turn works to protect you, especially if a disagreement occurs later. It strengthens the document if it is also signed and dated by a witness.

While it is imperative to record the details of the sale, the document proving you are the new owner is even more critically important.

Bill of Sale

This book provides you with a sample of a proposed *Long Rider International Equine Bill of Sale*.

This is a simple piece of paper that makes men honest and keeps them so. Thus, if you have no wish to be disappointed, summon to your assistance the aid of those powerful refreshers of memory, your allies, the pen, this document and a witness. Remember, an honest man will have no more objections to signing a written agreement than in making a verbal promise, and a prudent man will never take the latter when he can get the former.

Therefore, when concluding the agreement, never accept a verbal agreement on the sale of a horse. Don't shake hands and give anyone your money.

One Long Rider was ridiculed when he asked for a bill of sale.

"They told me to forget about the receipt because the horse was the receipt, and anyway, the old man couldn't write and nobody had a pen."

Make the seller provide evidence that he is the legal owner, is entitled to sell the horse and can provide every bit of necessary paperwork at the time of sale and never accept a promise to receive the papers at a later date.

Take care to note the horse's brands and distinguishing markings. When the document is signed, witnessed and dated, have it notarised if this service is available.

Depending on what country you are in, you may need to register the sale with government office for agriculture. For example, in Argentina you must register the sale of your horses with the SENASA office. This requires you to obtain an official "certificado" from the local justice of the peace registering the sale and documenting you as the new owner.

Also, be sure that you keep separate copies of these papers, so that you can prove ownership if you lose the originals.

Just because the papers are signed, that doesn't necessarily mean the deal is concluded. When Canadian Long Rider Bonnie Folkins bought horses before riding across Mongolia, she learned that the first-time owner and his foal share a powerful bond. When such a meaningful relationship comes to an end, significant rituals are involved. The purchase and delivery of the animal to a new owner is a slow process wherein the seller is courted with vodka and gifts. Before the sale is complete, and to memorialise his past attachment to the horse, the original owner cuts two locks of hair from the mane and tail that he keeps for the rest of his life.

Buyer's Remorse

Finding a great road horse isn't simply a matter of saving or spending money.

There should be an intangible element to the animal which makes you eager to set off with him on your exciting mutual journey.

Thus, even if you've received a good deal financially, to offset any trace of buyer's remorse you should ask yourself two questions before sealing the deal.

Despite any cultural or regional prejudices do you believe you have chosen the best horse you can afford? Are you willing to trust your life to this animal?

The ease with which a person can lose his loyalty for a horse is notorious. That is why the old saying goes, "The horse has only two faults, one that it takes a long time to catch him in the field, the other that he's not worth a damn when caught."

Trust is more important than money. If you don't trust the horse, don't close the deal.

Summary

In 1667 the famous English horseman, William Newcastle, wrote, "I must tell you, there are good and bad horses in all countries in the world; but there are more bad than good. If you have found the right horse, it is heavenly. But if you have mounted the wrong horse, it is hell."

Despite this grim warning, equestrian travel proves that if you persevere, you'll find the right horses. That's what Keith Clark discovered when he arrived in Argentina, determined to ride across the Andes Mountains into Chile. His troubles began when the local who had promised to help Keith locate horses admitted he hadn't actually been out into the countryside for ten years. This prompted Keith to begin his own investigations.

"I have seen so many really bad horses that I was beginning to wonder where the good horses were hidden. I've been bitten at, kicked at, run away from but I'm $1,000 dollars poorer and 2 horses richer. They aren't ideal. Nor are they as big as I would like. But they are well schooled, have worked on a regular basis, are calm, traffic wise, healthy, and best of all, have really good feet. Plus, they're both lovely to ride. They stop on a sixpence and neck rein, which is so much more convenient than the European style. I paid a bit over the odds for them but I'd been spending $40 a day in hotels, taxis etc in looking for horses so I think it was well worth it," the satisfied Long Rider reported.

Though the years have marched on, the buyer must still be wary. A horse market in Kyrgyzstan, then.

A horse market in Kyrgyzstan, now. Different horses, same tricks.

Chapter 16

Long Rider International Equine Bill of Sale

This sales agreement, dated the _____ day of _____, _____ between

_____

(Name of Seller)   of (Seller's City, Province and Country)

and

_____

(Name of Buyer)   of (Buyer's City, Province and Country)

is for the sale of one _____
                        (List sex of animal – gelding, mare or stallion)

Parties agree as follows on the following description of the equine including name, age, date of birth, colour, markings, breed and registry number.

_____

_____

_____

_____

Seller warrants that the equine is in good health with no known defects or injuries and will furnish Buyer with health records on the equine. Seller also guarantees that he is the lawful owner of the equine and has the right to sell the animal.

The total sales price for this equine is _____
                                        (List Dollars, Pounds, Euros, Pesos, Yen, etc.)

the receipt of which is hereby acknowledged.

_____

Witness/Notary

Chapter 17
Long Rider Horsemanship
Part One - The Philosophy

A Hundred Thousand Messages

In an effort to document the modern renaissance of equestrian travel, the Long Riders' Guild has carefully preserved every single email it has ever sent or received. There are hundreds of thousands of these messages, which arrived in a plethora of languages, and were dispatched from every continent except Antarctica. Though they cover a tremendous number of topics, I cannot recall a single one which asked the Guild about how a would-be equestrian traveller should ride!

That is surprising when you consider that the average proposed journey is usually 2,500 miles long. Moreover, not only do at least half of these potential Long Riders reveal that they have little or no equestrian background, many cannot yet ride when they initially contact the Guild for advice. Regardless, they routinely write to say that they are preparing to undertake a life-changing equestrian journey.

For example, before he set off to ride from Mongolia to Hungary, Tim Cope admitted he was afraid of horses and could barely ride. He remedied the problem by taking lessons before his departure and then rode into the history books.

An even more dramatic example is DC Vision, a Founding Member of the Guild who rode 22,500 kilometres (14,000 miles) on a four-year journey through the United States. While the mileage is impressive, what is astonishing is that DC had never even been near a horse before he swung into the saddle.

Yet what surely must be the most dramatic example of such amazing personal courage was exhibited by the South African Long Rider Ria Naysmith. Before setting off to cross the African continent with her husband, Gordon, the former nurse completely lacked any riding skills. Luckily, this basic deficiency was remedied by a helpful stranger.

"While we were camped on a farm to test the gear, a young man named Neil Peacock realized I needed help riding. One day he just came, saddled the two wildest ponies and took control. He said to me, 'Now Ria, this is a horse. That is the front. That is the back. You sit in the middle.' This I will never forget. For hours and hours he took me up and down gullies, over mountains and through rivers. He knew my life depended on that. Bless his dear gentle heart; he probably did save my life because he taught me so many little things about the horses, how to see what each individual liked, how to handle each one, etc.," Ria recalled.

Mongolia to Hungary? An epic journey through North America? A life-threatening ride across the entire African continent? Wouldn't you consider those monumental feats of riding?

In a modern horse world preoccupied with where you put your heels, what colour jodhpurs you wear or if your horse won a blue ribbon in the last show, acts of bravery in the saddle don't register. Why isn't riding across a continent granted the same respect as beating your neighbour in a competition?

The answer lies in a forgotten prejudice from our collective equestrian past.

The Roots of Long Rider Horsemanship

To find an answer to this riddle we must focus on the vastly different equestrian cultures of Europe and Central Asia, and study how these still-warring riding styles exerted different influences on mankind's mounted history, both past and present.

Any investigation into the earliest links between humans and horses must begin on the great grasslands which once spread along the Equestrian Equator, an invisible line which runs from modern Hungary to Mongolia.

Though King Hammurabi of Babylon first mentioned the horse nearly two thousand years before the onset of the Common Age, by 884 BC a relief in the palace of King Assurnasipal depicted mounted nomads wearing trousers and riding boots. Likewise the saddle and stirrup also originated among these original steppe riders. But it wasn't just equipment which coloured subsequent equestrian events. In fact the riding ability of these earliest horse herders was so extraordinary that the ancient Greek historian, Herodotus, wrote of the Scythians, "Their country is the back of a horse."

Nor was this skill restricted to one tribe or era. Though the Romans were not a mounted race, this didn't keep their historian, Sidonius, from recognizing true skill in the saddle when he also saw Central Asian horsemen.

"You would think the limbs of man and animal were born together, so firmly does the rider stick to his horse. Other people are merely carried by their horses. These people live there," the Latin author noted.

Yet if the riding technique of these steppe warriors had reached such a high state of perfection, why does the modern equestrian world choose instead to mimic the Romans, those fathers of prestige transport?

The Birth of Prestige Transport

While there were notable individual horsemen in Rome, especially Julius Caesar, history clearly demonstrates that the finest equestrians the world has ever seen originated in Asian nomadic societies. Ironically, it is not those original horsemen who are now looked upon with reverence. Instead it is the European heirs of those whom they conquered, starting with the Romans.

What the Romans did was to bequeath to the modern horse world the image of mounted majesty. Unlike the nomads who rode to live, the Romans turned the horse into an item of prestige transport. Thus triumphant Roman emperors met their victorious returning armies just outside town, mounted a sedate horse, and then rode to glory in front of the adoring mob of Rome. This type of egotistical display laid the foundation for the glamour horse industry still ruling the equestrian world in the USA and Western Europe today.

Early Admonitions

This isn't to say that the closing of the western mind didn't occur without warning.

It was Roger Pocock, that legendary horseman, author and Long Rider, who penned this adage wherein he lamented the prejudices too often found among so-called "civilized" horsemen.

"The human mind may be likened unto a stable with horses all in a row. That strong team, Tradition and Custom are overworked. Bias and Prejudice have plenty to do. Passion and Vice get an occasional airing and Vanity has daily exercise. But Reason is kept in his stall, the master's own mount, and stale for want of use. He is not popular with the other horses, he is not easily ridden, is heavy to handle, and goes painfully lame from having been kicked too much."

Having fought the Comanche and other expert Native American tribes during a long series of blood-soaked equestrian wars, the United States Cavalry also issued a stern caveat to young officers not to dismiss so-called uncivilized riding.

"You should realize that there are many systems of equitation and styles of riding, all of which have merit and a particular purpose," the manual cautioned.

Even so, regardless of Sidonius' praise, and in spite of Pocock's warning, most European riders have inherited the Roman belief that they are descended from a civilized people whose ancestors held violent mounted savages at bay. Given such a deep-rooted prejudice, it becomes easy to assume that if the Central Asian society was inferior, then its horsemanship must also have been barbaric.

Generations of riders have accordingly become encased in this cultural and equestrian bigotry, which grants unwarranted equestrian precedence to the Europeans.

There is an alternative equestrian philosophy, one which states that it is not one man's glory in the saddle we should be concerned with or wish to imitate.

The marvellous point of the human-horse equation was that a place, no matter how far away it might be, was within the grasp of a courageous horse-human, both then and now. That is why, though the legendary Silk Road was 10,000 kilometres (6250 miles) long, with its eastern terminus being the Chinese Pacific coast and its western Alexandria on the Mediterranean, thanks to the horse distances were not merely diminished, they were also defined.

The horse liberated any bold human from the shackles of gravity and the petty restrictions of the village mentality. Thus even the mysteries of the distant Mongol Empire could be experienced by a brave mounted teenager from Venice named Marco Polo.

The Equestrian Legacy of Genghis Khan

Let us consider for a moment some of the differing aspects of Mongolian versus European equestrian culture.

In the 13th century, so few goods penetrated into the far north of Mongolia, where Genghis Khan was born, that a man with a pair of iron stirrups was considered wealthy among the Mongols. In such a harsh environment riding did not evolve around the abstract concept of mounted esteem.

In this world, where every child could ride alone by the age of four and every male learned the mounted skills of war, only the riding mattered, not the style. This was in stark contrast to Europe, where horses were typically reserved for the wealthy and riding was for centuries the prerogative of the ruling male class.

One point which pedestrian scholars often fail to consider is the immense number of horses which formed a vital component of the Mongol empire. For example, by 1206 the still-youthful Genghis Khan ruled a vast territory the size of Western Europe which contained an estimated 20 million animals.

Was there ever a western commander who, like Genghis, ordered his troops to take the bits off their horses while on the march, so as to allow them to graze, and reinforced his orders with the draconian sanction that any soldier who abused this ruling was to be beheaded?

Scarcely; but then there was never a Western army that could match such enormous feats of strategic travel on horseback. While there is any number of equestrian feats one could discuss, a single battle alone provides what may be the definitive example of which equestrian style, Mongol or European, was more effective.

After the death of Genghis Khan, his third son, Ögedei Khan, continued the expansion of the empire by ordering the Mongol cavalry to conquer Europe all the way to the Atlantic Ocean. The five-year campaign which Ögedei launched in 1235 contained an estimated 150,000 hardened warriors and 750,000 horses who swept into Europe after having already ridden four thousand miles from their base in Mongolia.

One branch of this army made a feint into Poland and Germany, a ruse so effective that the Mongols killed off most of the northern Europeans sent to stop them. It was during the decisive battle of Mohi in Hungary that the Mongols not only defeated the flower of European knighthood, they also slew an estimated one hundred thousand soldiers, thousands of mounted aristocrats, a Catholic bishop and the fabled Knights Templar.

When Ögedei died, the Mongols withdrew so that the royal princes of the blood could be present for the election of a new ruler. Thus it was only Ögedei's death which prevented the invasions of Austria, Germany, Italy, France, and Spain, and the remaining small European principalities. Indeed, Mongol forces were moving on Vienna, and launching a fierce winter campaign against Austria and Germany in the first wave into Western Europe when the Mongol monarch expired. Some historians believe only his death prevented the complete conquest of Europe.

Thus an Asiatic equestrian system, which promoted men from the lowest social levels of society to the highest ranks of leadership based on their skills and achievements rather than birth, triumphed over a rival who dominated others thanks to a spiritual and military caste system. Also, for the first time the skills learned during a long journey were contrasted against the "art" of riding.

And while their husbands and sons were busy conquering Europe, the Mongol wives managed the largest empire in history from their own saddles. Mongol Queen Mandhuhai, for example, led her soldiers to mounted victory while pregnant.

Yet the equestrian wisdom involved in moving that many warriors and horses across so vast a distance is seldom considered in the context of today's horse world. What we are asked to focus on instead is the modern indoor horse, who lives in a house, has servants, is delicate and finely bred, not his rangy Mongolian cousin who lived outdoors and was empowered with immense gifts of scent, hearing and endurance.

What we should be asking ourselves is: how did these warriors ride? Did they focus on form or function? And how do the riding skills of these Central Asian horsemen translate into wisdom for the modern Long Rider?

Clashing Cultures

When the death of the Mongol emperor prompted the invading riders to return home, Europe did two things. It gave thanks to God for saving it from its pagan enemies. Plus, with the exception of the Hungarians, the majority of Europeans reverted to their recently-defeated riding style.

Unlike the rest of Europe, the Hungarians never forgot the ocean of blood which the Mongols had spilled at the battle of Mohi. They recalled that Mongol express riders, known as arrow riders, could gallop 150 kilometres (93 miles) a day, with numerous changes of mount, and deliver a message over the 4,000 kilometres (2,500 miles) from Peking to Kabul in six weeks.

While the Europeans obstinately galloped down the wrong historical track, the Mongols maintained an elegantly simple riding style which allowed their ambassador to ride 11,500 kilometres (7,000 miles) to England.

Yet as the defeat of the European knights faded from popular view, the feats of daring Mongol riders were replaced in the West with an increasingly fossilized riding style which confined itself more and more to ceremony. This distinction became painfully clear when the movements now associated with dressage were invented in Italy.

When King Ferdinand of Naples sent one of his equerries to Hungary to introduce these new dressage methods at the royal court, King Matthias sent him back with this message.

"With the horses we trained ourselves we defeated the Turks, subjected Serbia and vanquished all before us, honourably by means of our own horses. We have no desire for horses that hop about with bent hocks in the Spanish fashion; we do not want them even as a pastime, still less for serious business. What we want are horses that stride out and stand firm when required," he rebuked his fellow monarch.

Why had Europe forgotten the bitter life-and-death equestrian test it had failed to win at Mohi? And what equestrian system had the European monarchs favoured instead?

The Dressage Myth

The word dressage is derived from the French word for training. The fundamental belief enshrined in the system is that once a horse is mounted by a rider, the animal's normal balance and centre of gravity are disturbed to the point where the horse can prematurely damage itself with wear. Thus the theoretical aim of dressage is allegedly to remedy this imbalance by training the horse to rebalance itself with the weight of the rider. Sadly, history doesn't support this claim.

Despite the French name, most of the terms connected to the dressage movements known as *haute école*, the airs above the ground, such as the *passage, piaffe, capriole* and *levade* were created by the Italians, who are also credited with being the inventors of the rules and principles of this type of riding which became the prerogative of European aristocracy.

Federico Grisone was the Neapolitan nobleman who was not only the father of dressage; in 1550 he also authored, *The Rules of Horsemanship*, wherein he advocated the use of severe spurring and harsh bits. In this still-influential book Grisone explained how he routinely used other cruel methods to train and punish horses placed in his care. This included placing live hedgehogs under the animal's tail, punishing his horses by placing a cat, strapped to a pole, under their bellies, and forcing the horse's head under water to the point of near-drowning if it showed any fear of crossing water.

As we shall see, many dressage tactics were cruel then and remain cruel today.

During the Renaissance the crème de la crème of the European landed gentry were drawn to Italy to learn the sophisticated manners and graces needed to handle the sword, dance and ride. Thus, thanks to this invented Italian riding style, the last traces of any utilitarian equitation left intact in Europe from the Middle Ages was transformed into a rigorous ritual of riding.

This fixation in Europe on refined mounted manners not only undermined the very concept of equitation, thanks to an apostolic succession of riding connoisseurs including Gian Battista Pignatelli, Antoine de Pluvinel, Francois de la Gueriniere, William Cavendish, Francois Baucher, James Fillis and Alois Podhajsky, a myth was born which stated that this courtly mounted ballet was actually a deadly mounted battle drill.

Harsh Reality

By the late sixteenth century the armoured knight was a hazy memory. European noblemen were however still riding to battle. Only now upstart peasant foot soldiers were apt to yank them out of the saddle with cruel twelve foot long pikes. With no armour except a breast plate to protect him, the nobleman was suddenly fair game for any serf brave enough to get within sword's point.

According to a legend still being actively perpetrated by many dressage advocates and modern websites, it was during this time of conflict that the lords of Europe originated the art of *haute école*, so as to combat the armed serfs. This method purportedly taught mighty stallions a series of moves whereby they flew off the ground, lashing out with their deadly steel-clad hooves, kicking and killing anyone unlucky enough to come within the range of their blue-blooded riders.

A fine theory; yet noted equestrian historian, Dr. Elaine Walker, takes exception to this fairy tale.

"It seems very unlikely that in the terrible crush and chaos of battle there would be time to focus on the execution of elaborate caprioles and curvets. Also, while the drama of the capriole, with the horse leaping forward high above the ground, may in theory threaten the head of any man below, even in the refined atmosphere of a riding house, it is a difficult and specialized movement," Walker observed.

She also noted that an additional key consideration would have been the time and cost involved in producing the horse and rider combination capable of performing such intricate moves.

"Even allowing for claims of a short method of training, to produce one horse that could perform the most modest of airs would take many months, with two or three handlers involved in the training. Then the number of horses that had the skill and physique to perform the great leaps, the croupades and caprioles would be very limited and these would be highly expensive animals."

Walker also deduced that few noblemen would be eager to risk endangering the expensive stallions specifically imported from Spain for this hobby riding. Finally, thanks to the advent of gunpowder and firearms, the assumption of asking your stallion to help you leap out of the way of danger should have become an obsolete mounted myth.

Yet during the campaign of 1691 French cavalrymen rode into battle stubbornly adhering to this false fashion. According to an eyewitness, their horses were absolutely unable to adapt themselves to the harsh military conditions encountered in actual battle. These poor dazed and stupefied animals were barely able to drag themselves to the battle ground, and once there, they panicked and began performing bravura *haute école* exercises in the midst of the war.

Despite a resounding defeat the French cavalry, faithful to this Italian tradition, resolutely continued to fight in a style more appropriate to the carousel – and subsequently lost many more engagements. Voices were eventually raised in France against dressage-based equitation, but in vain, the result being that in 1757 thirty-eight Prussian squadrons, under the direction of Frederick the Great, put fifty-two French squadrons to the sword.

Such defeats emboldened a growing number of dissenters to denounce dressage. One such critic, General Ingelfingen, wrote, "Every circus horse knows how to perform elaborate movements, but no circus horse was ever in sufficiently good condition to do the work of cavalry horses. This system tends to turn riding into an art. But it has no real value and should therefore be reduced to a minimum, for all such performances are only proofs of the mastery of the rider over his horse, and are unnatural movements, carried out at the expense of the horse's power."

Ironically, though the Germans, French and several other nations retained their love of dressage, the questionable practice was eventually dropped by the Italians who started it. Thanks to the more practical riding style introduced by Captain Federico Caprilli, in 1892 the Italian cavalry turned its back on the riding style it had helped originate.

Fashion versus Function

While some might argue that refined horsemanship and rough and tumble equestrian travel can co-exist, no two men better represent the polar opposites involved in this long-running equestrian feud than Francois Baucher of France and Henning Haslund of Denmark.

Baucher began his riding career in the circus and then graduated to the big time when he became his nation's most controversial 19th century riding teacher. He is credited with inventing the flying changes, where horses change their lead at every stride. More importantly, Baucher used brutality to crush the instinctive forces of the horse. By driving the horse forward with the spur, and simultaneously holding it back with the bit, the unfortunate animal realized it had become completely trapped. According to his critics, Baucher's technique of severe mental domination, termed the *effet d'ensemble*, resulted in the horse becoming an "ambulatory cadaver." The Frenchman is not only still revered in the dressage world, one of his cruel training methods is currently at the heart of the modern dressage world's most appalling dispute.

In stark contrast to Baucher, Henning Haslund had the soul of a Mongol nomad, even though he had been born in Denmark. The foot-loose young man originally journeyed to Outer Mongolia in 1923, ostensibly to help run an experimental agricultural project. Yet it didn't take long for the call of adventure to out-sing the tune of the peasant's plough. Henning, who was an excellent horseman, was employed by Sweden's most celebrated Central Asian explorer, Sven Hedin. In the company of that great Historical Long Rider, Henning spent several years exploring the Gobi desert and learning the basics of scientific research. The young Dane also made an extraordinary ride which stands in stark contrast to Baucher's reportedly fantastic equestrian skills.

Delivering the mail – Baucher or Haslund?

Unlike Genghis Khan's resolute arrow riders, who faced every type of hardship without flinching, it is said that Baucher never ventured outside a circus ring or a riding school. On one occasion, a nobleman of high rank visited Baucher's school in Paris. Baucher was at that moment riding a beautifully-trained horse, on which he executed an elaborate performance for the benefit of his distinguished visitor. While they were talking together, the aristocrat suddenly remembered that he had forgotten to post an important letter which he had in his pocket. Drawing it out, he handed it to the champion dressage rider and asked him to ride the horse and deliver the letter to the nearby post office.

"Your Highness," replied Baucher, "I am overwhelmed with regret that I am unable just at present to obey your orders; but if you will wait three months, so as to give me time to train my horse to go outside, I will then be delighted to take the letter for you."

In stark contrast to Baucher, in his book *Mongolian Adventure*, Haslund recalled how he delivered the mail in Mongolia.

Because of the rarity of letters from home, the Dane set off for the closest post office. Unfortunately the only horse available was an untamed stallion named Hao. It took the combined efforts of two Cossacks and five Mongols to capture and saddle this wild beast, who Haslund then immediately mounted.

"I pulled on a pair of thick gloves, fastened the riding-whip to my wrist, put a handkerchief between my teeth and leaped into the saddle. And then things began to happen. Hao gave a mad scream and began a series of buckjumps into the air, each time landing on the ground with stiffly spread legs, curved back and nose far down between his forelegs. Each time he came down I felt as if I had been hit on the head with a club; things began to swim before my eyes and I lost one stirrup. At that moment an alert friend gave the bucking horse a mighty swipe over the hind-quarters which set him off across the steppe at a wild gallop," the young Long Rider recalled.

"I tried to reduce the gallop to a trot, but every time I pulled him in, Hao snorted and set off at increased speed. It grew so dark in the forest that I had trouble in keeping to the track that led to my goal. I wanted desperately to camp for the night, but perceived very well that if I dismounted I should never succeed in getting back into the saddle. I came to the place where the track divided into two or more, and I could only hope that the one we took was the right one. Dawn came, but still Hao did not slacken his gallop. The sun rose and its rays fell on the pounding, sweat-dripping horse. The sweat was running off me, and when I pushed my hat to the back of my head, it flew off, but I dared not stop to pick it up. But what the exertions of the wild journey had not been able to bring about the sun accomplished as it rose higher and higher in the sky. Hao several times slowed down to a canter, and at length I succeeded in pulling him up at a shady spot where there was rich grass. The exhausted animal gorged contentedly on this fodder, but I myself dared not get out of the saddle," the weary traveller wrote.

Sweating and dusty, Haslund and Hao finally arrived at the little log-house at the southern point of the Russian postal service.

"The first thing I asked the young Russian postmaster to do was to stamp a blank sheet of paper with the station postmark and the date and hour of my arrival. With this paper as evidence, I could prove I had ridden the eighty-two miles in fourteen hours."

Eighty-two miles, non-stop, on an unbroken stallion?

With such a mounted feat in mind, one can't help but wonder why the most formidable equestrian army in the 20th century chose instead to emulate the practices preached by Baucher.

Hitler's Horses

Though Adolf Hitler was only in power for a brief time, Germany was at war for six of those years. While many of the Führer's personal quirks are well known, records from his personal physician reveal that Hitler was afraid of horses. How ironic then that the Nazi despot fielded the largest mounted army in modern history, dispatched his mistress to glorify the temple of dressage and sponsored the most successful Olympic equestrian team in history.

Despite its legendary blitzkrieg, Hitler's German army suffered from a series of mechanical and cultural deficiencies which made its war effort equine dependent. Unlike the United States, where mass-produced inexpensive automobiles had encouraged the common man to become a driver, Germany had few drivers, and in stark contrast, a much smaller motor pool. These twin facts forced the Nazis to incorporate an enormous number of horses into their maniacal war machine.

Starting in 1939 with an estimated 855,000 German horses, the Nazis eagerly added approximately an additional 435,000 horses captured from Holland, Belgium, France, Poland, Yugoslavia and the Soviet Union. Another levy in the occupied countries brought in 1,450,000 more horses. Plus the Germans purchased 10,000 high quality animals from neutral countries. Thus the tyrant who unleashed Stuka dive bombers on Spain, sent his Tiger tanks roaring into France and hammered England with V1 rockets, kept his army on the move thanks to an estimated 2,750,000 horses and mules. This included using horses to reposition Luftwaffe planes on the airfield, to transport petrol to the Wehrmacht, to assist in removing corpses from the concentration camps and to maintain a ferocious cavalry.

Though the modern dressage world is keen to forget it, the pinnacle of this massive Nazi equestrian movement culminated in Vienna at the Spanish Riding School.

Originated in 1580 under the rule of Austrian Emperor Maximillian the Second, the *Spanische Reitschule* is the most famous example of a riding style that should have passed into history by the time Hitler came to power.

Milk-white Lipizzan stallions with their origins in Spain became the favoured mounts, hence the name "Spanish" riding school. In 1735 the Austrian emperor built an auditorium for the public display of these horses doing their airs above the ground. This ornate building became the Vatican of equestrian art, and while other countries moved on militarily, the Austrians maintained this riding school which revered 16th century ideals.

The horses were taught an equine ballet which included acrobatics normally never seen in the equine world. These included the *piaffe,* an in-place trot; the *levade*, where they balanced on bent haunches with their forelegs curved in mid air; the *courbette*, where they leaped from the *levade* position and finally, the *capriole*, a tremendous leap from the standstill with the forelegs curving inwards and the hind legs straight out.

Austria was annexed in 1936, only four years after Hitler came to power. Shortly after this invasion, the Nazis drafted the Lipizzaner stallions into their equestrian war machine by placing the Spanish Riding School under the direct command of the German Wehrmacht. When the current director, Count van der Straten, declined to cooperate with the Nazis, he was replaced by a political appointee, Alois Podhajsky. Other riders and staff were also dismissed, with the remaining Austrians being integrated into the German cavalry.

Given Hitler's love of dramatic display, the legendary riding academy provided him with a perfect theatre wherein he draped swastika-covered flags inside the school. Eva Braun, the Fuhrer's mistress, attended a performance to mark the Lippizan's forcible conversion into equine Nazis.

But it wasn't all high-jinks and high jumps in Vienna, as the Third Reich used the dressage school as a training ground for their most promising cavalry officers. One of the Germans who enjoyed such a perk was Georg Wahl, a Wehrmacht officer personally chosen by Alois Podhajsky. After the war both former German army officers remained involved with the School. Wahl became Chief Rider, while Podhajsky gained worldwide fame, largely thanks to an inaccurate Disney movie which white-washed his activities with the Nazi high command.

Though Vienna's ceremonial equitation was designed to portray the rider in an aura of dynamic glory, many horsemen instead considered the Spanish Riding School to be a purgatory for horses. Plus, numerous scholars have denounced the institution's training methods as being cruel and unnatural.

For example, in the mid-1970s the English equestrian historian, Anthony Dent, derided Vienna as being the home of "decorative riding" and said the goals of the school were utterly contrary to the horse's nature.

So why was the horse-hating Hitler so keen on promoting this contrived riding style?

Because it helped strengthen his obsession with proving the athletic prowess of his mythical Aryan master race.

Sportive Nationalism

As George Orwell warned, "Sport is war without weapons."

No one knew this better than Joseph Goebbels, the Minister of Propaganda for the Third Reich.

"German sport has only one task: to strengthen the character of the German people, imbuing it with the fighting spirit and steadfast camaraderie necessary in the struggle for its existence," Goebbels told the world prior to the 1936 Olympics held in Berlin.

By only allowing members of the so-called Aryan race to compete for Germany, Hitler's original goal was to use the international sporting event to promote his poisonous doctrine of racial supremacy. Additionally, he fielded the most successful, albeit controversial, equestrian team in the history of the Olympics.

The trouble began on the cross-country course where contestants from the other eighteen competing nations fell while trying to jump a fence which had a landing much deeper than anticipated. Strangely enough, every German rider landed successfully, suggesting that the host team knew the true condition of the obstacle and intentionally withheld this information from the other challengers.

Regardless, Hitler was delighted, as for the first and only time in Olympic history one nation, Germany, managed to capture all six equestrian gold medals in every event. They also carted home an individual silver medal in dressage.

Thus, when the Olympic flame was extinguished, the Germans had amassed 89 medals, including 33 gold. More importantly in terms of today's equestrian world, the triumph of Hitler's sportive nationalism helped establish the strong Germanic tradition of winning at all costs which now dominants modern dressage competitions.

Cruel Results

Back in 1913 America's first mass-market magazine advised its readers that, "the horse has become unprofitable. He is too costly to buy and too costly to keep."

Despite the advent of the motor age, the horse remains a constant reminder of nature to millions of urbanites forced to live in an artificial environment, with a minority keeping horses as companion animals, pets or for hobby riding.

Unfortunately innumerable horses are callously bred, brutally used and casually destroyed in the developed world because of the harsh conditions forced upon them by mankind's eagerness to compete in various types of mounted contests.

Though it likes to disguise its sordid aims under high-sounding nicknames, the four corners of the modern shrine dedicated to equestrian rivalry are money, ego, nationalism and competition. This theology encourages the use of domination and aggression to exploit the horse's athletic abilities. Additionally, thanks to corporate avarice, the horse has been denigrated into a prestige item which confers social status but makes the owner susceptible to numerous marketing ploys.

Thus, modern equestrian competition is a lifestyle game based upon the concept that for you to win, others must lose. This translates into a negative experience for the majority of competitors who invariably deal with public humiliation and personal disappointment. Paradoxically, while a silver trophy or blue ribbon may confirm someone is a winner, they do not prove he is a horseman.

Nowhere is this more evident than in modern dressage.

In his book, *Riding Towards the Light*, the dressage master Paul Belasik wrote that all dressage riders should have a complete disdain for force. According to this respected American author, the point of the mounted exercises was to transform dressage's "roots of violence, subjugation and war" and replace them with a "harmony with nature."

A worthy ambition. Yet David Mitchell, a reporter for the Guardian newspaper in Britain, expressed his perplexity and concern when he observed an Olympic dressage event in 2008.

"I've just been watching coverage of the Olympic dressage and I must say I'm absolutely baffled. In case you haven't seen it, let me explain what happens: people dressed in a sort of funereal version of fox-hunting gear take it in turns to go into a large sandy arena riding horses that seem to have been driven mad. The horses behave like the deranged dancing bears in those charity adverts, doing weird fidgety fastidious things that clearly aren't natural to them:

they hop from foot to foot, they walk on the spot, they stand still for a bit, quivering, before turning round in awkward timorous circles and walking diagonally across the arena. Quite what treatment these creatures have been put through to get them to be this odd I dread to think," the bewildered reporter wrote.

Mitchell's concerns and suspicions are well founded.

Deriding what he termed the "din of ambition" which infects modern dressage, author Belasik warned that if the exercises are used incorrectly they possess the potential to destroy the horse.

Perhaps Belasik was thinking about Baucher when he issued that admonition, as one of the French riding master's techniques involved severely bending the horse's neck towards its chest. This harsh and uncomfortable exercise, now known as hyperflexion or rollkur, is at the heart of an international animal cruelty controversy wherein the horse's pain is ignored in favour of Olympic gold medals.

The notorious rollkur technique caused an outrage when a Swedish Olympian, Patrik Kittel, was filmed riding his horse while dragging the animal's nose so low it nearly touched its chest. The public was even more shocked to see the horse's tongue, which had turned blue from lack of circulation, hanging out of one side of his mouth. In the video, Kittel halted the horse, leaned forward, adjusted the horse's tongue and then casually continued his ride.

It is commonly believed that so long as the horse is not being physically abused to gratify man's ego, then the horse's participation in athletic events can and should continue. However, we have a right to ask ourselves how Baucher's cruel training method crept into modern dressage?

It began in the 1980s when two German dressage competitors won Olympic gold medals aboard horses allegedly schooled using the harsh method!

This is why when British journalist, David Mitchell, sat down to write his layman's impression of the Olympic dressage competition he concluded with this query.

"…the fact that brilliance and incompetence are indistinguishable to all but the dressage cognoscenti does not speak well of the sport…… I'm perfectly willing to admit that it must be very difficult to make horses do that, but what's the point… what is the satisfaction in this tuneless dance, this effortful yet unentertaining capering about?" Mitchell asked.

Mitchell might have also asked, if whale bone corsets have lost their appeal, why do we continue to embrace a European riding style which flourished during the age of Mozart? Why do we ignore the minuet but still embrace the *capriole*? Is dressage about equestrian freedom or equine repression? If it is a defacement practised on the horse against its true nature on account of man's selfishness, then why is it still being practised? And how does the Euro-centric concept, that to be a good horseman a person should fit a certain set of mounted criteria, affect a Long Rider?

Protecting the Past

"At every crossway in the road that leads to the future, tradition has placed, against each of us, ten thousand men to guard the past," wrote Maurice Maeterlinck, the Belgian horse lover and Nobel Laureate author.

Though the equestrian world is notoriously averse to change, it needs to transform with the pattern of the times. Our collective philosophy should not be static. However, the answers we seek may lie where we least expect them.

I fear that too many of today's equestrian leaders assume they are going to find elucidation in the only place they know where to look, which is via the established equine practices of the past few centuries. They believe that the answers to 21st century problems lie in renewing an allegiance to European traditions based on commerce, competition, nationalism and social hierarchy.

There are instead unexpected lessons to be learned when riders venture out of doors. Not only do they develop their courage, but also, more importantly, they realize that riding isn't merely about detail, it is about individual accomplishment. Regardless of whether it is a minor weekend trail ride or a major Guild-endorsed equestrian journey, this new era of riders are learning that it isn't "Thou Must" but rather "This Is."

The time has come to free the horse and rider from the artificial restrictions imposed upon it by a long-dead minority of Europeans. It is time to issue a bold challenge which states that the equestrian values as practised by nomadic society offer more sense of personal liberation for horse and rider than those activities and values served up by the likes of Baucher!

History proves that the Mongols were brilliant natural horsemen. But what made them fantastic riders? Not the fact that they ever urged their hardy horses to perform a perfect ballet like some porcelain Lipizzaner. These were horsemen who rode to live. It was the MILES they rode that gave them supple hands, a tight seat, and a deep emotional bond with their mounts

We are left to ask ourselves, if the airs above the ground weren't of any actual military value, now or then, why is the myth of their military invincibility still being taught to naïve Europeans and eager North Americans? Who continues to embrace and promote this equestrian superstition?

Because the European loyalty to a renaissance equestrian tradition is symptomatic of a reactionary flight from modernity, allow me to float an idea for your consideration.

In his book, *The Centaur Legacy*, the Danish equestrian philosopher, Bjarke Rink, proposes that bio-mechanics and history prove that the act of riding a horse creates a finer, faster, superior human being. Therefore, if riding improves humanity, then who had a more beneficial effect on collective history, the Mongol horsemen or the European dressage masters?

Put another way, if Baucher taught the nobility, then Genghis Khan taught everyone else. So who, we must ask ourselves, rates as the greater horseman: the Mongol who changed the history of the world from the saddle or the Frenchman who taught a prince how to make his horse stand on its hind legs?

Should we not be asking ourselves, as equestrian scholars, why is a riding style which suffered a massive military defeat, continues to inflict immense pain on the horse and was designed to serve a tiny aristocratic nobility, persistently revered to this day? What did Genghis ask the horse to do? Only what came naturally, as man and horse were joined by mutual need and desire.

Thus, despite what that tyrant known as "custom" has long dictated, the time has come to stop deferring to ritual riding and look for truth where it began, with the original equestrian travellers of long ago.

A Nomadic Alternative

In 1993 the movie, *Free Willy*, helped draw the world's attention to the plight of orca whales forced to exist in small aquariums so as to provide entertainment for urbanized humans and a financial incentive for their money-hungry captors.

Considered one of the most culturally influential children's movies ever made, one viewer summed up its lasting appeal when he wrote, "We are so desensitised towards cruelty to animals that we are practically oblivious to their plight. When we go to water parks and see captive whales performing tricks we laugh and cheer and go back to our freedom and think nothing of the life that was destroyed when that beautiful beast was taken from its habitat. The movie demonstrates that we should not imprison these or any other wild animals."

Free Willy was not only a resounding financial success; it changed the views of modern society. So why isn't Hollywood racing to make a film about someone trying to rescue a Lipizzan stallion from the Spanish Riding School? If keeping a whale captive and forcing it to jump into the air is unethical, then why doesn't the same rule apply to Vienna's "dancing" white stallions?

Sadly, as the Spanish Riding School demonstrates, the majority of equestrian activity today is aimed at forcing the horse to do something which it would not normally choose to do in a natural setting, i.e. leaping over unnaturally high and life-threatening obstacles in a cross-country competition, walking like a stiff-legged zombie in a dressage ring, sliding to a screeching halt in a reining contest after first being spurred into a gallop, bucking in a rodeo after a strap has been tightened around its genitals, racing around a track while being whipped by a jockey or bounding into the air so as to perform *haute école*.

Moreover, in an age when a top level dressage horse can routinely cost more than $50,000 how many children can aspire to become riders? Contrast that to what a Long Rider needs to undertake a life changing equestrian journey: personal bravery and a trusting horse. That is a type of riding that even in these hard times is within the reach of all. It represents the alternative nomadic narrative which has been shunned or suppressed for too long.

The phenomenal growth of the Long Riders' Guild demonstrates that instead of focusing on mistakes and punishments, many human beings still aspire to fulfil a deep-seated longing for personal migration.

Inspire them. Teach them. Guide them. Point them in the right direction – and they will mount up and not look back at the villages they are leaving behind. That is the legacy which has lain fallow in our collective sub-consciousness for many generations, the knowledge that in this new century we need to have the courage to liberate the horse from the oppressions of the show ring, otherwise we can never liberate ourselves.

Yet this is nothing new. It is the ancient challenge that has washed across the book of human endeavour for ages. Here on one page can be found the Chinese hiding behind their "Great Wall" in a fruitless attempt to keep the rootless Mongols from rushing in and altering "imperial" history. This struggle has been called many things, but in its basic form it is the ongoing battle between sedentary and nomadic instincts. Yet nomad equitation is devoid today of its earlier manifestations of militarism. The need to acquire territory, slaves and cultural dominance has been tossed out of the saddle bags of history. What is left is a growing rejection of intensive commercialism in favour of individual freedom.

What does 6,000 years of mounted exploration do to human beings in general? Why do we still yearn for it? What have we lost? Where are the answers? Not in the mall, with its crowds of easily-ruled pedestrian consumers; nor in the show ring with its endless repetition of an equestrian treadmill.

Equestrian sport is aimed at overcoming false obstacles. Yet equestrian travel is not a game. It encompasses the ancient enterprise of survival wherein the only true obstacle to overcome is fear. Equestrian sport is about loyalty to a rigidly defined reality. Equestrian travel instead requires each rider to make use of their own skills, to develop a particular strategy for their journey and to strive for personal excellence. It encourages migration, change, tolerance, cultural exchange, human progress and an enriched life. The result is a more emotionally mature, generous, kind, patient and sympathetic horse-human. In a word; a Long Rider. And by definition, every Long Rider is a winner.

Mounted Messengers

James Fillis, the English dressage master, is credited with teaching his horses to canter on three legs and to canter backward.

When Long Riders gather they discuss surviving dangers, not what circus tricks their horses can do. This is because there are no tales of great travellers who were inept horsemen. History repeatedly proves that the skilful Long Rider isn't a horseman in the same sense as the ceremonial rider, James Fillis, claimed to be.

For example DC Vision and Tim Cope didn't know the difference between a crupper and a courbette before they set off. Yet they rode 32,000 kilometres (20,000 miles) between them and brought their horses in safely and in perfect health. Likewise, Gordon Naysmith rode 20,000 kilometres (12,000 miles) from South Africa to Austria, Vladimir Fissenko rode 30,500 kilometres (19,000 miles) from Tierra del Fuego to Alaska and Otto Schwarz rode 48,000 kilometres (30,000 miles) on five continents.

Though these three extraordinary horse-humans collectively rode more than 95,000 kilometres (60,000 miles), what can explain this indifference to technique in their world and the near-obsession with it in the other? Is it only common mythology which states that equestrian travel doesn't produce excellent horsemen when you have examples such as these? What these extraordinary Long Riders demonstrate is that true horsemanship isn't about style. It isn't about beating your neighbour. It's about competing with yourself and treating your horse with respect.

And while you're thinking about that, I must mention that this is not, as some people would love to believe, a group of rough and tumble cowboys who can't distinguish a *piaffe* from a pastry! For example, before he became the 20th century's most distinguished equestrian traveller, Captain Otto Schwarz competed at the Olympic level for the Swiss dressage team.

What these examples prove is that every generation bears a few Long Riders who slash away the chains of predictability and ride out into the world in search of the unknown, aboard horses fair and tall, freed from the restraints of gravity and the village. For equestrian travel offers an alternative to the competition-based, ego-dominated, sports-oriented horse world that exists today. Being a Long Rider is not about winning a ribbon in the ring. It is about making a lasting mark in your own life.

It is also about the eternal unification, and subsequent emotional influence, which the horse has on the rider. Two modern Long Riders exemplify this affect.

Ballet teachers don't normally spring to mind when you think of mounted heroines but that's what Bernice Ende did before her love of equestrian travel led her to set off in search of adventure and personal discovery. The willowy dancer is currently on her eighth extended journey and is nearing the 40,000 kilometre (25,000 miles) mark under her saddle.

And who helped open the door to these challenges? An eight-year-old Thoroughbred mare named, Honor, who didn't have a friend in the world. In fact, because the irascible former race horse had been passed from one owner to another, Honor was "deemed good for nothing but dog food." Luckily, Bernice saw something special in the grey mare.

By purchasing Honor and emotionally rehabilitating her Bernice gave the horse a second chance in life. Not only did the two became inseparable, thanks to Bernice's kindness and Honor's courage, they enriched the lives of thousands of people they met along the way.

However, Honor was born lucky compared to Misty.

When retired policeman Howard Wooldridge came across the Pinto mare, she had been ruthlessly run through the competitive reining world. Not only had Misty been physically exploited, the unfortunate mare had also lost her right eye after being kicked by another horse. Ugly, unwanted, and doomed, Misty was a horse with a one way ticket to an early demise when Howard made the rash decision to purchase her.

Then, despite Howard's lack of expertise and Misty's physical limitations, this unlikely duo set off to ride "ocean to ocean." Their 3,000 mile journey took them from the Atlantic to the Pacific, during which time they both recovered from the emotional afflictions which had been tormenting them.

When we consider Honor and Misty, their glory resides not in how they looked but in what they accomplished. Far more vital than the miles they conquered is the fact that these two damaged horses had managed to mend the souls of their Long Riders.

It is because of horses like these that Long Riders do not care about man-made miles or setting records, for horses do not concern themselves with such silly things. Like their mounted ancestors, intrepid souls such as Bernice and Howard swing into the saddle in a solitary movement of individual bravery. Theirs is not an obsession with form. It is instead a denial of death and a rejection of frailty. No one handed them the courage to change their own destinies or granted them the valour to define the perimeter of their lives.

These Long Riders shine like stars from their saddles because they know that we don't change the horse. Horses like Misty and Honor change us.

Inner and Outer Horsemanship

As I believe this chapter demonstrates, history has provided us with two types of riders. Those that hold up a picture and say, "Look at me," and those that hold up a mirror and say, "Look at you."

The world of competition and ceremonial riding is populated with masters and acolytes, all eager to participate in and endorse a rigid ranking system. Despite talk about "riding towards the light," the majority of these people focus on the body to the exclusion of the spirit.

There is nothing wrong with the concept of training. In fact, it is critically important that a Long Rider's road horse be calm, sensible, and reliable because, unlike a ring rider who is motivated by sport, a Long Rider's life is imperilled if his horse is poorly schooled. The danger lies in allowing technique to become so dominant, so restrictive, that the beauty of the equestrian experience is shattered by the rider's egotistical search for technical, not spiritual, perfection. Outer technique without inner guidance is a path leading nowhere.

That is why the rider must never forget the underlying grace of the horse and not denigrate its role to that of a mere machine. While technique has its place, it must not be allowed to seduce us. When it becomes a dogma we lose touch with the poetic mystery which first brought us onto the horse's back.

Long Riders know instead that the horse has no nationality. He simply answers your request because of the affection which resides in his nobler heart. The Long Rider views riding not as an art but as an indispensable accomplishment. He knows you can't have harmony in a competition, as they are mutually exclusive. He realizes that a *piaffe* is seldom remembered but a journey is never forgotten.

People who become manacled to tradition are encouraged not to acknowledge the horse's needs. They race, jump, preen, shine, show, and make him an extension of their egos. Such an animal is a slave, not a mentor. There can be no emotional equality with that type of horse. What you have instead are dependent horses, which are used for a few hours a week – if they're lucky.

The road horse invites you instead to feel, to respond, to reawaken your soul. He is concerned with riding, not rituals. He doesn't care how you ride but where you go.

The modern world also has an obsession with speed. The horse doesn't need it and I question whether we require it either. Being a Long Rider is about slowing down, not speeding up. A life-changing equestrian journey begins when you reduce your own biological clock down to the point where it fits into the harmony of the nature around you. The saddle should be a portal – not a seat in a speed boat.

That is why the Guild teaches equestrian travellers that the first goal is to slow down to the four-mile-an-hour pace of the road horse. Observation begins when you watch the road slide by – one small pebble at a time.

Riding Out is Riding In.

Summary

A coincidence occurred as I was writing this chapter. The Canadian Long Rider Bonnie Folkins emailed to say she had just completed her second expedition, a 1,600 kilometre (1,000 mile) exploration of Kazakhstan. It was while riding across the heart of the ancient Equestrian Equator that the modern rider encountered our nomadic mounted ancestor.

"We climbed even higher and rode along the flat top of a mountain with a scraggly expanse. I kept thinking there had to be a valley ahead or something on the other side - but there was never another side. Everywhere we looked there was only flatness. We were in fact riding on a gradual rise of land and the high altitude made me anxious. I took full responsibility for my restlessness knowing I had let them talk me into taking that route. But at that vast place we saw something so special and unexpected it made the entire trip worthwhile. It was the sight of a young shepherd galloping bareback. We tried to catch up with him over a terrain filled with stones and furrows and the wind blew so hard that when we tried to call him our voices would not carry. He rode like a feather and his horse moved like an animation. The shaggy-haired boy in his ragged deel let his arms fall loosely at his sides and his body seemed buoyant as they bounced along effortlessly - like one together - and in absolute harmony. It was as if they were dancing. When we finally caught up, he told us he was fifteen and the horse was three. Teasingly we asked if we could buy his horse, to which he answered, "I love my horse, I *really* love my horse. I will *never* sell my horse!" I was mesmerized and ever since that day I have dreamt about trying to go back to that place to find him - just to watch him ride," Bonnie wrote.

Thus in an ironic twist, as this chapter was being penned, the modern Long Rider had accidentally witnessed the essence of equestrian freedom which we have been investigating.

Yet when the chain of memory is broken, falsehood can masquerade as truth.

That is why the horse world today is largely geared to the preservation of an artificial equitation based on out-dated Eurocentric equestrian exercises that have no moral bearing on the good of either specie. As mankind travels into outer space, horses will be as irrelevant as a soufflé dish unless they revive their traditional roles as aids to exploration. This is the job nature designed them for. Thus, it's time to shift the equestrian emphasis away from collective competition and focus instead on individual accomplishment.

Long Riders represent a fundamental shift in how we view and define the human-equine interaction. Instead of relying on our brains to outsmart their muscles, we have opened our hearts to an inter-species understanding that was previously denied us. We Long Riders are not conquering the horse, not degrading the horse, not marginalizing the horse. We Long Riders are tossing aside our previous convictions, forgetting our national origins, ignoring our mother tongues, reaching deep inside ourselves to speak a new language - the language of the horse, the language of peace, the language of wanting and desire and unfulfilled longing and the ache of loneliness that only our horses and a never ending horizon can salve.

Perhaps the best-selling author and North American Long Rider Doug Preston summed up the basic, undeniable difference between the European ring rider and the far-roaming Central Asian horseman who forever changed equestrian history.

"Over thousands of years, human beings and horses developed a profound relationship, one that has probably become embedded in our very genes. Our ancestors used horses for travel, for war, for peace, for trade, for work, and for play. But of all the uses humans have put horses to, the greatest and wisest has been for exploration and discovery. From Marco Polo to Coronado and beyond, horses were almost always part of the great human adventure of exploration and long distance travel," Doug wrote.

In the early 1960s Lt. Col. C.R.G. Hope, editor of *Light Horse* magazine, warned, "The riders of tomorrow need something else."

Tomorrow has arrived and that something else is equestrian travel.

An example of prestige transport and military fantasy was provided in 1662 when Prince Philippe, the Duke of Orleans, attended a royal carousel given by his elder brother, King Louis XIV of France. In his regal finery, the European aristocrat was pretending to be the Shah of Persia.

In contrast, the hard-riding Mongol queen Mandhuhai led her nomad warriors to victory after victory, charging into battle even while pregnant. Her unparalleled triumphs prompted the Chinese into the most frenzied period of wall building in that nation's history.

Though he is still revered in the modern dressage world, the French riding master, François Baucher, was unable to deliver a letter to a nearby Parisian post office, pleading that his horse needed three months of extensive training before it could cope with going outside.

Yet when Henning Haslund wanted to pick up his mail, he galloped eighty-two miles non-stop across Mongolia on his unbroken stallion.

SPANISCHE HOFREITSCHULE
WIEN

Though the Spanish Riding School is anxious for the public to forget it, this institution was a highly regarded part of the Nazis' brutal equestrian war machine.

Likewise, Adolf Hitler's greed for Olympic gold medals led to the Third Reich's team winning all the equestrian events for the first and only time in history.

Man's ego then. Lashing a Lipizzaner stallion at the Spanish Riding School, so as to force it to learn how to do one of the "airs above the ground" invented in the 16th century.

Man's ego now. Using the infamous rollkur training method to force a horse's head into its chest, a technique attributed to François Baucher and now favoured by the Germanic dominated dressage world.

Though Thoroughbred mare, Honor, had been deemed worthless, she dramatically enriched Long Rider Bernice Ende's life; proof positive that such a horse takes its rider on a spiritual, as well as a physical, journey, the impact of which will never be forgotten.

Nor did it matter that Misty, the one-eyed Pinto, was facing a bleak future when she was rescued by Long Rider Howard Wooldridge. Unlike the famous stallions of Vienna, this humble mare mended the soul of her loving rider.

Chapter 18
Long Rider Horsemanship
Part Two - The Practice

Aimé's Silence

Aimé Tschiffely was the most influential equestrian traveller of the 20th century. He wrote three classic books about his equestrian journeys. Yet what this intensely private man never revealed was any obsession with technique, a topic which ring-riders focus on today. This is because Long Riders like Aimé have always had their true roots in the worlds of travel and exploration, not in the competitive equestrian scene.

Thus, it would be presumptuous in the extreme if I attempted to dictate the manner in which you should ride, for I can't and won't tell you exactly how to do so. I can only make gentle suggestions, based on many years in the saddle, many travels, many experiences of other equestrian cultures and many books. What we can also do is use the accumulated wisdom of other Long Riders so as to arrive at a harmonious set of principles which keep you and your road horse safe, despite all of the various hazards awaiting the two of you.

The Roots of Riding

Though the arbitrators of equestrian rank have established a codified practice of pretence, riding is no longer a part of workaday life. Thus a comparison of equestrian performances, past and present, is not an absolutely feasible task, for it could only be valid if based on identical conditions. Yet regardless of his departure point, the Long Rider undergoes a different type of contest, one which demands a daily trial of strength, requires constant attention in the face of danger and calls for superb dexterity in the saddle.

The first thing then is to appreciate the difference between riding and horsemanship. Many people regard the terms as synonymous. Yet a linguistic investigation of the two words reveals a distinction.

The word "ride" derives from the Anglo-Saxon word "rad" (the same root as road), meaning "to be conveyed on a smooth place." In this way a ship "rides" at anchor in a roadstead; and when one "rides a horse," strictly speaking, "one is a rider conveyed by a horse on the smoothed way." In sharp contrast, "horseman" is a composite word, meaning "man-*and*-horse together making one whole."

Accordingly, the goal of Long Rider horsemanship is to achieve a state wherein two separate biological entities merge into a single harmonious Centaur, one representing the horse's strength and the human's intelligence.

Riding and Horsemanship

While it is comparatively easy to write about that type of riding, it requires patience and practice to obtain the necessary skill needed to maintain the tempo of travel.

To begin with, remember that none of the riders linked to the world's greatest equestrian cultures, i.e. the Hungarian Csikos, American Cowboy, Russian Cossack, Mongol Nomad, Argentine Gaucho, Comanche Indian or Australian Wrangler were taught to ride or believed riding was an art. Their riding was natural, with a perfection of grace rarely seen among civilized ring-riders. That is why the judicious Long Rider author and frontiersman, Roger Pocock, advised equestrian travellers to "forget everything learnt in riding schools and be comfortable in the saddle."

Pocock knew what he was talking about because after retiring as a Canadian Mounted Policeman, he made the only solo journey along the length of the notorious Outlaw Trail. Not only did this hidden trail take him from Canada to Mexico, it required Pocock to ride through some of the most hostile horse country on the North American continent. The highlight of this astonishing journey occurred when Pocock met Butch Cassidy at his Hole-In-The-Wall hideout. Here Pocock learned that in order to elude pursuit after a bank or train robbery, the legendary outlaw leader had constructed a secret equestrian "underground railroad." This system allowed Cassidy and his followers to gallop across the Old West in record time. Racing from one state to another, they would arrive at a prearranged hidden band of horses, quickly change their saddles to a fresh mount and then continue their mad dash along the most dangerous trails imaginable so as to out-distance their confused and weary pursuers.

Cassidy not only routinely survived scores of mounted dangers, he proved to Pocock that riding is a habit, not an art form, and that people who became obsessed about technique were mere shadows of the authenticity which occurs naturally among the earth's wild riders. The light-weight English saddle, for example, was designed to allow a rider to be thrown free when a horse fell while fox hunting or jumping, while in contrast desperado riders like Cassidy were required to sustain their seat at all times – or lose their lives.

Therefore, it is not to be expected that Long Riders be perfect riding masters, nor that their road horses should perform *haute école*. What is required is that every Long Rider should have his horse under thorough control at all times and be able to ride him with confidence and pleasure.

Yet how do we achieve this objective?

Our First Goal - Safe Riding

Before we deal with the specifics of how we realize our goal, let us place foremost in our minds the primary purpose of Long Rider horsemanship, namely accident-free riding.

It may surprise you to learn that international studies confirm horseback riding is more statistically dangerous than motorcycle riding. With an estimated thirty million people riding horses annually in the United States alone, the rise in accidents is directly linked to the growth of equestrian sporting events.

While all riders face an inherent risk, because the horse is emotionally unpredictable, sports riders place themselves in even greater jeopardy. When they climb into the saddle their action not only places their heads approximately nine feet off the ground, they routinely gallop and jump at unrestrained speeds of up to forty miles per hour. The result is that during the course of their riding careers, approximately one in five of these riders will suffer a serious injury. These will usually be severe head and neck trauma, such as occurred to the actor, Christopher Reeve, or fractures to the upper extremities.

Most of these grim injuries are linked to falling or being bucked off a horse, with the majority of equestrian injuries occurring to white females and the largest number of accidents taking place either at a recreational sporting facility or at home.

A major distinction between accident-prone sporting events and equestrian travel is that the latter is largely calamity free, regardless of the enormous mileage involved. This is because Long Rider horsemanship minimizes the risk of the horse shying and is aimed instead at preventing horse and rider from falling. Unlike break-neck show jumping, the objective of Long Rider horsemanship is to safely traverse any type of terrain, thereby overcoming all obstacles with the minimum amount of fatigue to horse and human.

We should remember that the horse too longs for safety. Unhappily, in their eagerness for another trophy, far too many sports riders become addicted to the thrill of winning, all the while overlooking the pain being inflicted upon their mounts. Such events result in a treasure-trove of fees for veterinarians brought in to rescue and remedy injured equines.

Thus, our first goal should be to realize that a safe ride is the most pleasant experience for horse and human.

Riding the Road Horse

A hundred years ago the average equestrian traveller had been raised around horses and possessed a strong natural sense of riding, whereas today's citizen usually resides in an urban environment, may be afraid of the horse and lacks the muscles and balance required to ride well.

Therefore an equestrian traveller should realize that the initial objective in Long Rider horsemanship is not the ability to sit any horse under all conditions. This book isn't intended for horse tamers and buck jumpers. Nor should a Long Rider be wondering how to hurl himself over the highest jump. A Long Rider's first lesson with the horse is the constant need for patience and understanding, as the best-natured and tamest horse in the world can be ruined in minutes by a brutal rider.

Luckily, nearly everyone can become a competent rider. The purpose of our study is to turn out a skilful Long Rider who can sit skin-tight at all gaits, through forest dense as a hair brush, down hills, across streams, through rough country. A person who can thus control the entire horse, from the head to the hindquarters, will feel confident enough to cross tricky bridges, make their way through heavy traffic, swim a river or avoid dangers.

Whereas dressage riders rely on a teacher to help them solve a riddle in the ring, Long Riders confront challenges alone. This requires them to find answers on the spot, all the while remaining calm in the saddle.

So, what then are we seeking?

To sit a horse equally well though all his paces.

To control his impatience fearlessly, yet soothingly.

To manage him at speed with a firm, light, steady hand.

To keep our seat, while preserving our balance with ease.

To have the animal entirely at our command, as if both were infused with a common intelligence.

These are the essential attributes.

As a pastime pursued for its own sake, equestrian travel leaves the ring far behind. For travel provides you with hard riding and open air, the glorious sweep of an unknown country, and the sharp intoxicating spice of adventure, without which a ride will ever afterward seem to you like a loveless marriage.

The Seat

No Long Rider in history knew more about equestrian travel and classical dressage than Captain Otto Schwarz. Before the Second World War, Otto was preparing to represent Switzerland in the 1940 Olympics. When the Nazis threatened to invade his homeland, Otto joined the Swiss cavalry and spent the duration of the conflict leading cavalry patrols through the Alps. After the war, Otto became the most widely-travelled Long Rider in the 20th century, racking up nearly 50,000 kilometres on five continents.

Otto combined the best of East and West, in that he rode with the grace so revered by the European dressage world, all the while his journeys required him to routinely ride half-wild mounts in distant countries. Yet this Olympic rider turned explorer had realized that though his personal journey had started under the stern eye of a European dressage master, that isn't what modern Long Riders need do.

"It's true that you will recognize the true rider by his seat in the saddle. Yet riding in the dressage ring is not a necessary preparation for the Long Rider because one can, in spite of many surprised faces, learn to sit with ease without going round and around in circles. That is why many Long Riders who master riding are far superior to the four-corner riders, particularly in terms of relating to the comrade-horse," Otto wrote in his classic book, *Reisen mit dem Pferd*.

But what fundamental principles are involved when we place our bodies in the saddle and above that of the horse?

Maintaining your balance in the saddle provides you with the highest degree of stability and safety.

Your body is in equilibrium in the saddle when the various forces acting upon it balance one another. The responsive and relaxed sitting gained from being evenly balanced in the saddle becomes the foundation for every accomplishment gained by you and your horse. But the horse's forward movement constantly destabilizes your centre of gravity in one direction or another, thereby placing you in continual peril. This problem becomes critically important during fast paces, when your body is pushed forward by the tremendous impulsion generated by the horse's hind quarters. That is when your centre of gravity is most often displaced and you face the greatest danger. It is this non-stop disturbance of your equilibrium which is thereby in constant need of being restored. Thus when we sit on the horse we can not only feel his different movements through our seat, it is through the saddle that we establish a primary contact and control with the horse. The ultimate expression of this contact is when the Long Rider sits with attentive confidence while the horse is moving freely. And it is through the seat that we attempt to achieve the mutually balanced horse and human.

So, you must be asking yourself, how does the Long Rider achieve this fantastic sense of balance?

You should sit relaxed, completely erect and perfectly square in the deepest part of the saddle.

Your body's weight should be placed over the exact centre of the saddle, which also places you directly above the centre of the horse's spine, which is located at the 16th vertebra.

Your head should be held in a naturally straight position, without sticking your chin out.

Your eyes should be looking over the horse's ears at the horizon.

Your shoulders should be completely relaxed and squared, as tension in the shoulders creates stiffness in the upper body, neck, arms and the lower back.

Your upper arm should rest comfortably against your body.

Your elbows should be allowed to be close to your body, without touching it.

Your lower arm should be relaxed.

Your wrists should be supple.

Your hands should be carried vertically, so that the thumb is the highest point.

Your upper leg should be in continual contact with the saddle.

Your knees should be pressed gently but firmly against the horse.

Your lower leg should hang softly and provide an essential contact with the horse.

Your feet should be parallel to the ground.

Your stirrups should be adjusted so that your leg is not quite straight, with the ball of your foot able to take your weight.

It is the duty of every Long Rider to continually correct your position in the saddle. The most essential point is that you always remain sitting straight up in the saddle and never lean your weight back against the cantle. Such an action places enormous pressure on the horse's kidneys and causes severe saddle sores.

Additionally, you should realize that the seat can be used as a weapon against your horse.

This is because the weight of the rider, pressed down aggressively against the horse's back, can impose a harmful effect and create great tension in the horse.

Long Rider Jeremy James warned, "Poor riders rely on the bit and spur. With their legs they push the horse on and with their hands they pull him back. They treat the horse as a mechanical contraption."

When you ride, you should always be looking for ways to conserve your horse's strength. An erect position in the saddle transforms you into a Long Rider, not a slouching passenger who bounces in the saddle. Though it takes time and practice to obtain a secure seat, the balance so essential to your safety is connected to this part of your equestrian quest. Thus every moment spent in practice, before you depart and during your journey, will help you to harmonize with your horse.

The Breathing

A Long Rider's actions in the saddle can also be influenced by his breathing.

Short, choppy breathing toughens your position in the saddle and transmits the wrong signal to the horse. By breathing deeply, the air entering your lungs compresses your organs, which in turn lowers your centre of gravity. Calm, steady breathing also forces us to sit up straight in the saddle. While these physical benefits are desirable, the tranquil breathing of the Long Rider can result in the horse and rider quietly reaching a state of serene co-respiration during their travels.

The Hands and Reins

Your soft hands and flexible fingers act as the communication centre which transmits suggestions and commands along the reins to the horse. The impulses you convey through these reins reach the bit. This in turn sends signals via the sensitive portion of the horse's palate, along his nervous system and into his brain. Such a silent exchange of ideas allows you to communicate your desires and needs to the horse. This exchange of simple truths between human and horse is monumental in its implications, as this is the doorway which allow the two animals to merge into a new entity.

The reins should exert an easy control over the mouth. While maintaining a light contact with the horse's palate, they transmit a message of confidence and compliance.

Like the seat, your hands can transmit the wrong message to the horse. The reins should never feel heavy in your hands. They run like silk ribbons to the horse's mouth, while resting lightly in your fingers.

The Bit and Bridle

In this mechanized age, finding the perfect road horse is extremely difficult. That is why it is important to remember that the bit is made of iron and this valuable animal's mouth isn't made of steel. What many people fail to remember is that the bit can cause excessive pain to the horse. Thus it is exceedingly wrong to constantly pull on the bit and it is imperative that your hands must never be used to punish the horse by tugging on the bit.

The safety of the road horse depends a great deal more on the manner in which he puts his feet down, than on that in which he lifts them up. If he should start to fall the horse uses his head to maintain his balance in a manner similar to the way humans use their hands. By maintaining a constant gentle impression on the bit, the Long Rider encourages the horse to carry his head up and maintain his centre of gravity.

Yet every horse is apt to stumble and therefore comes the golden rule of riding with the bit. Never trust to your horse's sense of balance. Always maintain a light contact with his mouth via the bit. If he begins to stumble, use a gentle pull back on the bit to help the horse pull his head up, which in turns helps him regain his balance. You will thus be able to give the animal valuable assistance before he falls too much off balance.

Bear in mind that the bit must fit. This is often a problem in overseas countries. Do not use a double-bridle when travelling. Make sure that the throat lash on the bridle is adjusted so that the fingers on your hand placed edgewise can slide between it and the horse's throat. If using a curb bit, never over-tighten the chin strap.

The Gaits

The Long Rider must concern himself with three gaits, the walk, trot and canter. These paces enable the traveller to advance, turn in both directions and in an emergency, move backwards. The aim of Long Rider horsemanship is to maintain control during all three gaits.

The walk, the most important gait used by Long Riders, averages four miles per hour. The posting trot averages nine miles per hour, while the canter averages twelve miles per hour. The walk and trot are the principal gaits used by equestrian travellers.

When walking, it is better for the horse if the Long Rider dismounts and walks alongside his mount. This provides much needed rest for the horse and allows the rider to stretch his own muscles. If time is of the essence, the most constructive combination of gaits is for the Long Rider to canter a short distance, dismount and walk beside his horse, then repeat the procedure.

Many travelling horses were originally amblers, which meant that they walked at a rapid, shuffling pace which quickly outdistanced the normal rate of an average horse. But by the dawn of the 19th century the much-admired amblers had vanished from memory in Europe. At the same time, the construction of metalled roads demanded a different pace from equestrian travellers, as the new roadways were unsuitable for galloping. It was the outriders, known as postillions, who rode one of the lead horses on long-distance coaches, who developed what is now known as the posting trot. Rising to the trot provided the postillion with a tolerable means of progress. Thus, it was the introduction of these hard roads which brought about the most significant change in the face of equestrian travel, until the motorized vehicle invaded the roads at the dawning of the next century.

Stirrups

Regardless of which gait the Long Rider uses, the genius of the stirrup is that it provides the human with an artificial platform upon which he can defy gravity, maintain his centre of balance, travel at great speed, raise his eyesight ten feet above the ground and swing a weapon in both directions without fear of falling.

The Aids

In addition to his seat in the saddle, the other natural tools available to assist the Long Rider in guiding his horse are any combination of the use of his voice, hands, legs and heels.

The lower leg and heels are used to ask the horse to move forward. Spurs act as the heel's enforcers. They can be of critical assistance if, for example, you are on a busy road and a fast moving truck is bearing down on you. In an emergency such as this, you need the horse to react instantly, so as to save you both from peril. However, most Long Riders prefer not to rely on these thorns of pain, as they are seldom needed. Thus, they should only be employed by skilled riders facing extraordinary circumstances.

While a situation might arise when you need to use a switch as a temporary riding crop, most equestrian travellers do not carry any sort of riding whip.

Always remember this. The horse's original residence was on the wide open steppes. This freedom-loving animal was not designed to reside in a small stable, like a hamster confined in a cage. Therefore the horse carries in his genes an instinctive desire for freedom, as well as a need for exuberant movement. Thus strong aids are seldom needed by equestrian travellers, as they are mounted on road horses that are equally eager to journey towards an exciting horizon.

Discipline

All too often the twin concepts of fear and punishment are based on species domination, individual ego, and the corrupting power of money.

Yet, though history is replete with examples of the cruelty inflicted upon horses by humans, it is encouraging to realize that an equal number of enlightened horse-humans have agreed that the infliction of needless discipline is counter-productive.

"Punish yourself rather than hurt him, for you are more likely to deserve any blame than he is," the equestrian scholar, Blundeville, cautioned in 1609. "Because few riders can correct with discretion, I would wish him rather to use no correction at all, but only to win him by gentle means, by fair speaking, and by feeding him by hand. For truly unless there be mutual love between the rider and the horse neither can profit. Above all things, be merciful. Be generous with the way you demonstrate that you cherish him, by the voice, which should be delivered smoothly and lovingly, and then by the hand, by clapping him gently on the neck and buttock. The hope of reward, and the fear of punishment, governs the whole world, not only of men but horses too."

Before he raced to his death at the head of the "charge of the Light Brigade," the progressive Irish horseman, Captain Louis Nolan, completed a startling horse training book in 1852, which contained a similar revolutionary phrase.

"If the horse does not understand what you want, and you punish him because he has not understood you, will he then understand you better?"

Nor was this progressive ideology restricted to the West, as in his book, *The Byerley Turk*, Jeremy James documents how the grooms employed in the massive cavalry of the mighty Ottoman Sultan viewed the subject of equine discipline.

"The groom will use neither whip nor stick for fear of setting up a system of response to pain, which is an evil route to follow. He teaches the horse by encouragement and reward alone. There is no such crudity as the need to break a horse. There is only the skill to make one. If you get it right now it will always be right. All the time the groom maintains the horse's confidence and trust because this is the bedrock of the art of the horseman."

This philosophy of tolerance, Jeremy noted, is an example of how "East meets West on an equine spine."

Travel invokes an enormous sense of loyalty between horse and human. Consequently, if the Long Rider and his horse are moving freely as one, why would the equestrian traveller punish the other half? If you don't ask the horse to do anything artificial, then how can he react badly to a reasonable request? I cannot even think of any major equestrian travel author, over the course of 500 years of equestrian travel literature, who discusses the need to punish a road horse. Why? Because the road horse is advancing forward wholeheartedly and this freedom of movement produces a happy animal. Thus, by its very nature, equestrian travel largely withdraws the problem of disobedience.

If problems do arise during your journey, how and why do you need to discipline your road horse?

First recall that the horse has a distinct social and personal nature which you must never neglect to take into account.

Socially, the horse belongs to a herd. This public interaction teaches the individual animal that he has a part to play in the larger equine community. The group maintains a strict hierarchy which issues on-the-spot punishments to offenders, by means of bites and kicks. As a consequence of being raised in a herd, every horse learns that he must submit to stronger horses in power, all the while he in turn can dominate horses who are weaker than he is.

Thus, while the animal kingdom does have some herd animals which display a sense of gentle communal accord, every horse in contrast has a strong feeling of personal entitlement which encourages him to be self-centred. This perspective on life results in various types of insensitive behaviour, including greed and aggression, coming to the forefront if the horse is not disciplined by his new herd leader – you!

If left to his own devices, a horse can misinterpret overt kindness on your part as weakness. He can, and will, not only seize the leadership initiative, he will attempt to physically dominate you. When this occurs, either intentionally or by default, it can lead to serious injuries as he will behave as aggressively towards the Long Rider as he would to a submissive horse.

That is why it is critically important that the road horse be well-mannered and evenly disciplined, as these are the bedrocks of respect and safety. The horse must not be defiant. He should recognize that during the journey, the Long Rider is the herd leader. This requires the traveller to maintain discipline, especially when his road horse is confronted with fearful challenges. You can be kind, but confident, considerate, but strong. The result is that when a horse adapts to the authority of the Long Rider a sense of mutual confidence is born.

Although discipline is part of travel, the road horse is your companion, not a sports instrument. He should obey out of love, loyalty and curiosity. You should always attempt to avoid a quarrel with your horse. If you absolutely must punish him, then do so with wise restraint, for nothing is worse than breaking his trust.

The moral here is that your personal pride is like rust. It can seize and stiffen your journey, especially if you over-discipline your horse. But the oil of kindness can smooth your problems in such a way that horse and rider move as one.

Bucking

There are many types of fine horsemanship but in equestrian travel the main consideration is the ability to stick to the saddle.

Yet the world is full of a multitude of potentially-frightening objects, sounds, and smells, any one of which can cause your normally even-tempered road horse to shy or buck. A horse that buck jumps out of occasional fear can be forgiven. One who routinely bucks, especially as you are mounting, should never be relied upon as a road horse.

The good news is that most European and Asian horses do not buck like their cousins from North or Latin America. These horses are notorious for placing their heads between their legs, doubling up like a jack-knife, and trying to tear the rider's liver out via a system of tricks with names such as sun-fishing and pile-driving.

In the 1920s Thurlow Craig spent years riding in the jungles and pampas of Latin America. During these explorations he developed the theory that horses in the Americas develop a stronger bucking instinct because they are often attacked by predatory cats, such as the puma, panther or jaguar.

"The puma is so fond of horse-flesh, that in certain parts of the Cordilleras it is impossible to let horses run free. The explosive quality of the range-bred horses' bucking is the result of generations of negative experience with these mountain lions. The puma, when attacking a colt, generally jumps from slightly behind, gets one arm over the withers and the other over the nose, usually breaking the horse's neck. I have seen horses with deeply scored withers and claw-marks over the nose, and can quite believe that the only way a horse could get free from such an encumbrance would be by bucking. Hence the difference between European horses and American," Thurlow observed.

Regardless of why your horse starts to buck, if the Long Rider is thrown off, especially if the horse also falls, the traveller must get away from the horse without delay. If you hit the ground, roll away from the horse before you even rise to your feet, as the horse may injure you in its panic to rise.

I was once flung from the saddle in the midst of a mad gallop. When my gelding tripped in a rabbit hole at a dead run, the speed at which we were travelling launched me through the air like a cannonball. Though I hit the ground with an immense impact, the momentum of the fall continued to push me violently across the ground. Even in my shocked state I knew I had to roll or be crushed, because I could hear the huge body of my horse tumbling head over heels right behind me. The horse and I both came to a halt, then arose dazed, dusty, but uninjured. If I had not managed to roll on ahead of him, the horse would have inadvertently crushed me.

The safest place for a Long Rider is in the saddle but if you are thrown get away from the horse as soon as possible.

Verbal Commands

Though he does not share your linguistic skills, the horse is always communicating with his environment, other horses and the traveller. It is the Long Rider's job to detect these non-verbal signals, decipher what the horse is trying to impart, avoid, approach, desire or fear, then reach an understanding between what the horse needs and the human wants.

Many Long Riders become intensely attuned to their road horse. For example, when DC Vision rode across North America, he became so synchronized to his Shire mare, Louise, that he rode her with only a halter and loose reins, all the while developing an intense sense of non-verbal cues which resulted in a serene trans-continental journey.

So in addition to his physical education, don't neglect the psychological schooling of the road horse, which will quickly get used to the Long Rider's voice. The proper note and volume makes the difference. Make it easy for your horse to know what you are telling him. Your voice can urge him on or be calming, rewarding or slowing. This principle should also be used to teach him to stop on a word of command, so as to offset emergencies en route.

Uniformity and Justice

Horses are not machines. Thus the Long Rider should never attempt to elicit a robotic response from the road horse. There is no place in equestrian travel for the cruelties perpetrated on dressage horses which are asked to over-bend, artificially extend, and jump on their hind-legs like tortured equine birds.

For example, though he was an Olympic level dressage rider, Captain Otto Schwarz rode a vast array of horses during his various equestrian journeys on five continents. Though some of these horses were raw, rough and barely trained, the Swiss Long Rider dealt with each individual horse and problem in a quiet, restrained, temperate manner, stressing gentle, uniform requests and thereby creating a sense of equine justice between Long Rider and road horse.

Likewise, Jeremy James recognised the unity of man and mount when he wrote, "The horse must know that he always has a friend – not a master – a friend, an ally, someone to trust. In this way horse and rider will become united. Who is doing the thinking will merge and very soon, they think the same. They will be one. They will be one because the rider will show the horse what's best for them and the horse will do it because it is."

Respect

When you set off on your journey, there is far more at stake than the mere gaining of miles. The trip is designed to create a lasting emotional bond with the horse, which is brought about because of the admiration and confidence enjoined between the road horse and Long Rider.

Where there is no compassion, there is no trust. Where there is no trust, there is no respect.

Ride the horse as though you were part of him, all the while allowing the horse to express his true nature. This is the way of Long Rider horsemanship.

Joy

Civilised horsemanship deals with the indoor horse, which lives in a house, is a delicate eater, cannot withstand severe temperatures, must be clothed and requires constant attention. Long Riders interact with the outdoor horse, which is notable for his endurance, stamina, appetite, temper and courage. The Yakut horses of Siberia, for example, routinely thrive in minus sixty degree winters.

An indoor horse's sense of smell and hearing are dulled. His eyesight is often poor. Such a horse tends to stumble, which in turn requires constant attention with bit and rein. The eyesight of the sharp-eyed outdoor horse easily guides his feet over every type of obstacle. His smell and hearing are far beyond human range. This type of road horse steers the course suggested by the Long Rider with nothing more than a simple bit and a loose rein.

Too many show jumpers and ring-riders are devoted to an endless search for perfection. This human obsession takes the form of pushing their luckless horses into joining them in finding the perfect circle, the ideal figure eight or the fault-free race over large painted sticks. These are horses whose lives are designed to enhance the self-esteem of their riders, not instil a joyous sense of mutual achievement.

For example, the great Cossack stallion, Count Pompeii, whom Basha O'Reilly rode 4,000 kilometres (2,500 miles) from Volgograd to London, faced the last day of that journey with the same sense of immense enthusiasm as he did when he first galloped away from his native steppes.

Responsibility

Too many people view the horse as a disposable commodity, a plaything with legs, an ego booster, a rare collectible, a way of establishing their tribal identity. They forget that the horse has biological, emotional, sexual and cultural needs, preferring instead to confine him for the majority of the day in a small stall, buy him clothes which nature did not intend for him to need or wear and forego his requirement to be a free animal, not a domestic drudge. This focusing on the exterior ignores the horse's personal needs.

For example, when John Egenes rode "ocean to ocean" on his small Quarter Horse gelding, Gizmo, countless people remarked not on how shiny the little horse was but on the transparent immensity of his "heart."

A Test of Basic Skills.

In terms of creating confident riders, by cutting out the element of monotony in training in a ring, riding afield introduces excitement and an element of surprise for horse and rider. Released from all bullying, nagging and fear of punishment, one month's training for the team, along trails in the open, is equal in value to five months in an indoor riding school.

But regardless of how you arrive at it, you must be a competent horseman capable of achieving the following list of equestrian goals before you depart.

You must be able to confidently catch, handle, halter, lead and tie the horse.

You must be able to groom, brush and clean his hooves correctly.

You must be able to saddle and bridle and know when the saddle and tack are properly adjusted.

You must be able to judge stirrup length correctly.

You must be able to mount from both sides.

You must be able to maintain quiet hands, soft reins, a strong sense of balance and the correct position in the saddle.

You must be able to control the horse at the walk, trot and canter.

You must be able to halt, back up and travel up and downhill.

You must be able to recognize if the horseshoes are in order and be able to remove one if required.

You must be able to off-saddle and recognize the signs of saddle sores.

You must know how to feed, water and bed down the horse.

You must know how to clean your tack.

The Mutual Reward

In addition to being the most famous naturalist of all time, Charles Darwin was an avid equestrian traveller. The noble Long Rider admonished us when he wrote, "Animals, whom we have made our slaves, we do not like to consider our equal."

Modern consumer society encourages the idea that selfishness and self-advancement are commendable. When individuals worship self-absorption their unbridled self-interest overwhelms any sense of belonging to a larger community or caring for its environment.

Yet horses require empathy, not self-interest. They are capable of performing acts which are not directly in their own interests. This arose when I was unconscious and dying of hepatitis in Pakistan. My mare, Shavon, saved my life by carrying me unaided through the mountains to the nearest doctor.

That is why Long Rider horsemanship is based upon the ethical doctrine of altruism, fairness, gratitude, self-sacrifice, loyalty and inter-species co-operation.

This philosophy was beautifully expressed by the Swedish Long Rider, Renate Larssen.

"After a two-month-journey which took us through Syria, Turkey, Bulgaria, Romania, Slovakia, Hungary and into the south of Poland, I arranged for a horse transporter to take my mare, Serena, and I across the Baltic Sea and back home to Sweden. Our equestrian journey was one of great physical, emotional and spiritual exertion. And though our bodies and souls will bear the marks for the rest of my life, I regret not a single day or a single step we took together. Serena showed me that true loyalty and love really will conquer everything, from treacherous marshes in Romania, to dangerous truck drivers in Slovakia, and attempted armed robberies in the mountains of Syria. Not once did she falter, stumble, or show exhaustion. She carried me through the bog of multiple-byway-crossings in early morning traffic, galloped away from motorcycles through a rocky desert, climbed onto tiny carts without hesitation when we managed to hitch a ride with a passing farmer, watched over me as I slept between her legs in cramped sheds, and stood close by my side in the middle of a Carpathian thunderstorm. All credit for the completion of the journey should be hers."

As Serena proves, we don't teach our horses anything, compared to what they teach us.

Summary

Too often riding becomes devoted to the concept of prohibition, not permission. Modern riding places an emphasis on competition and commercialism. It views riding as the application of a method, not a vehicle of inspiration.

Because of this inherited species arrogance, most humans concentrate on perfecting the skills needed to become a dominant rider, all the while ignoring the many non-verbal lessons on offer from their horse. This results in a one-sided working relationship. In contrast to this philosophy, the Long Rider is attempting to become a fluid and unrestrained Centaur, not an overlord.

For example, when Aimé Tschiffely rode into New York after completing his journey from Buenos Aires, no one commented on his "seat." They marvelled instead at the tangible emotional ease the Swiss Long Rider shared with his hardy Criollo gelding, Mancha.

We are discussing a type of horsemanship that satisfies the human soul, that interacts with and respects the horse and that reflects a mutual initiative. It's about connection, not collection.

There is no sense of nostalgia in the Long Rider for bygone days; no longing for the warm glow of romance; no muttering about the passing of a noble memory. Though certain basic techniques may have changed, Long Rider horsemanship has never passed away. It has endured because it is based on the élan, courage, and panache which come from riding across, over, under and through every imaginable factor the environment can throw at you. This is the ancient art wherein you have to rely on your own equestrian resourcefulness to thrive and survive.

Thus there is a difference between an obsession with technique and the attainment of complete self-confidence in the saddle. One is a method used by blind men to achieve mechanical results. The other is a harmony of body and spirit that communicates itself to the horse, removes both animals' fears, and results in the Centaur.

Unlike the dressage world, which is all don't, don't, don't, being a Long Rider is all about live, live, live. Jeremy James put it best when he described the Long Rider and the Road Horse as being, "Two Hearts, Two Minds, One Will - Straight out of the soul of the steppe."

Statistics demonstrate that competitive sport riding is more dangerous than motorcycle riding, with one in five riders suffering a serious injury.

Compare the dangers of modern sport riding to the equestrian achievement of the North American Long Rider George Beck and his Morab gelding, Pinto, who journeyed 33,000 kilometres (20,352 miles) without an accident during their three-year journey to all 48 American states.

In the 1930s Captain Otto Schwarz competed in dressage and jumping for the Swiss Olympic team.

Yet thanks to the years he spent patrolling the Swiss border during the Second World War, Captain Schwarz discovered a love for equestrian travel which resulted in him riding nearly 50,000 accident-free kilometres on five continents.

During her journey through through Syria, Turkey, Bulgaria, Romania, Slovakia, Hungary and Poland, Swedish Long Rider Renate Larssen learned to have complete trust in her mare, Serena.

Chapter 19
Getting a Horse Fit

Hot-House Horses

In regards to the fitness of your horse, just because you buy it doesn't mean it's ready for the road.

Horses that have not been rigorously exercised prior to your departure must not be asked to suddenly perform hard labour. An animal which has been treated tenderly, and has been warmly bedded in a cozy stable, cannot be turned out onto the cold road without negative consequences. Such horses have been treated like hot-house plants. Not only are they weaker, more delicate and tender, they are susceptible to a vast number of infirmities. For example, a horse in soft condition is always liable to get a sore back just as a man who has not ridden for some time is apt to chafe on the saddle.

Unfortunately, not only do most horses lack conditioning, just as worrying is the fact that their riders mistakenly believe they can build up the strength of the animal during the course of the journey. This is a flawed philosophy. Regardless of how stout and healthy the horse appears at the commencement of a journey, if he is ridden hard when first setting out, he soon becomes exhausted and every additional mile adds to his physical discomfort.

This is all the more important if the horse has been regularly stabled and has previously worn an outdoor coat to protect him against harsh weather. If this is the case, then he should be prepared by diminishing his clothing and gradually accustoming him to all weathers. Such a soft horse should be brought into work slowly. Nor should he be asked to carry great weight for long periods until his muscles and back have hardened.

War horses in England, for example, were given four or five weeks tough training prior to a campaign, so as to ensure they were in good condition. That is why it is critically important that your road horse be healthy, strong, trained and part of a well-oiled equine-based alliance before you set out.

A training regime should therefore be launched prior to leaving on the journey. This will not only reduce the chance of causing possible pain to your road horse during the first few days, it may also offset serious injuries and delays.

Beware the Trainers

Strangely even though the modern horse world is awash with trainers, few of them are familiar with the traditional methods used to bring a road horse into shape.

What most trainers have forgotten is that the horse is capable of freeing us from the confining mentality of the safety-loving pedestrians who inhabit our ancestral village. Consequently, to "train" a horse, only to return horse and rider to the ring or the barn, makes no more sense than having your mechanic repair your automobile, then suggest you park your car back inside the garage, rather than set out on a liberating drive down the road. You wouldn't think of listening to a mechanic who told you that. But thousands of so-called "trainers" make their living telling horse owners to do just that all the time.

In fact, history proves that the best teachers are other horses, with the older, wiser animal training the beginner.

But lacking such a wise equine elder, how can you turn a plump pasture pet into a rugged road horse?

Paper Tigers

Like all aspects of equestrian travel, preparing the road horse requires a sense of devout pragmatism.

The majority of horses will be fat, not fit. Not only are the horse's muscles soft and flabby, the rest of his body is also in remarkably poor condition for travelling. When first exposed to severe training his blood-vessels soon lose their elasticity, his heart fails in driving power; his lungs cannot sustain rapid breathing and his joints complain at the unexpected exercise. Although an inexperienced horse is jumping out of his skin with excitement at the beginning of the day, a very moderate amount of road work will leave him rapidly fatigued. At the end of a hard day's riding you will be left wondering how the ground-eating tiger you mounted in the morning was transformed into the weary stumbler now beneath you.

The Long Rider doesn't need a highly-strung sprinter. He requires a hardy workaday horse. That is why thorough fitness is absolutely essential. The only guaranteed formula for such success is healthy exercise and good food, judiciously combined, for one month prior to your departure.

That was a difficult lesson which Long Rider Clay Marshall learned. Having planned to undertake a journey through the mountains and deserts of the American Southwest, Clay overlooked the need to get his horses into shape prior to departure.

"I had read of Aimé Tschiffely. My heart, mind and commitment were so intent on beginning the ride as soon as I got out of the military, that I failed to grasp the significance, necessity and longevity of horse preparation and conditioning. Therein was my greatest mistake of this ride. I know now, even if I'd had the full three weeks, it was nowhere near enough time to condition a horse for such a ride. Of course I should have known better. If I were competing in a marathon, triathlon, or hiking the Appalachian Trail, I would have to train, condition, and work my way up to such an undertaking. My joints, muscles, lungs, and heart simply wouldn't be able to handle such an event without the proper conditioning and preparation. It is the same for a horse, but I was blinded by my goal, blinded to the logic of it, and it quickly caught up to me," Clay recalled in his book, *Ninety Days By Horse.*

Training the Road Warrior

The simple fact that you have introduced the horse to fresh air, invigorating work and an unknown trail will improve his body, excite his emotions and arouse his curiosity.

To begin with, you should ride the horse for a minimum of two hours a day, with one day a week off. This time in the saddle should gradually be extended over the course of the training period until the horse can easily do four hours of rapid road work without showing signs of distress.

As the majority of your travelling will be done at the walk, this is the pace which you should concentrate on. When training, encourage your horse to maintain a brisk, steady, mile-eating walk. Never allow him to stroll or stumble, as he's working, not picnicking in the country.

A moderate amount of trotting should be included in your training routine, with the proportion being three parts walking to one part trotting. Don't be afraid to combine trots, and a strong walk, over as wide a variety of terrain as is possible. A collected canter will help develop his wind. But bear in mind that the walk and trot are the essential gaits for any journey.

Never sprawl in the saddle. Like the horse, you too are getting in shape for what's to come. Break up the ride by dismounting, walking alongside for a brief time and then re-mounting. Plenty of steady walking, and a reasonable amount of trotting, should provide enough healthy exercise to get you, and your horse, into working condition.

But be careful. Your training program should never be so severe as to exhaust the animal, as his muscles will suffer and he will lose weight. Never work a tired horse. He will be prone to falls and injuries. Create instead a training program that increases the horse's condition, all the while being careful to never overburden him.

Vary the Exercise

In addition to hardening his muscles, the exercise regime should stimulate your horse's intelligence and steady his nerves as well. While being careful not to attempt anything too hazardous, you and the new road horse should attempt to explore narrow trails, go up and down hills, cross shallow streams, traverse bridges and travel along traffic-laden roads.

If your journey will require you to cross urban areas, then it is imperative that your training rides include places where your horse will encounter cars, crowds and noise, as you need a horse that is comfortable in traffic.

Though you want to maintain a brisk walk during these rides, the first miles should be covered slowly, so that the horses can feel their feet, stretch their legs and empty their bowels before they are called upon to trot, and the last mile should also be walked so that they return to their stable cool.

As the training programme progresses, the road horse should be fully loaded for the duration of that day's ride. This is to ensure that the skin and muscles of the back become fully hardened to the pressure and weight of your saddle and gear. Without this pre-conditioning you run the risk of causing saddle sores.

It is also essential not to follow the same monotonous route every day. A horse has the remarkable ability to recognize and memorize his surroundings. Thus if he discovers he is heading for home via a predictable path, he will often hurry, fidget and sweat during his return. This nervous effect may usually be avoided by choosing a different daily direction.

The Result

As the needs for training will vary widely depending upon each horse, your efforts will need to be guided by keen observation and practical experience. Yet regardless of the degree, to produce a well-conditioned road horse you must adopt an overall strategy which includes full feeding and fair work. No other combination is guaranteed to achieve the desired physical condition. The result will be a horse whose previously fat, flabby flesh has been transformed into hardened muscle.

Once this muscular development has been attained, the work encountered during a journey will not only be carried out with comparative ease, such exercise will add to the quality of the horse's overall physical condition. Hardened horses are capable of sustained exertion without becoming greatly fatigued. Add in the healthy appetite brought on by a day's trek, and the former soft horse can now travel indefinitely.

The value of the road horse is never based on his looks or pedigree. His significance is founded on service.

Tips

There are a handful of suggestions which may be helpful when you begin to road-train your horse.

Because the two of you will be in a different place every night, it is important that your horse establish a bond of trust and friendship with you. Though it may seem obvious, it is the repetition of small acts of kindness aimed at the horse which will win over his affections.

Regardless of local custom, always approach the horse from the left side. Never frighten him, either by your actions nor voice. Speak softly. Move quietly. Work efficiently.

Place the saddle blanket forward of its intended position and pull it backwards into place in order to align the hairs on the horses back properly. The front edge of the blanket should be about the width of a hand in front of the saddle.

Always check that the saddle is properly adjusted before mounting. The front of the sidebar should be about the width of four fingers behind the point of the horse's shoulder blades. This will prevent the sidebar from interfering with the free movement of his shoulder.

Mount smoothly, making sure you don't pull the saddle off-centre. Because of the vagaries of travel, you may find yourself forced to dismount on a steep trail or onto a hillside. That's why it is important to teach your horse to permit you to mount from either side.

During the training period, when you dismount to walk alongside your horse, make sure he is trained to maintain a safe distance. His trust in your judgment should be so profound that if you are in the lead, he will follow you through, across, over, under or around a challenging obstacle.

Make sure the road horse is trained not to take fright if you open a map, pull on your rain coat, adjust your hat, reach for your canteen, etc. He should stand rock solid when you stop him.

Once the horse has reached his peak condition, calculate his rate of travel at both the walk and trot. This will allow you to estimate how long it will take you to reach each day's destination.

Fear

Fear is an emotion whose painful appearance is prompted by something that appears dangerous, threatening or supernatural.

Horses are like humans. Anything can scare them. In most cases the causes are entirely external, including a loud noise, a scary smell, or a terrifying shadow on the trail. You never know. Who has not heard of a horse suddenly seized with fear by the unexpected arrival of a treacherous flock of pigeons, a perilous paper blowing by, a mysterious reflection of light, a bush swaying in the wind, a man suddenly standing up or a mischievous dog running out of a house?

Some horses panic at the unanticipated sight or smell of other animals, including llamas, peacocks, pigs and camels.

Likewise sudden noises, such as a car back-firing, a rifle being shot or a loud truck horn blaring may frighten the horse. While these sorts of noises are to be expected, equestrian travel may present you with sounds out of the ordinary too.

For example, upon being confronted by a particularly wicked-looking bridge in Pakistan, I decided to dismount and walk across alongside my mare, Shavon. Luckily I had taken the reins firmly in my right hand, because the bridge had a startling surprise in store for us.

Being too poor to rebuild this remnant of the British Raj, the Pakistanis had attempted instead to strengthen the rickety wooden structure by nailing flattened out five-gallon tin cans onto the wooden planking. It was, if nothing else, a shiny solution. The problem was my horse and I had just spent weeks travelling along dusty mountain trails, all of which had provided us with many miles of silent trekking.

Unfortunately the moment Shavon's steel-clad shoes struck the tin cans, it sounded like a Jamaican steel drum band had suddenly starting playing right beneath our startled feet. The result was that my formerly placid ride became a race across the bridge, as Shavon attempted to flee from the frightening noise. Of course the noise, and her panic, grew with every step as her hooves pounded the tin cans. That's how I crossed the bridge in record time. With no guard rails and a long drop down to the stone-encrusted river bed below, I hung onto the reins, trying to control the frightened palomino as she sprinted from these noisy demons.

Regardless of the cause, a frightened horse's action is sudden and can be dangerous. The way to overcome fear is be prepared for its unanticipated arrival. Consequently, you must always be alert, especially if your horse is timid or shies easily.

If your horse panics while you are in the saddle, he may break into a deadly run. If this occurs pull strongly on one rein until you force him to turn his head. This will compel him into a tight circle and stop his headlong rush.

Horses are not innately vicious. As Shavon proves, a horse that panics is experiencing genuine terror. That is why a wise Long Rider always remembers that mercy should go hand in hand with justice. Thus, even if the horse requires correction, mildness will, in most instances, accomplish your purpose.

Shoe before you go

Never shoe your horse just before you start. You must be certain that the nails have not lamed him and that the shoes are firmly in place. Therefore, have your horse accurately shod some days before you set out on a journey.

Problems overseas

The Long Riders' Guild website and this book are akin to a caravanserai, where equestrian travellers ride in, share their vital information, then journey on. There are countless examples of cultural diversity embedded among this geography of ideas and experiences.

For example, when Ella Sykes set out to ride across Persia in the late 19th century, she made this startling discovery.

"Men prefer to ride mares, ignoring stallions to the point of starvation. Yet they would spend any amount in order to keep the mares in top shape. Mares being such valuable property, they are bought and sold in a peculiar way. The whole animal is seldom purchased by one man but three or four buyers have each an interest in one or more of its legs. The man to whom the forelegs belong has the task of stabling, feeding and exercising the creature and he will, if possible, buy out the possessors of the hind legs by degrees."

But modern equestrian travellers such as Keith Clark learn that not only do you have to take care of all four legs, it's often hard to do so when you are attempting to make your first ride in a foreign country. During his journey in Argentina and Chile, Keith realized that getting a horse ready for a journey is often complicated by exotic and sometimes unknown local rules.

"When Chico introduced me to his friend, I was very specific in describing what I was looking for. The horse had to be well trained, healthy, a decent size and from six to twelve years old. The friend said the estancia owner had two horses that were perfect for me

So the next day we drove forty kilometres over really rough tracks. When we arrived at the estancia, a gaucho went looking for the herd which contained the first horse chosen for me. When he came back with the herd, the horses were put into a corral. After half an hour, my horse was finally caught. That's when the interesting task of saddling it began. First the horse was hobbled and blindfolded. They wouldn't let me put my saddle on it. But they needed my bridle as it was very head shy and they couldn't get one of their bridles on. Mine can be disassembled, so we broke it down and put it back together around the horse's head. Then they insisted that the horse be left hobbled and blindfolded, while we went to the house for an hour long lunch.

When we emerged, they announced that we would all ride out and find the other horse chosen for me. My saddle was placed on a horse which wasn't for sale, while the gaucho was ordered to ride "my" horse. During the lengthy search for the missing horse, I could see that the gaucho was having difficulties with the original animal. He was sawing on the bit and dragging the horse's head around in order to control it. But after an hour of such treatment the gaucho thought the horse was sufficiently tired for me to ride it. After we swapped saddles, I soon discovered that the horse had a mouth made of cast iron. It wasn't long before I was getting blisters from the reins.

We eventually found the other bunch of horses and started them back to the estancia. Of course this meant galloping, which was a bit worrying as I had next to no control over my semi-wild mount. Despite my best efforts to control it, the horse galloped straight through bushes and over ditches.   Eventually I realised that my best option was to let him join the herd, while I went along for the ride. This worked well until we slowed down to approach the estancia. That's when he decided he didn't like me and began trying to bite chunks out of my legs. When we finally got back to the estancia, the horse's owner came out.

'Isn't he a great horse,' he said. If only I knew how to swear in Spanish! I managed to tell him what I thought of the animal. The owner then claimed that the horse had misbehaved because he was only four and had just been broken in. Even though the white hairs and healed sores under the saddle area indicated that this was no youngster, a quick glance at its teeth showed that it should have been collecting its pension.

Caught out, the owner replied that the horse was just frisky and hadn't been ridden a lot. I had a look at the bars in its mouth. They were thick and calloused from being brutally handled for so many years. When I pointed this out, the Argentine owner became defensive and claimed I hadn't been able to control the horse because my bit was from Chile. He asserted it was too soft. If I wrapped wire around it, he assured me, everything would be ok and I could ride the horse with ease.

Does gringo equal stupid, I wondered silently? A full day wasted but it was interesting and there have been a lot of days like that," Keith reported to the Guild.

Identifying Problems

One thing to keep in mind; it is during the training period that you should confirm that your potential road horse is well and truly able to undertake your mission. Despite your best intentions and constant efforts some horses are simply unable to adapt to the rigours of travel. If you make this discovery, the horse should not be taken on your journey. In such a case, many people are hesitant to sell the horse. Yet a financial loss is easier to bear than being injured by riding an unsuitable animal.

Summary

As this chapter explains, you can seldom just set off.

This is especially true if you have a fat, unconditioned horse fresh out of pasture, as it would be cruel to expect him to put in strenuous days on the road without reasonable preparation. The four cornerstones for this physical training must be patience, consistency, kindness and forgiveness.

The cumulative power of such conditioning means that you can not only demand a reasonable amount of work from a seasoned horse but that it actually does him good.

Any attempt to employ horses without advanced preparation risks failure of the journey.

Finally, few people have transformed pasture pets into road horses. Such an animal is to be treasured. That is why it is essential that the Long Rider should set out on his journey with a fixed determination to take it easy, to enjoy the beauty spread out before him, and not to labour under the constant notion that he must accomplish a certain number of miles within a specified time.

Before he left to ride across the Andes Mountains in Chile and Argentina, British Long Rider Keith Clark made sure his horses were physically prepared for the journey ahead.

Clay Marshall discovered that it is imperative to give your horses time to become conditioned to the hardships of the ride.

Chapter 20
The Pack Horse

Why a Pack Horse?

After having completed his incredible 29,000 kilometre (18,000 mile) solo equestrian journey around the entire perimeter of the Australian continent, Long Rider Steve Nott made this apt observation about one of the most commonly-misunderstood aspects of equestrian travel, the necessity of using a pack horse.

"Hollywood would have us believe the erstwhile western hero can travel for weeks on end, all the while covering hundreds of miles with just his saddle bags and a blanket. All too often when night arrives the cinematic rider has mysteriously produced a coffee pot, frying pan and enough food to fabricate a hearty evening meal. In fact even a brief list of camp necessities, let alone the food, soon makes it apparent one needs a pack horse and pack saddle," Nott warned other travellers.

Likewise it was another set of Aussie Long Riders that reinforced Nott's cautionary note. Iain White and Michael Bragge rode 4,000 kilometres (2,500 miles) from Brisbane to Melbourne. They expressed another fundamental misconception about pack horses.

"Most people believe that an unsatisfactory riding horse can still be used as a pack horse. This is a myth. The admirable qualities of a good riding horse, confidence, composure, balance, strength, willingness and flexibility are necessary in a pack horse too."

As these wise men of the saddle prove, if you are planning an equestrian journey of any distance, you need to consider the weight you will be asking your road horse to carry. If you find that geographic and climatic challenges force you to bring extra food for you and your mount, as well as cooking gear, a tent and additional clothing, then you should not overburden your mount. The answer lies in using a pack horse to carry every extra ounce of weight that you can relieve the road horse from carrying.

Not only is it kinder on the road horse, additionally a pack horse also grants you a tremendous sense of independence. You can take more equipment along if you have a pack animal; you can travel further without resupplying; and horses, being very gregarious, enjoy themselves much more when in company.

There are negative alternatives if you decide not to use a pack horse, as was discovered by the British Long Riders Vyv and Elsa Wood Gee. During their journey from Scotland's John O'Groats to England's Lands End, their two Fell ponies carried only essentials.

"Determined to be totally self-sufficient and travel independently without a back-up team, we carried everything we needed in our saddle bags but with weight and space limited to the bare minimum, we were dependent on constantly replenishing our stocks," Vyv cautioned.

As this chapter explains, there are many reasons to consider using a pack horse, including lightening the burden of your road horse and greater independence. While these are noteworthy reasons, what is usually overlooked is that the hard-working and humble pack horse is one of mankind's most misunderstood, albeit historically important, creatures.

Pack horses made history

Throughout mankind's journey through history he has drafted a wide variety of animals, including elephants, camels, llamas, yaks, oxen, goats, sheep, donkeys and dogs, into carrying his burdens. Legend has it that Australians even thought about using kangaroos, but they couldn't figure out a way to keep the loads from falling out of the pouch when the animals jumped.

Yet who first thought to turn a horse into a beast of burden?

English equestrian historian Anthony Dent theorized that early humans kept tame horses as ready supplies of meat and milk, but that an accident happened while travelling with these horses which altered history. A critical step occurred, Dent said, between the milking of the mare and riding her.

"The gap was spanned by a period of pack carriage – the most primitive form of horse transport. Imagine a man and his family and his little band of mares migrating over the steppe from one waterhole to the next. The day is hot and the going soft from the spring rains. Even the most primitive people acquire luggage – bedding, weapons, tools, and tomorrow's food at the least. Plodding along laden beside the mare, it occurs to someone that she is carrying nothing. So, at least drape that heavy hide sleeping-bag across her back, and there you have it, the working horse."

It was this same placid pack horse, Dent believes, that provided mankind with the inspiration to ride.

"Among the essential baggage of all foot-nomads are their offspring who cannot walk as fast or as far as the adults. Sooner or later someone will put a footsore toddler up on the mare along with the cooking-pots. Now the child is riding, probably not enjoying the experience. Yet another idea is born, and grown men will also aspire to ride – on a sound horse, not a lame milch animal, and to that end some of this year's crop of filly foals will be spared the cooking-pot this autumn, and in due course will grow up to carry a living human load. Thus slowly over the centuries horse-manship comes to birth."

While we can't be certain when the horse first carried mankind's burdens, there is ample evidence demonstrating how important this development was.

In his book, *Horses*, English Long Rider Roger Pocock lamented that scholars had neglected to appreciate the historical importance of the pack horse.

"While chariots and cavalry were mainly engaged in killing civilization, the unobtrusive pack pony did almost as much as the ship in spreading culture along the channels of commerce."

From China to the Atlantic, and from the northern taiga to the Indian Ocean, the old world was threaded all over with pack trails snaking from water to water over the deserts and pastures, the forests and hills. Except in the very dry districts where camels were used for transport, the pack horses did all the carrying overland.

Elizabethan England, in particular, enjoyed a thriving pack horse system, as the citizens of that era lived in the horse-borne rather than a horse-drawn culture. Despite the wide publicity that the coach enjoyed on its first introduction to the country, its numbers were few during Shakespeare's lifetime, nor was it widely distributed, with the majority of coaches in England remaining concentrated in London and its immediate environs.

The same was true of commercial traffic. Shakespeare's carriers, such as those that were robbed by Falstaff's gang, relied on packhorses, not carts. Plus, regardless of whether the cart was humble or the carriage royal, it was not possible to travel on wheels during certain seasons, such as those of the autumn and spring rains.

Because of these obstacles to travel and commerce, a network of pack horse trails criss-crossed England, Cornwall, Wales and Scotland. From the port of London, for example, a pack trail starting at Tower Hill ran westward along Newgate, Holburn, Oxford Street, and Bayswater Road, crossed the Thames at Oxenford, then branched to the gold mines of Dolgelly and went on to the tin deposits of Cornwall.

The nation's commerce and culture flowed along these localized equestrian arteries, while even greater trade routes could take a bold traveller, and his trusty pack horse, on a three-year journey to faraway Cathay.

So if England was once a nation held together by a cobweb of pack horse pony tracks, how did it manage to lose this vital part of its equestrian heritage before the end of the Victorian era, and how does that nation's loss affect modern horse travel?

The Disappearance of the Pack Horse

When Queen Victoria ascended the throne in the summer of 1837 the ringing of pack horse bells would have been a routine sound heard from one end of the island nation to the other. That merry chiming came about thanks to the lead pack horse, which carried a loud bell warning other pack trains travelling along the narrow trails to wait in wider passing places, lest both caravans come to grief.

Thus before other means of locomotion existed, the pack horse was not only employed in agricultural and ordinary road work, but as the medium of carrying supplies to the inhabitants of outlying holdings on the moor and wolds. Though thought of today as being a service provided by any strong horse, the English Pack Horse had become a designated breed of national importance.

This breed was powerful and sure-footed, two properties which the ancient pack horse possessed to a very considerable extent. Though debates were common about the origin of the pack horse, the indisputable fact remains that the breed was regarded on all sides as being so essential to the existence of the inhabitants of the countryside that it would have been a rash, if not reckless individual who would have ventured to prophesy in 1837 that the pack horse would soon become little more than a national memory.

Yet when the Crystal Palace Horse Show of 1897 was held to celebrate Queen Victoria's Silver Jubilee, it was popularly believed that no specimens of the breed could be found. Various factors associated with the rise of the Industrial Age, including the development of wider roads which permitted wagon travel and the advent of railroads, had combined to bring about the demise of England's pack horse. In the space of a single generation, one of the most valuable horses in English history had vanished.

Professor J. Wortley Axe, an English equestrian expert at the time, expressed his regret, saying, "It is unfortunately rather to the discredit of British horse-breeders that so useful a variety as the Pack Horse, which at one time was so commonly met with in many parts of the country should have become practically extinct; but the fact remains that until the occasion of the Queen's Horse Show it was popularly believed that no specimens of the breed could be found."

After a great deal of trouble, a single stallion and a lone mare were discovered, and by permission of their owners were included in the Diamond Jubilee parade of British horses, which was arranged in honour of Her Majesty Queen Victoria's long reign. The reproach remained that one of England's most important breed of horse had been allowed to die out.

How does the demise of a long-ago English pack horse affect modern equestrian travel? That question was indirectly answered by an American cavalry officer in 1952, when he predicted, "The General Staff may have made a very serious error in eliminating the pack unit because in a few years there will be no men left who can train a pack train when we desperately need them."

With the United States and its military allies recently scrambling to resurrect the art of pack transport, so as to assist their military operations in Afghanistan, the old cavalry officer's prediction has come true.

As machines replaced pack transport, valuable breeds and generations of collective human knowledge were lost. England suffered the most, with the majority of all packing techniques and technology having been unknown there for at least a century. Meanwhile, though the United States retained the basic concepts of pack travel, thanks to the efforts of private packers, many of that nation's most important advancements, including the development of the army's most sophisticated pack saddle, have been lost to posterity.

It is in the light of this intellectual vacuum that we must consider how best to use the pack horse and his specialized saddle when we set out on a long and difficult equestrian journey.

An Ally, not a Machine

It would be a mistake to think that the pack horse is a lowly beast of burden.

But not all humans recognize the basic dignity of this important animal.

Charles Brand journeyed to South America in 1827. While preparing to cross the Chilean Andes, he noted how cruelly the local pack horses were treated.

"They lace the loads on as if the horses were made of iron. Frequently I have seen two men with their feet against the horses' sides, drawing the rope of hide until it has literally been hid in its belly and the poor animal would stand and cough with pain."

Any Long Rider who has ever journeyed alongside a pack horse will be the first to tell you how strong, clever, patient, and above all, loyal they are. I can speak from experience when I say that there have been days when the sun was boiling down and I wondered how my road horse and I could carry on. That was invariably the moment when my pack horse would choose to rub his weary head on the right leg of my trousers. When this occurred I knew that no matter how hard my road horse and I were struggling, the devotion and sacrifice of the other animal walking beside me was greater than either of our burdens.

In an effort to understand the pack horse, let us begin by realizing that one shouldn't compare dogs and horses. The former will admire his master almost to the point of slavishness. The pack horse, on the other hand, keeps his honour by maintaining a degree of detachment. While you can easily command a dog to kneel, there is about horses a personality that reacts to true feelings and remembers poor treatment. Such a singular animal should never be degraded to the status of a drudge.

Thus, it is imperative that the pack horse be treated with great respect, as because his burden is greater than the road horse's, the maintenance of his trust is of even more concern to the Long Rider.

Since much of the modern world suffers from collective equestrian amnesia, amateur travellers routinely abuse these valuable animals. Such people forget that this is not a four-legged rental truck or some hair-covered soulless contrivance designed to be over burdened then cruelly used. This is a highly intelligent animal whose ability to assist you must never be exploited. Sadly, that is what has happened in recent years when heartless and foolish people drove pack horses to their deaths.

Two recent examples both occurred within a space of a few months in the United States, and though popular myth would have us believe that women are more kind to their horses than men, these pack horses were slain by female owners.

The first incident occurred when a woman with no equestrian travel experience lost her job in Florida. Being at a loose end, she decided to immigrate to Texas in search of work. Not being content to just ride there on an unconditioned horse, she loaded what looked like a small apartment's worth of possessions onto a pack horse and proceeded to urge the animal to follow her into the sunset. It died.

The second woman bragged to all and sundry that she was going to undertake a nearly three-thousand mile long ride along the torturous Pacific Crest Trail that stretches from Mexico to Canada, "in one season." Her horses were underweight and prone to stumbling before she started.

The ruthless tyrant drove the horses hard through the mountains. Due to her ignorance, she was rescued twice by the authorities but, claiming that God wanted her to continue, she drove her animals on regardless. Eventually she came to a large, clearly-posted detour sign erected by the national Forest Service. It stated that the trail ahead had been effectively destroyed and was too dangerous for any animal traffic to proceed. She chose to ignore the sign and, having dismounted, forced her horses to ascend a tiny track. Having broken the cardinal rule of never tying your road horse to the pack horse, this woman's unlucky animals soon fell hundreds of feet off a cliff to their deaths.

Both these examples illustrate how out of touch vast numbers of modern so-called riders are with the fundamentals of pack transport. Thus the first lesson to remember is that because the pack horse is more prone to injury than the road horse, as his duty is always more wearisome, his need for protection is all the more acute.

The Long Rider who lives with his horse twenty-four hours a day, and takes time to study him, will soon notice that there are no dumb horses as is falsely claimed. Pack horses remember cruel treatment, never forget beatings and can sense when someone approaches with malicious intent. Thus your actions are all the more important to the pack horse, as he is not the recipient of the small acts of tenderness which the road horse receives during the course of a normal day.

Regardless if your journey takes you to Patagonia or Pakistan, the play of the pack horse's ears, the attitude of his body, how he carries his tail, the way he moves during the course of a day's travel are all indicators of his state of well being. Experience teaches you if he is melancholy or mistrusting. You will learn his weaknesses and his character faults. You will discover how far you can push the limits of his patience.

What you must never forget is that a bad person can literally work a horse to his last breath. While he will never be a craven peon, a pack horse cannot speak when feeling pain or being overburdened. Thus you must never degrade him.

The Perfect Pack Horse

Let us consider how we physically define such a noteworthy animal? Though it is a bit like trying to identify the perfect mate, here are some reliable guidelines.

Breeds: a Long Rider focuses on deeds not breeds. When the English Pack Horse became extinct, the last equine specifically bred for this purpose passed into legend. What you need is physical strength, mental agility and deep emotional devotion, not papers proving an illustrious pedigree. An inexpensive mustang, a sturdy farm mule, or perhaps a former logging horse are the type of blue collar worker you require for a journey.

As for sex and age, the requirements for a pack horse are similar to those of the road horse – see Chapter 11, That Rare Thing, the Road Horse.

Body type: unlike the flexible weight carried by the road horse, the pack horse is burdened by a relentless dead weight which always bears straight down onto his body. This is why your pack horse should have a short back, well-defined withers, well sprung ribs, strong chest and good loins. A short back and pronounced withers are especially important as they work together to keep the pack saddle in place.

Height: the pack horse should not be more than fifteen hands high, as you must lift the pack saddle and panniers on and off the animal twice a day. Thus, choosing a taller animal only adds to your workload as you must lift the heavy pack boxes up onto the pack saddle.

Motivation: don't think that just because a horse is physically imposing, he will automatically make an enthusiastic weight carrier. The Australian bush packers warned, "An ounce of blood is worth an inch of bone." Thus, a massive Percheron, with his heavy bone, may prove to be reluctant to travel hard all day, while a more hot-blooded horse will accept the challenge.

Emotions: a pack horse must be a quiet, gentle, and manageable animal. You require emotional reliability, not a case of equine nerves. That is why a pack horse must have two reliable characteristics, trust and obedience. He should exhibit his trust by allowing you to quietly load him. He must demonstrate his obedience by calmly following you through every type of obstacle, including down steep trails, through timber, alongside busy roads, over streams and away from danger. He must learn to trust the road horse to warn him of any hazards ahead. His emotional mission is to ensure that your supplies are safely on hand when the sun sets.

Intelligence: most people overlook the fact that work horses receive directions from the reins or are guided by the rider's hands, while pack horses are required to make independent decisions. For example plough and logging horses are both guided by long reins. While a pack horse spends much of his time hooked to a lead rope, occasions will arise when the animal may be asked to make his own way over, around or through obstacles along the trail. Unlike the unburdened plough horse, the pack horse must not only overcome these challenges without assistance, he must do so while maintaining and balancing the load on his back.

Agility: pack horses are often confronted with downed trees, sizeable rocks, intimidating mud holes, narrow trails and watery obstructions, any one of which will force the horse to weave his way around danger. This ability is all the more important when you remember that the road horse will see the problems rising to confront the Long Rider. Yet the same obstacle will often take the pack horse by surprise because his view is partially blocked by the road horse. When this occurs, your pack animal should have the skill to side step peril.

Endurance: a pack horse should always be physically robust. He must be a hardened horse who is able to ignore the elements, overcome slight thirst, bed down anywhere and eat everything. What you don't need is a soft, sensitive, stable-bred animal that requires special food and inordinate amounts of emotional attention. A pack horse should thrive on living out of doors, delight in spending his night in a strange field and eagerly devour a dinner of fresh grass.

Training: a pack horse must be easy to catch, enjoy being groomed, allow his feet to be handled and stand still while being loaded. He should never lay back his ears, show the whites of his eyes, and threaten to bite or kick you. Replace such an animal prior to your departure. Your pack horse must be calm when handled, unruffled when being tacked up and serene on the trail.

Such an animal is a recipe for success.

An Intangible Quality and Specific Skills

While it's all well and good to discuss the physical attributes of the pack horse, let's not lose sight of the fact that your journey cannot be successful if you set off with an unreliable animal. Such a horse is as dangerous to have on the trail as a defective companion. Some Long Riders say that the right pack horse has an intangible quality about him, a look in the eye that denotes a calm confidence which in turn leads to him doing the correct thing on a regular basis.

This isn't to say that a pack horse isn't required to have specific skills. It is imperative that he be able to manage difficult terrain. This includes watching where he puts his feet and being so surefooted that he never trips over obstacles. He must also be able to avoid crashing his load into trees or other obstructions.

Such an animal works in a businesslike manner. He should be practical, hardy, a keen eater and above all, able to look after himself. In parts of Africa, Central Asia and especially Mongolia, you should look for animals that are still fat after a harsh winter. A different home every night should be of no emotional concern to a reliable pack horse.

Training a pack horse to neck rein prior to your departure is time well spent, as you will be able to control both animals with a minimum amount of effort and no wearisome pulling on the lead rope. A well trained pack horse should be able to follow your road horse like a faithful shadow, keeping close to you, all the while he neither crowds the road horse nor crashes the pack saddle painfully into your leg. It takes time, and plenty of patience, to train both horses to travel so effectively and quietly.

Conformation

If we were to describe a perfect pack horse, he would have a deep chest, hearty lungs, big level back, deep middle, and powerful quarters; his legs too are short, heavy in bone, and carry a good deal of muscle. No long backs will do, for long backs do not carry weight. His must have a back broad enough to keep the pack saddle in place.

There should be no trace of tubbiness in the barrel, nor should he have a thin ewe neck. If possible, he should have a massive, well-sprung rib cage which will spread the load more evenly than on a narrow-chested horse, for a comfortable pack horse not only travels easily and well, he can go further.

Because he is used in mountains, moors and all types of difficult terrain, the surefooted pack horse is comfortable negotiating the steep declivities and stony paths which come his way. Given today's motorized age, he must also be able to travel quietly alongside heavily trafficked roadways, ignoring roaring lorries and considering honking cars as no more than a routine nuisance.

Often a bay, many times a brown, occasionally a black, his colour isn't as important as the strength of his legs and toughness of his feet. Regardless of what colour he is, a pack horse must stand quietly, behave sensibly, load easily and follow loyally.

In addition to his strength he must be patient, docile, gentle, free of vicious habits and be a paragon of common sense. In addition to his regular duties, a good pack horse should also be broken to ride and able to perform that role in case of an emergency.

Young horses are never suitable for packing. Their bones have not fully developed and they generally lack the emotional maturity required for such a responsibility. Mature horses between the ages of seven to twelve generally work best.

Size and Strength

A solid pack horse should weigh at least 1,000 pounds and be a tremendous eater. This is another reason to avoid excessively large pack horses, as the availability of food in the countryside you will be travelling through will have a direct impact on the pack horse's performance.

Food means energy, which in turn translates into daily progress towards your goal. Therefore never purchase a pack horse that isn't already in strong physical condition. A horse that isn't a good feeder doesn't belong on the road, as a skinny horse will never put on weight during a journey.

You must never forget that your pack horse works twice as hard as your road horse. This is because the moveable live weight of the Long Rider does not bear down as harshly as the crushing dead weight of the pack saddle. The weight on the road horse is always moving. The weight on the pack horse is fixed and unrelenting.

Thus, in terms of overall effect, fifty pounds of live weight on a riding horse equals one hundred pounds of dead weight on a pack horse.

Because of this, it is easy to overburden your pack horse. Just because he can stand up under the load, doesn't give you the right to overload him. Such a scene was witnessed in Montana, when a father and son team of amateur riders purchased horses from a horse rescue operation. These men were from Georgia and had no experience with horse travel, so they drove the heavily-burdened animals into the mountains, then failed to feed or water them adequately. One of the pack horses was found abandoned on the trail, dying of thirst. Thankfully the American authorities arrested these scoundrels and imprisoned them for animal abuse.

What you need is an animal that starts strong and then holds his condition during the journey.

Gait

Pack and road horses cannot work equally if they are not similar in size and temperament, posses the same basic strength and have an equal pace.

Your own balance and safety in the saddle depends on having a pack horse who is an eager, helpful and happy partner. Never match a fast road horse alongside a wearisome, obstinate pack horse determined to drag you out of the saddle. Like your road horse, your pack horse should have a long, smooth, mile-eating gait. Thus they should not only be closely matched in size but in gait too. Otherwise every day's travel becomes a plague wherein your right arm is tugged out of joint, the lead rope burns your hands when it is yanked backwards or you are pulled out of the saddle when the pack horse balks.

Margaret Leigh learned this during her ride from Cornwall to Scotland. She wrote, "The pack horse should be smooth paced and at least as fast as the road horse. For a led horse always tends to drag, and if he is a slow walker, the whole troop will be delayed."

Larger horses not only require more feed, they tempt the Long Rider to carry more weight. Often excessively large horses, though emotionally willing, cannot maintain the pace of a lighter, faster road horse. Thus, while strength is essential in a pack horse, he must also possess enough speed and stamina to match the everyday pace set by the fast-walking road horse, as it is the slower horse that will set the pace.

Ironically, a fast-moving road horse will become the one who wears down first and becomes demoralized by being teamed to a slow-moving pack horse. His keenness and energy will have been wasted if the slower pack horse is constantly trotting to keep up, which is something to be normally avoided as any time a pack horse trots, he is more prone to injury and saddle sores.

This is not to say that throughout history various cavalries did not require their pack horses and mules to trot so as to reach the action without delay. However, most Long Riders do not trot their pack horses, though the rare occasion may arise when you decide to do so. At such times it is critically important that the pack horse have a smooth, steady gait and be eager to move alongside the road horse without any delay or deception.

What is more important than the speed of the pack horse's trot is his overall ability to perform his tasks despite adverse weather and minor daily problems. The pack horse must be eager to travel alongside the road horse, for if a led horse tends to drag, pulls back on the lead rope or if he is a slow walker, the Long Rider's daily progress will be delayed and his enthusiasm dampened.

Unacceptable Behaviour

Unlike the average riding saddle, a pack saddle and panniers can frighten an untrained horse or mule. Therefore before purchasing a potential pack animal, it is imperative that you test his physical skills and emotional capabilities. Will he follow you easily when you lead him on foot? Will he stand quietly when you load him? Will he move alongside another horse quietly, without nipping or pulling back on the lead rope? If he doesn't follow you and your road horse like a quiet shadow, your life on the road will be a constant heartache.

While a physically strong, fast-walking animal can be trained to be a pack horse, you should automatically rule out any animal which exhibits severely negative habits. Thus, never purchase a horse that is hard to catch, runs away when approached or turns their heels to kick. Unhappily for Keith Clark, he accidentally employed such a horse in Chile. After they had stopped for a brief break, and Keith had stepped down from the saddle, the pack horse bolted. It took three hours to catch him, by which time Keith's camera and gear was lost on the pampas.

Avoid horses which are barn sour or herd bound. Your pack horse should be emotionally mature and as eager as you are to make the journey. Horses who have become overly attached to either their home or companions are prone to fight the Long Rider in an effort to return. Such horses seize every opportunity to begin pulling, bucking and even rearing, prior to running back home.

Above all, stay away from horses that pull back while being led. Horses that resist the lead rope fall behind, and then rush forward, often times banging the panniers into the rider's leg. This is not only painful; it can throw the Long Rider off balance, which is dangerous.

Mules

Just as I have previously acknowledged how some people and cultures prefer to ride mules, likewise there are many people and cultures who favour mules as pack animals. While the choice is yours, there are a few things to keep in mind.

To begin with, there's the biology. A mule is produced by breeding a mare horse to a stallion donkey. The result is a mule. If you reverse the order, by breeding a stallion horse to a mare donkey, you obtain a hinny. The latter tends to look more like a horse than a mule. While mules are commonly found world wide, hinnys are less common. Both animals carry many of the emotional characteristics of their donkey forebears.

The size of the mule depends upon the breed of the dam. For example, if a Belgian mare is bred, the resultant mule is exceptionally large. Thus mules, like horses, vary in size based upon their parentage. Once again, the same basic requirements of size, speed and strength which you look for in a pack horse should likewise be applied to any potential pack mule.

There are many positive aspects to mules.

Their conformation is often a great help to a Long Rider packer, because many mules have high withers. This helps keep the pack saddle in place, especially when travelling in mountainous areas.

Mules are renowned for their stamina and strength, which generally allows them to carry a heavier load than a similarly-sized horse.

Because of their hybrid vigour mules are less susceptible to colic, withstand hot weather well and enjoy a reputation for being hearty eaters.

Many mules have a strong walk, an excellent sense of balance and enjoy a well-founded reputation for being extremely sure footed.

The shape of a mule's hoof is slightly different than that of a horse. Mules' hooves are generally narrow and their feet are normally tougher than a horse's more oval hooves. The narrower hoof of a mule enables it to walk carefully across treacherous ground, a critically-important asset when travelling.

Mules are renowned for their keen sense of smell and will alert you if a strange animal is in the vicinity.

Because of their mixed parentage, mules are normally sterile hybrids. On rare occasions a mule may give birth. However, mules are not normally distracted by mares in heat, amorous stallions or sexually confused geldings.

Unlike a horse, which generally retains a degree of independence, a mule is more apt to be a follower, which is why large numbers of these animals are traditionally used in large military caravans.

Now the bad news: mules have some serious disadvantages, especially if you are an inexperienced Long Rider.

While mules can generally carry a heavier load than the same-size pack horse, the hybrid mule is a stubborn animal that may baulk.

Mules are often described as being smarter than horses. This may result in an animal that is willing to challenge your authority or intimidate you.

Though certainly capable of individual affection, as a rule mules seldom grant the same degree of trust to a human which a horse will. The result is that when he is challenged by unforeseen problems, a mule may be reluctant to respond to the Long Rider's commands as quickly as a horse will. This often results in an already-grievous situation becoming even more complicated.

While the horse has a musical neigh, the mule produces a harsh bray which has never been described as melodious.

Mules dislike dogs and will often attack them.

Mules are not available in many parts of the world. When encountered they are often more expensive than a comparable pack horse, with a good mule often selling for fifty percent more than his equine cousin.

Many mules dislike being shod, a problem which needlessly complicates a journey.

Last, but certainly not least, mules are potentially more dangerous than horses. Here again, the hazard is linked to the mule's supposedly superior intelligence. What seems fairly certain is that more so than horses, mules long remember an injustice and will carry a grudge against the offending human. Such resentful mules are known to bite their handlers.

Even worse, mules are known to be vicious kickers that are capable of striking out in any direction, even sideways. Unlike a horse, who will lash out wildly with his hooves, an offended mule will skilfully take aim and inflict a well aimed kick at the packer. Such kicks have been known to severely injure or kill people, so extreme caution is required.

Mighty Mules

The issue of mules is akin to similar issues which involve a person's personality, and the needs which confront him at the moment.

The history of equine travel is filled with stories of Long Riders who either rode or packed mules with great success.

Long Rider Sir Auriel Stein, praised the mules of Persia.

"My halt at Shiraz enabled me to arrange a needful transport in the shape of a dozen and a half of hardy Shirazi mules, essential for the rough journey before us. Already in 1915 I had learned to appreciate the excellent qualities of these animals, when travelling during the war along the Perso-Afghan border to Sistan. Ever since I had looked out for a chance of travelling with those plucky muleteers from Shiraz who know so well how to look after their animals. My expectations in regards to these transport arrangements were fully justified. In the course of my tour, which covered aggregate marching distances of some 1,300 miles, I never experienced the least trouble on their account, however bad the stony tracks were or however difficult to secure adequate fodder. Nor was a single mule ever found to suffer from serious sores," Stein recalled.

Such legendary endurance is still present today.

What surely must be the most successful modern use of mules as pack animals was undertaken by the Argentine Long Riders Raul and Margarita Vasconcellos. During their journey from Arizona to the Argentine, they were faithfully served by two small, matching, sturdy pack mules named Pelusa and Fifi. The diminutive duo of mules marched more than ten thousand miles without a lost day or a sore back.

Another fan of the mule was the renowned North American Long Rider Virl Norton. In 1976 Virl entered the Great American Horse Race, a 5000 kilometres (3000 miles) epic endurance event which ran "ocean to ocean" across the United States. Though the field abounded with tough Arabian horses, and many other seasoned equines normally associated with endurance racing, Virl won the legendary race by riding his big mule to victory. Yet in 1979 Virl made a solitary equestrian journey from Illinois to Washington DC, and this time he chose to ride an Arabian horse.

Thus, the choice is yours, and may well depend on which of the animals, horses or mules, you find locally available, better trained and properly priced.

If you decide to use a pack mule, do not be tempted to buy one of the massive and exceedingly tall mules now favoured by many American farmers. These animals, though attractive in the extreme, are usually bred from blonde Belgian work horses, and are too big for equestrian travellers.

A Long Rider pack mule should be from 14.3 to 15.1 hands in height and weigh from 1,000 to 1,200 pounds (about 500 kilograms). He should be compact, stocky and have a short neck; short, straight, strong, and well-muscled back and loins; low withers and croup; large barrel with deep girth; straight, strong legs; and short pasterns and extremely strong hooves.

In addition to these desirable physical proportions, it is essential that pack mules should be gentle and have friendly dispositions. They should have no fear of man and should be free of vices and vicious habits. They should walk and trot freely and boldly over varied terrain. There should be little movement of the back and a minimum of side swaying of the body while the animal is in motion.

For the sake of brevity, I have intentionally confined the wording in this chapter to use the words "pack horse." This is not meant to overlook the suitability, nor certified historical record of use, which pack mules have offered to mankind. There are countless people who prefer to use mules as pack animals. The arguments, both pro and con for mules, are many, long standing, and are often based on subjective personal experience or opinion. As Long Riders our focus should be on the journey, not the species. What works is what counts.

Other Pack Animals

Even though we have been discussing horses and mules, we need to acknowledge the fact that because of the world's diversity, you may be presented with other pack animal options.

Burros and donkeys may be used as pack animals, if led by pedestrians. However, because they are slower than horses, they do not make suitable pack animals for fast-moving equestrian travellers. Also, if tired, a burro or donkey may decide to lie down and refuse to travel on.

Llamas have traditionally been used as pack animals in the Andes Mountains. They eat less than a horse, do not have to be shod and thrive in cold weather but there are no examples of modern Long Riders mutually using equines and llamas. Like the burro, if tired or over burdened, a llama will lie down.

There are several successful examples of 19th century Long Riders who routinely used camels and horses on long journeys. Sven Hedin of Sweden and Gabriel Bonvalot of France both spring to mind. They rode horses but had their equipment carried on Bactrian camels. More recently, when Tim Cope rode across Mongolia, he packed his gear on a Bactrian camel.

The problem with camels is that the majority of horses are not used to them. Therefore it is not uncommon for the sight or smell of a camel to send many horses into a panic. If circumstances dictate mixing horses and camels, then use extreme caution, make sure the animals are all used to each other prior to your departure and do not attempt to lead a camel from horseback. In Tim's case, for example, he employed a Mongol herder to lead the Bactrian pack camel, while he rode alongside.

As a rough rule of thumb, a small donkey will usually carry no more than 50 pounds, a large burro 70 pounds, a small mule or an average horse 100 pounds, a yak 120 pounds and a camel 300 pounds. Any of these animals can be burdened with more weight but a greater load will be detrimental.

Summary

Regardless of whether you decide on a pack horse or mule, the defects of conformation to be avoided in the selection of pack animals are:

(I) Withers-too thick, too flat, or too thin.

(2) Back-too short, too long or swayed.

(3) Chest-broad-ribbed, draft type.

(4) Barrel-excessively large.

By incorporating a pack animal into your travel plans you are able to extend your geographic possibilities and re-inforce your emotional and financial independence. Yet most first-time travellers are tempted to overload their pack horse. Thus the basic law of equestrian travel still applies, whether you are using a pack horse or not. The more you know the less you need. However, if you need it, then put it on your pack horse. Don't overburden your road horse!

Also, never consider your pack horse as an inferior member of your expedition. It is your duty to cherish and take care of this special animal. After all, who will carry your expedition through thick and thin as this horse or mule will? Therefore be to his faults a little blind, be to his virtues ever kind.

If you find that geographic and climatic challenges force you to bring extra food for you and your mount, as well as cooking gear, a tent and additional clothing, then you should not overburden your mount. The answer lies instead in using a pack horse to transport every extra ounce of weight which you can relieve the road horse from carrying.

Since much of the modern world suffers from collective equestrian amnesia, amateur travellers routinely abuse these valuable animals. Such people forget that this is not a four-legged rental truck or some hair-covered soulless contrivance designed to be over burdened then cruelly used. Just because he can stand up under the load doesn't give you the right to overload him.

If we were to describe a perfect pack horse, he would have a deep chest, hearty lungs, big level back, deep middle, and powerful quarters; his legs too are short, heavy in bone, and carry a good deal of muscle.

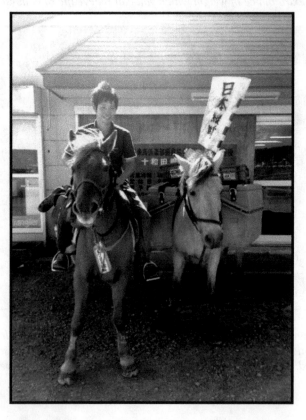

Before setting off in 2014 on a journey across Japan, Kohei Yamakawa carefully chose two geldings which were physically strong and emotionally mature. Because of their short stature, loading the pack saddle on Road Snow (right) was made easier.

Pack and road horses cannot work equally if they are not similar in size and have an equal pace. This larger pack horse outpaced the smaller road horse, which caused constant trouble for Indonesian Long Rider Nirwan Ahmad Arsuka on his first journey.

It would be a mistake to think that the pack horse is a lowly beast of burden. The unobtrusive pack horse did almost as much as the ship in spreading culture along the channels of commerce. One man who understood this was Sergeant Robert Seney. His mounted career stretched from the last days of the horse soldiers to the age of the modern Long Riders.

In 2001 Long Riders Edouard Chautard and Carine Thomas set off with their road and pack horses to make the first mounted exploration of the Pacific island of New Caledonia. Their journey took them more than a thousand miles through the dense interior.

Syrian Long Rider Adnan Azzam made three historic rides, including a journey from Spain to Mecca. During his trip across North America he used a pack horse.

Thanks to the historical motivation provided by Aimé Tschiffely, Argentine Long Riders Raul and Margarita Vasconcellos (above) set off to ride from Arizona to the pampas of Argentina in the early 1980s. They relied on two diminutive pack mules named Pelusa and Fifi to carry their gear.

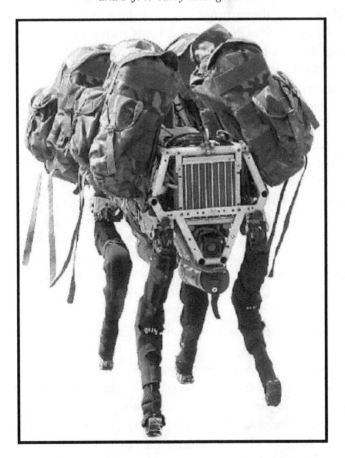

Having lost the vast treasure-trove of knowledge connected to pack animals and pack transport once possessed by its military experts, the United States government has provided millions of dollars to develop a robotic pack animal instead.

Chapter 21
Pack Horse Training

Boy Scout Secrets

Most people don't know that thanks to the British Long Rider Roger Pocock a forgotten chain of equestrian events link the Boy Scouts to the Long Riders' Guild.

Though born in England, in the 1880s Roger Pocock became one of the early volunteers for the newly-formed North West Canadian Mounted Police. After suffering severe frost bite during a campaign against political rebels, Pocock was invalided out of the elite force. It was at this time that he learned that a Cossack Long Rider, Lieutenant Dmitri Peshkov, had just completed an amazing 9,500 kilometre (6,000 mile) winter-time ride across Siberia.

In his book, *Following the Frontier*, Pocock explained how he believed Peshkov's journey along a road would never be equalled, so the Englishman determined to make the longest equestrian journey along a trail instead. This is how the former mounted policeman set out in 1890 to make his historic ride along the length of the Outlaw Trail. According to London newspaper accounts, Butch Cassidy was amazed when the unarmed Pocock boldly rode up to his Hole-In-The-Wall hideout.

After having completed this 5,000 kilometres (3,000 miles) ride from Fort MacLeod in Canada to Mexico City, Pocock learnt of the outbreak of the Boer War. He promptly sailed to England and enlisted for service in a mounted unit. When this conflict ended Pocock returned to London. There he contemplated how ill-prepared his country's military and government had been prior to the outbreak of hostilities. One tactical problem, he realized, was that large sections of the vast British Empire were not serviced by a telegraph. As the Boer War proved, Britain's enemies could be counted on to exploit this communications breakdown, so as to encourage rebellion and attack unsuspecting garrisons. The answer, Pocock believed, was to form a league of hard-riding volunteers. Such seasoned sharp shooters could relay emergency messages and alert the garrisons scattered along the Empire's various frontiers.

Thanks to his travels and military service, Pocock was friends with a diverse crowd of colourful cowboys, exotic soldiers of fortune, seasoned sailors, big game hunters, polar explorers and travel writers. These were the type of "frontiersmen" who could be England's vigilant eyes and ears during peacetime but would spring into action in times of conflict. Thus in 1904 Pocock launched the Legion of Frontiersmen. Though originally based in London, the idea took off like wildfire, the result being that in a short period of time Frontiersmen were eagerly offering their unique equestrian, tracking, hunting and espionage skills to the government.

Though the Legion was primarily a mounted militia, this didn't discourage a wide variety of adventure seekers from joining Pocock's band of hearty amateurs. The result was that the Legion's early roster reads like a "Who's Who" of Edwardian bravery. Big game hunter Frederick Courtney Selous quickly signed on, as did Prince Louis of Battenberg and various other nobles. Writers such as Joseph Conrad, Arthur Conan Doyle and H. Rider Haggard eagerly threw their hats into the ring. And though they couldn't agree on the South Pole, Sir Ernest Shackleton, and Captain Robert Falcon Scott both sent in their applications. Even that dashing Long Rider, "Gentleman" Harry de Windt, who had journeyed from Paris to New York via Siberia, became a Frontiersman.

In a nod to their hard miles in the saddle, the uniform of the Frontiersmen consisted of a neckerchief, khaki shirt and breechings and tough riding boots. Crowning the Frontiersman was a Stetson styled after that worn by the Canadian Mounted Police.

Within three years Pocock's idea had spread across the British Empire. Then a chance meeting changed the course of non-military events as well.

In 1904 Roger Pocock was invited to stay at Louther Castle, the stately home of Lord Lonsdale, one of the English nobles who belonged to the Legion of Frontiersmen. Lord Lonsdale's other prominent guest was Robert Baden-Powell. Like Pocock, Baden-Powell had seen military service during the Boer War. During the Siege of Mafeking, Baden-Powell's small force had been surrounded by a Boer army of 8,000 men. Despite the odds, Baden-Powell's beleaguered outpost withstood the siege for 217 days. During the blockade Baden-Powell employed a group of boys to carry messages and stand guard, so as to free older men for active duty. With the memory of those boys in mind, and having witnessed the success of the Legion of Frontiersmen, it was no coincidence that Baden-Powell discussed the formation of a "Legion of Boy Scouts" with Pocock.

When Baden-Powell founded the Boy Scouts in 1907, the influence of Pocock's Frontiersmen was publicly acknowledged. The Boy Scout uniform, most notably the distinctive Stetson, was modelled after the Legion's. In fact, the A.W. Gamage Company in London was responsible for providing uniforms for both organizations. While such exterior links mattered, the wisdom and frontier knowledge of the Frontiersmen were also critically important to the fledgling scout movement.

When Baden-Powell published his classic book, *Scouting for Boys*, in 1908, he praised the Frontiersmen as "scouts for peace," and urged his young followers to read Roger Pocock's masterpiece, *The Frontiersmen's Pocket Book*. Published in 1906, the older book covered vital topics such as riding, navigation and bush craft, which quickly became standard Scout practice.

Because so many Frontiersmen volunteered to become the original Scout Masters, Baden-Powell also extolled their immense positive influence. Even in far-flung outposts of the Empire, links between the two groups were encouraged. For example, even though civil unrest was causing trouble in China in 1912, a Frontiersman took time away from his duties in order to be quickly married in Shanghai. A troop of Boy Scouts lined the aisles of the church.

Yet the roots of Pocock's idea for a mounted volunteer force could never be disconnected from the war clouds hanging over nearby Europe. Perhaps it won't surprise you to learn that the patriotic and brave Frontiersmen were largely exterminated during the horrors of the First World War. In an age which valued courage and patriotism so highly, Pocock's Frontiersmen enlisted to fight before Great Britain had officially gone to war with Germany. According to legend, the first English troops to see action against the Kaiser were a group of mounted Frontiersmen who had sailed at their own expense from Manchester to fight alongside the beleaguered Belgian army. While that tale is open to debate, what isn't disputed is that nearly 10,000 Frontiersmen lost their lives during the Great War. Many of them won the Victoria Cross, along with a host of other decorations from the Allied commands. Yet when the guns went silent, the Legion of Frontiersmen lay decimated.

They still exist of course. There are a few tiny bands of Pocock's dream scattered in New Zealand, Australia, and Canada. But surely the true legacy of the Frontiersmen is not one of military daring but the example of self-sacrifice and personal bravery which they bequeathed to the fledgling Scouting movement. For those principles are as needed today as they were the night Baden-Powell and Pocock discussed them at Lord Lonsdale's castle.

That is how Peshkov's ride across Siberia led to Pocock meeting Butch Cassidy, and how those rides inspired the English Long Rider to form the Legion of Frontiersmen, which in turn motivated Lord Baden-Powell to found the Boy Scouts. And all of these exciting events were swirling around the streets of London when a young man named Aimé Tschiffely arrived in that city, having left his native Switzerland and come to England in search of adventure.

Little Long Rider

Of course I had no way of knowing all this when I eagerly joined the Boy Scouts in 1965. All I knew was that my pack was overloaded because I had followed all the rules.

Throughout my first three months as a Scout, it rained during every campout. During the course of those endless soggy weekends, my iron-hard Scout Master required me to hike for many miles along muddy tracks. To add to my woes, I was burdened to death because of the Scout's motto, "Be Prepared." In my case this meant that due to inexperience, I had faithfully packed everything which the Boy Scout manual urged me to carry in case of an emergency. It took more than fifty miles of water-logged hiking before my little eleven-year-old mind began to realize that no matter what the manual said, I wasn't likely to need a needle, green thread and extra buttons in the immediate future.

Ah, but the guilt.

I can still recall the night, when prior to leaving the next morning on my fourth campout, I debated about the need to follow the rules laid down in the manual. Did I really need all this kit, I wondered? After all, none of it had even been taken out of my backpack during those long hikes. Should I instead follow my common sense and jettison some of the weight that was breaking my back?

The buttons and thread were left at home.

The extra clothing went next, followed by every single ounce and item I could manage to do without. Of course if wise old Roger Pocock had been there, he could have warned me before I walked fifty miles to learn this painful lesson the hard way.

The moral of the Boy Scout story is that the more you know the less you need. But, to bring it all back to equestrian travel, the less you know the more you pile on your poor pack horse. In other words, the less a man knows about horses, the greater is his idea of its powers.

That is why the critical law of Long Rider packing is to never place one single item or ounce on your pack animal if it can be avoided. Not an extra packet of food. Not those warm socks. Not even those little Boy Scout green buttons you think you might need in an emergency.

Your road horse is designed to carry you, your saddle, rain gear, map and any essential paperwork. Everything else goes on the pack animal.

But remember, when you try to turn an out-of-shape pasture pet into a road horse, it suffers. When you try to draft an untrained animal into being a pack horse it can lead to serious injury or death.

So if you're going to get it right, what do you do?

The first thing is to avoid the danger of romance!

Romantic Notions

In 1855 Francis Galton made a critically important observation in his classic book, *The Art of Travel*.

"The art of good packing is to not overload the pack horse, to balance the pack boxes accurately and to secure the load so that it does not slip. Up to 120 pounds of cargo, a pack horse keeps pace with a mounted man, swims rivers, crosses swamps, penetrates bush, and climbs mountains."

This law of common sense still held sway at the dawning of the 20th century when the American cavalry cautioned, "In general, the pack loads accompanying a combat column should not exceed twenty-five percent of the weight of the pack animal which, for small mules and horses, would mean a maximum pay load of about one hundred and thirty pounds. One hundred pounds is considered an average load. This is a general rule and the load must be varied to meet the condition of trails and the condition of the individual animal."

By the time the Second World War rolled around, the laws of good packing were so pervasive that even the United States Marine Corps warned, "Pack animals must not be overloaded."

Earlier in this book I cautioned you not to accept advice from anyone who had not ridden a minimum of five hundred miles in a straight line, explaining that weekend riders do not understand the rigours and dangers encountered in an equestrian journey. Likewise, you should be extremely cautious about accepting advice from people whose packing experience is limited to guiding trail riding tourists or participating in short hunting expeditions.

That was the valuable lesson which Michael Bragge and Iain White learned in 1982 before they rode from Melbourne to Brisbane, Australia.

"Although lots of people in the bush had some packhorse experience back then, none had ever lived with the packhorse for long periods while travelling 140 kilometres per week. We found that we needed to listen carefully to advice but invent our own solutions," Michael recalled in an email to the Guild.

The worst example of what happens when you listen to the wrong packer occurred in 1999 when two inexperienced foreign travellers attempted to follow in the hoofprints of Butch Cassidy and the Wild Bunch. Lacking any experience, these novices sought the advice of a so-called expert in New Mexico. Though he looked the part, with the standard battered Stetson, cheek full of chewing tobacco and unshaven face, the packer had no long distance travel experience. What he did have was a low bank account and a wagon load of bad advice. The tourists were not just trusting, they were eager to pay. Thus the stage was set for an equestrian disaster.

Things began badly. Four horses were tied closely together inside a stout corral. A fifth animal, with no packing experience, was led into the centre of the corral, where one traveller held the lead rope, while the packer cinched a pack saddle in place. The problems arose when hard sided panniers were draped along both sides of the unsuspecting animal. Perhaps it was a deeply implanted genetic memory of a predatory big cat suddenly landing on his withers that drove the horse into a blind panic? We'll never know. What is certain is that the would-be pack horse broke free, and with the panniers clanging and scaring him, raced towards the other horses in search of safety.

Sadly, that's not what he found. The frightened horse galloped alongside the corral fence, shearing off the four lead ropes and sending the other horses into a terror-stricken retreat. In an instant screaming horses were scattering in all directions. But before wheeling away, the largest of these horses lashed out with his mighty steel-clad hoof. The blow hit the pack horse full on the shoulder, pulverizing the bone and instantly crippling the beleaguered animal. Thus the wrong animal had been involuntarily drafted, terminally frightened and fatally injured in less than five minutes. Because of his agonizing wound, the horse was destroyed on the spot.

But the pack master's lessons were far from over.

Not being content with his original deadly mistake, the amateur packer proceeded to bury two more horses under two hundred pounds of gear a piece. This didn't include the Coleman stove and fuel he placed atop one of the already burdened animals. Armed with this mountain of weight, the overloaded travellers set off across the harsh South Western deserts and over the unforgiving Rocky Mountains. They eventually reached the Canadian border, but not before one pack horse plunged to its death off a cliff, all the animals routinely suffered from saddle-sores and thirst and the pack horses struggled to stand under their crushing loads.

How did things go so wrong?

The amateurs had forgotten the wisdom from the past.

St Francis of Assisi said, "If you have men who will exclude any of God's creatures from the shelter of compassion and pity, you will have men who will deal likewise with their fellow men."

That is why, even though genuine cowboys and ranchers en route routinely advised the travellers that their horses were overloaded, they chose to ignore this valuable advice and press on with their immense pile of gear.

While some may argue that an army pack horse or mule did occasionally carry loads of up to 250 pounds, such weight was the exception, not the rule. Nor were the military animals in question involved in long-distance travel. They were primarily used for the short-distance transport of military goods and weapons.

Our concern, as Long Rider packers, is never to vindicate how much weight we can theoretically place on the pack horse. Our objective is how to always protect the delicate health of our pack animals by travelling with a minimum of weight.

As the example from New Mexico proves, it is imperative that the pack horse be taught his trade at home.

Fundamentals

As you now realize, it's not easy being the pack horse. Not only does he always work harder than his companion, the road horse, in case of an emergency on the trail, the pack horse must also be able to operate using his own initiative and common sense.

This led Australian Long Rider Michael Bragge to caution, "It is a fundamental misconception to think that an unsatisfactory riding horse can be used as a pack animal. This is a myth. The admirable qualities of a good riding horse, confidence, composure, balance, strength, willingness and flexibility are necessary in a pack horse too."

With this in mind, when inspecting any potential candidate for the position of pack animal, be sure to ensure that you can lead him quietly while on foot, that he stands quietly while being loaded, and that he will travel alongside the road horse without biting or pulling back. If any of these primary rules are violated, your journey will be an ordeal.

Therefore, if an equestrian journey is to progress smoothly, there are many critical elements in a pack horse's education which must be addressed prior to your departure.

Tutoring for the trail

Even if he has been previously ridden, a new pack horse is faced with a bewildering assortment of challenges. The creaking and swaying of the panniers may frighten even a calm horse. The weight of the load may throw his balance off. The bulky pack saddle no longer allows him to casually make his way between trees, around obstacles or along a narrow cliff side trail.

Instead the pack horse finds that he is carrying a great inflexible weight. Rigid panniers may poke him. Breast collars and breeching often scrape him. A crupper under his tail may frighten him. A lead rope pulls, rather than directs from behind like the riding reins he is used to.

Is it any wonder that a horse or mule might express his distaste or fright at this series of new intrusions? When so many things might go wrong, unless you relish the idea of seeing your gear scattered down the trail, you should choose a safe place to begin training the pack horse.

Standing

First and foremost, the pack horse must stand like a rock, not just when being packed, but during the course of his normal working day as well.

Unlike tacking up the saddle on your road horse, which swings into place with ease on the near (left) side and does not require the Long Rider to walk to the off (right) side, the moment the first pannier is hung on the near side of the pack saddle, the load immediately become unbalanced. Even if there are two Long Riders working efficiently, the assistance of the pack animal is critically important at this moment, as he must remain calm, hold his position, maintain his balance and not interfere with the loading of the second pannier.

It is also important that a pack horse learns to come to a halt, and stand still, when the Long Rider stops his road horse and dismounts. This can be accomplished by attaching a strong long lead line to the halter. To bring the pack horse to a halt, the rider says "Whoa," and reins in his road horse. He dismounts quickly, and carrying the length of coiled rope in his hand, moves quietly away from the pack animal, paying out the rope as he goes. If the pack horse attempts to move, the Long Rider discourages any movement by a sharp quick tug on the long lead rope. This process should be repeated until the pack horse learns that when the road horse stops, so does he. When this occurs, the extra long lead line is then replaced by a normal length lead rope.

Saddling

Before the pack horse is ever fully loaded, it is critically important that he should be allowed to become thoroughly familiarized with walking about with only the empty pack saddle on his back. When he is accustomed to wearing the pack saddle, take him on very short training rides alongside your road horse. This allows him to become used to the feel, sound and smells associated with carrying the unburdened pack saddle on his back.

Only when you are confident that he has no need to fear wearing and carrying the pack saddle can you carefully introduce him to the concept that low hanging panniers, or other luggage, will be placed on his back and may hang down along his ribs.

Loading

Instead of starting with hard sided panniers, which may frighten or rub him unexpectedly, you should begin by hanging two soft straw-filled bags off the pack saddle. Allow him to stand quietly, growing accustomed to this strange, low hanging, but unbreakable load. Then begin walking him calmly in hand. Always make sure that you stand well to one side so that if he becomes frightened, he will not unintentionally injure you by shoving, running or jumping past you in a panic.

Lead him alongside, past or through objects which will touch the straw bags. To demonstrate how he needs more space than he is used to, walk him between two trees which provide six inches of clearance on each side. To accustom him to the unexpected sound of panniers scraping, walk him beside a barn wall. To build up his balance, walk him up and down a short steep trail. These exercises will build up his confidence, all the while reinforcing important new lessons: more space is needed to move safely forward: strange scraping noises emanating from the panniers are not life threatening and the sense of balance can no longer be taken for granted.

If possible, keep the road horse in sight so as to reinforce the pack animal's emotional security.

When you feel he is ready, set off on a short training ride. But be ready to stop, halt, dismount, and calm the pack horse at the first sign of any trouble. If need be, drop his load and return empty, rather than frighten him. Next, substitute two hay bales in place of the straw bags. Though still unbreakable, they will teach him to accept a large firm load. Walk him through his exercises again, making sure to praise him upon his success.

Once the straw bags and hay bales have been accepted without trouble, take the next step, which is to carefully hang the empty panniers onto the pack saddle. It is often the noise, or unusual sensation of panniers unexpectedly scraping his ribs, which sends nervous horses into a panic, so proceed cautiously. Once the empty panniers are accepted without protest, once again walk the animal peacefully on a short lead rope. Always allow the new pack horse as much time as required to become accustomed to these strange new burdens.

Only after the pack horse has learned to stand quietly to be loaded, and will let you walk him with the pack saddle and panniers in place, should you begin to gradually add equal amounts of weight to both panniers. Training rides should be kept short.

Nor should you forget that the unaccustomed sounds of the gear being carried in the panniers might startle the pack horse. The result may be an impromptu rodeo on a narrow trail which sees your gear smashed and scattered. Even worse is when a panicked pack horse becomes a runaway, streaming gear behind him as he disappears into the distance. When travelling you must always ensure that any objects loaded in the panniers are padded, so as to diminish the sound of rattling or banging which might frighten an inexperienced pack animal. The training period is when you forestall this problem by intentionally placing a small tin can holding stones, or some other suitably noisy, small and indestructible objects in the bottom of the panniers. Walking the pack horse by hand, sooth his concerns when the noisy load begins to shake, rattle and roll. Repeat this procedure on your trail ride, using the noise to reassure the pack animal that any sound emanating from the panniers is of no physical or emotional concern to either of you.

Never rush any part of this training and make certain these exercises are accomplished slowly, so as to avoid frightening the animal.

Leading

The moment you introduce a pack animal into the equestrian travel equation you automatically diminish your own personal safety by half. This is due to two factors which do not arise when you travel with just your road horse.

A Long Rider normally sits erect in the saddle, with his eyes on the horizon, his shoulders square, his hands on the reins, his hips loose, his legs long and the balls of his feet resting lightly atop the stirrup. He and the road horse are a single unit moving in the same direction.

But the pack horse instantly throws the Long Rider out of balance. This occurs when the Long Rider shifts the road horse's reins into his left hand and holds the pack animal's lead rope in his right hand. The effect is that the Long Rider's body is always slightly off centre, his balance is compromised and his attention is now diverted in two directions. He is literally a man in the middle.

The true danger is that if a pack animal baulks and the road horse unknowingly continues to move forward with alacrity, the Long Rider can be pulled backwards out of the saddle without warning. I witnessed such an accident in Pakistan. It happened so quickly that the rider didn't even have time to release the lead rope. He was yanked straight out of the saddle and came crashing down on his back at the feet of the obstinate pack horse that had caused the mishap.

Thus the lead rope becomes an instrument for your potential destruction if your pack animal is not properly trained to lead quietly.

Therefore, once the animal has been taught not to fear the pack saddle and panniers, the next critical part of his further education is to teach him to travel faithfully behind the road horse, not to pull back on the lead rope during the course of the day's travel and never to stop without warning. Once again, this training must be completed prior to your departure and the first part of such training begins on the ground.

Ideally the pack horse should walk along freely, maintaining a constant space of three feet between the rider's leg and his head. But it takes time and practice for the pack horse to learn to respect your personal space.

Such training is vital, as a horse that invades your personal space is not demonstrating affection. He is attempting to dominate and intimidate you. That is why you must not confuse your feelings of emotional loyalty with any display of his physical bullying. Any invasion of your space afoot is a strong indication that you'll have diminished respect in the saddle. That is why you have to begin by establishing that you are in firm control when you stand near the pack animal.

Your safety on the ground is immediately jeopardized if the horse is allowed to come too close without your consent or invitation. He can now tread on your feet, smash you with his head or bite you. That is why it is essential that a horse never be allowed to crowd you. Though you may decide to stand next to him, or demonstrate signs of affection such as stroking his neck, he must not be permitted to intrude into your space uninvited.

This is a dilemma which the well-informed Stan Walchuk grappled with on many occasions. During his years of riding through the Rocky Mountains, Stan needed to train numerous pack horses. He quickly realized how critically important it was to teach these animals to maintain a safe distance. To do so, Stan developed a daily practice which has surprising historical connections to another equestrian culture.

"When you walk alongside the horse's head, hold the lead rope close to the halter with your arm straight. It feels odd at first to have your arm straight, but in a short time it becomes an easy habit," Stan said.

But why keep your arm straight?

Because Stan accurately deduced that by straightening your arm, you create a solid buffer between yourself and the pack horse.

"If you do this you will not get your feet stepped on," the wise Long Rider said.

Ironically, it wasn't only the Canadians who hit upon the idea of creating a safety space between pack horse and rider. During the Second World War, the German cavalry used an item known as the leading stick. One end of this three-foot-long, lightweight, wooden staff was clipped to the pack horse's halter. The cavalry rider held the other end in his right hand. The leading stick not only maintained the pack horse's distance, it ensured that the heavy gear, i.e. machine gun, wooden ammo boxes, etc., did not smash into the rider's unprotected leg.

Thus, though the country and year differ, Stan and the German cavalryman both confirm the necessity of teaching the pack horse to maintain a safe distance from the rider. Though no modern Long Rider has yet to resurrect the concept of the leading stick, the principle is sound and such a stick would surely prove to be an excellent way to teach a young pack horse to maintain the proper distance.

The German leading stick demonstrates another point about leading horses. Namely, where you ride may determine how you lead.

The distance and the placement maintained between the road and pack horse may be influenced by the culture you are travelling through. For example, in North America it is common practice to have the pack animal follow close to the Long Rider's right leg, while in Russia pack animals are taught to follow behind the tail of the road horse. For our purposes, we shall focus on the Euro-American practice of keeping the pack horse on the off side of our road horse.

Teaching the pack horse to follow the road horse correctly is a matter of practice and patience. Training should always be done at the walk. It is not uncommon for an inexperienced pack animal to show signs of confusion, or to hang back, when you and the road horse move forward. The first time this occurs you will feel the tension spring into the lead rope. If a stubborn pack animal is allowed to repeatedly pull back during the course of an entire day's travel, the pressure on your right arm and shoulder will become agonizing.

Begin by placing the pack horse's head close to your right leg. Holding the coiled lead rope in your right hand, urge the road horse to move forward slowly. Ideally the pack horse will follow the more experienced animal in front of him. If he continually baulks, dismount. Wrap the lead rope up alongside the right side of the pack animal's cheek, running it over the bridge of his nose, down the opposite cheek and back under the halter. The lead rope will now encircle the pack horse's face. By placing the lead rope across the pack animal's nose in this manner, it will have been converted into a mild hackamore which will exert a slight pressure on the bridge of the nose. Remount, bring the pack animal up close to your right leg and set off again, making sure that the lead rope is kept sufficiently tight so that it exerts pressure on the animal's nose if he pulls back.

This temporary hackamore instantly transfers a mild message to the pack animal. It is far better to follow along quietly, for should he decide to pull back the slightly uncomfortable pressure on his nose will be constantly applied until he learns to relieve it by resuming his correct position in line. Most horses are intelligent enough to take on the importance of this fundamental lesson and quickly learn to faithfully follow the road horse.

As with all things, there is a tender balance here too. While you wish to keep the pack horse close enough to hand, so as to not pull your arm out of its socket, equally you do not want him smashing the pannier into your leg or the road horse's flank. This is why it is imperative that you and your team practise leading until all of you are sufficiently well versed in this vital daily aspect.

With a well-trained pack horse, the lead rope should act as an indicator of direction transmitted from the Long Rider.

When travelling along roadways, the pack horse should follow the road horse on the off side, so as to keep him away from traffic. The major exceptions are in countries where the cars travel on the left of the road, such as Britain, Australia, New Zealand and Japan. Never allow the pack horse to stroll along and then trot to catch up. The pace of the pack horse should always match that of his companion. If the pack animal becomes fatigued, do not enter into a tug of war with him. Dismount and rest the animals.

When leading the pack horse over level ground, there should be a constant, reassuring pressure running along the lead rope. It should never be a tug of war. When pack animals are led down short slopes, they should be discouraged from trotting. When confronted with steep slopes, the pack animal is given his head as much as possible so as to allow him to seek his own footing and maintain his balance.

Pack animals should never be encouraged to jump over obstacles, such as logs and ditches, as this may dislodge the pack saddle or cast the panniers out of balance. If you encounter such a problem, proceed cautiously. Stay far enough ahead and out of the way if your pack horse is required to jump an obstacle.

If the terrain becomes rough or steep, you may decide to allow the pack animal to follow the road horse freely, as he can be caught as soon as the obstacle has been passed. However, you should have avoided placing yourself and your horses in such a precarious position to begin with.

Straying

Pack horses die when they fall off trails. They fall off trails when they stray out of line. They stray out of line because they're improperly trained before the journey begins.

Disasters hit you when you can least afford them. This is especially true in the mountains, where help is usually far, far away.

Most pack horses fall because they try to overtake the road horse. Their eagerness, curiosity or stupidity causes them to hit an unexpected obstacle, to lose their balance, to round a corner too quickly. Regardless of why, the result is that the unforgiving heavy load on their back is snatched by the force of gravity, and then, in a heartbeat, the pack animal is either falling through the air, or more likely, rolling down the mountainside, all the while you listen in horror to the sound of his big leg bones snapping like dry twigs. If he's unlucky enough to survive the fall, he'll be lying crippled at the bottom, in indescribable agony, while you're still perched on a trail high above, trying to figure out how to dismount from your scared road horse.

That's what happens when a pack horse strays out of line.

Never take inexperienced pack horses into the mountains, never take them along high, narrow trails and never allow them to stray out of line. If your pack horse isn't courteous, disciplined and smart enough to have grasped the life-saving meaning of this lesson, he doesn't belong on the journey – nor do you.

Gaits

The cavalry trained their pack animals to not only march rapidly, but to also be able to trot, and in the face of a tactical emergency, even to gallop a short distance with a full load.

Long Riders, however, are not in any danger of being attacked by Apaches. Consequently, our primary pace is always a fast, smooth, mile-eating walk. If the terrain and weather are not adverse, a well-matched team of road and pack horses will cover four to five miles an hour on average.

If you put your horses into a trot a number of unfortunate things may occur. You greatly increase the possibility of upsetting the load. Gear may work its way loose, thereby creating noises which causes the horse to panic. Additional pressure will come to bear on the withers, which may cause saddle sores. Greater fatigue will require a longer period of recovery.

The short answer is, if you're trotting your pack horse, then you've probably made a mistake in some other part of your daily travel planning, i.e. you misjudged the distance to be travelled and are facing a rapidly-setting sun. But unless there is a concern for your collective safety, do not add to your troubles by trotting your pack animal.

Training Rides

Most horses will soon realize what is expected of them in this new role. Given the proper training they learn to stand still while being loaded, negotiate between obstacles and not crowd the Long Rider on the trail. When these goals have been achieved, every effort must be made to physically condition the pack animal for the trials ahead.

Such conditioning can be acquired by making training rides which require your pack horse to practise carrying a full load over varied terrain. This is also when you ingrain good discipline by introducing him to the wide variety of sights, sounds and smells which might startle him. This includes automobile traffic, blaring horns, noisy crowds, loud music, low-flying aircraft, train whistles, barking dogs and irritating children. Once he learns that none of these disturbances will cause him any pain or harm, his docility and good conduct will be assured.

Additionally, the pack horse's sense of equilibrium must be encouraged. He should be challenged to undergo small trials which build up his confidence and reinforce his sense of balance. Carefully lead him across narrow bridges, along constricted trails, next to streams, between trees in a forest, beside a traffic-laden road, up and down a steep incline. He must walk along confidently behind you, following you without hesitation wherever you decide to lead.

Never demand long trial rides from your unconditioned pack horse. Initial training rides should be short and then gradually lengthened as the animal's physical condition improves. Your goal is to have the pack animal ready to travel with a full load for five days a week.

Training Schedule

The gentling, training, and conditioning of an expedition's pack animals should begin as soon as possible. A horse without pack training may be nervous, soft, overfed, and under worked. To prepare him for an extended equestrian journey his muscles must be hardened, his body accustomed to hard work and his nerves seasoned.

The following thirty-day training programme, using the pack saddle and equipment needed during the trip, will allow the animal to be educated and conditioned prior to your departure. It also requires you to alternately ride the pack horse. The result will be a gentle, dependable and willing pack animal.

Day 1 – This is the introductory day for pack horse and Long Rider. The goal is to establish a strong emotional bond with the horse and win his confidence. The Long Rider should talk to the horse, hand feed and pet him. Hand feeding will teach the horse not to fear you and to associate you instead with acts of kindness. The horse should be quietly groomed, brushed lightly and his feet cleaned. All your actions should be quiet, patient and firm.

Day 2 –After grooming, begin the day by walking the horse quietly around the corral. Begin to teach him voice commands. Say, "easy," when you want him to slow down and "whoa" or "halt" when you want him to come to a complete stop. While walking, reinforce the need for the pack horse not to invade your space, by keeping him at arm's distance or by using your lead stick. Next, introduce him to the strange things which now make up his daily work equipment, including the pack saddle, panniers, saddle pads, breast collar and crupper. Let the animal see, smell and investigate every article. Once he's familiarized himself with the equipment, rub a saddle blanket across his back and down his legs. Then lay a rope across his back. Let it dangle over his back and then withdraw it slowly. Move it back onto his haunches, letting it fall down along his tail and heels. Reassure him verbally while these exercises are under way and reward him when the work is completed.

Day 3 – After grooming, place the pad and pack saddle on the animal's back. Cinch it lightly and then walk the animal. Remove the pack saddle and replace it with your riding saddle. After you are mounted, drape your rain coat first on the pommel and then on the cantle, walking the horse quietly so as to allow him to become used to feeling strange objects brushing his body while he's moving.

Day 4 – After grooming, cinch the pack saddle securely and carefully place the empty panniers on the animal's back. Slowly walk the animal in the corral, halting frequently and reinforcing his need not to crowd you. Let him grow used to the feel of the panniers moving along his ribs. Next, replace the pack saddle with your riding saddle, then practise mounting and dismounting from your riding saddle on the near and off sides. Practise asking the horse to walk and halt.

Day 5 – After grooming, mount the horse and then exercise him at the walk and trot. Practise turning right and left in both gaits. Urge him to stand still when he comes to a halt. Next, allow a rope to drag behind as you proceed at the walk. Let the rope touch his flanks and ankles as he walks. Next, replace the riding saddle with your pack saddle and panniers and then work on the walk, halt and keeping his distance. Praise him for his good work.

Day 6 – After grooming, mount the horse then practise turning and halting at the walk. Replace the riding saddle with the pack saddle and panniers. Repeat the exercises on foot, being sure to lead the horse from both the near and off sides. After coming to a halt, drop the lead rope and step back for a few moments, emphasizing the need for him to stand still. Repeat this exercise as needed.

Day 7 – Meticulous grooming and feet cleaned in the morning, then allowed to rest the remainder of the day.

Day 8 – After grooming, mount the pack horse, then set off cross country on the first training ride. Walk briskly over easy ground away from the corral for the first half hour, then walk and trot alternately for the next hour. If possible, make a wide circle so that the horse does not return over the same ground. During the ride, halt the pack horse and practise reading a map or looking through your binoculars, while asking him to stand quietly.

Day 9 – After grooming, mount the pack horse and make a five-mile journey along a quiet road. Pick easy footing which allows the horse to focus on moving easily, without fear of stumbling. Never sprawl in the saddle. Keep the walk brisk and trot sharply. Alternate your gaits. Halt frequently and urge the horse to stand quietly when motor traffic passes. When he's halted at a safe place away from traffic, take off your hat, move it in the air, then replace it on your head.

Day 10 – After grooming, mount the pack horse and make a seven-mile journey, alternating between travelling across country and along a fairly busy road. Walk, trot and halt en route. When you reach a safe place, halt, throw your hat on the ground, then dismount, put it on and remount on the off side.

Day 11 – After grooming, place the pack saddle, empty panniers, breast collar and crupper on the animal, cinching it securely but not too tightly. Then mount your road horse and lead the pack horse at the walk for an hour along a moderately well-travelled road. Halt frequently. Emphasize staying in line. Even if the pack horse crowds you, practise patience. Upon your return, praise his hard work and reward him with a hand-fed treat.

Day 12 – After grooming, tack up the pack and road horses and then perform a ten-mile training ride with empty panniers. If possible, alternate between a trail and alongside a road. Focus on keeping both horses moving at a brisk walk. Halt the horses frequently and require them to stand still until you give the go-ahead. When walking, emphasise the need for the pack horse to maintain his distance from you and the road horse. If possible, and you deem the situation safe, lead the pack horse around trees and down an incline.

Day 13 – After grooming, tack up the pack and road horses then perform a five-mile training ride with empty panniers through difficult country. Look for low hanging branches or bushes which will scrape the sides of the panniers and make unexpected noises. During the ride, dismount and secure your road horse. Then lead your pack horse over an obstacle such as a small bridge, around a boulder or over a ditch. Require him to practise stepping over several big logs. Remember not to let the pack horse leap over any obstacles. This is especially dangerous in tough terrain because if he jumps unexpectedly, the pack horse may tear the lead rope out of your hand, drag you off your feet or bolt.

When he's clearing the obstacles, emphasize his balance, composure and discipline. Praise him in the field when he accomplishes his tasks correctly.

Day 14 – Meticulous grooming and feet cleaned in the morning then allowed to rest the remainder of the day.

Day 15 – After grooming, place the pack saddle and empty panniers on the pack animal. Then mount your road horse and lead the pack horse at the walk for thirty minutes along a busy road. Halt frequently, letting the pack animal become accustomed to the sounds of the traffic. Return early. The remainder of the day the pack horse rests, after being praised for his hard work. By now he should be in good health and unquestionably on the way towards becoming conditioned. Our goal is for the pack horse to be able to travel twenty miles a day, under a full load, for five days a week.

Day 16 – After grooming, mount the pack horse and set off on a seven mile training ride cross country. Walk and trot briskly. Halts and standing still emphasized en route. During the ride, practise dismounting and re-mounting from the off side. Do this repeatedly.

Day 17 – After grooming, tack up both horses. Today the pack horse carries his first load. Divide a total of fifty pounds in both panniers and then make a five-mile training ride across country. Make sure the footing is level, as the emphasis is on letting the pack animal get used to the weight of his new burden.

Day 18 – After grooming, tack up the pack horse and place fifty pounds divided between both panniers. Then set off on a seven mile training ride along a quiet road. Remember to use your packing scales to ensure that the panniers are properly balanced. Emphasize the need to halt during the journey, to stand quietly when halted, maintain distance when travelling and walking briskly.

Day 19 – After grooming, increase the load in the panniers to seventy-five pounds. Pack everything carefully, taking care that nothing in the panniers rattles during transit. Today's emphasis is on safe travel, not rapid progress, as today's exercise is to encourage the pack horse to start using his own initiative. Set off on a ten-mile training ride which includes crossing numerous obstacles and difficult terrain. Negotiate steep inclines, narrow trails, go between trees and ride along a noisy road.

Day 20 – After grooming, set off on a ten-mile training ride along a busy road. Take a break at the five mile mark, allowing the horses to stand, relax and grow used to the noise of the traffic. At the completion of the ride, give extra attention and praise for the pack animal's good performance.

Day 21 – Meticulous grooming and feet cleaned in the morning, then allowed to rest the remainder of the day.

Day 22 – After grooming, increase the load in the panniers to one hundred pounds, carefully ensuring that each pannier carries fifty pounds. Make a ten-mile training ride across country. Today's load should accurately reflect the normal amount of gear you will actually be using. Even distribution of the weight is essential. Walking briskly, keeping proper position en route, halting and standing should now be established.

Day 23 – After grooming, a one hundred pound load and a fifteen-mile training ride. This should be a combination of cross country and road work.

Day 24 – After grooming, tack up the pack animal. Equally divide a fifty pound load between the panniers. The emphasis today is to accustom the pack animal to unexpected noises emanating from the panniers. Place noisy metal objects next to each other. Insert a metal can full of pebbles on top of the load. Keeping in mind the onset of the noise, walk the pack animal carefully, being sure that he doesn't run over you or pull away in fright. Halt frequently, reassuring him that the noise is nothing to be afraid of. When he appears to have accepted the noise, take him on a thirty minute training ride with the noisy load in the panniers. Upon your return, praise and hand feed him.

Day 25 – After grooming, a one hundred pound load and a fifteen mile training ride cross country. Halt halfway through the ride; loosen the cinches, allowing the horses to rest with their loads and saddles in place.

Day 26 – After grooming, mount the pack horse and ride him along a quiet road for twenty miles. Halt halfway, loosen the cinch and let him rest.

Day 27 – After grooming, a one hundred pound load and a twenty-mile training ride along the same quiet road. Halt halfway, loosen the cinch and let him rest. Upon your return, praise and hand feed him.

Day 28 – Meticulous grooming and feet cleaned in the morning, then allowed to rest the remainder of the day.

Day 29 – After grooming, a one hundred pound load and a twenty-five mile training ride along a quiet road.

Day 30 - The pack horse should be physically conditioned, emotionally equipped and mentally ready for travel.

Tips

Every hour spent educating and physically training your pack horse prior to your departure decreases your chances of having an emergency during the journey.

Make sure that the pack horse is properly shod one week prior to departure.

Because of the irregular stabling awaiting you on the road, your pack horse should be grazing and spending as much time as possible outside prior to your departure. Establish a regular time to feed him his morning and evening meals, so as to reinforce the importance of these emotionally important rations.

The pack horse is a sensitive animal, employed in a back-breaking job, who should never suffer from bad treatment. Most punishment is superfluous and must only be used in those rare cases when absolutely necessary.

Because of the difficulty of his carrying his heavy daily burden, psychological rewards are even more important to the pack horse than to the road horse, who routinely receives a string of small comforts and reassurances from the

Long Rider during the course of a day's ride. Therefore, reward your pack horse with praise and attend to his physical needs with great care.

Trust comes from mutual understanding. If you respect the pack horse, he will repay your kindness a thousand times over.

The Great Taboo

I have chosen to include this information in a special section, so as to emphasize the dreadful consequences which may arise if you ignore it.

In 1931 Thurlow Craig wrote about the many misadventures he had survived while exploring the infamous Chaco jungle of Paraguay. While recalling various episodes involving jaguars and bandit chieftains, Thurlow made this critically important observation.

"A horse that hangs back on the leading rope nearly tears your arm out, but you cannot take a turn around the saddle horn, as this is the surest way of injuring the back of the horse you are riding."

That's just the half of it. If you get lazy and wrap the lead rope around your saddle horn you have effectively tied your pack horse to your road horse. The consequences of this act of stupidity are dreadful and multi-faceted.

Should you become slothful and wrap the lead rope around the saddle horn, the lightest punishment you can expect is that the pack horse will snap off the saddle horn if he suddenly stops.

That's what happened to Bryan Brant.

"We had to cross over a ditch and my horse Abbey decided at the last minute to jump. But the pack mule Jack didn't want to. Abbey and I were stopped in mid air of the jump as Jack jerked back hard enough to rip the pommel and horn from the saddle. I remember seeing half of the saddle coming right back at me with very little time to react. I stood in the saddle as it was folded in half just barely clearing it as it went under me."

Should the lead rope be lying across the top of your leg when the pack animal baulks, the rope will squeeze the top of your leg like a vice, effectively pinning you in the saddle, all the while a 1,200 pound pack horse is acting up or rearing behind you.

That's how John Beard was nearly killed. He made the mistake of attaching the pack horse's rope to the horn of his saddle. When the pack horse panicked, the lead rope trapped Beard in the saddle.

"Before I could get the rope freed from the saddle horn, the pack horse had passed around behind my horse, bringing her rope across my thighs, passed it under the back of my saddle, and pulled the saddle, with me in it, under the side of my horse. I tried desperately to untie the rope but found it impossible. I tried to reach my knife from a back pocket to cut the rope, but it, drawn tightly across the pocket, prevented me. The rope was beginning to cut deeply into my thigh and my grip on the reins with one hand and on the saddle horn with the other began to loosen. It looked as if I was in for a pretty bad smash up when my wife, at imminent risk to life and limb, managed to free me."

Should you make the mistake of wrapping the lead rope around the saddle horn, and then let your hand rest on top, when the pack horse snaps the rope back, it will amputate your finger or thumb as effectively as a pair of surgical scissors.

Should you be ignorant enough to dismount, and then tie the lead rope to your saddle horn, you have instantly placed the lives of both your horses in tremendous peril. That's what a criminally neglectful traveller did in the Sierra Nevada Mountains. When her road horse slipped off the perilous mountain trail, he pulled the pack horse to his death as well.

As Thurlow Craig aptly pointed out, the best of these terrible scenarios is that tying the lead rope to the saddle horn greatly increases the chances of giving your road horse a terrific saddle sore.

Never tie the lead rope to your saddle!

Never wrap the lead rope around your hand!

Carry the lead rope in your right hand in countries where cars travel on the right.

If you break this taboo, you and your horses may suffer severe injuries or die.

Ana Beker was seriously injured on the first day of her ride from Argentina to Canada, when the inexperienced traveller tied her pack horse to her road horse. In front of a crowd of well-wishers, the pack horse suddenly tugged with all its strength, startled Ana's mount and the latter threw her.

"The impact of my fall was so violent and unexpected against the hard surface of the road that I lost consciousness and only came to in hospital."

French Long Rider Philippe Rustenholz also learned this lesson the hard way when he came within an inch of losing his life because of this mistake.

"I packed the mule with barely a hundred pounds and loaded my spare riding horse, Flecha, with the oats and the saddle bags. Then I set off whistling, looking towards the mountains. I rode Flauca, who is the fastest, and was leading Flecha, who is the boss, and to whom I tied the mule. I hadn't gone very far when I heard something behind me, and turning round, I saw the terrified mule had pulled back on her rope which, luckily, broke.

But this action had upset the saddle onto which I had put the oats and now Flecha was all tangled up, with the packing rope caught between his rear legs. Before I could stop him, Flecha overtook me at the run. Unfortunately I had tied his leather lead rope to my saddle. When this rope caught my riding horse, it pulled my saddle straight over Flauca's body, (I had not tightened the girth very much). The rope also ripped my saddle-bags loose, which then smashed into my horse's leg. Luckily the breast collar did its job and stopped my saddle from turning completely upside down.

But I now had all my weight on the left stirrup. To make matters worse, Flecha's leather rope had trapped me tight in my saddle. That's when I found myself caught between two now-galloping horses.

Flecha already had his saddle under his stomach and the packing-rope tangled round his legs (a brand-new rope which I had only bought the day before). Plus, any second my saddle was about to give way and slide further down. If that happened, I would fall between the two horses who were now galloping flat out with only fourteen inches between them.

In an effort to save myself, I spoke to them, trying to calm them with my voice, all the while I was busy trying to pull my saddle back into place. Then the horses stopped. The first thing I did was to untangle the lead-rope and dismount. Then I freed Flecha from the packing rope which had wrapped itself around his hind legs. After this, I took care of Flauca, whose saddle was barely held in place by the breast collar. When I looked behind me, I saw that my kit was spread across two hundred yards.

With these thoughts in my head, that's the moment my mule chose to come rushing up to joyfully rejoin her companions. But not before jumping a deep, wide rocky ditch which brought her load banging down on her back. At least the cinch on the pack saddle held and the panniers weren't broken," Rustenholz reminisced grimly.

Disasters - Avoidable and Otherwise

Because we're discussing equestrian travel, not flying or driving, I must reiterate the fact that unlike those largely predictable modes of transportation, there is always a strong element of chance present in equestrian travel. This means that no matter how much time you have spent carefully training your pack horse prior to departing, surprises often occur once you're travelling.

While a single Long Rider and road horse must always be cautious, as I previously emphasized, the introduction of a pack horse increases the danger level for all concerned. This law of the trail becomes apparent when something unexpected occurs. A bird flying out of the bush may scare a pack horse. Stepping on a yellow-jacket nest hidden in the trail is guaranteed to put a pack horse into a bucking spree. The unexpected sight of a fearsome animal, be it a camel, llama, peacock, yak, dog or pig, may throw the pack horse into a panic. You must always be ready for such an unforeseen occurrence suddenly to terrify the previously calm pack horse.

Keith Clark learned this lesson when he began his journey in Chile.

"On the very first day I had a really dodgy moment. As we were climbing a steep trail the pack saddle slipped loose and slid underneath Lucky's belly. I really thought I was going to lose him because the off-balance pack saddle was about to pull him right over the edge. But he stayed still whilst I got off. Fortunately, he didn't kick or panic while I carefully unloaded him, because he would have gone straight to the bottom of the mountain if the pack saddle moved. I guess I named him right when I called him Lucky," Keith recalled.

As Keith's experience proves, things can and do go wrong suddenly when pack horses are involved.

That is why Frank Heath, who rode to all 48 American states, wrote, "I am a strong advocate of the idea that a horse has more intelligence than he is generally presumed to have. But for her own safety as well as mine, she must let me be the judge."

Horse Harmony

The life of a Long Rider is always full of habitual vigilance, inflexible work, constant concerns and daily negotiations. The labour of packing and unpacking your gear is a time-consuming chore. Keeping your equipment in proper order is never ending. Making sure that everything you own is carefully preserved against the unending movement of the pack saddle, not to mention the climate, is a serious challenge.

That's why you don't want to further complicate your life by setting off on a journey which lacks a sense of horse harmony. Because equines maintain a strong pecking order, they require time to formulate their social policy. The last thing you need alongside a busy road is to have an alpha pack horse biting the flanks of your intimidated riding horse. Because your days and nights are always preoccupied with a host of other concerns, it is critically important that the road and pack horses work, eat and sleep together without any difficulty.

The horses should live together peacefully, if not as friends, at least with a sense of mutual tolerance. It helps if they are roughly the same size and walk at the same pace. Ideally, they should be able to inter-change their duties, with both horses being obedient enough to ride with one hand, while the other is led.

Not only should you be careful about your own horses showing signs of temper, when travelling you must always take care that other horses do not kick, wound or injure your animals. When approached by other ridden horses, always take care that neither you nor your animals are kicked unexpectedly. Medical care for you can probably only be found in some distant city. Sadly, if one of your horses is seriously injured, he may have to be put down on the spot.

Carts and Wagons

A word of caution. If you make a mess of it, and find that your pack animal is unsuitable, ill trained, belligerent or dangerous, don't be tempted to think you can resolve your problems by changing a pack saddle for a cart or wagon.

The most notorious example of this miscalculation occurred in the late 1980s when an American was trying to cross Patagonia. Having no experience with packing, he reasoned that an ancient two-wheeled cart could be dusted off and drafted into carrying his gear. The local gauchos were willing to cooperate, so the gringo's Criollo reluctantly agreed to be backed between the shafts of the cart. A set of old harness was draped across the body of the increasingly nervous animal and then attached to the cart. But the experiment came to a brutal conclusion when the American attempted to lead the Criollo. The moment the old cart began to creak and groan it sent the horse into a terror-stricken panic. The result was that first the lead rope was ripped out of the astonished gringo's hand. Then the horse sprang straight into an insane gallop and attempted to escape the churning, groaning old wagon behind him. Sadly, no matter how fast the Criollo ran, he was relentlessly chased across the pampas by the wagon. According to eye witnesses, the horse didn't stop running until there was nothing bigger than a matchstick left of the wagon.

A horse that has never been in harness is totally useless in a moment of emergency for the purposes of draught. Driving is a science and falls outside the scope of this book.

Summary

The pack horse should be sedate, reliable, gentle and strong. Bad-tempered equine bullies will never do. The efficient progress of the Long Rider's journey depends on the prior training, physical conditioning and emotional behaviour of his pack animal. Pack saddles and panniers, tough terrain and scary traffic, it all has to be second nature to the pack horse before you hit the road.

Don't think you can use the pack animal as a pickup truck. Remember, it's not the kilometres that will kill your horse, it's the kilograms. Never overload the pack horse with a single ounce of extra weight.

Though his burden is heavy, you must never forget that the pack horse has much to contribute beyond mere conveyance and convenience.

Regardless of whether you use a pack horse or a mule, both should be treated with kindness and patience. Rough treatment of any kind must be avoided.

The final word on the subject comes from the poet, Bloomfield.

> A man of kindness, to his beast is kind.
> But brutal actions show a brutal mind;
> Remember, He, who made thee, made the brute,
> Who gave thee speech and reason, formed him mute;
> He can't complain, but God's omniscient eye
> Beholds thy cruelty – he hears his cry!
> He was designed thy servant, not thy drudge.
> But know – that his Creator is thy judge.

Roger Pocock served in the North West Canadian Mounted Police, made the only solo journey along the Outlaw Trail from Fort MacLeod in Canada to Mexico City, organized the civilian militia known as the Legion of Frontiersmen and helped Sir Robert Baden-Powell form the Boy Scout movement.

Before setting off on their 2,500 mile journey across Australia, Iain White and Michael Bragge made the mistake of thinking that a riding horse could be quickly and easily drafted into the role of pack animal. As these pictures, taken by Michael in 1982, demonstrate, Iain learned that "confidence, composure, balance, strength, willingness and flexibility are necessary in a pack horse too."

Choosing the proper pack animal depends on more than just muscle. Louise, the Shire mare seen on the right completed a 22,500 kilometre (14,000 mile) journey across the USA. But Vicky, a retired harness racing horse seen on the left, lasted only one day as a pack horse before being found psychologically unsuitable.

Prior to riding from the Atlantic coast of Maine to the Pacific coast of Washington, North American Long Rider Deb Yavorski made certain that her Appaloosa pack horse, Wolf, was physically fit and emotionally ready for what lay ahead. They completed their journey without any problems.

English Long Rider Tim Mullan *understood the importance of carefully training the pack horse prior to riding across Mongolia in 2013.*

This was especially vital in Tim's case because neither the native horse nor the Mongols had ever seen the type of pack saddle, panniers and breeching which Tim had obtained for the trip.

During the Second World War, the German cavalry used a wooden lead stick, which allowed the cavalry soldier to maintain a safe distance between his riding and pack horse.

Close-up of the Wehrmacht lead stick.

Mules are renowned for their stamina and strength, which generally allows them to carry a heavier load than a similarly-sized horse. They have a strong walk, an excellent sense of balance and their hooves are normally tougher than a horse's. However they tend to baulk and have a reputation for kicking with remarkable accuracy.

Chapter 22
Long Rider Packing

Justified Concerns

Before setting off on a great journey, it is not unusual for would-be Long Riders to quietly question their equestrian qualifications. Such silent pondering usually focuses on a lack of riding ability. Yet there is a graver issue involved in equestrian travel, one which has caused far greater pain and scuttled more journeys than all the basic riding mistakes put together.

I refer to the expertise needed to pack a horse successfully.

Howard Saether and Janja Kovačič are perfect examples of first-time travellers who worried about transporting essential goods into the geographic unknown. How could they solve this knotted riddle in the short time they had before setting off to ride from Uruguay to Texas? Nor were they amateur adventurers. Prior to taking to the saddle, they had been deep-water sailors. Plus, having spent his youth in Norway, Howard was also a seasoned Arctic dog sled traveller. These were hardened travellers who had already survived far more escapades than the vast majority of first-time Long Riders. The infamous Chaco jungle lay across their proposed route and they needed pack horses to get through.

"I must admit that we didn't have the slightest idea about packing horses before this trip. We are both experienced sailors, so we are used to ropes. But when we started to look at the traditional ways of putting cargo on a horse, which involved dozens of meters of rope and intricate knots, we were quite terrified. Not to mention, we couldn't imagine doing all this work several times a day. We also heard all the horror stories about the horses being scared out of their wits when cargo slipped to one side or under the belly of the horse," Janja explained.

Luckily, an answer to this equine dilemma had been discovered in Canada by the Long Riders' Guild.

Defining Packing

Before we put any equipment atop our imaginary horse, let us consider what we are trying to accomplish.

First of all, pack systems are like politics. They're always local. A cowboy in the Rocky Mountains will rely on his 1960s Decker pack saddle. A gaucho in Patagonia will throw a 1890s style sawbuck pack saddle on his Criollo gelding. While a Chinese trader heading towards Tibet will place the girthless pack saddle developed in Asia long ago atop his sturdy mule.

Because equestrian practices are based upon generations of obstinacy and tradition, if you ask any of these seasoned packers for advice, they will invariably find fault with any system other than the one taught by their forebears.

Such an incident occurred when Tim Mullan and Sam Southey took the finest pack saddle and equipment available to Mongolia. The local horsemen decried these foreign innovations.

"The Mongolian people helping us decided this way was no good and insisted on making something up on the spot," Sam wrote.

This resistance to change is not intellectually surprising but it doesn't help a Long Rider on a practical level.

The vocation of packing is nearly as old as civilization itself, so whereas we can allow for debate between different equestrian cultures, let us start with the truths involved in packing horses in any part of the world.

To begin with and as previously stated, the dead weight of the pack saddle is a harder burden to bear than the live weight of a Long Rider. Hence our need to ensure that the pack saddle we choose is as gentle and effective as possible.

Next, while it is true that a loaded pack animal can normally travel anywhere a man can walk without the use of his hands, what is seldom considered is that leading a pack animal is far more difficult than riding a lone road horse.

Packing horses requires special skill and unremitting care if the system is to be employed successfully. If you make a mistake it may result in serious injury due to badly-fitting saddles, wrongly-adjusted panniers and loads being allowed to remain on the animals for too long of a period.

Thus, it is mandatory that you pay strict attention to the essential principles of packing, i.e. weight, balance, stability and pressure. Regardless of where you travel, the load should always be as light as possible. No matter how many times you load your pack horse, the correct balance of the panniers is of paramount importance. Early detection of a problem may prevent injuries to your pack animal, which in turn will ruin your trip.

Jobs not Journeys

There are two more basic lessons to consider and they both come to us courtesy of Down Under.

When Michael Bragge and Iain White set off across Australia they sought advice from an Outback legend, Harry Downe. During the Second World War, many of Australia's remote lighthouses could not be reached by sea because of the danger of Japanese naval mines. To keep the lighthouse-keepers supplied, the government recruited Harry to lead a large team of pack horses through the bush.

"Twenty two horses lined up every second morning to pass through a loading pit Harry had dug to relieve his back from lifting the loads on to the horses. They then followed him nose to tail as he blazed a trail to the lighthouses," Michael explained in an email to the Guild.

Lighthouses and twenty-two pack horses?

That's a job, not a journey.

Likewise, the people likely to offer well meaning-advice to a Long Rider are usually also employed in one way or another. This includes the cavalry packer with his leather-covered pack saddle designed to carry machine guns, the forestry packer whose caravan of heavily-burdened mules keeps remote ranger camps operating, or the professional hunter who guides clients into a base camp serviced by large numbers of pack animals carrying everything from safari tents to cocktails.

While all of these professionals can relate to many of the primary equine problems encountered by Long Rider packers, there are some fundamental differences. Their pack animals are asked to carry very large loads. They travel over well-known ground. They and their animals return home after a brief period in the field. And asking advice from such people is fraught with trouble.

This isn't a new discovery or a recent problem.

In 1925 Clyde Kluckhohn set off to ride through the stony wastes of Arizona, Utah and New Mexico in search of a geographic legend known as "The Rainbow Bridge," a giant multi-coloured arch of stone rumoured to be located in a remote part of the desert.

Having been born in Iowa, young Clyde didn't have a clue on how to load a pack horse. So he sought the advice of local "experts." What he discovered was not encouraging.

"I received much advice from old-timers. In particular I was told the best way of tying a pack saddle. At first I absorbed all the information greedily, but soon the magic wore out. The principle cause of my disillusion was the discovery that the authorities were not in perfect agreement."

Long Rider packers travel light, move fast and they don't go home.

A perfect example of this new type of equestrian pack traveller is Tim Cope. He had no previous equestrian experience but he rode 6,000 miles along the Equestrian Equator, following the hoofprints of Genghis Khan's mounted warriors from Mongolia to Hungary.

He had no packing experience but he took his pack animals across Central Asia, Russia and into Europe with no problems.

How?

By using time-honoured methods and cutting-edge new technology, the combination of which allows a beginner rich with enthusiasm but lacking hands-on experience to become a successful Long Rider packer.

Labour

To begin with, prepare for hard work.

Equestrian travel is always hard work. Because of the long miles and harsh weather, it beats you on an anvil of physical pain. It taxes your emotions to the breaking point by confronting you with a host of dangers, delays and challenges. And that's before you add in the daily work involved in grooming, watering, feeding and tending your road horse.

But when you bring pack horses into the travel plan, you've not only increased the expenditure of energy needed to take care of more animals, what's worse, you have now created a rod of iron that will beat your back every morning and evening, as you struggle with the packing, balancing, loading, and unloading of your equipment.

In the comfort of your home, you may view the accumulated kit sitting on the parlour floor and believe you've reduced it to a minimum. But the morning you depart, your world changes. First you must work to keep everything reasonably protected. Sharp edges which may break or cut another object must be taken into account when you're loading the panniers. Anything which can spill or leak has to be wrapped with care. Potentially noisy objects, which might cause a pack horse to panic, must be padded.

Even after you've vigilantly packed your belongings, you'll be aware that every time the pack horse sways down a hill, trots to keep up or smashes the panniers into a tree, your worldly possessions are being subjected to the equestrian equivalent of a tumble dryer.

And don't forget the physical labour and time required to carry it from the camp to the panniers, to pack the panniers, to carefully weigh them, to hang them on the pack saddle, and then repeat the entire procedure in the evening, after you've had a long, hard day in the saddle.

When you put things into perspective perhaps it won't surprise you to learn that you, the solitary Long Rider, have taken on the jobs of no less than four men. In addition to helping each other load the pack animals every day, these men each had specialized duties in the cavalry's pack team.

The Packer, who reported to the Cargador, was responsible for the care of the pack animals and for preparing the cargo prior to loading.

The Cargador, who reported to the Pack Master, was responsible for repairing damaged pack saddles en route and had to inspect the cargo prior to departure to ensure each load was balanced.

The Pack Master, who reported to the Caravan Commander, had his hands full, as he was responsible for the care and maintenance of all pack equipment and animals in his unit. Prior to departure, he was required to oversee all packing to ensure that the loads had been properly packed to avoid injury to the animals' backs. During the day's journey, he was required to ride along the entire column in order to check all loads and observe the condition of the men and animals under his command. In his abundant spare time, he was required to train the men in the proper method of saddling, adjusting, and packing the pack saddle.

The Caravan Commander was responsible for the entire pack train when on the march. He organized personnel and animals at stream crossings and required proper maintenance of the pack equipment, cargo and animals under his control.

As a Long Rider Packer, you do it all!

The Dangers of Pack Saddles

Sore backs are a plague which can cripple or even kill a pack horse and historically, before the Guild was formed, nothing ruined equestrian travels more often than pack saddles.

The back of a horse should be smooth, firm and flat. If you run your fingers along the spine, moving from the withers to the dock of the tail, there should be no trace of lumps, sore spots or heat. Injuries to a horse's back occur because of friction and pressure. Friction rubs off the hair and outer surface of the skin, and pressure, partly or entirely, cuts off the blood supply. The result is injuries to the back, shoulders, withers, or other part of the body. One clue as to the existence of such wounds will be white hairs on the pack horse's withers or along his back. The hair turns white as a result of the flesh underneath having suffered a trauma or wound.

Do not think that a pack saddle has to draw blood to injure your animal. When the skin of an unconditioned pack animal is subjected to the unaccustomed pressure of a pack saddle, it is liable to be bruised by even moderate work. Even after the back is hardened to contact with the pack saddle, it may become inflamed by continued or uneven pressure. Regardless of the cause, once the animal's skin is broken, it will never heal thoroughly during the remainder of your journey unless you take an extended break.

A bad pack saddle is a curse on the poor animal unlucky enough to be forced to wear it.

Traditional pack saddles have two inflexible bars which lie alongside the animal's back. When the animal moves, these bars press deeply into the horse's withers, shoulder blades and on his upper rib cage. Now imagine what happens when you place a heavy load on top of these bars. With every stride taken, the hard bars push, dig, cut or damage the flesh beneath.

Many injuries also occur if the front arch of the pack saddle is too narrow in the neck. If there is excessive swelling in the wither area from a narrow pack saddle, the pack horse will develop a critical infection known as fistula of the withers. This large hump swells, eventually erupts and pus is extruded. In extreme cases, this painful injury can lead to death.

Orient and Occident

The principles of fitting the pack saddle are identical with those of the riding saddle. Yet as the description of these wounds proves, poorly fitted pack saddles routinely caused terrible saddle sores for Long Riders all over the world.

In the third section of this book entitled "Equipment," I explain how the Orient and Occident developed two diverse philosophies of pack travel which are as different as chopsticks and forks. Though the end result is the same, the equipment and practices are very different.

In that upcoming chapter, I also provide a detailed history of the pack saddle, explaining the historical sequence of events in the Occident which led to the development of the aparejo, sawbuck and Decker pack saddles. Just as importantly, I also reveal the secrets of the cavalry's now-lost Phillips pack saddle and explain how the girthless Asian pack saddle operates.

But that's history and what concerns us first is hands-on knowledge. Therefore the most vital point for you to grasp is that regardless of what type of pack saddle you are using, they are all capable of causing dreadful wounds on various parts of your pack horse's body. To reduce the already high risk of injury to the pack animal's fragile withers and back, it is imperative that crude, improvised or antiquated pack equipment never be used on an equestrian journey.

Consequently, before you depart, carefully confirm what pack saddles are available in the local equestrian culture where you plan to ride. If proper equipment is not an option, and it seldom is, then you must purchase a safe pack saddle in advance and transport it to your destination.

And if we want to reduce the immense damage which cheap, ineffective pack saddles can inflict, then we need to look for the answers in Canada, land of the adjustable pack saddle.

The Canadian Adjustable Pack Saddle

Unlike ring riders, who can telephone for help in case of an emergency, the life of a Long Rider often depends on his equipment. That is why the Guild never endorses any product until it has been rigorously examined in the field by various trusted Long Riders.

The single most successful piece of equipment ever tested is the adjustable pack saddle made by Custom Pack Rigging in Canada. It has done more to reduce equestrian travel injuries than any other article in modern history. Because it is lightweight, strong, durable, inexpensive and can be adjusted to fit any equine, Long Riders have successfully used it on equestrian expeditions all over the world.

Unlike the rigid pack saddles used in previous centuries, the Canadian adjustable pack saddle can be adjusted to fit any animal's conformation. There is more to this statement than meets the amateur's eye. The rigours and hard work encountered during a journey will quickly sweat the fat off any horse or mule not used to hard travel. Thus, despite the best of care, the actual shape of your pack horse will very likely change according to the availability of rations, how far you've travelled, etc.

In the past, when the pack horse lost weight the cavalry packer would add, or adjust, saddle pads so as to further cushion the animal's back. The adjustable pack saddle allows you to continually and accurately fit the pack saddle to the animal as his body changes shape.

Stan Walchuk is Canada's best known Long Rider. He made a perilous solo equestrian journey across that nation's most daunting mountain range, the Cordilleras. Afterwards he opened a renowned outdoor equestrian school where he teaches wilderness and packing skills. Stan routinely takes mounted groups deep into the Canadian backwoods. During those trips his pack horses are always equipped with the adjustable pack saddle.

"Some traditionalists do not like the idea that modern adjustable plastic pack saddles have bars that swivel. They feel that the load may rock more or extra pressure may be placed on one bar more than the other. We cannot tell that it makes a difference. Adjustable saddles definitely fit a wider variety of horses better than wooden sawbuck pack saddles. We also believe that the metal cross frame, used on the adjustable pack saddle, is less likely to break than wood," Stan explained.

There is another benefit too.

Because they are adjustable, one pack saddle can be fitted to the various sizes and shapes of horses encountered during an extended journey. This is a significant consideration for Long Rides, who may be forced by circumstances to change their pack animals as they cross through various countries.

Tim Cope proved how adaptable this pack saddle can be. Not only did he fit it to a number of horses, at one point he even used it to pack his gear across Mongolia on a Bactrian camel.

"Pack horses can be a Long Rider's Achilles heel. Yet with the pack saddle from Custom Pack Rigging, I never had a saddle sore or rub of any kind. I had two of these pack saddles. They are adjustable, light, unbreakable, and never broke despite the incredible strains they received during the journey. What's more they are so adjustable they can be fitted to camels and yaks as well. Plus, when you need to ship your gear the pack saddle breaks down into a very handy little package. My adjustable pack saddles were crucial and lifesaving," Tim said.

Meanwhile, on the other side of the world, before he set off to ride across the Andes Mountains, Keith Clark made another critical observation about the adjustable pack saddle. They make more financial sense than the locally-made alternative.

"About the pack saddle, as far as I'm concerned there is only one way to go and that is the saddles and panniers from Custom Pack Rigging. They are hardly more expensive than the pack saddles found here in South America but are far better. Go for the one where the arch bolts in the middle. Then it will fit just about any horse or mule."

Saddle Pads

Because of the dead weight bearing down on the pack horse's back, he requires a thicker saddle pad than the one you place under your riding saddle. A good pack saddle pad is usually twice as thick as a riding saddle pad.

In addition to hand-making each of their adjustable pack saddles, Custom Pack Rigging also offers many of the other critically important items needed by a Long Rider Packer, including the thicker pack saddle pad. One very good option is the pad which is open at the top and can be attached to the pack saddle.

During his ride across Mongolia, Tim Cope reported, "The CPR pads are the envy of all the nomads. It has worked a treat along with all the other CPR gear."

Panniers

In the past, packers transported goods in baskets hung on the sides of their pack horses. By the late 19th century the American and European cavalries had devised a method wherein objects were wrapped in thick canvas cloths, securely tied shut, then lashed to the sides of the pack animals using a set of long ropes and a series of complex knots. By the mid 20th century, as the size of loads was reduced by civilian packers, soft-sided canvas panniers began to be hung off pack saddles. In the beginning of the 21st century a nearly indestructible pannier was constructed out of thick plastic.

Because they are equipped in the rear with stout nylon loops, the modern hard-plastic pannier can be easily hung onto the adjustable pack saddle. This has largely eliminated the need for the long rope and hitches that once made up such an important part of 19th century packing.

One of the other great improvements of these panniers is that their smooth sides are curved to fit snugly alongside the pack horse's rib cage. This greatly reduces chances of the pack animal being wounded or rubbed by the load. The panniers also have closely fitting lids, which can be equipped with locks so as to protect your gear.

Because they are water proof, the panniers can be taken through rivers with no problems. If crossing a waterless areas, a spigot can be fitted. This turns the pannier into a large canteen capable of keeping horse and human alive.

Long Riders have reported one drawback, which is that in extreme heat the panniers may lose their shape if packed too tightly.

Custom Pack Rigging offers two sizes of these panniers and regardless of where they travel Long Riders have suggested that the larger size pannier be chosen. The additional room helps ensure that you won't have to place extra gear in a top pack. It also makes it easier to balance the panniers.

It is critically important that you practise packing the panniers prior to your departure, as you must know where every item is kept. You do not want to fumble in the dark looking for cooking gear, a first aid kit or warm clothing. While it may have dawned on you that there is a need to separate your gear according to size, shape and weight, Long Riders have learned of another factor. The need to separate the kitchen from the office,

Long Rider Otto Schwarz learned a similar method during the Second World War. He and his mounted Swiss troopers had two large leather pommel bags attached to the front of their cavalry saddles, one of which carried essential items needed by their mount, while the other bag contained the few items each man was allowed to carry.

Long Riders have learned to divide the panniers into two separate units, the contents of which are kept strictly segregated. One pannier should be marked with the letter P for provisions. Anything of an organic nature, including food, cooking gear, horse brushes and hobbles should be kept in this pannier. The second pannier should be marked with the letter E for equipment. This box contains anything which might potentially poison your food and water, including your lap top, camera, first aid kit, stove and fuel.

Once you've marked your panniers, rehearse packing at home until you know where everything is and how it fits inside each box. Where do your clothes go? Can you easily reach the items needed to set up camp? Are heavy objects set securely at the bottom of the pannier? Have you made sure that fragile electronic equipment won't be crushed? What about leaking cans, bottles or ointments? Are your maps handy?

As you can see, the internal arrangement of your panniers is a significant duty which requires thought, care and practice before you leave. Nor can you say your duties are done once you've fitted all your gear into your carefully-marked panniers, because it's not enough to fit it all in. You must always ensure that each box has been carefully weighed and is balanced within a few ounces of its work mate. Even the difference of a few too many ounces heavier on one side may pull the saddle off side. This in turn creates pressure, which causes saddle sores that can ruin a trip.

Pack Scales

It's simple, really.

If the panniers are equally balanced, you immediately reduce the chances of your pack horse getting a saddle sore. Balanced panniers also decrease the likelihood of a load slipping to one side. Thus you must confirm the equality of the load's weight.

To do this, you need packing scales.

When Long Riders think of essential equipment, this inexpensive tool doesn't usually spring to mind. Yet it costs very little, provides an accurate measurement every time it's called into service, will last for years and will save your pack horse a mountain load of sorrow. Though a good pack scale can handle weights up to 150 pounds, it is a small sturdy instrument which has a tab that automatically notes the exact weight of the pannier.

There are different ways to weigh panniers.

Traditionally, two people weighed the panniers using brute force. A rope was tied between the nylon straps, so as to provide a way to hang the pannier from the pack scale. One person then lifted the heavy box off the ground, trying to hold it steady in the air while the partner attempted to get an accurate reading. Not only is this physically tiring, when weighing a pannier it is important the pannier is raised gradually, not jerked up into the air, as this sort of abuse can break the pack scale.

There is an alternative method which not only does away with the problem of repeatedly lifting the heavy box; it can be done by one Long Rider.

If you're in the field, and cannot hang the pack scale from a convenient strong nail, tie a rope to a tree. Then throw the rope over an overhanging limb twice, so as to keep it from slipping back. When the rope is pulled tight, tie your pack scale securely to the end of the rope. Using a smaller piece of rope, tie the pannier's nylon hanging straps together. This provides you with a way to hang the box from the pack scale. Finally, hang the pannier from the scale and check the weight twice so as to insure the accuracy of the measurement.

In an emergency, balance a long pole on a tall object, such as a large rock, tall tree stump, corner of a corral, etc. Then hang each pannier from the ends of the pole and carefully arrange your gear in the two boxes so as to make the load as evenly balanced as possible.

It may be tempting not to bother how carefully you balance the panniers. When you discover a saddle sore on your pack horse's back, you'll be so filled with regret that you'll wish you had paid more attention to this fundamental lesson.

Top Pack

The top pack is a large square canvas bag which rests on top of the pack saddle's panniers. The obvious problem is that this big luxurious space tempts you to fill it with paraphernalia, all of it apparently needed, yet adding to the overall weight the pack horse has to carry.

The other drawback to top packs is that they raise the pack saddle's centre of gravity. Normally, the weight of the panniers ensures that the centre of gravity is fairly level with the top of the animal's rib cage. But a top pack places a hefty chunk of weight directly atop the pack animal's back. This in turn can cause the pack saddle to rock, become destabilized and pull the pack saddle off to one side.

Thoughts differ among Long Riders who have used top packs. For example, Tim Cope used one with great success when he rode along the Equestrian Equator.

"One of my most useful pieces of equipment that I had custom made before I left is a huge canvas bag. It is tough, weatherproof and has multi uses. It is big enough to easily fit my saddles, blankets and general tack when travelling by plane, car, truck whatever. When riding, everything that is cumbersome and does not easily fit into the panniers is thrown into this bag, which I then strap to the top of the pack saddle. I would definitely recommend that all riders get some kind of bag like this."

In contrast, Keith Clark decided against using a top pack.

"I suggest using the largest panniers, never load your pack horse with more than fifty kilos (110 pounds) and keep the top of your pack horses free of a load. When riding in Chile I found it was hard to find feed. By keeping the top unloaded, and the horses relatively lightly loaded, it's easy to load a small bale of hay or a sack of feed on top when you find it."

Pack bags

Though we have focused on panniers, an occasion may arise when you wish to hang soft sided, but tough bags from a second pack animal. Stan Walchuk recommends using two strong canvas duffel bags, as they are inexpensive and can be equally balanced with relative ease.

Tim Cope had similar canvas bags made after his journey was well under way. Like Keith Clark, Tim used these bags to stock up on essential grain for the horses.

"My second horse was dedicated mostly to grain. Generally I would load him up with fifty kilos of grain, either oats, barley, wheat, or corn, whatever was available, which would last my horses for five days."

Lash Rope

The lash rope is a long rope with a hook on one end. Though the length and diameter may vary, it is used to keep the panniers from swinging out of balance, or bouncing up and down when covering hard ground. A lash rope becomes critically important if you decide to use a top pack, as the rope will keep the canvas bag in place.

The lash rope is placed over the top of the panniers and top pack and then brought underneath the stomach of the pack horse. The rope is run through the lash rope hook, then pulled gently to tighten it snugly under the horse's stomach. The rope is then tied off. Any excess rope is securely fastened to the pack saddle. Inexperienced pack horses may panic if the lash rope is pulled too tight or if a rope end is allowed to swing loose while travelling. So practise using the lash rope before your departure.

Like the adjustable pack saddle and pad, the lash rope is available from Custom Pack Rigging.

Hitches and Knots

Pack animals used by cavalry and back country packers routinely carried large, awkward, extremely heavy cargo. These loads were traditionally wrapped in thick canvas cloth packages called manties, which were then tied shut. Two men lifted the manties into place alongside the pack horse. Then a series of complicated knots, known as hitches, were used to lash the cargo onto the pack saddle.

These traditional packers employed so many varieties of rope work that the result was a Gordian's knot of hitches.

The squaw hitch tied up a single load. The Phillips hitch was employed for double box loads. A single diamond hitch held double loads of normal size but a double diamond hitch was brought to bear if there was a triple load. The basket hitch secured odd shaped loads. And we must not forget the Nagle hitch or the sweet diamond hitch.

In short, there was a hitch for every day of the week and every type of cargo imaginable. The only problem was that it took a professional to master them all. This might all seem a bit daunting. It certainly intimidated deep-water sailors like Howard and Janja, who expressed their doubts at the start of this chapter.

Yet Thurlow Craig knew a thing or two about knots and his advice on the subject may surprise you.

"Do not worry about what you may have read regarding complicated pack knots such as the old diamond hitch. Any one of them, particularly the diamond hitch, will take a tenderfoot weeks to learn, during which time he will tie himself up in knots in his nightmares."

If you use a lash rope, learn one standard hitch to secure your load. Regardless of which knot you choose, these are the rules regarding their use.

Work quietly to avoid alarming the animal. Always keep the lash rope away from the pack horse's feet and legs. Form the hitch rapidly. Three minutes is sufficient time to complete any hitch. When completed, make sure all parts of the hitch are as tight as possible. Check to make sure the load is balanced before and after tightening the hitch. Always ensure that no part of the rope is fouled up on the pack saddle and that the loose end is secured.

Breast Collar, Crupper and Breeching

When you encounter steep terrain, there are three pieces of equipment which keep the pack saddle from sliding either forwards over the horse's withers or backwards towards his tail, i.e. the breast collar, crupper and breeching.

The crupper and breeching are different varieties on the same theme, i.e. a strap designed to keep the load from moving forward or backward, depending upon the terrain. This is especially important if the pack animal has low withers.

Whether you use a crupper, or the heavier breeching, depends on your horse and destination. For example, if you're travelling across hundreds of miles of flat land, then neither the crupper nor breeching are required. But if the terrain is mountainous, then one should be chosen. Regardless of which one you pick, care must be taken when saddling up the pack horse. Because the crupper fits under the root of the animal's tail, a timid pack horse has to be trained not to be frightened when it is put in place.

In addition to stopping your pack saddle from sliding in hilly country, there is another advantage to securing your pack saddle in the front and back. It allows for a slightly looser girth on the pack saddle. This is an important point, as great care must be taken not to pull the girth too tightly.

If the cinch, breast collar, breeching or crupper are fitted incorrectly, then friction and pressure will cause serious wounds, including having the animal's hair rubbed off, followed by severe abrasions. You should be able to fit one or two fingers under the breast collar and breeching, so as to confirm that it is not too tight. Because cruppers can cause a painful friction burn under the horse's tail, always ensure that they are fitted properly, and checked often during the day's journey.

Breast collars and breeching can be obtained in either leather or durable nylon. Because of the excessive horse sweat caused by packing, the latter is easier to clean, cheaper and very tough. Leather however is less likely to cause friction burns.

Lead Ropes

The last piece of essential equipment for the Long Rider Packer is the lead rope, which should be eight feet long and an inch in diameter, so as to provide a strong and comfortable grip. Be prepared for bad rope in bad countries.

Now, with our equipment ready, let's examine how we go about loading the cargo on the pack horse every morning.

Preparation of Cargo

To begin with, don't interrupt the pack horse's breakfast until you've prepared his load for travel.

Even if you have two large panniers, and a top pack, there is still a limited amount of space within which everything has to fit.

Therefore, because every ounce counts, dispose of all surplus commercial packaging, placing food instead in tightly-closed cloth sacks or sturdy zip lock bags. Telescope everything you can, so as to minimize the space needed in the panniers. Wrap anything breakable. Make sure any pots or metal items that might rattle en route are carefully padded. Don't mix food and fatal, i.e. keep provisions away from potentially lethal equipment and fuel.

Place the heaviest items at the bottom of the pannier. Pack your cargo tight to make sure it can't shift when you're travelling. Try to roughly balance the weight of each pannier as you load it. When both panniers are loaded, use the pack scales to confirm their weight is evenly distributed. Not only do the panniers have to weigh the same; they also have to be balanced from front to back.

Now let's get the horses.

Prior to Packing

The goal of your morning packing is to close camp, load the horses, and set off, as quickly and efficiently as possible. But the morning's work cannot be hurried. In order to make this system work, you have to be disciplined and organized; otherwise your horses suffer because of your inefficiency. Though this takes practice, your goal should be to have your horses saddled, loaded and on the road in thirty minutes.

To begin with, it's important that you have found a quiet, level place where you can pack and saddle your horses. Lifting heavy panniers is hard enough without struggling to hoist them uphill onto a pack saddle or losing your footing when your hands are full. Carefully choose the location where you will work.

The left side of the pack horse is known as the near side. The right side is known as the off side. Because most horses are mounted from the left side, they are easier to pack from the left. One person can pack a horse but it is much easier for two people.

Don't pick up any equipment unless you know it can be trusted. Make it a part of your morning and evening ritual to inspect your riding and pack saddles. This includes the girths. Make sure that they, and the saddle pads, are absolutely clean of anything which might rub or injure the horse's sensitive skin.

Before you begin saddling your animals, place their equipment in a neat pile behind where you plan to tie and work with them. Riding saddle, pad, bridle, saddle and pommel bags should be ready for your road horse. Pack saddle, pad, breast collar, breeching or crupper, lash rope, panniers and top pack likewise should be ready to be loaded without delay onto the pack horse.

Be sure you leave plenty of room between the horses, so that you can move between them safely. Also, make certain that neither horse can step backwards onto your equipment.

With your ground chosen, your horses safely tied and your gear ready, begin by saddling your road horse, which will be carrying the lighter load. Use this opportunity to adjust the bridle, make sure the stirrups look in order, and secure the pommel and saddle bags. If you're carrying a rain coat, or any extra gear, tie it in place too. Finally, before moving on to the pack horse, make sure the road horse's girth is not too tight, leaving it just snug enough to keep his load in place while you're busy with the pack horse.

With your road horse ready, promptly move on to the pack horse.

Fitting the Pack Saddle

Not only does the pack horse carry a greater physical burden, he is enclosed in more complex equipment, so extra care is always needed.

To begin with, when grooming your pack horse, be quiet, systematic, patient, observant and consistent. Before saddling, use the saddle pad to smooth his hair, front to rear, two or three times.

Placing the saddle pad in the proper position is the first test of the day. When a pack horse sweats, the wet hair encourages the saddle pad to slide towards the tail. Additionally, there is a great deal of movement around the horse's shoulder blades, which also encourages the pad to retreat. Finally, if the girth or lash rope become loose, they too allow the saddle pad to move off centre. The combination of constant movement, slick sweaty hair, loose girth and steep terrain results in the pack saddle slipping backwards during the day's travel. That is why it is a common mistake to not place the saddle pad far enough forward when you begin to saddle up.

Thus, when the horse is groomed, place the front of the saddle pad one hand's distance in front of the rear edge of the shoulder blade. The result should be that about three inches, or one hand's width, of the saddle pad are left exposed when you place the pack saddle on the horse's back.

Placement of the pack saddle is also critically important. Always place the pack saddle gently on the horse's back. The forward edge of the pack saddle bars should be placed far enough to the rear of the shoulder blades so as to allow the latter to operate without restraint. A distance of about three inches is usually enough. In addition to placing the pack saddle in the centre of the horse's back, and far enough behind the shoulder blades, you must also ensure that it is not leaning to either side.

Once the pack saddle is properly placed, lift the front edge of the saddle pad snugly up under the forks. This is to ensure that the pad is not riding on the horse's spine. A tight saddle pad can cause tremendous damage by rubbing off the hair, breaking open the skin and pressing down on the fragile spine. Additionally, if the pad is too tight up front it encourages the load to rock back and forth. This swaying in turn also encourages injuries to the horse. Lifting the pad also allows cool air to circulate along the horse's heated back.

With the pad and saddle in place, turn your attention to the girth.

A minority of pack and riding saddles use a second girth, which is placed behind the horse's stomach. The second girth was originally designed to be used by cowboys who were required to ride unruly horses during the course of their normal day's work. If such a buck jumper began to throw a fit, and the girth broke, then the unfortunate cowboy could be killed in the resultant crash. That is why saddle makers in the late 19th century began offering the option of having a second girth on high-backed western saddles. The idea of having a spare girth was also transferred to American pack saddles at the same time, with the idea again being that a second girth could help offset an emergency.

But Long Riders are not riding buck jumpers. That is why they do not need a second girth on either their riding or pack saddles. It is needless weight, whose use cannot be defended in the remote possibility that it might, some day, be needed.

Because the pack saddle covers such a large portion of the horse's body, fitting the girth properly is a vital part of your morning routine. A common mistake is to pull the girth too tight. This can induce a feverish sweat, interfere with breathing, cause galls under the girth, injure the back and leave the animal exhausted.

Girths are dangerous, not only because of the injuries and distress they can cause, but because they can interfere with the horse's locomotion. The hind legs propel the horse forward, while the hind quarters move side-to-side and up-and-down. A tight girth inhibits these movements, which in turn affects your day's travel.

Depending on the conformation of your pack horse, the girth is normally positioned approximately four inches behind the point of the horse's elbow. Learning to tighten the girth takes time and practice. The basic test is to draw it tight, until it reaches a point of resistance against the animal's body. Do not yank, struggle or apply too much pressure. Also, be sure not to disturb the hair underneath the girth, as this may cause saddle galls.

Once you believe the girth is snug, secure it. The pack saddle should now be safely in place, well balanced and firmly set on top of the horse's back. If you have positioned it properly and it is not too tight, you should be able to slide two fingers between the horse's body and the girth.

Some pack animals learn to blow out their chest, prior to having the girth tightened. This is a defensive measure, designed to protect them from the agony of having the girth pulled too tightly. Make sure the girth is properly fitted to begin with, but don't over tighten it because of the horse trying to trick you in this manner. The pack saddle girth will receive a last-minute adjustment prior to your departure.

With the saddle in place, place the breeching or crupper in its proper position. If you are using a breeching, make sure that there is one inch clearance between it and the horse's hind quarters. If a crupper is required, make sure that it is not too tight and lies at the base of the horse's tail.

Next comes the breast collar. Place it above the point of the shoulder and make sure that it never restricts the movement of the front legs.

Now, with everything in place, walk around the pack horse and make a careful examination of how it all looks. Is the saddle straight? Have you pulled the saddle pad high enough under the pack saddle? Is it far enough forward to keep it from sliding back? Did you place the girth in the right place? Does the crupper or breast collar look too tight? Can you see any hair being pulled out of place by the equipment?

If it all looks good, then give the girth a final adjustment, pulling it snugly into place. By adjusting the girth just before you leave, you decrease the chances of the load slipping to one side.

With your road horse standing by, and your pack horse saddled too, it's time to load the equipment.

Packing Up - Morning

Your panniers should be already packed, weighed, balanced and ready to be slung on the pack saddle.

If you are working in a team, have one person stand on the right side of the pack horse. They hold the pack saddle in place, while you lift the left pannier onto the pack saddle. With the first half of the load on, it is your turn to hold the left pannier up, keeping it from pulling the pack saddle off balance, while your friend in turn lifts the right pannier and secures it to the pack saddle. Both panniers should now be resting securely from the pack saddle, thanks to their sturdy nylon straps.

Should you be required to load the pack horse alone, have both panniers sitting close by, ready to be instantly loaded. Lift the left pannier in place, then quietly but quickly move to the other side of the horse and hang the second pannier without delay.

Regardless if you have help, try to ensure that the pack saddle has not been pulled off balance, that the saddle pad has not moved, and that none of the horse's equipment has been jarred out of position. If you need to use the lash rope, don't tug or jerk the load out of balance. Pull steadily instead.

Distribution of the Load

With the panniers in position, take a moment to check your work.

Step back and see if the centre of the pack saddle lines up with the pack horse's back. Are the panniers placed too high on the ribcage? If so, they will pull the saddle off balance. If they're too low, his breathing will be constricted. If they're too far back they will interfere with his progress.

Now walk behind the animal and see if the bottoms of the panniers look even? Finally, ask yourself, does the pack horse appear composed, comfortable and confident? Is he ready to take on the challenges of the day?

If you have decided to use a top pack, this is when it should be carefully lifted on top of the pack saddle and lashed into position. Never overload the top pack, as it can cause the load to tilt to one side or may damage the adjustable pivot on top of the pack saddle.

Should you need to carry pack bags, bedrolls, duffle bags or a tubular tent, place the objects lengthwise, making sure they are tied close to the pack saddle.

Ideally the pack horse now has his load equally divided, with 40% on both sides and 20% placed on top. With this load evenly distributed, a robust pack horse should be able to carry one hundred pounds in the panniers and an additional twenty-five pounds in the top pack. The pressure from the load will also have been properly distributed over the weight-bearing surface of the horse's back.

Many Long Riders like to cover the finished load with a top tarpaulin. This can either be a regular piece of canvas which you tie into place or a specially made top tarp designed to cover your top pack. Regardless, a top tarp not only guards your top pack from bad weather and sharp branches, it has other useful functions around camp.

Diminishing Weight

One heavy object often carried by Long Riders is grain or some sort of food supplement for the horses. Michael Bragge recalled, "We were sponsored by a horse feed company. They gave us enough hard feed for the trip. We picked up a forty-five kilo bag of this mixed feed at towns along the route. We had one packhorse purely for hard feed. We would load up heavy at the start of a stretch between towns and the load lightened over an average four or five days. Some of the gear from the other pack horse would be swapped to the feed horse to even the effort. We travelled very light. Our own food was very plain and sparse. We lost many kilos; in fact I was quite faint at times and extremely thin when I returned."

Right. With both horses ready, prepare to mount and move.

Get it Tight and Set it Right

You should begin your departure routine as soon as the road and pack horses are ready.

First, give your pack horse a final once over and then check his girth. You may find that the weight of the load has already pressed the pack saddle down onto the saddle pad, which in turn has released the tension of the girth. If it is loose, then re-tighten it.

Next, before you mount the road horse, glance around your camp to make sure you haven't forgotten anything. Are your important travel documents safe? Have you confirmed the directions, have your maps handy and know which road you will be travelling on today? Have you visited the toilet before you swing into the saddle for the rest of the day?

If you are travelling with a friend, don't swing into your saddle until they are also ready to leave. Then untie your road horses and mount at the same time.

Before you mount, place your road horse so that he faces your pack horse. Hold the lead rope in your left hand, next to your reins, then mount with reins and rope on the near side of the saddle. This method keeps you from swinging into the saddle and finding the lead rope wrapped around your waist. As soon as you are firmly in the saddle, turn your road horse in the direction you will be travelling, shift the lead rope to your right hand, and draw the pack horse close to your mount. You should now be ready to travel.

If you don't do it right in the morning, you'll surely suffer later in the day. Good packing and loading at the beginning means time and trouble saved all through the journey. Waiting up ahead could be bad weather, a dangerous trail, terrible traffic or dreadful people. That's why you must get it tight and set it right before you leave camp.

However, even if you discover a last-minute problem, no matter how time-consuming or depressing, don't lose your temper around the horses. When you're a Long Rider Packer you will discover that loads shift, ropes stretch and girths loosen. Practice will soon resolve the vast majority of your initial problems.

Now let's ride towards the horizon.

Leading the Pack Horse

In theory you can lead a pack horse over practically any type of country except heavy bush and swamps. While that's an encouraging thought, the first few minutes after you mount are often the most difficult.

Your goal is quiet, trouble-free riding. That's why your first challenge is to make sure that your horses are in the right emotional order. If you are riding alone, with just two horses, then chances are your horses are comfortable working with each other. However if you are riding with another person, and there are additional horses to consider, then determine which horse is the dominant animal, which horse might kick if it is crowded, which one might panic in case of trouble, etc. Thus, the order in which you ride can be affected by the emotional disposition of your animals. Determine these emotional factors before you leave.

Once you're all under way, the lead rope becomes both a blessing and a burden.

Always set off at the walk. Make sure your pack horse has taken his proper place slightly behind your road horse. The horse uses his head to maintain his sense of balance, as humans do their hands. If you hold the lead rope too tight, the pack horse cannot maintain his stability.

Keep the lead rope slightly taut. If you let it go slack, your pack horse may move to one side, bringing the lead rope under the road horse's tail. This will result in an instant rodeo. The lead rope should never be allowed to drag on the ground, become wrapped around your boot or get tangled under either horse's feet. Never place it between your leg and saddle. If the pack horse bolts, and the rope is under your leg, it will yank you out of the saddle. Hold it firmly in your hand, letting the slack rest on top of your leg. If you're riding in mountainous terrain, keep the lead rope on the downhill side.

Let me remind you again, no matter how tired you may become, never tie your pack horse to your saddle. This is the equestrian travel equivalent of playing Russian roulette. If the pack horse slides off the trail, you'll be pulled to your death. If he jerks back, and your hand is resting on top of the saddle horn, the rope can cut your finger off like a hot knife. If the pack horse takes fright and runs around the far side of your road horse, you'll be trapped under the rope and effectively tied in your saddle with panicking horses beside and under you. You risk death and disaster if you ignore this rule.

Traditional packers in North America sometimes tied the lead rope to the tail of their riding horse. The problem with this method, known as tailing, is that eventually all pack horses pull back. When this occurs you will end up with a riding horse that has a sore tail, if you're lucky, or even worse, your horse will have his tail snapped off.

It is also inadvisable to let your pack horses follow freely behind you. This practice is known as trailing. Like tailing, it used to be a common practice in the American west. Because of the collective emotional nature of equines, caravans of pack animals do indeed tend to follow their mates. Yet with the fencing of the once-wide-open spaces, this romantic practice is now rarely encountered. Because free-roaming pack horses damage trails, the practice is illegal in many American national parks. The risk of allowing your pack horse to run free anywhere near a busy road is obvious. Always keep your pack horse under close control.

If you encounter a problem, you may decide that it is better for you to dismount and lead your horses by hand. If you do decide to lead your horses, never wrap the rope around your hand. If a horse panics the lead rope can dislocate your shoulder. If he slips off a trail he can pull you to your death. Hold the rope firmly but be ready to let go.

Breakaway String

If a situation arises where you are alone on a narrow trail but have to lead both horses, then you should employ what is known as a breakaway string. This is a light string, strong enough to keep your pack horse attached to your road horse, but weak enough to allow the pack horse to pull back and save himself if the first horse encounters trouble. The breakaway string is something you should keep where it can be reached in case of emergency.

Never tie the breakaway string to the saddle horn or the tail of the road horse. Tie it in a large loop to a D ring on your saddle. With this looped string now in place, tie the lead rope to the riding horse with a half hitch, then guide your riding horse and pack horse in this temporary team fashion. Don't allow the pack horse too much slack. Give him enough of the lead rope not to trip but not enough to get into trouble.

On the Trail

There are rules of the road, after you've begun to ride.

If you are travelling with a companion, you must be able to see and speak with each other at all times. On good ground the distance between riders may lengthen but when bad terrain is encountered, shorten up the distance and decrease the pace. Otherwise the horses left behind may become upset at being separated and try to catch up with their companions. Similarly, if one of you needs to stop for any personal reason, then you should dismount and wait until he or she is back in the saddle.

Never allow the horses to bunch up, as a nervous or irritable animal may kick out. Keep your distance between riders. Make sure you can always see the hooves of the horse in front of you. If water is encountered en route, and the horses wish to drink, you should always try to accommodate them. However, you make this decision, not them.

Under no circumstances should anyone hold on to the saddle, breeching or a horse's tail to assist themselves in walking.

The Pace of a Pack Horse

In an emergency, a pack horse can trot, gallop, even jump if properly loaded. Yet rapid gaits, such as the trot or gallop can quickly injure the pack animal. During the normal course of events, you should never trot a pack horse. If you're in a hurry, you made a mistake in some other part of that day's planning. Unless you find yourself in an emergency, don't compound your error by risking injury to the pack horse when you force the pace.

You must adjust the speed of your progress depending on the obstacles you encounter. If you are riding with a companion, and you come across a stream, sharp turn, road hazard, etc., the first rider must not proceed until all the horses are safely reassembled.

Even when the road isn't trying to outwit you, it is necessary to keep your attention focused on your pack horse. The combination of placing the pack saddle, saddle pad, crupper, breast collar, panniers and top pack on top of a moving animal is a recipe for trouble. Add in a dash of challenging terrain and you will spend half your time looking backwards, instead of dreaming about the beautiful landscape.

Saddle pads slip backwards. Panniers slide over to one side. Hitches come loose. Formerly-secured ropes suddenly drag along the trail. With so many potential disasters waiting to frighten or harm the hard-working pack horse, you must be constantly vigilant.

Taking a Halt

Half an hour after you've started, plan to take a ten minute halt to check and adjust the load.

During the rest of the day, keep your horses moving at a steady pace, taking halts to rest the horses as and when the opportunity arises.

Stan Walchuk has a recommendation regarding slowing and stopping your horses.

"Use the word 'whoa' only when you know you are going to stop. To slow down say, 'easy, easy.'"

When a halt is called for, be sure to move your horses well away from the roadside. If you are riding along a trail, move your animals off the trail so as to keep it clear for other travellers. Regardless of where you stop, be sure the location you have chosen is safe. Look for low-hanging branches which could injure an eye, sharp objects which can slice open a leg or roots which can tear off a shoe. Then tie your horses up short, to make sure they cannot get tangled up. Unless you want to run the risk of having your reins destroyed, always secure your horses with lead ropes.

Just because the horse is resting doesn't mean you can. Every halt demands a careful inspection be carried out before you can relax. Have the panniers gone out of balance? Has the top pack shifted? Is the lash rope still secure? Is the saddle pad still in place? Have the breeching or breast collar rubbed?

If you decide to allow the pack horse to graze, care must be taken that the pack saddle doesn't slip forward onto the withers. Should the halt exceed thirty minutes, you should take the opportunity to off load and rest the pack horse.

Before you ride on, scatter any manure. And it is illegal to smoke during fire season in some countries.

Meeting Other Travellers

It's not always true what they say about the "good old days." That's what Aimé Tschiffely discovered when he rode into the Andes Mountains of Peru.

"The trail was cut out of a perpendicular mountain wall. The river below looked like a silver streak. There had been incidents where two riders happened to meet in such a narrow dangerous place and the man who shot first was the man who rode on, for there was neither turning back nor crossing each other in such a trap."

Luckily the basics of trail courtesy have progressed since Aimé's day. But any time you meet other horses on the trail you and your animals are placed in peril.

Though traditions differ depending on which country you are riding in, the custom in many nations is that horses travelling uphill have the right-of-way in the morning, while those travelling downhill retain that privilege in the afternoon. When two groups of mounted travellers meet on the level, the smaller group yields to the larger party by moving off the trail. Should the caravans be similar in size in steep country, the one travelling downhill yields to uphill traffic. Regardless of their size, if one group has a chance to pull their animals off the trail safely, they should let the other party pass first.

If you have to reverse your horses on the trail, keep their heads pointed downhill when you turn them. Allowing your horses to keep their eyes on the trail helps decrease the chance of them accidentally stepping off the edge. Because of these dangers, it is wise to train your horses to turn around on a narrow trail prior to your departure.

Nonetheless it's not just horses and gunmen who you'll find lurking on the trail. National parks, popular trails and pilgrim routes routinely have hikers, mountain bike riders, back packers and ATV riders travelling along them. Many of these people do not know how to react when they encounter Long Riders. They should be asked to step off the trail on the downhill side and remain quiet until you pass.

Trouble Up Ahead

Equestrian travel, like life, is filled with dilemmas. That's why you have to mount a two-part defence against unexpected adversity. First, take every precaution. Second, when trouble arrives, and it will, stay calm.

The easiest way to reduce the possibility of overt risk is to not wander off the trail. Should you lose your way, don't blunder ahead blindly. Dismount, secure your horses and scout ahead on foot. If you are travelling with a friend, one person should stay behind with the horses. Do not let stupidity, stubbornness or pride override common sense. If the trail appears treacherous, turn around, rather than risk the safety of your trusting horses.

Because you are travelling with a pack horse, the possibility of trouble increases dramatically. The dead weight of the panniers can be knocked off balance, causing the pack saddle to slide under the pack horse's stomach. The lead rope might slide under your road horse's tail in a tight turn. A sudden noise might frighten both horses.

Your job is to be ever vigilant. Never take it for granted that the riding and pack saddles don't need to be adjusted. If either horse appears to be worried, pay attention and look for the cause of his concern.

If you detect a problem, find a safe place to stop and resolve the issue immediately. Remember, a pack saddle can ruin a horse's back in an hour. Don't risk the animal's health and the outcome of your journey by neglect.

Even though you've done your best to balance the panniers, they may need to be re-adjusted on the trail. It pays to keep one item on hand which can be easily transferred from side to side after you've started to travel. The Long Rider Michael Bragge kept a small axe strapped outside the panniers, which could be moved to help the load find its equilibrium.

Should the ground become treacherous, causing your laden pack horse to fall, his head should be held down to prevent him struggling. The panniers must then be removed before he is allowed to get up. If the ground is very difficult or dangerous, the pack saddle should be removed as well as the load.

Never forget that the smallest Shetland pony is stronger than you, and any horse can injure you in an instant. If a pack horse starts bucking, use extreme caution when you approach him.

Dangerous Trails

Pack horses learn how to avoid knocking the panniers into trees, how to maintain their balance on narrow trails and how to step over obstacles. You may arrive at a stretch of trail that requires you to dismount and proceed on foot. Do not let the pack horse crowd you on the trail. Keep him well behind you.

If you encounter rough country, slide your feet out of the stirrups and be ready to dismount quickly. If the trail looks dangerous, stop immediately. If you are alone, secure the horses and then proceed cautiously on foot.

Never let your horses wander over to the edge of the trail, as it may give way. Train them instead to always stay in the centre of the path. If the trail starts to break away underneath your road horse, jump off on the uphill side. Removing your weight from the saddle might save his life.

Such an accident occurred to the Robert Seney.

"I had a trail give way while riding my horse Trooper. Fortunately, he was strong enough to power his way back onto the trail. But Trooper and I could have been seriously injured or died if I hadn't jumped out of the saddle."

Many well-known trails in the United States take Long Riders through heavily-forested areas. Should you come to a deadfall, i.e. large broken trees fallen across the trail, do not try to ride across without scouting ahead. Long Rider Ed Anderson encountered so many fallen trees that he resorted to carrying an extremely sharp, collapsible saw which he used to clear the trail. Always secure your horses before you scout ahead or work to clear the trail.

Nor were fallen trees the only hazards Ed encountered during his ride from Mexico to Canada along the Pacific Crest Trail. At one point he found himself on a high, narrow trail. A protruding boulder made it unsafe to proceed, either in the saddle or on foot.

"I tied Primo, and, hiking ahead, explored and identified, a cross-country possibility to get safely past the obstacle. I had to climb about 300' and cut some small trees and branches with my large folding saw to open the route. I then returned to Primo and backtracked to the other end of my detour. We got around the boulder safely on this detour."

However, Ed encountered other problems including gates so narrow that he had to remove the saddle bags before his road horse could squeeze through.

"If you try to get your pack horse through a place wide enough for your riding horse, but marginal for your pack horse's panniers – and he scrapes or gets stuck, this could trigger a panic reaction and result in an accident," he warned.

Should the trail require you to climb either up or down hill, make sure you stop to check that your load is properly secured and centred. After the descent or ascent, check that the pack animal has no injuries to its withers or back.

Safety

There are basic safety rules which should never be forgotten.

Don't ride with loose reins. You should always have contact with your horse's mouth, otherwise you risk losing control in an emergency.

Don't shove your boot all the way forward into the stirrup. The ball of your foot should rest on the stirrup, otherwise you risk being dragged to death if you are thrown and your foot becomes trapped.

Don't let your road horse move about when you are mounting.

If either your road or pack horses spook on a regular basis, thereby putting your life at risk on the road, sell or replace them. Your safety is more important than your sense of emotional loyalty.

Unless your name is Roy Rogers, and your horse is called Trigger, never shoot a gun off a horse that hasn't been trained to handle gunfire.

Always ensure that someone knows your travel plans.

Packing Up - Evening

Tomorrow's ride begins tonight.

You must develop a system for stowing, checking and preparing your pack saddle and gear for the next day's ride. Not only does this reduce the chance of losing valuable equipment, in case of rain or emergency it allows you to lay your hands on vital equipment in the dark without delay.

The first requirement at the end of the day's ride is to locate a safe place to off load and stable the horses. People who neglect this basic step wake up to find a disaster. This is what happened to the American who rode after dark. Too tired to take proper precautions, he tied his horse to what he believed was a harmless wire fence. The next morning he awoke to discover his horse's face covered in blood, because he had tied it to a barbed wire fence.

Once a safe location has been found, keep your horses together for safety's sake. While the road horse began your day, the pack horse now receives preference. Remove the panniers and loosen the girth. But do not remove the pack saddle. Exposing the heated area of a horse's back to cold air can cause injury. With the pack horse unloaded and standing easy, use a sponge to clean his eyes and nostrils with cool water. You can then offer him some hay, but no water for an hour.

With the pack horse eating quietly, loosen the girth on your road horse, sponge off his face too and give him a ration of hay as well. Once again, don't water him nor remove his saddle.

While both horses are preoccupied and relaxing, scout your campsite. If you have been invited to put your horses in someone's barn, check to make sure there are no sharp items close to where they will sleep. If the horses are going to reside for the night in a strange field, check it for dangers. If you are pitching a tent, try to locate it close to the trail you arrived on. If horses become frightened in the night, they tend to run back in the direction from which they last travelled. Should you awake to the sound of horse bells rushing by your tent, at least you'll know in which direction to look for your horses in the morning.

Only remove the pack and riding saddle after the horses' backs have completely cooled. You can check by placing your hand underneath the saddle pad. If the back feels cool to the touch, then you can remove the saddle. This might take an hour or more.

If circumstances demand that you offload the saddles without taking this precaution, then be prepared instead to wash the horse's back with a bucket of cool water the moment the saddle is removed. The horse's back should be briskly massaged with the water and all traces of sweat removed. Some Long Riders such as Jeremy James prefer this method. However, the availability of water and the weather also affect this decision.

With the pack saddle and its equipment, as well as the riding saddle, removed, arrange your gear so that it is ready for the morning. Panniers, lash rope, breeching and the other gear belonging to the pack horse should be resting next to the pack saddle. Likewise the riding saddle and gear are also carefully prepared for the next day's ride. Never set the bottom of your saddles in the dirt, as grit and sand can tear a horse's back to ribbons.

Even though your gear is now sorted, you must not forget to carefully check it for any signs of dirt or damage. It doesn't take much to cause a pressure point on a pack horse's back. When completed, all of your equipment should be assembled neatly and arranged the night before for the next day's work.

Where you store the equipment overnight is also of importance. Hell on earth starts when you awake to wet or frozen ropes. What's worse is to discover that a salt-loving porcupine has chewed holes in the saddle's sweaty girth. Or perhaps a wandering bear has dropped by to stick his nose in your panniers. These sorts of early morning discoveries cause some Long Riders to carry a small collapsible tent which they store all their equipment in.

If you don't want to carry the extra weight of a spare tent, you can hang your saddles and gear from a tree branch. Regardless of what you decide, protect your precious gear once the sun sets.

Only by careful planning the night before can delays in packing up the next morning be averted.

Summary

All this talk of dangerous lead ropes, bucking pack horses and heavy panniers might tempt you to think that taking a pack horse is more trouble than it's worth. You may wonder why you don't employ a supply vehicle and a back up driver instead.

In the late 19th century a Long Rider made this observation about compromising your independence.

"Be independent of a servant. A servant following or preceding with a pile of trunks, the contents of which will never be needed and can easily be dispensed with, is a nuisance to all those who would enter into the true spirit and freedom of a journey in the saddle."

Substitute "truck" for "servant" and you have your answer. When you set off to explore the world on horseback, you slow down. You begin to notice the sights, sounds and smells of nature which are denied to pedestrians locked in their steel cocoons. You watch the stars at night for signs of the next day's weather. Your body slows to match the rhythm of your horse's quiet pace.

The key to your equestrian independence is the pack horse. Granted that you treat him with respect, and protect him from injury, he will serve you as faithfully as your road horse.

The art of packing is probably the oldest connection between horses and humans. It is a noble craft which need not frighten us and can be done successfully by first-time Long Riders.

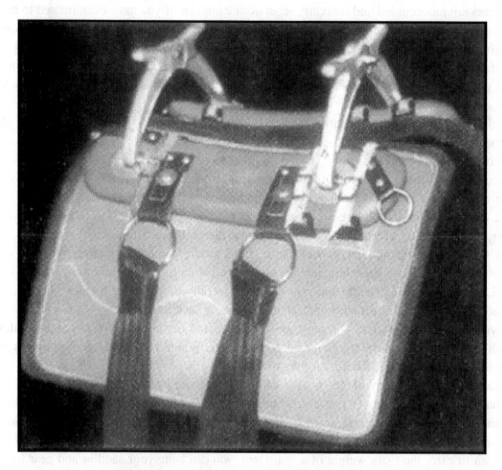

The adjustable pack saddle created by Custom Pack Rigging.

In his book, Cordillera, Canadian Long Rider Stan Walchuk described his historic solo ride from Alberta, Canada into Alaska alone via the Cordillera region of the Canadian Rocky Mountains. The renowned Long Rider offers clinics on equestrian mountain travel, including lessons on how to use the adjustable Canadian pack saddle. He taught Filipe Leite about packing before that young Long Rider rode 16000 kilometres (10000 miles) from Canada to Brazil.

Tim Cope on the last day of his ride from Mongolia to Hungary; six thousand miles and no problems with the pack horses or pack saddles.

Tim never set off without having first used the pack scales to carefully weigh and balance the load in his two sturdy panniers.

Side view of Tim's cargo. Note how he wrote the large letter "E" on the pannier, so as to separate "equipment" from the "F" pannier, which held his food.

A view of Tim's pack horse loaded with the adjustable pack saddle, panniers and top pack.

The top pack, which carried light weight items on top of the panniers. Also note the extra thick saddle pad which Tim has placed well forward of the pack saddle.

Tim's adjustable pack saddle was even successfully used on a Bactrian camel in Mongolia.

Brazilian Long Rider Filipe Leite completed his journey from Calgary, Canada to Sao Paolo, Brazil on August 23, 2014. Like Tim Cope, Filipe used the adjustable pack saddle which ensured that his pack horse travelled through ten countries without any trouble from saddle sores.

Chapter 23
Caring For Your Horse

When we set out to become Long Riders, we enter into a life of adventure and adversity. We also undertake a serious duty to our horse.

Thus, though it is easier to ask a question than answer it, let us attempt to understand the basic care which your road and pack horses require.

Horse History

As time passes and the older that this *Encyclopaedia of Equestrian Exploration* becomes, the further will humanity have moved from the age when the skills needed to keep a horse happy and safe were a day-to-day state of affairs. Having been born in the middle of the 20th century, I was privileged to spend my youth with horse men and women who had links to the previous equine dominated world. Their wisdom and warnings to me had, in turn, been painstakingly gathered from their own teachers, who had ridden in the late 19th century. And what an equestrian age that was.

To put the magnitude of this vanished equine knowledge into perspective, let us look at the city of London.

At the dawn of the 20th century, there were an estimated 300,000 horses living and working within the city limits of Great Britain's capital. We are not speaking of horses lodged in farms in the nearby country that travelled in and out the city. London's inner-city horses were owned by private individuals, public companies and governmental agencies. The accommodations for this enormous urban herd were as varied for the horses as the humans who employed them. Horses lived in everything from tiny huts in dark alleys to multi-storied stables which held several thousand horses under one roof. If it was true that the sun never set on the British Empire, it was equally true that it employed millions of equine subjects to defend, feed and maintain social order among its human citizens.

Ironically, though London's streets were thronged with horses, few of them were used exclusively for riding. This was instead a massive four-legged work force, the likes of which today's mechanised humans can neither remember nor relate to.

An estimated forty thousand carriage horses pulled father to work and the children to school.

Mother went shopping on the omnibus, of which 22,000 horses drew more than 2,000 vehicles across London every day. These companies employed 11,000 men to look after their animals' needs.

If the family couldn't afford a carriage, they could always travel by horse-drawn tram. London had 135 miles of horse drawn tram lines. Every year these tram horses collectively travelled twenty-one million miles through the crowded city streets. The North Metropolitan Tram Company alone employed 3,500 horses.

Before the days of UPS and FEDEX, private companies delivered household goods to the family home from nearby railway stations. One company engaged 2,000 horses, which they kept stabled at twenty depots strategically placed around the great metropolis.

The concept of rental cars has its roots in the stable too. The Tilling Corporation maintained an inner-city herd of 2,500 horses which they rented to anyone, including washerwomen, the fire brigade and police.

Meanwhile, the sturdy coal horses kept everyone warm by moving an average of thirty tons of coal a week each.

The doctor, the duke and the drayman all relied on hard-working horses, who routinely laboured ten hours a day for six days a week. From the Lord Mayor to the beggar boy, the horse influenced the daily lives of every Londoner.

Knowing how to feed, water, clean, groom, shoe, medicate, harness, saddle- and work-horses was an everyday occurrence to hundreds of thousands of Londoners.

A Horse's Needs

It is the doom of men that they forget. Thus the accumulated equine expertise which was so recently a part of London's daily life has been lost. Differing views of this sad fact were recently revealed by two of England's celebrated television stars.

James May was one of the hosts of an automobile programme called *Top Gear*. Though he is associated with cars by the programme's 350 million viewers, May is a keen craftsman, who has derided what he calls a culture of incompetence. These are the members, he said, "of a useless generation who have lost the practical skills practised previously."

In stark contrast to May, the programme's other host, Jeremy Clarkson, expressed no sympathy for the passing away of traditional skills.

In a rebuttal to his co-host, Clarkson wrote, "The point is that if you cannot do something, get someone to do it for you. Mr. May says children should be taught basic skills at school. I disagree. Teaching someone how to rivet is like teaching someone how to do cave paintings. It's simply not relevant. The only engineering a child needs today is how to transfer a tune from one computer to another."

The problem with Clarkson's view of the world is that rivets and paint don't suffer when amateurs make a mistake. But horses do.

Long Riders have been living with, and learning from, their horses for thousands of years. For example, during his 1930s ride through the Chaco jungle, Thurlow Craig noted, "A horse travelling as my horse Bobby had been doing gets very lonely and is always anxious to meet and greet other horses to exchange news."

What Craig saw, and people like Clarkson have never known, is the evidence of the complex social life which horses have. Nature originally intended for these animals to spend the majority of their time involved in social grazing in immense open areas. This communal experience strengthened societal bonds, reinforced collective needs and taught individual responsibility. Thus, though horses and humans share a sense of extended family, there is a critical difference in that horses have a physical need to move, run and roam across wide grasslands, while historically humans have sheltered in dark dwellings.

By forcing them to spend the majority of their time in solitary confinement in unnaturally small stalls, we remove horses from their companions and natural environment. The result is a dramatic increase in psychological problems, such as restless pacing, chewing the stall door, ceaseless weaving, unremitting pawing and severe emotional depression.

There is a minority of modern urban dwellers beginning to voice a well-meaning but misguided opinion that travelling with horses is harmful to the animal. Restoring an animal to its natural environment is helpful in the extreme, not only physically but emotionally. Moreover, as the hard working horses of old London proved, horses take pride in their daily tasks.

The Task at Hand

Keeping a horse healthy and happy is a challenge, even in a modern stable with all the necessary feed, tools and tack close at hand. The difficulties increase when you ride into the unknown. Common sense, resourcefulness and ingenuity are required to overcome the problems which await you.

Because you have chosen to take him away from his home, the road horse relies on you to provide a much-needed sense of security.

That is why you must always think of your horse first. You feed him before you feed yourself.

Although the horse is strong of bone and muscle, he is an animal of delicate constitution that is as liable to coughs and colds as any human being. A healthy horse gives little trouble if he is treated with ordinary care. Yet to ensure this his food should be of the best, his bedding should be kept scrupulously clean and he should always have a supply of good water. Though these are basic rules, they present daily difficulties when travelling.

Only a fool takes pride in dirt and disorder, thereby mistaking what he calls 'roughing it' for self-assurance. A real Long Rider is known by the way he maintains a strict regime of compassion, cleanliness and competence when dealing with his horse.

The Long Rider must live for his horse, who acts as his legs, his safety, his honour and his reward.

The bravest men, living through the worst conditions, have expressed this sort of tenderness towards their mounts.

"My horse was dead tired after the great work that he had done for the previous week," wrote an American correspondent sent to ride with the Cossacks, "so that I walked a good deal on foot. I was probably more tired than he was, but then he was absolutely necessary for my safety. It is extraordinary what a lot of interest one takes in his horse during war-time. It becomes a part of one's own body and is looked after with corresponding care. You are more alarmed at your horse's appetite falling off than at your own. You take a far keener interest in its hoofs than you do in your own painful feet. You frequently examine its back to see that it is not getting saddle-sores. You arrange the blanket under the saddle with the same care as you would arrange a shawl on the shoulders of a fair lady. I can now understand why statues to great warriors always represent them on horseback."

Your Horse Pays the Price

One trait of the past was that no man laid a hand on another person's horses unless he wanted a fight. It was a rule that the horse's owner tended his own stock so long as he was not ill or injured.

In the century since cars took control of the world's roads, mankind has not only lost the majority of its collective equestrian wisdom, this lack of daily know-how has opened the door to horse hustlers, video professors, clinicians and other assorted scam artists.

One of the greatest dangers every Long Rider faces is the unforeseen need to involve strangers in helping feed, water and shelter your animals.

When Lucy Leaf made her journey, occasions arose when she was forced by circumstances to entrust her horse, Igor, to strangers.

"I had to trust the care of my horse to others many times, and you can be sure, things weren't always perfect," Lucy wrote.

She got lucky. Many other Long Riders did not.

After riding from the Arctic Circle to Guatemala, one weary equestrian traveller was invited to share dinner with a local minister. The hungry rider was urged to entrust his horse to the minister's servant, who accidentally killed the animal by giving him the wrong food.

Richard Barnes was hosted one evening by someone who appeared to be a keen horseman. Having recommended Richard enjoy a hearty dinner at the local pub, the Long Rider was horrified upon his return to discover that his host had cut the mane and most of the tail off his road horse.

Never overestimate your allies. Never trust a drop of water, a bucket of grain, a syringe full of medicine or a night's accommodation to a stranger.

Fair Play

The horse never forgets injustice or error. His memory matches that of the elephant. He remembers everything, which explains how he can follow the exact route he took outward so as to find his way home.

Patience and tolerance must always be uppermost in your mind.

There are many little kindnesses which help to ease the labour of your loyal horse. Never forget to pet him, so that he learns to look forward to being emotionally rewarded. When local conditions allow, give him treats such as sugar, apples or carrots and he will ever be nuzzling at your pocket. In return for this emotional investment you will be rewarded by his low, soft greeting when he sees you approach. This is not given to a person who thinks of a horse as "it."

Summary

You can see what's on the inside of a man by the outside of his horse.

When the road horse and Long Rider live together, the servant, like a mirror, reflects his master's qualities. To courage, energy, cheerfulness, and kindness, a horse responds with confidence, endurance, contentment and love.

That mighty mounted warrior, Genghis Khan, knew this. According to legend he said, "Take care of the horses before they lose condition. For once they have lost it, you may spare them as much as you like, but they will never recover it on the march. Don't overload the riding horses, and no horse on the march is to use a bit. If these orders are disobeyed commanders are authorized to behead offenders on the spot, so as to protect the welfare of the horses."

Though the modern world is populated by television hosts who don't ride or care to remember our common equestrian heritage, remember what Genghis ordered.

First the horse, then yourself.

If you are ever in doubt, look at the special position we have jointly occupied throughout history. They of noble shape, fair and tall, were not given unto our care to denigrate but to uplift our souls and to free us from the restrictions of our two tiny legs in our individual search for wisdom.

The end of the equestrian era. London mail delivery horses on their last day of work.

Welsh Long Rider Thurlow Craig and his Criollo gelding, Bobby, survived a host of wild adventures in South America.

It doesn't take a genius to become a compassionate horseman. Russian Long Rider Vladimir Fissenko had no prior knowledge of horses, but that didn't stop him from riding 30,500 kilometres (19,000 miles) from the tip of Patagonia to the top of Alaska.

Though her sturdy road horse, Igor, wasn't an expensive, blue- ribbon winner, North American Long Rider Lucy Leaf rode him for 13,000 kilometres (8,000 miles) on a life-changing equestrian journey.

Chapter 24
Securing Your Horse

If, for the sake of argument, man has been riding for six thousand years, then he has spent five thousand years of sleepless nights worrying that his horse might run away and come to grief.

That's what happened to the North American Long Rider Hans Asmussen, who chased his hobbled horses for thirty-two miles through the mountains of Montana.

Was it the frightening smell of a predator lurking in the undergrowth? The terrifying sound of a twig snapping in the night? The allure of luscious grass passed earlier in the day? The enticing sexual excitement of a wild stallion? They have all caused horses to panic, bolt or escape into the night.

Thus, regardless of what age, country or climate we ride in, mounted mankind has always needed to secure his horse against the possibility of the animal running away. Because the majority of the modern horse world keeps horses strictly confined in stables or sealed off behind strong fences, they do not appreciate the heart-sickening feeling of waking up to find your beloved horse is gone.

Yet when a Long Rider sets off into the unknown, there is no guarantee of a safe fenced-in pasture or a snug stable awaiting his horses that night.

By contrast, the only thing you can depend upon is that after a long day of hard travel, your road and pack horses need water, food and rest, in that order. The problem is how to accommodate their needs, while maintaining a sense of security which will guarantee you're not afoot in the morning? As I shall explain, mounted man has devised a variety of intriguing answers to this never-ending dilemma.

When things go wrong

Horses, like children, can land themselves in a life-threatening muddle in a remarkably short time. Close your eyes and they're gone. Slip into sleep and you may awake to a disaster.

That's what happened to one inexperienced traveller on her very first night out. She tied her untrained horse to a picket pin and then retired for the night. Upon her return next morning, she discovered the animal had managed to wrap the picket rope tightly around one of its rear legs. The horse had panicked and pulled back in anger at being restrained. The relentless rope grew tighter. No one heard the horse scream as his anger turned to fear, then into pain. When the sun rose, and the owner returned, she discovered the horse's hoof had been nearly severed by the merciless rope. The unfortunate horse had to be destroyed the same day.

Nor is it only the untested whose horses come to harm.

In 1951 the seventeen-year-old North American Long Rider Tex Cashner was making his way from Ohio to Texas on his treasured horse, Streak. Because the duo had ridden hundreds of miles without any previous problems, Tex hobbled Streak with no misgivings and then went to sleep. The trusting Long Rider had made the basic mistake of believing that, thanks to a pair of hobbles, his worries were over. In the predawn light Tex was taught a cruel lesson that stayed with him the rest of his life.

"When I went to bed that night little did I realize that next morning would bring disaster.

I had stopped in a grassy field which lay alongside the road I had been riding along. To avoid flooding, this road had been built up twenty feet higher than the surrounding country. Looking across the grass, I could see a fence and then a railroad track approximately two-hundred yards away. It was nearly dark when I made camp, and as there were no trees, instead of tying Streak I made a pair of crude hobbles from rope. He was quietly grazing a short time later when a train came by, the result being that the bright lights and loud noise spooked Streak. He found out right away that by lifting both front feet at the same time he could run, and run he did, right up the hill towards the road. I went and got him and led him back close to my bedroll. Then I opened a can of beans for supper. After eating, I checked Streak's hobbles, made sure he was safe and then rolled up in my blanket. Because I had ridden for ten hours, I was very tired and was soon sound asleep.

Some time in the early hours before dawn I was awakened by another train passing by. I remember hearing the horn, and the light blinding me for a second, but despite the noise I fell back to sleep at once.

Two or three hours later, I was awakened again, this time by a large thumping noise up on the road. It was still pitch black, no moon. Then I heard a semi-truck start up and drive away. I was now more or less awake, so I sat up and shone my flashlight around. Streak was nowhere in sight, but I figured he had moved out of the range of the light. I lay there for a short time listening to the night sounds, then fell back to sleep. Looking back on this now, I think I may have known what happened but I was afraid to admit it to myself, an eternal optimist.

When I awoke again, it was daylight. I raised my head and looked around. Streak was nowhere to be seen. I stood up and looked toward the road. That's when I saw what looked like a mound of dirt beside the road. I knew at once it was my horse. Suddenly I was numb. I sat back down on my bedroll in a state of shock and stared out across the field at the mound. After a time I finally got up and started walking toward my worst fear. My mind was telling me that it was a pile of dirt, but my gut was telling me that it was Streak. I reached my horse's body and stood there looking down at him. The hobbles were still in place.

The tears did not come at first. As I stared at him I thought I saw him breathing. I reached down to touch him. But it had only been a cruel illusion. Streak was cold and he was gone. Traffic was moving by me on both sides. Cars would slow down and then move on, the drivers staring at me and my dead friend, then hurrying away once their morbid curiosity had been satisfied.

Streak is dead, I said to myself. Yet I couldn't believe it. He had always been full of fire and life. Now Streak was dead. He was my true friend and loyal companion through many hardships. Now he was dead and I didn't know how to accept that terrible truth. I finally realized that even though he was gone, I had to finish the trip we started. Even if it took my life too, I know Streak would have had it so."

Standing alongside that desolate American roadside, the inexperienced Long Rider vowed to ride on. Though the youngster did complete his trip to Texas, he never forgot that his misfortunate night's sleep, which had seemed so alluring, had cost Streak his life.

So don't think they're angelic little beings, these horses. In fact, most of the problems start and end with your mischievous equine companions.

Awake in the Night

Horses aren't like Long Riders. At the end of a hard day in the saddle, you'll be able to fall asleep anywhere. As the weary Tex learned, even if a train roars by a few hundred yards away, no bed will be too lumpy, no patch of ground too rocky, to prevent you from falling into a slumber so deep that it would take a burning house to rouse you.

Meanwhile, your horse hardly ever sleeps. In fact he only spends 12% of every twenty-four hours dozing. That's less than three hours a day. The rest of the time he's perfectly capable of getting into trouble.

And there is a long list of potential dangers and distractions waiting to send him hopping in hobbles or galloping with his picket rope trailing behind all the while you snooze on peacefully.

For example, a road horse worries when he loses sight of the Long Rider. He becomes distressed if his equine companions disappear. Being a grassland animal, he will fuss if you picket him in dense trees where wild animals might be hiding. Or he may become upset if you've left him alone in what he thinks is a scary spot for the night. An absence of food can be an agony for your horse. But poor food can vex him too. A lack of night-time grazing will leave him disturbed and ready to look elsewhere for a meal. Your horse will become alarmed if he detects predators which a sleeping Long Rider may not be aware of. He suffers great anxiety if insects attack and he can be counted on to get into difficulty if you tie him too tightly or restrict his movements.

All the same, you may be saying, that's why some clever Bronze Age horseman invented hobbles, to keep the horses from running away? Yet a smart horse can reach the sea overnight, even if he's wearing hobbles. One Long Rider crossing Kazakhstan was followed for three days by a stray horse in hobbles that followed the traveller's horses. The determined escapee was only stopped when a local agreed to catch and restrain the clever animal.

Therefore, if we have to sleep, how do we use common sense and equestrian history to keep ourselves from waking up as pedestrians?

Different Options

Should you list all the way humans have tried to restrain their horses, it might sound like a little Long Rider's nursery rhyme.

Pick a hobble and a picket pin for one horse. Picket lines or electric fences work for many. A South African anchor will keep them quiet on the veldt. Perhaps a Peruvian blinder will stop them from wandering across the treeless pampas. Don't forget that the German coupling strap will latch two of them together. Never neglect the Italian tethering ring when you've got an even dozen. And if you've nothing else, then tie him to a Tibetan dead man before you sleep.

As this silly verse demonstrates, there are a number of ways to restrain your horse. Each has its drawbacks, proponents and dissidents. What you do depends on a variety of factors, including the horse, local accommodations and weather conditions.

But before we begin to examine our night-time options, let's spend a moment remembering how essential it is to safeguard the road horse when we climb down from the saddle at the end of long day.

Tying your reins at camp

When you secure your horse by the lead rope to a tree, bush or fence, he should be tied so that he cannot injure himself or break the rope by walking on it. Any knot used should be capable of being tied and untied quickly, and should not become unfastened if the horse becomes restless. The following is a useful method for securing a horse to a bush or small tree. Take a suitable branch or bunch of branches, place the loop of the reins under and round it, then double back the end of the branch, breaking it if necessary, and pass it through the reins and tighten up. You will find this quick and handy knot provided in the special appendix entitled "Long Rider Knots," which is provided in the *Horse Travel Handbook* by the same author.

Hobbles

To put it bluntly, hobbles are handcuffs for horses. Though they allow the horse to take small steps, they restrict him from running freely. Their appearance varies, as they can be constructed from rope, leather, nylon, burlap, rags, vines, anything soft and handy which can be used to prohibit the horse's escape.

A standard hobble usually consists of two cuffs which are joined in the middle. The construction of the cuff, and the adjoining connection, differs greatly, with opinions regarding the best way to construct hobbles being as diverse as any religious debate.

One American Long Rider who rides through the northern Rocky Mountains noted his preference when he wrote, "Our hobbles are made from two inch wide leather with buckles and a swivel attached to one of the centre rings. Since bull snaps and other swivel snaps cannot withstand the force of a horse in motion, we use a rope with a bowline knot to the swivel D."

Further south in Arizona, another Long Rider registered a completely different view on the same tool. He wrote, "We discovered that commercial leather hobbles don't work well long term. They can sore the horse. What we found works really well instead is to take a ¾ or 1-inch cotton rope, unbraid it, and then rebraid it in a three-strand braid to make an excellent, soft pair of hobbles. This works in country that does NOT have burrs or sticky seeds, which will catch up in the hobbles and cause chafing."

Not only does the construction vary, so do the number of hobbles used. Though Occidental riders traditionally secure their horses with two front leg hobbles, Central Asian horsemen prefer to tie a third, rear leg hobble, to the front pair. Often known as a sideline, this third hobble decreases the chances of a horse bunny-hopping away from camp or travelling a great distance should he decide to escape.

But no matter where you find yourself, never assume your horse has been trained to be hobbled. Untutored horses who suddenly find their movements restricted by hobbles will react differently. They may freeze in fear or try to bolt. They may rear in anger or pull against the hobbles out of frustration. Regardless, you must never place hobbles on an untrained horse, then let him loose, as he may panic, fall or injure himself.

When you first put on the hobbles, keep a light grip on the lead rope and be ready to step forward and calm the horse. Give him ample time to practise moving cautiously. When he seems confident, drop the lead rope and step back a few feet. Increase your distance as he gains confidence and proficiency. Only when he can graze quietly, and move with self-assurance, can you leave him unattended in hobbles.

Tim Cope had good luck when he used hobbles.

"I used different kinds of hobbles, from three legged ones in Mongolia, to simple Kazakh rope hobbles, and even Australian leather hobbles held together with chain. They were crucial out on the open steppe, because I could let the horses graze freely without being tied. This meant that if they got frightened they would only run two kilometres away, not ten!"

Yet hobbles are far from foolproof and sometimes dangerous.

If the countryside is rough, they can trip a horse. If they are used for long periods of time, they may sore the horse's pasterns or cut his heels. More importantly, clever horses learn how to bunny-hop, travelling for miles even though their feet and legs have been theoretically restricted by hobbles.

Certainly the most dangerous and foolhardy thing you can do is to hobble your horses before you water them. If a thirsty horse is hobbled, he may lose his balance at the creek or lakeside, and drown before you can cut him loose. Never hobble your horses before you water them.

The Picket Pin and its Equipment

Another successful method of securing horses is to attach them to the ground. Traditionally a strong metal stake, known as a picket pin, served to restrain the horse, while the long rope tied to his halter or leg allowed him to graze freely.

Many Long Riders are strong advocates of the picket pin system.

Richard Barnes, for example, recalled how he successfully used a picket pin and rope to allow his Cob, Remus, to graze at the end of their day's journey.

"Coming down a dip towards the bridge over Blue Lins Brook, I saw a grassy place by the stream. Nearby wood and water promised comfort, so I tethered Remus by the stream and sat back against the saddle bags, watching him. Every day had this unspeakably pleasant moment, when the work was over, and horse and rider could relax. A horse that has worked is happy on the tether, walking about, eating and dozing at will. Tonight, Remus' stake was in soft ground by the water's edge: he could have pulled it out with an easy flick of his neck, but strolled about instead, munching."

Though the picket pin and long rope offer solutions, they also present Long Riders with several concerns, starting with the pin itself.

Many cheap picket pins are constructed from soft iron and often have a ring welded to the side of the pin. A soft metal pin may work in a grassy pasture close to home but it will never survive the unbreakable soil awaiting a Long Rider. Driving a soft picket pin into hard ground will dull the tip or break it. The pin must be constructed from steel and have a sharp point. The head of the picket pin must be big enough to survive fierce blows from your hammer. Likewise, having the ring welded in place invites a horse to create an instant disaster by wrapping the picket rope around the pin. To stop this fundamental problem, the picket pin must be equipped with a stout ring that swivels.

Either a strong hammer or axe is indispensable when you try to drive the picket pin into rock-hard or frozen ground. Armed with your hammer, and a robust picket pin equipped with a stout swivelling ring, your horse can graze in a wide area.

Except you must consider the method whereby you attach the horse to the picket pin, for that too is also open to discussion and cultural considerations. In order to deter theft, parts of the Muslim world preferred to attach their horses to the picket pin by the use of a chain. This method could also be found in the sections of southern Europe, such as Albania and Bulgaria, which were once part of the Turkish Caliphate. Yet if for no other reason than the weight, picket chains are not a viable option for Long Riders.

Equestrian travellers in the Occident will be able to purchase a proper picket pin, as well as the rope which is also needed, without any problems. Yet it may surprise you to learn that strong, flexible, durable rope is a rare commodity in many countries. A local alternative is often poorly constructed from hemp. Though supporting native craftsmen is an admirable idea, trying to untie a soggy knot constructed from cheap rope is no fun; nor is finding that the rope has frayed and allowed your horse to escape. Inexpensive rope stretches and seldom lasts long when subjected to the intense physical trials demanded by an equestrian expedition. In many nations the only alternative is to purchase plastic rope imported from China. Yet this rope is usually extremely inflexible, making your daily task of tying and untying knots a nightmare.

Many Long Riders have come to realize that if you are riding in a country where top quality rope is unavailable, then the best alternative is to purchase nylon mountain climbing rope before you leave and pack it alongside your pack and riding saddles. An 8 millimetre (0.3 inch) thick climbing rope will provide tremendous strength, can be quickly tied and untied, won't be frayed by rubbing against the steel picket pin, and can be wrapped and stored with ease. The length of your picket rope is a personal decision, though Long Riders have noted that a picket rope which is fifteen to twenty metres (about 50 feet) long will provide plenty of room for their horses to graze. The thing to remember is that horses are far more likely to become entangled on a short line than a long rope.

If you are not going to use the rope for any purpose except for tethering, then you may wish to secure a heavy-duty metal snap, equipped with a strong swivel, on one end of the rope. This will enable you to tie one end to the picket pin and snap the other end onto the metal ring at the bottom of the horse's halter.

If you decide to use expensive climbing rope on your picket lines, then pay close attention or this rare commodity will be stolen in rope-poor countries.

Training with the Picket Pin

You may be wondering why you should bother training your horse to use the picket pin? After all horses aren't stupid and how hard can it be to walk in a circle around a steel pin stuck in the ground?

There are two primary justifications to train your horse to use the picket pin properly. First, if your horse lacks training he may wrap the rope around his leg while grazing and panic. If you're lucky he will only receive a serious rope burn on the back of his pastern, a wound which may incapacitate him for several days. More worrying is when the horse lifts his rear leg to scratch and the rope becomes snagged under the rear edge of his horse shoe. Now he's caught with his hind leg up in mid-air, which can pull his tendons or cause him to fall and injure himself. In either case the rope becomes his instant enemy. But it gets worse.

If your horse panics while grazing, pulls the pin free and runs away, this sharp steel object being dragged behind has been transformed into a deadly projectile capable of wounding you or blinding him.

This is why wise Long Riders always train their horses to graze on the picket pin before they start their journey.

To begin with, make sure that your horse is hungry before he starts his training, as this will encourage him to focus on grazing. Choose a hazard-free pasture as your training ground. Make sure there are no obstacles, rocks, sharp objects or barbed wire fences which might cause an injury if he becomes tangled in the picket rope.

Take the horse to the centre of the pasture, snap your long pliable rope to his head collar and then slowly walk away until you've reached the end of the line. Allow the horse to begin grazing, but every so often tug the rope gently. Next, while being careful not to let the line become entangled in his feet or legs, walk behind the horse, keeping the rope off the ground, then pull it lightly until the horse shifts his position to accommodate you. Your goal is to accustom him to the feel of the long rope, to teach him not to get tangled in it, not to panic if this occurs and to accept the idea that there is an immoveable central position from which he cannot wander.

Once he has taken this information on board, the next step is to let him trail the rope with a dead weight attached to it.

North American Long Rider Doug Preston made a historic journey to retrace the route taken by the Spanish conquistador, Coronado. But before Doug set off on this ride across the harsh deserts of Arizona and New Mexico, he ensured that his horses were taught to respect the picket pin.

"The picket pin is essential for any horse being taken where there are no corrals or where the horse has to be tied up to bushes, rocks or trees. I start the training with a 30 foot heavy cotton rope on the horse's halter, tying the other end to a heavy tire that the horse can move only slightly but not drag. Then I put the horse in a big field and let him work it out. He'll get tangled up but because the heavy tire moves slightly he'll be able to free himself -- usually. (Keep an eye on him, of course, but let him do most of the work.) Eventually, he'll be so clever with long ropes that you can tie him high, low, on a fifty foot rope with brush all around -- and he'll never have a tangle. I had a horse who knew ropes so well that if he got a rope wound around a leg, he would lift up the leg and give it a little shake, dropping the loops right off. It's so important for a horse being taken on a long ride to know all about ropes," Doug recommended.

However, the time required to train a horse to accept the picket pin varies. Some horses master the concept in half a day and remain rope-smart from then on.

But British Long Rider Jane Dotchin needed more time to accomplish this essential part of her road horse's training.

"Sitka was taught to accept a tether by a simple method. I tethered him to a large, heavy, block of wood. This means that when the rope inevitably became wound round his legs and he pulled to get free, he would avoid rope burns on his legs. With his instinct telling him to gallop away from anything alarming, there was a time when Sitka would run flat out around the field, 'chased' by the wooden block on the end of the tethering rope. When he saw that the block was not going to give up the chase, an exhausted Sitka would begin to slow down. Low and behold ! He then discovered that his 'Pursuer' would slow down, too. Eventually, he learnt how to avoid getting the rope wrapped round his legs and at this stage he was ready to go on a proper tethering pin with a swivel. Even though it took Sitka several months to learn how not to get tangled in the rope, it proved invaluable when we were camping," the experienced Long Rider recalled.

Whether it takes your horse a couple of days or a couple of weeks, you must ensure that he is confident and capable of being attached to a picket pin without coming to grief. The first test is to ensure that your horse can graze quietly, while not getting tangled in his long unsecured lead rope which is trailing along behind as he walks. Next, he has to have learned to respect the restrictions placed upon his freedom by the picket pin. Only then are the two of you ready to depart.

Tying off the Picket Pin

There are two problems when you begin your journey and want to picket your horse for the night. Where do you attach the rope to the horse and where do you place the pin in the ground. Let's start with the horse first.

Different equestrian cultures take strong views on where you secure the picket rope to the horse. These options include snapping the rope to the bottom of the halter, snapping it to a single hobble on a front leg, snapping it to a single hobble on a rear leg, snapping it to a loose collar around the horse's neck. There is no perfect answer to this question. What you do is determined by the cultural background of you, your horse and the nations you will be riding through. However, there are considerations for each option.

For example, horses raised on the pampas of South America are often secured by a rope attached to a neck collar or halter. Because they are accustomed since birth to this system, they know how to avoid getting tangled in the picket rope.

But a horse who is wearing a rope attached to his halter is prone to trouble, as every time he raises or lowers his head the rope can become misplaced. This may result in the horse's head becoming restrained or his legs entangled. Even worse, it is common for a horse wearing a long halter rope to get the line wrapped around his rear hoof, which instantly causes the rope to burn his pastern. Thus, tying the picket rope to the halter is not a perfect solution.

Some nations prefer to attach the picket rope to a soft hobble placed on one front leg. This method reduces the chances of the rope becoming entangled when the horse moves his head while grazing. Furthermore, it greatly decreases the chances of the horse's rear legs becoming entangled in the rope. While this method may appear to save a great deal of trouble, there is a concern that if the horse panics, he could dislocate his shoulder by pulling on the picket rope.

Snapping the picket rope to a soft hobble, attached to one rear leg, has many advocates and few apparent drawbacks, as it withdraws the problem of the horse's head moving the rope into the wrong position and does not place the front shoulders in peril.

As these various options demonstrate, deciding and training your horse in advance is critically important.

Hammering in the Picket Pin

Before you drive in the picket pin, make sure there are no obstacles, especially roots, rocks, logs or tree branches, which will catch or snag the rope.

If you are picketing more than one horse, ensure that there is a large border of empty space between the horses. Once your horses are picketed, walk them to the end of the rope before you depart, so as to confirm they can not become entangled in your absence.

Regardless of how careful you have been, never leave picketed horses unattended for long periods of time. Even experienced road and pack horses can snarl a rope or take a wrong step that places them in peril. Check on them with clockwork regularity. If you are in doubt about the safety of the ground, etc. then you may wish to allow your horses to graze on a picket pin during the daylight hours, then move them to a picket line before the sun sets.

If your horses are going to be picketed in one place for many hours, you must move them on a regular basis. Otherwise, once they have eaten the grass down, their constant movements in this restricted area will reduce the ground underfoot into what appear to be large, barren helicopter landing pads. A long line reduces the chances of this occurring and increases the animal's chances to obtain the maximum amount of grazing.

Because of the intensely strong herd ethic which arises among travelling horses, you may decide to combine hobbles and picket pins, so as to allow the animals varying degrees of freedom.

Though they were riding on opposite sides of the Earth, Keith Clark in Chile and Tim Cope in Mongolia employed this system successfully at the same time.

"A typical campsite on the steppe saw me picketing two of my horses during the remaining daylight hours, while allowing the third horse to roam free. Each horse was picketed on a 15 meter long rope that was attached to a picket pin driven into the ground by my axe. With these two horses secured, the third horse was allowed to wander free on hobbles. The only drawback to this system is that if the hobbled horse wandered out of sight, the other two became anxious and began whinnying for their companion to return. Turns at being the free horse were rotated. But before sunset, I always tethered all three horses as close as possible around the tent at night," Tim explained.

While Keith used the same system on the other side of the world, he also made a critically important observation.

"I came up with a compromise for my two horses, which was to tether one and let the other one loose with/without hobbles depending on experience. But it's important to remember that if you are dealing with more than two horses, you always have to tether the number one horse, otherwise it will lead the others away. That's the problem I had when I left Nispero at a farm for his back to heal. After being away for two weeks, when he returned the dynamics of the herd had changed and he discovered he wasn't the leader any more. But because I hadn't realized this, the first night when all the horses were reunited again I tethered Nispero as usual and let Papaya and Manzano graze loose in their hobbles. But the new leader, Papaya, promptly led Manzano off to greener pastures, which meant that I had fun chasing after them while riding Nispero bareback," Keith remembered.

Doug, Jane, Keith and Tim are among the many Long Riders who have used picket pins to allow their hard-working horses to graze, as opposed to being tied up all night. But remember, never leave your horse unattended on a picket pin, nor fail to check on his safety on a regular basis.

Tibetan Dead Man

In this age of plenty, it is difficult to appreciate how zealously our forebears guarded their tools, saddles, and ropes. A saddle was designed to last a man's lifetime. Though tools or ropes were inanimate objects, they held their own stories and were accorded respect. Likewise, hard-won lessons were passed on from one generation to the next.

A case in point is the dead man. In soil which is unable to hold a picket pin, horsemen buried a "dead man," which secured the horse and kept it close to camp. The principle is to dig a hole at least eighteen inches deep, place an object in the bottom of the hole, tie the picket rope to it, bury the object and sleep on top of the "dead man."

For example, Gabriel Bonvalot observed this practice in Tibet during his epic journey from Paris to Saigon in the late 19th century. While riding across the treeless Tibetan plateau Bonvalot observed and noted, "The Tibetan riders dig a small hole in the ground about two feet deep. Then they tie the halter rope to a rock, bundle of sticks or even a bag of sand. They place the bundle and rope end at the bottom of the hole, fill it with sand and tread it down firmly. The result is a mode of fastening horses which offers much more resistance than one might be inclined to think," Bonvalot noted.

At the same time, over on the treeless pampas of Argentina, Don Roberto Cunninghame Graham observed a strikingly similar practice being put into effect by the gauchos.

"When sleeping out on the pampas in places where there were no trees or bushes, horses were fastened up for the night by scraping out a hole in the ground. When this had been done, a bone, or a piece of wood (carried for this purpose), was inserted into it, and forced into a horizontal position at the bottom of the hole. To the bone or piece of wood was fixed the lasso to which the horse was tied. Then the hole was filled with earth, which was stamped down and usually the riders, for more security, lay down to sleep over the place where the horse was, as it were, anchored. If anything frightened the animal during the night, the sleeper was awakened by its snorts and by the jerking of the rope."

Though there are no known cases of modern Long Riders using this method, its historic reliability seems to ensure that, should the right circumstances arise, it might be used with great effect.

South African Anchor

In 1860 Sir Francis Bond Head, recorded how Boer horsemen in Africa had devised a unique method to secure horses in a treeless environment.

"In South Africa, farmers and sportsmen of all descriptions have long been in the habit of what they term anchoring their horses by a lump of lead, from three to five pounds in weight, carried in a small pocket buckled to the outside of their left saddle bag. To this anchor is attached a piece of cord about ten feet long, which, passing and running freely through both rings of the curb bit, and hanging from them like a loose rein, is fastened to a D or ring on the off-side of the saddle. No time need be lost in displacing the lead from its pocket when necessary, as it can be jerked out on the ground in the act of dismounting. When a horse has been thus anchored, if he attempts to move on, his nose is brought down to his breast by the cord, which, tightening equally on both sides, acts exactly like a bridle in the hand of a rider; and as the pressure of the curb-chain ceases so soon as he stops, he soon finds out that the best thing he can do is to stand still and graze."

As the cord was not fastened to either ring of the bit, but merely run through both, the pressure it exerted when the horse tried to move was equal on both sides; and therefore, on the pulley principle, a lead of four pounds weight made it necessary for the horse to overcome with his mouth a steady and continuous pressure of eight pounds on the extremity of the bit lever before he could move forward. On mounting hurriedly the cord was grasped with the reins, the anchor was raised, and while galloping away was placed in its pocket.

The Boer system of anchoring horses was so successful that the German cavalry later adapted this method.

Ground Tying

While we are on the subject of Boer horsemen, let me remark on the manner in which they taught their horses to ground tie.

The Boers used the anchor to teach horses to stand on the veldt. At first the Boer horseman would attach the reins to the anchor. With his head secured by the lead weight, the horse quickly learned to associate having his reins placed on the ground with being attached to the actual lead weight. With the passage of time, the use of the anchor was reduced, until the point was reached where the rider could dismount, drop the reins on the ground, and the horse would stand still, believing that he was still tethered by the anchor.

There is no doubt that teaching a horse to ground tie can be tremendously helpful if you find yourself in open country. The South American gauchos also taught their Criollos to ground tie.

But dropping the reins on the ground, and hoping the horse remains stationary, though immensely useful, has not in fact secured your mount in any meaningful manner. Don't risk your saddle, and all the rest of your gear, on the strength of a psychological trick practised on the horse.

The Ground Picket Line

The practice of attaching horses to a picket line is a custom most often found in Canada and the United States. There are two types of picket line, the high line and the ground line.

History demonstrates that when horsemen from various cultures travelled across a treeless environment, they experimented with how to attach their horses to the ground. These experiments resulted in picket pins, anchors, etc. being used. Likewise, the mounted men who roamed the desert country of North America also used a ground-based security system known as the ground picket line.

The ground picket line consists of a strong rope stretched tight, flush with the ground, which is held in place at either end by two steel picket pins. Horses are then tied to the ground line at regular intervals.

It's a fine theory and Hollywood made the most of it in a John Wayne movie entitled *The Train Robbers*. Accompanied by the beautiful red-headed actress, Ann Margaret, the Duke and five fellow cowboys set up camp amidst the glistening white sands of the Mexican desert. With a romantic camp fire blazing, and the requisite big metal coffee pot bubbling away cheerfully, the group's seven riding horses and two pack mules are shown standing quietly, side by side, tied by their lead ropes to a ground picket line.

Mind you, these are not mere mortal equines like you and I ride. They are low-maintenance saints who no one has bothered to feed or water since they left Texas and rode into Mexico. And though this is a dry camp, without a blade of grass or a drop of water, and regardless of the bumbling gun-toting killers sneaking about close by in the adjoining darkness, to heighten the illusion of domestic equine bliss the nine tireless animals never fidget. Nor do they bite one another, act irritable, scream or kick. No horse steps across the magic string which seems to have glued them all into place. And none of them would dare to empty his bowels or urinate without permission from John Wayne. They are, in a word, pretty pony pictures, created by that fantasy factory, Hollywood, and divorced from reality.

The ground picket line is seldom used now, though the theory remains valid. The problem is that the horses must be taught in advance how to use the system. They must never be tied so tightly that their heads are lowered by force. Their lead rope must be long enough to allow them to stand with their heads in a natural position. Horses tied to this line must have ample space between them and the next animal. And though John Wayne slept the night through alongside his mythical animals, if you place your precious horses on a ground picket line you had better check them with great regularity, being ready to quickly untangle or calm them.

The High Picket Line

The use of the high picket line is restricted to certain parts of the horse world. You will, for example, find it commonly applied in parts of the western United States and Canada, but many African or Asian horsemen will never have heard of it. Yet regardless of where you may ride, the high picket line can be easily adapted to local conditions and horses. However there are strict environmental restrictions which must be followed at all times if you use this system.

The basic concept consists of attaching the high picket line between two trees and then tying the horses' lead ropes to the picket line. There are several parts to a successful high picket line, including the tree-savers, the knot eliminators and the actual rope.

The two nylon tree-saver straps are fitted around the bole of the two trees between which the picket line will be placed. These wide nylon straps, which have large metal rings at each end, prevent the rope from damaging the trees.

It is important that you choose the right type of rope for a high picket rope. Like a picket pin rope, a top-quality climbing rope is powerful and flexible enough for this purpose. Many climbing ropes are non-stretch, braided for extra strength, and are capable of holding hundreds of pounds.

It is not only time consuming to tie your horses to a high picket line via a traditional knot, it also enhances the chances of a problem, should the animal get in trouble and you must quickly untie him. Instead of tying each lead rope to the high picket line, stainless steel in-line swivels, commonly known as knot eliminators, are placed at regular intervals along the high picket line to which the horses are attached. These swivels ensure that the animals do not twist the overhead picket line or become entangled with each other.

Where you decide to place the high picket line requires careful attention. The spot chosen should not have roots, stumps, rocks or plants underfoot which might trip the horses. Two stout trees serve as the twin bases of the high picket line. The tree-savers should be placed on each tree as far above the ground as you can reach. This allows the horses to move freely or lie down beneath it, whereas setting the line too low may result in a horse becoming entangled and injured.

For safety's sake, each horse's lead rope should be attached to a knot-eliminator, which will allow you to free the animal quickly in case of trouble. For comfort's sake, the lead rope of each animal must be equal to the distance from the horse's muzzle to the ground as it stands at its normal head height. This allows the horse enough slack to be able to move, eat hay off the ground and lie down to rest.

The high picket line must be kept tight, though it is inevitable that it will flex as the horses eat and move.

How you position the animals along the high picket line is also crucial. Take note of the animal's social order, placing the most dominant horse at the head of the high picket line and the most timid animal at the more secure end.

The Trouble with Trees

There are twin dangers when you mix horses and trees.

Any time you tie a horse to a solid, immovable object, such as a tree, you place your animal at risk. If he panics, pulls back, and finds himself severely restrained by the halter, lead rope and tree, the combination could be injurious or fatal. If you must use a tree, then tie the lead rope to a break-away string to reduce the risk of injury.

What is more common is that if you tie your horse to a tree, the animal will strip off the bark, devour the tender leaves, expose the roots by pawing, destroy the fragile undergrowth and leave a long-term scar on the landscape. Because of the damage done to trees by thoughtless horse campers, the United States Forest Service enacted Wilderness Regulation #36CFR261.6, which states that the owners of horses caught damaging trees or vegetation are guilty of a federal violation and will be fined.

The U.S. Forest Service also requires horse campers and travellers to use tree-savers so as to prevent the high picket line rope from cutting into and damaging the tree's bark.

Just as importantly, a high picket line must be placed in a durable site if you want to assure the security of your horses and minimize damage to the camp area.

Even though high picket lines are associated with minimum impact horse camping, the reality is often quite different. Unlike John Wayne's patient horses, real animals are mischievous and will pass the night pawing the ground or breaking off branches within reach. There is also the problem of manure and urine. For these reasons, place the high picket line on a spot that offers hard soil and natural drainage. Place the tree-savers as high as possible around two strong trees and then secure the picket rope on both ends with a quick-release knot. Make sure the picket rope is tight, then place the knot-eliminators so that there is at least six feet between each animal and at least eight feet between the trees at each end.

Always try to place your high line picket in an area that has already been used for this purpose or will suffer the minimum amount of damage from the horses' hard hooves. Even if the trees are not harmed, the horses' constant movement will reduce the ground to dust in hot weather or into a muddy patch when it rains. Knowing about this possible damage in advance, you will appreciate the need for caution when a local person offers to let your horses rest for the night on their property. The last thing you want is to awake to an angry host, who has discovered their formerly green garden has been desecrated, every blade of grass stripped and young trees reduced to matchsticks.

To minimize this type of damage, you should always guard your high picket line, making sure that your animals remain properly tied, preventing them from entangling and injuring themselves and keeping hay under the centre of the picket line. You should also remove manure promptly. Even if there are no obvious problems, you should move the high picket line occasionally if you plan to camp in one place for any length of time to allow the previous spot to dry.

One equestrian traveller who mastered the high line picket was Steve Nott. In the 1980s he made a journey around the entire perimeter of the Australian continent. During that marathon journey Steve used a high picket line. However, because in-line swivels and knot-eliminators were not available, he came up with another way of keeping his horse from becoming entangled on the picket line.

"Tied tight between two trees, my picket line had two sticks tied across about six feet out from the trees. With my horse's lead rope looped over the rope, he could feed the length of the rope but the sticks stop him going round the tree and becoming tangled. The lead rope should be just long enough for him to put his head comfortably to the ground," Steve said.

Electric Fence

If you are travelling with a pack horse, then you might wish to consider using a portable electric fence kit, which can be fitted into the bottom of a pannier.

This system is lightweight and runs on small batteries. Fibreglass rods are driven into the ground to make up the portable corral. A highly-visible tape is strung between the rods. The small charger will keep the batteries serviceable for a month. A standard kit weighs approximately sixteen pounds (8 kilos). A single strand fence will create a temporary pasture measuring 50'by 50' (15 metres square), which should safely accommodate four horses. A double strand fence measuring 25' by 25' (7.5 metres square) will still provide a large area for two horses.

The key to an effectively powered electric fence is a good ground. While a portable fence allows your horses to graze freely, they must still be trained to respect the polytape before you begin your journey. Place the horses inside the portable fence while you are still at home, allowing them to graze and spend several nights inside the polytape. Because of its efficiency, it won't take long for your horses to acquire a healthy respect for the fence. They will quickly learn to stay away from it even if the power is turned off.

Peruvian Tapa Ojos

One of the most unusual methods of securing horses occurs in Peru, where aristocratic hacienda owners devised the *tapa ojos*.

Because of the similarity in their names the larger Peruvian Paso is often confused with his cousin, the Paso Fino horse of the Caribbean. Though both horses share a common Spanish origin, they are different breeds who do not have the same four-beat lateral footfall.

The Peruvian Paso is a strong working horse who is a direct descendant of the horses imported into the Andean kingdom in the 16th century. The original mission of the Peruvian Paso was to provide a fast amble which allowed their riders to cover up to eighty kilometres a day on level ground. Yet while riding from one hacienda to another through rocky and remote country, there were many portions of the mountainous terrain where there was no place to tie the horses.

In addition to breeding exceptional horses, the Peruvian hidalgos were also connoisseurs of exquisite riding gear. Finely hammered silver and braided leather were used to create a unique type of equine artwork. The tapa ojos are part of this tradition.

The Peruvian bridle, known as a *jato*, consists of three pieces, the headstall, reins and the eye covers. These moveable blinders, which are made from soft leather, normally rest along the side of the horse's head while he is on the move. However, should the rider wish to secure his valuable mount in a treeless locality, he need only slip the *tapa ojos* down over the eyes of the Peruvian Paso, at which time the horse is trained to stand perfectly still until his vision is restored.

German Coupling Strap

Thanks to the ongoing military research made by the Belgian Long Rider Robert Wauters, the Long Riders' Guild was informed of the German cavalry coupling strap.

The German cavalry had a method of securing horses which consisted of a leather strap 412 mm (16 inches) long and 25 mm (1 inch) wide. It had a sturdy metal clip at each end. One clip was attached to the bit and the other to the rear of the second horse's saddle. An ex-German cavalryman confirmed this method was used.

The former cavalryman warned that if the horses were left unattended for too long, they might chew on the leather saddle out of boredom or because the sweaty leather tasted of salt. He also informed Robert that it was vitally important that you only couple compatible horses. The Belgian Long Rider has tried this method and had good results.

An emergency method which incorporates the same principle is to tie the reins of each horse to the right stirrup of the other. Horses can be securely coupled in this manner for short intervals but care must be taken that the reins, when tied, are not more than six to eight inches long. This head-to-toe position suits them well because it is a position they naturally assume in summer, so as to use each other's tails to keep away the flies from each other's faces.

Neither of these methods will work with laden pack horses, unless the panniers are first removed.

With three horses, one can be tied to the head collar of either of the two horses so coupled. Four horses are secured by tying a horse to each of the two originally coupled. No horse should have more than one foot length of rein, and the best knot to use is a slip knot round the rein itself.

Italian Tethering Ring

The Italian cavalry devised a unique way to secure large groups of horses. This was done by attaching the lead ropes of several horses to a small eight-inch (20 cm) iron ring. The lead ropes would be passed through the holes and then knotted to prevent the horse from pulling free. Horses thus tethered must bunch together with their heads inwards; consequently if they attempted to proceed in any one direction a certain proportion of them would have to move backwards. Stampeding en masse is therefore practically impossible.

Runaways

If you fear losing your horses, don't allow all your animals to graze at the same time. Keep the most reliable horse tied close to camp, in case you need to ride out to find and return any runaways.

Once they've had an hour or so to graze, many horses will have appeased their appetite and may become curious about what lies over the hill. You should anticipate this moment and be ready to bring them back to camp.

Horses that have learned to anticipate grain or salt will be more likely to follow you willingly so as to ensure their evening meal.

Should a horse begin to run away when you approach, don't attempt to grab its lead rope and stop it. The power of a running horse will pull you off your feet and drag you across the ground.

Even if a pasture is available, don't relax your guard. It is better to hear bells than count tracks. Always put different-sounding bells on your horses. This will enable you to listen to the movements in the dark, and if they run away, be able to determine in which direction they fled.

If your horses have vanished, don't waste time trying to figure out how they got loose, concentrate on finding them. The first necessity is to determine where they went, and most of the time the loose horses will have returned in the direction from which you travelled the previous day.

That lesson was demonstrated in 1628 during an equestrian journey from Transylvania to Constantinople, when all but one of the horses of Prince Janos Kemeny ran away in the night. Awakened by the neighing of the tied up animal, the Prince set out to look for his other horses in the pitch-darkness. Instead of trying to mount and ride the animal in the dark, the clever Prince tied a long rope to the halter of the one remaining horse, the end of which he held firmly in his hand. The horse followed the smell and tracks of the runaways to the place where the previous evening they had been watered by a stream outside a village.

If for any number of reasons your horses escape, the first thing to do is to circle your camp and look for outbound tracks. Because horses haven't changed since the days of Prince Kemeny, you may well find that your animals have also headed back across ground travelled the day before.

Summary

The last thing you want to discover after you have begun your journey is that you have an equine security problem.

A traveller riding across Canada in 2007 overlooked the necessity of training her horse prior to departure. Soon after the ride began the horse was tethered to a picket pin. During the night the animal became so badly entangled that the rope severed the horse's tendon. When a veterinarian was summoned the next morning, it was discovered the wound was so deep that it was leaking sinovial fluid, which lubricates the joints and allows for ease of movement. Because the horse was in great pain and there was virtually no probability of recovery, the decision was made to euthanize the animal immediately.

As this case illustrates, it is imperative that your horse be trained to use some type of restraining system before you leave the safety of your home.

Once you're on the trail, don't assume that a hobbled horse can't escape. As Tex Cashner learned, even a moderately-constrained animal can run straight into trouble.

If you decide to use either type of picket line, listen for any signs which might indicate that your horses are in trouble. Check on them with great regularity, if only to reassure them that all is well and that you are near by.

Traditional latigo leather two-strap hobbles can be purchased from any good outfitter supply company. Care must be taken that the leather does not harden and chafe the horse's pasterns.

These heavy duty hobbles, made from harness leather and chain hobbles, have a soft lining which can be replaced.

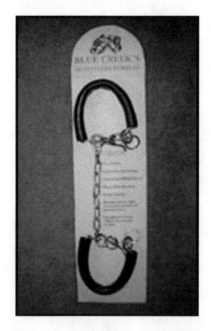

Sturdy chain hobbles, with soft neoprene rubber cuffs, can be purchased from Canadian Long Rider Stan Walchuk at his Blue Creek Outfitters Supply Company.

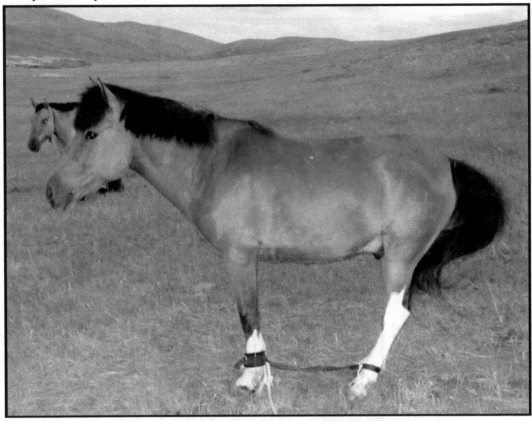

The sideline helps reduce the chances of a hobbled horse bunny-hopping away from camp. English Long Rider Sam Southey used this method during her journey in Mongolia. Canadian Long Rider Stan Walchuk offers this type of three-legged hobble at his Blue Creek Outfitters Supply Company.

Before North American Long Rider Doug Preston rode from Arizona to New Mexico across the Despoblado Desert, he taught his horses how to use the picket pin and rope.

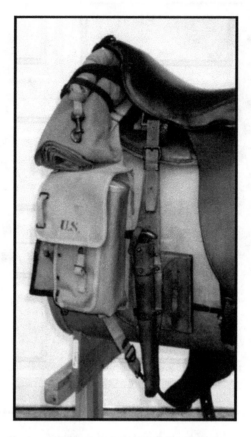

A traditional picket pin can be seen in its regulation leather holder (centre) on this U.S. cavalry McClellan saddle. Photo courtesy of the Society of the Military Horse.

The picket pin kit offered by Outfitter's Supply contains a steel picket pin with a swivel head that reduces the chances of a horse becoming entangled in his picket rope, a neoprene hobble and a thirty-foot picket rope.

Swiss Long Rider André Fischer's horse grazing quietly on his picket line in Patagonia

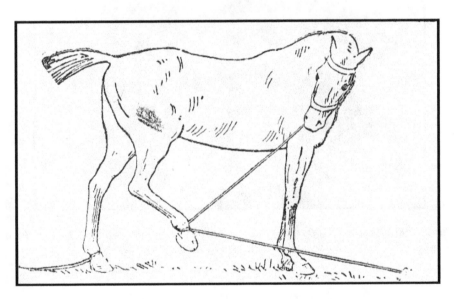

When you attach the picket pin's rope to the horse's halter, you run the risk of the animal receiving a severe rope burn on his pastern.

Before he set out on his 29,000 kilometre (18,000 mile) ride around the Australian continent, Long Rider Steve Nott taught his horse how to stand quietly on a picket line.

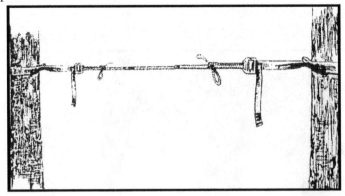

If you are travelling in a country which does not have tree-savers available, you can use old nylon seat belts to save the trees at both ends of the high picket line.

It is critically important that the horses cannot reach the trees at either end of the high picket line.

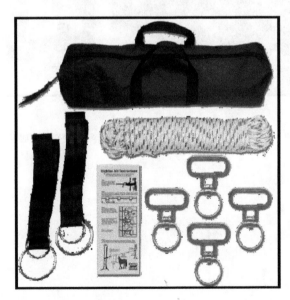

A four horse picket line kit, complete with tree savers and in-line swivel knot-eliminators, from Outfitter's Supply.

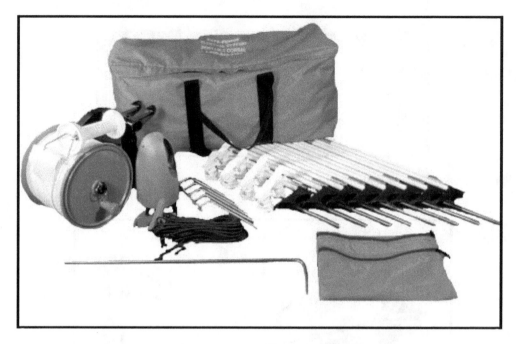

An electric fence kit from Outfitter's Supply Company.

British Long Rider Mefo Phillips used a portable electric fence with great success during her ride from Canterbury, England to Santiago, Spain.

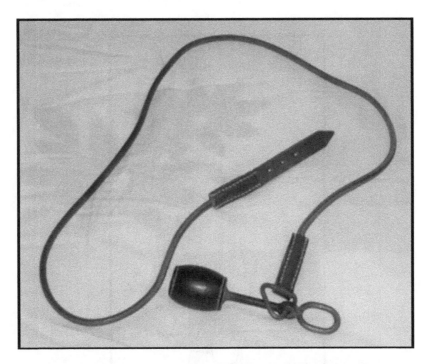

This lead horse anchor was used by the German cavalry, who adapted the original concept from Boer horsemen in South Africa. Photo courtesy of the Society of the Military Horse.

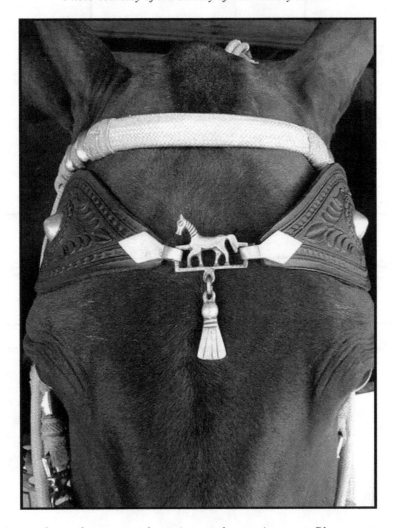

The Peruvian tapa ojos can be used to secure a horse in a treeless environment. Photo courtesy of Santa Barbarian.

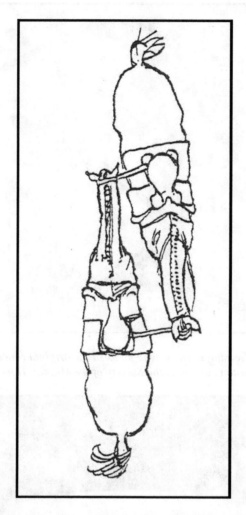

While doing military research, Belgian Long Rider Robert Wauters documented how the German cavalry also used the coupling strap to secure two army horses.

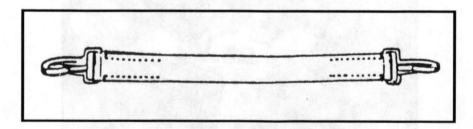

Though no modern Long Rider has yet used it, the German army coupling strap could be easily reproduced using a leather or canvas strap and strong metal snaps.

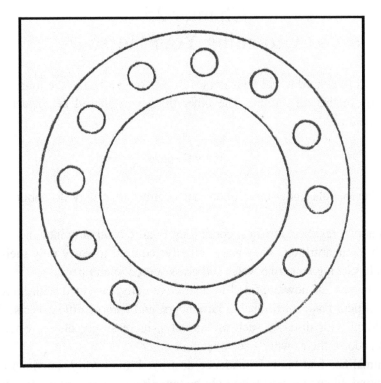

Because their heads were all facing into the centre of the Italian cavalry's tethering ring, large groups of horses could not stampede.

Many environments do not have trees to which a Long Rider can tie the horse; i.e. the pampas of Argentina and the treeless Tibetan plateau. In such a situation horsemen dig a hole at least eighteen inches deep, place an object in the bottom of the hole, tie the picket rope to it, bury the object and sleep on top of the "dead man." This photo, taken in 1911, shows an American Indian using this method to secure his horse in the desert.

Chapter 25
Grooming Your Horse

Despite the fact that you worked hard to get your horses fit before you began the journey, at the outset you should expect the rigours of the trip to tire the animal. The other thing you should be expecting is to spend more time grooming than you did at the barn.

Why Groom

In this motorized age when people know more about carburettors than they do about Criollos, it makes sense to state the obvious.

The majority of modern horses reside in artificial conditions. Nature originally intended them to spend most of their time grazing, so as to obtain their nutrition. They were initially required to carry only their own body weight. Their only exercise was restricted to moving from one water and grass source to another.

Unhappily, innumerable horses are now confined in restrictive cells, provided with large amounts of high energy food which is far in excess of their basic nutritional requirements, and receive little exercise. The result are millions of idle pasture ornaments, riddled with diseases such as laminitis, increasingly obese, whose lives serve little or no practical purpose, except to endorse their owner's social status.

Thus, this once-wild animal has had his independence destroyed, his bodily functions jeopardized, and his emotional needs altered by mankind. In such a world, it might be tempting to disregard the fact that keeping your road and pack horses properly groomed is one of the fundamentals of ethical equestrian travel.

There is a certain irony involved in any discussion about grooming road horses versus their pampered cousins in the show ring.

Ring-riders obsess about the physical appearance of their animals. These people happily spend millions of dollars every year so as to purchase expensive shampoos, tail conditioners, chemicals to brighten hoofs, *ad nauseam*. The object is to eradicate any trace of the "wild," to obliterate dirt, to eliminate unsightly hairs, to artificially colour coats stripped of their natural oils. The goal is the creation of an equine Barbie doll, all curls and spice and everything nice.

The road horse's health depends on being expertly groomed. If not, he, the Long Rider and the journey all suffer. Yet, in contrast to the ring rider's pretty pony, a road horse would be considered dirty by the uninformed. This is a mistake common to people who are used to treating their horses like their cars; i.e. eager to spend Sunday afternoon washing the fragile skin of the animal as if it were the robust metal exterior of their Ford Mustang.

Painstaking grooming is more important to a road horse than any desire to merely improve the mount's outward appearance. But grooming the road horse differs dramatically from that of the ring horse.

Grooming and Travelling

The sun rises and sets with a Long Rider grooming his horse.

There are no physical secrets between these two.

Like a parent who has brushed his child's hair over and over again, a Long Rider comes to know every funny bump, gentle hollow, soft curve, sore spot and ticklish place on his horse. The whorls embedded in an out-of-the-way place on the horse's coat, the knots which always mysteriously appear in the same spot in his mane, the one hoof that seems to be forever dirtier than the other three, these are the sort of little things which any Long Rider spends his time paying attention to, but seldom speaks of to others.

Though every horse has to be expertly cleaned every day, the best way of testing if a horse has been well groomed is by passing the fingers the reverse way through the direction of the hair, particularly under the belly. If the horse is dirty, they will be covered with grey scurf.

The amount of grooming will depend on the conditions you encountered during that day's travel. The harder the day's work, the greater amount of care will be required to keep the horse's skin in perfect condition.

Hard travel increases natural perspiration through the skin of the horse. Good grooming removes the dirt and dust which would otherwise clog the pores of the skin. It increases the flow of blood to the skin and surface muscles which carry the saddle and rider. Also, it keeps parasites away.

Hearty road and pack horses spend their time in the natural elements as nature intended, the result being that rain, wind, sun, cold and heat are all things which a horse's coat can deal with during the normal course of a journey. The Yakut horses of Siberia, for example, routinely survive winters where the temperature dips to a chilly minus sixty degrees. Other horses survive in harsh deserts, thrive in treacherous bogs, and inhabit various untamed corners of the planet where they require no artificial care from man.

To keep the horse healthy, grooming must be done every morning and evening, with careful attention being paid to the horse's outward state at all times.

One thing working in your favour is that the hard work and exercise produced by the journey will help keep the road horse in peak fitness. By contrast idle, grain-fed horses are more prone to scurf and grease than their hard-working cousins on the road.

The Necessities

Before we investigate the details of grooming, let us carve these two rules in stone.

Never saddle a horse that has not been perfectly groomed.

Never conclude your day's travel with a hot horse. Later in this book I will discuss the normal course of a Long Rider's daily events. Yet for the moment, let me say that when your day ends, your horse should under no circumstances be dripping with sweat. Regardless of where you bed down, don't arrive at that night's destination with a heated horse. If the horse is hot at day's end, he should be walked until he cools off and is dried.

If the horse is wet from rain, don't remove his saddle. Remove his bridle, replace it with the halter, tie him, loosen the girth, then rub him down with handfuls of loose straw or a towel, using brisk friction to warm and dry him.

In normal dry-weather conditions, once you have determined where your horse is to be quartered for the night, lead him into the stable, or tie him securely, then loosen the girth on his saddle. Remove his bit and bridle, place his halter on, then give him as much water as he will drink. In cold weather, or if the water is from a deep cold well, make sure the bucket of water has had a chance to be left in the sun so that it may not be too cold. Once he has slaked his thirst, take the time to observe the horse's frame of mind and to be looking for any abnormalities in movement, behaviour, the condition of his back, etc.

When he has finished his drink his feet should be picked out to see that no stones have lodged in them. Then his nostrils, mouth, eyes, dock, and sheath, in fact all the hairless parts, should be washed carefully with a gentle sponge dipped in cool water, then dried with a soft towel.

Don't be in a hurry to unsaddle him. The sudden exposure to cold air on the hot flesh under the saddle is liable to cause injury to the delicate skin, nerves and blood vessels. Be patient and allow the back to resume its normal temperature. The time required will differ, depending on the climate, that day's work, your saddle and your horse. After having allowed the horse to relax, slide your hand under the saddle pad to determine if the horse's back has cooled down. If so, then the saddle may be removed and any remaining sweat on the horse's back should be dried at once. It is a good idea to rub the back vigorously where the saddle sat, so as to restore the circulation in the skin.

Next, use a curry comb to remove loose hair, mud and any objects that become tangled in the horse's coat. Then employ a stiff brush to remove dirt and dust from the coat. Always move the brush from front to back in the direction the horse's hair naturally lies.

Take note. You are attempting to remove dirt, mud, dust and insects, not the natural grease and oil which serves as a protector to the horse's skin and helps keep him warm. By stripping the coat of its natural oils, you leave the horse standing stark naked in the sun and rain. Remember, this is a large, outdoor animal, a representative of a species who has spent hundreds of thousands of years living wild without the benefit or interference of mankind. Remove the dirt, not his body's defences and dignity.

There is no need to brush forcefully beneath the horse's knees. This area will gather dust and dirt again as soon as the horse is travelling, so merely keep the lower legs clean, not glistening.

In addition to sponging and brushing, standard grooming procedures should include checking the eyes, ears and teeth for abnormalities. Also, always keep a sharp out for any type of saddle sore, horse bite or insect sting.

Horse Hair

In the artificial world of the show ring, Arab horses not only have all the hair cut off their noses, but the animal's muzzle is then greased to make it shine. Not being content to strip away the desert dweller's hair, there are reports of owners who have enhanced the artificial dip seen in the forehead of some Arab show horses. These animals are reportedly operated upon so as to enhance their chances of winning top-dollar competitions.

Never cut the hair of a road or pack horse.

Any horse, even a poor Arab show animal, needs the bristles on his nose. These feelers provide information to the horse in the same way a cat's whiskers do. The bristles on a horse's nose help him graze at night and to feel his way in the dark through unfamiliar surroundings. Removing them is akin to cutting off your fingers. You have removed the animal's sense of touch. To do so may appeal to a human's vanity, but it is a crime against nature.

The hair which lines the external ear should also be allowed to remain untouched. Likewise, do not tamper with the hair around the pasterns, which acts as a shield against water that otherwise will enter the folds of the foot and cause cracks.

Mane and forelock hair is vital to serve as a shield against excessive sunlight and harsh wind on the horse's eyes.

Above all, it is absolutely essential, if you want to keep horses in good health and condition, that a road horse's tail should never be shortened or cut. By doing so, you deprive him of nature's protection against insects.

Stables and pastures are excellent breeding-grounds for flies. When the horse is required to stand in the open he must be equipped with his best defence, a long tail. If it is too short for him to reach his flanks with it, he will be kept in perpetual agony by his annoying air-borne enemies.

Washing

Visit any contemporary stable in the developed world and you will probably find a wash rack reserved for wrecking the coats of horses. This is a recent practice based upon a misplaced modern tradition and the custom of doing what others do without questioning the health effects on the horse.

The washing of horses as a general practice is to be strongly condemned.

As previously explained, the horse's skin contains essential oils and grease which protect the coat and flesh beneath. That is why travelling horses take no harm from the rain and may be ridden through water with impunity, because the natural greasiness and subsequent exertion of the journey keep up the circulation and warmth of the wetted skin till it is dry again.

Because they do not appreciate the importance of this natural defence, many horse owners eagerly subject their horses to a forceful bath as soon as the day's short ride is concluded. A sign of sweat and into the wash rack goes their horse. The owner then lathers up the animal like nanny washing baby in the tub. After the suds are rinsed away thanks to the powerful water hose, expensive ointments are slathered on the denuded coat and then thick globs of gelatine are brushed through the animal's mane and tail. The result of this shower of artificial chemicals is a perfumed equine whose body has been stripped of its natural defence system, but one that smells good, and even more important, looks shiny.

Using soap on a horse removes a great proportion of the usual greasiness in the coat which serves as a protection from cold. Thus, despite your best intentions, should you wash your road horse in cold and changeable, temperate climates, it may very easily lead to sickness, and even in warm and equable temperatures its practice is not always without danger. This in turn necessitates the animal being guarded against chills by protecting him in a thick, expensive, artificial coat designed to protect him from the weather. Wrapping baby in a warm coat may work back home at the show stable but not for Long Riders and their road horses.

The dangers which washing may give rise to are not however only due to the wetting of the skin but to want of attention in the subsequent drying. In all cases where it is found necessary to wash, too much care cannot be bestowed on making sure that the animal is thoroughly dried and the warmth of the skin restored, otherwise a chill may follow.

Washing the legs and belly in order to get rid of mud is frequently followed by stiffness and cracking of the surface. This is more likely to happen if warm water is used or when the weather is cold and especially where there is a keen wind. If, at the end of the day, his legs are wet, you should dry them carefully.

Heels should not be washed as a rule. To leave the heels damp is to invite such diseases as cracked heels and grease. If heels become soiled and have to be washed they should be very carefully dried.

It has been stated that animals with white legs are more frequent sufferers from cracked heels than others, and this is no doubt the case; but it is not on account of weakness or peculiarity of the white skin, but owing to the fact that it is more frequently washed.

Washing the hooves both round the wall and on the sole is occasionally required as a matter of cleanliness after the feet have been picked out. It is not necessary to do it as a matter of routine and whenever possible it should be done outside the stable.

The only purposes for which the use of water, or soap and water, is necessary on the body of the healthy horse is for the removal of dirt stains which will not groom off, and for the occasional cleaning of the mane and tail and hoofs. If the legs and belly are covered with mud it should be left to dry and then be brushed off.

Otherwise, washing of the body should be prohibited as a rule, except for the special purposes mentioned, and should it be necessary at any time to break the rule, the greatest care should be taken to dry the skin thoroughly, ensure the animal is warm and kept out of draughts.

Clipping

After having twice ridden across the Andes Mountains in the early nineteenth century, Sir Francis Bond Head picked up his pen and made a note of the interesting bits of equine history he had learned during his many travels. He recalled, for example, how the French Emperor Napoleon was indirectly responsible for the English gentry to begin clipping the hair off their horses.

"During the Peninsular war against Napoleon's armies in Spain, the English observed that Spanish muleteers gave their animals apparent relief by rudely shearing off the hair that covered their bodies; and on the idea being imported into England, commenced the practice of clipping. Soon afterwards the practice arose whereby English hunting horses were denuded of their coats, being shaved as bare as the hide of a pig that had just been killed, scalded and scraped," Bond Head wrote.

Cutting all the hair off your horse to maintain a fashion from the Napoleonic age may appeal to English fox hunters, but should never be inflicted on a Long Rider's road horse.

Summary

Grooming a road and pack horse is a serious business. On the best of days, it requires a great deal of hard work. The attempt to dry and groom a muddy, soaking, heavy-coated horse after a long day in the saddle is a wearisome finale to a day's ride.

It is as necessary to rub their sweaty backs as it is to attend to their hungry stomachs.

Select the right tool and don't rush while grooming.

What a road horse needs from a Long Rider at the end of the day is a brush not a bath. Though horse owners mean well, they are not doing their horse a favour when they wash away all of the natural oils which normally protect the animal's skin from the elements.

Chapter 26
Watering Your Horse

Water is the life-blood of the journey. Yet Long Riders normally never carry it.

According to the time of year, his size, and the difficulties of that day's travel, the road horse will need eight to ten gallons (about 40 litres) of water every twenty-four hours. Yet a single gallon of water weighs ten pounds. When every ounce counts, that's an impossible burden for a road horse. Plus, chances are that if you refresh your thirst from a canteen, you will overlook the equally dire needs of your parched horse.

So if you don't carry water, what do you do and when do you do it?

Precious Water

The Long Rider must be ever observant. Pay great attention to your horse's drinking habits and remember "little and often" in terms of watering him.

But the world is a vastly different place, isn't it?

That's what the Canadian Long Rider Bonnie Folkins discovered when she rode across the dry steppes of Mongolia.

The landscape was so dehydrated that local animals were driven mad by thirst.

"One time we set up camp by what we thought was a working well. A small herd of cows came running over hoping we would pump water for them but the pump was broken. They stood with their tongues hanging out. We tried and tried to get it working. It was a terrible feeling watching the helpless animals wander away."

The thirsty Canadian had to ride two miles from camp before she eventually found water for her horses.

Because so many people live in rain-rich countries, they might find Bonnie's desperate search for a drink surprising, but she learned quickly enough that if she was going to survive, she had to ask the Mongol nomads she met where the water was. And when she found some, she couldn't afford to be picky.

"You have to approach the nomads' gers and ask the shepherds where the water is. There are miles and miles between water, so you learn to rely on the smallest streams, tiny water holes, even puddles are a welcome source," Bonnie reported.

Why Water

When horses around the world worked for a living, there was a common belief that the more a horse was of northern ancestry, the more he needed to drink. According to this theory, an Austrian Haflinger, for example, would drink more than a desert-dwelling Moroccan Barb.

As Long Riders we are concerned with the basic safety requirements of the horse. Consequently, the importance of water to your horse's health cannot be over-emphasized.

Water does more than ease a horse's thirst. He must, on average, consume ten gallons of water a day just to keep his various body functions operating properly. For example, six pounds of hay passed into his digestive system will absorb six quarts of the horse's saliva. And though he drinks ten gallons of water a day on average, only a gallon of liquid will normally be lost through urination. The rest of the water is absorbed into the horse's hard-working body. Thus, even in pleasant weather and easy country, horses must always be properly watered.

When you factor in the additional challenges encountered in an equestrian journey, a lack of water can create a life-or-death situation for your horses.

The equestrian expert and Long Rider Jeremy James has made a long and careful study of how critically important water is to a road horse.

"First of all, the world is full of thirsty horses and whoever set about the maxim that horses should have their water restricted has been responsible for more equine misery than any other single piece of misinformation visited upon horses since man first sat upon them," he said.

Horses need a lot of water: plain and simple. If horses are denied water, no noticeable effect may be seen immediately but over a long period it will tell and the horses will exhaust more quickly than a horse allowed free access to water. If in doubt, try it yourself: increase your water intake and you'll notice a doubling of energy.

But, Jeremy warned, there are a lot of myths surrounding the watering of horses, lots of misinformation about colic and so forth but actually the world is full of dehydrated horses.

If in doubt, he suggested, try the skin pinch test.

"Pinch a little skin on the horse's neck and if it stays tented for a second or two, that horse is 3-5% dehydrated. He's got 2% more to go until he's on the critical list. Don't skimp on this or you will have a very bad time trying to persuade your horse to go in one direction while its senses tell it that water lies the opposite way."

"If not careful," Jeremy wrote, "something called anyhydrosis can set in whereby the horse goes well past its requirement and actually cannot drink. This is when people add electrolytes to water but I would strongly advise against that. Water should never be contaminated by anything at all, especially some chemical compound or electrolyte. So the rule should be let the horse drink as often as he likes."

Essential Water

Traditionally getting a drink for a wild horse also meant risking his life. Beasts of prey waited in the nearby shadows. The muddy bank might trap and drown an unwary horse. Deadly snakes slithered in the thick grass. Deep-seated memories of danger and sudden death lurked in the background every time a horse eased up for a drink. That is why wild horses never went deeper into the water than absolutely necessary. Horses didn't frolic in the water. They drank and ran.

In the wild, a horse drinks while he can hold his breath, lifts his nostrils to breathe deep and fill his lungs, then takes a second drink, perhaps a third, and turns away abruptly.

This explains why the structure of the horse's bowels is adapted for taking in large quantities of water at comparatively infrequent intervals.

Regardless of where you find it, be it a mountain stream, a farmer's water trough or a suburban garden tap, the water should ideally be fresh, pure, free from taste, smell and colour. Water should also be a temperature between 10 and 14 degrees Celsius (50 to 60 degrees Fahrenheit).

Yet Long Riders don't often deal with ideal conditions. That is what the French Long Riders Marc Witz and Marie-Emmanuelle Tugler discovered when they rode across Bolivia.

"When we reached the estancia, we were received by a gang of hunters. One of them led us to a well, which was the only water source on the property. The bees buzzing around it didn't frighten us for long. We had to have that water. Its yellowish colour and earthy smell didn't put us off either. We and our horses drank it anyway. And we came to no harm," Marc recalled.

Water in the Morning

It is absolutely necessary that you do not set out unless you have watered the horses.

Although most horses are disinclined to drink early in the morning, especially in cold weather, every effort should be made to make them drink before starting that day's journey.

This is critically important in countries where water is scarce, as this early-morning watering may be the only opportunity they have to drink for hours.

How much Water?

You should attempt to water your horse at least three times a day. If the weather is warm, increase his daily watering to four times a day, minimum.

Normally he will spend five minutes drinking three or four gallons at each of these opportunities.

Watering while Travelling

Watering while travelling can be difficult. Never pass up a chance to water your animals, especially on hot days. Never ride for more than four hours without watering the horses.

A small quantity taken frequently is far better and more refreshing than copious draughts, taken before or after rest, and, more important than all else, far less dangerous.

Before you water the horses, remove the road horse's bit and loosen the girths on both the riding and pack saddles. Don't allow your horses to move faster than a walk to and from the water.

Your horses should be watered quietly, without confusion. Never attempt to hold more than two horses at a time when watering. Do not let them crowd or push each other.

If you are using pack mules, care must be exercised to insure that they do not lie down in the water and damage their loads.

Horses should not be made to move faster than a walk for a quarter of an hour after a full drink. If fast work is required from your horses soon after watering, they should not be allowed to drink more than six to ten swallows.

Watering from a Trough

Though they seem like a quaint remnant of the previous equestrian age, the few remaining water troughs, set up by various municipalities, are not the artefacts of our kindly forefathers. In fact, it took a major social campaign in the latter days of the 19th century for city fathers to recognize that the horses employed in their vast urban herds were suffering needlessly due to a lack of clean drinking water. As horses had the unfortunate habit of dropping dead when overworked, money was raised through public subscriptions to install these much-needed water troughs.

There was only one unforeseen drawback.

The water troughs soon became prime breeding grounds for every type of nasty infection lurking amongst the thousands of equine employees. Runny noses, hacking coughs and weepy eyes were all too often the result of taking a cool drink from the public trough. The risk of contagion became so well known that cavalry officers were warned about watering army horses from such public sources.

American officers were told, "Public watering troughs should be avoided owing to the risk of contagious disease being introduced."

Their British counterparts were ordered, "Be careful about allowing the horse to drink from public troughs to which other animals have access as diseases are often contracted by neglecting this precaution."

The date on the calendar may change, and watering troughs may only hold flowers in today's big cities, but when you ride in out-of-the-way places, your thirsty horse will come face to face with the same risky water source faced by his four-footed forefathers.

If this happens, never let your horse drink out of a trough if the water appears dirty. Better to water him from a pail or a canvas bucket, which you should be carrying for this sort of emergency.

If you decide the water in the trough looks suitable, be sure the trough is of sufficient height and that the rim does not present any sharp angles or corners.

Never let too many horses crowd the trough.

Regardless if your animal is taking a drink from a trough or some other water source, horses need ample time to drink their fill. They should never be hurried or led away quickly.

Don't make the mistake of thinking that he has finished drinking merely because he has lifted his head. Horses drink, pause for a breath and then resume drinking.

Also, don't allow an animal to be taken away from the trough till all have finished drinking.

Water in Hot Weather

Heat means the animals should be watered more often. Particularly in the summer, thirst tires a horse out more drastically than hunger. A horse may become placid after a heavy drink on a hot day.

If the animal is hot, sweaty and overheated when you stop to water him, he may be given a few sips to quench his immediate thirst. Then he should be walked slowly until he has cooled off, before being allowed to completely satisfy his thirst.

Water in Cold Weather

There are two things to remember about horses and cold water.

One, horses will seldom drink very cold water freely. Two, drinking cold water can sometimes be harmful to horses.

Thurlow Craig warned, "About the only rule I make with water is never let a hot horse drink cold water. A single bucketful of very cold water on a heated stomach can play the devil with the toughest horse."

Thus, if the horse is hot and sweaty, don't let him fill up on cold water. Take the chill off the water by placing the bucket in the sun, or by adding a pint of hot water to it. The goal is to have the temperature of the water match the outside temperature of the air in the stables.

Travelling on horseback in cold weather provides an additional difficulty, which is to provide your horse with a drink of warm water. In order to maintain his normal body temperature your horse must be encouraged to drink his fill. The problem is that because equine thirst is more elusive than hunger, your patience may be tested as you try to keep his water from freezing until he finally decides it's time for a drink.

No matter how much trouble he causes, giving your horse warm water is important, as if he drinks cold water he will use up precious body heat and valuable energy heating it internally. Cold water will also cause him to shiver, which reduces his vigour and drains his resistance to cold.

The problem with watering your horse in cold weather is that his thirst is not as predictable as his appetite. Therefore providing him with fresh warm water, and then convincing him to drink it before the water in the bucket has frozen solid, can present you with a frustrating cold-weather problem. If cold weather is a factor, allow for extra time, rather than compromise your horse's safety by not allowing him the time needed to ensure he has had a long, deep drink of warm water before you set off across the cold landscape.

Also, once you are en route, don't be tempted to think that snow can resolve your horse's need for fresh water. Regardless of how pure and moist it appears, snow leaves a horse dehydrated. Horses left without water in a snow-covered environment may die of exposure.

Water at the Day's End

Before you off-saddle, every effort must be made to obtain your horses a plentiful supply of good, clean water. Stagnant water should be avoided if at all possible.

If that night's water supply is supplied by a stream, places should be designated for drinking and cooking, watering animals, bathing and washing clothes. Be sure you water the horses upstream, away from any kitchen or bathing soap.

Since it is customary to pitch camp and groom before watering, this allows time to cool the horses thoroughly. Water drunk too fast is dangerous and can cause colic. That is why care must be taken at the conclusion of the day's journey.

After he has slaked his immediate thirst, feed him some hay. Once he is cooled, he can have a long drink before his dinner.

Dangers of Watering

Let me make this clear. Horses should always be watered first and fed afterwards. If you get the sequence of watering and feeding wrong, your horse can die. It's that brutally simple.

This is what happened to the Argentine Long Rider Ana Beker. After having met Aimé Tschiffely, the petite woman was inspired to ride from Buenos Aires to Ontario. During her journey, she entrusted her horse to a stranger, who fed the horse first, then watered it. The animal died of a painful colic soon afterwards.

The mechanics of a horse's stomach help explain why water can be dangerous.

Unlike a cow, who is an herbivore equipped with more than one stomach so as to digest vegetable matter efficiently, horses are omnivores with only one stomach. Your road horse's stomach is equipped to hold two to three gallons of water. But the horse normally drinks four to five gallons of water at once. If you feed the horse first, then water him, the fluid passes straight through the stomach, flushing the food along with it into the intestines, where it often becomes lodged. The decomposing food, which cannot be passed, becomes gaseous, decomposes, causes unbelievable amounts of gastric pain, and often, as was the case with Ana Beker's horse, results in the horse dying a slow, agonizing death.

Because of this deadly combination, you must always water the horse at least half an hour before you feed him, never after.

If you are travelling, and at least an hour has passed since the horse was fed, then the animal may be watered as usual.

But there are other dangers lurking in the water.

Water which is dirty and motionless can kill your horse. That is what happened to the equestrian traveller Dane Hartwell. Upon reaching Los Angeles, Dane pitched camp along a trickle of a stream which ran through an obscure corner of the giant metropolis. Little did he know that there was a camp of illegal immigrants further upstream. The water was severely polluted and Dane's horse died from an E-coli infection.

Plus, there are other pollutions to wary of. Be careful of water that may have been contaminated by pesticides that have been washed out of farmers' nearby fields.

During her journey across the plains of Canada in 2012, Catherine Thompson was warned that the water sources were heavily polluted because of such chemical pesticides.

"I have just spent two weeks travelling through farm country that is heavily sprayed, dodging farms where the sprayers were out in full force and trying to figure out the best places to get water. I was given the good advice to never get water for me or horses from canola fields and other heavily sprayed crops. It is safer to try for hay fields which are generally not sprayed."

Also, avoid letting your horses drink from a water source shared by sheep. The woolly animals carry a parasite which can infect horses and cause a serious health risk.

No Water

Finally, what if you're not worried about any of these problems? What if you find yourself, like Bonnie Folkins, in a part of the world where there is no water?

In cool weather, and if they have not been travelling hard, horses can drink only twice daily, as under such conditions they get a good deal of moisture from their grazing.

Yet, if you find that you have to make camp without water, let the horses graze, but don't give them grain or any dry food.

Emperor Napoleon said an army marches on its stomach. Yet as this photo of American cavalrymen proves, keeping your road horses watered is of critical importance. This photograph shows the horses being watered in a moveable canvas trough, which was set up in the Texas desert.

Though they were originally hailed as a humanitarian victory, many of the civic water troughs erected in major cities were responsible for spreading disease among the local equine population. This photo shows one such American water trough, which was still being used in 1927.

How you water depends on where you ride. These Hungarian Csikos are watering their horses from a log trough on the puszta (steppe).

Australian Long Rider Nic Cuthbert is watering his horses on the steppes of Mongolia.

Though it may appear tempting to ride your thirsty horse into what looks a cool lake or stream, like this Argentine gaucho did, you should resist the temptation. First check that the footing next to the water is safe. Lead your horse to the water on foot, keeping him quiet and under control. Don't allow your horse to go any deeper into the water than is necessary to let him drink. Don't rush him, letting him drink his fill.

Canadian Long Rider Bonnie Folkins encountered a lot of difficulties when she rode across Mongolia, one of which was the lack of water.

These Mongol horses are licking ice to assuage their thirst.

Billy Brenchley's horse Rahaal drinking from the Nile River.

Though the plains of Alberta looked beautiful, Catherine Thompson learned that pesticides sprayed on nearby fields had polluted the local water sources.

Chapter 27
Feeding Your Horse

Challenging Our Conceptions

A man may be as clever as a professor in one sphere of life and naïve as a schoolboy in another.

To put it another way, though you may know a great deal about feeding a horse in your native land, you will be surprised to learn how other cultures have solved this riddle.

One of the most incredible examples of feeding a road horse dates back to the Atomic Age. It involves Frank Bessac, the last known Long Rider to ride a meat-eating horse. Sadly, Frank died as I was writing this book, but not before sharing his astonishing story with the Guild.

In the immediate post-World War II period the Soviet Union began work on its own atomic programme. In order to monitor their progress the newly-created CIA sent their agent, Douglas MacKiernan, to Urumchi, a city in China's western Sinkiang Province. Working from that consulate MacKiernan investigated the Soviet mining of uranium in northern China and secretly planted electronic sensors to detect the Soviets' first atomic blast on August 29, 1949, in Kazakhstan.

When the Communists seized control of China MacKiernan was ordered to evacuate. But conditions in the east had deteriorated so seriously that MacKiernan had only one option, escape by horseback across one of the worst deserts in the world and ride on to the still-free Tibetan capital of Lhasa. Accompanying him on this wild mission would be Frank Bessac, a young American academic who had been trapped while studying in Mongolia.

Ahead of them lay the notorious Takla Makan Desert, which they managed to cross because they were mounted on specially trained meat-eating horses.

Nor were these animals the first of their kind, as meat-eating horses had been previously used by Long Riders to explore the Arctic Circle, Tibet and Antarctica.

Yet before we delve into the lesser-known corners of equestrian travel history, let us examine the more widely recognized facts regarding how we feed our travelling horses.

Precious Food

Before you set out on your journey, you must ask yourself these basic questions.

What will your horse eat? Will you expect him to survive on grass alone? How much time will you allow him to graze every day? Will you give him hard feed? Where will you obtain it? Will the local population sell their own horse food in order to help you? Will you be forced to arrange for food drops in remote areas? Who will transport the food in such a case? Will you be required by cultural and climatic circumstances to give your horse food which you never expected?

These concerns aren't new.

After having traversed the icy Andes Mountains, Aimé Tschiffely plunged down into the fiery hell known as the Matacaballo ("Horse-killer") Desert. There his two horses struggled and sank in merciless sand dunes which rose one after another like huge ocean billows. Yet before plunging into the desert, Tschiffely had arranged to have truck drivers drop hay at strategic spots along his forthcoming route.

More recently, when Christy Henchie and Billy Brenchley began their ride through Sudan's Saharan desert, they followed the railway line south, relying on the trains to drop off food at the stations along the way.

If you remain close to home, riding in your own country, through a recognizable equestrian culture, then your horses may not encounter such severe dietary challenges. Diet can even influence the type of horses you buy, as Keith Clark discovered.

"I saw a lot of good horses in Argentine but I've learnt my lesson well. Never buy town horses that have been raised on hay and corn. My two horses, Nispero and Papaya, have taught me that what's needed are range bred horses with the gut capacity to utilise rough fodder. Nispero is a mountain bred horse, whilst Papaya a village bred horse. Nispero is older and bigger but he eats less and is always in better condition than Papaya. I think it's more of how horses are reared than what breed they are. After all, Brumbies and Mustangs are only a few generations away from coddled stable horses."

Diet has another large part to play in any equestrian journey. Even with the best of intentions and a great deal of hard work, you may discover that your road horse must eat what is locally available. This translates into radical changes in his diet. He must adapt to anything and learn to eat everything.

Jeremy James noted, "It is almost impossible to get a Fijian Jungleee to eat an apple, although he will readily eat a guava. By the same token, you'll be hard pushed to get a Welsh pony to eat a guava but it'll happily chew up a turnip. In a sense it would be a question better asked the other way round, which is what will a horse refuse to eat or should not or cannot eat."

Thus, what you feed your horse will depend largely on where you ride him and what you can find. For example, when French Long Rider Pascale Franconie rode through the Jordanian desert, she fed her Arab stallion "a meagre stew of cold beans in colder mutton fat."

Likewise, before I purchased my Pakistani army horses, their daily ration was based on the traditional cavalry diet of hay and grain. By the end of our journey they were consuming bread, gobbling apricots off tree limbs, were in love with rice and would grudgingly accept damp straw mixed with wheat flour.

That's the good news. Horses are far more adaptable than most people realize.

The bad news is that when Long Riders venture far afield, they occasionally discover that it can be almost impossible to find adequate horse food of any description. This occurred when a landslide in the Karakoram Mountains of northern Pakistan trapped me and my horses. Local farmers were extremely reluctant to sell me the hay they had carefully harvested for their own animals' winter-time needs.

Ultimately, contrary to common belief, you will find that your travelling horse's diet can be changed dramatically as circumstances demand with no ill effects. Regardless of where you ride, finding daily nourishment for your horse will become a major preoccupation and task.

Looking for Food

When you travel you will learn that you face a serious nutritional challenge. Your journey cannot proceed without a well-fed horse. Yet regardless of your desire, it may prove difficult to keep the animal adequately fed. Thus, because conditions are constantly changing, keeping a road horse healthy is harder than maintaining an animal at home. That is why no opportunity to feed the horse should be passed without the animal being cared for. In order to accomplish this, you must develop a sharp eye for opportunity.

Because of its size and weight, hay cannot be transported by Long Riders. Your horse requires bulk food, even if its daily discovery cannot be relied upon. If you have a chance to buy hay, don't think twice. When an opportunity to graze occurs, it should become second nature to stop and take advantage of it. If you encounter a standing crop which will act as fodder, don't hesitate to attempt to make a purchase. Empty nosebags should be kept full, no matter what the contents, so long as they are eatable. Cocoa, sugar and even meat may be made use of to help us keep up the balance of nourishment and the strength of the road horse.

Every Long Rider should be fully aware of their duty in this respect. We must also examine what, when and who can feed your horse. Yet first we must understand the link that exists between the horse's food and his emotional well being.

Emotional Concerns

We have acknowledged the physical importance of keeping the horse well. But there is another element at play here: the emotional importance of the food.

Because the horse has a small stomach, he needs frequent meals, and under the strain of long-distance travel should have a varied and luxurious diet. As we have already seen, because of a variety of factors it may not be possible to give the road horse either a large feed or the food he is used to receiving in a traditional stable. This situation is complicated by the fact that, in addition to his physical requirements, the road horse develops an enthusiasm for his food which a pampered stable animal seldom demonstrates.

When horses are on a long journey, they inhabit an environment where there are very few factors upon which they can rely. They awake in a strange place. During the day they are constantly exposed to frightening noises, suspect strangers and potentially dangerous animals. At night they are asked to sleep in a fear-provoking new location.

Having been asked to inhabit such a worrisome world, is it any wonder that a road horse exhibits such intense loyalty to the Long Rider? During the day he provides the horse with a sense of protection and reliability. As the sun begins to drop, the Long Rider is the comrade who can be counted on to provide a reassuring evening meal. The longer the journey, the more emotional weight attached by the horse to his food.

That is why the building of confidence between horse and rider is imperative.

Under no circumstances do the needs of the travelling horse come second. He must be convinced that in an uncertain world, full of chance and circumstance, you are the dependable ally who will always protect his interests. His well-being must always take precedence over yours. He must be the first to be fed, first to be watered and must have the best bed available. Such a sensible policy ensures that a self-assured horse will enjoy better digestion, which in turn allows him to travel further.

The foundation of this principle is trust.

This need not mean that you must adhere to a slavish routine. The hardships of travel do not encourage precise time-keeping. What matters is that the road horse knows that when he stops, you will feed him.

Those who ignore this critical rule of travelling are more likely to risk an equine breakdown and journey failure than those who remain sensitive to the emotional realities which food represents to the travelling horse.

So if food is important, physically and mentally, let's investigate how a horse's digestion works.

Equine Digestion

Unlike cattle, horses have a fast digestive process. Yet the horse's small equine stomach cannot contain large quantities at a time like that of the ox. Nor is there a gall bladder to store up the bile, which flows constantly from the liver directly into the bowel, but the bowels, which are seldom less than thirty-five yards long, are capable of accommodating a large quantity of food during slow digestion.

It is normal for a horse to spend the majority of every day grazing, with small amounts of food taken in constantly and chewed slowly before being swallowed. This food remains in the stomach for a short time before it is passed on into the intestines, from where it can be converted into needed energy. Nor does the horse stop eating at night, preferring to spend part of each evening grazing instead of sleeping.

This "feed little-and-often" point is one to remember, because as we know when our own stomach is empty, we feel languid. So does the horse. When travelling long distances, he must be allowed to eat every few hours as his small stomach must be frequently replenished. Otherwise he will lose condition and excess acid will build up in his empty stomach.

Amount of Food

Because of his small stomach, a horse cannot eat very much at one time without impairing his digestion. On the other hand a horse has very large intestines; and bulk, such as grass or hay, is, therefore a necessity in his diet.

Horses will thrive indefinitely on grass or hay if not worked too hard. But you cannot maintain a healthy horse if it is deprived of hay or other bulky matter, no matter how much grain you may give it. Nor can a horse's digestion support an unlimited ration of grain unless a sufficient amount of bulk fodder accompanies it. This is a notable fact in the practical feeding of horses and must not be lost sight of.

To determine how best to accomplish this let's look at the math involved in feeding horses.

The enormity of the previous equestrian age is hard for modern readers to grasp. One way to understand the scope of that lost world is by concentrating on the logistical aspects involved in mounting, working and feeding horses. Here are a few examples.

In 1901 Lt. Colonel Rimington was ordered to lead 9,000 mounted troops into combat against the Boers fighting the British Empire. That cavalry column stretched 54 miles across South Africa.

Nor did peace time demand fewer equestrian logistics. Up to 180,000 horses changed hands in Chicago every year. One American military depot alone housed ten thousand horses. And the horses in five major American cities, New York, Chicago, Boston, St. Louis and Cincinnati, consumed 1,073,199 tons of hay in 1899 alone.

When you stop to consider the effort of feeding this many horses, you will understand how hay was the 19th century equivalent of 20th century oil, a precious commodity which enabled the world's military, postal, transport and travel industries to function smoothly.

The United States cavalry estimated that 300 calories were required for each 500 pounds of horse per level mile and that 34% more was needed if the horse was climbing an 11% grade. To achieve this level of proficiency the cavalry fed each mount 12 pounds of oats and 14 pounds of hay per horse all year around.

This dependence on horse power inspired scientists at the US Department of Agriculture to study the connection between food and efficiency. In 1903 they determined that "a horse walking 5.8 miles per day neither gains nor loses in weight on a regulated daily ration, but that when the speed was increased the animal lost weight."

The scientists realized that because roads and work are not uniform, it was necessary to adjust a horse's ration according to the work done. At that time a popular standard for maintaining horses was to allow 10 pounds of hay and 10 pounds of grain per 1,000 pounds of live weight, the proportion of grain and roughage being about equal, pound for pound.

Then in 1911 a special farmer's bulletin was issued by the U.S. Department of Agriculture. This study detailed how different horses, doing different work, in different parts of the world, had all been successfully fed.

In December, 1909, a 1,000-pound driving mare at the United States Morgan horse farm, averaging 20 miles daily, consumed the following ration:

Pounds	
Hay	10
Whole oats	1
Ground oats	1½
Cracked corn	6½
Mixed feed	3

The mixed feed consists of corn, oats and bran in about equal parts.

During November, 1911, a 950-pound mare at the Bureau of Animal Industry experiment farm, averaging 12 miles daily, consumed the following ration:

Pounds	
Hay	6½
Whole oats	6½
Ear corn	1½
Cowpea hay	3
Corn stover	3

The cowpea hay contained a good percentage of grain.

Street car horses in Bremen, averaging 1,150 pounds in weight, consumed the following ration:

Pounds	
Corn	14.3
Oats	2.2
Peas	1.1
Hay	8.8
Straw	2.2

Ration of driving horse at Wyoming Station, weighing 1,200 pounds:

Pounds

Alfalfa   21.25

Straw   3.2

This concept of feeding horses bulk and supplemental food was accepted practice when Countess Linde von Rosen rode from Stockholm to Rome in 1929. She made sure that her horse, Castor, was fed hay and grain.

At the end of a day, Linde would locate a suitable inn with a stable. She began by carefully grooming her horse, then provided him with, "as much hay as he will eat, usually around 5 kilos (11 pounds)." Linde then allowed Castor "to drink as much water as he wants." She then fed him 3 kilos (6.6 pounds) of oats. At nine p.m., after having had her own dinner, she returned to the stable and fed him another 4 kilos (9 pounds) of oats. At five the next morning, Linde fed Castor 3 kilos (6.6 pounds) of oats before setting off for the day.

Seventy years later, when Jean-Claude Cazade was riding to Arabia, he fed his Arab stallion 10 kilos/22 pounds of grain a day, as and when he could locate it.

Rules of Feeding

Given that this is an international study, one must bear in mind that what works in England may be unacceptable in Ethiopia. For example, the question of feeding your horse grain might depend on what nations you ride through, as some equestrian cultures never practise this custom. Therefore, what must concern us are the laws of equine health, biology and nutrition which can be relied upon no matter where you travel.

There are in fact rules of feeding which must never be broken no matter where you journey.

First, provide water.

Second, feed hay or grass.

Third, feed grain, when circumstances permit.

Fourth, do not work horses immediately after a full feed.

Fifth, feed often and in small quantities during the day.

Let us consider each of these critically important rules individually.

First, Water

A horse drinks very rapidly and in large gulps.

As this occurs, the water runs quickly through the gullet, stomach and into the small bowel. If you place your ear next to the side of your horse, you will hear the rush of the water while he is drinking. If the horse's meal is only just finished, it may not be sufficiently mixed with the stomach's gastric juice. As a consequence digestion will be incomplete.

A serious danger arises when a stream of water passes through such a full stomach, as the water is capable of washing a considerable portion of the horse's undigested grain into his bowels. When this occurs, not only does this mean a loss of nourishment, it also raises the threat of indigestion, colic, and in extreme cases, death.

Second, feed hay

Bulk fodder, i.e. grass or hay, serves as the horse's primary daily diet. If placed on grass, you must allow adequate time for the horse to graze. If fed hay indoors, avoid grooming, saddling, etc., so as to leave the horse undisturbed while he eats.

Third, feed grain

Never give your horse grain before water.

It must not be imagined however that "water before feeding" means "do not give any water till the next meal." The horse's stomach is, as a matter of fact, never really empty, some food usually remains in it; but within an hour of feeding water may be given if desired; and when left constantly with the horse it will be found that a sip or two is frequently taken, but not a long draught.

It does not pay to feed cooked, cut, ground, or soaked feeds except in cases of poor teeth or faulty digestion. The teeth should be in good condition to masticate feed properly.

Horses that are jealous of their food should be fed separately.

Fourth, do not work horses immediately after a full feed

Allow the horses plenty of time to eat and digest their food.

Immediately after a meal the stomach and bowels are actually bigger than before, they contain more water and food and are perhaps slightly distended by gases resulting from the digestive process, consequently they occupy more room than was the case just previous to feeding. The extra room is provided by a little filling out of the belly generally and also – and this is the important point – by the bulging forwards of the stomach against the diaphragm.

On the other side of the diaphragm (midriff) lie the lungs; any pressure on them impedes their power of expansion, and it is for this reason that strong work immediately after a meal causes instant blowing and distress. The lungs cannot expand and contract with sufficient facility to get rid of their contained blood and provide the amount of fresh air necessary for the animal. Laboured breathing is the result. If hard work is persisted in under these conditions either the lungs get choked with blood or the digestion stops; the latter is most serious, rupture of the stomach as a result of gaseous distension being not uncommon.

Fifth, feed often and in small quantities during the day

The equine digestive system is constructed to encourage a horse at pasture to spend most of his time leisurely grazing, the only variations being when he allows himself an occasional short gallop, an infrequent drink and a few hours' rest. The bulk of the food does not stay long in the stomach, but once it is about two-thirds full, passes through at the rate that it is taken through the mouth, until feeding is finished.

In contrast, a road horse, whose stomach works best when it is about two-thirds full, learns that he has a short period of time in which to eat rapidly. Yet extreme care must be taken not to over-feed the horse. He must be allowed enough time to consume his food quietly and thoroughly.

If his morning and evening feeds, which require a good deal of digestion, are too large, there is a danger of the animal over-distending the stomach and incurring indigestion. Should this overloading be excessive the stomach is stretched to such an extent as to be incapable of effort, the food soon ferments, gas is given off from it, and acute indigestion, which may lead to rupture of the stomach, ensues.

To off-set this danger, horses should be fed bulk food in the morning and evenings, and be allowed to graze, as circumstances and time allow, during the day's travel.

Also of importance, the horse should never be fed more than he will readily eat, nor should he be fed when very hot.

Three Square Meals

The road horse that has not been fed and watered properly in the morning is not ready to travel, so make it a rule to give your horses their food two hours before you put them to work.

Ideally, a horse should have three feeds a day, the first at six, the next at eleven and the final one last thing at night. Of these breakfast and dinner are the most important.

To provide a large dinner after great exertion is counterproductive. So the best policy is to prepare the horse for that day's labour by keeping his strength up. That is why a healthy morning meal is especially important, as with his stomach and digestive system inadequately filled from a small breakfast, the horse will tire quickly. Yet care must be taken. Horses receive slightly less food in the morning than in the evening because it is injurious for them to do fast or severe work when gorged with food. They also have more time to eat and digest their food quietly during the night.

Whenever possible, don't miss any opportunity to try to feed the horse some hay, or a third of its grain ration, at lunchtime. At this habitual feed time the horse's digestive juices start working. And as they proceed on the journey there is an onset of the feeling of hunger. That in turn makes a horse feel enormously tired and sapped of energy. If nourishment is not provided, then Nature will set the digestive juices working, which may cause colic if the horse is not fed. Even a few handfuls of oats will stop the exhausting feeling of hunger. Adhering to the policy of feeding little and often will sustain the power of the road horse in a way that may surprise you.

The evening routine should begin with water. After three-quarters of an hour, give the horse hay. Then give him his oats or grain. It is enough if a part of the hay ration has been eaten before the oats, as this prevents them from swimming along with the water and helps them stay in the stomach. This is unfortunately the case as the animal often over-drinks and then tucks into his oats.

Don't over feed your horses in the evening. Overly tired animals won't eat or, if they do, the changes in their digestive juices will make it impossible for them to absorb the nourishment properly. The food will then be partly wasted.

Because horses have small stomachs compared to other animals, it is natural for them to eat in small quantities and often. If your horse misses a feed, do not give him a double ration as it may result in colic or another illness of the bowels.

When possible, feed the horse three meals – morning, lunch and evening, and dispense the food as follows:

Ration	Morning	Lunch	Evening
Oats	One-third	One-third	One-third
Hay	One-fourth	One-fourth	Two-fourths

When keeping a horse at home, it is customary to always feed at the same time of day.

However, Long Riders have discovered that this is not always possible. For example, when Doug Preston made a difficult journey across the deserts of the American Southwest, he adapted his feeding schedule to meet the requirements of the harsh climate and dangerous terrain.

"I have found that feeding horses on a rigid schedule is not a good way to prepare a horse for a long ride, when they might be turned out to graze at any time of the day or night or given feed at unexpected hours. Riding in the desert, you never know when you're going to come across a beautiful patch of grass or when you're going to pass by a ranch where you can buy oats. If you feed a horse on a rigid schedule he will be much more likely to colic when his feeding schedule is disrupted on the trail. What's worse, a horse fed on a strict schedule becomes highly anxious on the trail when the feed times are delayed or changed or when there isn't enough feed. So I try to alter feeding times and, once in a while, I actually skip a feeding time."

Who Feeds Your Horse?

There are three primary concerns involved with allowing someone else to feed your horse. The horse's food may be stolen. The horse may be given substandard fare. The horse may be killed because of negligent feeding.

Let's begin with the lesser of these evils.

Since the 14th century it was traditional to allow an ostler to feed and care for your horse at an inn's stable. Like his modern counterpart, the parking lot attendant, ostlers often took advantage of their clients, using a series of deceits designed to enrich their pockets at the expense of the horse's stomach.

One such common practice was for an ostler to make a show of pouring in an ample ration of grain into the horse's manger. The moment the weary traveller left to seek his own supper, the ostler removed the grain and the mute horse stood hungry.

Therefore, don't trust the most honest face in the world in the matter of feeding and caring for your horse!

Though times have changed, a Long Rider will always feed his horse himself, rather than risk placing the animal in the care of another man. It is better to sit with the horse and wait, rather than risk deception. See the hay and grain put into the manger, and stay in the stable until your horse is done eating. Get your own dinner afterwards, for you are of less importance. If your table is not properly served you can complain. Your horse cannot.

Another ostler trick was to charge the traveller top dollar for second rate rations.

No matter where you stop for the night, the feed in every stable has to be thoroughly inspected. Make sure there are no rat droppings in the oats. Check that there is no gravel in the grain on which your horse might crack his teeth. Confirm that the hay does not smell mouldy. Ensure that the water is not stale.

Do not trust to anyone to see to these matters but yourself, especially as regards the quantity and quality of the grain given, which should always consist of the best your money can buy. Otherwise it is very possible that you may pay for what you did not receive, to your own detriment and especially to that of your horse.

Why does this matter? Because the horse's condition is crucial on a long ride and you must monitor his appetite. The more he eats, the better his condition and the greater your chances of geographic success.

Verne Albright made this discovery when he made the first modern equestrian journey on Peruvian Pasos, going from Peru to California.

"Because grain in Peru is thrashed with stones and hooves, the result is that considerable residue inhabits the finished product. I soon discovered it was necessary to carefully clean each day's grain ration of stones, dead insects, bits of manure, and other foreign objects which were always mixed in with it."

Finally, in previous centuries it was considered rude to interfere with a man's horse, so long as the rider was healthy enough to stand. Nowadays it is more common for trusting travellers to allow strangers to feed and care for their animals. In one such case, a traveller arrived at a hacienda in Guatemala. The owners promptly invited the tired and hungry man in for dinner, assuring him that their servant could be trusted to feed the hungry horses. After enjoying his own hearty meal, the traveller emerged to discover that the ignorant native had killed one of the horses by mis-feeding it.

To avoid these risks, always tend to your own horses.

Grazing

Mankind has been involved with grazing horses for millennia, yet few riders have ever thought to study it. Long Rider and equestrian author Roger Pocock was an exception. He made these remarkable observations regarding grazing horses.

"A horse's neck is exactly long enough for grazing on level ground but I never saw one try to graze downhill. Neither does he readily graze directly up any steep place, preferring to quarter along the hillside, rising very slightly. His first rule in grazing then is to crop uphill. But the moment the air stirs he applies his second grazing rule, which is 'feed up wind.' If he had man's way of reasoning, he would argue thus, 'If I graze down wind I smell myself, the grass and the dust. But if I graze up wind I get the air clean to my nostrils, and can smell an enemy in time to fight or run.' His third rule is to graze if possible homeward or toward shelter. If the grass is plentiful he feeds quickly, and has time for rest on warm sheltered ground or in the lee of timber. If food is scant, he gets no time for rest."

More recently, Jeremy James gave serious thought to the importance of the grass itself, recounting how it can help or harm a horse.

"All that is green is not always good. Most large tropical grasses are fast-growing, sharp-edged, and carry little nutritional value. In some countries, i.e. Fiji, you will find horses standing belly deep in rolling acres of mission grass unable to eat it. Not only isn't it designed for them, it also contains, as do many tropical grasses, oxalates which strip calcium. Even the kikuyu grass is a dodgy feed for horses. Setaria grasses are actually toxic to horses as they contain glycoside setarin, which when found in hay will kill a horse. But most grasses can be eaten by horses although they will select carefully, avoiding the less nutritious or least palatable," he wrote.

"Remember, even the energy content of grass varies according to the season." Jeremy continued. "In Spring the grass is very juicy and nutritious. From May to July the grass has its richest nutritional value. In late Summer and early Autumn it loses its seed and begins to dry, losing its nutritional value. In winter any nourishment value is very low indeed."

As Jeremy noted the lower the quality of grass, the longer the time you must allow for the grazing of your road horse. Yet what if you cannot discover the precious grass?

That was certainly a terrible lesson which William Holt learned when he made his way across industrialized England in the mid-1960s. His horse, Trigger, had spent years pulling a cart through this rapidly-urbanizing landscape. After years of living on the road with various owners, Trigger had a heightened sense of survival. He would eat almost anything, and because he was constantly in traffic, had nerves of steel. Yet even his uncanny ability to survive on scant food and tough conditions was sorely tested when Trigger and Holt reached a true concrete jungle.

Holt wrote, "Towns were so close together it was impossible to see where one ended and another began. I felt hot and uncomfortable in a world dusty and dry. Less and less grass, more and more houses. Poor Trigger! Not a blade of grass at all now. I made inquiries but nobody knew where fodder for a horse could be bought. I begged a bucket of water in a public house. Then we went through miles of dreary streets. It took all the rest of the day to get through the city of Birmingham."

As Bill and Trigger learned, it is necessary that rest-breaks on the journey be adapted to the grazing that you find.

Howard Wooldridge practised this philosophy of practicality when he rode "ocean to ocean" across the United States.

"Near midday I would stop and let Misty graze for an hour on any grass near the road, i.e. the post office, a cemetery, McDonald's, etc. "

Unobservant, careless or untrained travellers may pass an opportunity for a brief bite. Yet even though Bill Holt and Howard Wooldridge travelled on different continents and in different centuries, they both realized something of incredible importance to any Long Rider.

Never pass up the chance to let your horse enjoy good grazing!

You cannot expect a hard-working road horse to maintain his weight and condition if you only allow him to graze for a few hours in the morning and evening. Therefore no chance should be neglected. No grazing, however short, is unimportant. Whenever dismounted allow your horse to graze.

This normally serious rule becomes life-threatening if you stray into the wrong country. When Bonnie Folkins recently rode through Mongolia, she found the steppes had been stripped of its legendary grass.

"There is a stocky variety of grass in Mongolia that grows in clumps and looks like straw. It can be seen from a distance in long pale yellow lines. That stout grass got us through many miles, especially in the last days of the ride. But over-grazing in Mongolia is a serious problem due to globalization of the cashmere industry and the exploitation of cashmere goats. As nomads have tried to produce more wool, the condition of the land has degenerated. Because of this over-grazing, it was almost impossible for us to find grass for days. We were constantly on the lookout for it and our horses got agitated when they did not see it," Bonnie wrote.

Keeping weight on your horse requires a constant effort on your part.

Regardless if you are in an urban environment or in some hostile natural landscape, the rule remains the same. Because you never know where and when you will find good grazing, never ride by grass thinking that you will find better pasturage further down the road. If you come upon good grass, stop travelling and let your horse graze for an hour or so. If the grass is rich and the camping fine, cease that day's journey early so as to allow your horse the chance to replenish his energy and rest.

Before you depart, study the grass of the country through which you will be riding, as the more you know the less chance of letting your animal graze on dangerous vegetation. Train yourself instead to look for tender young grass en route, as older grass is less palatable, less nutritious and requires more chewing. Grasses that have been slightly frosted contain a high percentage of fructose, which horses are fond of. Never let your schedule take precedence over good grazing. In good pasture, horses feed quickly and rest early; in scant feed, they take more time to feed.

Also, stacked, warmed, wet and, worst of all, ripe grass is bad because it can cause a dangerous colic.

Hay

The world once ran on hay.

Immense amounts of labour went into planting, growing, harvesting and transporting it to the hordes of hungry horses who resided in cities. Fortunes were made by savvy dealers who sold that vital greenery to the desperate horse owners who depended on hay to power their delivery wagons, cabs, fire engines, beer wagons, hearses, carriages, stage coaches and omnibuses. In such an environment, hay was gold and America in particular couldn't get enough of it.

For example, that nation's 1888 hay crop was the largest ever raised. It had to be because by then there were millions of horses in the nation's urban work force. To feed these hungry animals in one year alone New York imported 411,374 tons of hay, Chicago 197,778, and Boston 184,510 tons from the adjacent countryside.

As the equestrian age reached its peak, enormous portions of the American landscape had become dedicated to growing the hay which provided the power needed by these vast herds of hard-working horses. Agricultural historians have estimated that in 1910 America had 325 million acres of harvested cropland. Yet nearly a third of the country's entire agricultural output was reserved for feeding horses, with 16 million acres being used to feed urban horses and another 72 million acres designated to feed farm horses and mules.

The spread of automobiles, trucks and tractors not only sparked the equinocide which destroyed these vast urban herds, those machines also shattered the American nation's dependence on hay, replacing it instead with today's addiction to petroleum.

In a world where the words diesel and biofuel have more relevance and recognition than lucerne or fescue, we need to appreciate and understand the hay which powers our road horses and helps fulfil geographic dreams.

When judging hay for purchase, there are a number of important factors to consider including smell, touch, taste and time of harvest.

Hay consists of dried grasses and other plants which have been allowed to mature. The fragrance of good hay is due to the aromatic grasses contained in it, which combine to create a pleasantly fragrant chemical called coumarin. This pleasant characteristic is generally spoken of as the nose of the hay; it becomes fainter with age, but persists as long as the hay is good.

It was formerly the custom to speak of hay as upland, lowland or water meadow. Thanks to this ability to determine its geographic origin, it was previously possible to identify which type of hay it was by a simple inspection. However modern farming methods produced hay on land which had been laid down to this particular purpose. This in turn resulted in new standards and definitions.

There are a number of well known grasses used to make today's hay and these vary according to each country. In Great Britain, for example, these include Fescue, Timothy, Rye, Yellow Oat, Orchard, Sweet Vernal, Yorkshire Fog, Red Clover and Lucerne. Regardless of which country it originates in, excellent meadow hay can be distinguished by the large variety of grasses and by the superior aroma.

Good hay can vary in colour from pale green to pale gold. If it is dull yellow or dark brown it may have been damaged by rain. If too gold, it may have been too dry when harvested.

The best way to check the colour of hay is to inspect the heart of the bale, not the exterior, which can be bleached by sunlight. Don't be put off by a bale with part of its exterior bleached. Chances are it has simply been placed on the outside of a haystack. Though the bleached area may have lost its vitamin A content, most of the important nutrients will still be there. If you're not able to cut a bale open to check its interior, thrust a hand inside the bale as far as you can and pull out a fistful to check its colour, smell and feel. It should feel crisp, be sweet to the taste and have a pleasant aroma.

Pay close attention to when the hay crop was harvested. Hay is harvested at two distinct periods of growth. Each cutting has a different objective and can affect the nutritional value of the hay you feed your horse. If he wishes to produce the finest possible quality of hay, the farmer cuts the hay early when the majority of the grasses are in full bloom or just after the flower has disappeared. If he desires to provide his land some help from the seed, he cuts the hay late, so that a large proportion of the already well formed seed will fall out and help restore the next crop.

From the traveller's point of view, young hay, known as the first cutting, is far preferable to late, or second cutting, hay, as the appearance of seeds means that the hay plant has become woody and is less nutritious than the succulent hay harvested during a first cutting.

You should always inspect the hay carefully prior to purchase. If properly harvested the hay's stems should be flexible and its leafy matter soft. If it is hard, dry and coarse, your horse will find it an unpleasant experience. The best hay has plenty of leafy matter and flowers, not stalks and mature seed heads. Make sure there are no weeds, thistles or rubbish in the bale.

Rain destroys the aroma of good hay very rapidly. It can also cause the hay to become musty or mouldy. Hay which is stacked damp from rain is likely to turn musty, and if the dampness is pronounced, to become mouldy. Musty hay is sometimes dark brown or bright yellow in colour, has a characteristic unpleasant odour and a bitter taste. Moist hay provides perfect growing conditions for mould, which can be toxic to livestock. When mould is visible it appears as white patches in the bale, and the surrounding portions are generally deep brown or black in colour.

When inspecting hay, your nose is of tremendous help. Though the bale may appear to be fine from the outside, cut it open and thrust your nose into its heart before the surrounding air can dilute any odours of mould. In such a case the absence, rather than the presence, of a musty smell is to be desired. If the bale has a sharp, unpleasant, musty smell, then the hay has been infected with mould and is naturally unfit for fodder.

Lucerne hay is a favourite of horses, but it can be expensive, especially in parts of the country where it doesn't grow well. However, the hay will vary as and where you ride. Hay, as made in England, is not often found in India. Yet

Long Riders report that the desert countries of Tunisia, Egypt, Libya and Sudan have freshly cut alfalfa hay which is high in protein. One thing to keep in mind in dry climates is that if the hay is dusty, sprinkle it lightly with water prior to feeding.

Regardless of where you travel, it is of great importance that the hay you buy must be good quality; if not, then no matter how much of it a horse eats, his condition will still be poor and his energy low.

Chaff

Not all horses are slow and dainty eaters. Those who routinely reside in stables often learn disagreeable habits, one of which is to bolt their food. The practice of feeding greedily is often encouraged by the close proximity of other horses. In such cases, a great deal of waste may occur, as greedy horses pull long hay out of the rack, and in their haste to feed, drop much of the hay to the floor and soil it underfoot.

Regardless if you're in the stable or on the road, the principle of feeding hay as chaff discourages such waste, ensures the thorough mastication of the food and promotes economy.

Chaff is made from hay which has been cut short, about one inch, but not so short as to make it a dust. While hay may be the only ingredient, chaff is often composed of a mixture of hay and straw. Good oat straw, for example, can form one-half of the roughage part if fed with good hay.

Though chaff has its place in the stable, the traveller may encounter various versions of chaff in a wide variety of countries. India and Pakistan often rely on chaff, which is commonly known as chopped feed in those countries. While hay is supposed to be the primary ingredient, poor horse owners may mix chopped straw with water and flour. Extreme cases have even seen straw mixed with old bread. Neither of these provides much nutritional value and should be avoided unless there is an emergency.

Another latent threat involved with using chaff on the subcontinent is that it often incorporates sorghum. There is a danger in that young sorghum plants contain a great deal of prussic acid, which can be injurious to your road horse.

Also, chaff might contain mould. Therefore smell the chopped feed to confirm that it does not smell musty. If you have any doubts, do not feed it as horses cannot tolerate these toxins.

Alfalfa Cubes

Alfalfa cubes are found in North America and are made up of alfalfa hay which has been chopped into particles and then compressed into small squares. The cubes retain much of the nourishment found in hay, so some horse owners use alfalfa cubes as a replacement for traditional hay.

Because cubes are sold in large bags, which are extremely heavy, there is little chance that a Long Rider will carry them on an extended journey. However you may encounter them, if invited to place your horse for the night in a Canadian or American stable. If this occurs, and your horse has never dined on alfalfa cubes before, then proceed cautiously.

Some horses may choke on the dry, hard cubes. To prevent this, the cubes can be soaked to help the horse chew and swallow the feed. Yet caution is advised, as feeding a horse a full ration of alfalfa cubes with no transition may cause a case of fatal colic. If possible, give a reduced feed to provide sufficient nutrition, and allow the animal's digestive system to become used to the new food.

Oats

Throughout the last few centuries, oats were the preferred grain feed for horses. Although many other grains are successfully used as horse food, wherever oats can be obtained they are universally acknowledged to be the best.

As already mentioned, grass is the natural food for the road horse and it will serve as the basis for his nourishment. Horses will instinctively choose the grasses which are good and nourishing. But one thing is clear; the hard-working road horse needs additional sources of energy and the Long Rider must learn to incorporate whatever energy-rich food is locally available.

Horses are able to consume and digest a larger quantity of oats then any other grain, without special preparation, and without their digestion becoming upset. Oats build strong muscles and are less fattening than corn. They invigorate and add temperament to the horse. They are widely available and are the easiest grain to feed.

Oats should be big, hard, dry, without any smell, and should be snow-white when broken. As far as possible, they should be free from dust. Though oats may be given whole it is a decided advantage to have them bruised previously, not because the horse is unable to grind them with his teeth, but to ensure that the husk of each individual grain is split so that any which escape mastication may be readily acted upon by the gastric and other fluids during the process of digestion.

The amount of oats fed will depend on the condition and work rate of your road horse. Provided that a suitable quantity of bulk fodder, either grass or hay, is provided, the amount of oats may vary from 8 to 16 pounds (3.6 to 7.3 kilos) of oats per day. Traditionally Long Riders fed their road horses four quarts (4 litres) of oats in the morning, two at noon and six at night, and with all the hay that the animal cared to eat.

While oats can provide a tremendous dietary advantage, care must taken when using them.

In many countries oats are threshed haphazardly, which allows a certain quantity of earth and small stones to be included in the feed. You must ensure that the oats are cleaned; as such debris can damage a horse's teeth or produce digestive troubles. Also, oats may be extremely expensive in some countries. In certain Muslim nations, make sure people do not think you are purchasing oats to make illicit alcohol. Finally, oats contain an enzyme which may cause some horses to react badly to this feed. As and when you encounter oats, feed them cautiously until you can determine how your horse will react to this high-energy food source.

Corn

Corn produces excellent results when carefully fed to horses. Traditionally, it formed part of the horse's winter ration. Corn goes by various names, including mealies in South Africa or maize in Europe. Yet regardless of what it is called, it should have no distinct smell, be perfectly dry, have a bright colour, not at all brown, be quite hard and when bitten it should taste sweet.

If horses are accustomed to being fed corn, they may and do consume it whole without ill effects, but whenever possible it should be crushed, as it is hard, difficult to masticate and takes a comparatively long time to digest. Limit it to two pounds (1 kg) a day, and when fed, bear in mind that owing to the slowness of digestion horses should not be watered until a considerable time has elapsed after feeding.

In some countries, it is often customary to give it on the cob as this is said to increase its feeding value and digestibility. If fed fresh on the cob, first remove the soft hair from the cob. The leaves and corn stalks are also appetizing.

Barley

Though seldom used in England, barley is a very good horse food often used in the East.

However, the toughness and indigestibility of its husk is such that it can only be consumed with impunity by animals native to the country and not always even by them. For all others it must be prepared by crushing, parching or boiling, or it rapidly gives rise to indigestion and colic. Due to its hard husk, crushed or boiled barley must be fed in smaller quantities than oats.

Rye

Rye is generally in such demand for other purposes that it is hardly worth while considering it as a horse feed. Yet some countries have traditionally fed rye to horses, including Belgium, Denmark, Sweden and Russia.

It is inferior to oats, and in countries where it is fed as a daily ration, it is often coarsely ground or cooked, then mixed with chaff. Rye has several shortcomings. When fed in large quantities, it can cause diarrhoea. If allowed to stand long after cooking, rye can rapidly ferment. This grain is extremely liable to suffer from the growth of ergot fungus, which may be recognized as a small body about half an inch long and of a purplish black colour.

Wheat

Wheat is generally used for many other purposes so it is seldom used as a horse feed. In England it is looked upon as being unsuitable for horses. This prejudice is, however, largely due to a lack of experience as other countries and cultures make good use of wheat as a horse food. In India, for example, wheat flour known as *atta* is constantly given to horses which have undergone severe exertion.

When feeding wheat, it is essential that the grain should be quite dry as it is otherwise extremely indigestible. If possible, it should be crushed or parched, then mixed with some other forage in order to ensure thorough mastication. It is only mentioned here as an emergency ration, should only be utilized when no other grain is available and must be fed in small quantities

Rice

In Burma and the rice-growing districts of India, notably Bengal and Assam, horses are fed on unhusked rice and though it is indigestible for animals unaccustomed to its use, for those constantly fed upon it, it is a serviceable grain and keeps them in good working condition

It should be crushed or boiled, but should not be fed without the husk, as the removal of this renders it unsuitable for horses owing to its want of woody fibre. It should be fed in small quantities.

Beans and Peas

These grains are exceedingly nutritious but owing to the fact that they are very heating foods, cannot be given in large quantities under any circumstances. In England it is claimed hunting horses fed beans and peas can be recognized by their increased endurance. However they are not advised for travellers unless the horse is working hard and there are no other options.

Beans should be hard and dry, sweet to taste, light brown in colour, and free from weevils, a tiny insect which commonly infests dry beans and peas. Peas should also be dry, sound and free from weevil.

The amount which it is advisable to give in addition to other forage is probably not more than 4 or 5 pounds (about 2 kilos), should be given in at least two meals and this only to big horses that are doing severe work. They should always be split on account of the extreme toughness of their husks.

Fruits

Many places and cultures encourage horses to eat different beneficial fruits. This food source not only provides a horse with sugar, fructose and energy, it can add a welcome diversity to an otherwise boring meal.

While it is common practice to feed horses apples, they also enjoy eating pears, figs, pomegranates, guavas, mangoes, papayas, paw-paw, apricots and dates. Horses quickly learn to drop the stones from fruit like apricots, dates, etc. My Pakistani army horses, for example, needed no encouragement to eat ripe apricots from trees. Dates are another excellent fruit for horses, as they supply mineral salts and fructose in greater quantity than any other fruit.

You can feed watermelon to horses that are dehydrated, as it provides sugar and much-needed fluid.

Don't expect fruits to provide Vitamin C to your horse, as he makes his own. But what fruit does is to provide interest, sugar, fructose and energy to an otherwise boring ration. Fruit helps retain your horse's interest in eating whatever comes along. And the faster your horse adapts to a varied diet, the better he will be.

Nuts

Horses are essentially browsers as well as pasture grazers. So they will crop shrubs, ivy, oaks, walnuts etc. to good purpose. Although it has been claimed that horses cannot eat black walnut and that acorns will kill them, this depends upon the individual horse and how well fed he is to begin with. If a poorly-nourished horse eats acorns, the tannins might indeed prove fatal. On the other hand, a long-term well-nourished horse can eat them with safety. The same is true of walnuts. Moreover, walnuts are a good natural purge. Ivy is not poisonous to horses and acts as a natural de-wormer.

Other Options

A great many nutritional trials are conducted with horses that are kept under ideal conditions which no road horse will ever experience. But scientific theory and daily practice will often end up poles apart because the Long Rider's world is made up of unexpected challenges. This holds true for his road horse too, who learns to put up with enormous changes in his diet. Therefore it would be a mistake to place all our faith in clinical tests which do not take into account the various ordeals a travelling horse will face.

Are there alternatives for a keen-eyed Long Rider and his adaptable road horse? Certainly. When it comes to feeding the road horse in other countries, a great deal depends on how much you know about as wide a variety of foods as possible.

It is equally important to encourage the horse to enjoy various types of food, rather than restrict his diet to one or two favourites. Not only do single-feed diets delimit mineral and vitamin uptake, a horse that refuses to adapt his diet may colic when exposed to a new food source. The best type of animal is one who will eat anything, is interested in whatever is on offer and has no dietary idiosyncrasies.

Luckily the horse is, like man, an omnivore who can and does eat a wide variety of food.

There are, for example, a great many agricultural products which can be fed to horses to good effect. Potatoes are utilized for horses in Ireland and parts of England. They should be cooked before use, as they are indigestible raw. Turnips can be fed raw or, after boiling, mixed with other food and fed as a mash. Rutabagas, mangelwurzel and sugar beets can well be fed in limited amounts to produce a laxative and cooling effect on the digestive apparatus. Carrots are a traditional delicacy for horses.

Further afield, military travellers who took horses and mules through Burma in 1944 discovered that the animals were capable of consuming bamboo leaves. The bamboo leaves had little nutritive value and when fed in too great quantity seemed to cause intestinal impactions in the animals.

Sugar cane stalks have been used as horse feed too. In an emergency sheep and cattle feed might be used, but not pig feed. Long Riders have also added raw eggs and salt to chaff.

What these examples demonstrate is how adaptable the horse is. Yet before inviting him to partake of these various foreign delicacies, don't forget to have his teeth properly checked and make sure that he has been wormed before the start of your journey.

Sugar

Sugar as a food is both sustaining and fattening, and is especially useful during exposure to cold and hardship; as an addition to otherwise insufficient rations, it may be used under these conditions. Linde von Rosen found it beneficial to give her horse a few hundred grams of sugar per day (about 20-30 sugar cubes).

Molasses is also of great value. A by-product from the manufacture of sugar from sugar cane, it is relished by horses. When added to an otherwise low quality feed, it will introduce a considerable beneficial energy factor into an otherwise low-quality meal. For example, by adding molasses to corn stalks, you will more than double the nutritional quality of the meal. A small amount of molasses may also be added to the horse's drinking water. It may be slightly constipating but produces a sleek coat and increases weight.

Salt

A travelling horse should always have access to salt. It purifies the blood, reduces disease and helps rid the horse of worms. When travelling in hot weather, horses, like humans, sweat out their body-salt. If not replaced, the horse will suffer from lassitude and weakness. Placing a teaspoon of salt in the horse's nosebag adds interest to his meal and helps him maintain this valuable mineral.

Meat-Eating Horses

Contrary to popular belief, which states that horses are passive herbivores, horses have the biological capability and desire to consume a wide variety of meat. These equine omnivores have been found on every continent including Antarctica and have been known to consume eighteen different types of flesh, including antelope, beef, birds, chicken, fish, goat, hamster, horse, human, moose, offal, onager, polar bear, rabbits, seal, sheep, whale and yak.

Mankind has known about meat-eating horses for at least four thousand years. Hercules is said to have conquered a notorious band of meat-eating mares. Alexander the Great's mighty stallion, Bucephalus, was a meat-eater. Likewise the Japanese god of war rode a meat-eating horse. Shakespeare, Kafka and Faulkner wrote about them and equestrian cultures in Scandinavia, Africa, South America and Central Asia knew of their existence.

Nor was the evidence restricted to dusty legends, folklore or works of fiction.

Meat-eating horses were used to escape from the Apaches and outrun the British army. They fought in Napoleon's invasion of Russia and competed in the Olympics. More recently Long Riders have provided eyewitness accounts of modern meat-eating equines in England and Wales.

A widespread equestrian amnesia has largely erased mankind's collective memory of these animals. This denial has been encouraged by an international multi-million dollar industry serviced by horse whisperers, glossy magazines and popular culture who collectively preach that horses are meek prey animals that fear predators and eat only grass.

This modern mythology ignores mankind's previous definition of the horse, which has been accurately described as "the savage horse, the most terrible and cruel in its anger of all creatures on earth."

Horses, in fact, have a strange family history. They belong to the Perissodactyla order of animals which includes odd-toed ungulates that browse and graze, such as horses, tapirs and rhinoceroses. Horses digest their food in one stomach, rather than in several, as cows, camels and sheep do. The equine digestive system makes use of a single stomach, intestines, cecum and the colon, much like another omnivore, the human.

To differentiate them further, horses and mules have an enzyme which cattle lack. This enzyme breaks down and allows the horse to digest coarse cellulose. In unfortunate circumstances, horses are often able to survive harsh conditions on poor feed such as twigs, bark and dead grass.

And, we might ask, meat?

The modern equine mouth provides a clue to this intriguing possibility, because in addition to the flat herbivore teeth residing there, horses have canine and wolf teeth as well. Conical canine teeth are used on meat, not plant life. Oddly enough, these canine teeth are shared with humans, not carnivores.

Additionally, the jaw of a modern horse can move side to side, to chew vegetation, or front to back, for consuming meat. Once again, humans also have this adaptable mandible capacity. Thus, like their human riders, horses possess teeth, jaws and digestive systems which would allow them to be omnivorous.

Why are meat-eating horses of concern to modern equestrian travellers? Because these incredible animals were previously used to explore Central Asia and the polar regions of the world. Not only had Historical Long Riders crossed Tibet and Central Asia on such animals, more importantly, the last living Long Rider to own, ride and feed meat to his horse, died as I was writing this book.

Himalayan Clues

Thanks to a ten-year study undertaken by the Long Riders' Guild Academic Foundation, incredible incidents involving meat-eating horses were discovered buried in the history of equestrian travel. This special study can be found in the book entitled *Deadly Equines – The Shocking True Story of Meat-Eating and Murderous Equines*.

First the Guild confirmed that the nomadic Hor-pa tribe of Tibet nourished their horses on meat mixed with ground barley. The Hor-pa nomads were descended from Mongol soldiers sent by Kublai Khan to set up post stations. After the collapse of the Mongol empire, the Hor soldiers remained in Tibet. It was their routine practice in winter, when snow covered the grazing, to nourish their ponies with dried or powdered meat, tsampa (puffed and ground barley), and tea.

Sven Hedin made use of these horses during his journey across Tibet in the late 19th century. On his two-year journey through the remote highlands of Tibet, Hedin reported, "The two small Tibetan horses, which travel with us, take a great interest in the horses we rode here from India; but they do not seem quite sure that our animals, which are so thin and wretched, are really horses. At this day's camp, No. 63, the Tibetan horses ran up to their masters for two large pieces of frozen antelope flesh, which they eagerly ate out of their hands like bread. They are just as fond of yak or sheep's flesh, and the Tibetans say that this diet makes them tough and hardy. We cannot help liking these small shaggy ponies, which live to no small extent on the offal of game, are at home in the mountains, and tolerate rarefied air with the greatest ease. The cold does not trouble them in the least; they remain out all through the night without a covering of any sort, and even a temperature of -22.7 Celsius (-4 Fahrenheit), does not affect them. Though they are not shod, they run deftly and securely up and down the slopes, and the men on their backs look bigger than their horses."

But it was the detailed eyewitness notes made by Gabriel Bonvalot which really shocked the Guild, as this Long Rider had not only witnessed meat-eating horses, on March 7th, 1891 he obtained and rode them in Tibet.

"We have had some small Tibetan horses given us which are full of go, and which feed on raw flesh, as we have seen with our own eyes. These carnivorous beasts have marvellous legs, and are as clever as acrobats; they balance themselves with the greatest care on the ice or amid dirty bogs, and then, gaining the path with a bound, carry us along at a rapid trot, to which we have long been unaccustomed. Anyone would imagine that they find us to be as light as feathers, and we certainly look far more like lean hermits than fat monks."

Nor were these animals restricted to the Himalayan Mountains.

Meat-eating Horses at the Poles

Throughout history various cultures realised that horses could consume meat. The Turcomans were in the habit of giving their horses balls of meat. Certain African tribes fed their horses animal and human flesh. Marco Polo reported that the horsemen of southern Persia fed their horses dried fish.

At the dawning of the 20th century meat-eating horses were employed in the Arctic Circle and Antarctica. A British Long Rider, Frederick George Jackson, began this strange episode in equestrian travel history when he employed a Siberian mare in the Arctic Circle. That horse ate polar bear meat.

Though it has now been forgotten, shortly afterwards the British War Office published *Animal Management*, a manual prepared by the veterinarian department for His Majesty's Cavalry and Artillery. The index of this official book had a listing for "meat as horse food."

When the Irish explorer, Sir Ernest Shackleton, set out to explore Antarctica in 1907, he took eight Manchurian horses with him. Although it was later learned that horses will eat seal meat, Shackleton had no way of knowing this prior to his departure. Thus, he determined to enhance his horses' normal diet with a special meat-based supplement known as "Maujee Ration." This was a distinctive type of equine pemmican developed at Aldershot, one of England's most important military establishments.

Sir Ernest noted, "It consisted of dried beef, carrots, milk, currents and sugar, and was chosen because it could provide a large amount of nourishment while weighing comparatively little."

It was so nutritious and enjoyable, that the horses preferred it over traditional fodder or corn. History was made on 3 December, 1908, at 7 p.m., when Sir Ernest and his pony, Socks, pitched camp – and shared this same meat-based food for their dinner.

Sadly, Shackleton did not gain the Pole, though he and one of his sturdy horses came remarkably close to that elusive geographic goal. He was followed by equestrian explorers from Great Britain and Germany, both of whom also used meat-eating horses on their quest to the Pole.

In 1912 Germany's Kaiser Wilhelm II authorized explorer Wilhelm Filchner to travel to the South Pole. The young German had already made successful explorations across Central Asia, most notably when he rode from Baku to the Pamir Mountains in the late 19th century.

At the same time, Captain Robert Scott was heading up a team of British explorers who were also heading towards Antarctica. Both expeditions used horses, some of whom eagerly ate dried fish, blubber and raw seal-meat.

Nor did the use of meat-eating horses stop there.

Exploring Greenland

Prior to leading an expedition to cross Greenland in 1912, the Danish explorer Johan Peter Koch had made a careful study of the methods, techniques and equipment Scott and Shackleton used in Antarctica.

Like other explorers of that era, Koch believed that using teams of dogs and horses made tactical sense. In addition to his four human comrades, he enlisted the aid of sixteen Icelandic horses.

In his book entitled, *Through the White Desert*, Koch explained how he consulted with Professor Harald Goldschmidt on how to feed the horses in the frozen grass-free environment of Greenland.

Goldschmidt taught at the Royal Veterinary and Agricultural University, where he held the post of Chair in Animal Husbandry from 1903 to 1922. He was considered Denmark's leading equine nutritional expert.

Knowing how Shackleton and the British army had created the Maujee Ration, Goldschmidt created a special "power fodder" devised to provide extra energy for Koch's horses. Like the British, Goldschmidt's recipe was a mixture of grain, sugar and meat; which consisted of 35 parts corn, 25 parts peas, 20 parts molasses, 10 parts wheat and 10 parts tallow (a form of beef or mutton fat).

In many ways Goldschimdt's power fodder resembled a Danish version of the Native American food called pemmican. Because his specialty was the digestive system of the horse, the professor would not have put anything into the power fodder that was detrimental to the horse's health. It also demonstrates that the leading equine nutritional expert of that day had no hesitation in prescribing an animal meat based product as part of a horse's diet.

When Koch's ship sailed for Greenland it carried 6 tons of hay and 4 tons of Goldschmidt's power fodder for the horses.

Not only did the Icelandic horses eat the power fodder with great gusto, but Captain Koch remarked, "Overall it seems the horses are taking on omnivore characteristics, as they even eat frozen horsemeat, including bones and gristle. Besides that they are happy to eat meat-chocolate, butter, biscuits, hard bread, pemmican, blood pudding, lemon-bonbons, sugar, oat porridge, and sausages. Only the liverwurst was not eaten as it was too spicy. The horses even relished the fatty water we had used for washing our dishes".

Another interesting point noted by Koch matched previous eyewitness evidence seen by the British explorer, Jackson.

Like the horses used by Jackson, Koch wrote that his Icelandic horses were also "crazy for polar bear fat."

But the last Long Riders to use meat-eating horses did so in faraway Tibet.

Ride or Die

In the spring of 1950 an American academic, Frank Bessac, became trapped while studying in Mongolia. In order to flee the oncoming Chinese communist army, Bessac joined a caravan headed by the American Consul, Douglas MacKiernan. Their plan was to escape on horseback across the deserts of Western China, over the Himalayas and on to the safety of faraway Lhasa, Tibet.

Having initially eluded their Chinese pursuers, when the equestrian escapees reached the desert, Kazakh nomads advised the travellers that, because there was no pasture ahead, they could only proceed if they rode specially-trained, meat-eating horses. The Kazakh chief, Hussein Taiji, said that such horses were rare, and would cost twice as much. The diet of these extraordinary horses was another equine, the wild ass of Central Asia.

It took three months to find these rare meat-eating horses. When located, the Americans discovered the horses wouldn't eat just any kind of meat – they would only eat the liver of the wild ass, known as the Gobi Kulan. They also learned they couldn't feed them liver every day, or it would have killed them, so they were fed liver every few days.

Mounted on the meat-eating horses trained by the Kazakhs, the Americans set out to ride along a route never before travelled by foreigners. There was indeed no grass on the entire trip and only the horses which ate the liver survived. Shortly after reaching Tibet, MacKiernan was murdered and beheaded by Tibetan border guards. Bessac however survived, went on to become a noted professor of anthropology and a Member of the Long Riders' Guild. Professor Bessac died while I was working on this chapter of the *Encyclopaedia*.

What is also of importance is that shortly after Bessac escaped, the nomadic Kazakh tribe which raised these meat-eating horses also fled from the advancing Chinese communist army towards the safety of India. The Kazakhs too rode across the grassless deserts of Central Asia mounted on horses which could be fed on meat obtained en route. This escape of an entire tribe was later documented by National Geographic magazine in their November, 1954 issue, who, though they specifically mentioned the meat-eating horses in their article, did not understand the global significance of what they had just printed.

As Steve McQueen stated in *The Reivers*, the film about a fish-eating racehorse, "Sometimes you have to say goodbye to the things you know and hello to the things you don't."

Such an awakening occurred in 1960 when Jane Goodall witnessed a chimpanzee colony capture, kill and eat a colobus monkey. Goodall was the first person to prove that chimps, like horses and humans, are omnivores. Likewise, the modern equestrian world needs to set aside sentiment and look at the facts involved in the topic of meat-eating horses. In the interim, Long Riders need to be aware that equestrian travellers in the recent past have encountered, purchased and ridden meat-eating horses.

As I stated at the start of this chapter, though you may know a great deal about feeding a horse in your native land, you may be surprised to learn that other cultures have solved this enigma by feeding their horses various types of meat.

Are you liable to encounter such a horse today? Probably not. Are you likely to meet someone whose horse has been known to happily consume different types of meat, including meat sandwiches, turkey, salami, sausage, hotdogs, roast beef, ham and Kentucky Fried Chicken? Very likely.

Cultural Considerations

As the meat-eating horses demonstrate, the topic of equine nutrition is fraught with complications, some of which are connected to local custom, regional difficulties and legal restrictions. For example, Bonnie Folkins discovered that her Mongolian horses would not accept grain, even when they were hungry. She had to buy hay to supplement their daily diet.

Yet when French Long Rider Nicholas Ducret made a journey through the Pamir Mountains at roughly the same time, he had great difficulty finding grass.

"Grass was effectively non-existent, hay rare and jealously guarded for the winter. I was lucky enough to obtain 285 pounds of barley from the Kirghiz people on the shores of Lake Karakul which enabled me to be self-sufficient."

During her journey from Argentina to Canada, Ana Beker constantly struggled to find food for her horses.

"It is not easy for others to imagine the extent to which food for the horses becomes an obsession. I dreamed of bundles of fodder and vast plains of lucerne. I would not wish my worst enemy to suffer what I felt when I had to watch my poor beasts starving. I have seen them seizing anything green or straw-coloured that protruded between the rocks. During our long wanderings the horses had to eat the most extraordinary things, including roots, maize-leaves, carob beans, cuttings from jujube trees and bananas as their only food for days. In Ecuador often times they were obliged to swallow the leavings of the soldiers' meals in the military mess hall."

Thus, in many cases what you feed your horse will depend on what it knows and what you can find.

Plus, you may have to consider the legal implications of feeding your horse.

Many travellers in the United States incorrectly assume that the back country is rich in grass and water. Unfortunately many wilderness areas have been overgrazed, have limited water or restrict access to horse travellers. It is imperative that you contact the proper authorities for information on what lies ahead for you and your animals. One such example involves the legal use of grain and feed.

In the past some American packers and horse travellers brought in supplemental feed for their horses and mules. It was later discovered that some feed contained seeds for noxious weeds such as spotted knap weed and leafy spurge, which can spread and destroy grazing for stock and wildlife.

Because of this environmental threat the United States National Forest now prohibits the use of non-certified forage and non-certified hay, so as to limit the introduction and spread of poisonous weeds through forage and straw onto USFS controlled land. Once a person enters USFS land, a person cannot possess any non-certified forage, straw or mulch. Baled or compressed hay and forage (hay) cubes are considered forage. Possessing non-certified forage, straw or mulch on USFS lands is subject to penalty.

Nosebags

Many Long Riders use nosebags to feed their horses grain. If you decide to do so give all the feed bags at the same time so your road and pack horses don't get impatient.

Be sure the nosebag is properly fitted. If put on too long, it will make feeding difficult. Either the horse will throw his head back to fling the grain into his mouth, which of course means he will spill them, or he will put the nosebag on the ground, thereby dirtying the bag and its contents. If the nosebag is put on too short, the horse will get his nose in the food, which will also make feeding difficult.

As soon as the ration is finished, the nosebag must be removed, otherwise if the horse tries to drink with the nosebag on, he could drown. Plus, if left in place the empty nosebag is often damaged and will be soiled by saliva and nose secretions. This is particularly important where the horse has any sort of respiratory problem.

Even normal spittle will mix with the leftovers and result in a smelly, sour mess which ferments in the bottom of the bag, so clean the grain bag after each feeding as if it were your dinner plate. Otherwise the saliva, together with uneaten grain, may start fermentation. Turn it inside out and clean it with hay, grass or leaves. Wash it out and sun it when you can.

If you don't use a nosebag, don't feed grain on the ground, otherwise your horse may develop sand colic. Place the grain on top of a flake of hay or a canvas tarp, then hold the horse by the lead rope until he has finished his meal. In an emergency, you may use a saddle blanket for this purpose. If so, place the grain on the top of the blanket, otherwise hair may become mixed with the food or grain which may irritate the horse's back when you saddle him.

Toxic Food

Just as the world is full of appetizing options, the road horse must also be protected from toxic plants or contaminated feed.

Horses may consume poisonous rations for a variety of reasons. Hunger and ignorance of local conditions are often the main causes.

While a horse will turn away from a toxic plant at home, he may accidentally consume one in a foreign clime. That's what happened in 1903 when the British military invaded Tibet with 185 riding animals and 1,372 pack ponies. Of those, 24 riding ponies and 899 pack ponies lost their lives through a simple mistake.

With grazing on the Tibetan plateau always scarce, the English soldiers believed they were allowing their down-country horses to eat what appeared to be a harmless local plant. In fact many of the horses died during the Tibetan trip as a result of eating aconite, a poisonous plant better known in the British Isles as wolfsbane.

Some toxic plants are very well disguised. Indigofera, for example, resembles clover but destroys a horse's liver when eaten. Most problems of toxicity arise from hungry horses gorging on what is available. Forty horses recently died in Queensland, Australia after consuming a poisonous plant there.

While it's true that a Long Rider's horse must be prepared to adjust his diet, it is equally correct to point out that a travelling horse must be protected from poisonous food encountered along the way.

Water

Though I have devoted a special chapter to watering the horse, allow me to stress again the need always to allow your horses the chance to drink. Never walk past water without giving them this option.

Let the horse drink as often as he likes. Remember, without water, no spittle, without spittle, no digestion! For drinking, "little and often" again is the rule. In hot weather it is good to drink a second time in the evening between 8 and 9 p.m.

You may have to teach your horses to drink when presented the chance, as water may not available again for a long distance.

Before Doug Preston made his journey though the blazing deserts of the American Southwest, he trained his horses to drink.

"In the wild, horses tend to drink twice a day, in the morning and at evening. It is good to train a horse to do without water, so they learn to drink well (but not over- or under-drink) when water is available. So at home, I let the horses only water twice a day and do not give them free, all-day-long access to water. On the trail, the horse does not get anxious or panicky at not having water all day, and when we do find water (I've done a lot of desert long-distance riding) the horse knows that he should drink well when he has the chance."

Remember, your horse needs a great deal of water, so always make sure he is well hydrated.

Summary

This is by no means a full account of what a road horse can be fed. Rather it is designed to alert the Long Rider to the many options which exist in terms of feeding the horse. Though the topic is extensive, common sense and caution will help you make the proper choices.

In this motorized age, it is important to recall that your horse is not like an auto, which can be filled easily and effortlessly. What will help in foreign countries is your ability to improvise. Thus a Long Rider must be very resourceful if the feeding is to be consistent.

To begin with, before you depart determine how much hay, grain and water your horse normally consumes. Once you are on the road, always keep a careful eye on the horse's condition. If he begins to lose weight he is being pushed too hard, isn't being properly fed or could be exhibiting stress caused by flies, ticks, thorns, etc.

Feed little and often. Water before, not after feeding grain. Give enough bulk to keep the digestive tract working. Always give the largest meal in the evening when the horse has the most time to digest it. Try to give the horse an hour and a half to eat. Leave him alone to enjoy his meal. If he refuses to eat check to see if he is tired, suffering from colic or chill, or if the food is unclean or bad.

In any event, a committed traveller will always keep a keen eye on his horse and will pick up on the smallest of signals if and when something goes wrong. By attending to the problem immediately, you have a good chance of going a very long way with your road horse.

Mary Bosanquet, wrote, "The warmest and most delicious dinner will have no charm whatever until one has been released by the sight of the horse's contentedly feeding."

It may sound arcane to those who have not experienced it, but once you have earned the confidence of a road horse, you will have an animal who will go anywhere and eat anything because, in his eyes, you are worthy of and have earned a trust which is never given lightly.

At the dawning of the 20ᵗʰ century the United States military fed 10,000 horses at one of their army remount depots.

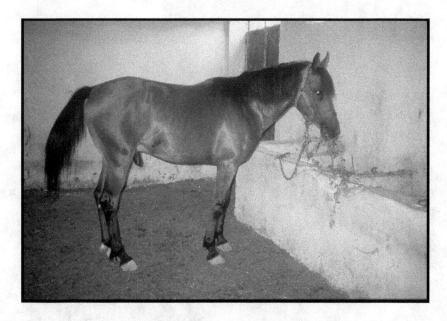

When British Long Rider Gill Suttle rode through Syria in 1998, her Arab stallion was lucky enough to be able to feed on delicious local hay and other nutritious food stuff.

The world once ran on hay. In 1910 the United States had 16 million acres being used to raise the hay needed to feed urban horses and another 72 million acres designated to feed farm horses and mules.

When French Long Rider Thierry Posty rode across part of Japan in 2007, local villagers provided this carrot treat to his horse. While common today, the use of feeding carrots to horses was first noted in 1776 by the British Long Rider Arthur Young, who observed the vegetables being fed to farm horses in the Midlands.

Many countries and cultures encourage horses to eat different beneficial fruits. This food source not only provides a horse with sugar, fructose and energy, it can add a welcome diversity to an otherwise boring meal. During his ride across Mexico, Orion Kraus documented how local horses eagerly ate ripe papayas.

Though originally from Tunisia, Christine Henchie's horses Nali and Chami learned to adapt and consume what was on offer in the ten countries they travelled through. Here they are seen eating mangoes in the Sudan after spending 27 days floating down the Nile River on a barge.

Finding adequate food for your road horse can often be very difficult. Because of their isolation, local farmers in the Karakoram Mountains of northern Pakistan were reluctant to sell the author this hay for his horses.

Further down country, corn stalks sold in the Pakistani bazaars are used to feed horses in the hotter Punjab and NWFP provinces.

This Manchurian horse, Socks, was one of those who accompanied Sir Ernest Shackleton on his expedition to Antarctica in 1908. Socks, who ate the meat-based Maujee ration designed by the British army, joined the ranks of other horses used by explorers in the Arctic Circle and Antarctica, who also consumed raw polar bear meat, blubber and penguin skins.

Even though Captain Robert Scott's horses lacked the tasty Maujee ration used by Shackleton, eyewitnesses recorded that at least one of Scott's horses was an avid meat-eater. "One of our ponies, Snippets, would eat blubber and so far as I know it agreed with him," Apsley Cherry-Garrard wrote.

German Long Rider and scientist Alfred Wegener accompanied the Danish explorer Johan Peter Koch to Greenland in 1912. Wegener's horse, Little Fox, was one of the Icelandic horses which eagerly ate Professor Goldschmidt's "power fodder." Wegener later became known for advancing the theory of continental drift in which he hypothesized that the continents were slowly drifting around the Earth.

North American Long Rider Frank Bessac fed his Kazakh horses raw Onager liver when he rode across the Gobi Desert in 1950.

Chapter 28
Shoeing Your Horse

An Everlasting Dilemma

Until the dawning of the twentieth century, you could still see one of mankind's oldest consecutive equestrian customs being practised in rural Japan. To understand how that might be, we have to look at archaic horse history.

The tradition of guarding horses' hooves did not simultaneously originate alongside riding. In fact hoof protectors didn't become essential until paved trails and hard roads began causing frequent damage to the animals' feet. Thus it was the advent of artificial terrain, such as cobblestones and gravel, which helped stimulate early man's research into equine foot security and even these initial attempts at horseshoeing were not practised for many centuries until after the horse himself was in general use.

The first defence of the horse's hoof was based upon the rider's foot. Using his own foot as a model, man created leather socks and fibre sandals for his mount. Neither proved to be a great success.

For example, if forced to ride through a stretch of deep mud, it was not uncommon for the leather socks to be sucked off and lost in the mire. They were, therefore, seldom put on the animal for the whole journey. Because sandals were tied in place, they were also insecure.

Nor did fibre sandals prove adequate to protect the hoof from injury. This was demonstrated in 72 B.C. when Rome's deadly enemy, King Mithridates, had to withdraw his 6,000 cavalry horses from the siege of Cuzicus because the monarch's sandal-shod horses had sore hooves which were becoming badly worn.

Next to the inventive powers of men there is nothing as remarkable as their want of ingenuity, and the obstinate way in which they will continue from generation to generation, doing something absurd from mere force of habit and utter want of thought.

This point is illustrated by the fact that, regardless of the drawbacks, Japanese pack horses could still be seen wearing straw sandals at the dawning of the 20th century.

Many years passed before the Romans thought to incorporate a slab of metal into this pony puzzle. Known in Latin as the *selene*, because it resembled a crescent moon, a Roman horseshoe involved strapping a metal plate to the horse's hoof. First the fragile hoof was wrapped in cloth or leather and then it was placed atop the plate. Metal eyelets attached to the side of the plate allowed the Roman rider to tie the *selene* into place. At least that was the theory.

What do you think happens after you have tied Roman metal plates to the hooves of a galloping horse? No one had bothered to find out, until the answer was discovered in 2006. That year a team of British archaeologists employed a leading English farrier to duplicate a set of Roman *selenes* for the television program, *Time Team*.

Using examples of actual *selenes* found in museums, master farrier Cliff Barnes re-created the Roman horseshoes, which were then tested. The results proved that the *selene* was uncomfortable and unsuitable for long journeys.

"I don't think you would want to work a horse over a long distance wearing these shoes," Barnes reported. "Turning would be very difficult with the loop at the front and wings – the horse would probably stab itself with them. The only use I can think of for them is a veterinary purpose – to hold a poultice in place. I certainly feel it confirms that the shoes were not for everyday use."

Armed with this eyewitness information, the British archaeologists realized that the *selenes* were probably only worn by draught or pack horses that never went faster than a walk, and which probably travelled along paved Roman roads.

Like the saddle, and so many of the other fundamental tools which we now take for granted in the equestrian world, no one knows the name of the innovative human who discovered that because the outer hoof wall held no living tissue, it could hold a series of small nails.

What we do know is that there is no trace in either Roman art or literature of a horse being shod with a nailed-on shoe. For example, the equestrian statue of Caesar Marcus Aurelius, who died in 180 A.D., depicts his horse as being shoeless.

Just as we don't know who invented the nailed-on horseshoe, we are also uncertain where it originated. We know where the first horseshoe in Europe was found. In 1653 the tomb of the Frankish king, Childeric I, was discovered in

Tornai, Belgium. Inside were valuable coins, a priceless sword and 300 small gold bees. King Childeric's industrious insects later became the royal symbol for Napoleon's French empire. But more importantly, inside the Frankish king's tomb was the first iron horseshoe and all its nails.

Though early horseshoe history is still vague, what is certain is that things began to pick up speed after Childeric shod his horse sometime before his death in 481 A.D. By 1000 A.D. Europeans were commonly nailing on bronze horseshoes. During the Crusades (1096 – 1270) iron horseshoes were accepted in lieu of coins at tax time. The practice of heating horseshoes began in the 16th century. At the dawning of the 19th century an American invented a machine capable of producing sixty horseshoes an hour.

Ironically, though mankind has ventured into space, earth-bound Long Riders must still contend with the never-ending problem of how to protect the hooves of their road and pack horses from excessive wear and sore feet.

And A Never-Ending Debate

Regardless if you were riding alongside the Roman Master of the Horse, Mark Anthony, in 47 B.C, or attempting to ride from Rome to Russia in 2011, one thing still holds true for any Long Rider.

Miles mean trouble.

Keith Clark discovered this harsh truth when he rode across Chile.

"The horses are getting shod yet again! All this road work is expensive in horse shoes. The heels are fine but the toes get worn down very quickly," he noted wearily.

How do we travel far and wide on our horse, while protecting its feet, not just from harsh terrain but from equally dangerous and incompetent farriers? Who do we believe when it comes to deciding if we should nail on shoes, put on boots or let the horse go barefoot? What sort of cultural traps await an unsuspecting Long Rider who seeks to have his horse shod in faraway countries?

Realizing that your journey will be halted if the hoof fails, let us examine this problem carefully, using reason and history to try and find an answer.

But even before we attempt to solve that prehistoric riddle, we first have to investigate a debate which has raged for centuries. Do we send our horses out barefoot or shod?

Barefoot is Best

Let me begin by stating that history is on the side of barefoot horses.

Genghis Khan led his cavalry to victory on barefoot horses. Likewise the galloping warriors of the Scythian, Parthian and Cimmerian kingdoms triumphed over their enemies without the help of farriers.

These wide-ranging military campaigns were accomplished on horses that carried humans across the grasslands stretching along the ancient Equestrian Equator, as such firm ground was ideal terrain for the horse's hooves.

Times change and so did the perceptions of the horsemen alive in each age. When Napoleon invaded Russia in the summer of 1812, his Grande Armée was accompanied by an estimated 150,000 horses. These equine warriors departed from France after having been shod with 600,000 horseshoes, held in place by 4,800,000 horseshoe nails. Despite this initial metal protection, as the harsh Russian winter progressed, and the military situation deteriorated, the majority of those horses who returned to France were unshod.

With such a conflicting equestrian history, it is no wonder that mankind became needlessly involved in a debate which continues to antagonize, wound and distract horsemen to this day.

By the late 19th century a dispute was raging in Europe and the United States. It pitted barefoot believers against horseshoe disciples. The barefoot brigade challenged the horseshoe advocates to explain how man, (i.e. farriers equipped with horseshoes), could improve on what God had invented: that natural wonder, the horse's hoof? It was a good question, which went largely unanswered because with millions of horses working in cities, pulling and trotting across hard metalled roads, the majority of Victorian era horse owners simply ignored the vocal minority who advocated a return to the past.

Then in 1881 an English horseman named J.T. Denny published a controversial book entitled, *Horses and Roads: How to keep a horse sound on his legs.*

Denny didn't waste time trying to be polite to farriers. Using history as an intellectual battle axe, he attacked the entire industry of horseshoeing.

"No foot, no horse. Whoever hath care of a horse's feet hath care of his whole body," he began.

He continued, "From time immemorial it has been recognized that the foot of the horse is the part of him which calls for the utmost care and attention. Fortunately our ancestors did not shoe their dogs and cats or in all probability most of us would do so in the present day. Yet advocates of shoeing scorn to retreat, will not make an advantageous peace, desert a silly custom or discard an ancient usage. Like a crab on the march they cannot deviate from the line which they have adapted. All this trouble however might at any moment be avoided if the human race would only stoop to employ a little reflection."

Denny then provided evidence to support his argument.

"In Mexico, Guatemala, Ecuador, Peru and Brazil horses were not shod. In the wilds of Exmoor and in the mountains of Wales horses ran over rocks, through ravines and up precipitous ridges unshod and to the evident advantage of their hoofs. The steppes of Russia, the grass runs of Australia, the prairies of the USA, the savannahs of Uruguay and Argentina all possess vast tracts of grass-covered plains, on which horses live and work unshod. In Spanish Puerto Rico horses go barefooted whilst in English Jamaica they are shod. Thus climate has nothing to do with the question. Hernando Cortes did not invade Mexico with anvils, forges and iron. In the retreat from Moscow the horses lost all their shoes before they reached the Vistula. Yet they found their way to France over rough, hard, frozen ground. Likewise during the mutiny in India many cavalry horses went unshod because they could not get shod and never went better in their lives."

He carried on by saying, "Of course the remark that the horses are enabled to go unshod because they have not to travel over any hard ground is only due to a popular delusion, the real fact being that it would be much better for them if they took all their walking exercise over good hard roads. Their feet would then become sufficiently toughened to enable them to dispense with the last remnant of iron. Unshod horses enjoy almost a total immunity from diseases of the feet and legs and thrush is effectively cured by removing the shoe from any horse that suffers from it. The frog is a natural calk but it must have fair play. It is pointed in front like a plough shear to offer resistance in one direction."

"All of these ideas lead up to the main point, which is that the freer the hoof is from iron the better it does. An unshod horse feels his feet and knows what he is doing with them. The unshod horse will not slip on asphalt or even ice because the natural healthy hoof is rough enough and tough enough to hold on a smooth surface. It has been widely proved that the naked foot of the horse is as much at home on any kind of hard road as on another and can pass over all of them alternately without wearing out or inconveniencing the horse. The unshod horse can successfully deal with all roads," the crusading Denny concluded.

Despite his sincere efforts at educating the horse industry, Denny and his friends were largely forgotten by the time the First World War began.

When it comes to equestrian travel, this is no mere parlour argument, for what goes under your horse's hoof will affect how far forward he moves. Thus, it would please J. T. Denny if I shared the greatest modern example of his barefoot philosophy. Yet the tale of that journey must be told by Gordon Naysmith, whose barefoot Basuto ponies, Norton and Essex, made a legendary ride.

"Late in 1970 I departed on a 20,000 kilometre (14,000 mile) horse trip that was to take me from Lesotho, Africa to Austria and take nearly two years. A great problem was that of horseshoes. Going north from southern Africa there is a long ride before reaching Kenya, where shoes are available. Carry enough shoes? Ouch! Much discussion arose, with the vast majority saying that the shoes were needed. Then I thought of all the wild horses and wondered how they got on without a smithy to visit. When I made up my mind to forego the shoes the riding fraternity called me mad, stupid and worse. But, I decided, no shoes for the horses!" Gordon wrote in his thrilling book, *The Will to Win*.

"The decision taken, I went and bought horses in Lesotho where the vast majority are unshod. I looked for horses with black hooves, because of their legendary hardness. The idea was to start the trip slowly and give the hooves time to get to their hardest. At the end of each day a mark was made on the hoof with a file, one inch up from the front of the hoof. To start with the marks were in the wrong direction as the hoof wore faster than it grew. In two months the hoof was strong enough for us to ride for eight hours on a daily basis."

The aftermath of the journey is of concern and importance to Long Riders.

Gordon wrote, "It may be of interest that after arriving in Germany, the horses were retired to a farm. The new owner insisted they should be shod and called in the smith. The blacksmith was unable to make any marks on the hooves with his rasp. In fact the horses were not shod for more than a year, until such time as the hoof had grown softer. After that, to keep the horse's hooves in shape the farrier used a grinder on the hard hooves. For the new owner could not afford the time to ride the horses enough to keep the hooves worn down."

Ironically, because hammering metal to the bottom of horse's hooves had become so widely accepted by the late 20th century, the modern horse world paid little attention to the tremendous implications of Norton and Essex's epic expedition. In fact, the debate about barefoot horses had been largely forgotten by the time those diamond-hard-footed Basuto horses arrived in Austria. It wasn't until the mid-1980s that a variety of factors slowly rekindled the embers of this long-dead debate.

After being nearly driven into extinction in the 1920s by agents of the Ken-L dog food company, and others seeking to make a profit from the sale of horsemeat, the wild horse was once again on the rise in the United States at the end of the 20th century. This new interest and sympathy inspired studies to be launched into the history and preservation of the mustangs. One aspect of this rediscovered compassion was a comparison between the wild barefoot and the shod domestic hoof. It wasn't long before the 1881 war cry of J. T. Denny, "the best shoe is no shoe," was revived.

Puncturing the hoof with nails was unnatural, the public was told sternly by a new generation of experts. Meanwhile, a growing number of farriers began to offer their clients what became known as the mustang roll. This is a method of trimming the unshod foot which attempts to resemble the natural hoof, allowing the frog to expand as the hoof grips the ground. It was also reported that wild horses were less likely to suffer from navicular and lower leg diseases. Armed with these findings, advocates claimed the strong natural hooves of wild horses proved that shoeing was a manmade cruelty which was no longer needed in the enlightened 21st century.

Another contributing factor to the resurrection of this debate was the element of nostalgia. Since the death of Genghis Khan, the Mongols had continued the practices of their forefathers, which included rarely shoeing their horses. In contrast, the majority of mechanized citizens in the United States and Western Europe had become increasingly out of touch with the day-to-day equestrian knowledge once possessed by their own mounted ancestors. This is one reason why many determined mustang fans took a militant stand against horseshoes. Yearning for what they perceived to be a more natural horse, these wild horse advocates routinely denounced the horseshoe as a token of impurity.

One mustang advocate wrote, "Don't shoe your horse. If you have to, he probably isn't a Spanish mustang."

In justifying their beliefs, these activists silenced reason and ignored any genuine criticism of the barefoot philosophy. When so-called authorities make blanket statements such as these they neglect to recognize or respect the customs of other equestrian cultures. They fail to realize that none of us have all the answers. Our culture and time constrict our knowledge. What works in the limited confines of our known existence may be completely wrong somewhere else.

Why does this matter?

Because the horse suffers in silence when humans attempt to vindicate their personal pride and narrow national beliefs.

Thus, there are horseshoe fans who, with some degree of justification, denounce barefoot horses as little more than a holistic fad. Meanwhile, barefoot devotees continue to champion an anti-cruelty campaign.

And, once again, history proves that the barefoot minority are partially correct, as there are plenty of examples of knife-happy farriers who have ruined fine horses. If you don't believe me, consider this admonition about letting an ill-trained farrier near your horse.

Lieutenant J. P. Piggott wrote, "These people blindly pursue one established practice unsupported by any knowledge of the feet; they pare away the heel and frog to such a violation of nature that the coronet is brought nearly to the ground, thereby becoming tender and sensible to the smallest pressure."

Why is what Piggott said important? Because he issued that rebuke in Calcutta, India in 1794!

So where does this leave you, the potential Long Rider? Still in trouble, believe me.

But who's right? Do you set off barefoot or shod?

Ancient Hoof - Modern World

Barefoot advocates often rely on romance rather than science. They argue in favour of historical parentage, while tending to overlook modern facts. One typical commentator said, "How often did the Apaches shoe their Indian war ponies?"

But 19th century Indian ponies weren't required to travel where today's road horse must go, were they? And besides, is it even correct to say that wild horses possess such supernatural hooves? Not according to actual scientific studies.

The Australian Brumby and American Mustang, both of whom are free to roam on natural terrain, are often presented as examples of hard-footed horses that possess ideal hoof conformation. Freedom is not however an automatic guarantee of perfect hooves, as demonstrated by new research confirming that many wild horses have flawed feet.

For example, when New Zealand's Kaimanawa wild horses were lately examined, it was discovered that hoof abnormalities were surprisingly common. In contrast to popular myth, these feral equines had no consistent foot type. Moreover, problems such as hoof wall defects, frog abnormalities, contracted heels and medio-lateral imbalance were very much in evidence. The scientist leading the study at the Australian Brumby Research Unit, at the University of Queensland's School of Veterinary Science, concluded, "Clearly this group of feral horses should not be used to guide the direction of foot care practice."

In its original natural environment, the hooves of wild horses were shaped and trimmed by the constant wandering needed to find grazing and water. Little changed when our ancestors first domesticated and rode the horse as mankind continued to reside alongside their horses in a grassland environment. Though many centuries had passed, when Gordon Naysmith and his Basuto horses set off, they became perfect examples of those long-ago wanderers and their original tough-footed mounts.

Yet what happens when you take an animal designed to live on the clean dry plains and then confine him in a dung-filled stable? What adverse effects occur when you restrict his movements and pump him full of high energy food? Unfortunately, his hooves suffer. Whereas it is true that some wild horses are born with extremely hard hooves, if you remove that wild horse from his natural environment, then force him to travel on the hard surface of an artificial road for months on end, even his formerly-tough feet will begin to splinter.

Thus, as military and Long Rider history demonstrate, under certain circumstances a horse can work and travel without wearing shoes; but those circumstances are few and far between in this modern world.

So what is the deciding factor: personal philosophy or geographic necessity?

Let the Terrain Decide

As Long Riders, we're trying to protect our horses, not advocate a cultural belief.

And three equestrian travellers provide one common answer to our collective problem.

When my wife, Basha O'Reilly, set off to ride from Volgograd, Russia to London, England, her Cossack stallion, Count Pompeii, began the journey barefoot. Having commenced his life as a wild horse running free on the steppes, the mighty stallion's hooves became sore when he entered Eastern Europe and began travelling along paved roads. At that point Basha did the reasonable thing. She had him shod.

When Tim Cope set off to ride 6,000 miles from Mongolia to Hungary, his horses also started without shoes. But after travelling thousands of kilometres Tim had to have his horses shod when he encountered rocks and roads.

And who else used shoes?

Gordon Naysmith!

Though his Basuto horses made the vast majority of their 20,000 kilometre (14,000 mile) journey barefoot, Gordon didn't maintain an obstinate prejudice against hoof protection when the ground became aggressive. He realized that there was some terrain which would destroy his horse's hooves, if he chose to ride across it without protection.

This champion of barefoot horses wrote, "At one point in the north of Rhodesia we used strap-on shoes to protect the hooves where the ridge tops were broken volcanic rock. These emergency shoes would have been better if they were made with cloth ties instead of straps. But they did the job when they were required."

Basha, Tim and Gordon can be used as a measure for other Long Riders because their final decision, like yours, should always depend upon the terrain.

You are not riding a wild horse or asking a feral horse to carry your pack saddle. Free-roaming horses such as these don't spend their days carrying hundreds of pounds on their backs or walking on hot modern roads.

In order to keep your horse's hooves healthy, you have to take a variety of factors into consideration.

First, barefoot advocates are correct when they say that shoes can harm horse's hooves, especially if they are improperly applied. Yet as a Long Rider, your first duty is to always err on the side of caution. Hence the necessity and hence the benefit. If the way becomes rocky and rough, you shoe your horse or arrange to protect his hooves with boots or some other option.

But if we are in trouble by leaving our horses barefoot, are we home free if we ask a stranger to hammer a metal plate on their feet?

In fact, if you decide to shoe, your troubles may have just begun.

Whom Do You Trust?

Horseshoes are like religion. Everyone has an opinion on the subject – and many of them are mistaken.

Sydney Galvayne was a renowned Australian horse trainer who journeyed to England in 1884. There he devised a new technique of calculating a horse's age by studying his teeth. In addition to lecturing on horse training, Galvayne also wrote a warning to everyday horse owners, cautioning them to pay special attention to what happened at the blacksmith's barn.

"There is perhaps no question relative to the general well-being of the horse that has created more controversy than that of shoeing. Masters and men disagree, fellow-smiths in the same forge disagree; every smith can shoe a horse better than any other smith, and knows more than anyone else how it ought to be done. Yet horses are lamed and crippled daily by the bad shoeing of careless and ignorant smiths. The bad smith won't do as he's told. He will do as he likes, and he tells you so; and as you do not, as a rule, carry a forge in your saddle, you have to put up with what you get, and go away thankful that it's not worse," Galvayne advised

If Galvayne was right, then there were criminally incompetent farriers doing business at the height of the 19th century equestrian era. So what hope can there be for those of us riding in this mechanized age?

Recipes for Disaster

Before he set off, Gordon Naysmith's critics predicted the utter ruination of his horse's feet if he attempted to make his journey with barefoot horses. They were wrong.

Their antagonism demonstrates how the majority of horse owners will refuse to change the habits of their fathers, preferring to do things the way they were done, or perceived to have been done, in the old days. So if we agree to have an open mind, and to use shoes as and when needed, what are the dangers to our valuable horses?

There are three classic recipes for such a Long Rider disaster.

First, you ride into a country and are unable to locate horse shoes at any price because they do not exist in that culture. This is what happened to Raul Vasconcellos during his ride from Arizona to Argentina. Upon reaching Central America in the late 1980s, his horses were in desperate need of horseshoes but none were to be found at any price because, like in many portions of the globe, the practice of hammering metal onto an animal's foot was an alien concept. Raul's sore-footed horses couldn't debate the issue, so he eventually constructed make-shift shoes from pieces of old automobile tyre. After cutting the tyre to fit, he hammered it into place and the horses proceeded successfully.

Not being able to find a horseshoe is nothing compared to the second problem, that of locating a competent farrier.

Unlike the lack of horseshoes, this dilemma is not restricted to out of the way nations. For example, plenty of North American Long Riders have discovered that when they needed an expert, the only person on call was a local fraud armed with a knife, a hammer and a handful of steel nails. Journeys have been ruined by such incompetents who are eager to operate on your beloved horse's feet and then overcharge you for their services.

The damage done by such unqualified farriers was previously noted by Sir Francis Bond Head. In the early 19th century he warned horsemen to be extremely wary of bungling farriers.

"It is strange to say but the merciful protection of shoeing, which is found in many countries in the world, is all too often destroyed by mischief. If an ignorant clown were to drive a nail through a chronometer, he would only destroy an insensible and inanimate work of art. But when a man of wealth, intelligence and science, who happens to also be the proprietor of a valuable horse on whose safe going his comfort and life depends, allows his horse to be improperly shod, then the owner is inadvertently guilty of an act of barbarism."

Was Sir Francis exaggerating?

Two hundred years after that Long Rider explored the Andes Mountains on horseback, Keith Clark nearly had his journey through the Andes ruined by just such a fellow as Sir Francis warned of.

"I always get nervous when someone I don't know is playing around with my horses feet," Keith recalled in an email to the Guild. "When I asked for a farrier in one village, this old guy turned up. His eyes were bloodshot and he had the shakes really bad. So in order to let everybody save face, I pretended to take a last quick look at my horse's feet. After making this examination for show, I said that I had made a mistake and that the hooves were good for another fourteen days. But it's taught me the lesson that before I set off on my next trip, a horse shoeing course is on the books."

There is a final common problem.

You ride into a country that is equipped with horse shoes and has farriers, only to discover there is no one ready and willing to assist you.

This is what happened to Jane Dotchin as she made her way across England.

"The extra roadwork meant more wear and tear on Sitka's shoes, which were by now wearing thin. I decided that we had better find a blacksmith – but this was easier said than done. I started by asking people I met on the road if they could tell me where the nearest blacksmith was. The answers I was given were hardly encouraging. One person said their village hadn't had a farrier for thirty years. Another reported that shoeing horses was a dying trade. Most people just shrugged and said they couldn't help me. Eventually I was directed to a village several miles away where there was a riding school. When Sitka and I arrived, the boss explained that the blacksmith he used came from another village and would only come out when there were several horses needing attention. It was all very disheartening. Then he explained that there was an unqualified blacksmith living six miles away who might be able to help, so we plodded off in that direction."

A Once-Thriving Trade

Ironically, though Jane couldn't find a farrier in England, the country used to be awash with them.

When King Henry VIII journeyed from London to Yorkshire, on what was known as the Royal Progress, he was accompanied by approximately 5,000 various types of horses. That in turn translated into 20,000 horse shoes and a private army of horseshoers. Armed with forges, anvils and tools, they spent their nights keeping the monarch's horses shod and ready for the next day's journey.

Historically, shoeing a horse was an art, a profession practised by experts.

In 1887 a major New York stable employed 18 full time horseshoers, one for every sixteen horses.

In Boston 238 horseshoers pursued their craft in 1900.

In those portions of the modern horse world where horseshoeing once thrived, i.e. Australia, Western Europe and North America, finding a farrier to re-shoe your horse may not be a problem, although Europeans should bear in mind that anyone in the United States can call himself a farrier, without necessarily having undergone any training.

And therein lies an extreme danger to a Long Rider's road horse.

Dangerous Incompetents

As Jane and Sitka learned, one of the major challenges encountered by today's equestrian travellers is the time, and luck, involved in finding a qualified professional farrier.

But this isn't a new problem. Even in the early days of the automobile age Long Riders were learning that qualified farriers were fast disappearing. During his journey to all 48 states in 1925, Frank Heath learned the hard way about how quickly an incompetent farrier can harm a valuable road horse.

Throughout the course of his journey Heath complained, "One of my greatest problems was in finding a blacksmith to shoe my mare."

An especially harmful incident nearly ruined Heath's journey."

"I explained exactly how I wanted Gypsy Queen shod and then because I was very hungry I went in search of lunch while she was being shod. When I returned and looked at her feet I was so damned mad that I knew better than to open my mouth to say anything except how much was the bill. The foot had been shod exactly the reverse of my instructions. I determined to never again absent myself while Gypsy Queen was being shod.

Heath concluded, "In these days of autos the animal blacksmith has disappeared. In order to have proper work done, I learned to do it myself."

The horse's hoof is a complex piece of natural machinery. Though perfectly adapted by nature to its original task, the toe may grow too long, even during a journey involving hard work. In such a case the foot needs to be trimmed and shod with extreme care.

According to legend, nailing a horseshoe over a door will keep the Devil away. Yet all too often the superstitious shoe nailed over the doorway does less harm than the one hammered on by a hopeless farrier

Even if you locate a farrier, you should never be misled into thinking that the hard-won miles under your saddle will protect your horse's hoof from a knife-wielding knave. One equestrian traveller had ridden five thousand miles across the United States, when a so-called farrier cut his horses' feet so savagely the journey teetered on the edge of disaster.

The worried Long Rider was forced to cool his heels while his horses recovered. During this enforced layover someone said, "Whoever shod your horse must have been some kind of shoeing school dropout."

In fact, even though there are thousands of extremely competent farriers in that country, in theory America would let an unlicensed monkey hammer a shoe on a horse, as there are no legal requirements prohibiting an ape from calling himself a horseshoer.

This lack of official care stands in sharp contrast to Great Britain's Farriers Registration Act, which states that shoeing may only be undertaken by registered farriers who have completed an extensive course of training and then passed rigorous examinations.

"To qualify for registration as a farrier, people must, among other things, complete a four year and two month apprenticeship with an approved training farrier and pass the Diploma of the Worshipful Company of Farriers Examination."

The British law against unlicensed and unqualified farriers is rigorously enforced. In 2013 Dean Baker was arrested and charged with carrying out unlawful farriery because "he undertook farriery on a horse at a livery yard in Glanamman by removing the front and rear off-side shoes of a horse in readiness for the immediate reception of new shoes." Baker was found guilty and fined.

The following year Arlo Burton Coles was discovered to be neither a registered farrier nor an approved apprentice under the Farriers Registration Act. He was arrested when he "undertook farriery on a horse at a stables in Epworth, Doncaster, by finishing off the shoeing of a horse by clenching up the nails on a new shoe, which another had nailed to the horse's front left foot, and by filing the nails of the new shoes, fitted by another, on the front feet of the same horse." Coles was also found guilty and fined.

Likewise, France also insists that farriers and their apprentices are tested, licensed and insured.

There is a high degree of irony in any debate about placing shoes on horses.

On the one hand, as a traveller in a strange town or country, you must exercise extreme caution when dealing with farriers, too many of whom view the hoof not as a sensitive part of the horse's body but as an inanimate lump of horn stuck on to the end of the leg for the purpose of nailing a shoe on. The other extreme are those nations where horses are constantly over-shod, forcing animals at grass to carry shoes which serve no purpose except to enrich the farrier who placed them there needlessly so as to serve an entrenched social tradition.

The horse world is populated by lying horse sellers, patent medicine peddlers and toxic trainers, but they quail in comparison to that trickster, the bad farrier.

Therefore, when your horse requires to be shod, suffer no fools to touch him.

But what if you have no choice?

Following Your Orders

A critic once wrote, "As to farriers, it is useless talking to them, as some people can read nothing but print. He works on the assumption that he knows better what the horse's foot should be than the Creator of the animal does, for they are never satisfied until they have altered the natural foot into a form of their own, which they think the right one."

While protecting the hoof is a noble aim, altering it to suit the farrier's fancy is counterproductive.

An age-old problem has been when the farrier attempts to make the foot fit the shoe. After finding a shoe of the right approximate shape, a lazy blacksmith will whittle and rasp the hoof so as to accommodate the horseshoe. Having cut away everything he can without drawing blood, he heats the shoe until it is red hot and then immediately applies it to the bottom of the hoof. Nails are produced and the affected foot is now hammered to the iron plate.

Bad farriers are encased in selfishness, ignorance and prejudice which is averse to assault or discussion.

The health of the horse and the safety of the journey depend on you never allowing yourself to be bullied into silence by a farrier. If you are dealing with a licensed professional then you may assume there is a degree of scientific knowledge in evidence. However, if you are forced by circumstances to employ a backwoods blacksmith, you must never presume that, though the farrier can observe the outside of the foot, he has any knowledge of its interior anatomy.

Regardless of how educated he may be, when you take your horses to any farrier, in any land, make him follow your directions to the letter. If you suspect, for any reason, that your animal is being injured, order the operation to be halted at once. Better one poorly shod foot than four lame hooves.

Cultural Problems

Mind you, it could be worse.

In certain parts of the world the treatment afforded to horses in need of shoes involves a shocking degree of ruthless efficiency.

Kazakhs, for example, routinely throw a horse to the ground, tie all four feet tightly together and then roll the animal onto its back. While several men keep the animal from struggling, the hooves are quickly cut and shoes nailed into place as fast as possible.

Further east, the Chinese developed a method which is still in use. It involves placing the horse inside a strong wooden frame which has been driven deep into the ground. Once the horse has been pinned inside this chute, he is lashed securely in place. With the horse effectively restrained inside this wooden straightjacket, a farrier then sets to work.

This Chinese method was noted by Historical Long Riders who rode through that country, the last case being registered in the 1910s. But Steve McCutcheon recently confirmed that this is one method of shoeing which has never fallen out of favour. During his journey from Delhi to Peking Steve's horse was reshod by a Chinese farrier who used this technique.

"My horse, Boran, hated being strung up like a side of beef between two poles, but there was no other way to do it. The local experts knew what they were doing. Boran's front right shoe had snapped in two at the front whilst grazing and needed replacing. I had several spare horseshoes from Pakistan and since his other feet were fine we just replaced the one.

No horse likes its feet tampered with and Boran least of all. Yet Xingjian farriers have a ruthlessly effective way of dealing with this and spare no horse any leniency when it comes to getting the job done. Without giving him time to think, I led Boran between two large goal posts outside of the farrier's village shop. His bridle was quickly tethered to a crossbar above and a thick rope circled around his body. Two large loops were then passed under his chest and lower belly, suspending his weight off the ground and effectively immobilizing the equine.

The horse did all he could to escape, bucking, whinnying and sinking on his haunches to put weight on his front feet but he was tethered beyond movement and wasn't going anywhere. This was a procedure common throughout China and though I felt sorry for him, the farrier took only ten minutes to trim the hoof, level it off and place a new shoe on it. Given all the hassle I've had with previous horses, the whole operation was like lightning and I appreciated the work done," Steve explained.

Do It Yourself

Of course there is an alternative to tying your road horse between Chinese posts or letting an unlicensed hack hurt your horse. You can learn how to shoe your own horse.

Because of the time, study and money involved, this isn't an option which many Long Riders pursue. But there have been some resounding success stories.

Before he set off to ride from Uruguay to Texas, Norwegian Long Rider Howard Saether graduated from an American horseshoeing school. Howard was emphatic about how useful the course had been.

"I don't understand how people can undertake a long horseback trip without being able to shoe their own horses. Farriers did not exist along our route and what we saw of shoeing was basically horrible. That's why I'm sure it was a good investment to attend a horseshoeing school."

Prior to riding from Arizona to Argentina, Raul Vasconcellos also studied horse shoeing and like Howard he too praised the ability to work on his own horses. But while we should applaud both these Long Riders for their diligent efforts, it is simply not practicable or possible for everyone to either follow suit, or to be able to carry the necessary tools and horseshoes as you make your way through various countries.

Before riding across New Zealand the British Long Rider Mary Pagnamenta asked herself these basic questions, which in turn apply to any would-be equestrian traveller.

Have you acquired the basic skills needed to resolve an emergency with a horseshoe? Will you be able to tell when a shoe has become worn and needs to be replaced? Can you tell if the nails are tight? Can you determine if the shoe is loose? Can you remove a shoe without damaging the hoof?

Like any type of specialized equestrian knowledge, learning how to care for your horse's hooves is more complex than you might first believe.

Heavy Shoes

Regardless of who nails them on, you or the farrier, there is a major drawback to horseshoes, weight, which may influence your trip in two different ways.

The obvious issue is that an average horse shoe weighs from 1¾ to 2¼ pounds (about a kilo). So the idea of carrying the dead weight represented by extra horse shoes, nails and the tools required putting them on flies in the face of travelling light. This is especially true when you recall that it's not the kilometres which injure your horse, it's the kilograms.

But, though they provide protection, the shoes also deplete the horse's strength in a surprising second way.

Though today it is seldom remembered, medieval Islamic texts warned that one pound on the foot of the horse was akin to placing eight pounds on his back. The modern French Long Rider, Jean Francois Ballereau, revised this formula in the 1990s, warning that a one-kilo horseshoe drained as much energy from the road horse as seven kilos of dead weight.

Therefore, it is critically important that you use the strongest, lightest shoes available, as an ounce on the foot equals pounds on the back.

Because they carry the majority of the weight, the front feet suffer the most abuse from rocky ground, so one alternative is to only shoe the front hooves when trouble arises. Many equestrian cultures, and Long Riders, have used this method with good results. In stark contrast, no culture only shoes the back feet.

Another point to be aware of is that some cultures prefer horse shoes which incorporate a large metal clip which is fitted deep into the front of the hoof. In theory this clip acts as a giant horse shoe nail, clamping the shoe firmly to the foot. Yet the hoof has to be cut back in order to fit the clip. This severely weakens the hoof wall. Furthermore, the clip adds weight to an already heavy shoe. Clips may be favoured by farriers but are seldom needed by Long Riders.

If your journey is extreme and you feel you should carry one spare shoe, then it is recommended that you carry a hind shoe. Not only will it normally fit either hind foot, it may be adjusted relatively easily to fit a front hoof as well, whereas it is more work to fit a front shoe to a hind hoof.

No Hoof – No Journey

In a world which is all too often obsessed with a horse's pretty appearance, the humble hoof is often overlooked. Yet hard hooves made history and you need them too if your journey is to succeed.

The horse's hoof is akin to your fingernail, in that it grows continuously. This growth in turn demands that we provide adequate care for the horse's feet. But what does a good hoof look like?

Captain Otto Schwarz learned a thing or two about horse hooves during his time in the Swiss cavalry and later when he rode on several continents. Otto recommended that the hoof have strong, straight walls capable of holding a nail. Flaring or cracked walls would disqualify a potential road horse. The frog should be full, the heels broad and the bottom of the hoof concave. The overall appearance of a healthy hoof should be oily, not dry and never cracked. Because white hooves are often brittle, dark or black feet are an age-old favourite, he said.

Otto was a firm believer that if your horse had hard feet, you would save yourself trouble on the road.

So when do you shoe?

When to Shoe

Settled people determine when to shoe their horses by the calendar. The usual custom is to have the horse reshod every four to eight weeks, depending on the growth of the hooves and the wear on the shoe. A horse leading a quiet domestic life may not require a new set of shoes. In which case the old shoes should be removed, the hoof trimmed and the shoe carefully reset with new nails. When this is done extra care must be taken to ensure that enlarged nail holes do not damage the fragile hoof wall.

But during the same eight-week time-span that the pasture pet is grazing quietly, a Long Rider's road horse will encounter a host of challenges. This is why Long Riders learn to anticipate when their horses will need shoes and where to find them.

During his journey around the entire perimeter of England, Cornwall, Wales and Scotland, Richard Barnes hit on this solution.

"Because I knew that Remus tended to walk a hundred and sixty miles on his front shoes and twice as far on the back ones, I was able to make accurate calculations as to when I would have to find a blacksmith."

Likewise, the North American Long Rider Lynn Lloyd's horse used seven sets of shoes when she rode "ocean to ocean," from New York to San Diego.

Journeys such as these provide a would-be Long Rider with a model whereby you can learn to estimate the approximate mileage you will get out of each set of horseshoes. Once you learn to judge where and when you will need shoes, you can arrange for a farrier to be awaiting your arrival.

What you must never do is delay an appointment with the farrier. Don't procrastinate on this vital point of horse health or expect to find help miraculously awaiting you up the road.

The next question then must be: what are the rules of safe shoeing?

Long Rider Horse Shoeing

It is critically important that before your departure your horse's hooves have been properly trimmed and the shoes fitted precisely. This is not a job that can be delayed, as a newly-shod horse may have tender feet. This is especially true if one of the nails has pricked him. Riding a sore-footed horse is irresponsible. Setting off on a journey with one is even worse. Consequently, to ensure that his feet are in good condition, have your horse shod several days before you set off.

When she was making her 3,000 mile ride across Australia, Long Rider Sharon Muir Watson travelled with many horses. During that trip, Sharon made this important observation.

"Try to use horses with the same size feet as this will allow you use the same shoes. If you are travelling with more than one horse, it will make life much easier if they have similar-sized feet."

Regardless of how many horses you have, your morning begins with a careful examination of each and every hoof. Using a hoof pick and brush, look for stones, remove any mud, make sure the frog is clean and check for any signs of thrush. When the hoof is clean, confirm that the nails are tight and the shoe is snug.

If a shoe becomes loose during the day's journey, you will have to stop and remove it with care. Even if one or two nails have fallen out, simply pulling the shoe off with the remaining nails still in place may cause the nails to tear holes in the hoof wall as they are withdrawn. These large holes in the hoof wall will thereafter not hold a new nail very securely. When you have to remove a loose shoe, you must first loosen the ends of the nails and then carefully remove the nails so as not to damage the wall of the hoof. When drawing out the nails, check them separately to make sure there is no sign of blood or moisture on them.

Because the hoof is always growing, when the time comes to trim the horse's hooves, remember that many farriers blunder greatly by wielding their knives with happy abandon. You must ensure that the shoe fits the hoof. Never allow the farrier to cut the hoof to fit the shoe.

A horse's hoof is akin to a thick bamboo, in that its chief strength lies in the tough outer covering which protects the sensitive parts inside. Allowing a farrier to severely rasp off the outer wall of the hoof is as wise as removing the lids from the eyes. Likewise damage occurs if the bottom of the hoof is cut too severely. The ill-advised farrier who subtracts this part of the hoof is like a carpenter who cuts off the bottom of a post, which in turn weakens the pillar in the most essential way at the place where the greatest strength is required.

Thus, keep trimming and rasping to the hoof wall a minimum.

Likewise, don't allow the farrier to trim the frog severely. When horses walk, they do so from the heel to the toe, not from the toe to the heel. As they are walking the triangular-shaped frog comes into contact with the ground. This critically important portion of the hoof is designed to prevent slipping and concussion. Plus, unlike the insensitive hoof wall, the frog has nerves and can cause pain. Therefore the frog should not be touched if it is sound and firm. If it is ragged, then allow the edges to be lightly trimmed, otherwise the drawing knife should not be used.

Neither should the sole of the foot be interfered with except to remove the horn that has grown since the last shoeing. This should be done with a rasp, never with a drawing knife.

There are two types of shoeing, hot shoeing and cold shoeing. The latter involves nailing a shoe of the approximate size and shape onto the horse's hoof. Hot shoeing involves heating the shoe in a forge, then hammering it to fit the horse's hoof as closely as possible. Both require a degree of skill, with hot shoeing being practised in the Occident far more than in the Orient,

The construction of the horseshoes is also of importance. If the horse's hooves need trimming, but the shoes are still roadworthy, then have them nailed back into place. Steel shoes are best, if they are obtainable.

But as Dutch Long Rider Wendy Hofstee discovered, strong shoes may not be available.

"Undoubtedly the worst things we had to deal with were the horse shoes we had to buy in Ecuador. The steel was so soft the shoes wore down in two weeks, partly due to the cobblestone roads," Wendy explained.

To add to Wendy's problems, frequent shoeing tore holes in her horses' hooves,

"By the end of the ride our poor horses' hooves were riddled with nail holes and we had to rest up to allow for hoof growth."

Another problem to be aware of is how many nails the farrier drives into the hoof wall. Too many nails can ruin the hoof. Though an average horseshoe has eight holes, you should be able to get by with using six nails on each hoof.

If you must replace a shoe while travelling, make sure the points of each nail are sharp. The horseshoe nail is specially designed to turn outwards after being driven into the hoof. But you must ensure that the tip of the nail is pointing in the right direction before hammering. Be sure that the flat side of the nail is facing outwards; otherwise the nail will penetrate into the soft portion of the hoof, which will immediately injure the horse.

Once you have confirmed that the flat part of the nail is aligned correctly, drive the first nail into the third, or centre, hole on the outside of the horseshoe. Drive the nail so that the point emerges about an inch up alongside the hoof wall.

The sharp end of the nail must then either be snipped off with clippers or twisted off with the claw end of the hammer. But remember to retain enough of the nail to bend it over and drive it down towards the bottom of the hoof.

When the first nail is driven in, clipped off and set in place, then drive the second nail into the same hole on the opposite side. Continue back and forth in this manner until you have set all the nails in the horseshoe. Try and place the nails as high on the hoof as possible, so as to allow the old nail holes to grow down towards the sole.

Because it is important for the shoe to become firmly set, you should never oil a horse's feet after he has been newly shod, as the oil may seep in under the nails and allow the shoe to move.

Making Shoes Last

Don't think that just because you've managed to get your horse shod your worries are over. Harsh surfaces, hot roads, jagged gravel and ruthless rocks are all waiting to destroy your horse's hooves. That's what Jean Claude Cazade discovered when he began his journey from France to Arabia. Even though his stallion was wearing steel shoes, the horse had to be re-shod on average every twenty days.

This is a problem which has no geographic restrictions.

When Ivan Denton rode east to west across the United States, he noted, "The steel shoes wore out so fast that his hooves couldn't grow out fast enough for new nail holes."

Likewise when John Egenes rode across the United States in the opposite direction, his horse also suffered.

"It's only been two weeks since I shod him but the shoes are worn through and Gizmo's feet are breaking down from having so many nail holes in the same spot."

Further south in Chile the hooves of Keith Clark's horses were also being destroyed.

"It's only been three weeks since they were shod, and a week of that they spent idle, but the gravel roads are so tough that they already need new shoes."

Luckily these Long Riders discovered a way to save their horse's hooves. They had a farrier place borium on the bottom of the horseshoes. Borium is a generic name for tungsten carbide crystals, which when embedded in a carrier material, provides a protective hard wearing shield to steel horseshoes. Borium is sold in narrow rods. Small pieces are cut off the rod with bolt cutters. The shoe is heated and then the borium is applied. It melts onto the shoe. When it cools, the borium acts as a diamond-hard shield between the shoe and the road.

This material is so strong that after Jean Claude Cazade placed it under his stallion's shoes, the horse travelled 6,000 kilometres with only three changes of shoes.

Two Horseshoe Champs

The world of the Long Riders encompasses humanity and horses. The vast measure of this can be realized when you compare Gordon Naysmith, who championed barefoot travel, alongside Robert Seney, who rode across the United State on one set of horseshoes.

Sergeant Robert Seney, the former United States cavalry soldier, had been inspired to become a Long Rider by the amazing travels of the little Historical Long Riders Bud and Temple Abernathy.

On their first equestrian journey in 1909 the tiny travellers, aged nine and five, encountered a host of Old West obstacles, including wolves and wild rivers, when they rode more than 1,000 miles from Oklahoma to Santa Fe and back alone. The following year the valiant brothers set their sights on New York City, which they reached after a month of hard riding. In the summer of 1911 they rode from New York to San Francisco in sixty-two days without any adult assistance.

Having read about the Abernathy Boys when he was a child, after Seney retired the former horse solider set off to see all 48 states. He made six journeys in the United States during which he rode a total of 38,500 kilometres (24,000 miles). The majority of his rides were made on his famous horse, Trooper.

Because times had changed since the days of the Abernathy Boys, Sergeant Seney realized that Trooper's hooves needed extra protection. He was one of the first North American Long Riders to advocate the use of borium. In a special article, Seney recalled how he and Trooper made shoes last.

"Strange as it seems it is possible to cross the United States on one set of horse shoes. This may be accomplished by putting on two layers of horse shoe borium and a bead around the leading edge of the shoe and replacing the borium as it wears down and before the iron is worn too much to take a weld. The shoes should be re-set every six weeks and not more than two months. The iron will wear where there is no borium and the nail hole will become shallow. I go ahead and use them anyway until the iron becomes so thin you can almost bend it with your hands.

There are two reasons for putting borium on shoes, to make them last longer and to help stop slipping on the pavement. The tungsten crystals in the horse shoe borium will grip the pavement like a cat scratching wood when first applied, but they lose much of this quality as they become worn down.

When borium is applied for the sole purpose of keeping a horse from slipping, it is put on in small spots. This is fine for the purpose but it is useless if you wish to make the shoe last. It should be put on from front nail hole to front nail hole the width of the shoe, one layer on top of the other and around the leading edge of the shoe. About one inch is all you need on each heel. It must be put on with acetylene as electricity will not do the job.

Borium is expensive. I recently (1980) paid $86.00 for five pounds but it is worth it if it saves you from a hospital bill caused by your horse slipping on the pavement. I have found most farriers in the eastern United States carry borium and the equipment to apply it. This is not true in the West, although you will occasionally find one. Since I do my own shoeing, I carry borium and have it applied at a welding shop.

Horse shoes are hard to find when you are travelling on horseback. Fortunately, with the borium applied, you will not need very many. Farriers may be found in all parts of the US today but to find one when you need him is very difficult since they are very busy men and you may have to lay over a day or two. When I turn the clinches, I tap them down as far as possible and do not rasp them off smooth, rasping them down flush with the foot will weaken them, making it more likely that you will lose a shoe. The only times my horses ever lost a shoe on a long trip was when I would get careless and let the nail-heads get worn off till they would no longer hold a shoe," the retired cavalryman explained.

Not only is the Long Rider world vast, it also doesn't discriminate between the sexes. This was demonstrated when another North American Long Rider, Tracy Paine, also championed borium horseshoes during her 10,000 mile ride.

In a special report to the Long Riders' Guild entitled, *Long Lasting Shoes That Stay Tight*, the lady Long Rider explained how she had updated Sergeant Seney's original idea during her 1990s ride across America.

"I developed this method of shoeing out of necessity and through careful observation when I was travelling by horseback across the United States. It is very similar to the conventional method; however there are a couple of little tricks that will make shoes last longer and stay tight longer over any type of terrain, especially pavement.

I have never liked using horseshoes. In fact, when I first started my horseback journey, my horse was barefoot! I had no idea how quickly a horse's hooves could wear down when travelling on pavement (roughly 75% of the time). In less than three weeks, I was looking for a farrier to shoe my horse. Eventually I bought my own tools and packed them with me. Horseshoes are, at best, a necessary evil.

But borium is a must!

The most preferable shoe I have found for long distance horseback travel is a lightweight, flat iron shoe with no heel or toe calks. A shoe like this will wear paper thin and crack at the toe in only two weeks of pavement travel. Yet this same shoe, properly coated with borium, will last one year of pavement travel.

Welding borium onto a shoe is an art as well as a science and must be done properly to be effective. Anyone who knows how to weld can do the job. Borium consists of tungsten carbide chunks in a brass matrix. The shoe is preheated first. This can be done with a hot torch flame, a forge, or even a good campfire! When the shoe is hot, borium is applied using a torch with a low flame. If the flame is too high, the borium will burn and pop! This stuff melts at a low temperature. The borium should be applied in a thin single layer (not more than 1/8" thick) for the main purpose of protecting the shoe from wear. There is no need to build the layer of borium up thick.

Borium is also very effective for riding on ice and other slick surfaces such as parking lots coated with blacktop sealer! Because borium affords the shoe some traction, it is advisable that a horse not used to borium shoes be ridden on soft surfaces before riding on hard, unforgiving surfaces so as not to cause leg injuries," Tracy wrote in her report.

Modern Improvements

Sergeant Robert Seney and Tracy Paine were pioneers in their use of borium equipped horse shoes.

Luckily the remarkable ability of these long-lasting horseshoes has become increasingly well-known among the Long Rider community. As a result at least one farrier has established a shop which specializes in the creation of borium equipped horse shoes for equestrian travellers.

In 2009 Rick Blackburn set out with two horses to ride 3,500 kilometres (2,200 miles) from Canada to Texas. He immediately ran into problems.

"I was only able to keep horseshoes for 350 miles or two weeks before replacing them. This was a problem because the hooves were getting nailed too often, which was weakening the walls."

Luckily Rick had heard of Roger Robinson, who runs *The Blacksmith Shop* in Harrisonburg, Virginia. Roger is a master farrier whose expertise is creating horseshoes specially treated with hard-wearing borium.

After receiving two sets of these special shoes from Roger, Rick continued his journey. The Long Rider had the shoes re-set twice during the course of his ride.

"In addition to the extra traction the borium shoes provided," Rick wrote, "the shoes showed no sign of wear."

And even greater endorsement for this master farrier's work was provided by another Long Rider, Bernice Ende.

As I work on this chapter, Bernice is on her eighth consecutive equestrian journey. During the last ten years she has ridden nearly 25,000 miles in the USA and Canada. She is currently attempting to become the first person to ride "ocean to ocean" in both directions on a single journey.

After so many thousands of miles, Bernice has learned a great deal about horse shoes and farriers.

Like Seney, Paine and Blackburn before her, Bernice has now equipped her horses with special borium equipped horseshoes.

She too contacted Roger Robinson in Virginia, who created sets of horse shoes for Bernice's two Fjord horses. It didn't take long before Bernice announced how well these new style horse shoes performed.

"I have used hard-surfacing on the horseshoes before and for pavement riding it's a must. But Roger Robinson, at the Blacksmith Shop is an authority on hard-surfacing and when I heard about him I had to call and ask about his work. He sent me two sets of DuraSafe borium horseshoes. The shoes are giving me twice as much mileage from a set of shoes; that is important. Plus, there is no slippage on ice or wet pavement; none. I cannot tell you how much this helps. I am thrilled with the horseshoes," Bernice informed the Guild.

No Loose Shoes

Long Rider turned farrier, Tracy Paine, shared an excellent way to keep horseshoes from working loose.

"Horseback travellers should avoid loose shoes at all costs. A loose shoe is dangerous. It is easily snagged off the hoof and very often takes part of the hoof with it. Unfortunately, loose shoes are all too common, especially for horses travelling on a daily basis, on pavement, and especially if the horse is a draft horse! The heavy weight of the draft shoe and the tremendous repetitive impact will work the shoe loose in no time. I knew of a draft horse that suffered loose shoes repeatedly and consequently lost so much hoof material that her hooves could no longer hold a shoe!

The trick to avoiding loose shoes is finishing the nails properly. Most farriers will drive a nail into the hoof wall and then wring off the nail by using the hammer claws to twist off the sharp end of the nail close to the hoof wall. Don't do this. Instead, bend the nail over against the hoof wall and cut it off with nail cutters. Leave 1/8" of the nail projecting from the hoof wall. When all the nails are done in this fashion, they are then seated using a 'clinching block' or any other piece of flat metal. Carefully file away any burrs under the nail stubs, do not create a groove in the hoof wall or file away any of the nail, as this will cause weakening. The nail stubs are then softly hammered flat against the hoof wall, and the job is done (see diagrams below). Turning the clinches in this fashion (as opposed to cutting the nail stubs short and then using alligator clinchers) will not cause tearing in the hoof wall, and they will last much longer. There is no need to smooth the clinches with a file because this will occur naturally in a couple days. A shoe nailed in this manner will stay tight for a very long time. I had shoes stay tight on my horse for six months straight while travelling."

Bend nail over	Cut nail leaving 1/8th inch and seat	Gently, bend over nail stub

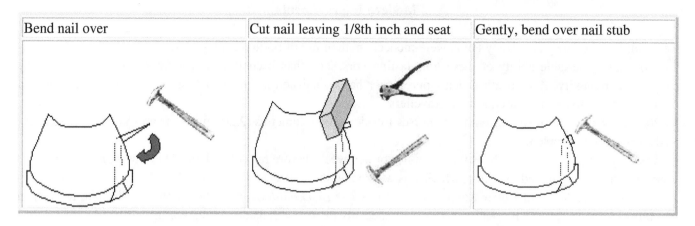

Boots

There is a third option. You can use horse boots.

As history proves, man has been strapping, tying, lashing and gluing various types of shoes, sandals, socks and boots on the bottom of hooves for countless centuries.

This concept has always had its proponents and critics, with Long Riders once again having played a historically significant role in this field of equestrian hoof care.

Though it wasn't exactly a boot, when the famous Swiss Long Rider, Aimé Tschiffely arrived in the United States, after having ridden 10,000 miles from Argentina, he placed rubber shoes under the feet of his geldings, Mancha and Gato, to help them stop slipping on the smooth American roadways.

Yet one of the most spectacular equestrian journeys did rely on rubber boots.

During their historic 30,500 kilometre (19,000 mile) ride from the tip of Patagonia to the top of Alaska, Vladimir Fissenko and his companion, North American Long Rider Louis Bruhnke, used Easyboots with great success.

Likewise the Belgian Long Rider Robert Wauters reported that the Dallmer boot was also successful

"I used them for 700 kilometres, 20 kilometres a day, in all kinds of terrain, tarmac, gravel, grass. They could have gone as far again," Robert said.

Made in Germany, the Dallmer Clog comes in four sizes to fit most horses. It has also been successfully tested by two Swiss women, Ursula Luethi and Marion Landert, who used them to ride from Zürich, Switzerland to Finland.

The problem with boots is that while the concept is faultless, no boot has yet been found which is perfect for all types of terrain or travel.

The Irish Long Rider Stephen O'Connor discovered this when he tested the expensive Marquis boot. Made in Germany, it has a very well deserved reputation. Yet the boots gave Steve problems.

"We set off that September in splendid sunshine. I had the Marquis Super Grip hoof boots on Murphy's front feet. We had tried them three times and they always seemed comfortable enough when I was only riding close to home. But soon after we began travelling, I put Murphy into a canter and one of the boots came flying off within a few seconds. I told myself that it might be that it was not done up tightly enough. The rest of that first day we were mainly on tarmac and covered about fourteen miles. On the second day we were walking along a grassy verge, when I noticed one of the boots was missing. Luckily it had just come off, so I was able to go back and find it. I learned it is a feature of this design that they come undone easily in long grass or scrub.

Then we really had trouble. We were only five days out when Murphy's feet got wet. That's when the boots began rubbing his heels. He became so sore that I took the Marquis boots off and didn't use them again. In fact, I had to let Murphy rest for a few days to let his hooves recover. When we set off again I switched over to a set of BOA boots. Luckily, they did not rub his heels. By the time we returned, Murphy and I had been on the road fifteen days and covered about 170 miles.

But in terms of hoof boots, I was very annoyed with how the Marquis Super Grip rubbed Murphy's heels. If I hadn't spotted the injury early, it could have ended the trek. Also, the fact they slipped off so easily is a major problem, especially considering how expensive they are. All I can say in favour of boots in general is that they will save a horse from going barefoot on tarmac. But even if they were more resilient, I have one other doubt about their constant use. What effect do these ungainly boots have on the horses' shoulders? My feeling is that boots are not the perfect answer for long treks," Steve reported to the Guild.

Though Steve had trouble, other Long Riders have reported covering many miles using various types of boots with few if any problems. If you do decide to use boots while travelling, you must confirm that the boots are a proper size and fit for your horse's hooves. Once they have arrived, begin by having your horse's hooves properly trimmed, as a long hoof may affect the boot's fit.

When his hooves have been prepared, tie your horse up safely and put the boots on carefully. If he has never worn boots before, walk the horse slowly, giving him time to adjust to the large objects on his feet. Once he has walked in a straight line, circle him slowly, being careful to watch for any sign that the boots may be slipping. Trot him and while you're running alongside, listen to ensure that his footfalls sound even. While you're testing him, keep a careful eye out for any signs of imbalance or distress.

Once you're happy with the fit, take a short training ride close to home. Stay on level ground, all the while paying strict attention for any signs of rubbing where the top of the boot comes into contact with the horse's sensitive skin. When one traveller detected signs of galling along the horse's hoof, he screwed a piece of soft rubber hose along the top edge of the boot to provide extra padding.

When you return to the barn, check the horse's hooves and legs carefully. If everything appears to be well, then mark the inside of each boot with which foot it fits. Before you depart, be sure you practise putting the boots on, and removing them. Better to make adjustments at home, than on the side of a strange road.

One other drawback about boots is that they are known to slip in muddy terrain. There have been cases where two horses, proceeding side by side up a muddy track, have had completely different experiences, with the steel shod horse climbing with no problem, while his plastic boot-clad companion was unable to proceed because he was slipping in the mud.

Preparing for the Worst

Regardless of who does it, you or the shoer, when the time comes to put on new horseshoes, expect to lose at least one full day of travelling. And don't forget, there have been several cases where Long Riders had to wait many days before the arrival of a farrier.

Even at the best of times a road horse may lose a shoe for a variety of reasons. It may be sucked off by mud. It might be pulled off by roots or rocks. The nails may slip, which might allow the horse to step on the loose shoe and pull it off. With so many possibilities for trouble, be sure you check each shoe or boot before setting off, especially if you are travelling through tough terrain that day.

Because of their weight, many Long Riders won't carry a spare horse shoe. However a handful of extra tough horseshoe nails weighs very little and can help when you're in trouble.

North American Long Rider Janine Wilder has thousands of miles under her saddle and during her travels she made this important discovery about horseshoe nails.

"The Mustad Company makes a specialty horseshoe nail that I have quite often used. Called Duratrac, these nails have a carbide welded top that adds durability and provides traction to the shoe. After using them off and on for over ten years they have proven themselves to be invaluable for long distance riding. I use four per shoe and this gives my horse just the right amount of traction for those areas of slick rock that can be tricky to navigate, especially when wet. They are also helpful in areas that are extremely rocky such as some areas of the Rocky Mountains," Janine advised.

One more word about horseshoe nails. Don't always expect to find them. An English Long Rider who lived and rode in Romania for many years warned, "Don't forget that local nails go with local shoes, so don't expect to find western machine-made nails or for them to fit handmade peasant horseshoes."

Regardless if you're carrying spare nails or not, if you detect any hint of lameness in your horse, stop and examine him immediately. There may be a stone stuck between the wall of the hoof and the side of the frog.

Should you notice nails sticking out from the bottom of the shoe, then you can pull them out, being careful not to damage the hoof wall. If this leaves the shoe loose, then remove it.

If you lose a hind shoe you can still ride at a gentle walk. But keep off the hard road as much as possible. But the rule is that if your horse loses a front shoe, dismount and lead him, even if it means a ten-mile walk to the nearest farrier. The equine foreleg is vulnerable to strain, so don't tempt Providence.

Emergency Hoof Care

Humans are a remarkably adaptable species. An example of this was provided by the English Long Rider Andrew Wilson, who rode the length of the Himalayan Mountains, from Ladakh to Afghanistan, in 1873. It was while riding in the wild Pamir Mountains that Wilson noted how local horsemen protected their horse's hooves from the damaging rocky ground.

"In Wakhan to the north of the Oxus," Wilson wrote, "there is the curious compromise of shoeing horses with deer's horn, which protects the hoofs, while presenting a surface less slippery than iron and one more congenial to the horse's tender feet."

Carrying a length of deer antler in your saddle bag is not recommended for modern equestrian travellers. That is why some Long Riders carry one Easyboot, much like a spare tyre. However these boots are large and fairly heavy. A lightweight solution is the Shoof. This is a classic emergency plastic shoe which can be easily carried in either a saddle bag or pack saddle pannier. Extremely light weight, it can be fitted to almost any size hoof, and goes on without any difficulty.

When forced to ride though rocky terrain, many Native American horsemen, including the Apache and Blackfoot, covered their horses' hooves in a leather hoof boot which was tough enough to protect the horse against sharp rocks and cactus thorns.

When his mustang mare ran into trouble during a recent ride through the Rocky Mountains, the North American Long Rider and mountain man, Conan Asmussen, relied on this 19th century repair to get him out trouble.

In a report to the Guild, Conan wrote, "First you cut straps to secure the boot with. Then you cut a piece of rawhide two inches bigger than the hoof all around. Get the rawhide a little damp and then stretch it to cover the entire hoof in a kind of sack. If possible, fit the boot below the coronet band. Next you punch holes in the top of the leather sack. Lace the straps through the holes from both directions so that there is a continuous lace visible on the outside of the boot. Now tie the knot in the back. Very quickly the boot will dry almost as hard as metal and will last for several months with ordinary wear. Once you get ready to take it off, you have to cut the edges with a hoof rasp, as it would take all day to whittle the rawhide boot off with a knife."

Conan's emergency rawhide boot stayed on "through sucking bogs and over steep rocky hillsides."

If you find yourself in a more modern setting, and don't happen to have any rawhide to make an Indian boot, then a roll of duct tape can be used to affect an emergency repair. Cover the entire hoof in a soft cloth wrap and then apply several layers of duct tape on the base of the hoof for tread wear. This creates an effective temporary boot. You can also use an old piece of rubber inner tube taped to the bottom of the hoof so as to create a temporary sole.

While rawhide and duct tape certainly represent the past and present, Steve McCutcheon effected a space-age hoof repair while travelling through the wilds of northern Pakistan.

This happened when Steve used a new material known as Superfast. Made by the Vettec Company in America, this is a revolutionary "shoe" which you make yourself by squeezing it out of a tube onto your horse's feet. This system has several great advantages, including the fact that because you make it yourself it will fit any horse, from a little Mongolian horse to a giant Shire!

Superfast is a fast-setting urethane material originally designed to help horses who had suffered damage to their hoof wall. Yet it didn't take long before someone realized that the material, which became rock hard in about two minutes, might be strong enough to replace traditional horse shoes in an emergency situation.

Having received positive reports about what might serve as a "spare tyre" for the world's equestrian explorers, the Long Riders' Guild made an initial test of Superfast in late 2003. However, due to the severe winter conditions, the results were indecisive yet promising.

Enter Steve McCutcheon, who was riding 10,000 kilometres from Delhi, India to Peking, China. No one had undertaken this extraordinary equestrian journey since Major Clarence Bruce rode the distance back in 1905.

Even though he was more than a thousand kilometres away from the Chinese border, and the winter snows were about to fall, Steve was confident that he could make it. The only problem was that in front of him lay the notorious Karakorum Mountains, one of the most geologically unstable mountain ranges in the world.

Shaky mountains tumbling down on your head? That's bad. No horse shoes? In the Long Rider's world that's even worse.

When he found himself miles from help and in need of horse shoes, this far-sighted English Long Rider pulled out the tube of Superfast he had been storing in the bottom of his pack saddle pannier for just such an emergency. And there, on the far side of the world, it appears that horse shoe history may have been made.

But let Steve tell us what happened.

"It was bitterly cold on the 10th of December. What lay ahead was nothingness. For long stretches we just trotted along barren rock. There was no grass, only scree and rock, rock and more rock. That word cannot be stressed enough. The Indus river flowing below became narrower and the mountains more ominous. The biggest worry to me was the lack of people. Villages existed, but in impossible locations far above and below the road. This was Indus Kohistan. The area was certainly remote, with little water and little life. It's a hostile place and the people are a reflection of that. Slightly wild, they see few outsiders. Few stop here. The land used to be called 'Yagistan' or 'land of the ungoverned' because cutthroats could hide in the many side valleys that riddle the region," Steve reported.

"It had only been four days since I had had new shoes put on my two mares but they needed doing again. I cursed the fool who had fixed such low-quality metal to my horses' feet. They turned out to have been locally made from re-inforcement iron. Yet I cursed myself too for not having had the foresight to purchase better-quality extra shoes back in Islamabad. And even though I did have spares with me, they were the same low quality as the ones presently being used.

But that wasn't my only problem. The only available farrier was 60 kilometres further along the Karakoram Highway at the village of Chilas and with winter coming on, time was not on my side. The logical solution would have been to go straight to Chilas and bring a farrier back with me and have the mares' feet fixed once and for all. Instead I decided to do it myself, right there on the side of the road. I was short on time but I had a solution. I had with me a product called Superfast made by a reputable company called Vettec in the USA. This hoof care product applies to the bottom of the hoof and sets in 2½ minutes," the Long Rider recalled.

"The reasons for its use here were simple. The Chinese border was due to close in two weeks. I was short on time and all eight shoes were completely worn down. The Superfast user guide seemed easy to understand and the gel would take only 3 minutes to apply to each shoe. As an emergency solution, there is little to rival the adaptability of this product. I was able to fit temporary shoes to the hooves under a variety of circumstances.

My route now lies through China where the distances are greater and the availability of farriers less. Superfast will be even more valuable to this expedition and given my prior experience I will be able to put this product even further to the test," Steve wrote from Chinese Turkistan.

Summary

Rawhide Indian boots or space age glue? What do you choose? Run barefoot or proceed cautiously with borium covered steel shoes? Which is better?

While you decide on how to proceed, what you must do is advance with intellectual caution. As I was writing this chapter, a New Jersey man was arrested for having duped investors out of nearly two million dollars. The money had been siphoned off to fund a scheme to manufacture a new type of horseshoe.

Men change with travel, manners change with clime, tenets with books and principles with time.

But road horses are working animals upon whose hooves your journey depends.

Thus, when it comes to protecting the horse's hoof, the future is as uncertain as the past – except when it comes to the never-ending debate about horseshoeing. As these various examples prove, there will always be shifting notions and conflicting beliefs on this subject.

I hope that this small study will open up your mind to the many alternatives.

During her 'ocean to ocean' ride across the United States, Sea G Rhydr made an important observation. Roads, such as this one which Sea photographed in Tennessee, may appear to be smooth and trouble free to a fast-moving motorist.

But, Sea wrote, "As we learned in Tennessee, certain roads that look really nice and smooth at a distance are actually 4 grit sandpaper under hoof – zillions of sharp little rocks steamrollered into tar is not quite as bad as gravel but certainly much worse than actual cement."

Rock-covered trails and unforgiving modern roads are capable of destroying the horse shoes of any road or pack horse in a remarkably short time.

This image shows the damage done to the hoof wall of a road horse taken over hard ground. You can also see the exit holes caused by the horse shoe nails.

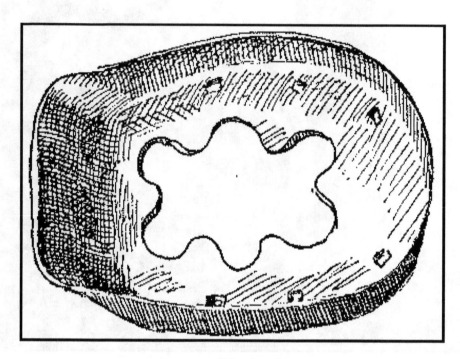

Horseshoeing is an art which developed alongside that of horsemanship. Yet down through the centuries concepts and practices have changed very little. This is a 12th Century Asiatic cap iron-sole horse shoe.

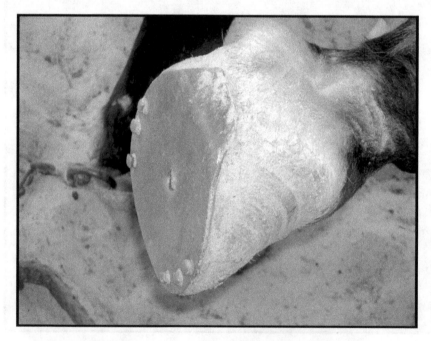

The 12th century horseshoe closely resembles this shoe, which was photographed in Libya in 2011.

English farriers have enjoyed a reputation for being skilled professionals since the days when King Henry VIII took along an army of skilled farriers to attend to the 5,000 horses who accompanied the monarch when he rode from London to York. The modern British Farriers Registration Act ensures that all the nation's farriers are licensed professionals.

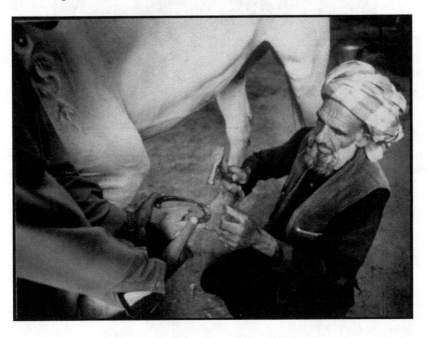

In stark contrast to the English farrier, this Afghan refugee who shod the author's horse in northern Pakistan, owned a hammer but had no horse shoes or nails and very little knowledge about the ancient art of horseshoeing.

Scottish Long Rider Gordon Naysmith trimmed the hooves of his barefoot Basuto ponies, Norton and Essex, every day during their historic 20,000 kilometres (14,000 mile) ride. By the time the horses reached Austria, their hooves were rock hard.

South African Long Rider Billy Brenchley was a professional farrier and a strong advocate of letting horses go barefoot when the terrain allowed. This photo shows the hoof of his horse, Nali, after travelling 4,300 kilometres (2,600 miles) across the mainly sandy terrain of Northern Africa.

Yet where you ride will determine if you use horse shoes or allow your horse to go barefoot. Like Gordon Naysmith, Billy Brenchley realised he needed to use horse shoes once his animals began travelling along hard roads. This image shows Billy making an emergency repair to his horse, Chami, along a busy road he encountered further south in Africa.

Though corporate-made steel horse shoes and nails are easily available in the Occident, many parts of the world are not familiar with the concept of horseshoeing, nor are shoes and nails easily obtainable. It took many hours for an army farrier to size, forge and fit this single set of handmade Pakistani steel horse shoes for the author's gelding.

Don't expect to discover the same procedures and products to be practised everywhere in the horse world. Like many other aspects of the horse world, the Orient developed a different procedure from the Occident for shoeing horses. This Chinese method of restraining a horse was used to control the horse of English Long Rider Steve McCutcheon.

In countries like Tibet, Mongolia, Kazakhstan and parts of Central Asia, native horsemen tie the horse's legs together and then roll the animal on his back before hammering on the shoes. These Kazakhs are shoeing Bonnie Folkins's horse.

When Swiss Long Rider Andre Fischer rode through Patagonia he discovered how local horse shoes were kept in place. Excessive toe clips such as this not only add to the weight of the shoe, they also mutilate the hoof.

During her 16,000 kilometre (10,000 mile) ride across the United States, North American Long Rider Tracy Paine learned how to shoe her mare, Dawn. An·early advocate of applying borium to horse shoes, Tracy learned she could make a single set of horseshoes last for six months of hard riding.

Thankfully, improvements have been made. In 2009 Rick Blackburn set to ride from Canada to Texas. He ran into problems keeping his horses shod for more than two weeks, until he learned about Roger Robinson, a master farrier whose expertise is creating horseshoes specially treated with hard-wearing borium.

Robinson, who operates "The Blacksmith Shop" in Harrisonburg, Virginia, has now equipped Bernice Ende with special borium-treated horse shoes to help her complete the first "ocean to ocean" ride in both directions on a single journey.

Another option is to protect the horse's hoof by the use of a boot. This is not a new concept, as can be seen in this 19th century photograph which shows a Japanese pack horse wearing protective boots made from durable bamboo.

Russian Long Rider Vladimir Fissenko used Easy Boots during his journey from Patagonia to Alaska.

Many companies are now offering protective boots. Sea G Rhydr reported excellent results with the Renegade Hoof Boots she used. "I'm really impressed with the new design. The V in the front means that they snug down closer to the hoof wall, the closed heel cup in the back keeps out dirt and detritus. There are no rub marks from the new boots and we made good time over roads we would have been avoiding if we were barefoot."

Other Long Riders have not been so lucky. Irish Long Rider Steven O'Connor discovered this when he tested the expensive Marquis Super Grip horse boot which is made in Germany. Steven discovered the boots came off easily, which meant he had to spend time looking for the lost boot. Plus, they rubbed his horse's heels badly.

The modern Shoof (left) is a classic "emergency" shoe which can be easily carried in either a saddle bag or pack saddle box. Extremely light weight, it can be fitted to almost any size hoof, and goes on without any difficulty. It is based upon the same principles used by Roman horsemen 2,000 years ago, whose hippo-sandal (right) was also designed to protect the hoof on rough ground.

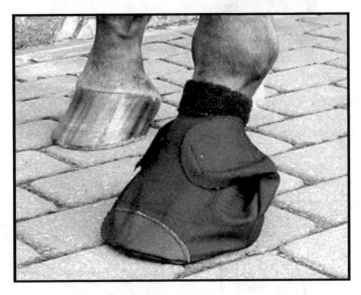

Another type of light weight emergency boot, this one held in place by Velcro.

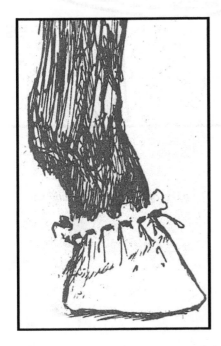

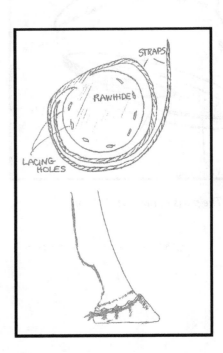

While riding through the Rocky Mountains, North American Long Rider Conan Asmussen's mare injured her hoof. So he created a rawhide boot, using a technique perfected by the Apache Indians.

English Long Rider Steve McCutcheon used a more modern solution than rawhide when he was forced to create emergency horse shoes under the harsh conditions found in Pakistan's Karakorum Mountains. He squeezed out the contents of a tube of Superfast, created by the Vettec Company, and created impromptu horse shoes in under five minutes.

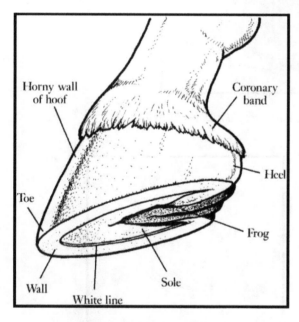

The parts of the horse's hoof.

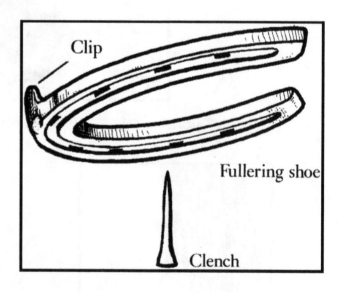

The parts of the horse shoe and nail.

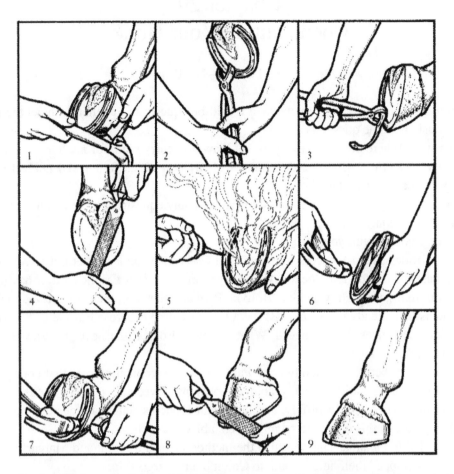

Steps in horse shoeing. Cutting off the ends of the nail heads. Removing the old shoe. Using the nippers to trim the hoof. Rasping the bottom of the hoof. Applying the hot shoe to ensure that it is properly seated and sitting flat on the hoof. Driving in the nails. After cutting off the excess nail, bending the end down towards the bottom of the hoof. Rasping the edge of the hoof. The result; a well set shoe.

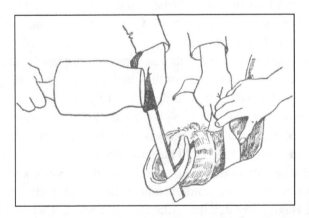

The German cavalry manual warned, "Just as the performance of Infantrymen depends largely on the quality of their boots, so does the performance of horses depend on the way they are shod." A useful tip for Long Riders can be learned from the German cavalry. The farrier had an assistant use a strap to keep a horse's hoof under control while the farrier removed the shoe.

Chapter 29
Documenting Your Horse

No Papers – No Trip

Regardless of where they are about to journey, when would-be equestrian travellers contact the Long Riders' Guild for advice they usually ask the same questions.

How do I plan my route? Where do I sleep every night? How do I carry grain for my horses? Should I take a gun?

What no one has ever asked is, "What are the chances of my expedition failing if I neglect to obtain the proper medical and legal paperwork for me and my horses"?

That is a question that should seriously concern you because many equestrian travellers have watched their dreams die on the rocks of legal objection.

Let me share just one example with you.

In 1982 French Long Riders, Jean-Francois Ballereau and Constance Rameaux set out to ride in the hoofprints of Aimé Tschiffely. The determined duo left Buenos Aires, Argentina with four Criollos. After having ridden more than three thousand successful miles, through Argentina, Bolivia, Peru and Ecuador, the team arrived in Columbia.

Because Jean Francois had already made successful equestrian journeys across Europe and North America, he was prepared for the physical challenges that lay ahead. What this wise Long Rider never foresaw was that his latest trip would be destroyed by paper.

The Darién Gap jungle lies between Columbia and Panama. It is a tropical morass that connects Central to South America. Inhabited by suspicious natives, deadly animals, poisonous vegetation and various types of blood-loving insects, it is no wonder that first Aimé Tschiffely, and later Jean-Francois Ballereau, decided not to risk the health of their horses by travelling through this one-hundred mile stretch of swampy hell.

In Aimé's case, he sailed to Panama. This was also the method chosen by Raul and Margarita Vasconcellos. When they reached Panama, they shipped their horses south to Columbia by cargo ship.

But cargo ships capable of carrying horses north to Panama from Columbia were no longer available, which forced Jean-Francois and Constance to instead fly their horses to Panama City. What happened next illustrates the type of bureaucratic nightmare which awaits any unwary Long Rider.

The French Long Riders had received the enthusiastic support of the Panamanian embassy staff in Columbia. Armed with what they believed was the proper paperwork, Constance and Jean Francois loaded their horses on the plane, and after a short flight, landed in Panama.

The horses were disembarked, standing on the hot tarmac close to the plane, when a lady in a dress and red high-heeled shoes walked out to inspect their arrival. According to Jean-Francois, she glanced at the papers and then promptly announced that the documents were not in order. When the French Long Riders began to argue that the papers had been completed by Columbian authorities, with the aid of representatives of the Panamanian government, the local bureaucrat took offence. She ordered Jean-Francois and Constance to load their animals back on the plane, and return them to Columbia immediately, or she would have the horses shot where they stood.

Talk of the three-thousand miles already ridden meant nothing to this governmental Medusa. Facing disaster, Jean-Francois and Constance reluctantly returned to Columbia, where they spent many fruitless months trying to arrange to move their animals into Panama. Having irritated the authorities in Panama City, the French Long Riders watched in horror as their funds dwindled and their dream died. Eventually they were forced to give their horses away and return to France.

Jean Francois Ballereau, one of the most successful and knowledgeable 20th century Long Riders had been stopped, not by jungles but the antagonism of rule-worshipping urban dwellers.

Thus, regardless if you're riding in Paraguay or Pennsylvania, being armed with the proper paperwork for your horses is of vital importance.

Paper Problems

The troubles faced by the French Long Riders have not disappeared. If anything, it has become more difficult to take horses across international borders.

That's what Irish Long Rider Hugh MacDermott recently realized. He bought his horse in Argentina, in preparation for riding across the Andes to Chile. That's when he discovered his troubles had just begun.

"An interesting point about buying this horse was the eventual cost of organising all his paperwork. That came to a third of the actual price. And to think we complain back home about red tape. I'm still waiting on his international passport," the disgruntled Long Rider wrote.

The necessary documents fall into three main categories. Regardless of where you ride, certain documents prove the horse belongs to you. Other documents validate the horse's identity. The last group of documents confirms that the animal is healthy, carrying no communicable diseases and can travel without infecting other horses.

Obviously, the required paperwork needed to establish these three legal and medical principles differs from one nation to another. Mongolia, for example, does not allow any foreign horses to be imported, nor will the government authorize that nation's horses to be removed by travellers. So straight away these sort of unflinching rules can ruin your travel plans.

You must investigate the legal and medical requirements of every state and nation you plan to travel through. Many countries maintain an agricultural department which deals with such questions. Only after you have obtained official clearance can you safely set off.

Just Say No

Yet, as Jean Francois learned, just because officials in one country say "Bon Voyage," that's not reason enough to believe trouble isn't waiting to ambush you up ahead. What an official tells you in one country may not be accepted by their superiors further down the road or across the border. Though they are often well meaning, these local representatives of their government, such as consuls or passport control, might not be aware of border restrictions, visa requirements or recently-passed equine health regulations, which are known to their more well-versed colleagues in the border, passport or veterinarian branches of the national government.

This assumes, of course, that the government officials, though ill informed, actually do want to help you. All too often, as Jean Francois learned to his dismay, government officers don't care how far you've ridden. To them, your grand journey is only confirmation of your eccentric nature and a strong sign that your judgment can't be trusted. The result is that the officials obsess over your horse's paperwork. Any deviation from the rules means they might get in trouble, which in turn could result in them losing their jobs. Your progress thereafter becomes connected to their career and financial well being. In such a case, mild annoyance turns into official suspicion, which results in personal fear and concludes with professional hostility.

That is why when a timid official is in doubt about how to handle you and your horses, the fastest and easiest thing for him to do is to simply say, "No."

Misplaced Trust

Remember, in this mechanized age horses normally show up at national borders either in a truck or aboard an airplane. Papers are glanced at, because the horses are traditionally classified as valuable athletes, cargo or meat. They are no longer transport. They are instead transported.

In stark contrast, when you ride up unexpectedly atop your horse, perhaps with a pack horse in tow, you immediately present a problem, an embarrassment, a departure from the usual quiet running of the government official's office and department. In the majority of cases, these bureaucrats have never had an opportunity to deal with an equestrian traveller before. Your unwelcome arrival means extra work, more forms to be filled in, rules to be reviewed, veterinarians to be consulted and worst of all, perhaps, the unwelcome interference of their department chief.

You are, in other words, someone who they want to get rid of. One way to do that is to reassure you that all your paperwork is in order, then hurry you down the road with a foolish smile on your trusting face, all the while they know, or suspect, that some other unlucky government border guard or official further along the line will be the one who has to break the news that your trip has come to an end because some form is not completed properly.

That is why the first lesson about paperwork is to never trust what appears to be well-founded and even well-meaning advice given by government employees stationed in another country. Accept this local help, by all means, as a good place to start. However, in addition, you must obtain the most up-to-date information directly from high-ranking authorities operating from legitimate offices located in the capital of the nation you are entering. These are the people who can actually authorize your horse's entry into that country. Once they know you are on your way, if you encounter a problem at the border, they are the ones you can telephone to ask for help and advice.

If you avoid this step, you imperil your journey.

A Plethora of Problems

To put this complicated situation into perspective, let's not forget some of the other types of legal challenges waiting to ambush your dreams.

Unrealistic Time Period

Because most horses are now transported by motor, nations offer medical papers which are only valid for a specified time period. For example, many medical documents are valid for ten to thirty days. Yet it is the rare Long Rider, and the brief trip, which can travel across an entire nation in less than thirty days.

Antagonistic Attitude

Some nations are now requiring that any foreign horse receive a medical examination every ten to thirty days. That's fine, if you've just flown your million-dollar show jumper in for the Olympics, and plan to be back home at your mansion at the end of the week. But it doesn't work for a slow moving Long Rider, does it? The German government, for example, insists that this medical inspection must be done by a nationally recognized government veterinarian. This means you have to find such a vet, arrange for him to meet you at some as yet undetermined place, pay for his services and any required lab tests, and then make sure the paperwork is provided to the home office in time.

Official Confusion

Don't be surprised to learn that the government's right hand doesn't know what its left hand is doing. Customs agents have one set of requirements. Border guards will look in your saddle bags for terrorists and contraband. National agricultural officers are frightened of allowing in diseased animals. Who reviews all these rules to find out which apply to your situation? Who finds out what papers will open the border and allow you across the country? Often, you do.

Sexual Prejudice

Because many nations are paranoid about sexually transmitted equine diseases, if you thought trying to take a mare or gelding across an international border was hard, wait till you discover how much more difficult it is to ride your stallion through a foreign country.

During her ride from Russia to England, my wife, Basha, entered Sweden with her Cossack stallion, Count Pompeii. The Swedes promptly locked the Russian stud in quarantine. While various officials argued about what was to be done, Pompeii was kept on a starvation diet. In order to confirm that the foreign horse was disease-free, blood tests needed to be done, during which time Basha was charged vast amounts to hold the kidnapped stallion.

After seventeen days of such bureaucratic torture, the authorities were threatening to euthanize the great horse because they couldn't reach a decision. Luckily, Basha managed to speak to the Chief Veterinarian of the European

Union in Brussels. Count Pompeii's life was saved when Europe's highest ranking equine medical officer intervened and ordered the Swedish government to release the horse.

Medical Dilemmas

Many horses in Central and South America are carriers of a tick-transmitted disease known as piroplasmosis. Though common from Mexico to Patagonia, the United States has not had a large scale invasion of the disease due to a stringent equine medical barricade erected along the entire length of the American-Mexican border. Because of this medical defence system, Long Riders attempting to ride from Latin America into the United States are routinely denied entry into North America if their horses are found to be carrying this communicable microbe. There is no known paperwork, medical tests or way to evade this remorseless legal requirement.

For example, though he rode his Criollo geldings from Patagonia to the Texas border, the German Long Rider, Günter Wamser was refused entry into the United States when his horses were found to be carrying, not the sickness itself but the antibodies to piroplasmosis, in their bloodstream. Any infected horse caught evading the medical border authorities will be destroyed and the owner risks imprisonment.

Even though we are entering a legal jungle, let us investigate what sort of documents you and your horse may need. Let's start with the various ways governments want us to prove who the horse is and who he belongs to: the Equine Identification Documents.

Breed Documents

Purebred horses registered in the record books of an international breed are provided with documents from that breed's headquarters. Along with a photo or accurately-drawn identification, this document presents the animal's detailed physical description, as well as his exact markings, specific colour, height, size, age, sex and details about the forebears. The name and address of the horse's breeder are also provided.

Microchips

An increasingly popular method of identifying horses is to implant a microchip in their necks. This is a tiny silicone chip which, when read by a scanner, not only provides the horse's identity number but information about his owner and home address. Microchips are effective because they cannot be readily detected by thieves. However, a suitable scanner must be available to read the chip. As this may present a problem if the horse is travelling between nations, you should discuss this concern with the proper authorities before you begin your journey. All horses residing and travelling in the European Union must be microchipped.

United Kingdom Equine Passport

Beginning in 2005 Great Britain passed a law requiring all equines to be issued with a passport. This document clearly identifies the animal, describes its age, and provides information about its owner and residence. The equine passport must be kept up to date and the horse, pony, donkey or mule cannot be sold or legally transported without this vital document. Do not attempt to purchase or travel on a horse in the United Kingdom unless the owner can provide the passport.

American National Animal Identification System

Following the success of the British equine passport system, the American government instituted the National Animal Identification System (NAIS). Though still a voluntary program, it allows state and federal authorities to identify and track stolen horses.

Once we can prove the horse belongs to us, what happens next? That very much depends on where you go.

Travel between Countries

Don't expect an easy time when you begin exploring the legal world of horses. For example, when Pascale Franconie was riding from France to Arabia in the early 1980s, she encountered unexpected trouble when she arrived at Belgrade, Yugoslavia. Given that horses were considered dangerous, local police fined the young Long Rider because she had broken a city ordinance by riding on the pavement and not tying up her horse.

Travelling between countries ranges from relatively easy to completely impossible. Some nations, such as Great Britain, Ireland and France are less restrictive as there is a tripartite agreement between the veterinary authorities in these countries. Any privately-owned horse must still have a valid passport and an export licence before entering the other countries. Likewise riding between Canada and the United States is fairly routine, though the countries only allow horses to enter and exit via certain specified border control posts.

Because of political hostilities, countries such as India and Pakistan do not allow horse travellers to take their animals across these national borders. Travel in certain countries, such as Russia, is drastically reduced to ninety days because of the short nature of the tourist visas offered to Long Riders.

Mongolia will not allow horses to enter or leave.

Horses are no longer allowed to travel in Antarctica.

Though the documents and regulations involved in allowing horses to travel over international borders vary, each nation will require entry and exit papers for each animal. Veterinary certificates stating that the animal is in good health are required. Customs declarations, such as the ATA Carnet, are often required to prove you do not plan on selling your horses after you arrive. Transit permits issued by the Ministry of Agriculture are strongly suggested. You must ensure that all of these documents are in the relevant languages of the countries you plan to travel through.

Travelling in the European Union

There are currently twenty-seven member countries in the European Union. Austria, Belgium, Bulgaria, Cyprus, Czech Republic, Denmark, Estonia, Finland, France, Germany, Greece, Hungary, Ireland, Italy, Latvia, Lithuania, Luxembourg, Malta, Netherlands, Poland, Portugal, Romania, Slovakia, Slovenia, Spain, Sweden and the United Kingdom.

To ride between EU nations, your horse will require an equine passport, export licence and health certifications. But be advised that border crossings may prove to be difficult because the majority of equines cross them inside some sort of motorized transport. Because these animals cross entire nations rapidly, many health certificates are only valid for a limited time, so plan your border crossing carefully.

Though Switzerland and Norway are part of mainland Europe, neither nation is a member of the European Union. If you attempt to cross these borders on horseback you are departing the EU, which may have unintended negative consequences. For example, if a horse from the European Union resides in a "third country" for more than thirty days, the animal is automatically classified as a "non-EU horse." Should this occur while you are travelling, EU veterinarians will require you to obtain new health certificates and be able to prove to the EU border authorities that your horse poses no medical threat. Here again, this sort of problem requires careful advance research and plenty of intelligent reconnaissance on your part.

Should you be returning with horses to the United Kingdom from non-EU countries, DEFRA (the Department for Environment, Food and Rural Affairs) must be contacted in advance. In addition to accurate health records and blood tests, such incoming horses, and all their equipment, must be accompanied by an ATA Carnet (see next page) issued in the horse's country of origin.

After you return to your home, keep all your equestrian medical documents carefully preserved, as local authorities may question the medical condition of your horse later on. And what sort of documents might they be?

Export Licence

If you are taking your horse out of Great Britain, ferry transport companies will ask to see the export license issued by the British government. This document, which is issued by DEFRA, documents the value and details of the animal. Ponies departing Great Britain require a different type of export license than horses.

ATA Carnet

The document known as the ATA Carnet demonstrates to custom officials that you do not plan to sell your horse after you have entered their country. The carnet serves as a financial guarantee which offsets the need for you to pay import and export taxes on your horse when you enter and leave a country. The carnet is issued by the Chamber of Commerce in your native country. Though it may not be recognized by some countries formerly allied to the Soviet Union, it eliminates the need for you to provide a cash deposit to the Customs authorities of the non-European Union country you are riding through.

Transit permits

Obtaining transit permits for road and pack horses is complicated because the Ministry of Agriculture may require you to declare your route, explain how long you plan to reside in the country, and list the places where you will be staying. Acquiring the transit permit may largely depend on whether you can arrange for someone sympathetic in the local government to assist you in completing the paperwork, etc.

United Kingdom Route Plan

If you plan to apply to DEFRA for a United Kingdom Health Certificate for your horse, that office will require you to provide details regarding your planned route, which roads you plan to travel on, the time needed for your journey, etc. This information is entered on a form which you send to the DEFRA office, along with the application for a United Kingdom Health Certificate. Upon receiving your route plan, the DEFRA office will stamp your route plan and return it with your UK Health Certificate. You must keep the UK route plan with you during your journey, remembering not to surrender it to any foreign officials. If any questions arise, DEFRA may require the route plan for inspection six months after the conclusion of your journey.

Medical Documents

North American Long Rider Lisa Wood summed up the best way to avoid medical entanglements.

"I got as many vaccinations for my horse as possible and I always carried my horse's medical records with me."

That philosophy certainly saved Howard Saether a great deal of trouble during his ride from Uruguay to Texas. He discovered the violent alternative which awaited horses that lacked the proper medical papers.

"Please advise everybody who plans to travel with horses down here to have their horse Health Certificate papers ready," Howard wrote from the jungles of Paraguay, the third country he and his horses had crossed so far. He went on to describe what happened to horses that lacked the proper medical documents.

"To enter the state of Santa Catarina, we needed special permission from the chief veterinarian. But thanks to some good publicity in the newspaper, the local mayor telephoned that vet on our behalf. The mayor's call persuaded the doctor to allow our horses to enter. Everything went smoothly after we proved their medical papers were all in order. But we had to disinfect the horse's hooves. Then we were allowed to ride into the state. But don't take any chances. Yesterday the chief veterinarian was called by the police to inspect a truck caught illegally carrying eighteen bulls into the state. Even though these were prize breeding animals, because the bulls lacked the proper medical papers, and could have carried a disease, they were killed on the spot. Horses that are found entering the state illegally go the same way too," Howard explained.

Make sure that all your veterinarian certificates of health are in the language of the issuing country and in the one of the country of destination. This document certifies that an accredited veterinarian has examined your horse and found it to be free of any diseases and all of its inoculations are up to date.

The health certificate must include an accurate description of the horse. His age, sex, colour, markings, registered name and breed identification number must also be provided. The vet may also note where you plan to travel with your horse. The health certificate may not be valid for more than thirty days in some American states and certain nations. Confirm this in advance and carefully check to ensure what blood tests are required by each country.

United Kingdom Health Certificate

Though you will not need a government issued Health Certificate to transport your horse between England, Ireland and France, other countries will require this document. To obtain the health certificate, either you or your vet should apply to the DEFRA office, though the document will be delivered to your vet's office. After the certificate is on hand, have your horse's medical inspection completed no more than 48 hours prior to your departure from Great Britain. The ferry company will want to confirm that your animal's health certificate is in order, but you will be allowed to retain the document. Be sure to protect this important document when you are travelling. Prior to your return to Great Britain, you will need to have a second health certificate issued from your country of departure.

Vaccination record

Whether you are travelling across state lines or international borders, Long Riders must have a vaccination record which confirms the horse is in good health and that all of his inoculations are up to date. For example, it is essential to prove your horse is not infected with the highly contagious and deadly equine disease known as glanders. Likewise, your horse must be vaccinated against tetanus, and flu. Certain European countries, such as France, require you to take additional precautions against piroplasmosis.

Don't forget to check how long the vaccination record is valid for in the countries or states you will be travelling through, as the length of validity changes from place to place and in America from state to state. Also, try to stay current about equine health conditions while you are travelling.

Though going across national borders is tough, taking horses across American state lines can also be challenging. You must determine what each state's medical requirements are in advance, so having the vaccination record up to date is the first step towards medical success.

Coggins Test

Having a valid Coggins test, proving that your horses do not carry EIA, is an absolute requirement in many parts of the world.

The Coggins test was devised to detect the presence of Equine Infectious Anaemia, more commonly known as EIA or swamp fever. Horses are infected with the highly communicable disease when they are bitten by blood-sucking insects, such as horseflies. If a horse is found to be infected with EIA, even if the animal demonstrates no clinical signs of illness, he is quarantined for life or euthanized, so as to decrease the chance of spreading the disease.

The Coggins test, which proves that your horse is not infected with EIA, must have been done prior to your departure. State and national requirements vary as to how long the Coggins test is valid. Regardless, you must be able to present a valid Coggins test when you arrive at stables, campgrounds or other public equestrian facilities. Because it often takes weeks to obtain the lab results proving a negative Coggins test, you must allow plenty of time to have this document completed prior to your departure. Certain American states, for example Washington and Oregon, maintain reciprocal agreements, while other states demand additional information, such as the horse's temperature, being recorded on the document.

Brand Documents

Branding a horse is an olden method designed to identify the horse as the property of a person, place or organization, i.e. the owner, his ranch, or the national army. Traditional branding was done by applying a heated iron against the horse's hide. The resultant mark left a permanent scar on the skin and hair. The more modern method of freeze branding uses liquid nitrogen to create a permanent mark on the horse's body.

The locations of where the brand was placed on the horse's body depended on the owner, organization or nation which has control of the animal. Cowboys traditionally hot branded their horses, either on the left flank or shoulder. The Pakistani army, which sold me horses, use a number of large brands to indicate the horse's year of birth, the cavalry depot where it is stationed, etc. In order to deter theft, many horses now have a series of small numbers freeze branded along the top of their neck. This identity number is then intentionally hidden under the animal's mane.

This identifying mark on your horse's body is noted on the brand inspection card. In addition to describing the actual brand, the document may also list the horse's other identifying features such as age, sex, colour, breed, microchip number and markings.

Travelling with horses in the United States and Canada will require you to be familiar with the brand card and ensure that your horses have this important document, even if they do not actually have a brand. Many American states employ brand inspectors to confirm that horses are not being stolen. To deter theft, brand inspectors inspect any horse which has been sold, has crossed a state line, or has been transported more than seventy-five miles within the state. When a brand inspection takes place, the brand inspector physically inspects the horse and documents and then issues a brand clearance which authorizes the transportation of the animal.

State brand laws vary widely, so it is imperative that you confirm the brand laws where you will be riding. For example, in western South Dakota you, as the animal owner, must have proof of ownership and obtain a certification from a Livestock brand Inspector before you leave that area. Failure to have your animal inspected is a misdemeanour and horse owners will be charged. Before you begin your journey, you should contact the brand control board in each state and request details.

The brand card becomes critically important once you cross the Mississippi river and continue to ride west. American state authorities will require you to carry health certificates, a Coggins test and brand inspection papers. When a brand inspector checks your horse, he will draw the horse's distinguishing marks on an outline of a horse pictured on the brand card. Notations are also made about the horse's colour, markings, age and sex. The brand inspector also confirms proof of ownership and ensures that the horse's health certificate is valid. After paying the brand inspector a fee, he will issue you with an official brand card or certificate.

State laws require that every horse have its own brand card. Because brand cards are valid until the horse is sold, brand inspections are usually done once a year. Some states offer a lifetime brand inspection which is valid so long as you own the horse. It is your responsibility to determine what the requirements are before you make your journey. Brand inspections and brand cards become of increasing importance when you ride your horse across state lines. Any time you see signs asking for animal identification, be prepared to provide your brand card to the local inspector. The United States Department of Agriculture may provide you with the most up-to-date information about brand requirements in each state.

Summary

Remember, it is the bureaucrats, not the bandits, who are your biggest challenge.

This is why it is imperative that well in advance of your departure, you obtain all of the equine identity and medical documents which every nation, or each state, will demand of you.

One potential source of information is a professional horse transport company; carrying horses across borders on a daily basis means they have to be completely up to date with each country's health and documentary requirements. You may have to pay a fee for their knowledge, but it would be money very well spent!

Raul and Margarita Vasconcellos were lucky enough to find a cargo ship which took their road horses and pack mules from Panama to Columbia.

But after having ridden more than 3,000 miles from Patagonia, French Long Rider Jean Francois Ballereau had his dreams shattered when his expedition was halted by government officials in Panama.

During her ride from Russia to England, Basha O'Reilly entered Sweden with her Cossack stallion, Count Pompeii. The Swedes promptly locked the Russian stud in quarantine. The authorities were threatening to euthanize the horse that is the flying symbol of the Long Riders' Guild before the Chief Veterinarian of the European Union in Brussels ordered the Swedish government to release him.

Though he rode his Criollo geldings from Patagonia to the Texas border, the German Long Rider Günter Wamser was refused entry into the United States when his horses were found to be carrying, not the sickness itself but the antibodies to piroplasmosis, in their bloodstream. Günter had to find homes for the animals in Mexico and purchase new horses in the United States before carrying on his journey to Alaska.

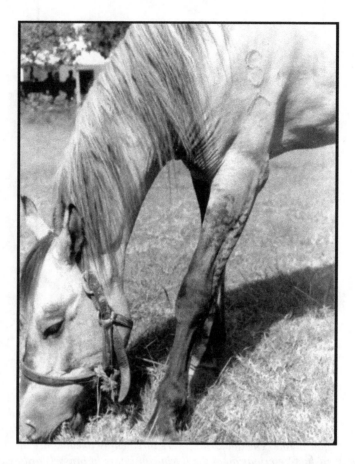

The author's dun gelding, Pasha, who was purchased from the Pakistani army. The arrow brand on his left shoulder confirms he is a military mount, while the large letter S indicates that he was quartered at the army remount depot located at Sargohda.

The brands on the right side of Pasha's body confirm his year of birth, 1984, and his military identification number, 104.

Chapter 30
Travelling Health Record

Animal's Name and sex

Birth date and place

Previous Owner

Date purchased

Colour and Markings

Normal weight

Normal respiration (at rest)

Normal pulse (at rest)

Inoculations (dates and vaccinations used)

Coggins Test (dates)

Travelling from

Travelling to

Statement of condition

Approval for further travel

Name, address and phone number of inspecting Veterinarian

Section Three
Chapter 31
The Equipment - No more, No less

A Prophecy

Colonel Thomas Orde-Lees accompanied Sir Ernest Shackleton on an ill-fated expedition to the South Pole in 1914. In addition to being a keen skier, Orde-Lees was also a pioneering parachutist who advocated linking technology and exploration.

In a prophetic statement regarding the future of exploration, Orde-Lees said, "No doubt the explorers of 2015, if there is anything left to explore, will not only carry their pocket wireless telephones fitted with wireless telescopes but will also receive their nourishment and warmth by wireless."

Though Long Riders cannot yet download meals from their mobile phones, Orde-Lees' vision reflects the remarkable technological advances which have changed the face of exploration in recent years.

Yet, while there is much to be excited about in terms of technological advancement, when it comes to the ancient art of equestrian travel, many original truths remain unchanged. One of the most important is how an equestrian traveller deals with the issue of equipment.

Liberty and Luggage

There is a sense of liberty which comes when you swing into the saddle and aim your sights at a distant geographic goal. To some degree you are liberated in that your world is now largely confined to what is securely stored in your saddle bags and on your pack saddle.

By placing your baggage on your horse's back, you at once achieve a sense of independence, which imparts an enthusiasm to the whole affair. You have been thrown upon your own resources, but you have been granted a terrific sense of freedom.

Nonetheless there are risks involved.

One can be self-contained without having to be a Spartan. Yet how do we decide what is required and what is superfluous?

If our journey is to be a success, not a button should be missing. But how do we realize the true spirit and freedom of a journey in the saddle if we are needlessly burdened with excess belongings?

A flood of Personal Possessions

Though his mileage may be long, a Long Rider's list of possessions is small. This stands in stark contrast to the prevailing philosophy which encourages the possession of a vast multitude of objects.

Things give us a false sense of security. They encourage us to go into debt. They clutter our lives and cause us worry. They must be cleaned, moved, protected and insured. They anchor us to the past. They become emotional icons, whose loss or damage causes us distress.

They plagued our ancestors, just like they continue to worry us today. Nor have all previous travellers been immune from bringing too much baggage.

Galloping Lions

In 1910 an American named John McCutcheon set off on safari in East Africa, today's modern Kenya. In addition to hunting various types of big game, the newspaper cartoonist was determined to "gallop lions."

According to McCutcheon, "This riding method is dangerous, for in it the hunter endeavours to round up or herd a lion by riding him to a standstill. When the lion is fighting mad he stops and turns upon his persecutor."

That was the moment, McCutcheon said, when the obituary columns back home usually listed the names of the unfortunate galloping lion hunter.

Prior to successfully chasing the king of beasts on horseback, McCutcheon had noted, "It is amazing how much stuff is required to outfit a party of four people for an African shooting expedition of several months' duration."

McCutcheon journeyed into the veldt accompanied by two transport wagons drawn by thirty oxen, one headman, four gun bearers, four scouts, one cook, four tent boys, four grooms, eighteen servants and one hundred porters.

Accompanying this vast herd of humans were sixty-five locking "chop boxes" of sixty pounds each. Made from wood, they were marked with bands of various colours to identify their contents. The vast number of items which McCutcheon and his fellow hunters took on safari is too extensive to list.

However, among other items the porters carried were dozens of cases of food containing sausage, bacon, ox tongue, kippered herrings, baked beans, German prunes, marmalade, tea, coffee, chocolate and Worcestershire sauce. Other cases contained ammunition, clothes, medicines, camera supplies, writing materials, soap, toilet paper and two-dozen bottles of Scotch whisky.

Each night camp was pitched and four large canvas tents were erected for McCutcheon and his friends. After the bwanas had washed away the day's dust in their canvas baths, cocktails were served, the table was laid, another diverse meal was presented and life in the bush took on an altogether comfortable pace.

Nor was it only the gentlemen who enjoyed themselves in the outback.

Prior to setting out to ride from Persia to India, the English Historical Long Rider Ella Sykes made sure that she had procured the services of a Swiss maid to accompany her on the arduous equestrian journey ahead. She also took along crates of china, silver, fine wine and delicious food.

Ella also had the foresight to enlist the services of a Persian, who rode the "luncheon pony" that carried her mid-day meal.

History and Horses

As McCutcheon and Sykes demonstrate, throughout history travellers have had to decide what to pack. In some cases, equestrian travellers had little choice.

For example, pity the poor knight's horse that had to carry an average of 436 pounds (nearly 200 kg.) of armour for himself and his steel-clad rider.

Compare this to the traditions of light-weight riding that originated with Central Asian horsemanship. In contrast to the cumbersome Europeans, Mongol warriors simply wore leather armour on their chest. Not only did this minimize the weight carried by their mounts, it also signified that they had no intention of being shot in the back while retreating.

Riders from lands along the Equestrian Equator were ideally suited to long distance travel as every man carried precisely what he needed but nothing more. The value of this philosophy was confirmed by the efficiency of the Mongol postal system, which routinely passed messages six hundred miles in a day, via hardy horses and tough riders who changed at every post house.

Russia Launches the Long Riders

Because of their historical interaction and geographic proximity, the Russian equestrian culture was heavily influenced by the hard-riding Mongols. Likewise, it is a Russian who is credited with inspiring the modern age of equestrian travel.

This came about at dawn on April 16th, 1889, when a young lieutenant in the Czar's cavalry, Mikhaïl Vassilievitch Asseyev, set off to ride from his garrison in the Ukraine to the newly erected Eiffel Tower in Paris.

"These days", he warned, "when a rider has covered 40 kilometres (25 miles) in a day, we think that's the maximum. If we ride 50 or 70 kilometres (32 or 45 miles), everyone thinks it's an amazing achievement. To cover a hundred kilometres (62.5 miles), the rule-book allows five days: four days' travel (at a walk) and a day of rest. It's insane! A military horse is designed to go to war, and war is no picnic!" Asseyev thundered.

To prove his point, on that early April morning, Asseyev mounted his mare, Diane, and chose another horse at random from the cavalry remount. He then set off for Paris. Thanks to the knowledge gained from Central Asians, Asseyev rode his horses "à la Turcoman." This was a system whereby the rider rode the first horse from dawn till noon; all the while the second horse ran alongside unencumbered. After a brief lunch break, he then shifted his saddle to the second horse, allowing the first mount to run alongside.

What Asseyev and the Turcoman tribesmen knew was that it was the weight, not the distance, that tired out a travelling horse. Hence, a horse could carry a rider and his luggage all morning, but could regain a great deal of his energy by travelling unimpeded during the second part of the day.

Thanks to this efficient method, Asseyev reached Paris after having travelled 2,633 kilometres (1,646 miles) in 33 days. His average had been nearly 80 kilometres (50 miles) a day.

Upon their arrival in the French capital, Asseyev's mares were in such perfect condition that the Society for the Protection of Animals decided to honour their owner. In front of a crowd of four thousand people, the President of the Society for the Protection of Animals (SPA) awarded the young Russian officer a gold medal.

When the Czar read the report on his subject's equestrian journey, he wrote in the margin "Brave young man! A very original journey!" and made him an officer in the Imperial Guard, after which Asseyev was never heard of again.

What was the key to the first modern Long Rider's success?

Determination? Certainly. Tough horses? Absolutely. Luck? Without a doubt.

But underlying it all was this critical fact. Asseyev's tack and baggage together weighed less than 20 kilograms (45 pounds)! It would hardly have been possible to travel lighter.

Killer Kilograms

When the English army invaded Abyssinia in 1867 they took 20,000 pack animals.

When the Czar ordered his troops to invade Central Asia in 1873 a troop of 170 men were equipped with six cast iron pots with lids, seven water vessels, seven pounds of pepper, four pounds of laurel leaves, 100 pounds of tobacco, nine bottles of vinegar, 100 pounds of onions, 10 pounds of horseradish, 200 pounds of salt, 300 fathoms of rope, 7 shovels, 170 wooden teacups, and much more besides. The total estimated weight for the unit was 1,600 pounds. Such a surplus of equipment required one pack horse for every two men.

Long Riders can't count on such an extensive support system.

Though Asseyev made his ride more than a century ago, his journey enshrined an equestrian principle known, understood, and followed by all great Long Riders ever since.

It is not the kilometres that kill your horse, it is the kilograms!

Long Riders with deep knowledge and great experience have known for centuries that the horse's greatest enemy is weight.

The burden which must be put on to the back of the road horse is so enormous that it is absolutely essential that it should be reduced by every possible means and to as great an extent as is practicable. Thus, every possible ounce must be removed from the horse's back.

This was the timeless lesson which the English Long Rider Sir John Ure learned when he rode across the Andes in the 1980s.

"Everything you carry must be for using, be it a knife or an article of clothing," he warned.

The more you lighten the horse's load, the less liable he is to develop a sore back or give way to fatigue.

Disregarding Comfort

Richard Barnes took these lessons to heart before he set out to ride his Cob, Remus, around the entire perimeter of Great Britain.

"What I learned was to chuck out everything extraneous, to leave out every luxury, to get the cooking utensils down to one saucepan and a cup. I posted maps home after I used them. I didn't shave, only had one book and did everything to keep the weight down. I learned to place as much weight forward on the horse's shoulders and to keep any weight behind the saddle as light as possible, to prevent pressure on the horse's kidneys and offset any chafing and friction on the hips."

Lisa Wood followed the same basic rule.

"My experience has been, don't bring it, don't bring it, don't bring it. The safety-mongers would have you bring farrier service and a vet-mobile with you, as well as pounds worth of camping, safety, and first aid gear. On both of my trips (one in 1993 and one in 2001) I brought no pack animal, so I had to pack extremely lightly on my saddle horse. It is incredibly important to lighten the horse's load, and I will make a few points about things I discovered I didn't need, as well as listing essential gear," Lisa explained.

"People will encourage you to bring lots of other stuff. They will give stuff to you as bon-voyage presents. These are people accustomed to stuffing their vehicles with Coleman stoves, hammocks, insulated pads, folding chairs, and other non-essential camping supplies. Even people who go horse camping, but only go for a few days or weeks at a time, do not know what it is like to live on the trail," she continued.

"Not only do you not want the weight on your horse, you don't want the hassle of loading and unloading it, or of digging through it to find something. I admit I did take one packet of glove-warmers with me, and I saved them to put them in the foot of my sleeping bag on a really cold night and was glad to have them. It was a nice treat. But be as firm as you can and say no to as much clutter as possible."

Long Rider Lessons

Learning how to pack your gear is one of the secrets of successful equestrian travel. Regardless of where you ride, the same rules apply. Carry only what is indispensable and distribute the weight equally. Failing either of these, you will fatigue or chafe the horse.

This is not a new concept.

In 440 AD Emperor Theodosius II of Rome issued an edict that limited the weight carried in a cavalryman's saddle bags to 35 pounds. To disobey this law meant the equipment would be confiscated.

By the early twentieth century the possessions of modern cavalry riders had been even more restricted so as to provide the horse with as much relief as possible. The average load was 6 pounds 14¾ ounces in front of the saddle in the pommel bags and 12 pounds 13½ ounces behind the saddle in the saddle bags.

Unlike the standardized cavalry, it is impossible to construct a list of items which will suit the various requirements of people engaged in expeditions of different magnitudes, as various climates, obstacles and dangers will shape the needs of the individual Long Rider. Still, we can consider what previous equestrian travellers have decided to take on their journeys to diverse parts of the world.

Before Harry and Lisa Adshead set off to ride from Wales to Jordan, they decided they wanted to be self sufficient.

"The degree of autonomy that you want has a major influence on the gear that you need. If you don't mind seeking out people every night, you might get away with no tent, stove, pans etc. If you want to get up in the mountains and have some time on your own, you'll need more stuff."

Harry and Lisa learned that the problem lay in learning how not to overload their pack horse and still live comfortably on such a long journey.

"The packhorse's load is a dead-weight and it's on all day," Lisa recalled at the end of their successful trip. "The riding horses get a break when we get off and walk but the only way you can help a packhorse is to make its load as light as possible. A rule of thumb for a dead load is that it shouldn't exceed 80% of the allowable live load, typically taken as 20% of the horse's weight. E.g. for a 500kg horse, the dead weight shouldn't exceed 80kg. Allowing 20kg for grain to give a few day's autonomy and say, 15kg for the pack saddle, pads, harness, girth etc, this leaves a 'baggage allowance' of 45kg – for two people and three horses this is not a lot," Lisa explained.

Though Stan Walchuk rode through the Canadian Rocky Mountains alone, he too sought to be self sufficient. Among the essentials were one change of clothes, a bed roll, rope and a hatchet.

"Things you need right away should be on top," Stan wrote.

Having ridden all over Europe and deep into Russia, few modern European Long Riders have made more journeys than Antoinette Spizzo and Dario Masarotti.

"We use normal English saddles. On the back of the saddle we fix a home-made water-resistant cylindrical bag for the sleeping bag and the tent. In front of the saddle another bag for a woollen blanket and a raincoat for the horse. The saddle-bags also hold clothes, toiletries, a pair of shoes, the topographic maps, a water bottle, some emergency food, medicine, a special tool for emergency horse-shoeing and spare horse-shoes. We also carry a good water resistant map holder, two nose bags for oats and a folding canvas bucket."

When Howard Wooldridge rode "ocean to ocean" across the United States, he kept the weight of his personal possessions in his pommel and saddle bags down to 7.75 kilos (17 pounds). His list of equipment and possessions included such essentials as an extra pair of socks, a light-weight sleeping bag and a one-person tent,

Tough and Light

Equestrian travel is like mountain climbing, in that we don't use a lot of equipment but our lives depend on what we choose.

Renowned explorer Colonel John Blashford-Snell realized that when he issued this admonition.

"Too many people imagine that safety is synonymous with good equipment. You cannot really buy safety. It is a state of mind, in which every danger is sensed and evaluated. It is a sense which when awakened, seldom becomes dormant."

It is hard to describe the rigours encountered during an equestrian journey. This is no day-ride you're on. Horse sweat, dirt, unrelenting friction from daily movement and constant exposure to the sun and elements will soon dirty, fade and then break down all but the very toughest of equipment.

The equipment you take – saddle, pads, pack saddle, panniers, bridles, halters, bits and bridles, feed bags, lead ropes – everything must be chosen with the idea that as hard as you can possibly imagine the rigours of the trip will be, it will turn out to be harder still. It is a safe rule to have everything three times as durable as you think necessary.

When you're trying to cover miles, not influence a show ring judge, your goal should always be function not beauty. That is why whatever you decide to pack, it must be light-weight and extremely tough. It is also a good idea to use bright colours, so as to make it easier not to forget anything when you're packing in the dim morning light.

Buy the Best

Every expedition has a budget but you must never succumb to the temptation to purchase second-rate equipment. Your horse's welfare always takes precedence over your bank book.

These aren't rental cars you're riding. You can't take them back and turn them in for a newer model. Money saved could mean you end up with horses with sore backs and festering withers.

But even if we agree that every item has to be of the best quality, you must be prepared for breakage and loss. For example, during his three-year journey Tim Cope had fifteen pairs of hobbles, six halters, five lead ropes, six tethering ropes, two tents, three torches and two petrol stoves worn out, lost or stolen.

Cultural Problems

One question which plagues Long Riders planning to ride in a foreign country: take your own gear or buy locally?

To find the answer you must investigate the options, some of which are decidedly unpleasant. What ever you do, don't take anyone's word that you can arrive in a distant country and find quality, affordable equestrian equipment. Long Riders have learned to their dismay that what passes as "good" gear locally would be considered horse-killing junk back home.

Keith Clark made this alarming discovery when he set off to ride through Argentina.

"I had always thought that the gaucho saddle, known as the *recado*, would be really good. It looked comfortable for the rider, so I assumed it would be kind to the horse as well. But since then I have seen horses with open sores caused by the *recado* that went from their withers down the length of their spine. Even though these wounds went deep into their backs, the poor buggers were still being ridden. I'm really glad I brought my western saddle with me," Keith reported.

Justine Oliver learned the same thing held true across the Andes in Chile.

"We got our saddles in Chile, as they were cheaper. But our poor horses had back problems during the entire journey."

Nor is this problem restricted to Latin America, as Long Riders in Mongolia have encountered the same difficulty.

Austrian Long Rider Evelyn Landerer recalled, "Mongolians change their riding horses every two weeks, so it doesn't matter if the "one-size-fits-all" saddle doesn't fit the horse perfectly. The bridle and halter are usually made of dried but unprocessed leather that doesn't last more than a year or two."

Other travellers have reported that it is difficult to obtain proper riding saddles and grooming equipment in West Africa.

But surely the Long Rider with one of the most harrowing saddle stories is Lisa Wood, as she was unlucky enough to encounter horrific equestrian equipment on both sides of the globe. This seasoned equestrian traveller had made two extensive journeys in the United States prior to her overseas ventures.

Luckily, thanks to her wealth of personal experience, Lisa had decided to use a military saddle instead of the native saddles normally employed in Tibet. Though this decision spared her horse from injury, she noted how Tibetan saddles had inflicted "ghastly" wounds on the other animals she encountered.

"The other horses all suffered huge open wounds caused by the terrible Tibetan saddles and inadequate pads."

Lisa likewise noted how the Tibetans routinely used "rusty, cruel snaffle bits" and secured their horses together at night with "steel shackles."

Yet surely what ranks in Long Rider history as the most incredible equipment story occurred on the Galapagos Islands. Here again, coming from a country which has a rich equestrian culture, Lisa Wood was unprepared for what was on offer in these remote islands off the coast of Ecuador.

While hiking to the top of a volcano, Lisa asked a local resident if she could rent his horse and ride it up the long trail. After agreeing to a small fee, he brought forth a mare. The stunned traveller discovered that the "saddle" was made from old inner tubes stretched over pieces of scrap metal. This amazing contraption was kept in place by pieces of rubber inner tube acting as a crude girth.

Badly fitting riding and pack saddles will injure your horses and ruin your journey, so ensure that you make the right choice in advance. Even if you have to pay custom duty to import your equipment, relying on poorly made local gear can be a painful experience for both you and your animals.

Sponsors

No matter where you ride, some things never change. Jeremy James recognized one such parable when he wrote, "The old maxim still holds true. What you always need is half the kit and twice the money."

That is apparently not a problem in the United Arab Emirates, where the press reports that horse owners in that country spend an average of $32,000 a year on equestrian gear and equine medicine.

Because of tight finances, some people attempt to solve this financial dilemma by obtaining free equipment from commercial sponsors. There are two problems with seeking such sponsorship: a loss of dignity and a loss of independence.

Lisa Adshead declined to follow this route. She recalled how, "Nobody gave us anything because we didn't write any begging letters asking for anything for free."

Yet when your budget is tight it seems tempting to badger potential sponsors to donate equipment. One British woman enticed several companies to donate expensive equipment in support of her "one girl, one pony, one dream" journey. The result was that the trip was a cloak for incompetence which ended in abrupt failure for all concerned.

Mixing money and adventure is always a dangerous combination, as complications arise at once. Take care before you enter into a marriage of convenience that ends in tears.

Summary

The world has changed a great deal since the Victorian poet, William Barnes, dubbed the recently-invented bicycle a "wheelsaddle."

Weight is still the greatest enemy of the road horse.

That is what the Swiss Long Rider Jessica Bigler discovered.

"After a month and a half on the trail, I took a lot of things out of my saddle bags because by then I knew that a Long Rider doesn't need much to be happy. One learns by experience that of all the stuff so carefully made ready, one quarter will be abandoned at the start and half be thrown away upon the march, for the happy Long Rider must know what to discard."

John McCutcheron travelled in relative comfort when he went to East Africa on safari to "gallop" lions

When English Long Rider Ella Sykes made her way from Persia to India she was accompanied by her faithful "luncheon pony."

In stark contrast, the first modern Long Rider, Mikhaïl Asseyev, rode his horses with a minimum of equipment from the Ukraine to Paris by using the "à la Turcoman" method.

A good example of local equestrian gear; this South American saddle consists of a rope, a skin, an old bag and some scraps of blanket.

Chapter 32
Riding Saddles

Nothing causes more pain to horses, and cancels more trips, than the riding saddle. Despite its fundamental significance, the purpose and mechanics of this essential item are all too often misunderstood. Therefore, before setting off, you need to be sure that what you place on your horse's back isn't going to undermine your chances of geographic success.

The Trouble with Bareback

To begin with, why even bother with a saddle? The answer lies back in the roots of riding.

Unlike the old riddle of which came first, the chicken or the egg, we know that man began riding before he invented the saddle. But it didn't take long for early horse-humans to realize that there were distinct disadvantages to sitting on a horse bareback.

Mounting without stirrups isn't easy. Once you're on the horse, staying there without a saddle is a risky proposition. Nor should we neglect to mention the often considerable pain caused to the human posterior when it is forced to sit on a horse's bony spine for long hours. Plus, riding bareback encourages the horse to sweat. The sweat stings and irritates human skin, which is likely to be chafed from the animal's constant movement. Such chafing results in painful open wounds on the human's legs and posterior. Plus the pungent smell of horse sweat permeates clothing.

Because our ancestors rode to stay alive, it is not surprising to learn that horse-humans along the Equestrian Equator invented pants to protect their legs and saddles to guard the horse's back. Yet there was another problem associated with riding bareback.

When a bareback rider sits on a horse, the majority of the human's weight bears directly down on a small space on either side of the equine spine. This places all of the human's considerable weight, many pounds per square inch, on a small portion of the horse's back. That pressure can damage sensitive tissue, bruise the muscles, injure the spine and harm the horse's kidneys.

As anyone would rather carry two buckets of water than one, because the load is halved by being properly distributed, so will the horse prefer a heavy load distributed over the whole rigid area of the ribs to a light load concentrated on a few square inches. Early horse humans realized that to reduce equine injuries the rider's weight needed to be spread over the maximum number of square inches on the horse's back.

Thus saddles not only provided a secure seat, they also distributed the rider's weight over a larger portion of the horse's body. This was a critically important development for man and horse.

In terms of equestrian travel, never ride your horse any great distance bareback. By not placing a saddle on your horse's back, you place every bit of your weight on two pin-pointed spots on his back. Even if your horse does not receive an external sore on his back, you are doing him no favours by placing your considerable weight near his kidneys and atop his spine.

Don't forget, a horseman's grave is always open.

So don't cut your chances of survival down by jettisoning the one piece of equipment that will assist your horse and may save your life.

Consequently, if a Long Rider needs a saddle, where does he start to look for answers? When dealing with the saddle, the place to begin is the horse's back.

Nature's Intention

If Nature had intended horses to carry humans it would have provided the animal with some form of protection. Not only do horses lack a turtle's protective shell, the construction of their back lends itself to injury and invites trouble.

To make matters worse, saddle sores are often caused by ignorance and indifference. One of the reasons saddles injure horses is because too many people fail to realize the extraordinary damage which a saddle may inflict in a very short time.

Thus the first step to offsetting injury is by possessing a basic knowledge of the horse's anatomy.

The Spine

We cannot consider how the horse carries weight without understanding the movement of the spine. The spine is composed of a series of linking bones. While their movement is limited, these sensitive bones are of the utmost importance. They arch from the neck and fall towards the hind quarters.

The object of this arched construction is to secure strength. Yet it is man's spine, not that of the horse, which is essentially designed to carry weight. Some of the individual links in a man's spine are actually larger than those of the horse. Because of this, man's vertical spine is far stronger than the horse's horizontal spine.

The upper part of the backbone is the part of the spine which can be examined and felt. Because they were not designed to bear man's weight, they form the seat of all the trouble which may be found in a bad or sore back. When these bones are exposed to pressure, even be it ever so slight, the parts become inflamed.

The Loins

Many people mistake the back and the loins. The back bones extend from the last bone on the neck to the last rib; the loins lie between the last rib and the hind quarters. The loins were never intended to support weight and no saddle should ever rest upon them.

The Forelimbs

People might assume that the forelimbs, which carry 60-65% of the horse's weight, are attached to the skeletal spine. They are not. Unlike humans, the horse has no collar bone for added structural stability, so the forelegs are not fitted to his body by means of a joint. They are attached by large masses of muscles. The body is therefore slung between the forelegs, and in this respect differs considerably from the hind legs, which are secured to the body by a large cup and ball joint.

When the foreleg moves the shoulder blade is put into motion. Attention must be paid to the fact that when the shoulder blade is moving forwards and backwards, no part of the saddle should ever press upon it or interfere with its movements; otherwise the length and safety of the horse's stride will be affected.

Skin and Muscle

The sensitive skin covers a large slab of muscle which runs the entire length of the horse's back; from the point of fitting the saddle, this is the most important muscle of the body. These muscles act as a buffer to the bones beneath and so prevent injury.

When horses are worked hard during travel, one of the first places to show muscle waste is the back. The muscles, which were previously convex, now appear to become concave. The whole shape of the back is altered. It is this meta-morphosis of the back which renders all previous saddle fittings useless, for the impoverished back is as different from the well-nourished one as can be possible; it is as though we compared the skeleton to the living subject.

Bone and Hair

The shape of a horse's back depends entirely on the shape of the bones which compose it. When the bones are short, the back tends towards flatness. When long, the withers are high and the ridge of the back prominent. No horse with high lean withers should be used for travel. Plus long backs are, as a rule, weaker and more prone to damage than a short back, which is stronger.

Likewise the shape of the ribs affects whether the saddle will stay in place. It the ribs are unduly curved, it will be impossible for the girth to be properly tightened and the saddle will slip forward towards the neck.

Spines and Saddles

The pressure of the saddle is never quite the same at any two points over the back. So long as there is a good deep bed of muscle the risk of injury is decreased. But as the muscle becomes reduced in bulk the saddle is brought day by day nearer to the skeleton.

Continuous pressure will kill anything. Running water, for example, will eventually wear away the hardest stone. Likewise the pressure caused by the unyielding saddle against the rigid bone soon destroys the skin and begins to wear a hole in the horse's back.

Injuries to the back tend to get worse instead of better, so curing a saddle sore cannot be hurried. This is why it is imperative that every precaution be taken so as to ensure that no part of the saddle rests directly on any of the hard structures of the back, be it the spine or ribs. It must only rest on those parts of the body well covered with muscle.

This also explains why the most perfectly conceived saddle can cause sore backs if worn for days, or even hours, with no relief from pressure. Armed with this basic knowledge regarding the horse's sensitive back, let us consider the saddle.

An Understated Masterpiece

Unlike automobiles, which are subject to the artificial dictates of corporate designers, the basic concept of the saddle has not altered for more than a thousand years. This is because the primary needs of today's horse and rider are no different than that of their ancestors.

From a human perspective, the saddle has two main purposes. First, it provides the rider with a secure seat which allows him to offset the pull of gravity and move in rhythm with the enhanced speed provided by his mount.

Furthermore, the saddle also provides the rider with stirrups. These two platforms enable him to remain in balance over the horse's centre of gravity, all the while engaging in any number of activities, including shooting a bow, chasing a cow, escaping from enemies, jumping over obstacles, racing at great speed or travelling great distances.

Though first developed and used in the East in about 400 A.D., the concept and benefits of using stirrups migrated westwards into Europe. As a result in 580 A.D. the Roman Emperor Maurice Tiberius made stirrups mandatory for his cavalry.

Centuries have passed, but when an emergency occurs the combination of the saddle's security and the stirrups' balance allows the Long Rider to respond instantly to any perceived threat. Thus, from a human perspective the saddle is the command centre which prevents a fragile rider from tumbling to the ground and coming to immediate harm.

Equally importantly, the saddle provides two vital services to the horse as well.

Provided he sits in the middle of the saddle, it evenly spreads the rider's weight over as large an area of the horse's back as possible. That is a tremendous physical benefit to the horse, which greatly reduces the likelihood of intense injury to the horse's spine. Likewise, the saddle allows the human to establish one of the sensitive methods by which he can commune with the horse.

The saddle is, therefore, far more than a mere lump of leather. It is one of mankind's remarkable achievements, in that it encourages the meeting of two species' bodies, hearts and minds. Communication between horse and human begins where the saddle starts. It is the bridge upon which rests the safety of you and your mount.

A Common Theme

Despite the many variations mankind has devised, classic saddles share certain traits, all of which were designed to protect the horse and stabilize the rider.

The saddle has two arches, one in the front and one behind the rider. The front arch forms the pommel, the rear the cantle. Either may be high or low, depending on the culture and need of the rider. Owing to the shape of the horse's body, the strain on the front arch is greater than that on the rear.

Both front and back arch rest upon and are secured to two bars placed parallel to each other. The arches ensure the spine is not pressed upon. The bars distribute the rider's weight along the horse's back.

Regardless if we are speaking of a Cossack or a cowboy saddle, one from the Mongolian steppes or Australia's Outback, the arch and bar are the twin themes upon which all great saddles are made. Every variation is designed to distribute the pressure created by the rider's weight evenly over the surface of the side bars.

Basic Considerations

Mahatma Gandhi said, "The greatness of a nation and its moral progress can be judged by the way its animals are treated."

So let us begin our investigation with the understanding that the safety of the horse and rider are directly connected to the saddle. That means it cannot be too well made.

Yet it would be foolish not to admit that our individual personality must also be taken into account when choosing a saddle. Nor can we dismiss the notion of national pride and equestrian tradition, both of which have validity in our considerations.

What we must not do is to allow romantic notions or cultural allegiance to overrule mechanics and safety. Regardless of what our forefathers rode, there may well be far better and safer options available to a modern Long Rider.

Weight of the Saddle

Let us begin by realizing that when choosing a saddle for a journey, the first thing to consider is the overall weight.

A saddle used in Thoroughbred racing weighs four pounds, while a traditional double-rigged, square skirted, high-backed Montana cowboy saddle might weigh forty pounds. There is a vast array of saddles, all with differing weights, in between these two extremes.

Long Riders find themselves in a dilemma when the topic of saddle weight is raised. A light saddle may offer too small a weight-bearing surface, which will encourage saddle sores. On the other hand, you must avoid an excessively heavy saddle.

You cannot forget that the strength of the saddle is a vital component of success. Thus, the more weight carried on the saddle, the stronger it has to be. Yet a stronger saddle is a heavier one.

The answer is that the saddle must be large enough to carry the Long Rider's equipment, strong enough to withstand the rigours of the journey and light enough to do the work.

The Saddle Tree

One of the heaviest components of the saddle is its tree.

Regardless of whether it is made from wood, metal, rawhide, fibreglass, or any combination of these materials, the tree is the foundation upon which every saddle is constructed. It distributes the rider's weight and reduces the chances of equine injury.

Depending on the needs of the rider, the tree may have a high pommel and cantle, or it may be little more than two sidebars, with a low arch in the front and back. These factors are reliant upon the activity to which the horse will be used.

That part of the side bar projecting beyond the front of the saddle is termed a burr. The projecting rear portion of the side bars is known as the fan.

The saddle tree must be long enough to distribute the rider's weight over the horse's back and to protect the loins from pressure created by the saddle bags. The heavier the rider and load, the more important is this weight distribution.

The front and back arches of the saddle tree are also of keen interest, as if they are too tight they will pinch and injure the horse.

Distribution of Weight

The greatest journeys have been made on a variety of weight-distributing saddles. Though various cultures created different saddles, these early saddle-makers all realized that for a saddle to work it had to adhere to basic principles. It needed to be as simple as possible, as complicated gear may go wrong in a sudden emergency. It had to be built for weight distribution, covering the largest possible bearing surface over the horse's eighth to sixteenth ribs. It needed a high arch which will allow a free channel of air to flow along and cool the spine. A rough leather seat gave a strong grip.

Such saddles have a large bearing surface which disperse the rider's weight over a large portion of the horse's back and are better for travel than the English pattern, which concentrates the burden over a smaller surface.

The problems and principles which inspired the creation of these saddles have not disappeared. If anything, modern riders face new dilemmas unknown to our ancestors.

At the conclusion of the cavalry age, it was common for mounted units to protect their horses by setting a maximum weight limit on the riders. For example, the German cavalry would not allow a rider to weigh more than 165 pounds (75 kg). The horses used to carry the cavalrymen were well conditioned, big boned, athletic animals capable of covering great distances.

Nowadays many modern horses are bred for looks, not long hours of riding. Their bone structure is lighter, and their bodies more delicate, than their predecessors'. Ironically, while horses grew weaker, humans grew heavier. There is a rule of thumb which states that a horse should not be asked to carry more than a fifth of his own weight. Yet with obesity a global concern, weak horses are being asked to carry corpulent riders.

Thus, a weight-bearing saddle is needed to protect the horse and assist the rider.

Load-Bearing Surface

Another critically important aspect is the saddle's load-bearing surface.

More than one and a half pounds per square inch is too much pressure to place on the tissues and capillaries of a horse's back. Seventy percent of the rider's weight bears down onto the horse's withers. Thus it is a fundamental mistake to reduce the weight of the saddle if you compromise the surface that carries the rider's weight.

Nor can a thick saddle pad alone negate pressure points. This problem is compounded when the horse loses weight while travelling, at which point pressure points may become festering withers. To offset the intense pressure caused by the rider's weight, the saddle must have a large load-bearing surface.

The correct load-bearing surface along either side of an average horse's back is about 22 inches (56 cm). A properly constructed saddle will ensure that the more of this area that is covered by the side bars, the less pressure there will be on any one part of the back. Cavalry, Cossack and cowboy saddles take advantage of this fact and have bars averaging between 20 and 22 inches long. However, the average English saddle can fall short in this regard, as it is not normally designed to carry equipment.

Fitting the Saddle

If properly used, a saddle can grant an immense sense of security in all critical situations. Yet there can be few more effective implements of torture than an ill-made and badly-fitted saddle.

While it is true to say that it is more difficult to find the right horse than it is to find the right saddle, many trips fail because of the overlooked fitting of the saddle. Unless a saddle is fitted with great care, a sore back will surely result from the weight of the rider bearing down on the delicate skin, causing a pressure point and harming the animal's back.

Trials have shown that only 15% of saddles in use are correctly fitted to the horse. As this evidence demonstrates, saddles are like shoes. One size does not fit all.

That is why English saddles were traditionally created for one specific horse. Each year an expert saddler would carefully examine the horse's back and then rearrange the stuffing under the saddle to ensure a perfect fit. Though times have changed, the problem remains. Do we purchase a saddle for the horse or a horse for a saddle?

The answer is never easy, but we can take comfort in knowing that when attempting to determine if a saddle fits, there are six timeless rules which should never be forgotten.

1 – The withers must not be pinched nor pressed upon.
2 – The spine must have no pressure forced upon it.

3 – The shoulder blades must have free and unrestricted movement.

4 – The loins are not intended to carry weight.

5 – The rider's weight must be placed upon the ribs through the muscles covering them.

6 – The weight must be evenly distributed over a surface which extends from the shoulders to the last rib.

We cannot determine if the saddle fits properly by merely placing it on the horse's back, as it may appear to do no harm when empty but become dangerous when the rider's weight is applied. Therefore ask a friend to mount your saddle while you carry out a careful inspection.

The following are the chief points of importance in checking the fit of the saddle.

To begin, make sure the saddle is sitting as evenly as possible in the middle of the horse's back. It must not dip either in front or back.

The front arch should be resting above the hollow behind the shoulder. Because the majority of the rider's weight is pressed down onto this front arch, you must determine that the horse's withers are free from pressure and not being pinched. Adding to the problem is the fact that a narrow gullet at the front of the saddle compresses and damages the withers. For these reasons, the saddle must afford at least two inches of clearance above the withers when the rider is in the saddle. This is critically important as later, when the horse loses weight while travelling, the front arch of the saddle will drop even lower on the animal's withers. The front arch of the saddle must be wide enough to admit your hand on either side of the withers, wide enough not to pinch the withers and high enough not to press on them.

The seat may also be a cause for concern, as when the rider's weight comes down directly onto the horse's spine an injury is likely to occur. The heavier the rider, the greater the damage inflicted. Confirm that there is no pressure on the horse's spine and there is no contact with any part of the bone. When placed on the horse's back you should be able to see daylight straight through from end to end when the saddle is girthed up. To ensure this, the saddle should rest on the broad muscle on each side of the backbone.

Next, make sure the side bars bear evenly on both sides of the back, so as to ensure that the weight is equal throughout their entire length and width. To do this, the sidebars should lie flat on the horse's ribs.

Another potential problem occurs when the sidebars are placed too close together, as if they are not kept sufficiently apart they will pinch the withers. As the withers are the most frequent place of injury, this is a serious concern.

The saddle should be placed on the animal's back so that the front ends of the saddle bars, the burrs, are approximately three inches behind the shoulder blades. A horse with thick low withers is particularly liable to injury from the burr. Yet when fat begins to melt away from hard travel, there is nothing to keep the burr from pressing onto the shoulder blades.

If placed too far forward, the saddle will interfere with the action of the muscles. Cinch (girth) galls may also result if the saddle is misplaced. Placing the saddle too far forward will also interfere with the movement of the shoulder blades. Check that the shoulder blades are under no pressure and have free and unimpeded movement. This is done by placing your hand under the saddle pad to test the play of the shoulder. If the saddle is pressing down on the shoulder blades, it will be difficult to slide your hand on top of the shoulder blade.

Assuming you can place your hand on the shoulder blade, have someone lift the horse's foreleg to its full extent. This should be possible without pinching the fingers of your hand behind the shoulder blade and side bar. If your fingers are pinched the shoulder blade will also be pinched, and the saddle must be raised by placing an extra fold of the saddle pad under it. Be sure to test both shoulder blades.

Unless care is taken, the burr can prove to be a serious obstacle to the horse's shoulder blades, as it is essential that they be able to move forward and backward. Even worse is when the shoulder blades are encased in a straightjacket caused by a combination of pressure from the burrs, the girth and the rider's weight.

The saddle must not be so long as to press on the loins. Make sure the fans at the end of the sidebars curve upwards or they may dig into the loins and cause a serious injury.

Finally, check the girth, which should be placed about four inches behind the point of the elbow. It should be sufficiently tight to keep the saddle in its place and no tighter. It should be tightened gradually, and not with violence, care being taken that the skin is not wrinkled. When buckled, it should be loose enough to allow you to slide your fingers in between the horse's skin and the girth.

It is critically important that prior to your departure, you make every attempt to ensure that your riding saddle fits your road horse. However, it must never be forgotten that no matter how much care we take in originally fitting the riding saddle, such fitting is only applicable to the condition the horse is in at the time. This is especially important when travelling, which requires that the saddle must be inspected as regularly as the horse's hooves.

Comfort

As the various tests demonstrate, it is critically important that the saddle not harm the horse. Likewise, the saddle must not only provide you with a sense of security, it must also be comfortable enough to allow you to ride all day long through various types of obstacles.

Because of its significance, do not hurry to purchase a saddle. Sit in various sizes and styles to determine what suits and fits you. The seat of a saddle varies in length from 13 to 18 inches (33-43 cm) and a common mistake is to purchase a saddle which is too large.

Regardless of what type of saddle you choose, make sure that you are able to stand in the stirrups and just clear the seat. When the stirrups are properly adjusted, your knees should be slightly bent. However you should still be able to see the tip of your boots while sitting in the saddle.

Potential Problems

The problem with purchasing a saddle prior to your departure is that it is very unwise to begin a journey with a new or untested saddle. Remember, a saddle can inflict an agonizing injury without drawing blood. If you do not carefully test your saddle well in advance, you run the risk of ruining your horse.

Additionally, horses that are in soft condition prior to their departure will be more prone to saddle sores and injury. Therefore, even though you will have worked to get your road horse into shape, it is still a good idea to begin your journey slowly, so as to allow the horse's back to harden and become accustomed to the daily exertion and pressure from the saddle.

The first thing to learn is that the position of an injury on the back is never a mistake. It is the result of a definite cause. The knowledge that in nearly every case of injury the cause can be clearly determined is valuable information, but only if we remove the cause.

When considering how saddles injure horses, we must realize that there is no part of the saddle which is not capable of producing an injury, although it is certain that some parts produce it more frequently.

Every injury is brought about by friction and pressure, or a combination of the two. The former damages the horse's body by rubbing, while the latter partly or entirely cuts off the blood supply.

To offset damage caused by friction, any equipment, gear or bags attached to the saddle should move as little as possible.

Regardless of what is carried behind the saddle it should be concave towards the spine in order that nothing touches it. A rear load that is clear of the spine when the horse has good muscle may end up resting on the backbone when he loses flesh.

There is no one perfect type of saddle, and there are too many variations to name them all. So we will concentrate on examining those which have been used successfully. As we shall see, there is a wide range of different types of saddles which might suit a Long Rider's purpose. The choice will depend on a variety of factors.

English Saddles

The term "English saddle" refers to a type of light saddle that has a narrow gullet and relatively small sidebars, not one specifically created in Great Britain. These saddles were originally carefully fashioned and individually fitted to the high-priced equine athletes used in fox hunting.

The English saddle has several drawbacks in terms of equestrian travel.

Unlike range saddles, the English saddle lacks either the raised pommel or high cantle which was designed to keep the cowboy in his seat at all times, lest he lose his life in a stampede. In stark contrast, fox hunting required the riders to jump high hedges at a gallop. Thus, in case of accident the small, light-weight English saddle was designed to throw the rider clear of a falling horse.

Being tossed from the saddle is not an advisable tactic for an equestrian traveller. The cantle provides long distance support for the rider's lower back and kidneys, while the pommel gives him additional support in case of a bucking horse or accident. The English saddle lacks both, provides little assistance during an emergency and requires a skilled rider to keep his seat.

Of equal importance in terms of the horse's safety, and again unlike work saddles used by cowboys, gauchos and Cossacks, the English saddle does not have a large weight-bearing surface. Nor does its small saddle tree spread the rider's weight over the maximum number of inches available along the horse's back. Because many modern English saddles further reduce their overall weight by severely constricting the size of the sidebars, this prohibits the load from being properly carried. Thus, the sidebars may not cover enough of the horse's body to reduce the pounds per square inch for proper support during an extended journey.

Also of importance, the English saddle was not traditionally designed to carry extra weight or equipment. The burrs at the front of the saddle tree and the fans at the back of the English saddle lack the dee rings to which saddle and pommel bags can be fastened.

Another point to consider, in terms of long-term comfort, is that English saddles use stirrup leathers that may pinch the rider's legs. A western style saddle has leather fenders which prohibit this from occurring.

This isn't to say that English style saddles have not been successfully used on many equestrian journeys. They have. But only if they were either reworked or designed to carry saddle bags. Even then, they provide little in the way of rider security and may compromise the horse's health if the saddle tree is too small.

Australian Saddles

The Australian stock saddle took the basic design of an English saddle and then incorporated many of the best concepts of the western saddle onto it. The result was a saddle which demonstrates the best of both parents.

Like the English saddle, the Australian offspring is fairly light weight. Yet like the cowboy saddle, the Australian has enlarged the bearing surface as much as possible so as to distribute the rider's weight.

The Australian drover, like the American cowboy, was also involved in long distance cattle drives which required him to ride across great stretches of dangerous ground. The greatest of these was Nat Buchanan, who was in charge of moving 20,000 cattle 3,200 kilometres.

In order not to lose his seat during an emergency, the Australians added two bucking rolls to the front of their saddles. These padded additions provided the rider with a greater sense of security.

Finally, because they were living from the backs of their horses, the drovers ensured that strong dee rings were added to the saddle tree, so as to enable them to carry their "swag."

This compromise of cultures produced one of the world's best all-around work saddles. Comfortable and practical, it spreads the rider's weight, protects the horse's back and carries both their gear.

Not surprisingly, when Australian Long Rider Tim Cope set off to ride from Mongolia to Hungary, he chose to use one of these excellent saddles. Though it needed to be repaired because of the difficulties of that rugged journey, Tim reported that it did an excellent job.

Cavalry Saddles

As we witness the dawning of the 21st century, we need to realize that the great collective wisdom represented by the world's former cavalrymen is now passing away and will soon be nothing but a memory. Whereas there is a concerted effort to rescue endangered breeds from extinction, few people appreciate the fact that the men who once rode into war atop their horses will soon cease to exist.

Sadly, the knowledge which they possessed regarding saddles, horse care, equestrian travel, etc., will most likely be lost without anyone having taken notice. Sergeant Robert Seney was one such example.

Seney was a member of the US cavalry when the Second World War broke out. He spent the early part of the war helping to maintain a mounted guard along the Mexican border. Upon his retirement from the armed services the former horse soldier worked in Olympic National Park as a professional packer.

In 1976 the ex-cavalryman set out to explore his homeland aboard his horse, Trooper. During their many subsequent adventures Seney and Trooper made six journeys between 1967 and 1980. Seney's combined travels through all 48 states exceeded 38,500 kilometres (24,000 miles) in the saddle.

With the modern world's fascination fixated upon machinery, it is difficult to understand how efficient the cavalry once was. Horse care was a topic well understood in days gone by, as seen by the fact that Genghis Khan issued strict orders regarding the humane treatment of horses. His cavalrymen faced severe punishment if their equipment failed to pass regular inspections.

Such devotion to equestrian duty resulted in the Mongol cavalry being able to cover immense distances. In 1221, for example, 30,000 Mongol cavalrymen rode 130 miles in two days without stopping for food or rest.

As can be imagined, because their lives depended upon the saddles beneath them, the world's cavalry devoted a tremendous amount of time to studying and perfecting the riding saddle. The history of cavalry saddles is too complex a subject to fully investigate here. However, the principal discoveries are still of great significance to Long Riders.

Because they lived on the grassy plains situated at the edge of Europe, the Hungarians found themselves on the cusp of two equestrian cultures, the fast riding horsemen of Central Asia to the East and the more ponderous Europeans to the West. The saddle developed by the Hungarian hussars reflected the necessity of staying alive along this militarized frontier. It made use of two sidebars, a sloping arch in front and back, and a suspended seat. When a sheepskin was placed on top, the result was an extremely lightweight saddle which was quickly adapted by European cavalries further west.

Germany, Sweden, Austria, France, Prussia, England and Switzerland were just some of the countries whose cavalries opted to use a light-weight, weight-bearing saddle. Though the military saddles of these countries undertook further changes, it was thanks to the Hungarian inspiration which saw the development of some of the world's finest serving saddles, many of which went on to be used to make extraordinary journeys both past and present.

The British Universal Pattern saddle was one such example. It featured wide steel arches at the front and back, which allowed the horse plenty of movement, and had large sidebars to disperse the rider's weight. Sturdy but lightweight, comfortable for both horse and rider, it was easy to repair in the field. After having served the mounted forces of Britain, Canada, South Africa, Australia and New Zealand for many decades, this rugged survivor last saw service in 1978 during the Rhodesian civil war.

Because of this residual English influence, when I set off to ride alone across northern Pakistan I discovered that the Pakistani military were still using British Universal Pattern saddles. My UP saddle did an excellent job during the subsequent journey and caused no injuries to my mare, Shavon. Likewise, the Italian Long Rider Simone Carmignani used a British UP cavalry saddle to explore Pakistan's Karakoram mountain range.

Another cavalry saddle which made a successful transition into equestrian travel was the one designed by the Germans. This saddle has an excellent weight-bearing surface and is designed to carry the essential equipment for horse and rider. Extremely well made, this type of saddle was used by a young German lieutenant, Erich von Salzmann, who rode 6,000 kilometres (3,700 miles) from Tientsin, China to Tashkent, Uzbekistan in 1903. He made this remarkable ride, including crossing the Gobi Desert, in only 173 days.

When John Egenes rode across the United States in 1974 he also chose a German cavalry saddle. "It was the only one that would do. It was lighter than a Western saddle and fit my horse better than any other kind."

Yet the military saddle which carries the most miles, and thereby provides the greatest evidence, is the Swiss cavalry saddle owned by legendary Swiss Long Rider, Captain Otto Schwarz.

Over the course of sixty years, Otto rode 48,000 kilometres (30,000 miles) on five continents, making him the most well-travelled Long Rider of the 20th century. Otto rode in a host of places including Japan, Europe, Africa, North and South America. During these travels he had occasion to ride in western, English, Mexican and Moroccan saddles.

However, it was his Swiss cavalry saddle which garnered the most miles. Made in 1916, the saddle originally saw service during the First World War. When Otto was ordered to lead cavalry patrols through the Swiss Alps during the Second World War, the veteran saddle was again pressed into service. After the conclusion of those global conflicts, Otto put the still-strong saddle to work as a superior Long Rider saddle.

Otto's saddle is a dragoon's saddle, not the more light-weight officer's saddle. The padded sidebars spread the weight of the rider over a wide area on the horse's back. The seat is comfortable and places the rider directly over the horse's centre of gravity. To ensure that the cavalryman remained independent, the saddle is equipped with special fittings which allow front and rear bags to be securely attached. Like one of the famous Swiss watches, at nearly one hundred years old Otto's dragoon saddle was built to withstand the ravages of time.

As these examples prove, traditional cavalry saddles can be very good for the horse and excellent for Long Riders, as they are immensely strong and practically everlasting.

The problem is that they are no longer being made, there are very few originals still available and the survivors may have not withstood the test of time. Before you buy a cavalry saddle inspect it carefully. Look for cracks, splits or signs of distortion in the wooden sidebars. Examine the stitching in the leather, the girth straps and the rigging very carefully, looking for signs of rot or excessive wear.

One final aspect associated with cavalry saddles is their hard seat. In today's world, where it is common place to see various types of soft saddle covers, all designed to protect soft posteriors, it is often forgotten that the less padding there is between you and the horse, the nearer you are to him, and the better you can feel and control him.

Like any subject, there are exceptions to the rule about cavalry saddles too. In this case one of the most controversial military saddles came from the United States.

McClellan Saddles

Equestrian travellers have used the American military saddle with various results. Some, like German Long Rider Esther Stein who rode across Africa with it, experienced no problems. Others, most notably the English Long Rider J. Smeaton Chase, encountered terrible problems because of the McClellan. As we will see, the results often depend largely on the build of the individual horse, not on the efficiency of this saddle.

Captain George McClellan designed the saddle after touring Europe as part of a military commission charged with studying the latest developments in cavalry equipment. During his year-long tour, McClellan had the opportunity to interview many European cavalry officers, study various cavalry manuals and observe several battles of the Crimean War. Following his return in 1855, it took the American Ordinance Department four years to test and adopt the proposed McClellan saddle.

According to McClellan, he claimed his new design was based upon the Hungarian saddle.

Perhaps he got his geography mixed up?

In point of fact, the Hungarian hussar saddle has a suspended seat, whereas the saddle McClellan designed relied upon the exposed seat preferred by nearby Mexican vaqueros. As saddle development was still in its infancy in the United States, neither the traditional cowboy nor his legendary saddle had yet to appear. The Spanish influence on American equestrian events was already notable. Thus, while it is well known that the cowboy saddle had Spanish roots, few Americans realize the origin of their cavalry saddle also lay south of the border.

Regardless of its murky geographic origins, the McClellan saddle was duly confirmed for a number of reasons. Thanks to its simple construction, it was inexpensive to make, proved light weight for the horse, and thanks to its high pommel and cantle, provided a secure seat to the rider. Plus, because it was constructed out of wood, rawhide and leather, it was easy to repair. Once enshrined, the McClellan remained in service until America's mounted soldiers were retired at the dawning of the Second World War.

Thereafter thanks to countless articles, books and films, the McClellan became permanently associated with the dashing American cavalrymen who rode out west. While this makes for great television, it doesn't translate into good equestrian travel. Because McClellan based his saddle on the exposed Mexican saddle tree, riders routinely experienced serious problems.

From a rider's point of view, the McClellan provides a very poor support system, as the open gap between the sidebars must be ridden with care. While this is a grave concern for a Long Rider, the most damaging feature connected to the McClellan is how it adversely affects the horse's body.

Unlike the wide sidebars of the Swiss cavalry saddle, the smaller sidebars of the American cavalry saddle are built at such an angle that only their outer edges support the rider's weight. This results in a drastic reduction of the number of square inches making contact with the horse's back, which in turn produces too many pounds per square inch. Serious bruising is often the result.

The other problem is that the burrs and fans at the ends of the sidebars often cause severe injuries. The sidebars on the McClellan are short and do not flare outwards. This results in the front of the saddle interfering with the movement of the animal's forelegs. It also places intense pressure on its scapula. Moreover, the rear of the saddle tree often places pressure on the horse's loins, digging into its body when in motion.

Because a McClellan saddle is capable of causing serious wounds to the horse's withers and loins, it has had a regular stream of critics.

In 1879, during the height of the Indian wars on the Great Plains, a great many complaints were registered by serving officers. Yet money and bureaucratic incompetence left the McClellan in place for two reasons. First, the Ordinance Department protested that no official complaints had come to light regarding any poor performance records using the McClellan. More important was the fact that the government still had 42,000 surplus McClellan saddles on hand.

Even though the famous cavalryman, General Sherman, recommended the adoption of a replacement saddle in 1884, the Ordinance Department found they still had 20,000 McClellans on hand. Once again they quietly left bad enough alone and the torturous saddle passed on into history as the supposed preferred saddle of the U.S. cavalry.

Yet it wasn't only government officials who were fooled into thinking the McClellan was a superior saddle. Because of the misconception about its performance, Long Riders have set out thinking they have made a wise choice of saddles. One such well-meaning traveller was Joseph Smeaton Chase.

In his book, *California Coast Trails*, Chase recalled how in 1910 his horse Chino came up with wounded withers half way through a trip from Mexico to Oregon. After noticing his mount's affliction, Chase took to walking to ease Chino's burden, applying medication and even giving the horse time off to recover. However it must have become apparent to Chase that Chino needed more than a long weekend in the grass in order to press ahead to the trip's conclusion.

Soon after, the author reluctantly traded his trusty mount for another horse. It was only after this trade that we get a clue as to why Chino was experiencing a sore back. Chase recalled how much he liked his McClellan saddle because it was light weight. But more importantly, he noted the many dee rings which made it easy for the Long Rider to attach his equipment. While this feature is indeed an excellent one, the author did not connect the McClellan to the subsequent saddle sores. Instead he inadvertently risked his horse's safety in exchange for a little convenience.

This was a case wherein an otherwise kind, observant and considerate horseman made an elementary mistake which not only caused his expedition financial loss, but more importantly, caused his mute companion a great deal of pain every mile of the way. Had he known this, the knowledge would have caused the author no end of regret.

While many traditional cavalry saddles perform admirably during journeys, I would strongly advise a Long Rider to choose another riding saddle in preference to the McClellan.

Randonnee Saddles

With so many reasons not to trust the original McClellan saddle, it might surprise you to learn that it inspired the creation of this century's most successful travelling saddle.

The Randonnee saddle is a rare example of an old idea which has been vastly improved. Having carefully studied the good and bad points of the original American cavalry saddle, a French artisan saddler named Aimé Mohammed set out to create a new saddle based upon his predecessor's concepts.

His remarkable creation, the Randonnee saddle has been one of the most important developments in modern equestrian travel history. Created in beautiful natural coloured leather, each saddle is skilfully handmade and weighs only ten pounds.

Unlike the narrow McClellan, the wider arch of the Randonnee does not interfere with the horse's freedom of movement, nor does it inflict wounds to the withers.

The original narrow sidebars, which previously caused so much trouble on the McClellan saddle, have been substantially widened on the Randonnee so as to greatly increase the load-bearing surface.

Equally important, unlike its American predecessor, whose wooden sidebar was covered with a single strip of leather, the wider sidebars of the new Randonnee have been amply padded with thick wool felt and then covered with high quality leather.

Another terrific improvement was the removal of the McClellan's notorious open seat. While this open gap provided plenty of air flow to the horse's spine, its sharp edges presented a continual hazard to riders. The Randonnee resolved this problem by covering the seat with thick leather. The Randonnee saddle, which comes in three sizes, has a high pommel and cantle which give the Long Rider a deep seat and creates an excellent sense of security.

Like its famous predecessor, the Randonnee retained the metal dee rings in the front and rear to which bags can be easily attached. The modern metalwork is made from rust resistant steel.

The result is that the Randonnee saddle has been successfully used by Long Riders from around the world.

French Long Rider Annick Armand reported, "I put the Randonnee saddle to the test in my ride across Turkey, and was delighted with it because it provided strength and complete comfort for both horse and rider."

When Long Rider Renate Larssen rode from Sweden to the Middle East she also found that the Randonnee was comfortable, "even after ten to twelve hours in the saddle."

Despite the distance undertaken during his journey from Wales to Turkey, British Long Rider Harry Adshead noted that the Randonnee caused no saddle sores and "Although of simple design the shape of the seat allows you to comfortably ride long and deep."

Having provided many Long Riders with a trouble-free trip, the Randonnee saddle deservedly receives the Long Riders' Guild's complete endorsement and is recommended for any equestrian journey.

Spanish Saddles

The Iberian equestrian culture is an excellent example of the interplay of ideas which passes between the international brotherhood of horsemen, as Spain received, then in turn shared, some of the world's most important saddle developments.

When the Moors invaded Spain in the 8th century, they brought with them their high-backed saddles. A variation of this saddle went with Hernán Cortez and the other Conquistadors when they in turn sailed to the New World in the 16th century. The traditions of Spain were later transferred to the Mexican vaqueros, whose saddles and equipment inspired the American cowboy.

The Spanish saddle has extremely wide sidebars, which are filled with horsehair and cotton. These padded sidebars provide excellent weight distribution along the horse's back. Nor was the rider's comfort neglected, as a prominent pommel, high cantle and thick sheepskin on top, combine to provide the rider with a safe and secure seat.

Though more than a thousand years have passed since the Moors brought a high-backed saddle to Spain, the concept has withstood the test of time. A comfortable variation of the original design is still being successfully used by modern Long Riders today.

Irish Long Rider Steven O'Connor is one of several equestrian travellers who have praised the Spanish saddle.

Western Saddles

One of the world's most popular saddles is the cowboy, or western, saddle.

There are variations on this theme but the original was designed to have a prominent pommel and high cantle. Though they provided cowboys with a deep seat, these early saddles could weigh between 40 and 50 pounds (about 20 kg.) without any equipment attached.

Another major fault in these early western saddles was in the sidebars, which were often far too short, extending but a bare two inches behind the cantle and still less in front of the fork. These short sidebars placed most of the rider's weight on the back points of the bars right over the weak points of the horse's back. The result was a horse with sore kidneys. Also the saddle's front arch was often too narrow which injured the withers.

Like the McClellan, the original cowboy saddle has been improved in many ways since its 19th century inception, the most notable advance being that today's version is lighter in weight. Ironically, starting in the 1950s the original high cantle which provides a rider with support and security was reduced to a minimum so as to aid quick dismounting in rodeos. Perhaps the ultimate deviation from practicality was the 1950s western saddle which was equipped with a built-in radio. Designed to let the rider listen to popular tunes while "riding the range," thankfully it was a short-lived experiment.

Despite these setbacks, the western saddle has been of tremendous help to Long Riders both past and present. One of the Founding Members of the Long Riders' Guild, the legendary Marshall Ralph Hooker, used a western saddle during his explorations of America. Countless other Long Riders have also had great success with western saddles. Plus, despite its American roots, this saddle has proved to be of great help to Long Riders further afield.

Australian Long Rider Steve Nott used a western saddle when he made his ride around the Australian continent. More recently French Long Rider Edouard Chautard used a western saddle when he made the first mounted journey through the Pacific island of New Caledonia.

There are several things to keep in mind when considering a western saddle for travel. Because the western saddle was originally designed to aid cowboys working cattle, it had options which would be a handicap for a weight-obsessed Long Rider. For example, many cowboys took great pride in owning a heavily carved saddle. While they were undoubtedly attractive, it is far easier to clean and maintain a saddle if the leather is unadorned.

Another favourite option of the old-time cowboy was the large square leather skirts which appeared on the plains saddle used in Wyoming. They weigh more, cover far too much of the horse and prevent evaporation of sweat. If choosing to ride a western saddle, it makes more sense for a Long Rider to opt for the smaller, rounded skirts which were preferred by the buckaroos of Nevada.

Starting in the 1920s cowboy saddles featured oversized pommels. Known as bucking rolls or swells, they were designed to aid a cowboy who was required to ride a bucking horse. While most modern western saddles no longer have pronounced pommels, a Long Rider should avoid this extra weight on his saddle.

Finally, the saddle horn was designed to anchor a rope while roping cattle. As Long Riders aren't in the business of chasing cows, the saddle horn is irrelevant except as a handle for mounting.

Contemporary western saddle makers have taken note of the needs of Long Riders.

One such example, the Tucker Saddle Company, has an excellent record of making western style saddles that protect the horse and provide comfort to the rider.

Bernice Ende, who has ridden 25,000 miles on eight consecutive journeys, swears that her Tucker saddle is great for Long Riders. On her blog she wrote, "I've ridden more than 18,000 miles on my Tucker saddle. That should tell you something."

New western saddles have retained the important high cantle, the deep seat and many of the other vital aspects of the traditional cowboy saddle, all the while doing away with the extra weight, the fancy carving and any needless options.

While these are encouraging developments, many mass-marketed western saddles use a saddle tree whose sidebars do not make proper contact with the horse's back. These sidebars are often too short, which places the majority of the rider's weight on the four corners. Another danger associated with cheap western saddles is that the front arch is too low, which may cause severe damage to the horse's withers. Remember, despite the many positive points associated with the western saddle; carefully check the fit of any potential saddle.

Gaucho Saddles

Given how many successful equestrian journeys have used cowboy saddles, a traveller could be forgiven for thinking that the gaucho saddle would also be an excellent choice. After all, Aimé Tschiffely, the most famous 20th century Long Rider, used a gaucho saddle to make his historic ride from Buenos Aires to New York.

Ironically, while the cattle-based equestrian cultures of North and South America share many similar traits, the adaptability of their saddles to equestrian travel is not one of these. The reasons for this are of importance to a Long Rider.

The cowboy saddle relies upon a saddle tree which distributes the rider's weight, keeps pressure off the withers and protects the spine. The gaucho saddle does not provide these critically-important protections. The saddle of the pampas goes by several names including *chaqueno* and *ricado*.

Unlike the cowboy saddle, the gaucho saddle does not have a horn for roping, nor pommels or a high cantle to help secure the rider's seat. In contrast to the Spartan simplicity of the western saddle, the gaucho saddle is a multi-layered construction.

Thurlow Craig lived and rode on the pampas for many years. Though he had the choice to adapt to local custom, he decided to use a western saddle instead. Yet he left a detailed description of how the gaucho saddle is constructed and used.

"This type of South American saddle does not have a saddle tree in the usual sense. They are messy and cumbersome, and, broadly speaking, are made up as follows. First two saddle blankets are placed on the horse's back. Then a heavy shaped flap of leather called the *carona* is put on to cover the blankets. It has holes on each side to which the stirrups are attached. The *carona* serves a double purpose of keeping hot sweat from soaking through to the rawhide covered bars of the saddle (which would soften and rot the rawhide) and also it keeps tropical rain from soaking through the saddle-blankets," he wrote.

Craig went on to explain, "Then the saddle proper. This consists of two leather tubes which have been stuffed with horsehair. Joined over the horse's spine by leather straps, these tubes are placed parallel to the horse's spine. After this the first cinch goes over the top part of the saddle. Next the gaucho puts two or three sheepskins on top of the leather tubes. This is followed by a soft leather cover known as the *sobrepuesto*. Over all this comes the *pegual*, or top cinch, and when it is all on the horse it weighs as much as, or more than, an American stock saddle."

Like all equestrian cultures, the gaucho saddle reflected the needs of its rider. Unlike the cowboy saddle, which was constructed to keep the rider in the seat at all times, the gaucho saddle was built to throw the rider free.

During the course of a normal day's riding, the gaucho was required to travel immense distances. As gauchos disliked the trot, this was usually done at the gallop. Because the pampas were riddled with holes, these galloping horses would frequently step into a hole and complete a somersault. When this occurred, the gaucho's life depended on his ability to fall free from the saddle. In order to be catapulted to safety, the gaucho learned to let go of his stirrups, lean backwards and let the momentum of the falling horse throw him clear.

The other point in its favour was that it made a comfortable bed.

While it may be soft to sleep on, the *ricado* was meant to be used on a series of disposable horses. Because the pampas was the home of immense herds of Criollo horses, gauchos could switch mounts as and when they liked. Thus even though the *ricado* did a poor job distributing the rider's weight, if the horse was seldom ridden the chances of damaging its withers and spine were decreased. Moreover, because the horses were considered largely disposable, injuring them via a poorly-made saddle was not a personal priority or a national obsession.

While it is fine to study a nation's historical equestrian roots, it is something else to try and adapt that country's equipment into equestrian travel.

Before his ride in Argentina and Chile, Keith Clark discovered how the *ricado* could inflict fearful wounds on a horse.

"A lot of native saddles are made, not because they work well or are good for the horse, but because of local culture and equestrian tradition," Keith reported. "The *ricado* has no gap along the spine as in a saddle with a tree, so when the horse gets older or loses weight all the weight is put on the spine. Since I arrived in Argentine I have seen very few horses ridden with a *recado* that weren't injured."

Nor should we neglect to appreciate how different people place their bodies in a saddle. The Mongols, for example, ride with extremely short stirrups. Likewise the stirrups on the *ricado* are hung further forward than most saddles. This will require a foreign rider to readjust his seat.

Keith Clark isn't the only one to experiment with a soft South American saddle. At the beginning of his journey from Patagonia to Alaska, North American Long Rider Louis Bruhnke also tried this option. He too learned that a Long Rider's saddle makes demands which a *ricado* cannot supply.

While it is certainly of historical importance, and if used properly on short rides will not harm horses, the *ricado* is not equipped to carry saddle bags, is overly complex and can cause tremendous wounds to a horse's back. It is, therefore, not recommended for Long Riders.

Foreign Saddles

Despite the shortcomings of the *ricado*, Long Rider history demonstrates that many other types of foreign saddles have been successfully used.

The most famous example was the Russian saddle used by Cossack Long Rider Dmitri Peshkov. This type of saddle uses a light-weight tree but provides the rider with a comfortable padded seat. Peshkov used such a saddle to make his ride from Siberia to St. Petersburg. The Hungarian saddle resembles the Cossack one and has also seen recent use in Europe.

Another foreign saddle which has provided excellent service can be found in Western Europe. The Camargue saddle of southern France was designed to be used on the horse of the same name. The Camargue horse has spent centuries living in the marshes and wetlands of the Rhone river delta. Like the better-known cowboys and gauchos, local riders known as *gardians* use the hardy Camargue horses to round up wild cattle. Because of the demands of riding through this swampy terrain, the Camargue saddle has a deep, comfortable seat.

The Camargue saddle provided excellent service to Robin and Louella Hanbury-Tenison. After purchasing Camargue horses in France, Robin and Louella rode their new mounts home to Cornwall. Following local tradition, they decided to use the local Camargue saddle on that original trip. The saddles performed so well that the Hanbury-Tenisons used them on various other equestrian journeys, including riding along China's Great Wall and through Spain.

Because the Camargue is a heavy saddle, it may not be suitable for all horses. So caution should be used when considering it for travel.

As these examples demonstrate, so long as the basic principles of proper saddle construction are followed, a Long Rider will discover that the options of what type of saddle to use are more varied than he thinks. Thus there are not as many bad saddles as there are bad fits.

There are distinct disadvantages to picking the wrong saddle. The first problem that may arise is that you may not be comfortable riding in a native saddle unless you were born to it.

For example, the saddles traditionally used in Mongolia, Tibet and China require the rider to sit very high over the horse's centre of gravity. At the same time they use very short stirrups. These saddles require the rider to sit on the horse in a way which is uncomfortable to a westerner used to long stirrups and a deep seat.

Some Long Riders have been forced by circumstances to adapt to local equestrian equipment. One such example was the New Zealand Long Rider Ian Robinson, who used a native saddle when he explored Afghanistan's Wakhan Corridor in 2008.

But beware of going to a foreign country and thinking you will find comfortable and well-made saddles. After arriving, many a Long Rider has discovered that the local equestrian culture does not share the same views on the horse's safety and the rider's comfort.

Henri de Büren was a Swiss Long Rider who journeyed to Peru in 1853. Prior to his departure he had the foresight to purchase a first-rate riding saddle. Sadly the other European members of the expedition had not taken that precaution and consequently they suffered greatly.

"Except for those of us who were prudent enough to bring our own saddles, all the other travellers had to sit on pack saddles instead of proper saddles during the gruelling three-month ride through the jungles of Peru," de Büren wrote.

Regardless if it is Peshkov in the 19th century, Hanbury-Tenison in the 20th, or Robinson in the 21st, a Long Rider's saddle must be lightweight, be able to carry the requisite equipment and not injure the horse.

Ironically, two Long Riders made a major historical contribution towards creating a saddle which did all three.

Flexible Saddles

Because each successive generation of mounted mankind encounters the same problems as did their ancestors, many of the same solutions are regularly resurrected with varying degrees of success. One such continual dilemma has been how to keep the saddle from wounding the withers?

As long as saddles have pinched, riders have been debating how to overcome the problem. One response was the development of an adjustable saddle. In 1916, for example, the British cavalry noted that there had been several recent attempts to "manufacture self-adjusting side bars, so as to enable them to follow the alterations in flesh which result from hard work."

There were other early attempts made by European cavalries. Yet the concept did not achieve global proportions until a remarkable pair of Long Riders revolutionized the modern saddle industry in the 1980s.

In 1982 North American Long Riders Len Brown and Lisa Stewart set off on what they believed was merely going to be a geographic journey across their homeland. Starting in New Mexico, the couple began a 3,000 mile ride through Colorado, Utah, Wyoming, Kansas and Missouri. During this rugged trip their two road horses and three pack horses were required to traverse mountains, cross deserts, and negotiate the plains.

Prior to their departure, the experienced Long Rider, Marshal Ralph Hooker, had warned the young travellers to take great care that their horses did not suffer from saddle sores. Despite their best efforts, this age-old curse did indeed wound their animals. Yet instead of going home, or switching saddles, when their horses became wounded, the young Long Riders began a mounted conversation that changed the course of modern equestrian events.

Throughout the history of mounted mankind, there have been moments when Long Riders fall into what I call "the long quiet." This is a tranquil inner space which occurs when you drift into deep thought, all the while you are rocking back and forth in the saddle. With plenty of time to ponder, it is amazing what Long Riders have conceived, written and discovered from the back of a horse. Lord Byron envisaged his greatest poem while riding through the Albanian mountains. Jonathan Swift was inspired to write *Gulliver's Travels* while riding across Ireland. Charles Darwin pondered the "origin of species" during his rides across South America, Australia and Africa.

Likewise, while Len and Lisa were riding through the backcountry of rural America, their conversations led them to a new insight about riding saddles. The result was that upon their return home, they created the Ortho Flex saddle. This unique concept allowed the sidebars to flex in four places. The result was a saddle which moved with the horse and a design which changed the equestrian world.

In an ironic development, the past and present history of saddles met thanks to the Ortho Flex. The North American Long Rider Louis Bruhnke had originally set off from Patagonia atop a primitive *ricado* saddle. Early in his journey, he sought the aid and advice of the Long Rider saddle inventors.

Len and Lisa provided Louis and his Russian Long Rider companion, Vladimir Fissenko, with two of their new Ortho Flex saddles. The result was that the two adventurers used the Brown's inventive solution with great success during their ride from the tip of Patagonia to the top of Alaska.

Len and Lisa have now moved on in search of new pursuits. Most notably Len has used his original research as the basis for a new type of saddle pad that reduces injury. While there continue to be variations on adjustable saddles, it was these two quiet wanderers who made technological equestrian history in an unprecedented way.

The Ortho Flex adjustable saddle, which is no longer owned by the Long Riders who invented it, has a very large weight-bearing surface and can be equipped to carry saddle and pommel bags. Unfortunately the saddles have been priced beyond the reach of the average Long Rider.

Treeless Saddles

As recent experiments with adjustable riding saddles demonstrate, previous equestrian developments are routinely "rediscovered" and then touted as being a startling breakthrough. One such current fad is the treeless saddle, the history and physical limitations of which are well known to equestrian historians.

It is worthwhile noting that scientists recently excavated horse skeletons dating back to the 1st century A.D. These animals were ridden by, and then buried beside, the steppe horsemen who rode along the ancient Equestrian Equator. Alongside the equine skeletons, archaeologists recovered the felt saddles used at that time. Not only do these primeval treeless saddles verify that the horses were ridden, they also confirm how this flawed piece of equipment inflicted wounds to the horse's backs. Despite their age, the equine skeletons display vertebrae which were fractured, indicating a poor distribution of rider's weight on the back of the animal.

Two thousand years later we witness a case of "plus ça change, plus c'est la même chose," or "the more it changes, the more it stays the same."

The German cavalry had six different sizes of saddles, five of which relied on a tree. Only the largest draught animals were occasionally fitted to a treeless saddle, because of their immense size. Thus the German cavalry, who then invaded Russia during the Second World War with the largest equestrian force in modern history, had two saddle choices. Either they could mount their thousands of riders on a light, weight-distributing saddle, or they could place them atop the treeless saddle.

They chose the traditional saddle because it worked.

In stark contrast, we need only remember the saddle used by the South American gauchos. The *ricado* is a form of treeless saddle which relies upon rawhide tubes placed alongside the horse's spine. As various Long Riders have confirmed, this version of a treeless saddle is capable of creating incredible injuries.

Nor did the results differ when Austrian Long Rider Horst Hausleitner tried to cross the African continent with a new version of the treeless saddle. The horse quickly suffered severe wounds and the expensive treeless saddle had to be replaced before the journey could continue.

Horst wrote, "I would not recommend it for a journey like ours, as it caused bad saddle sores along the whole backbone."

In stark contrast, his wife's traditional cavalry saddle created no problems during their 4,000 mile ride.

Disaster struck another expedition that also attempted to use a treeless saddle.

When Billy Brenchley and Christy Henchie began their ride from Tunisia to South Africa, they originally set out with treeless saddles. It didn't take long for them to realise the gravity of their mistake.

"This was not a successful experiment. We found that our seat bones simply applied too much pressure to our horses' backs and that there was no spine clearance," Christy explained.

Both Long Riders concluded, "You need a rigid saddle."

So why return to an item from the past that doesn't work?

Because a mixture of clever marketing and an increasing degeneration of global equestrian knowledge has encouraged confusion regarding the engineering purpose of the saddle tree. The result is that many well-meaning horse owners no longer understand the basic principles of why the saddle tree is important and why, when properly fitted, it works to preserve the safety of the horse and the stability of the rider.

Several new companies have sprung up to fill this intellectual vacuum, all of which promote a doctrine which states that the owner is doing his horse a favour by dispensing with the saddle tree. The allure of this inaccuracy is that by reducing the weight on the horse's back, the rider is aiding the animal. Nothing could be further from the truth.

Equine vertebrae are fragile and easily damaged. The saddle tree protects the spine by distributing the rider's weight over the horse's ribs and body. A treeless saddle encourages that weight to be concentrated in small, specific points directly above the sensitive spine.

Of equal importance is the fact that a treeless saddle applies immense pressure along the spinal column. This restricts blood flow and encourages injury.

A saddle tree allows a channel of cooling air to flow over the horse's spine. Treeless saddles lack the ability to create or maintain this channel.

Proponents of the treeless saddle argue that it does not restrict the movement of the horse's shoulders, conveniently forgetting that it allows the majority of the rider's weight to bear directly down onto the sensitive withers.

Another disadvantage is that the treeless saddle can shift while in motion. This encourages the rider to over-tighten the girth, so as to compensate for the lack of stability provided by a saddle tree.

For marketing purposes, treeless saddle advocates are quick to tout the rider's comfort. They neglect to explain that the rider's ease is gained at the expense of the horse's safety.

Ironically, in addition to encouraging equine injury, treeless saddles also perform badly for the rider. A treeless saddle cannot support the curvature of the rider's spine, which in turn encourages a strong secure seat. Without the support of a saddle tree over the withers, a treeless saddle will place the rider behind the horse's centre of motion, which in turn will place pressure on the horse's sensitive loins.

These alarming discoveries were confirmed in 2008 when the Society of Master Saddlers launched a thorough comparison between treeless saddles and those which used a traditional saddle tree. Their findings were conclusive. The treeless saddle exerted pressure on the spine, produced localized pressure on the horse's body, induced soreness and eventually led to tissue damage.

While any saddle tree can be ill-fitting or injurious, it is illogical to dispense with this time-tested tool for the sake of a fad which does not provide the support, stability, comfort and protection required by road horses and Long Riders. To do so drags mounted man two thousand years back to the days before science, technology, logic and generations of field trials proved the reliability of a weight-bearing saddle.

Thus as equestrian travellers we are left with this conclusion. Equestrian cultures from around the world long ago learned that the rigid saddle tree provides the utmost protection to the horse and stability to the rider.

A treeless saddle might not harm your horse on a Sunday trail ride. And it is conceivable that this piece of equipment might even be used on a journey without injuring the animal, especially if the rider is a light-weight person.

Yet the extreme rigours encountered during the course of an extended equestrian journey require you to provide your road horse with every possible advantage, before and during the journey. Therefore it is most strongly advised not to use a treeless saddle.

Sidesaddles

It may surprise you to learn that a saddle was linked to the social, political and equestrian domination of women. This did not, however, occur in the land of horses and free riders. It first occurred in "civilized" Europe.

Like their brothers, Central Asian women riders mounted up in order to participate in travel, sport, war and pleasure. Nor was it the fathers who taught Mongol children to begin riding at the age of three. That duty was reserved for the equally hard-riding mothers. The equestrian cultures of the Comanche and Hawaiians also took justifiable pride in the riding skills of their women.

Sadly, a distinctly patriarchal view of equestrian events dominated European and North American history, one which forced women and horses to endure one of mankind's most dangerous and disadvantageous pieces of equestrian equipment – the sidesaddle.

During the 1200s authors such as Chaucer wrote about women who routinely made lengthy journeys riding astride. The rowdy and earthy "Wife of Bath," depicted in *The Canterbury Tales*, was one such notable character. She rode a pacer astride, carried a whip and wore spurs. Other women also adapted split skirts or, if riding to war like Joan of Arc, donned armour.

Before the dawning of the fourteenth century it was common for western women to be found riding astride. Yet with the rise of feudalism, and its off-shoot, patriarchal politics, the need to secure a male heir was an affair of state and protecting the virginity of a potential royal bride became increasingly vital. One way to protect the royal hymen and off-set the accidental loss of virginity was to prohibit aristocratic girls from riding astride.

Thus sidesaddle riding was introduced into England in 1382 when Princess Anne of Bohemia travelled across Europe via this new mode of equine transport in order to wed King Richard II.

For those unfamiliar with the history of coaches and carriages, it is important to note that due to the lack of passable roads, driving a coach as a common form of transport would not take place until the dawning of the 19th century.

That is why, lacking a road, the virtuous virgin was transported to England in a chair-like affair that was based upon a pack saddle design. In addition to a padded seat, this new contraption provided a pommel in the front which could be used as a rudimentary handgrip. A wooden plank, wide enough to accommodate both feet, hung along the left side of the placid beast of burden. It was customary for the sideways-facing woman to sit on the near side of the horse, enabling her to use the right hand to hang onto the horse's mane.

The advent of the sidesaddle can be traced back to the English court and this Bohemian queen. For the next two centuries the sidesaddle became increasingly associated with "proper" behaviour, until by 1600 riding astride was no longer something a "lady" would do, as that ancient practice had taken on the aura of indecency.

A strong implication now dominated the European horse world. An unwritten law stated that only a woman as masculine as an Amazon, as libertine as the Wife of Bath, or as heretical as Joan of Arc, would have dared to ride astride. In this way by the end of the nineteenth century a philosophy of equestrian protection had become an entrenched social institution, one whose original purpose wasn't discussed in public, yet which exerted an immense influence across polite European and American society.

What the fans of the sidesaddle could not have foreseen was that as the 19th century drew to a close, this revered icon was about to become involved in a global equestrian debate which raged through the press and across the world of the Long Riders.

When Ella Sykes, the unconquerable English Long Rider, set out to canter across the deserts of Persia, it wasn't the local Muslims who almost slew her; it was the sidesaddle which nearly took her life on several occasions. In her book, *Through Persia on a Sidesaddle*, Sykes recalled quite honestly how she longed to ride astride, yet refrained from doing so because of her social position. The result was that she nearly lost her life because of the sidesaddle.

Luckily other lady Long Riders were ready to ride in defiance of the rules.

When she ventured to Hawaii in the late 19th century, English Long Rider Isabella Bird learned to ride astride thanks to her Hawaiian hosts. In addition to rounding up the wild cattle imported by the King of that island, the Mexican vaqueros had also taught the local women to ride astride. Bird not only adopted this technique, she used her vaquero saddle when she later explored the Rocky Mountains, Japan, Persia, Korea and Tibet on horseback.

Nor was a new generation of American women willing to quietly withhold their political and equestrian views any longer.

In September, 1910, Two-Gun Nan Aspinwall set off to prove that a woman could ride "ocean to ocean" alone. At that time many parts of the United States maintained laws which prohibited women from wearing trousers. Likewise it was considered socially rude for women to ride astride. During Two-Gun Nan's ride from San Francisco to New York, she wore a split skirt, shod her own horse, and rode astride.

Yet it was the tiny Alberta Clare, known as "the girl from Wyoming," who proved that women were no longer willing to follow the rules. In 1912 this diminutive pistol-packing Long Rider made a 13,000 kilometre (8,000 mile) solo equestrian journey across the United States. Clare publicly stated that she had two goals: to ride astride and win the vote for women.

In fact shortly after American women won the right to vote, they began abandoning the sidesaddle in droves in favour of riding astride. Thus, the fall of the sidesaddle is linked to the rise of female liberty, for it was the dawning of political freedom which brought about the overdue death of this repressive equine invention. By 1946, when Brian Vesey-Fitzgerald completed his masterpiece, *The Book of the Horse*, this encyclopaedic 880-page work lacked a single reference to the sidesaddle.

The horse turned "man" kind into a race of risk takers.

Yet today the sidesaddle is once again being described as a "romantic" way to ride, all the while its advocates remain reluctant to discuss the deadly side-effects associated with locking a human body into place alongside the left side of a galloping horse. The drawbacks include many dangerous disadvantages to horse and rider.

Concession to fashion ensures that the riding skirts are impractical for travel. Additionally, the sidesaddle is difficult to mount alone. Traditionally, a man could mount alone. Yet it took two men to help one lady get onto her sidesaddle.

It also handicaps the rider in another way: communications. Unlike male riders a sidesaddle rider can not apply the pressure of her leg to the right side of the horse, nor give her mount any signals with her thighs, knees, or heels. Even worse, in severe cases female riders could not drop their hands in order to turn or stop a runaway horse.

Sadly, if she was involved in an accident, a girl was more likely to suffer serious injuries in a sidesaddle. When fox-hunting men had riding accidents, the small English saddle was designed to throw them free of the massive horse. But when the horse of a female fox hunter fell, the heavy sidesaddle trapped the woman underneath the 1200 pound animal because she could not fall clear of the saddle. The result was that these women often had their backs broken and were invalids for the rest of their lives.

In addition, the sidesaddle was notoriously expensive to create and because it placed the majority of the weight on one side, it routinely injured the horse's back. Plus, because of the long flapping riding dress hanging along his left flank, a "lady's horse" had to be exceptionally well-trained, which translated into "expensive." Finally, because of its bad fit, grooms were known to girth a sidesaddle up so tightly that the horse had trouble breathing.

The result was that women, and horses, suffered devastating physical abuse.

A rider's longing for historical accuracy should never take precedence over the horse's safety. Just as women no longer bind their feet in the name of beauty, likewise there is no need to return to the equestrian past by incorporating the dangerous sidesaddle into equestrian travel.

Boutique Buyers

One of the unforeseen consequences of globalisation has been the increase in homogenous objects. From cars to clothes, the powers of the economy dictate that items need to be produced in a streamlined fashion. This philosophy increases profit but unfortunately destroys individual artistic endeavour.

Like various other everyday objects, the creation of today's saddle is all too often a victory of mass production over hard-won skill, a replacement of the handmade by the cheap-to-sell. The result is that the saddle, which has a long history of being carefully created by a special class of craftsmen, is now an object which can be bought off the shelf with no forethought, little knowledge and no questions asked.

Thus many modern saddles reflect a slavish effort on the part of manufacturers to cater to the perceived need of the public market. Look at any equestrian magazine and you will see ads for saddles designed for boutique riders. These people are obsessed with what's on top, the silver, and not what's underneath, the tree. Such saddles are seldom ridden hard or far.

A Long Rider can't afford this attitude. The saddle must be a work of art from an equine engineering point of view, not look like a leather masterpiece created by Gucci. The journey will either be a pleasure or an ordeal for you and your horse, depending on how comfortable, sturdy and functional the saddle is. Function, not flash, is what matters in a Long Rider's saddle.

Buy the Best

Beware of a clever sales pitch when shopping for a saddle. Never believe a salesman who says that a saddle will adjust to your mount or that a particular saddle fits a "normal" horse. As travel history proves, ensuring that the saddle fits properly is one of your first concerns.

Regardless of whatever style of saddle you decide upon, buy the best.

Cheap saddles are a mistake, first of all because your life is at risk if they break at a critical moment. Cowboys knew that when an emergency arose, a cut-rate saddle could get them killed. That is why when it came time to choose the piece of equipment upon which their lives depended, old-time range riders spent a great deal of time carefully choosing their saddle.

As a Long Rider what you're proposing to do is already so difficult that your mathematical chances of getting through are slim. If the bugs don't eat you, the loneliness doesn't get you, the sun doesn't bake you or the border crossings don't stop you, then you'll still have a host of everyday problems to overcome - any of which can end your trip.

Therefore when it comes to discussing how much you can spend on a riding saddle, cut economic corners somewhere else. Forego that extra luxury. Don't buy such an expensive sleeping bag. Forget the chrome-plated, magnetic, beer-can-opening flashlight that makes coffee in the morning, but never purchase a second-rate saddle.

Such savings are rooted in a horse's pain, for a badly-fitting saddle can result in serious injuries or even the death of your animal.

Summary

A good saddle is as important as the quality of the horse that carries it. Checking that the saddle continually fits well is as vital as the daily maintenance of the hooves.

The longer the ride, the more ideal the saddle must be. Prior to your departure you must confirm that the saddle is in perfect order, that the straps are all sound, the buckles work accurately and that it fits your horse's back.

Never brutalise your road horse with an ill-fitting saddle. If you leave knowing your saddle is liable to cause pains or sores, you're a scoundrel putting selfish desire before the decency and needs of a mute animal.

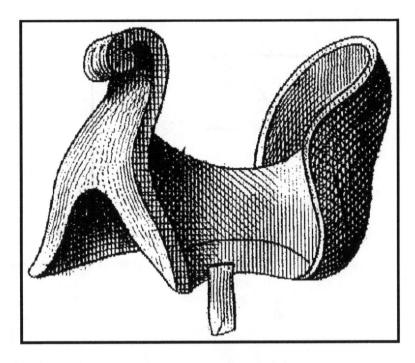

The basic concept of the saddle has not altered for more than a thousand years, because the primary needs of today's horse and rider are no different than those of their ancestors.

Though it looks primitive, the saddle tree of this modern Hutsul saddle from Romania is based upon ancient principles which are still in use today: i.e. a cantle, pommel and sidebars.

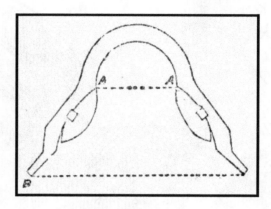

The front arch of a saddle is designed to keep the rider's weight off the horse's sensitive withers.

It is vitally important that a Long Rider test the fit of the saddle to ensure that it does not pinch the shoulder blades nor bear down on the withers.

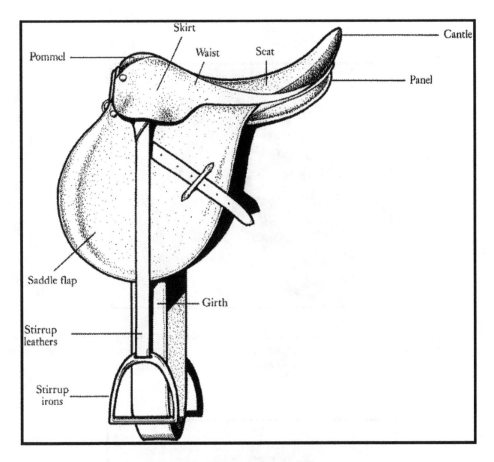

Parts of the English saddle.

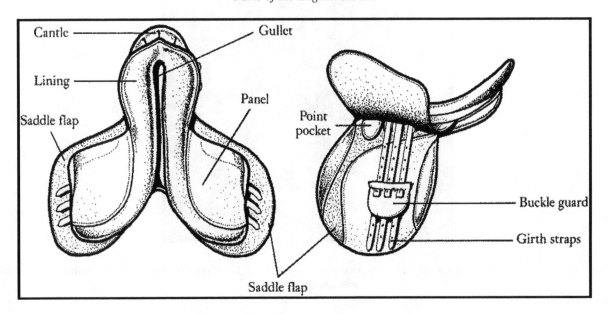

The underside of the English saddle.

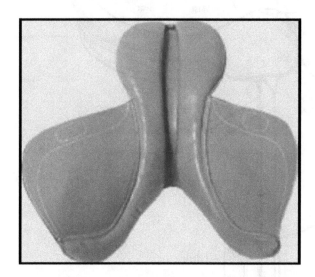

In addition to not being equipped with the dee rings needed to secure saddle bags, many English saddles have too narrow a weight-bearing surface under the saddle tree. This causes the rider's weight to press down onto a small area of the horse's back. Here you can see how extremely small the panels are.

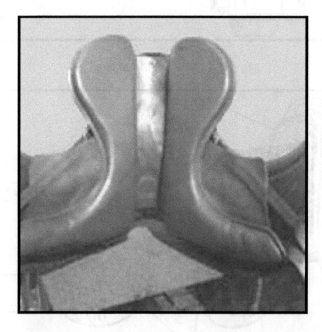

In contrast, this English saddle is equipped with wide panels which distribute the rider's weight perfectly; both photos courtesy of www.bentaiga.com

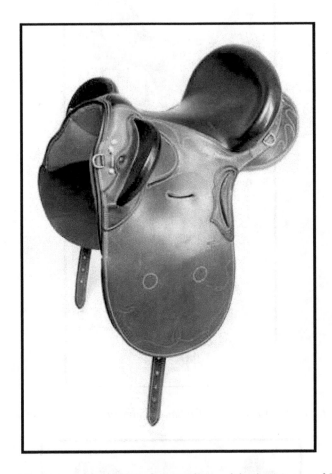

The Australian saddle features many of the best qualities of the American and English saddles.

Such a saddle was used with great success by Australian Long Rider Tim Cope during his ride from Mongolia to Hungary.

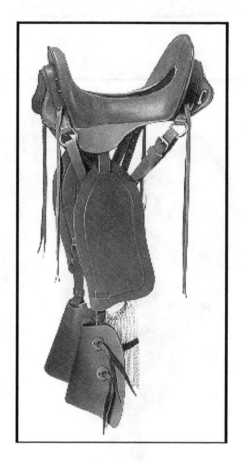

Unless fitted with care the American McClellan cavalry saddle may cause injuries to horses.

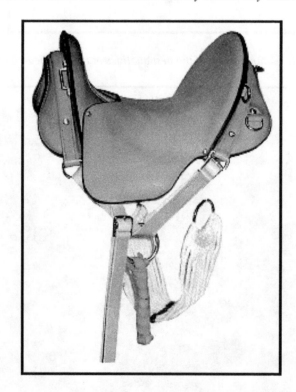

But the Randonnee saddle, which is handmade in France, is an improvement upon the McClellan saddle and has been successfully used by Long Riders in all parts of the world.

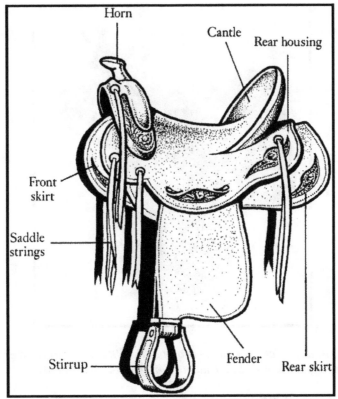

A traditional Western saddle; note the rounded skirts which reduce the weight and the high cantle which provides a secure seat for the rider.

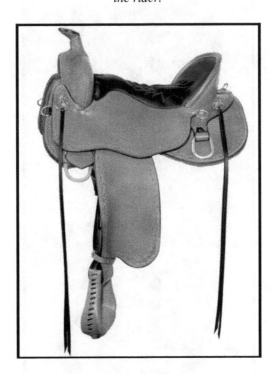

North American Long Rider Bernice Ende has ridden a Tucker Black Mountain western saddle for thousands of miles during her many journeys through the United States. The saddle is a popular modern choice for Long Riders who are seeking a western saddle which is comfortable for both horse and rider.

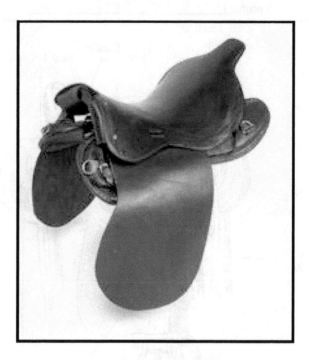

The British Universal Pattern cavalry saddle, commonly known as the UP saddle, provided excellent service to cavalrymen throughout the vast British Empire and was used by the author during a solo ride in Pakistan's North West Frontier Province.

Italian Long Rider Simone Carmignani also used a British UP saddle during his travels through the Karakorum Mountains of northern Pakistan.

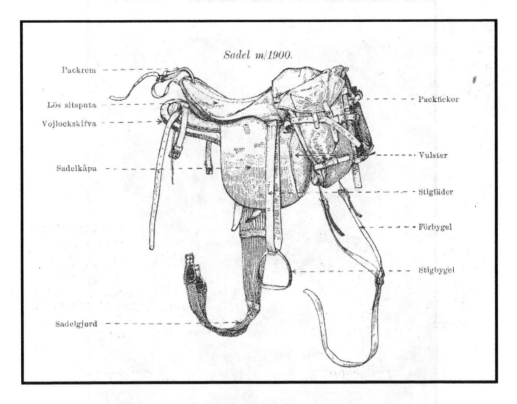

This Swedish cavalry saddle incorporated the features which European cavalry used with great success.

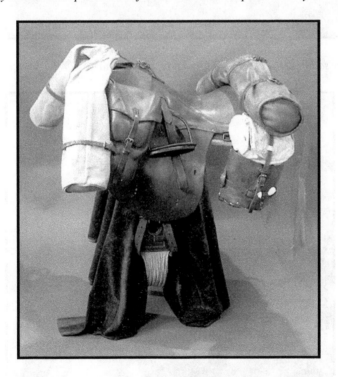

This Swiss cavalry saddle, created in 1916, saw service in both World Wars and was then used by Captain Otto Schwarz during his 48,000 kilometre (30,000 mile) travel career.

One of the best cavalry saddles was created in Germany; photo courtesy of the Society of the Military Horse.

German Long Rider, Lieutenant Erich von Salzmann, used such a saddle during his 6,000 kilometre (3,700 mile) ride from Tientsin, China to Tashkent, Uzbekistan in 1903.

A Spanish vaquero saddle protects the horse and is comfortable for the rider; photo courtesy of www.hue-hott.de.

Irish Long Rider Steven O'Connor used this type of saddle when he rode from Spain to England.

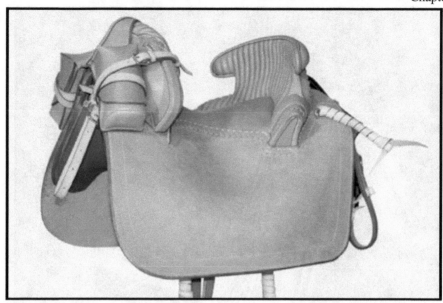

Though the Camargue saddle is very heavy, it provides a deep seat and is very comfortable for the rider.

Robin and Louella Hanbury-Tenison first used the Camargue saddle when they rode from France to England. They later used the French saddles when they rode across Spain, New Zealand, and as seen in this photo, along the length of the Great Wall of China.

Some equestrian cultures have developed saddles which work extremely well for equestrian travellers. For example a Cossack saddle has a soft seat for the rider and a wide weight-bearing saddle tree for the horse's back.

Cossack Long Rider Dmitri Peshkov used this type of saddle on his Siberian horse, Seriy, when they journeyed from Siberia to St. Petersburg.

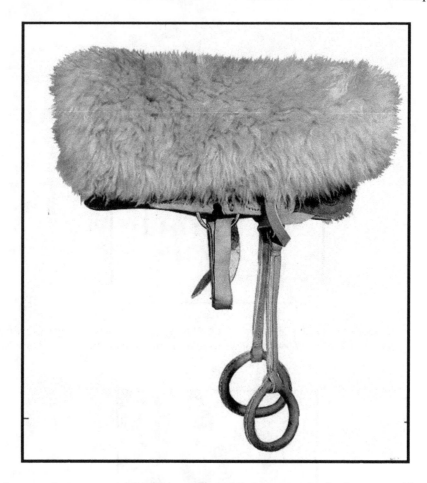

Other types of saddles have not been as successful. The gaucho saddle known as the ricado *was used by Swiss Long Rider Aimé Tschiffely during his ride from Buenos Aires to New York.*

When North American Long Rider Louis Bruhnke set out to ride from Patagonia to Alaska, he discovered that the gaucho saddle did not suit the needs of a modern equestrian traveller.

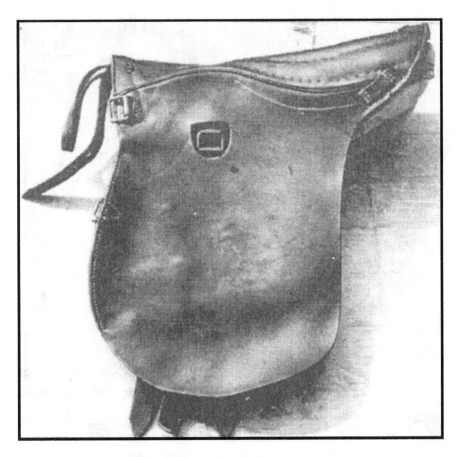

The German cavalry were well aware of treeless saddles. This particular saddle was used on rare occasions when large draught horses needed to be ridden short distances. Yet the majority of German army horses used a traditional saddle tree to offset injuries.

The unsuitability of treeless saddles was discovered by Billy Brenchley soon after he began his ride from Tunisia to South Africa. Both of his horses suffered saddle sores due to a lack of a weight-distributing saddle tree.

Though the majority of European women in the 19th century were forced by social convention to ride in the dangerous sidesaddle, English Long Rider Isabella Bird chose to explore the world astride her Mexican saddle. She is seen about to set off across Persia.

Cultural practices differ among nations. For example this Mongol saddle features many aspects found in Asian saddles, including a high pommel and very short stirrups. Such a saddle is extremely uncomfortable unless the rider is used to this style of Asiatic riding.

Long Riders should be extremely sceptical of thinking they will find suitable saddles in foreign lands. During a recent journey in Paraguay, Robin Hanbury-Tenison was surprised when circumstances forced him to ride this ill-equipped donkey.

Likewise, this Kazakh horse is wearing a homemade saddle that consists of old nylon webbing and bits of string.

Improvements to saddles continue, though not all are a success. During the 1950s clever salesmen attempted to entice the American public into purchasing the "radio saddle."

But a major breakthrough occurred in the late 1980s. During their journey across the United States, Len Brown and Lisa Stewart were inspired with the ideas which later led to the invention of the Ortho Flex saddle.

Chapter 33
Horse Equipment

Were you able to transport Aimé Tschiffely into the 21st century, he would once again seek the basic requirements of saddle, bridle and blanket, just as he did prior to his departure in 1923.

That is because even though new materials such as nylon, reflective tape and aluminium have been invented since Aimé set off for New York, when one considers how many centuries mankind has been interacting with the horse, remarkably few things have changed since our ancestors formalized the essential needs of equestrian riding and travel.

Yet every item is worthy of careful consideration, for mistakes are costly when the road is long.

Local Bargains

Before we investigate each of the vital components needed by a Long Rider, let us remember that, unlike a week-end trail rider, the equipment required to withstand the rigours of equestrian travel must be the best you can find and afford. Do not be tempted to arrive in a foreign country and think that cheaper local equipment will suit your needs.

The first thing you may discover is that your definition of equipment does not match what is locally available.

When Tim Cope arrived in Mongolia, he made this observation.

"The horse market is a bit of a shock if you are used to Western-made goods, as there is only rawhide in view. No buckles are to be seen because everything is done with knots here. And everything, including bits, halters and saddles are all one universal size."

Even if you are lucky enough to locate an item which you recognize, local standards may not match your needs.

Keith Clark experienced this while riding in Chile.

"I came into town for a few days to get dried off, cleaned up and to try and buy two waterproof rugs. They all sell the same ones and of course they guarantee that they are waterproof. Yet I wondered how they could be with all the stitching they put in them. One guy insisted they would stand any test, so we threw a bucket of water over one. Water went straight through. That's a faulty one, he insisted, try another. We tried four more before he gave up."

With examples like these in mind, it is easy to see why it is critically important for a Long Rider to purchase and test the necessary equipment prior to departure.

Saddle and Pommel Bags

One of the worst mistakes an equestrian traveller can make is to overload the road horse. That is why a primary goal of this book is to alert travellers to the ill-advised idea of placing enormous saddle and cantle bags on the back of your riding animal. Nothing is more likely to contribute to this fundamental mistake than the oversized saddle bags being sold by modern American manufacturers.

Genghis Khan understood the importance of restricting the weight on his soldier's riding horses. That is why he ordered that nothing be tied to the back of the saddle. Soldiers who ignored this edict were beheaded. If circumstances permitted, Mongols were allowed to tie a small water-resistant bag to the tail of the horse when fording rivers.

The concept of placing the rider's gear in a sack originated in Asia and spread west. Over time mounted warriors secured small leather pockets snugly behind the cantle. It was left to beasts of burden, such as the donkey, to carry bulky personal items and fodder in larger saddle bags. To designate ownership, these big sturdy cloth bags were embroidered with tribal colours and motifs.

Over the ages, the size of the saddle bag gradually increased, until by the early 20th century an American cavalry style saddle bag was approximately 14" tall and 14" wide (35 square cm.). There were two main drawbacks to this type of saddle bag – weight and storage.

Leather is heavy and requires regular maintenance. Many saddle bags are now made from durable cordura, which is lightweight, strong and washable.

Lisa Wood discovered it made sense to switch from leather to lightweight modern material.

"For the first trip I had beautiful leather saddle bags custom made. They provided the benefit of being waterproof but they had the disadvantage of being heavy. For the second trip I traded the leather bags for nylon and put anything that needed to be dry, for example maps and my journal, in a zip-lock."

The disadvantage is that some modern materials may cause the horse to sweat.

The other drawback to traditional saddle bags is they force the traveller to pack everything inside two large pockets, which hang down on either side of the horse and are subject to constant movement.

After making two journeys across Europe, Jeremy James lamented the drawbacks of this traditional system.

"Being basically sack shaped means that everything winds up in a bundle in the bottom of the saddle bags. Usually they are too deep and you can never find the thing you need. Your socks get muddled up with your maps and olives and a squashed pear perhaps, and some barley, a sodden notebook, screwed up veterinary papers and a damp shirt, plus a busted tube of toothpaste. We have all experienced it. Never again, we cry, swearing that the next time such a journey is undertaken it will be with saddle bags that are what they say they are: bags that stow goods in some kind of easily retrievable order."

Jeremy was not the first Long Rider to contemplate a solution to this bane of equestrian travellers. In 1938 English Long Rider and author, Edward Stebbings, noted that single-pocket saddle bags were a failure.

"They end up smashing everything into a big fat mess. The heaviest stuff goes to the bottom. It's just not an effective way to carry your material."

Though traditional saddlers had not grasped the importance of creating a saddle bag with internal pockets, Stebbings resolved the problem by designing a new system.

"My bags are of the hang-over saddle-bag type, with two inside compartments- size 11 inches by 12 inches and with rounded edges. These bags are made with a leather back; the rest consists of a light-coloured grey waterproof canvas, the edges bound with leather to add strength and prevent tearing. Halfway down the front edge of each bag is a looped strap through which the buckles of the girth are pushed before the latter are attached to the saddle straps. The bags have rounded ends, which are of importance, as if the bags are built square there is a greater danger of rubbing. The bags are connected by a leather flap, the hinder part of which is cut at the centre for some 2.75 inches deep and then cut outwards on a curve for some 6.5 inches so as to leave two separated pieces, to one of which is fixed a strap and to the other a buckle. The broader part of the flap is placed on the rear part of the saddle (a bag thus hanging on either side); the narrower, separated pieces of the flap, joined by the buckle and strap, fit under the cantle of the saddle, and thus hold the bags in position. Properly adjusted, the girth straps and the rear piece have eyelet holes for adjustment, the bags hang lightly and freely, and only the outward ends move up and down when going at a smart trot or a canter. I think the rounded ends to the bags are of importance, as if the bags are built square, there is, I think, a much greater danger of rubbing."

Though Stebbings had arrived at a solution, his ideas were never put into effect commercially. In 2004 a German rider, Frauke Nonnenmacher, discussed the concept of a multi-pocketed saddle bag with Jeremy James. Based upon Jeremy's ideas, Frauke designed a multi-pocketed prototype on paper. Yet it was the Italian saddle company, Prestige Italia, who not only created the modern multi-pocket saddle bag, they improved upon it.

The Italian system is made of strong, light-weight, washable material. The saddle bags contain the various internal pockets deemed necessary by Stebbings and James. Of equal importance, the weight of the saddle bags is kept off the horse's spine and kidneys by the use of a thin metal support bar which connects to the back of the saddle.

The support bar allows the passage of cool air to circulate under the saddle bags, thus stopping the bags from acting like a heat trap and soaking up horse sweat. It also places the weight of the saddle bags onto the projecting rear portion of the side bars known as the fans.

By providing a Long Rider with pockets in the saddle bags, and by then hoisting the weight off the horse's sensitive lower back, Prestige Italia solved one of the long-standing problems known to equestrian travellers.

In contrast, American companies adapted a "bigger is better" approach.

Because they are based upon flawed concepts, there should be a law against big saddle bags. A saddle bag should be kept small. By providing saddle bags the size of suitcases, the rider is encouraged to dispense with the pack horse and overload the road horse.

One American saddle bag maker justified the extraordinary size of his bags with these remarks.

"On my first attempt at horse camping, I experimented with the conventional packhorse, pack saddle and panniers combination. It didn't take me long to figure out that packing the old-fashioned way wasn't all that much fun. In fact, it was darn hard work. And why be tied down by having to lead another horse around, a constant distraction from enjoying the country I was out there to see?"

His answer was to create and sell extremely large nylon saddle bags which resemble army duffel bags. Thanks to their extreme size, many first-time travellers are tempted to overload the saddle bags, which in theory were designed to carry a few lightweight articles.

Additionally, these oversize bags ignore the horse's anatomy. They wrongly place the weight on the weaker part of the horse's back and over the animal's sensitive kidneys. This concentration of immense weight can lead to a sore back, can damage kidneys, which are difficult to heal, and ultimately result in spinal arthritis.

As if this weren't bad enough, the creators of these American steamer trunk style saddle bags also urge the rider to place an immense cantle bag behind the saddle. Not only does this add an obscene amount of extra weight over the horse's kidneys, it creates an immediate safety hazard for the traveller.

This vast duffel bag, which measures 24"x15" (60cm. x 38cm.), is lashed directly behind the saddle's cantle. The additional bulk makes it extremely difficult for the rider to swing his leg over this obstacle and gain entry into the saddle. Plus, the unnecessary bulk can create a hazard if the Long Rider needs to dismount rapidly in an emergency.

One Long Rider nearly came to grief when her horse began to walk off before she could swing her small leg over the massive saddle and cantle bags strapped to the back of her saddle.

"He walked off with me caught half-mounted with one leg stuck struggling over the cantle bag unable to get a firm grip on the outside rein, throwing me off-balance and walking straight onto the highway with an 85 mph posted speed limit, me hanging off the side of the saddle unable to either bail off or right myself," she wrote later.

Ironically, while the American cavalry accidentally inspired these oversize monsters, the European cavalry had taken careful note of the horse's anatomy and devised a superior system.

Because European cavalrymen were restricted to a bare minimum of weight, they were issued with two small saddle bags that strapped behind the saddle. The majority of allowable weight, for both horse and rider, was carefully packed in two large pommel bags which rested on that part of the side-bar projecting beyond the front of the saddle called the burrs.

This system placed the majority of the weight over the horse's strong shoulders, not over his weak kidneys. Richard Barnes used this method with great results when he made his ride around the perimeter of Great Britain.

"So as to prevent pressure on the horse's kidneys and allay any chafing or friction on the horse, I learned how important it is to place as much of the weight forward onto the horse's shoulders and to keep any weight behind the saddle as light as possible."

When carrying two day's spare grain ration, a European cavalryman would store it in a long canvas tube, which was secured atop the pommel bag, with one day's ration hanging down either side.

In summary, there are rules for saddle bags, just as there are for every aspect of equestrian travel.

Never overload the saddle bags. Place the majority of the weight over the shoulders instead of the kidneys. In order to ensure a safe ride, the saddle bags must be evenly loaded. Because of the constant movement of travel, never place sharp, hard objects on the side of the saddle bag that touches the horse's flanks, as this may cause pain and injury. Saddle bags should be made from tough light-weight material, have compartments, be securely mounted and rain-proof.

Remember to desensitize your horse to the sound of Velcro straps opening on saddle or pommel bags. Finally, place a strip of reflective tape on the back of the saddle bags so traffic coming up from behind will see you.

Saddle Pads and Blankets

Hard-riding horsemen from the past understood the need to ride close to the horse. That is why fast-moving equestrian cultures such as the Mongols used only one pad under their saddle, so as to protect the horse's back while not adversely affecting the balance of the rider.

"The balance of the rider is a necessity or you are continually fighting gravity and gravity always wins," wrote saddle pad inventor and Long Rider Len Brown.

The saddle pad is deceptively simple, yet tremendously important. It evenly distributes the pressure of the saddle and the rider's weight over the horse's back. It diminishes shocks and reduces pressure points. Because it is breathable, it absorbs sweat, while allowing air to circulate and cool the horse's back.

It should be large enough to allow at least two inches of pad to extend around the entire saddle. When fitting the saddle pad, it should rest up inside the gullet of the saddle, so as to allow a channel of cool air to flow along the horse's spine.

Because the saddle pad has to absorb shocks, and dissipate heat off the horse's back, riders have experimented with a number of different materials. History demonstrates that natural materials work best.

An extraordinary example are the saddle pads constructed from compressed horse hair.

When North American Long Rider Mary Ellen Eckleberg rode the length of the Mississippi river in 1976, she used a traditional Mexican saddle pad known as the *sudedero*. This lightweight pad, which was constructed from horse mane and tail hair, kept the horse's back cool.

Swedish Long Rider Mikael Strandberg spent the winter of 2004 making a record-breaking crossing of the frozen Siberian landscape. Upon arriving at the village of Nalimsk he discovered one of the world's most remote equestrian cultures. Despite the deadly temperatures, the hardy local Yakut tribal horsemen could be seen happily cantering their white horses across the snowy landscape in minus sixty degree weather.

"The Yakut saddle blanket is a work of art. It is made from woven horse hair and is thick and very comfortable," Mikael reported.

Though separated by thousands of miles from the Mexican *sudedero*, the nomadic horsemen of Kazakhstan also developed a horse hair saddle pad, which they named the *terlik*. Tim Cope was introduced to this extraordinary pad by a Kazakh herder, who explained its significance.

According to the Kazakh, despite years of constant hunting and riding, his horse had never had a sore back thanks to the springy horsehair pad. Not only did it cushion the horse's back, after swimming a river, the water drained away immediately.

Another traditional favourite is the wool blanket.

According to one cavalry manual, "A good thick blanket is a blessing, a thin blanket an abomination. A good blanket folds. A thin blanket wrinkles. A good blanket saves a back from bruising. A thin blanket is never satisfactory when horses are losing condition."

The thickness of the blanket prevents the ribs from becoming bruised due to the rider's weight and long hours under saddle. A good blanket is also a means to immediately replace artificially the amount of flesh a horse loses during the journey.

The traditional wool saddle blanket is not a square. The length is five feet five inches (165 cm.) while the width is four feet eight inches (142 cm.). The size when folded is two feet by one foot eight inches (60 x 50 cm.).

There is a specific method of folding the saddle blanket. First, fold the blanket in half. Next, fold lengthways so as to make three folds of equal width in the length of the blanket. Finally, fold one end over 24 inches (60 cm.) and then fold the opposite end on top.

It is then placed on the horse's back with the thick end near the withers and the front edge about two fingers' width in front of the rear of the shoulder blade. Be sure the blanket is raised well off the withers so as to allow air to circulate under the saddle.

Traditional wool saddle blankets allow a traveller to compensate for irregularities and problems which occur on the horse's back. Plus, by changing the fold every day, a clean surface can be placed on the horse's back for 12 days before the blanket needs to be washed.

Additionally, wool saddle blankets dry easily, can be used to keep the horses warm at night and are useful in camp.

Another natural fabric which works well is felt but it can difficult to keep it clean.

Though wool and felt work well in extreme cold, the best materials to use when travelling in hot weather are linen and cotton. Long Riders in Africa, India and Greece have successfully used linen tablecloths, thick towelling and cotton sheets to absorb sweat and cushion the saddle. All of these materials are folded in the same manner as the traditional wool saddle blanket.

In contrast, a wide variety of saddle pads which might work for a few hours exercise on a dressage horse will never suit the needs of a road horse. Unlike natural materials, manmade fibres break the hair and increase the chances of saddle sores on hot days,.

Air pads were patented in the 1890s and have proved to be ineffective.

Gel pads are heavy and the material moves away from pressure caused by the saddle. Neoprene is hot, can scald a horse's back and collapses when compressed. Plus, horsehair sticks to a neoprene pad, making it difficult to clean. Both gel and neoprene pads slip when covered in sweat, making it difficult to keep the saddle in place. Pressure-sensitive foam can be crushed by the saddle.

In an ironic twist of fate, when road horses on three continents were injured, the Long Riders' Guild discovered an American corporation was responsible for selling one of the most damaging saddle pads ever conceived.

These events had their beginning in 1971 when the American-based 3M Corporation decided to expand into the animal care industry. The company produced equine leg wraps, bandages, etc. But in an astonishing display of corporate cunning, 3M decided to repackage a material previously sold as an indoor-outdoor floor mat as a saddle pad.

According to the 3M Corporation's Technical Data on Safety-Walk Wet Area the product is porous matting made from vinyl filaments. The mat is designed as a cushion for bare feet in wet areas. Authorized applications include saunas and locker rooms. It is not recommended in kitchens or greasy, oily areas. There is no mention of any equestrian application listed.

Resembling a kitchen scrub pad, the plastic mat was cut into saddle-sized sections and advertised in leading American equestrian magazines, all the while its true origins were carefully concealed from the public.

Soon after 3M began selling the floor mat as a saddle pad, company representatives attempted to enlist North American Long Rider Lucy Leaf to use the product during her ride through the United States. Suspecting the abrasive nature of the material, Lucy declined.

The corporation eventually stopped directly marketing the material as a saddle pad, yet continued to sell the product to private suppliers, who cut it into saddle-sized pieces and then resold it at a handsome profit.

These facts became known when road horses belonging to Long Riders in Chile, America and Kazakhstan all suffered injuries.

It might be thought that if the natural tendency of the saddle is to slip forward, then the same must hold true with the saddle pad. Yet the opposite is true, as saddle blankets tend to work backwards and come out at the rear of the saddle. Many attribute this to the direction of the horse's hair, i.e. the pad slipping with the hair not against it.

This problem is aggravated when 3M's synthetic, chemical-based compound becomes slick with sweat. When this occurred, the 3M saddle pad worked its way out from underneath an American Long Rider's saddle. The pad fell off the back of the horse without the rider's knowledge, the saddle slipped over and the traveller was thrown without warning.

Though that traveller was not severely injured, horses belonging to other Long Riders suffered serious wounds. For example, a Long Rider crossing eastern Kazakhstan reported, "First the no-sweat pad rubbed the hair off my horses. Then it rubbed them right down to the skin. My horses ended up with raw spots where the no-sweat pad rubbed them so badly."

Likewise during his ride across Chile, Keith Clark's horses were also rubbed raw by the floor mat.

The truth behind the saddle pad's murky origins would have remained a closely guarded corporate secret, had Keith not discovered the so-called saddle pad being used as a door mat outside a supermarket in Chile. An interview with the local supermarket manager prompted an emergency telephone call to their corporate headquarters. These people informed Keith that they had no knowledge of any horse saddle pad and that the product sitting in front of their supermarket's front door was a licensed 3M product.

The international equestrian scandal was exposed when a 3M spokesman at the company's corporate headquarters in St. Paul, Minnesota confirmed to the Guild that the company knew horses were being scarred and injured by the misuse of their product.

In a lengthy telephone conversation, this 3M customer service representative revealed how he had personally fulfilled orders for years to an American company, who he knew was reselling the floor mat as a "no sweat" saddle pad. The corporate employee also volunteered the information that 3M was aware that horses had suffered injuries as a result of having commercial floor mats placed on their backs by unsuspecting owners and that 3M was aware that the floor mat had "scarred some horses."

During the subsequent inquiry Long Riders in five countries discovered that the 3M product known as "Wet Area Matting 1500" was being knowingly sold by the corporation to individuals who cut the coarse synthetic material into saddle sized pieces. The disguised floor mat, which 3M describes as being suitable for high traffic areas in sports centres, hotels and hospitals, was then remarketed as expensive saddle pads in the United States, England and Australia.

An example of this practice was uncovered when a colleague of The Guild telephoned the English offices of 3M to enquire if the company sold a saddle pad. A 3M spokesperson immediately supplied the name of a well-known London saddle shop. At no time during the conversation did the 3M representative advise the caller that the product in question, now being called a "cool breeze saddle pad," was in reality a floor mat.

Despite the Guild's repeated requests that the company issue a public warning to horse owners worldwide, the 3M Corporation refused to publicly acknowledge these documented concerns. Furthermore, following The Guild's requests for action, the company's website was altered and incriminating photographs which might link the floor mat to the so-called saddle pad were removed by 3M. Finally the Long Riders' Guild issued a plea to legal authorities on three continents to investigate how a 3M corporation product, originally designed as an abrasive floor mat, was being resold as a saddle pad to unsuspecting horse owners

According to the American company headquartered in Florida, which is mainly responsible for selling the product to unsuspecting horse owners, the floor mat is a "no sweat vent pad… as soft and comfortable as an old flannel shirt."

Under no circumstances should a Long Rider use this mislabelled product, which is being billed as the "no sweat pad" in America and the "cool breeze" saddle pad in England.

While science was misused in this case, one experienced Long Rider matched his knowledge of equestrian travel with equine biology. The result was a new type of saddle pad known as the Corrector.

After completing a 3,000 mile journey, Len Brown invented the remarkable adjustable Ortho Flex saddle. But Len believed that too many saddle pads were ineffective.

"If the saddle does not fit properly, no amount of padding will correct the problem after a saddle sore has occurred. I developed the Corrector saddling device which lets you use any saddle on any horse without having saddle sores. It is polyester felt and fleece, has a large elliptical opening at the top and is therefore very cool." Len wrote. This new type of saddle pad is being tested by Long Riders as this book is being written.

Regardless if you are using an ancient *terlik* horse hair pad, a traditional wool blanket or a modern alternative, keeping the saddle pad clean and dry is vitally important.

Saddle Strings

While there is a wide variety of riding saddles to choose from, many Long Riders use a traditional western-style saddle. These saddles were originally equipped with long leather strings designed to tie bedrolls and saddle bags in place. Unfortunately the problem with many modern factory-made saddles is that the strings are for looks, not work. These saddle strings are usually too short to be of any practical purpose, are not properly attached and are often constructed from inferior leather.

During her ride across the United States, Long Rider Tracy Paine resolved this problem.

"There are many different varieties of saddles out there. I used a plain old western saddle on my horseback trip; however, this method should work with just about any kind of saddle that is big enough and strong enough to hold saddle bags. Most conventional, store-bought saddles are made cheap. The flimsy saddle strings are usually stapled on! They do not hold up when travelling on an extended horseback journey. One of the first things I did to strengthen my saddle was to get new saddle strings. It's best to have long and tough strings. I used 7' long strings made of thick latigo leather. The strings are only as strong as their attachment to the saddle. The best way to attach them is to drill holes clear through the saddle and pull them through. Then hammer them flat on the inside (horse side) of the saddle while pulling on them from the other side," Tracy advised.

And Canadian Long Rider Stan Walchuk also warned about poorly-made, short saddle strings.

"A feature you're going to want on any saddle are strings to tie your gear to the saddle with. The strings of western saddles are used in the construction of the saddle to tie the tree to the component parts. Yet I've seen strings on western saddles so short knots could not be tied in them. I think you should at least start out with strings a yard long. They should be of thick alum-tanned latigo, not oil tanned. The alum-tan is very flexible and you can tie good tight knots in it."

Stirrups

Many people underestimate the importance of the stirrup, which accomplishes two fundamental tasks. It allows the rider to safely mount and provides a platform which helps him to maintain his balance during the ride.

Saddles predate stirrups. Romans, for example, rode in a saddle which had no stirrups. They managed to stay in place thanks to leather horns which jutted out over their hips and legs, effectively locking them in place.

The Greeks lacked a saddle and relied instead on a simple pad. When called upon to ride, these spearmen invented a singular manner of mounting. They tied a piece of rope to their spear, thereby forming a loop which was as high as their knee. They leaned the spear against the horse's neck, placed their foot in the rope loop and then tried to swing onto the horse's back.

While this pogo stick approach required a certain sense of gymnastic finesse, it was safer than trying to vault into the saddle while fully armed. In 522 B.C. King Cambyses of Persia died when he accidentally stabbed himself while trying to leap onto his horse.

Thus, though mankind had been riding the horse for centuries, getting atop the animal's back remained a challenge. Tree stumps, tall rocks, stools and a helpful push from a friend were all employed over the ages.

That is why the first stirrup was designed to provide the rider with a secure mounting platform, and why stirrups were originally only hung from one side of the saddle. The old English word, "stirrup," provides a clue circa 1,000 A.D., as it comes from *stig* (climb) *rap* (rope).

In addition to mounting, the stirrup provides a platform upon which the rider can maintain his balance. This in turn places us deeper into the saddle and ultimately grants us an immense sense of physical and emotional security.

The first step in this equestrian evolution took place in the second century B.C., when horsemen in India created the toe stirrup, a loop of rope which held the big toe. Though the toe stirrup restricted the use of shoes, it was an important early step in helping to stabilize the rider.

Centuries passed until stirrups were used in pairs on a saddle. The first example of paired stirrups was discovered on a Chinese pottery horse, dated 400 A.D. The use of paired stirrups appears to have then begun slowly travelling west across Central Asia and finally into Europe. Stirrups are said to have finally arrived in England about 1,000 A.D. This critical invention was brought to England by Scandinavian Vikings, who in turn had adapted it from the steppe nomads they had encountered while sailing down Europe's great river systems.

Having two stirrups transformed riding, travel and warfare. Stirrups allowed humans to ride further, faster and safer. They allowed a horseman to sit securely in the saddle while shooting a bow or throwing a lance.

Though stirrups originated ages ago, they still have an important part to play on an equestrian journey. The steadiness of the rider's seat depends greatly upon the stirrups being adjusted to the proper length. The length of the stirrup leather differs radically from one culture to another. In Mongolia, for example, the stirrup leathers are kept extremely short, whereas the stirrups on a traditional cowboy saddle were set much longer. When a cowboy stood up in his stirrups, there was about one inch clearance between his crotch and the seat of the saddle.

Unlike a cavalry or English saddle, which can be easily adjusted via a traditional buckle, stirrups on western saddles were very difficult to adjust, as they were usually laced into position. In the 1950s a sliding mechanism known as the Blevens buckle made altering the length of a western stirrup much easier. Yet until the advent of this buckle, young riders were warned to never let anyone else use their saddle because of the need to readjust the stirrups.

There are now as many different types of stirrups as there are equestrian cultures. Even so, a Long Rider's stirrups must meet certain criteria.

A lightweight metal stirrup swings away and is hard to catch if your foot slips loose. Long Rider stirrups should be heavy enough so as to make them easy to catch when the horse is in motion. The stirrups should also be wide enough to accommodate your riding boot. Finally, padded stirrups ease the pain in your knees which can occur after an extremely long day in the saddle.

The construction of the stirrup is also important. According to the German cavalry, there were three reasons to use wooden stirrups, as opposed to metal ones: less weight, better in cold weather, reduced noise.

Whether your stirrups are metal or wood, many traditional stirrups have a circular hole in the base, which allows water to drain out.

If you are going to be riding in cold weather or through dense brush, then you may wish to equip your stirrups with *tapaderos*. These are leather covers which fit in front of the stirrups. Cowboys riding in winter would often line their tapaderos with sheepskin. Travellers going through thick undergrowth report that the *tapaderos* protect their boots from being scraped. *Tapaderos* also protect your boots from morning dew and rain.

Girths

While it is commonly known that saddles can injure a horse's back, the girth can also inflict wounds on your road and pack horses. Girth galls are caused by friction. Buckles can wound a horse's sensitive skin via abrasion.

Like the saddle pad, the girth should be non-abrasive, so as to reduce the chance of chafing while in motion. It should be soft, supple and dissipate heat. It must be easy to clean and quick to dry.

Many Long Riders prefer mohair string girths, as they fulfil all these requirements. Though neoprene girths are easy to clean, they become hot, retain heat and induce sweating.

You cannot pay too much attention to the adjustment of the girth, for if it is not properly secured, the saddle may turn round, and the life of the rider will be instantly endangered.

In the 1930s, French Long Rider Léa Lafugie was in Tibet on her third journey. Even though she had ridden thousands of miles through the Himalayan Mountains on an assortment of mounts, it only took one tiny mistake to nearly end her life.

"I had hardly got onto my pony when he rushed off at a rapid trot, took the wrong path and bolted like a lunatic. It was impossible to hold him, he reared and suddenly I was hurled onto the rocks beside the trail which was hanging over the ravine. My head hit the rocks. I could feel a ribbon of blood dripping down my neck. My clothes were torn and my back a mass of contusions."

Lafugie soon discovered that the worn-out girth had broken. The moment the saddle began to slide, the nervous horse took fright and her fall was inevitable.

The problem is how to tighten the girth just enough to stabilize the saddle, without cinching so tight that it pinches the sensitive skin. The answer is that when properly adjusted the girth should allow two fingers to be placed between it and the horse's body. If done properly, the skin beneath the girth will be carefully smoothed and free from wrinkles.

Long Rider and equestrian inventor Len Brown has created a new girth known as the "Never Tight." This girth has a core of aircraft plastic moulded to the shape of the horse. The girth's inside lining is soft shoe sole crepe. The outer layer is Hermann oak leather. The hardware is stainless steel. The result is a girth which holds the saddle stable without pinching.

Because of the rigours normally encountered during a journey, many horses lose weight while travelling. If your girth is too long, it becomes hard to adjust it properly. That is why many Long Riders use a 28" mohair girth, as it is a size which provides more adjustment.

Breastplate and Crupper

The breastplate and crupper are not as a rule required except when travelling in mountainous country, so many Long Riders dispense with the extra weight.

However, in rugged terrain the breastplate and crupper are particularly useful, as the breastplate prevents the saddle from slipping back when travelling uphill, while the crupper keeps the saddle from sliding forward when going down steep trails.

The problem with both pieces of equipment is that they must not be too tight. There is nothing more distressing for a horse than to be harnessed up with either a riding or pack saddle held rigidly in place. An unyielding breastplate can quickly cause abrasions between the forelegs and cause saddle sores over the withers. A too tight crupper will rub the root of the horse's tail, causing a nasty sore which resembles a rope burn. This type of wound is hard to heal and painful.

For these reasons, the breastplate and crupper should be adjusted so that the saddle can move freely a few inches forward and back.

Both the crupper and breastplate must be kept meticulously clean.

Should a horse make a false step, he uses his head to maintain his balance, much like a human uses his arms. For this reason a standing or running martingale should never be used on road or pack horses, for it affects the animal's ability to recover his balance.

Bridles and Bits

Once early humans realized that powerful horses could transport them over great distances, a 6,000 year technological struggle began to direct and control the fast-moving animal.

Some equestrian cultures never adapted the bit and bridle. For example, when the Carthaginian general, Hannibal, attacked the Roman Empire in 218 B.C., he employed Numidian horsemen from Africa. These warriors preferred to guide their horses by the use of a small stick, which they employed along the animal's neck like a riding crop.

Though Hannibal's North African riders ignored the bit, the topic of direction and control had already preoccupied mankind for thousands of years. Early riders restrained their mounts by use of a rope looped around the horse's lower jaw, or placed over the sensitive nose like a hackamore. Because they are subject to decay, biodegradable equestrian evidence used to make early bits and bridles, such as leather, rope and horn, has been hard to locate and substantiate.

Yet evidence has been found. Archaeologists excavating in the Ukraine discovered horse skulls, dated from 4000 B.C., which bore traces of bit wear on the teeth. Other artefacts, including pieces of antler which may have served as cheek pieces, were discovered at a site near the Black Sea.

More durable metal equestrian artefacts which survived demonstrate that the first primitive snaffle metal bits originated in the Near East circa 1500 B.C. The more technologically advanced curb bit was developed circa 400 B.C.

Archaeologists are still struggling to document the exact history and development of the bit and bridle. Yet in 1889 the English Long Rider Henry Savage Landor discovered that one of mankind's most primitive equestrian cultures was still riding in the Bronze Age.

Soon after arriving in Japan, the young traveller left to make an equestrian journey through the largely unexplored Island of Hokkaidō. There he befriended the indigenous Ainu, a tribe of hunters and fishermen who predated the arrival of the Japanese by thousands of years. These robust natives were also horse riders who still employed one of mankind's earliest bits and bridles.

In his remarkable book, *Alone with the Hairy Ainu*, Landor made a careful note of how the Ainu riders constructed what might have served as the prototype for one of mankind's earliest bits and bridles.

"A curious method is adopted for directing the animal. It is as simple as it is ingenious. The necessary bit by which we control our horses is dispensed with, and it is replaced by two wooden wands about twelve inches long and two inches wide, tied together at one end, allowing a distance of three inches between them. In the middle of these wands a rope is passed which goes over the pony's head behind its ears, while the wands themselves, thus supported by it, rest one on each side of the pony's nose. Another rope, five or six feet in length, and acting as a rein, is fastened at the lower end of one of the wands, and passed through a hole in the other, thus allowing this simple contrivance, based on the lever principle, to be worked exactly in the way as a nut-cracker, the pony's nose being the nut. The disadvantage of the system is, that having one rein, this has to be passed over the pony's head each time one wishes to turn to the right or to the left, as by pulling the rope hard, and thus squeezing the animal's nose, its head is turned in the direction in which it is pulled, and it is soon taught that this is the way it must go. Furthermore, should the pony bolt, it can be stopped by pulling its head close to its haunches, thereby making it impossible to continue its race."

Though Landor had discovered that the equestrian clock had stopped on isolated Hokkaidō, the rest of the horse world had been busy making technological progress.

The original snaffle bit consisted of a bar that lay across the horse's lower jaw. By pulling on the ends of the bar, the rider could direct his horse. A substantial improvement occurred when the bar was cut into two smaller pieces. A small metal ring connected the bars, which now allowed the snaffle bit to flex. This two-sided bit, which became known as the broken snaffle, gave rise to the concept of the hard and soft hand. One side of the snaffle, usually the left, would be kept smooth, while the right side bar would be intentionally grooved or serrated so as to cause the horse pain if he resisted pressure from the rider's hand. Though these types of snaffle bits are one of mankind's earliest equestrian inventions, they are still commonly used in Afghanistan, where they are favoured by the riders who ride stallions in the wild game known as buz khazi.

Because of the severity of these early bits, the nomadic general, Genghis Khan, ordered his soldiers not to require their horses to wear bits during the march. This order achieved two things which remain of great concern to the modern Long Rider. By removing the bit, it kept the horse's mouth sensitive. It also allowed the horse to eat as and when it could during the course of that day's travel.

Over the course of time different types of bits were developed, each of which affect a different part of the horse's anatomy. The mediaeval warhorse, for example, was often ridden with a curb bit. This bit simultaneously presses against the roof of the horse's mouth, at the same time the long shanks create pressure on the top of the horse's poll. A third system, commonly known as the hackamore, does not affect the mouth but applies pressure instead across the bridge of the horse's sensitive nose.

Because they can be misused, the bit and bridle should never be used to inflict pain. Long Riders know instead that it is essential that the horse be allowed to hold his head high, to move forward freely and to take as much of the reins as the situation and safety require.

It is thanks to the bit and bridle that horse and human can achieve a subtlety of movement without the use of spoken language. The rider transmits his wishes via the reins. This in turn alerts the horse, via the pressure of the bit, to the needed change in speed or direction. The result is a silent symbiotic progress of two species.

Bits have been successfully used since Kikkuli, the first recorded horse trainer, recommended them 3,500 years ago. Yet there is a growing fashion in America and England to denounce all bits as barbaric. Advocates of what is called the bitless bridle ignore the fact that like any tool, bits can be misused. Nor is this modern version of the hackamore without its faults too.

When Irish Long Rider Caitriona O'Leary tested a bitless bridle in 2011, she ran into trouble.

"An update on the natural bitless bridle that I have been using. I tried it out in the fields for the first time yesterday. Bear in mind that the horse I ride is an old ex-racehorse who still thinks she is five. The bridle worked great in the school and made it possible to perform very precise and smooth transitions and my first two canters in the field were nice and controlled. Then Mina realised that if she arched her head a certain way she could jimmy that little noseband up and she bolted across a field, round a corner and almost into a wire fence with me. I only stopped with the help of a man walking his dog and then dismounted and walked back to get a bridle with a strong bit."

Caitriona later realised that the bitless bridle had not been properly adjusted; as a result she lost control of the horse.

"I had put the noseband too high, going for the look of a normal bridle. It only works if it's in a lower position where the nose is more sensitive."

Tragically, Caitriona died in 2012 after suffering fatal injuries during a riding accident in England. The runaway horse she was on had been wearing a bitless bridle. However the coroner's inquest was not able to determine if this piece of equipment had malfunctioned or had contributed to the accident.

What Caitriona sought, she said, was a happier horse. That is an admirable goal, one which Long Riders throughout the centuries have also tried to obtain.

Whether you go bitted or bitless is beside the point. Any equestrian implement can be cruel if misused. What needs to be remembered is that a Long Rider and a road horse have separate but equal needs.

Horses do not respond well to force. In an ideal situation they seek emotional stability and physical comfort. Ask and they will give. But you cannot cross a continent on a horse who won't obey a simple command to stop or turn.

Likewise, a Long Rider's life is placed on trust when he swings into the saddle. Unlike ring riders, equestrian explorers often find themselves facing life-threatening challenges. When such an event occurs, the rider must be able to make an instant decision, so as to protect the life of both parties.

The issue, therefore, is how best to achieve this delicate balance of comfort for the horse and safety for the rider.

There are as many bits and bridles as there are equestrian cultures. Your challenge is to carefully judge what works best for you and your horse. What you must not do is fall prey to a cultural fad or condone cruelty.

Throughout history Long Riders have recorded their amazement at the intensity of the emotional relationship which developed between them and their road horse.

At the conclusion of his 803-day journey from Canada to Brazil, Filipe Leite expressed how deeply attached he had become to his three horses.

"Frenchie, Bruiser, Dude and I were a herd in every sense of the word. We slept next to one another, woke up together, travelled all day."

When you eat, drink, sleep and travel with another biological entity for months and months, is it any wonder that language becomes a needless luxury?

Because of this intense knowledge of each others habits, some Long Riders have dispensed with any type of bit and bridle. Though John Egenes, DC Vision and Tim Cope collectively rode nearly 25,000 miles, each of their horses only wore a halter and reins. DC's Shire mare, Louise, was reportedly so alert to her rider's desires that she would respond to mental signals.

The Long Rider is seeking to transmit orders via the most subtle movement of the hands and fingers. However, not all horses are as gentle as Louise and you may well find yourself in a life-threatening situation which requires you to issue a command which must be instantly obeyed.

The key is to choose the gentlest bit which works for you and your horse. To begin with, discard the idea of using a double bridle and reins. One set of reins is quite enough for you and your horse to contend with.

Many Long Riders have had excellent results with an egg-butt broken snaffle. Great care must be used if you decide to use a curb bit. Unlike the primitive snaffle, which applies pressure to the horse's lower jaw, the curb bit acts as a mechanical fulcrum which can create incredible pressure and pain. That is why the curb chain must never be overly tight.

Regardless of which type of bit you choose, it must be carefully adjusted so that the bit rests on the bar of the mouth and does not jar against the horse's teeth. Make sure the bit is nickel plated so as to avoid rust. If you are riding in extremely cold weather, remember to warm the bit before putting it into the horse's sensitive mouth.

A traditional alternative to the bit is the hackamore. This system ignores the horse's mouth, preferring to use a noseband which is adjusted to lie just above the nostrils where the bone is thin and soft. A horse is very sensitive there, so responds well to commands. A hackamore is also good for travel because it allows the horse to graze and drink more freely.

French Long Rider Evelyne Coquet used a hackamore during her journey from Paris to Jerusalem.

"They learn very quickly and are much more obedient. If they had to wear a bit every day, for weeks and months, they might get sores at the corners of their lips. This way, they can graze whenever we stop to look at the map. We aren't asking for any fancy tricks. They don't need to be collected, we just want them to walk, and the hackamore does a very good job," Evelyne recalled.

Likewise, when British Long Riders Harry and Lisa Adshead rode from England to the Middle East, they too equipped their horses with hackamores.

"They worked perfectly, allowing horses to eat and drink all day without anything getting in the way."

Another excellent alternative is the halter-bridle combination, which eliminates the need to employ two separate pieces of equipment. The snaffle bit can be easily detached, leaving the horse free to graze and drink. The key to this system is to make sure the halter and bit are properly fitted prior to your departure.

Whether you decide to go bitless or bitted, the system you choose must be as efficient and tidy as possible. Many Long Riders prefer to use bridles made from nylon webbing, as they are easier to keep clean in the field. The problem with nylon is that it is very strong and in an emergency a nylon bridle will not break, like a leather bridle will, if a horse becomes trapped and panics.

Another essential decision must include your reins. Heavy reins do not encourage sensitive commands. Your reins should be tough, but rest lightly in your hands like ribbons. They should be long enough to allow you to easily lead the horse. Split reins are safer because they cannot become caught. Woven nylon reins work well because they are durable, lightweight and can be snapped on and off easily. The Mexican vaqueros are credited with inventing a system to keep the reins out of the water when a horse was drinking. They attached a thin 12 inch long chain between the bit and the reins, which kept the reins dry and clean.

Like any sort of guidance, there are no hard and fast rules regarding bits and bridles. Your decision on what system to choose will depend on which country you travel across, what equipment options are available there and how sensitive your horse is. Regardless of what you decide, remember to never apply more pressure to the horse than is absolutely necessary. Every command should be as light as possible. Patience, not brutality, must always be your guide.

Halters and Lead Ropes

The halter is one of those everyday items which is in constant use but seldom receives adequate consideration. It must be easy to put on, strong, flexible, simple to clean and fit well. Because it is seldom removed during the journey, it must not rub the horse or have abrasive parts which might injure him.

Like bridles, halters were originally made from leather but this material is heavy and hard to maintain. That is why many modern halters are now constructed from flat sturdy nylon fitted with a steel ring and tongue in the buckle. Nylon halters can also be easily repaired.

The drawbacks of a nylon halter are that if a horse becomes caught on an object, he cannot break free. Also, a nylon halter which is fitted too tightly will wear the hair off a horse's muzzle or behind his ears.

Many Long Riders have had good results with rope halters, which are light and have no abrasive metal parts that might rub a horse. If need be a rope halter can also be used as a hackamore.

A halter can be created from rope by the following method. Tie a small loop at one end of the rope. Four inches further along tie a similar loop. Make sure that both loops are only large enough to admit the free passage of the rope. Next, pass the free end of the rope through the first and second loops. If you need to adjust the halter, another knot may be added at each loop to prevent slipping.

The other element associated with the halter is the lead rope. You should always secure your horse with a lead rope and never by the reins. The problem is that lead ropes are under constant strain and frequent abuse. Horses walk on them. Sharp rocks tear them. The result is that lead ropes must be replaced every few thousand miles.

Unfortunately many countries do not sell top-quality rope. For example, Pakistan and parts of Africa are forced to use cheap coloured nylon rope from China. This rope is so stiff that it is difficult to tie a knot, and once tied, knots frequently slip loose. The pink, blue or green dye rubs off on your hands and your horse's neck. It becomes stiff in the rain, frays easily and is impossible to repair. That is why Long Riders often choose to bring their own rope with them.

Even though cotton rope is gentle on the hands, a horse can quickly damage it by dragging it on the ground, stepping on it, or rubbing it against rough surfaces.

Marine-grade synthetic rope is stronger, more durable and just as flexible as cotton. Climbing rope works well for equestrian travellers, many of whom choose a ½ inch (1.25 cm.) diameter as it is easy to handle and tie.

A lead rope should be eleven feet (4 m.) long. Many are equipped with a strong metal snap clip on the end, which allows you to instantly detach the rope from the horse in case of an emergency.

Stan Walchuk advocates the button loop lead rope instead of the metal snap. This simple system uses a button which slips through a loop on the lead rope. Stan can provide high-quality rope halters and button loop lead ropes from his outfitting company.

Top quality rope is also necessary to tether your horses, make a highline, erect an emergency corral or construct emergency reins. Each tethering rope should be at least 25 feet (9 m.) long, so carrying spare rope to cover these contingencies is something to consider. One problem is that top-quality rope is often stolen. For example, many Long Riders crossing Mongolia have had their lead ropes pilfered.

Teaching your horse to be rope wise prior to departure is an important lesson. If you are concerned about tying your horse, attach the tethering rope to a breakable loop of twine. This provides a weak link that can be snapped in case the horse panics.

The alternative to a lead rope is to adapt the lead stick used by the Swiss and other European cavalries. The lead stick was designed to stop pack horses carrying ammunition boxes from bumping into the rider's leg.

The lead stick is made of wood, is 1.10 meters (about a yard) long and 30 mm. (1½") wide. At one end there is a leather loop, which is designed for the rider to place around his wrist. At the other end there is a sturdy metal clip to attach to the horse's halter.

Belgian Long Rider Robert Wauters was the first to suggest that this tool could keep an inexperienced pack horse at a distance, which it is not possible to do with only a lead rope.

"Obviously you must not let go of the stick or an inexperienced horse will go crazy at this terrifying object swinging under its head," Robert warned.

Feed bag and Water Bucket

Not only does feeding grain keep your animals in top condition, the sound of the grain rattling in the feed bag acts like a magnet and brings a horse running. Some Long Rider horses become so sharp-eyed that they linger near camp if they even see the feed bags.

Yet feed bags can be difficult and dangerous. Because of the mixture of saliva and grain, the bag must be washed frequently, otherwise it will ferment. A feed bag can also accidentally kill a horse. This occurs when the horse is done feeding and tries to drink. If the feed bag fills with water, the horse may drown. For this reason, a feed bag must have holes placed along the edge to allow water to flow out.

The best option is the cavalry-style mesh feed bag which is constructed from durable vinyl-coated mesh and comes with adjustable nylon straps. Not only does this eliminate the danger of drowning, the bag is constructed in such a way that the horse does not have to toss his head to reach the grain, which slides to the bottom of the bag and is in easy reach. The excellent feed bag eliminates spills while remaining breathable and is available from Outfitter's Supply.

Long Riders are often required to carry grain during their journey. The traditional cavalry grain sack carried two day's ration. This small canvas sack measured 36 inches long and six inches wide (1m. x 15 cm.). Both ends were rounded and closed. A longitudinal slit in the middle was used to pour in the feed. The grain ration was equally balanced, then the sack was strapped across the pommel of the saddle.

Several modern companies offer durable bags which can be adapted for carrying grain. Ortleib's Dry Bags, for example, are lightweight, washable, inexpensive and have a rollover top which keeps the grain secured.

Another item which is often overlooked is a collapsible bucket. When Gordon Naysmith crossed the Arabian Peninsula, he and his horses nearly died of thirst. The only water was in a well more than sixty feet deep. Luckily, he was able to draw up the precious liquid one small bucket at a time.

Collapsible canvas or cordura buckets do not weigh much but are of great importance. The French have improved on this system by creating a remarkable collapsible bucket that cannot be tipped over by a thirsty horse. Regardless of which style you choose, remember not to smash the bucket against a hard surface as you will tear the material or damage the waterproofing.

Bells

Riders have been attaching bells to horses for 3,000 years. From a practical point of view, bells alerted pedestrians to move aside. Because of the narrow trails connecting villages, 18th century British packers used bells to warn one another of an approaching caravan of pack horses. Bells were also believed to ward off bad luck, a concept which still resonates in modern equestrian travel.

Early Roman horse bells were made from iron. By the 14th century the English were making bells of tin. These bells, the predecessor of today's well-known sleigh-bells, were created by closing four petals over a tiny ball. These melodic bells were so pleasing that several of them would be placed on a strap which fitted around the horse's neck.

Horse bells became a staple of the American Industrial Revolution, when William Barton launched the sleigh-bell industry in East Hampton, Connecticut. Thanks to machinery, two skilled workmen could produce 500 bells a day. According to the census of 1850, East Hampton alone created nearly three million bells a year.

Like much of the former equestrian world, the horse bell industry was destroyed by the appearance of the automotive. In 1908 a Ford Model T automobile sold for $950. By 1918 the price had dropped to $280. With more than 15 million cars being sold per year, demand for horse bells disappeared.

Though time has marched on, bells are more than a cheerful link to our past. They are of tremendous practical value to a Long Rider, whose movements are dictated by the sun and moon.

During the day bells provide a musical complement to your horse's gait. They transmit a reassuring message to passers-by that you have nothing to hide.

A small bell known as the saddle chime was sometimes hung from the horn of a western saddle to achieve this effect. During the course of twenty-two years and 17 movies, actor Jimmy Stewart rode the same horse. Stewart's long-time cinema partner was named Pie. To commemorate this forgotten part of his nation's equestrian heritage, the Hollywood legend attached a chime to his saddle, which can be clearly heard in many of Stewart's cowboy films.

While attaching a bell might seem like a bit of romantic fluff, ancient horsemen knew that bells could, in a sense, drive off bad luck, especially if that bad luck came in the shape of a bear.

Many riders who travel through heavily-infested bear country know that the sharp peal of a loud bell will help prevent a surprise meeting. This is especially important if you are travelling downwind, and a bear or another animal cannot smell your approach.

While bells are helpful during the day, they are even more essential at night.

In a perfect world our horses would spend their night quietly grazing, prior to setting off in the morning on another placid day of travel. Yet as anyone who has spent time with horses can attest, they can take fright easily. A rustling noise in the underbrush, the smell of a strange animal or even the mischievous urging of one of their fellows may result in you being awakened to the sound of your horses running off into the night.

As North American Long Rider Jeff Hengesbaugh said, "It's better to count bells than tracks."

Horses that travel together become emotionally bonded, with one animal assuming the leadership of the group. Some Long Riders hobble or picket this horse close to camp, knowing that the horses will graze close by during the night.

Yet chances are that despite your best efforts, at some time during your journey your horses will take the opportunity to escape. For this reason, you should always bell your horses at night.

The sound of the bells allows you to hear animals grazing peacefully during the night. This rhythmic noise keeps you constantly aware of the reassuring close proximity of the horses. Any sudden movement on their part, a quick jerking of the head because of a scary noise in the bushes for example, will also warn you that something, at least in the horse's mind, is going on. Without even leaving camp to investigate you are already alert to trouble.

You will learn that you can hear the bells even in your sleep. The soft sound of the bells during the night provides a comforting confirmation that your horses are grazing close by. That sound induces a sense of calm in you and the horses.

If things go wrong, the sound of the bells will tell you what direction the horses are headed. Because a good bell can be heard for a great distance, it will also help you track the animals if they have been stolen. Plus, after a horse runs away, he may rest, or intentionally stand still so as to avoid detection. A bell will alert you to his presence in the dark.

When horses run away in the dark, they may be seeking water, grazing, or trying to avoid a perceived danger. Regardless of the reason, they usually return in the direction from which you have been travelling. The only exception may be if they encounter another group of loose horses, in which they may fall in and follow the leader of this herd. In such a case, listening for their bells will help you recover them.

Keith Clark learned how useful bells were when his horses disappeared one night in Chile.

"I put bells on my horses at night when I camp. It's nice to hear them tinkling in the background as I know the horses are there. Before I had bells I was forever waking and looking outside.

One night I camped next to the Rio Murta. There was a spot with a lot of grass but only room to tether one horse, so as usual poor old Nispero got the duty. The two loose horses wore bells and as I slept I kept an ear open for them. I woke at midnight and no bells. Stuck my head out of the tent and no Nispero either. The rascal had slipped his head collar and they had all disappeared. I wasn't too worried as the road is either fenced or is bordered by impenetrable forest or bog. So they either went north or south. I decided to look for them northwards, back the way we had come. I heard the familiar tinkling and there they were in a patch of grass set back from the road. No trouble to catch and I've a feeling that they were as glad to see me as I was them. Alls well that ends well."

If you are going to equip your horse with night bells, they have to be loud enough for the sound to carry. A small saddle chime won't serve this purpose. Some Long Riders place different sounding bells on each horse, so as to help identify them at a distance.

If you strap a bell around your horse's neck at night, make sure the strap is just tight enough so that it cannot get caught while he is grazing, or slip over his head. You should be sure to train your horse to wear his bells prior to your departure.

Grooming equipment

Though it is important to reduce weight whenever possible, keeping your horse clean is a priority. A curry comb, a brush and a strong hoof-pick are necessities.

Do not venture overseas without confirming that these items are available locally.

You would also be well advised to carry a small mending kit which you can use to make emergency repairs to your tack.

Hoof Care and Vet Kit

When Margaret Leigh set off to ride from Cornwall to Scotland in 1939, she said, "I had intended to take spare sets of shoes and nails, but the weight was formidable, and they were not really necessary."

A compact emergency shoeing kit for travellers is now available. It contains a hammer, rasp, nippers, 16 nails and two horseshoes. Wrapped in a leather case, the entire kit weighs 1.7 kg. (3.75 pounds). A multi-purpose farrier's tool has also been invented which combines all of the functions needed to change a shoe with one piece of equipment.

You may think that carrying a small medical kit is a luxury. But emergencies happen fast and are frightening. Make sure that you have bandages, antiseptic spray, an anti-inflammatory gel, a course of antibiotics if available, and a broad-spectrum de-wormer.

Horse Rugs

It is hard enough keeping a travelling horse in top condition on available forage without asking him to expend vital energy staying warm. The American cavalry knew that a shivering horse is never happy. Plus you shouldn't put a saddle on a wet horse. So they used a saddle blanket and slicker to keep their horses warm and dry.

Weather, climate and topography will affect your decision to consider carrying a light weight, waterproof coat for your own animals. Long Riders caught in the open have adapted a number of things into ad hoc coats to keep their horses warm and dry, including sail cloth, bed sheets and large tropical leaves.

Tropical Protection

Because of their substantial muscle mass, horses create an immense amount of heat and will sweat profusely when worked hard in hot temperatures. When this occurs they are susceptible to dehydration, heat exhaustion and heat stroke.

A dehydrated horse has lost precious body fluids and will exhibit extreme fatigue. Horses suffering from heat exhaustion will have increased heart and respiratory rates, sweat profusely, and as the condition advances may collapse and go into convulsions. The most lethal of the three, heat stroke, occurs when a horse's ability to cool himself internally has failed. If not treated immediately, the horse will die.

One of the most unlikely pieces of equestrian equipment, the Bombay horse hat, was created in the 19th century to protect vulnerable horses from the potentially lethal effects of the tropical sun, which often reaches nearly 110 degrees Fahrenheit (43 degrees Celsius) in that city.

Caring for the Tack

One of your daily tasks will be to keep your tack as clean and dry as possible.

Neglected gear will always be a source of trouble and may well cause injury to you or your horse. Saddles, bridles and halters are most likely to wear out along the stitching or where straps and dee rings are attached. Prior to your departure, the stitching on every piece of equipment should be carefully examined to ensure that no portion is giving way.

Long Riders should carry a small cleaning and repair kit which they can use to maintain their saddle and other tack. Because it becomes soaked with sweat, the girth is particularly vulnerable. Clean it as often as necessary to keep it soft and resilient. Be sure to wipe sweat and mud off your stirrup leathers everyday. Also make sure the underside of the saddle is always kept clean.

Once you are under way, giving your tack a serious cleaning should be a pleasurable task. Always observe the condition of the leather. Soft and pliable leather is good. Dry stiff leather is a recipe for trouble. This means the saddle should periodically be disassembled, inspected, cleaned, oiled and then carefully reassembled.

All of the leather on your saddle and bridle should be cleaned with glycerine saddle soap. Using a small sponge and warm water, work up a good thick lather. Rub the lather into the leather, work it in well and then wipe it off. During the course of cleaning, examine every piece of equipment carefully for signs of stress or rot. Minor defects in the leather or bridle should be attended to at once. Stitching should be tested, as the life of thread is shorter than leather.

Many Long Riders keep a small bag in which they carry saddle soap, sponge, waxed thread, an awl, duct tape and a spare buckle.

Summary

Though it involves vigilant maintenance, given the proper care your saddle, bit, bridle and other equipment will provide you with years of service.

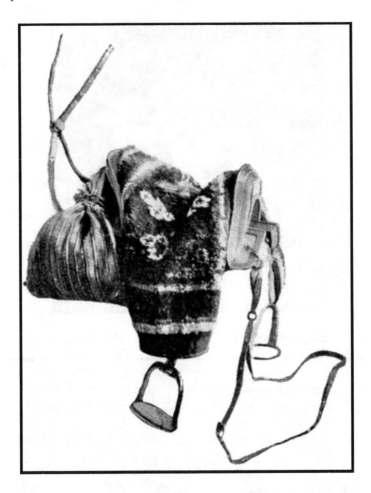

Genghis Khan's warriors carried their personal items in a small water-resistant saddle sack. The same system was still being used by the Tibetans in the late 19th century, as can be seen on this Tibetan saddle.

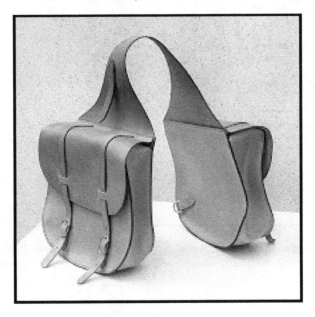

The heavy leather saddle bag used by the American cavalry meant that everything ended up being crushed together in the bottom of the bag.

In 1938 English Long Rider and author Edward Stebbings invented this saddle bag which had separate interior pockets.

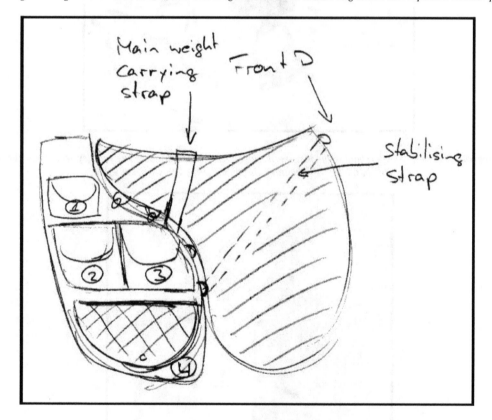

Though Stebbings' bag was never commercially produced, the concept was still being discussed in 2004, when Jeremy James and German equestrian traveller Frauke Nonnenmacher conceived plans for a multi-pocketed saddle bag.

Prior to riding from Italy to Russia, Italian Long Rider Dario Spizzo constructed his own multi-pocketed cordura saddle bags. Note the high-quality nylon rope which is easily accessible on the pommel bag.

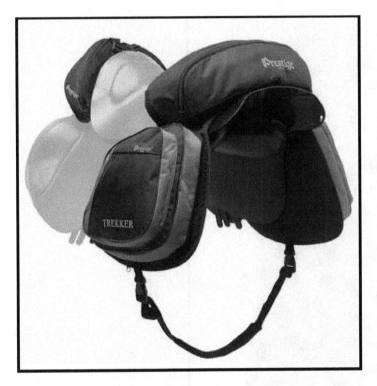

Top quality multi-sectional saddle bags are now available from Prestige Italia

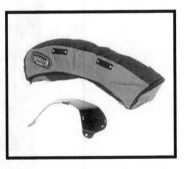

The Prestige Italia saddle and cantle bags receive extra support from a lightweight metal bar which fits across the back of the saddle. This device keeps weight off the horse's sensitive kidneys and allows cool air to circulate over his back.

Knowing how much to carry on your road horse is vital. North American Long Rider Susan O'Hara Bates rode from Mexico to the Canadian border with a minimum of weight on her horse.

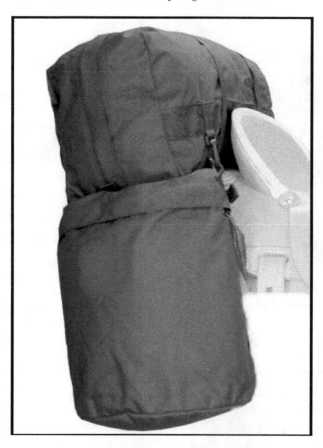

In contrast, American companies have produced saddle bags and cantle bags that resemble army duffle bags. These poorly-designed bags encourage the rider to dispense with the pack horse and overload the road horse. They also present a safety hazard as it is very difficult to swing into or exit from the saddle.

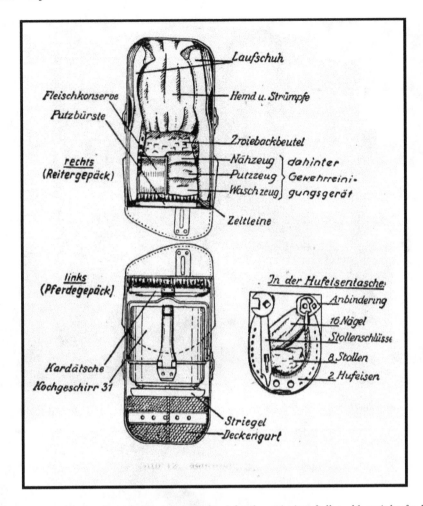

Because European cavalrymen were restricted to a bare minimum of weight, the majority of allowable weight, for both horse and rider, was carefully packed in two large pommel bags which rested on the front of the saddle. This system placed most of the weight over the horse's strong shoulders not over his weak kidneys.

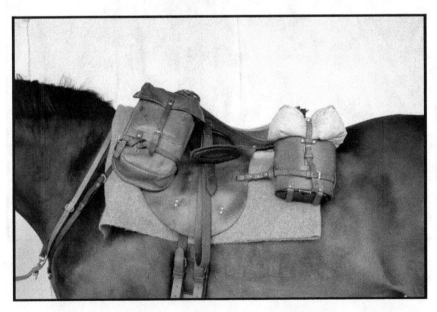

These Swiss cavalry pommel bags carried everything needed by horse and rider. The rider's mess kit and the horse's feed bag were attached behind the saddle; photo courtesy of the Society of the Military Horse.

The nomadic horsemen of Kazakhstan developed a lightweight horsehair saddle pad (right), known as the terlik which kept the horse's back cool.

Ironically, though they are separated by thousands of miles, the Mexican vaqueros also created a similar horse hair saddle pad which they called the sudedero. North American Long Rider Mary Ellen Eckleberg used a sudedero with excellent results when she rode the length of the Mississippi river, in both directions, in 1976.

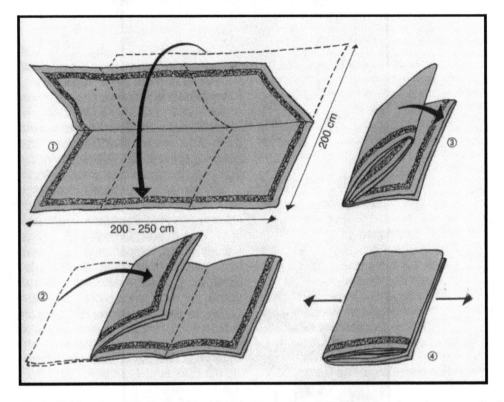

There is a specific method of folding the saddle blanket. First, fold the blanket in half. Next, fold lengthways so as to make three folds of equal width in the length of the blanket. Finally, fold one end over twenty-four inches and then fold the opposite end on top.

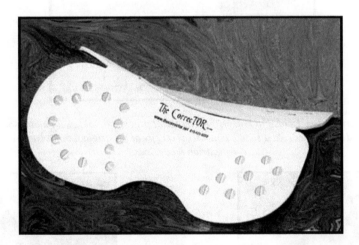

The Corrector saddling device was invented by North American Long Rider Len Brown. Made from polyester felt and fleece, it is designed to reduce saddle sores and keep the horse's back cool.

smart new way to saddle up

Animal Care Products 3M

In 1971 the American based 3M corporation decided to repackage a material previously sold as an indoor-outdoor floor mat as a saddle pad. Though the corporation later denied it had ever sold a saddle pad, this is a copy of the original 3M advertisement which appeared in American equestrian magazines.

According to the 3M Corporation's Technical Data on Safety-Walk Wet Area the product is porous matting made from vinyl filaments. The mat is designed as a cushion for bare feet in wet areas. Authorized applications include saunas and locker rooms. It is not recommended in kitchens or greasy, oily areas. There is no mention of any equestrian function listed.

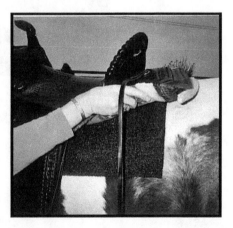

Resembling a kitchen scrub pad, the plastic mat is cut into saddle sized sections and advertised in leading American, English and Australian equestrian magazines using terms such as no-sweat and cool-breeze, all the while its true origins have been carefully concealed from the public. Horses belonging to several Long Riders have been injured by this product.

Long Rider stirrups should be heavy enough to make them easy to catch when the horse is in motion. The stirrups should also be wide enough to accommodate your riding boot. Finally, padded stirrups ease the pain in your knees which may occur after an extremely long day in the saddle.

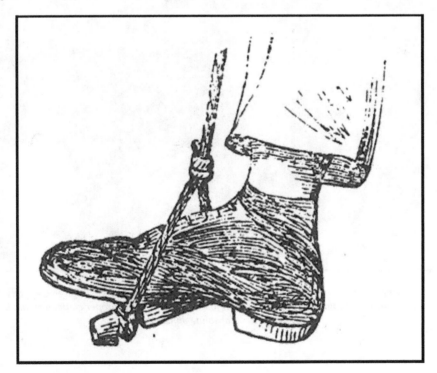

Famous 19th century explorer, Francis Galton, devised this emergency stirrup, which can be readily constructed from a piece of rope and a stick.

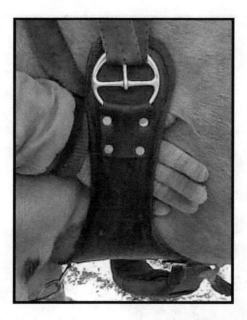

Equestrian inventor Len Brown has created a new girth known as the "Never Tight." This girth has a core of aircraft plastic moulded to the shape of the horse. The girth's inside lining is soft shoe sole crepe. The outer layer is Hermann oak leather. The hardware is stainless steel. The result is a girth which holds the saddle stable without pinching.

Roland Berg and Sabine Matschkus made two lengthy journeys through Europe. First they rode through Germany, Poland, Russia and Lithuania. Next they rode through Portugal, Spain and France. On each journey they used the proper equipment and kept the weight carried by the horses to an absolute minimum.

In 1889 the English Long Rider Henry Savage Landor discovered the Ainu natives of northern Japan were still using one of mankind's earliest known bits and bridle.

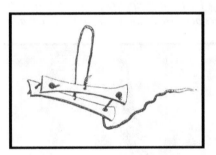

In an emergency, this simple system could be duplicated by a Long Rider.

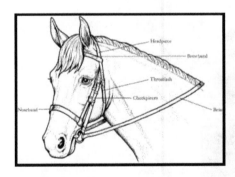

The snaffle bit, which applies pressure to the bars of the horse's jaw, has changed very little since it was invented thousands of years ago.

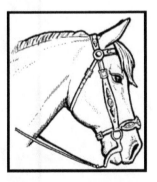

Because the curb bit can create immense pressure, it must be carefully adjusted and used with care.

North American Long Rider Tom Fairbank used a hackamore during his ride across the American west. Unlike a traditional bit which operates within the horse's mouth, the hackamore applies pressure across the sensitive bridge of the nose. This system is favoured by many Long Riders because it allows the horse to eat and drink easily while travelling.

The halter-bridle combination is an excellent option for Long Riders because it eliminates the need to employ two separate pieces of equipment. The snaffle bit can be easily detached, leaving the horse free to graze and drink.

Irish Long Rider Caitriona O'Leary rode in India. Upon her return to England, she used a bitless bridle which malfunctioned and resulted in her horse running away. Caitriona was killed in a riding accident in 2012.

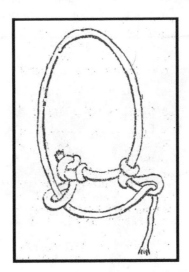

In an emergency a Long Rider can create a head collar/halter out of a single piece of strong rope.

There are a great many benefits gained by placing bells on a horse. Famous actor Jimmy Stewart used a saddle bell when he rode his horse, Pie, in many Hollywood western movies.

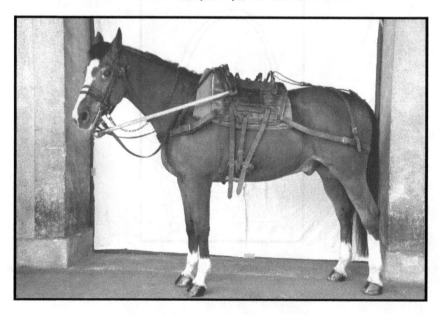

The Swiss cavalry used a lead stick to keep the pack horse from crowding the rider; photo courtesy of the Society of the Military Horse.

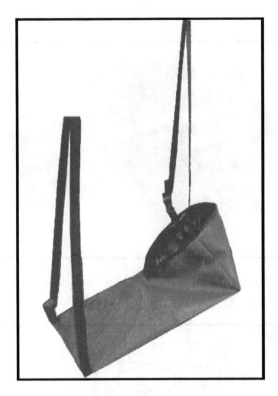

The cavalry-style mesh feed bag eliminates spills while remaining breathable.

While various types of collapsible water buckets are available, this French model will not tip over while the horse is drinking.

A travelling farrier kit contains the essentials needed to change a horseshoe in the field.

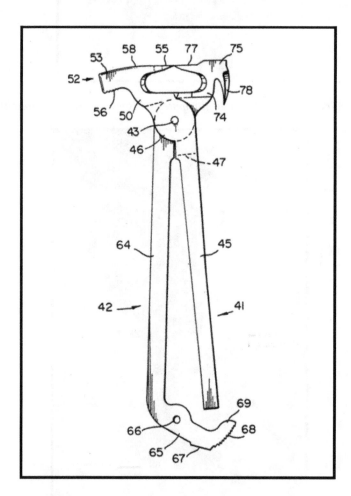

The replacing of a horse shoe on a horse involves many separate tools, each performing a different function. A recent substitute is a multi-purpose farrier's tool which provides all the tools in one.

When French Long Rider Thierry Posty rode through the rainy jungles of Fiji, he equipped his local horse with this impromptu raincoat.

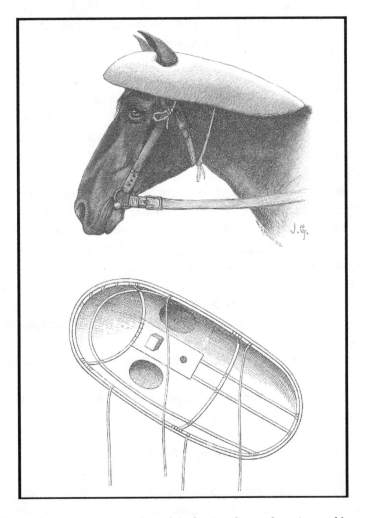

The Bombay horse hat was designed to protect horses from dehydration, heat exhaustion and heat stroke. Modern Long Riders can use the same concept, should they need to create similar protective head gear in an emergency.

Chapter 34
Pack Saddles

While the majority of the modern horse world continues to obsess about competitions, at the dawning of the 21st century an unreported revolution changed one of the fundamental aspects of equestrian travel. This occurred when Long Riders around the world began using the Canadian adjustable pack saddle. Until the advent of this remarkable piece of equipment, pack horses were routinely injured, and journeys destroyed, by outdated, ineffective pack saddles.

Yet this shift in equestrian perception didn't come about overnight.

Evidence indicates that man's earliest mounted exercise was on the reindeer who reside at the northern edge of the Equestrian Equator, above today's modern Mongolia. It was a natural step for early nomads to transition from riding the docile reindeer to the faster horse.

While this was a fairly straightforward evolution, mankind spent thousands of years puzzling over how to best transport objects on a horse's back.

Occident and Orient

During the passing millennia humans residing in those parts of the planet known as the Orient and the Occident developed different ways to accomplish a simple task. Forks, for example, were used in England instead of the chop sticks preferred in China.

Likewise there were equestrian differences, the most common being the long stirrup favoured by Westerners, as opposed to the shortened stirrup leather adapted by Central Asian nomadic horsemen.

While short stirrups and chop sticks are well known, what is seldom remembered is that different pack saddle systems developed on opposite sides of the planet.

A Radically Different View

Anyone who has witnessed a cowboy movie will be familiar with the idea of lashing cargo to a pack mule. Countless crusty old prospectors have made their way across the silver screen, followed by a trusty equine companion bearing a weathered sawbuck pack saddle.

While the Occident spent millennia experimenting with ropes and pads, an entirely different pack saddle system developed in the Orient. The girthless Oriental pack saddle consists of four main components. One, a thick pad rests atop the pack animal's back. Two, on top of the pad sit two thick wooden arches, which are kept in place by four strong wooden slats. Three, a lighter wooden framework is designed to fit snugly inside the larger wooden arches. Four, attached to this frame-work are two sturdy baskets designed to carry the load.

There were variations on this theme. For example the Japanese used small ropes to act as a rudimentary breast plate designed to keep the saddle from slipping backwards. Yet regardless if it was located in China, Viet Nam, Japan, Korea or Burma, the Oriental pack saddle also had another impressive improvement over its Western counterparts. This was the improved crupper.

The Western crupper is a hard leather band which can cause a friction burn under the horse's tail when the animal is travelling.

The Oriental crupper, on the other hand, is made of leather discs, or small leather balls. These circular objects are designed to roll along under the horse's tail while the animal is on the move.

Among the Ainu

When Henry Savage Landor made his equestrian journey through the remote northern Japanese island of Hokkaido in 1889, he learned that the original aboriginal inhabitants, known as Ainu, were dedicated horsemen.

Landor discovered that Ainu men regarded running as unbecoming after childhood.

"'If we must go quick, why not go on horseback?' says the practical Ainu, who is as perfect a horseman as the Indian. When riding, he is able to cover a distance of fifty-five miles easily in one day on a good pony and about seventy miles if he changes his quadruped four times."

The Long Rider discovered that both Ainu men and women rode astride. Though they used the Oriental pack saddle to carry wood and seaweed, the Ainu often rode on it as well. Landor copied this technique and rode the pack saddle during his exploration of Hokkaido.

Likewise, German Long Rider Otto Ehlers used the Oriental pack saddle when he rode from Burma to French Tonkin in 1892.

With the outbreak of the Second World War, Allied troops used the girthless pack saddle in 1944 when they took indigenous Chinese horses from the Salween River in Burma over 11,000 foot passes and into China. One American soldier noted, "The saddle permitted quick removal of the load in emergencies."

Rediscovered

Though it had given centuries of quiet service, with the advent of the motor age, the remarkable Oriental pack saddle might have faded into folklore if Jeremy James had not discovered it still being used in the mountains of northern Viet Nam. While doing field work for an equestrian charity, James was stunned to see a hardy hill pony come trotting out of a remote jungle.

The pony belonged to Hmong tribesmen. On its back was a pack saddle unlike anything he had ever seen before. Not only was it not secured with the traditional girth and lashings of rope, the pony was gaily carrying two large water casks, both of which were sloshing their heavy, unstable load on either side of the pony.

Though James managed to obtain a photograph of the elusive Oriental pack saddle, it might have remained an elusive equestrian artefact if one of this centuries most unlikely equestrian travellers had not used it to complete a remarkable journey from China, across Tibet and on into India.

The Tea-Horse Trail

For centuries the Chinese had been loading pack mules with bales of tea and then dispatching the heavily-laden caravans along the Tea-Horse Trail. This ancient path began in China, wound its way across the mountains, and concluded at Lhasa, the capital of distant Tibet. Yet since the advent of the Communist government, the Tea-Horse Trail had been largely forgotten and unused.

In April, 2006 British traveller Daniel Robinson learned that the first modern Chinese tea caravan was about to re-open the Tea-Horse Trail. The special expedition was organized by the Pur Tea Company, one of the oldest tea firms in China.

After negotiating with the caravan leader for permission to travel along the Tea-Horse Trail, Robinson not only became the first foreigner to do so, he was also the first modern traveller to purchase and use the girthless Oriental pack saddle.

There were 100 fully-laden mules on the expedition and they used the traditional Oriental pack saddle. Daniel travelled from China to Lhasa with the caravan. He then continued on a solo journey which took him across Tibet, over the Himalayan Mountains and into India. Thankfully for posterity, he recalled how the Oriental pack saddle operates.

How it Works

"First comes a blanket, then the pack saddle, which had a pad attached to it."

In a surprising change from western methods, this pad was filled with grain, which meant that it could be adjusted like a bean-bag chair to keep the animal comfortable.

According to Robinson, the saddle and pad together weighed about twenty kilos (44 pounds).

"It was quite heavy because it was made from hard, solid wood. The main front and back arches were a couple of inches thick and the slats on the sides were half an inch thick."

The result was a wooden framework that fitted snugly over the back and down along the rib cage of the pack mule.

"It was what I would call agricultural construction. Not only could it take a lot of daily abuse, it was built so strong that you could throw it off a cliff and it probably wouldn't break."

Unlike the modern Canadian pack saddle, the Oriental system does not allow for any adjustment. However, Robinson noted that its long-ago inventors had foreseen that problem and had adapted the thick saddle pad to compensate for this necessity.

"Because there were two plus inches underneath the saddle, the pad itself moulded to the shape of horse."

Robinson's pack saddle had a crupper which was equipped with wooden rollers.

"They varied in size, with the largest close to the tail and smaller further up the body. The crupper stayed attached to the saddle. It could be taken off but nobody ever did."

Yet the system was deceptively simple, so much so that even though Robinson had no previous pack saddle experience, he learned to break camp, load his gear, tack up both his mules and be on the road in little more than an hour.

While designed not to need a cinch, as is customary on Western pack saddles, Robinson's Oriental pack saddles had two loose cinch straps which could be used in the mountains to help keep the load in place. However the use of the cinch seems to depend on the terrain and was not necessarily used by other Oriental nations who made use of this system.

Military Might

It would be a mistake to believe that what might be deemed a quaint type of pack saddle once used by caravans had passed out of existence.

In 2014 film footage was released that proved the girthless pack saddle was by no means obsolete. The film showed modern Chinese army troops, clad in camouflage and carrying state-of-the-art weapons, making their way through mountainous terrain. Walking alongside the troops was a team of large pack mules.

Each mule was carrying heavy ammunition boxes. The total load on each animal must have been at least 150 pounds.

The film clearly shows the mules, equipped with the girthless pack saddle, scrambling up mountain trails and making their way through jungle-like terrain. At the conclusion of the film, footage shows two soldiers lifting the wooden pack saddle off the mule with one smooth coordinated effort.

Thus this ancient and reliable system, made from inexpensive and easily-obtainable local materials, which requires no complicated knots to be kept in place, and can be used without special training, is still being employed by one of the world's largest armies.

But somewhere back in the mists of time, as Oriental packers were experimenting with cruppers with rollers and girthless pack saddles, Occidental horsemen were busy developing an alternative system of packing horses.

Rome to the Rescue

In the famous Monty Python skit, the question is posed, "What have the Romans ever done for us"? In addition to sanitation, medicine, education, wine, public order, irrigation, roads, a fresh-water system, public health and peace, they could have added pack saddles.

As the art of riding spread from east to west, early man also studied the problem of how to carry his possessions on horseback. The ever-efficient Roman army tackled the dilemma by using a sawbuck style cross-tree pack saddle. Whether they invented it or not isn't known. Yet a Roman tombstone in Pannonia, modern Hungary, depicts a draught horse carrying a pack saddle. The Romans also brought the pack saddle into Britain.

Because of the poor roads and high hedges, the pack train reigned supreme in England until the railway replaced it as a means of transporting goods. Pack horse caravans carried every conceivable type of goods including bricks, coal, fish, flowers, leather, limestone, produce and wine. Special bridges, known as packhorse bridges, were constructed with low parapets so as to allow the horses to make their way over without dislodging the baskets carrying their loads.

Queen Isabella's Mules

While Queen Victoria witnessed the demise of the pack train, Queen Isabella of Spain observed its birth.

The next important step in pack saddle development for Westerners was the result of an import. This came about when the concept of the *aparejo* saddle pad was introduced into Spain by the invading Moors. The Spanish were quick to grasp the importance of protecting the back and withers of their pack animals. By placing the straw-filled *aparejo* under the primitive sawbuck, progress seemed to have been made.

This fact was confirmed in 1486 when Queen Isabella of Spain attacked Granada. In support of her army, she dispatched 14,000 pack mules. With the Moors conquered, Spanish conquistadors carried their sawbuck and *aparejo* on the ships which sailed to South America and Mexico.

Yet there were fundamental problems with the *aparejo*. It was difficult to keep the load in place and it required an expert to keep it properly stuffed with straw and individually fitted to each pack animal.

The Sawbuck

Further north British trappers working for the Hudson Bay Company took the wooden sawbuck pack saddle across North America. It was during this early stage of northern colonial development that French trappers came up with the term "panniers" to describe the deep baskets they hung from the sides of the sawbuck.

In 1849 the famous California gold rush brought another important change. That was the year Americans are credited with using a lash rope to tie the load tightly against the pack animal's body.

As the American military sought to subdue the Native Americans, the use of pack trains became increasingly important. During the 1886 campaign against the Apache chief, Geronimo, General George Crook realized he would never capture his elusive adversary if his cavalrymen relied on slow-moving supply wagons. Known as the father of modern pack service, Crook depended instead on large pack trains to support his now rapidly-mobile troops.

It was during this rugged campaign that the army's master packer, Dick Closter, improved the soft-sided Spanish aparejo. He did this by inserting wood slats into the pad. The slats helped form a uniform arch that spread the weight of the load over the pack animal's ribs.

Other army packers marched their animals into the record books. Famed army packer Charles Post took his pack train 100 miles in 26 hours, with one halt of ten minutes and one of two hours at a camp by water. At the finish one mule broke into a trot as it recognized the station some three miles away and trotted up showing little sign of fatigue.

As the 19th century was nearing its end, another army pack master, Henry Daly, discovered the cause of bunches while stationed at Fort Apache, Arizona. A bunch is a puffing up of the skin which is caused by unevenness in the filling of the pad. If no action was taken to relieve the animal of its misery, constant use would result in a saddle sore which would destroy the horse or mule.

The traditional wooden sawbuck pack saddle has changed very little since General Crook was chasing Geronimo. Though a strong leather breast collar, two stout cinches, and a robust series of leather straps known as the breeching, encompass the animal's body, it is still necessary to use ropes to tie the load securely in place.

Lashing on the Cargo

There are inherent problems connected to tying large, heavy objects to the body of a moving pack animal.

First, it is difficult to secure the cargo. In theory two loads of equal weight were held against the pack animal's ribs and were then lashed into place with a long rope. The idea of a rope securing the load in the middle is akin to the cinch which secures the riding saddle. But a rider's weight is fluid. It swings and moves in conjunction with the horse's progress.

In direct contrast to a rider's movement, packers wished to keep the cargo stationary. To achieve this they used a long rope and invented a series of complicated knots which were designed to strap the cargo into an immovable position.

The result was that the weight of the cargo pressed down relentlessly onto the pack animal's sensitive tissues, fragile muscles, weak withers and delicate spine. To further complicate the problem, the rope limited the animal's ability to breathe. The result was that the cargo became a hot, heavy, restrictive, agonizing straight-jacket. Together, the rope and the dead weight created a dreadful combination which all too often resulted in painful, often lethal, saddle sores.

Thunder Mountain

Thus, from Caesar to Geronimo, the sawbuck and its supportive pad, the aparejo, underwent very few changes. The next improvement occurred when gold was discovered in a remote portion of the Idaho wilderness known as Thunder Mountain.

In 1902 many Idaho packers took part in this search for El Dorado. Located in the remote mountains just north of the Nevada state line, the lure of easy riches inspired veteran miners and enthusiastic amateurs alike to travel over a hazardous track known as the Buckhorn Trail.

In these pre-mechanized days every type of supply had to be transported to the gold camp by pack animal. If a man was going to find a fortune, he had to be able to pack his tools and supplies onto an animal and make his way into the wilderness. This meant that knowledge of pack saddles, and pack animals, became vital commodities.

Like previous gold strikes, there were those who sought gold in the ground and those who got rich by providing supplies and services to the miners. One clever fellow made his wealth by teaching greenhorns how to tie the complicated diamond hitch used to secure a load on the sawbuck pack saddle. When he realized his pupils were as naïve about horses as they were about knots, the clever teacher increased his profit by selling the novice miners old work horses for a 300 percent profit.

With the lure of gold pumping adrenalin into their veins, a horde of eager miners began making their way through the wilderness towards Thunder Mountain.

According to one eyewitness, "There was a stream of people pouring into that huge mountain empire. And the things that were carried in over those trails! I saw a piano crated and slung between two stout horses slowly creeping up toward the snowy summits. Of course, there were quite a few accidents to pack trains. Some of those trails wound around over precipices so steep that they'd make a goat dizzy. Once a horse slipped it was finished. The animal became a total loss, together with his load of flour, bacon, powder, whisky or whatever he happened to be carrying."

Packers carrying supplies to the Thunder Mountain gold camp used tightly lashed aparejo and sawbuck pack saddles, the result being that their pack animals often suffered from galled backs in the hot weather.

The Nez Perce Indians, whose homeland included Idaho, are famous today for their association with the beautiful Appaloosa horse. Few remember that their saddle was the inspiration for the next stage in pack saddle development.

Their riding saddle had a high pommel and cantle made in the shape of a wooden hoop. These high wooden hoops not only provided the rider with a secure seat, they could provide a better system to carry goods on a horse's back.

An Idaho packer named C.S. MacDaniels is credited with being the first to change the sawbuck's wooden crossbeams for two strong steel hoops from which loads could be hung and ropes secured.

In 1906 an Idaho blacksmith named Oliver P. Robinette began producing the new pack saddle. He improved upon the sidebars too. A cottonwood log would be hollowed out and packed with rock salt, which resulted in the moisture being withdrawn from the wood. When cut to shape, the hardened cottonwood sidebars were so tightly grained that they never split.

Robinette's enhanced pack saddle became immensely popular in Idaho, Montana, Oregon and Washington. Because he burned his initials into the wooden sidebars, this led to the pack saddle being known as the OPR. It's more famous name, the Decker, wouldn't become official for another twenty years.

The Decker

The Decker brothers had a reputation for being excellent packers who took cargo into wilderness areas of Montana and Idaho. Based upon their own experiences, they attempted to patent their improvements to the sawbuck pack saddle. However their attempt to copyright the changes was not granted.

In 1930 the Decker Brothers reached an agreement with Robinette, and thereafter began producing the pack saddle now commonly known as the Decker. This system includes the breast collar, breeching and half-breed.

Once the Decker was in place on the animal's body, a thick pad known as the half-breed was slipped over the steel arches. Constructed of strong canvas, the half-breed has thick felt pads inside, designed to protect the animal's ribs, as well as oak side boards, which help distribute the weight of the load.

While a Decker provides more protection, it greatly increases the weight. A fully equipped sawbuck typically weighs 15 pounds (11 kg.), while a Decker equipped with half-breed, breast plate and breeching weighs about 25 pounds. As the overall weight of the equipment affects how much cargo a pack animal can carry, this is a vital concern to Long Riders.

Plus, there are other worries.

It was common for two men to be required to load a Decker and a complicated system of knots was used to tie the cargo in place. Even though the Decker pack saddle replaced the sawbuck's wooden cross beams in favour of steel hoops, it retained the same principles and failings. Unless vigilant care was taken, the immense pressure on the pack animal's body could cause severe saddle sores.

The Forgotten Pack Saddle

It sometimes happens that circumstances cooperate in such a way that mankind is able to effect a significant change. In these rare cases the status quo is overthrown thanks to an explosion of intelligence, teamwork, patronage and luck.

One such example began in 1961 when President John F. Kennedy expressed his belief that America should land a man on the moon before the decade was out. On July 20, 1969 an estimated 600 million people, one-fifth of the world's population, watched a live transmission showing astronauts from the Apollo 11 space craft becoming the first humans to walk on the moon.

Experts have concluded that the Apollo lunar programme is arguably the greatest technical achievement of mankind to date. Though horses have yet to venture into outer space, earlier in the 20th century a previous American technological effort had resulted in a ground-breaking equestrian development. The result was the most sophisticated and successful pack saddle the world had ever seen.

With the dawning of the 20th century, the development of the machine gun squad had prompted the United States army to consider how best to transport this effective but heavy weapon and its ammunition. In 1908 the War Department authorized an official comparison field test between two machine gun squads. One team would use the cumbersome sawbuck and crude *aparejo*. The other team would be equipped with an English army pack saddle. After three years of field work, neither system was found to be effective, but much valuable information was obtained as a result of these tests.

The need for a suitable pack saddle was keenly felt when American troops fought Pancho Villa's Mexican revolutionaries in 1916 and the problem remained unresolved with the arrival of the First World War.

When that conflict ended, the War Department once again contemplated how the American army would transport modern weapons of war. In addition to machine guns, there was an urgent need to move early radios, demolition equipment, wounded soldiers and mobile kitchens. While mechanized transport had its proponents, equine pack transportation was still a priority. Moreover, the army needed a pack saddle which would enable pack animals to accompany cavalry at the canter, while heavier cargo was moved at slower gaits.

To place the importance of the pack saddle into perspective, the First World War concluded in November, 1918. Upon the return of American troops from France, extensive tests of pack equipment began in earnest in 1919.

Like today's Long Riders, the War Department was looking for a system that would protect the pack animal and could be used by inexperienced troops after a short period of training. After having ruled out existing domestic and foreign pack saddles, the army concentrated its interest on a new type of pack saddle designed by Lt. Colonel Albert E. Phillips of the cavalry.

Beginning in 1920 a test was conducted by the Infantry School at Camp Benning. In 1922-23 a mountain artillery test was undertaken which consisted of marching the pack animals more than five hundred miles. Meanwhile, three separate tests were conducted by the 1st Cavalry Division. They marched their pack animals eleven hundred and fifty miles. In every test the Phillips pack saddle was found to have performed perfectly.

When the 1st Cavalry reported to the War Department, it stated that during their rigorous test of the Phillips saddle, "No tail sore, side sore or bunch occurred on any animal during the entire period of the test."

As a final result of all tests, the Phillips pack saddle was adopted for the Cavalry service on July 26, 1924. Though brilliantly designed, it was destined to disappear nearly overnight.

The Phillips pack saddle represented the highest development of the pack saddle. It consisted of two pads and a frame, with specially designed accessories of breeching, breast strap and girths.

The metal frame was scientifically designed so as to be light weight and to withstand hard usage. Four small hooks on each bottom bar acted as a foot rest in each corner. Not only did these foot rests keep the pads clean when the pack saddle was removed, the hooks allowed a rope to be easily passed around and tied off.

Two thick pads were stuffed with long curled horsehair, which retained its resilience indefinitely. Each pad was moulded to fit either the right or left side of the animal's body.

The Phillips pack saddle could carry cargo either by hanging it from the metal hoops or by using a traditional lash rope. Hanging cargo could be quickly and easily loaded onto the saddle thanks to attachments. The loads for which they were designed were simply placed in these hangers, which then held the cargo firmly in place.

With a traditional *aparejo* under an old-style pack saddle, the weight of the load was carried not only on top of the back but well down the animal's sides. This required very tight cinching in order to keep the pack saddle in position and to prevent the cargo from overturning. The cinch was centrally placed so that pressure was exerted over the barrel. The animal was thus held in a corset-like grip between the *aparejo* and the cinch. In the Phillips the weight was borne almost entirely on the back and cinching was therefore only tight enough to prevent overturning.

Another improvement was the Phillip's quick release buckle. Instead of relying on the tradition of tying off the girth, a leather belt came up from the girth and was threaded through a specially-designed buckle. This allowed the soldier to gently pull up on the leather belt until it felt snug. The buckle not only prevented the leather belt from slipping, it eliminated the need to encircle the animal with a rope and pull as hard as possible to safeguard the cargo.

At the end of the day, the soldier could release the leather belt quickly by simply pressing the buckle between his fingers. This greatly decreased the stress and time needed to unload the pack animals.

When unloaded, the metal Phillips pack saddle and its two thick pads were heavy enough to require two men to lift it into place. However, this was not an uncommon practice in the cavalry. For example, in order to decrease the chance of injury, Swiss cavalrymen assisted each other in lifting their riding saddles onto and off the horse's back.

Despite its weight, the Phillips was a marvel which could be used for long distance travel, during which time the pack animals suffered few if any injuries.

The Phillips was such a success that it was used by American troops in far-flung parts of the world. Though manufactured in one design, it came in four sizes, so as accommodate the different sized pack animals encountered overseas. The cargo-artillery type was designed for large American pack mules. The cavalry type was designed for the average American horse. The pony type was designed for the Philippine and Chinese pony. The Caribbean type was designed for the Central American mule.

Not only did the Phillips not injure these pack animals, if turned upside down and covered with canvas, a dozen of the buoyant saddles could be turned into an emergency boat.

The US army disposed of all these valuable pack saddles at the conclusion of the Second World War.

As a result of this short-sighted decision, when the Pentagon dispatched the modern US army to Afghanistan American soldiers were forced to revert to the primitive sawbuck pack saddle used by their 19th century ancestors.

Why did the 2004 Special Forces manual advocate the use of the sawbuck pack saddle? Because the War Department apparently forgot that the US Army had once invented the greatest pack saddle yet seen. The result was akin to equipping 21st century soldiers with a bolt action rifle from the First World War.

Past and Present

With the advance of the motorized age, the wisdom and most of the equipment gained from thousands of years of packing were vaporized. England's once-thriving packing culture became a distant national memory. In Europe equestrian travellers were reduced to scavenging for early 20th century pack saddles once used by continental armies. Across the Atlantic, Americans moved back into the past by forgetting that the Phillips ever existed. A handful of Australians salvaged pack saddles used during the First World War.

Under these conditions, equestrian travellers riding overseas increasingly resorted to using native equipment.

The advantages of native equipment were that it was still generally available, was relatively cheap and was often lightweight. The trade-off was that such pack equipment had several defects. Packing and unpacking required a comparatively great length of time. It could not be adjusted easily on the trail and wore out rapidly because of the strain of constant travel. Due to their crude construction such pack saddles often inflicted injuries to the animal.

Complicating the issue was the fact that in those few countries, like America, where pack saddles and equipment were still to be found, the system might vary from one part of the country to another.

Under such conditions, conclusions that once appeared legitimate became questionable. The result was that over the last part of the previous century, the price of loyalty to outdated equipment was saddle sores and terminated trips.

Even though there were those who continued to uphold their belief in a romantic past with more tenacity than judgment, an increasing number of people defended the old ways with less and less ardour. The result was a final surrender of these unprofitable prejudices and a willingness to embrace new ideas in the new millennium.

A Modern Answer

With the dawning of the 21st century, the Occidental style pack saddle underwent its last critical improvement. This came about with the invention of the Canadian adjustable pack saddle.

The inflexible aparejo and adjustable pack saddles are entirely different in principle as well as construction.

The sidebars of the Canadian equipment, which are made of unbreakable ABS plastic, are textured on the underside to grip the saddle pad and come in two shapes. One is flatter so as to fit mules, while a second type is designed to fit horses. Thanks to its adjustable nature, this pack saddle may be changed from one animal to another without refitting. The result is that the Canadian pack saddle can fit any pack animal ranging from a tiny Shetland pony to a massive two-humped Bactrian camel.

This adjustability is important even if you use the same pack animal during the length of your trip, because it also allows you to alter the pack saddle to fit your animal's back as it changes shape during the journey.

Light-weight and extremely strong, the Canadian pack saddle is equipped with a wide mohair string girth that is attached to the saddle by nylon webbing, a combination that allows for precise adjustment of the girth. A large wool or felt saddle pad provides excellent protection for the animal's back. A leather breast collar and rear breeching are available to keep the equipment in place, should you travel through mountainous terrain.

The hard plastic panniers are curved to fit alongside the pack animal's rib cage. Each pannier is equipped with straps which allow it to be easily hung on either side of the pack horse. Unlike the sawbuck or Decker, this simplified system does not require a traveller to be an expert in handling lash ropes or tying complicated knots. The result is a pack saddle which can be easily loaded by one person.

Another benefit is that when you need to ship your gear this system comes apart and can be compressed into a very tight package.

Because it does not hinder the natural movements of the animal this affordable pack saddle has revolutionized modern equestrian travel. In the last decade Long Riders have used it to travel great distances in diverse countries and it is currently involved in an unprecedented ten-year field test during which Guild members will use it on expeditions in every part of the world.

Able to withstand hardships, functioning in all climates, capable of fitting every type of pack animal, having nearly eliminated saddle sores, requiring no special training and affordable, this pack saddle has eliminated the need to use previous systems.

Packers

In today's computer-dominated world, many forget that being a packer was once a career choice which offered plenty of travel and lots of outdoor adventure. Though it is commonly known that the United States cavalry was eager to enlist men to ride and fight, a group of skilled civilian packers was also on call to assist the army when it took to the field in the late 19th century.

According to standards of the time, the essential conditions in the selection of a packer were that "he must know how to read and write, be sound in mind and body, not addicted to the excessive use of intoxicants, never display ugly temper, be honest and humble in all his dealings, be imbued with an 'esprit de corps' and never tie the pack string in front of a saloon."

Charles Post, one of the army's master packers, recorded that an army pack train consisted of 50 pack mules, 1 bell mare, 14 riding mules, 1 master pack master, 1 cargo assistant, 1 blacksmith, 1 cook and 14 packers.

While the job description might have changed with the times, the value of the pack animal has never lessened.

Initial fitting of the saddle

Purchasing a new adjustable pack saddle may be the first step in the right direction. However, care should always be taken when fitting a pack saddle and panniers to your pack horse or mule.

It is essential that the Long Rider observe a new pack saddle very closely prior to departure and that he promptly makes any adjustments which appear prudent.

The new pack saddle may fit some animals sufficiently well that few initial adjustments of the pad will be necessary. In such cases the saddle pad will shape to the animal's back after a small amount of use. However, the new pack saddle may fit some animals so poorly that the saddle pad should be altered, and the fit of the saddle carefully adjusted, so as to ensure a more accurate individual fit before the saddle is used on the road.

The steps for ensuring a properly fitting pack saddle are as follows.

The animal should be saddled without the pad and the fit observed from the front, sides, and rear. The front of the saddle should fit smoothly against the animal with no compression of the withers. The sides of the saddle should not be pushed outward excessively. The rear of the saddle should follow the body's natural curved lines without pinching.

When viewed from the front and rear, it should bear uniformly along the weight-bearing muscles of the back. Excessive bearing or compression at any one place is especially undesirable. The bottom of the sidebar should be horizontal or inclined slightly downward and forward; never downward toward the rear. Once you have checked the pack saddle, if necessary, remove it, and make any adjustments.

Next, saddle the animal with the pad in place, making sure the saddle is in the correct position.

The character of sweating under the saddle is explained by the simple fact that pressure on the skin lessens the blood supply to the sweat glands and the excretion of sweat is diminished. If the pressure is very excessive, there will be no sweating.

Cinch the pack saddle snugly and place evenly-balanced panniers on either side. Walk the animal until he shows signs of sweating and then remove the load and saddle.

Remove the saddle pad very carefully so as not to disturb sweat markings on the back. Wet surfaces on the back under the saddle pad indicate normal or little bearing from the saddle. Excessive pressure is indicated by a definite area or areas on which the hair is considerably drier than on the surrounding areas, or which is free from any evidence of sweating. The hair over these areas will be either ruffled or compressed depending on the movement of the saddle.

During a journey horses and pack mules lose flesh when worked hard for long periods of time. As a result, the contours of their backs change considerably. When this occurs you must adjust the pack saddle to compensate for these changes. By acting promptly the chances of an injury will be minimized.

Panniers

Traditional cavalry packers enclosed their cargo in a large piece of canvas known as a mantie. Tying a mantie securely closed required knowledge of special knots. It then had to be hoisted on the pack animal and secured in place with a carefully-tied lash rope. Not only was this time-consuming, but when cargo came loose on a difficult trail it could be dangerous to secure it back into place.

Modern plastic panniers are nearly indestructible and can be loaded by one person.

But packing the panniers is an art which requires that both sides of the load be equally balanced. Each pannier must weigh nearly the same as its companion otherwise the load will slide off-centre when the pack horse begins to walk.

Available in brown, green or florescent orange, the latter colour works best for Long Riders because it can be seen easily by drivers when circumstances force you to travel along a busy road. It is also a very good idea to place reflective tape on both ends of the pannier to increase your visibility.

These sturdy plastic boxes can withstand being cracked into a tree and can be cleaned easily. Some panniers can be rigged into a table and one pannier always makes a handy stool in camp. One pannier can also be fitted with a threaded female inlet for a shower-hose attachment.

If you are travelling through bear country, then you will need to obtain special panniers which are equipped with tops that cannot be dislodged by hungry prowlers. But even if you are not worried about bears, you should always be concerned about leaving your possessions in an unlocked pannier.

Keith Clark solved this problem when travelling through Chile.

"The panniers don't lock but are fastened using a webbing strap, so what I did was get a couple of hardened thin steel cables with eyes that just go around the box. If they are fastened length wise so that the cable goes between the protrusions that are meant for a diamond hitch there is no chance of slipping the cable off. Each cable is then fastened with a small padlock. It's not going to stop someone running off with a pannier but it certainly will deter a sneak thief."

To offset that danger, Keith obtained an extra cable which he used to padlock both panniers to an immovable object.

Pack Saddle Pads

Because of the dead weight suspended from a pack saddle, great care must be taken when choosing a saddle pad.

To ensure adequate protection against pressure points, a pack saddle pad must be bigger and thicker than a normal riding pad. A typical pack saddle pad is at least 30" x 40" (75 cm. x 100 cm.). Custom Pack Rigging, which makes the Canadian adjustable pack saddle, also offers an excellent selection of top-quality saddle pads. Some are constructed of soft, thick felt, which is lined on the top with smooth leather. These pack saddle pads are hard-wearing, soft, cool, and easily washed.

As one Long Rider noted, "My pack saddle pad is the envy of all the nomads."

Always avoid placing any type of abrasive material, such as canvas, against the pack horse's back and make sure the pack saddle pad is always kept scrupulously clean.

Other Equipment

Breast collars and the breeching are designed to keep the pack saddle in place when travelling up or down steep hills. They should be adjusted so as to be comparatively loose at the walk and trot.

In addition to panniers, some Long Riders like to keep soft goods, such as a sleeping bag or a warm coat, handy by placing them in a zippered bag which fits across the top of the pack saddle. At the end of a day's travel, the top pack containing your personal items can be easily carried to the tent.

These top packs, which are usually constructed from sturdy cordura, have two compartments. Though providing extra storage, they should never be overloaded, as they may pull the pack saddle off-centre.

You should also be aware that the metal bars on top of the adjustable pack saddle may rub a hole though the bottom of the top pack. North American Long Rider Tom Fairbank corrected this problem by placing two small pieces of rubber hose pipe atop the pack saddle's metal bars.

Some Long Riders have also used soft duffel bags atop the pack saddle. However, care must be taken that nothing hard comes into contact with the pack horse and that this weight is kept carefully balanced.

A rain cover is an excellent and low-priced bit of protection that will fit snugly over the top pack and keep your clothes dry.

While traditional packers often used two girths, this is not necessary for equestrian travellers.

The lash cinch is a short girth with a ring at one end and a hook attached to the other. It is used in conjunction with the lash rope to keep the panniers from swaying. Both pieces of equipment are available from Custom Pack Rigging and can be purchased with the adjustable pack saddle.

A final consideration may be to include a thick plastic tarpaulin. It can serve as a groundsheet at lunch and will keep the dew off your gear at night

Loading

Our motto at the Long Riders' Guild is, "The more you know, the less you need."

Almost everybody starts out with far too much gear and jettisons most of it along the way. Obviously what you actually need depends on whereabouts in the world you are travelling. For example, the requirements for a Long Rider travelling in the Himalayan Mountains differ from one riding in Europe.

Yet regardless of where you ride, experience shows that it's not the kilometres that are the enemy of the pack horse, it's the kilograms.

In some countries it is quite common to see horses and ponies literally buried under their loads, to the point where they appear to be walking mounds of hay or strolling brush piles.

Or you may meet people who recite tales about army mules who could carry a 300 pound pack for twenty miles. In both cases, what these people are quick to forget is that a horse can't complain. If you overload him, he becomes a mute victim of your incompetence.

We must remember that the army had multiple pack animals. You only have one. It is also wise to remember that if an army mule was forced to carry an extraordinarily heavy cargo, such an example represented a military emergency, not a daily duty. If repeated, it usually spelt the end of the pack animal.

Thus, don't let hoary tales of long ago tempt you to overload your animals, as you will quickly end up with a pack horse suffering from saddle sores and a sore back.

With this admonition in mind, you should not ask your pack-horse to carry more than a hundred pounds (50 kg.) of gear, as this dead weight is comparable to a 200 pound rider.

Balancing that load correctly is of the utmost consequence.

If one pannier weighs 52 pounds and the other 48 pounds, this will increase the expenditure of energy and cause discomfort to the animal. If the difference in weight is ten pounds or more, you risk injuring the animal. This is of such supreme importance that no care can be too strict regarding the balance of the load.

According to one folktale, if a load was out of balance, a packer would add rocks to the lighter side so as to balance the load. Whether this is true or not, it is an unacceptable practice. Never add an ounce of extra weight to an already-burdened pack horse. Nor should you ever guess at the weight of the panniers. Use a pack scale, which registers up to seventy-five pounds, to distribute the weight as evenly as possible.

Great care should be used when packing. Many Long Riders mark their panniers with the words "food" and "equipment," or use the letters F and E to denote what is in each pannier. This practice not only helps you to make a quick search in the dark, it also ensures that no poisonous object leaks or comes into contact with anything edible.

Don't pack cans or glass bottles, both of which represent additional weight. Whenever possible, decant any food into zip-lock plastic bags. Mark each bag so that you can tell chocolate from coffee in the dark. Choose foods which provide a healthy diet, provide lots of energy, are easy to pack and last. Rice, beans, lentils, nuts, oatmeal, sugar, salt, coffee and tea all serve this purpose. Place each type of food in a separately marked zip-lock bag. Bread, vegetables, meat and fish can be added to your diet as and when you find them.

If you carry cooking oil, be sure you pack it in an aluminium bottle that can be securely closed. Likewise, fuel for your stove should be kept in a tightly-sealed metal container, which is always stored separately from your food.

Because your clothes, personal possessions, equipment and food are always in constant motion, they are likely to be damaged or become wet. Chances are if you mark individual plastic bags with words, you may later want to use that bag for another purpose. If you use light weight nylon bags instead, which are available in a multitude of colours, you can sort your possessions easily.

When loading the panniers, place heavy objects at the bottom and towards the front. If you use a top pack, make sure that any odd-shaped object lies flat and never presses against the body of your pack horse.

Should you be forced to swim a river, line your panniers with thick plastic bags so as to further protect your possessions.

After the panniers are carefully weighed and placed into position the pack saddle should be properly centred on the horse's back. This means that the bottom bars of the pack saddle should be level or incline slightly downward and forward. The pack saddle should never tilt downward and towards the rear, as this may lead to injuries.

If the pack saddle and panniers are properly loaded, there will be no need to tighten the girth excessively.

When loading and adjusting the pack saddle, work quickly and quietly.

Using these rules of common sense, and thanks to modern equipment, an average person can become a competent packer in a short period of time.

Travel with the pack saddle

Fully-laden pack animals should not trot but must be able to move quickly and turn to either side without being interfered with by the pack saddle.

After the animal is on the road for a few miles its belly draws up and the saddle, under the weight of the load, settles in place. These two movements require a further adjustment of the girth at the first halt.

At each long halt, the girth should be loosened and afterwards properly adjusted before resuming your travels. Never tighten the girth any tighter than necessary. Always confirm that the pack saddle is centred after adjusting the girth.

In warm climates, avoid travelling during the heat of the day. Always allow your horses the chance to drink when an opportunity occurs. They travel better as a result.

Avoid taking an extended break when travelling. It is better to complete the day's march quickly and then make camp, as this allows the pack horse to be unloaded.

Preventing Pack Saddle Injuries

On occasion a pack horse may be hurt by defective equipment. Most injuries are a result of friction or excessive pressure caused when the pack saddle presses against the horse's sensitive body.

Never wait until a rest stop to correctly position a misaligned pack saddle or adjust a pannier. An injury can occur within minutes that will take days to heal.

To prevent injuries, make sure the pack horse was carefully saddled and that the panniers were properly loaded. Never over-tighten the girth, as this will restrict the animal's breathing and may cause girth galls. Yet be sure the pack saddle is securely in place, as a loose girth will allow the equipment to shift while travelling, the result being friction that will wound the animal. If out-of-balance panniers are detected, correct the problem immediately.

Summary

The pack saddle remains one of mankind's most important inventions and the pack animal has provided loyal service for thousands of years.

As the Chinese army's use of the girthless pack saddle proves, some techniques and equipment can be relied upon century after century.

In contrast, since 2005 the United States military has spent an estimated 62 million dollars developing a robotic mule which is powered by a go-kart engine. Equipped with an on-board computer and gyroscope, the unit is remotely controlled by a soldier via a hand-held joy stick. Estimates for producing each robotic mule run as high as $100,000.

In his thought-provoking book, *Hunters, Herders and Hamburgers*, Professor Richard Bulliet investigated human-animal relations. Bulliet argues that we live in an era of "post-domesticity" in which people live far away, "both physically and psychologically," from the animals whose food and hides they rely on. Bulliet contends that in our current era civilized man has undergone a sea-change in terms of his relationship with animals. People remain dependent upon animal products, even though they no longer have any daily involvement with actual producing animals.

In the specific case of the American military, because the majority of raw recruits lack the elemental interspecies dynamic enjoyed by their ancestors, basic knowledge of animal actions has been replaced by a Disney-esque view of horses and an absence of all knowledge connected to pack animals.

Thus, is it any wonder that in an age when a newly-recruited private grew up using Twitter and an Ipod, but doesn't know a hackamore from a halter, that his military masters are exploring such a cultural alternative?

Luckily, modern Long Rider history proves that an inexpensive pack horse, equipped with an adjustable Canadian pack saddle, will allow the average person to become a proficient packer and traveller.

The Long Riders' Guild teaches, "The more you know, the less you need." A road horse carrying an excessive load is a sign of a poorly-educated equestrian traveller.

Because they lack guidelines regarding proper packing technique, inexperienced travellers often treat their pack horse like a rental truck and overload it with needless items and excess weight.

During his exploration of Hokkaido, Long Rider Henry Savage Landor was the first foreign equestrian traveller to use the Oriental pack saddle. Like the Ainu horsemen, he both rode on it and used it to carry his belongings.

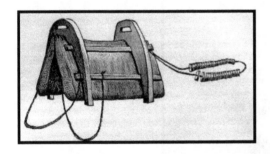

While the Occident experimented with ropes and pads, the Orient developed an entirely different system which resulted in the girthless pack saddle.

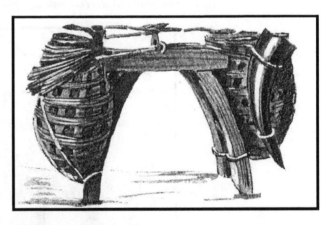

The five components of the Oriental pack saddle are a thick saddle pad, a stout wooden arch, a wooden frame which sits securely inside the arch, two sturdy baskets and the crupper.

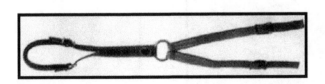

The Western crupper is a hard leather band, which can cause a friction burn under the horse's tail when the animal is travelling.

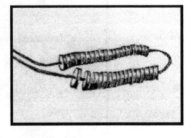

In contrast, the Oriental crupper is made of leather discs, or small leather balls. These circular objects are designed to roll along the horse's back and under its tail while the animal is on the move. This style of crupper was drawn by Henry Savage Landor while riding in northern Japan.

Jeremy James was the first modern Long Rider to see and inspect the girthless Oriental pack saddle. This hill pony, belonging to Hmong tribesmen in Viet Nam, had no problem carrying two heavy water casks through mountainous jungle terrain. After the casks were removed, Jeremy took this photograph of the basic pack saddle.

The girthless pack saddle was still being used by Japanese packers in the late 19th century. Note that this pack horse also wears bamboo hoof boots.

A recently-released film showed the modern Chinese army using the girthless pack saddle to transport cargo through jungles and across mountains.

The Chinese army crupper equipped with rollers to decrease the effects of friction on the pack animal.

Time marched on but pack saddles seldom improved, as is evidenced by this modern pack saddle from Paraguay. It is similar to those employed in the 15th century by Queen Isabella's mule teams.

Though they are separated by thousands of miles, these two late-19th century images depict American (left) and Russian packers both lashing the load to a pack horse using methods first tried during the California Gold Rush of 1849.

The traditional wooden sawbuck pack saddle has changed very little since General Crook was chasing Geronimo. Though a leather breast collar, two stout cinches, and a robust series of leather straps known as the breeching, encompass the animal's body, it is still necessary to use strong ropes to tie the load securely in place.

The riding saddle used by the Nez Perce Indians, which was equipped with loops made from antlers, may have provided the inspiration for the improved pack saddle created by Idaho packer, O.P. Robinette.

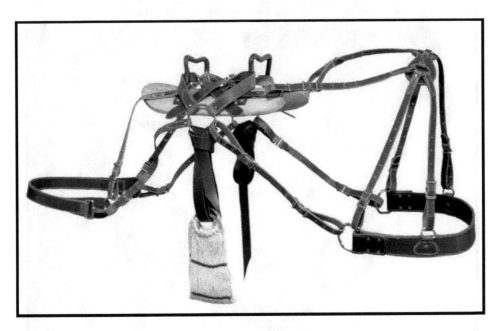

Even though the Decker pack saddle replaced the Sawbuck's wooden cross beams in favour of steel hoops, it retained the same principles and failings.

Once it was in place on the animal's body, a thick pad known as the Half-breed was slipped over the steel arches. Constructed of strong canvas, the Half-breed has thick felt pads inside, designed to protect the animal's ribs, as well oak side boards, which help distribute the weight of the load.

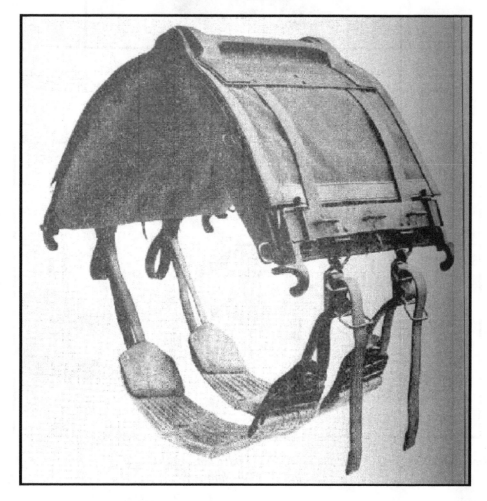

The Phillips pack saddle was a technical marvel which could be used for long distance travel, during which time the pack animals suffered few if any injuries. The metal frame had a hook in each corner which acted like a foot rest and kept the saddle pad clean.

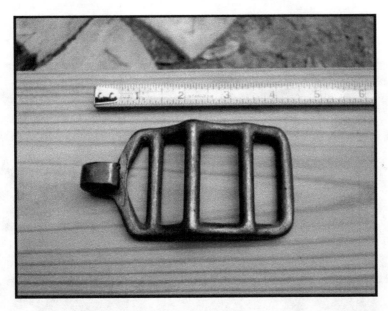

Another innovation on the Phillips pack saddle was the quick release buckle. This allowed the packer to carefully adjust the girth, without over tightening it; photo courtesy of John Ruf, Society of the Military Horse.

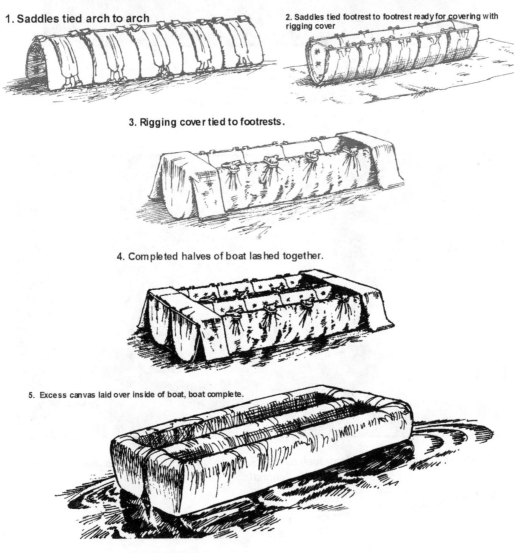

1. Saddles tied arch to arch

2. Saddles tied footrest to footrest ready for covering with rigging cover

3. Rigging cover tied to footrests.

4. Completed halves of boat lashed together.

5. Excess canvas laid over inside of boat, boat complete.

Not only did the Phillips pack saddle not injure animals, if turned upside down and covered with canvas, a dozen of the buoyant saddles could be turned into an emergency boat.

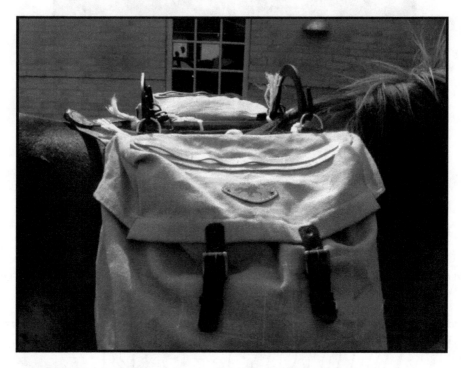

As a result of the loss of valuable knowledge, equestrian travellers in the early 21ˢᵗ century struggled in a vacuum. Some resorted to scavenging cavalry pack saddles which were nearly a hundred years old. Lacking access to modern equipment, one European traveller handmade these canvas pack bags.

Other Long Riders discovered that local equipment, such as this Guatemalan pack saddle, was inappropriate and wounded their animals.

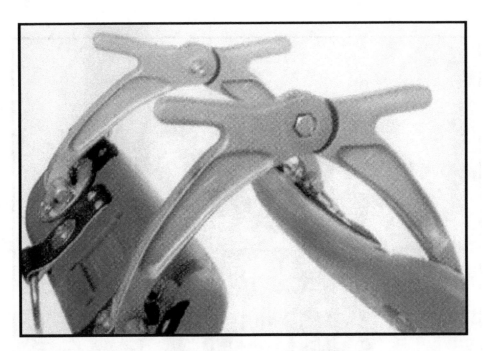

Strong, safe, and affordable, the Canadian adjustable pack saddle can fit any pack animal ranging from a tiny Shetland pony to a massive two-humped Bactrian camel.

This particular adjustable pack saddle is currently involved in a ten-year field test, during which Long Riders will use it on expeditions in every part of the world. Filipe Leite used it from 2012 to 2014 to complete his 12,000 kilometres (7,500 miles) journey from Canada to Brazil.

English Long Rider Steve McCutcheon used the Canadian adjustable pack saddle when he travelled through Pakistan's remote Karakorum Mountains.

Yet it is just at home in a more urbanized environment, as was proved when North American Long Rider Stan Perdue used it to travel from Georgia to Arizona.

Great care should be used when packing. When loading the panniers, place heavy objects at the bottom and towards the front. Mark the panniers with the letters F and E to denote "food" and "equipment." This practice not only helps you to make a quick search in the dark, it also ensures that no poisonous object leaks or comes into contact with anything edible.

Because the panniers are light weight, British Long Rider Elizabeth Hill had no problem loading them by herself.

Elizabeth's pack horse, Dino, became the first horse to take part in the ten-year field test of the adjustable pack saddle by making a 1,000 mile journey through Wales, England and Scotland.

Some merchants sell plastic panniers which can be converted into a camp table. Others sell panniers which have special bear-proof locking tops.

Chapter 35
Long Rider Equipment

Since the dawn of that long-ago day when the first human swung onto a horse and rode towards the distant horizon, equestrian travellers have needed a good reason for everything they wear or carry.

Unlike ceremonial riding, the goal of Long Riders was to be practical, not picturesque.

This timeless lesson was first recorded in a relief erected in the palace of Assyrian king Assurnasipal (884-859 B.C). It depicted mounted nomads wearing clothes that would be recognized by any modern traveller, i.e. loose trousers, comfortable shirts, protective head covering and tall boots.

Unlike ring-riders, our lives and those of our horses depend on our gear. If a piece of equipment fails in the middle of the Amazon jungle, while riding over the Himalayas, or fording a Russian river, we can't load up our pony and go home. You don't get ribbons or trophies when you're a Long Rider. If you do it right, you and your horse make it through in good health.

The clothing worn by a Long Rider depends on the journey, the season, and the countries being ridden through. Because these factors vary, it is impossible to be dogmatic or specific. Yet as the 3,000-year-old Assyrian relief demonstrates, some basic elements of equestrian travel have remained constant across the ages. Our duty then is to decipher what works when worn in the saddle.

At Ease

It was said long ago that there is no such thing as bad weather, only bad clothes. Because equestrian travellers have successfully ridden in every type of clime, ranging from minus 50 degrees in Siberia to well over the 100 mark in the Sahara, records indicate that proper clothing contributes to a traveller's success.

But if mankind is clever, he is all too often vain as well. That is why history likewise reveals that fashion not only rules but far too often accustoms our eye to a great deal of nonsense.

For example, a late 19th century exploration guide warned English explorers to be sure to pack their tuxedo and medals prior to crossing Africa. "A dress suit is necessary everywhere; to this, as occasion demands, may be added the medals."

I would impress upon you to leave your medals at home. The necessity for any Long Rider is that ease is indispensable and the reduction of weight is essential.

When considering what to wear, everything should be avoided that may cause discomfort on horseback. Your sleeves should never be too tight or the easy movement which is so necessary to the arms when riding will be impeded.

You should avoid wearing anything that may flutter in the breeze, for no sooner will your horse change from a quiet walk into a brisk trot than your clothing will begin flapping up and down.

Though comfort is a necessity, what about the local culture?

Culture or Comfort

No matter where you find him, man is most comfortable in the clothes he wore by birth and tradition.

Yet do we wear what pleases us or others? Are there repercussions if we place comfort over culture? Can we afford to disregard the animosity which our clothes might inadvertently inspire?

North American Long Rider DC Vision learned this lesson the hard way when he set off to explore the United States in 1990. Because DC was born and raised in the state of Maine, which is known for its hardy seamen and rugged loggers, he opted for comfort not culture. Consequently, instead of donning a cowboy hat and jeans, which felt alien to him, DC chose to wear loose cotton trousers, comfortable walking boots and a variety of hats designed to protect him from the sun.

At first all went well as he made his way south to Florida. But when he entered the western portion of America, he began to encounter hostility from the locals. Despite the fact that DC had ridden thousands of miles, they were uncomfortable with his appearance because it did not match their cultural definition of what a roving "cowboy" should look like.

Thus throughout history Long Riders have recognized the need to honour local tradition and harmonize with their surroundings.

Captain Charles Colville Frankland was a Long Rider who adapted to his environment. The young English officer set out in 1827 to explore Europe, the Ottoman Empire and Egypt. During the course of his two-year journey he wisely wore Turkish riding clothes, so as to reduce cultural hostilities and increase his ease in the saddle.

Shirts and Trousers

Granted we must not overlook cultural considerations, as globalization advances Long Riders are aided by the fact that humans are increasingly donning more standardized clothing.

Yet riding clothes must first and foremost be comfortable and functional. Any kind of tight clothing which cramps your limbs is an abomination.

If you choose to wear western style jeans make sure they are not too tight. Traditional jodhpurs were invented in India and originally had voluminous space for the rider's legs. In sharp contrast, modern riding breeches are skin-tight, have no pockets and are unsuitable for equestrian travel. Loose sturdy trousers are favoured by most equestrian travellers, especially if they are equipped with large cargo pockets, as you can carry essentials such as matches, light, compass and cash on you at all times. Regardless of what type of trousers you choose, break them in before you depart.

Long-sleeved shirts can be rolled up in hot weather and provide additional protection in the cold.

Many Long Riders have discovered that clothes made for mountain climbers offer waterproof protection and breathable comfort to horse travellers too. Some new clothes are created from cloth which has a built-in bug repellent.

Remember, everything you wear while travelling must be easy to wash.

Riding Skirts

Women have traditionally endured specialized problems. Like their male companions, they sought comfort as well as protection from the sun and elements. Yet in certain countries, it was imperative that their clothes not display their bodies.

Previous lady Long Riders, such as Freya Stark, solved this problem by wearing a long pleated riding skirt. Not only did this preserve her modesty when travelling in the countryside, it allowed her to obey the call of nature discreetly.

Although a split skirt allows a lady to mount and ride easily, it is not appropriate for travel because it ends up in the dirt around your ankles when you undo it.

Colours

After crossing Yemen in disguise, George Wyman Bury advised English explorers to avoid wearing white clothes and "do not blow your nose in public because it startles people."

Though you are now permitted to blow your nose in most countries, dark colours are still preferable to white. However, do not wear camouflage as it may get you shot by mistake or arrested as a spy.

Not taking precautions with these seemingly-small matters may cause you concern or inconvenience later.

Vest

The Long Rider has three places to carry gear – on his person, the riding horse and the pack horse.

In 1939 English Long Rider Margaret Leigh became the first to carry her valuables in a small back pack. Margaret did this because she did not have access to a pack horse. Since then, other equestrian travellers have occasionally resorted to this idea.

It is a mistake to carry anything on your back. Not only does it get hot and heavy, even worse, it can throw you off balance in an emergency.

The best way to carry your personal essentials is to place them in a multi-pocket waistcoat or vest. These pockets can carry the small, light weight items you may need quickly or in an emergency. The Kakadu Company in Australia makes a durable oilskin vest which has more than a dozen pockets.

Because you could accidentally forget your vest, or it might be stolen, you should always carry your most valuable documents in a small thin bag which you keep hidden under your shirt. This bag replaces the need for a traditional wallet, which might fall out while riding or create a large lump between you and the saddle.

Boots

Historically the tall English leather riding boot prevented the stirrup leathers from chafing or pinching the rider's calves. Such boots were made-to-measure and lasted for years. These tight-fitting boots were pulled off with the help of a wooden tool known as a boot jack. Carved wooden boot trees, which were shaped to the owner's foot and leg, maintained the boot's form when not in use. While English boots were fine for fox hunting, they were not designed for long distance travel.

Cowboy boots were also durable works of leather art that could provide years of service. Yet they too had a limitation, in that the traditional slick leather sole on a cowboy boot can slip. Because a Long Rider is required to lift heavy panniers, he needs the traction provided by a composition sole.

One of the most common injuries is when a horse steps on your toes. That is why boot-makers on both sides of the Atlantic agreed upon the need to protect the rider's toes, foot, ankle and calf. For this reason alone, don't wear soft-topped shoes, as your boot must provide a degree of protection.

Another fundamental need was expressed by the U.S. cavalry, whose standard marching drill was "walk a mile, ride a mile." Road horse and Long Rider both benefit when you walk, as the animal receives a rest from carrying your weight and you do not become stiff from staying in the saddle too long.

For this reason, Long Riders' boots must be comfortable enough to ride, hike and run in. One traditional option which met many of these requirements was the packer boot.

Unlike the loose-fitting cowboy boot, which is pulled on, the packer boot is laced up. This type of boot ranges in height from 10" (25 cm.) to all the way up to the rider's knee. The packer boot has an angled heel and provides support to the ankle. They are cut from thick leather, which is waxed on the flesh side to aid in waterproofing them. Not only are they able to accommodate different thicknesses of socks, depending upon the weather, they protect against snake bites and their textured sole provides traction when walking or loading.

Yet while the concept of the packer is brilliant, the reality is that many modern packer boots are made for looks, not long-term wear. Some Long Riders seek a compromise by wearing a light weight hiking boot which offers the protect-tion and traction of the packer, yet is made for durability. The Blundstone boot company in Australia is one such company. They offer work boots which are tough on the outside and comfortable on the inside.

Regardless of which style boot you choose, make sure the heel is substantial enough to prevent your foot from slipping through the stirrup. This is another reason not to wear smooth-soled walking shoes.

If your boots do not reach far enough up your leg to protect your calves from being pinched by the stirrup leathers, you may consider wearing leggings to protect yourself. Leggings will also keep your legs dry and protect you against brush.

Always break in your boots prior to departure.

Hats

According to one of the earliest court histories of Japan, the first shogun of Japan, Saka-noue no Tamuramaro (758–811), was described as having "a red countenance and a yellow beard." Another official known as Yamato Yakamaro was depicted as a "barbarian with a ruggedly honest character."

How did "barbarians" arrive in early Japan?

Apparently they rode there after following the Equestrian Equator east.

Clay figurines known as haniwa provided a clue. When a burial site in Chiba City was excavated, equestrian statues were discovered that depicted bow-legged fully bearded men wearing riding trousers, leather boots and broad brimmed hats. This archaeological evidence suggests that Central Asian horsemen migrated to early Japan, bringing with them many customs, including their tall conical hat.

The wide-brimmed, high, conical Central Asian hat is still worn today in Tibet. In fact, the state crown of the Dalai Lama is a cone-shaped hat.

The shape and size of a hat is as varied as the many equestrian cultures which still wear them. The Mexican sombrero provides excellent protection from the sun. The Australian Akubra has been protecting horse travellers since 1912, while the famous Stetson has been around since the 1860s.

Regardless of where they are made, hats are still critically important because they help moderate your body temperature. The tall crown provides insulation. The wide brim protects your face. A light-coloured hat will keep you cool. But a black hat retains heat and can be twenty degrees hotter than a white hat which reflects the sun.

The best cowboy hats were traditionally made from felt obtained from beaver fur. These durable hats shed water and never lose their shape. Cheap hats were known as a Woolsey, because they were largely made from wool. Unlike water-resistant beaver felt, a wool hat absorbed the rain. It then began to droop and eventually lost its shape. Many Long Riders spray scotch guard on their hats to help make them more waterproof.

A Long Rider's hat should be equipped with a stampede string. This is a string that encircles the crown of the hat Two small holes punched in the brim of the hat allow the string to hang down alongside either side of the rider's face. A small button can be slid up the two strings. This keeps the hat snug on the rider's head and ensures that it is not blown off in a wind or lost while galloping.

Though not strictly a hat, history has demonstrated the amazing versatility gained by wearing a turban. Like its cousin the hat, turbans instantly relay a great deal of information about the wearer's personality and origins. Not only is the style an indicator of the person's character, it often reveals clues about the wearer's tribal and national origin.

Turban styles differ radically from Yemen to Afghanistan, with the former looking more akin to a small towel worn around the head, while the latter are often thirty feet in length when unwound. It takes a great deal of skill to wrap an Afghan turban, but once in place it provides shade, insulation and acts as a rudimentary helmet.

I was once kidnapped by renegade Afghans while riding alone in Pakistan's North West Frontier Province. The brigands pistol-whipped me. Luckily my thick turban absorbed most of the blows.

Not only does a turban allow you to merge into the local population, but it also works well when riding through the desert as it provides excellent protection from sun and wind. Plus, by wrapping the tail of the turban around the lower part of your face, you retain moisture and protect yourself from damaging sunburn.

Unlike a hat, a turban has many other uses. It can be unwound and used to lower a bucket into a deep, inaccessible well. Depending upon the emergency, I have used my turban to create a lead rope, a halter or a set of hobbles.

Helmets

The issue of wearing a helmet is nothing new to Long Riders.

Beginning in the late 19th century, the renowned explorer, George Wyman Bury, spent years travelling incognito through the mountains of Yemen. His success at staying alive in such a hostile environment was based upon the fact that he adapted a fool-proof alternative native identity. When travelling under his native name, Abdullah Mansur, Wyman Bury grew a full-length beard, wore ragged local clothes and adapted to every native custom, no matter how obscure. He was so successful at passing for a native, that when the First World War erupted Wyman Bury's adventures inspired "Lawrence of Arabia" to follow suit.

Though not every traveller wanted to delve so deeply into a foreign culture, Wyman Bury warned explorers that there was a danger in being identified as a foreigner from a distance. At the top of his list of incriminating items was the pith helmet. Also known as the solar topi, this light-weight hat was made from cork and covered with khaki-coloured cloth. Though effective at protecting the wearer from the sun, it also became a symbol of colonialism.

Nowadays helmets no longer carry the stigma of politics. Yet they still instantly identify you as a foreigner in many foreign climes. Such identification may lead to you being defined as a rich tourist and subsequently robbed.

Most people now equate helmets in terms of preserving their personal safety.

Since he began riding more than twenty years ago, North American Long Rider Ed Anderson has become a committed believer in wearing a helmet.

"I had one friend, an experienced rider, who was killed in her own driveway when she somehow fell off her horse. Her head hit the pavement – she was not wearing a riding helmet. She was alone. No one saw this happen."

Ed's advice is, "Never mount a horse without first putting on your riding helmet."

There is an alternative school of thought which believes that wearing helmets encourages reckless riding by creating a false sense of inviolability and encouraging over confidence. This line of thinking argues that safety zealots act within the framework of the law but outside the parameters of common sense.

What helmet proponents seldom discuss is how it might actually contribute to injuries.

Don Andrews is a sports medicine expert who specializes in professional rodeo. He expressed a concern that adding the weight of a helmet to the rider's neck magnifies the snapping motion generated by a bucking horse or bull.

"The solution isn't as simple as it appears. What we've found is that with helmets, we see a greater rate of spinal injuries. Whenever there's a force delivered, it has to be transmitted to another area. The helmet takes the force, but it transmits it to the spine. When you increase the load on the end of a lever, the head in this case, you're asking for a neck injury."

This raises the possibility that the actor Christopher Reeve might not have suffered his spinal injury if he had not been wearing a helmet. As a result of this research many rodeos actually prohibit competitors from wearing helmets.

While helmets can provide a heightened level of protection, they were never designed to be a panacea which encourages irresponsible riding. A Long Rider should always strive to be in control of the horse. Despite everything, no matter what lengths you take to swathe your body in safety, riding will always be a risky affair.

This was recently demonstrated when an English woman was killed while riding near her home under normal conditions. The 47-year-old mother was wearing a helmet and protective body armour when her horse spooked. When the animal reared, it threw the experienced rider onto a wooden fence post, which impaled her through the neck between her helmet and body armour.

Gloves and Bandannas

"Nothing surprises the natives so much as my gloves," wrote James Richardson in 1846, when he encountered Tuareg tribesmen in the Sahara desert. Though the desert raiders had seen Europeans before, the concept of wearing gloves was one that delighted them.

"I am obliged to put them off and on a hundred times a day to please people. They then try them on, look at them inside and outside, in every shape and way, expressing their utter astonishment by the most sacred names of Deity. Some, also, have not seen stockings before, and examine them with much wonderment. But the gloves carry the palm in exciting the emotion of the terrible. One said, after he had put the glove on his hand, "Ah, that's the hand of the devil himself."

Gloves protect your hands from sunburn, prevent blisters caused by the reins and reduce the chance of injuries. Soft buckskin gloves are extremely comfortable – so long as they remain dry. When leather gloves get wet from snow or rain, your hands will feel like blocks of ice. Change to insulated, waterproof gloves as and when the weather dictates.

Bonnie Folkins was surprised to discover that Mongol riders did without gloves. They wear the deel, a long warm overcoat.

"The deel is simply amazing. It's so warm and nearly reaches the ground. You tie the deel at the waist and that gives the rider support in the saddle. It also creates a pocket for odds and ends. Mongolians do a very smart thing. They wear very long sleeves. That way they don't need gloves. Being a Canadian, I would not have thought it possible to not wear gloves. But on my last trip there, in February, the weather was sub-zero and thanks to my deel's long sleeves, I didn't wear gloves at all."

A large cotton bandanna is a versatile item. Besides protecting your neck from the sun, it can double as a washcloth, bandage or tourniquet.

Rain Gear

A day once dawned which threatened to wash away my dreams.

After an already-dangerous journey, I found myself in a remote village in the uppermost reaches of northern Pakistan. As the morning dawned, not a strand of sunlight could be seen. The road leading to my faraway destination disappeared into a tunnel of mountains topped by a pitch-black sky.

Yet I refused to be delayed. I mounted and within a mile became engulfed in a storm of such magnitude that it sounded as if the genies were fighting above me on horseback. No trace of man existed in those bleak mountains. On my left ran a river which snapped in watery fury at the track. Adding to my discomfort, the rain soaked my turban, ran down into my boots, and trickled past the neck of my poncho. Resigned to this watery distress, my horse, Pasha, and I rode on.

I can speak from experience when I say that rain is the one thing above all others calculated to make a life in the saddle unpleasant.

There are few experiences as bad as finding yourself atop your horse, with the sky bucketing down upon your heads. At that moment, when you're wet to the bone, your horse's head is drooping with fatigue, and another uncertain day is still ahead, all the morale born of your sunny dreams is washed away in the subsequent flood. On such a day, when you and your loving horse are victims of a merciless road and the pounding rain, you will understand the insignificance and temporary nature of your life.

Staying dry won't automatically keep your spirits up but it will go a long way to helping you press on.

Encountering wet weather is unavoidable. What you must do is make a fundamental decision before you leave. Do you become soaked through and change into dry clothes later or do you deal with the elements before they strike?

Before I tell you what works, allow me to recall from personal water-soaked experience what doesn't.

Hollywood lied, again, when they encouraged us to imitate Clint Eastwood and don a poncho. The stony-faced Clint starred as "the man with no name" in a number of "spaghetti westerns."

Of course as young movie-goers, we all held our breath when Clint flipped back his poncho, dramatically exposing the lethal Colt revolver he was about to use to dispatch a village full of inept gunmen to their graves. Mind you things would have been different if they hadn't been filming on a sunny day in Spain. Had it been rainy and windy Clint's career as a gunman would have been considerably shorter.

You may have been told that because the poncho is made of finely woven wool, it sheds water and keeps you warm. Nonsense. Such advice was written by stay-at-home authors who never attempted to ride twenty miles through a rain storm with a wet sack alternately clinging to their freezing body or threatening to frighten their horse to death when it blows up into your face The reality of a poncho is that it was designed to drape over a Boy Scout and his backpack, not protect a mounted traveller.

That was a lesson which Jane Dotchin learned the hard way.

"I got out my waterproof cape, slipped it over my head and down over my knees so that it covered my legs and saddle bags to keep everything dry. That was the theory anyway. But sudden gusts of wind kept sending the bottom of the cape flapping upwards, making my horse Sitka nervous. He leapt forward and the cape flapped even more. In the end, I had to tuck the cape in around me, which allowed the rain to run down onto the saddle – leaving me sitting in a puddle. The wind became stronger as we headed north and emphasized how unwise I had been to buy a lightweight waterproof cape. It flapped about too much in the wind, letting the rain soak into my clothing and the packs, and frightening Sitka."

Jeremy James had an equally dismal experience while riding in a poncho.

"The army poncho did two things. First of all it frightened the horse and secondly it let the wet in. Then when it had done that, it did another two things. It kept the wet in and then made you sweat. So not only did you get wet from the outside but you got wet from the inside as well. Then when you were really drenched, it had a final trick, which was to freeze you."

Regardless if the poncho is made from waterproof canvas, rubberized cloth or wool, don't take it on a trip. Because it is open ended, it will leave your arms and legs exposed to the elements. Being loose and floppy, it encourages a cold wind to blow around your body. Even worse, when a poncho begins to flap in the wind you will find yourself in the saddle, trying to pull the accursed bed sheet out from in front of your face, all the while your horse has decided to bolt. In such a situation, you're not wearing protection from the rain. You're draped in your shroud.

There are two safe alternatives for Long Riders: rain suits or rain coats.

What we think of as rain gear was invented in 1823 when a Scotsman named Charles MacIntosh created a waterproof material using naphtha and crude rubber. The advantages of this technological breakthrough were quickly adapted by the British navy, which began providing sailors with foul weather gear.

Like many a good idea, MacIntosh's innovation crossed the Atlantic and eventually arrived in the American west. Rubberized raincoats, known as slickers, were cut long enough to drape over the saddle and down to a cowboy's boots. While these yellow raincoats were highly visible, they had several drawbacks. Instead of keeping the cowboy warm, they became stiff in cold weather and retained frigid air inside. In hot weather, the rubberized material's same inability to breathe meant that the cowboy roasted.

The Australians improved on the American slicker when they constructed a full-length raincoat from oilskin. The added length grants protection down to the stirrups and these coats have the benefit of providing a cape across the shoulders which ensures additional protection in the rain.

While the design can't be faulted, the verdict is out in terms of using an Australian slicker during a long ride.

New Zealand Long Rider Ian Robinson, who rode solo across Mongolia and Tibet, swears by his.

"I can recommend an Australian company called R.M. Williams, which started out making clothing for Australian outback stockmen. The founder was one himself I believe. I used their oilskin coat in Tibet for six months, where I wore it daily in rugged conditions. But at the end of the trip it was still in good repair. I found it excellent and very hard wearing."

No doubt the Australian gear has now come into vogue. However what must be recalled is that it was designed for riding in the heat of the tropics. If the weather turns cold, these coats become stiff and heavy.

While Ian's experiences are encouraging, not all Long Riders have been as lucky when they chose to wear an Australian slicker.

Edouard Chautard, a Long Rider from the Pacific island of New Caledonia, has explored many parts of the globe on horseback. His encounter with the Australian raincoat was not a pleasant one.

"I bought an Australian-style rain coat. It looks very nice but I have never used such a bad raincoat! It is not efficient for hard riding in the rain, nor does it cover anything when you are in the saddle. For example, on a Long Ride in Canada I got completely soaked. I have not yet seen a rain coat that could cover everything, as a Long Rider needs. Maybe I'll have to make one myself but I'll have to find good material for that," Edouard advised.

There is a final element involved in deciding whether you don an Australian rain coat or not. It depends on where you're riding. While it doesn't matter to Long Riders "down under," equestrian travellers crossing the Canadian Rocky Mountains need to remember that oilskin is a bear attractant.

What an increasing number of Long Riders are opting for are light-weight, water resistant, Gore-tex rain suits made from highly reflective material. A jacket and trousers can be compressed and stored in a very small sack which fits into your saddle bag. Both should be bought oversized, so as to allow you to wear warm clothing underneath. This outer shell will not only keep you snug and dry; it will also help alert motorists to your presence on a dark and rainy day. Warm, waterproof gloves, with long cuffs, are also a boon on a wet and windy day.

In the end, if you want to stay dry, choose reality over romance.

Staying Warm

John Codman was never shy about sharing his opinions. Walking, he said, was a "solitary entertainment." He dismissed the bicycle as being "unnatural."

The former sea captain was in fact an avid Long Rider and, even though he was nearly eighty years old, Codman had no hesitation about riding across his native New England in the winter of 1887.

Having been raised to respect the region's legendary cold weather, Codman knew that riding his trusty mare, Fanny, would be a bone-chilling experience if he wasn't properly equipped. When he departed he wore a warm coat, high thick boots, heavy gloves and a hat equipped with ear flaps. The result was that he had an enjoyable winter journey.

In this respect, nothing has changed. Your cold-weather gear should be designed to offset the season, not be a fashion statement. Walking beside your horse during part of the ride will help keep you warm. But once you're in the saddle your circulation will diminish and the cold will creep in.

Riding across Tibet in winter proved to be a bit chilly, so Ian Robinson's first line of defence was his thermal underwear.

"In cold conditions I have always used thermal underwear from a New Zealand company called 'Ice Breaker.' They make thermal underwear, vests, etc., from 100% pure merino sheep's wool, specially treated to make it soft. They absorb sweat and can be worn for months on end without stinking! Hard wearing as well, they are used by Antarctic sailors and mountaineers down here," Robinson said.

While riding in Canada's cold mountains, Long Rider Stan Walchuk advised travellers to don a warm vest that comes far enough down to cover your lower back.

During his winter crossing of Kazakhstan, Tim Cope wore a fur hat with ear flaps, thermal underwear, thick Russian winter trousers, wind stopper gloves and a down coat. He also carried ski goggles to help him see during the frequent blizzards.

One of the most important discoveries Tim made was in connection to his winter boots, which were made in Canada by the Baffin Company. Tim reported his feet stayed warm in the stirrups, despite minus 30 degree weather. Baffin makes boots for polar explorers which are rated to minus 100. The only drawback for Long Riders is that you must take care the large boots do not get hung up in your stirrups.

Tim also passed along this tip about keeping your feet ice free.

"My Baffin boots worked well for walking and riding. But if you're going long days across wild regions with rare chances to dry your boots, always wear a vapour barrier on your feet, either over or under your socks. This can be as simple as a plastic shopping bag. This way your boot liners will stay dry and warm and you just have to live with wet socks at the end of the day. In the morning, just shake the ice out of your shopping bags and you are ready to continue."

Travellers crossing Siberia in winter may wish to use the traditional Russian *valenki*. These boots are made from thick felt and keep your feet very warm in temperatures as low as minus 30. However, you should cover them with rubber galoshes to provide a better grip in the snow.

Other Long Riders have also made excellent use of traditional winter clothing, most notably the Kazakh Long Rider Dalaikhan Boshai. He spends his winters in the saddle, riding across the frozen steppes in search of game. Instead of a gun, Dalaikhan hunts with the aid of a giant golden eagle, which has been trained to bring down wolves and foxes.

Because the temperatures are routinely minus thirty, Dalaikhan wears a large fur hat which has flaps that can be brought down and tied under the chin, thus protecting the rider's face. He wears thick sheepskin pants, which have the fur on the inside. His upper body is kept warm by a long sheepskin coat, called a *shuba* in Russia or a *ton* by the Kazakhs, which reaches down to his stirrups.

Chaps and Chinks

Traditional cowboy chaps came in three styles, straight-legged shotguns, flared batwings and fur covered woollies. Each was designed to protect a cowboy from being scraped by brush, injured by sharp mesquite thorns or freezing on the prairies, none of which should be encountered during the course of a well-organized equestrian journey.

Another drawback is that traditional chaps are secured by a sturdy belt that buckles in the back and a leather lace which connects the front of the chaps together. Cowboys were sometimes killed when their horse began to buck and the front of their chaps got caught on the horn of their western saddle.

Even though becoming trapped in the saddle in this manner may be an unlikely problem, there are more immediate considerations. Because of the weight of the leather, chaps and chinks are both heavy, especially when the weather turns bad and they become soaked with rain.

There is an exception. Billy Brenchley made excellent use of modern smooth-surfaced chaps which were constructed from a durable lightweight material.

"They protected my clothes and gave me an extra layer on cold desert nights."

Sash and Faja

The most useful but overlooked item from the horseman's original list of equipment is the long cloth which was wrapped several times around the rider's waist. Whether it was called a sash in English or a *faja* in Spanish, the result was the same.

By wrapping himself tightly, from the bottom of his rib cage to his hips, the rider kept his internal organs in place, strengthened his lower back and fortified himself for extremely long distances.

Central Asian horsemen, who wore a broad sash that was often fifteen feet long, claimed it gave them additional strength and offset nausea.

When Thurlow Craig journeyed to Paraguay in the early 1920s, he quickly adapted the *faja*.

Craig reported, "After I had worn a *faja* for about five years, I felt perfectly helpless without one. They give a great feeling of strength around the stomach, especially when riding broncos or doing other hard work. They are however a habit which once learned cannot be laid aside easily."

Spurs and Crops

Because road horses should be well trained, forward moving and emotionally stable, few Long Riders carry a crop. The long whip associated with dressage, is unthinkable. Likewise, the crop used during fox hunts, which allows a rider to reach down from the saddle and open a gate without dismounting, is equally unnecessary.

Though it is not a good idea to burden your hands, equipping your heels is another matter.

Long Riders epitomize freedom of movement for both horse and human. Knights of old were not so lucky.

In the mid-16th century a knight and his horse were both required to cover themselves in metal. A knight's armour weighed on average 55 pounds. That of his horse weighed nearly a hundred pounds (40 kg.). But bearing up under the load wasn't the knight's primary problem. He was too busy trying to stay in control to worry about how much his armour weighed.

Encased in steel from head to foot, the knight looked out at the world though a narrow slit in his helmet's visor. To make matters worse, a knight didn't ride on his saddle. He rode in it. The result was that the knight was literally wedged on top of his horse.

Because of his limited sight, the knight could not see where his horse's head was, nor could he determine how the animal was reacting to external stimuli.

With his right hand supporting a long, heavy lance, the knight tried to communicate to his horse via the reins in his left hand. As if he needed any additional challenges, because of the armour on his legs and along the horse's body, the knight could not feel the sides of his horses. He was, in a word, encased in a tin can, sitting on a bomb.

The idea of a tournament was for two knights to meet each other at the gallop. In theory one would be lucky enough to strike his opponent with the lance, thus unseating him and winning the day. The reality was that many horses objected to galloping at the on-coming clanking apparition. Tournaments were often delayed due to such horse antics.

To encourage their steeds to run forward, knights wore eight-inch-long spurs which ended in razor sharp rowels. These thorns of pain demonstrated the remoteness of these ruling-class riders.

Long Riders do not require their horses to act in an artificial manner. Theirs is a pragmatic approach, not an elaborate performance.

Travel is usually about allowing the horse to proceed forward freely. The daily requirements normally consist of stopping on time and yielding at the correct moment.

Yet because the world is full of dangers and trickery, you must be ready to meet physical chaos and emotional confusion. When this occurs, there is no time for your horse to contradict your commands. Nor must you try to coerce him into obeying. He must instantly respond to your directions to increase speed or turn sharply, otherwise you may both be lost.

It is in such a moment that spurs come into play.

Spurs are not just a symbol of cavalier rank. Used properly they are an effective aid which can alert a horse to peril, encourage him to react and guide him out of danger.

Jean Francois Ballereau, warned, "If misused, spurs can be a razor in the hands of a monkey."

That is why to be safely used without cruelty the rowels of the spur must be blunted or removed. Blunt spurs can bring a horse to attention, aid in steering him through a difficulty and do not harm.

John Beard, who wore a set of humane spurs during his ride along the Oregon Trail in 1948 wrote, "A horse seems to be able to think of only one thing at a time. A touch of the spur will help him to change his mind. When rightly used they help the rider to keep control. Spurs are not cruel unless the man who uses them is brutal."

Compass and Telescope

When asked what equipment she always carried when exploring the Sahara, Dutch camel traveller, Arita Baaijens, replied, "A compass and a Sudanese amulet against scorpions."

Most Long Riders need not concern themselves about Sudanese scorpions, but carrying an accurate compass is a valuable and potentially life-saving bit of advice. It should not be confused with having a GPS, which is subject to mechanical failure. A compass, no matter how small, is ever alert.

One of the many things Bonnie Folkins learned while riding across the inhospitable steppes of Kazakhstan was how often the local horsemen relied upon their small monocular.

"It is extremely important to travel with a tiny telescope. All the nomads use them to help locate shepherds, yurts, and to help demystify the landscape. A few times we were able to establish very distant roads by being able to pick up on dust trails from faraway traffic."

Knives

One dark night in Kafiristan, I learned that horses, ropes and panic don't mix.

My four horses were picketed side by side on a flat bit of ground. The moon hadn't arisen, so it was very dark. After a gruelling day, I thought my problems were over. They hadn't even begun.

The pack horse had been ill earlier in the day. While I stood there, speaking to him softly, the horse suddenly collapsed. When he fell, he landed across the picket rope of his nearest companion. Finding himself suddenly brought up short, that big horse retreated in terror, only to find himself held fast by the rope.

Luckily I always carry a razor-sharp knife. In less time than it takes to write this, I had sliced through the rope and freed the frightened horse, who sought refuge with his nearby companions.

There are two types of knives, fixed blades and folders. Both have their advantages. Each has been used by Long Riders. Either should last you a lifetime.

During the day a knife will be called into play for a variety of routine duties. As my experience illustrates, chances are you will have little warning when an emergency strikes. For this reason, you should never be far from your knife. Sleep with it close to hand, so if the need arises you can bound out of bed and put it to instant use.

Tools

Mongol troops carried fishing line, a file for sharpening arrowheads and needle and thread. Likewise, you will be required to effect repairs, mend clothing or patch tack during your journey.

There are several varieties of multi-purpose pliers now on the market. These square-nosed pliers can be used to withdraw a horse shoe nail, pick up a hot pot, pull a needle through heavy fabric or cut a wire fence. Like your knife, this is a small but important part of your gear which should always be on your person.

Whether you are carrying a knife, tool, pistol or camera, you would be well advised not to strap it to your belt. Should you be thrown, you can break your hip if you land on the equipment. English Long Rider John Labouchere was the victim of such an accident. When his horse fell on top of him, John was impaled by the long lens on his 35 mm camera.

Carry your knife, compass, telescope and pliers in your vest pocket, not on your hip.

Canteen

The average cavalry canteen weighed nearly four pounds (2 kg.) when filled. That is a great deal of weight to burden your road horse with.

An experienced Long Rider will travel along a well-watered route. He will drink when his horse does. Full canteens, like lariats, belong on the open range as seen in Hollywood films, not on a Long Rider's hard-working horse.

Personal Items

You have to consider that each item, no matter how small, still weighs something.

While conditions will vary, depending upon country, topography and climate, these are the items which Long Riders have consistently brought in their saddle and pommel bags.

Halter, lead rope, brush, curry comb and hoof pick. Toothbrush, toilet articles, soap and metal mirror. Sunscreen and sunglasses. Torch, maps, camera, diary and writing utensils.

During his ride across the African continent Billy Brenchley made this observation and suggestion. "Men, let your beard grow over your lips to protect you from the sun. It also makes you look older and therefore people are more respectful."

Emergencies

As Ed Anderson learned, equestrian travel is fraught with unforeseen hazards. While riding from Mexico to Canada along the Pacific Crest Trail, Ed experienced one emergency and learned of another.

"Primo's nemesis turned out to be llamas. We came upon three of them unexpectedly in Washington and he was terrified. Fortunately, I had time for a quick dismount. He ran in circles at the end of his extended reins, snorting loudly. He knocked me down, breaking loose, and then ran off at a gallop. Fortunately, I was able to track him down within about two miles. He could have gone much farther," Ed wrote later.

Even though Ed and Primo survived their emergency, others were not so lucky.

In 2009 an incident occurred along the same trail. An inexperienced equestrian traveller made the rash decision to take her two horses on a section of the trail which had been clearly marked as being dangerous and unsuitable for animal travel. To make matters worse, the woman had tied her pack horse to the riding animal. She was leading the two horses along a perilous stretch of trail, when the unfortunate animals lost their balance and fell hundreds of feet onto the rocks below.

To add to her problems, everything she needed to survive was at the bottom on her dead horses. Faced with such an extreme option, she decided to make her way down the mountainside to retrieve the bare essentials.

Ed Anderson later wrote, "On the way down the slope she found things that were not hers. She was to learn later that a hiker had recently fallen at that same spot. He had broken his neck, was lucky to have been rescued, and ended his hike in the hospital. The rider did find both horses dead, and with great difficulty, was able to retrieve what she needed."

Because you are travelling light, everything you carry must be kept to a minimum. Yet you must be prepared to face a challenge instantly and alone.

To begin with, you must always be able to stay warm. Don't rely on a cigarette lighter to do this vital job. In order to light a fire you need to place the flame underneath the tinder. Not only is it difficult to place a lighter under the tinder, if you hold the lighter on its side too long it may explode. Lighters also get too hot to hold, if you attempt to keep them lit for too long. The answer is to carry strike-anywhere matches in a waterproof container.

Finding dry tinder to make a fire may be difficult on a cold or wet day. A Wet Fire starting cube only weighs 36 grams (1¼ oz.), comes in a waterproof aluminium packet and can be lit under the most adverse conditions.

Other emergency items carried by Long Riders include an LED flashlight, energy bar, personal first aid kit, metallic reflective blanket and local currency.

Summary

When it comes time to pack for your journey, your guidelines should be realism and practicality.

Dress for comfort in the saddle and safety on the road.

If in doubt, arrange your proposed possessions in three stacks.

In the first, place all the things you will have immediate need for. In the second, place all the things you cannot do without. In the third, and smallest, place the things you would rather not do without. Bring half of all this and it will be more than you will ever have to use.

Long Riders have always had to balance their need for comfort with honouring local traditions. Jocham Östrup was a young Swedish Long Rider who did both. In 1891 he adapted local clothes, mounted an Arabian stallion and rode 4,500 kilometres (2,800 miles) through Egypt, Syria and Asia Minor. His adventurous journey is recounted in his excellent book Växlande Horisont.

This philosophy still holds. When the Slovakian Long Rider Janja Kovačič rode from Uruguay to Bolivia, she wore the comfortable clothes preferred by gauchos. This included a wide felt hat and the loose trousers known as bombachas.

In contrast, Israeli Long Rider Kareen Kohn made a point of donning clothing that would please his native hosts when he explored the Incan ruins in Peru and rode north to Mexico.

The Kakadu vest provides enough pockets to carry the essential items which a Long Rider should always have close to hand.

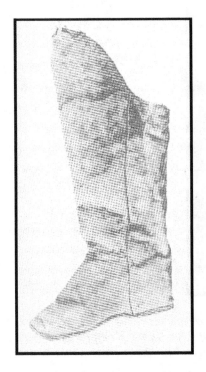

Despite the passage of millennia, the basic equestrian equipment used by Bronze Age riders is still in use today. One such example can be seen in the remarkable similarity between the four-thousand-year-old riding boot (left), worn by a mummified horseman in 1800 B.C., and the riding boots (right) worn by French Long Rider Louis Meunier when he crossed Afghanistan in 2007.

Khampa horsemen in Tibet are still wearing conical hats similar to the ones discovered in ancient Japanese graves.

Many Long Riders have chosen to wear a traditional cowboy hat. One notable example was Long Rider Virl Norton. After winning a 1976 trans-continental endurance ride which stretched from New York to California, Norton set off on another adventure. In the winter of 1979 he rode a thousand miles from his home in Illinois to visit President Jimmy Carter at the White House in Washington D.C.

When German Long Rider Eberhard von Westarp rode across the Ottoman Empire and Persia in 1913, he opted to wear the traditional pith helmet favoured by soldiers and some explorers during the colonial period.

North American Long Rider Ed Anderson wore a helmet when he made his ride along the difficult Pacific Crest Trail from Mexico to Canada.

Regardless of the age, equestrian travellers have always had to contend with riding in the rain.

As the author learned during his travels in Pakistan, ponchos are not suitable rain gear for Long Riders.

British Long Rider Alan Lucas is a great example of how modern fabrics can assist equestrian travellers. He is wearing comfortable boots that allow him to walk and ride. His calves are protected by wrap-around leggings. His riding pants are easy to wash. His waterproof jacket provides plenty of room to move. He has opted for a protective helmet that also shades his face from the sun. Modern, lightweight and durable, his clothing is ready for an extended journey.

Even though he was nearly eighty years old, Captain John Codman rode his horse, Fanny, across New England in the winter of 1887. Thanks to his warm clothing, he suffered no discomfort.

Kazakh Long Rider Dalaikhan Boshai (left) and his friend Tugelbai use golden eagles when hunting on the steppes. Because the weather is frequently minus 35, these hardy native horsemen wear traditional sheepskin trousers, as well as a sheepskin coat that covers their legs.

Ladakhi Long Rider Ghulam Rassul Galwan made expeditions in Chinese Turkistan and through the Pamir Mountains. He was one of the many equestrian travellers who wore a sash to aid them when riding.

Welsh Long Rider Thurlow Craig also wore a sash, known as a faja, when he explored the notorious Chaco jungle of Paraguay.

One aspect of clothing which should not be overlooked is safety. William Reddaway made a unique journey to the four corners of England in 2014, during which time he visited 30 historic cathedrals and abbeys. Because of the heavy traffic, he made sure to equip both himself and his horse, Strider, with bright reflective clothing.

When he rode from Zaysan, near the Chinese border, to Egindikol, in central Kazakhstan, Long Rider Alpamys Dalaikhan always kept a monocular in his coat pocket to help him make his way across the steppes of his native Kazakhstan.

Chapter 36
Electronic Equipment

Equestrian exploration is where tradition and technology meet.

In an age when preschoolers are exposed to words like Google, Twitter and Facebook, it is tempting to think our generation of cool hipsters wrote the book on savvy gadgets. How easy, and inaccurate, it would be to overlook the spirit of intellectual innovation that accompanied previous Long Riders.

One of the most dramatic examples occurred, not in a laboratory, but where you would expect to find an equestrian explorer, in the wilderness.

Riding the Radio Waves

In 1924 American Long Rider Lewis Freeman set off to explore the roof of the Rockies.

A seasoned traveller, Freeman had already ventured into remote parts of Africa and Asia. He also helped make technical history by demonstrating that radio waves could be broadcast and received from the bottom of the Grand Canyon.

In the early years of the 20th century, radio was in a comparable state of development to the internet in 2000. The men who had pioneered the new technology were still alive and fast fortunes were being made by those quick enough to develop the commercial aspects of radio. Yet important questions remained unresolved. For example, experts believed Canada's Rocky Mountains presented an insurmountable barrier to the passage of radio waves.

Freeman was determined to be the first person to receive a radio signal from within this high altitude "dead zone." To assist him, he had sixteen horses and some colourful companions.

The plan was to ride north from Banff in order to reach the distant Columbia Ice Field. Surrounded by 12,000 foot peaks, this remote wonder had only been glimpsed by mountaineers.

Covering an area of 130 square miles, the ice has a depth of 1,200 feet, comparable to the height of the Empire State Building, and is the largest ice mass in North America south of the Arctic Circle.

Though he was an experienced traveller, Freeman lacked the equestrian knowledge needed to reach the isolated glacier. To help him in his quest, he hired a renowned Canadian packer, Soapy Smith, as well as a wrangler and cook. The final member of the team was Bryon Harman, a pioneer in wilderness photography.

It was because of the weight of Harman's photographic equipment that Freeman and Smith were required to use so many horses. The carrier pigeons were another issue. They were Freeman's link to the distant world of radio.

In an age when tiny telephones take photographs and send text messages to all parts of the globe, it is hard to sympathise with the challenges faced by our predecessors. Freeman's radio is one such example.

He had chosen a RCA Radiola Model III. Priced at an affordable $24.50, the reliable unit was the gadget of its day. Measuring 'only' 8" (20 cm.) wide, 7" deep, and 7" high, the Radiola was housed in a cabinet made of solid mahogany. Tough, simple, inexpensive and, for its time, small, it was the perfect radio for Freeman's mission. But his job wasn't an easy one.

Two tubes acted as the audio amplifier and the radio wave detector. In lieu of speakers, Freeman used headphones to listen for the elusive radio signals. Because frequency numbers had not yet to be invented, Freeman had to use the station selector knob, which was marked with a simple 0 to 10 scale, to try and find radio stations. After locating a radio station, he would write down its numerical location in his "station log," in the hope that it might be located again.

Prior to his departure, Freeman recalled, "After getting the best technical advice available on the possibilities and limitations of radio under the conditions we expected to encounter, I had bought the set in New York and brought it to Banff. There I had a wooden box built around the set and the batteries connected up for us by the local electrician."

Because no one knew if the Radiola could receive radio signals behind the mountain barrier, Freeman also brought along homing pigeons. These trained birds would carry messages from the Long Rider's camp back to several powerful stations who "had promised to make a special effort to reach us in the event the Rockies did not prove to be entirely dead."

But it was horses, not birds, which occupied Freeman's immediate interest.

"The horses, picked long in advance, had been kept off the trail all summer to conserve their strength for the arduous and punishing work ahead. They all knew how to paw aside snow and find grass. But travelling though the snow would demand all their stored up strength."

Even with strong horses, and a capable crew, Freeman had been told that his plans to take the horses across the inhospitable mountains and onto the ice field, was, "verging closely upon the impossible."

The experts were nearly right. It wasn't inaccessible, but conditions were terrible.

In the valleys they struggled through swamps, where the horses were continually bogged down in stretches of treacherous glacial mud. They forded torrential streams, narrowly avoided landslides and travelled over scarred mountains. One day they thought themselves lucky to have covered nine miles in six hours. The cook fell into a crevasse. A four-day blizzard trapped them in camp. They fought through snow in minus 10 degree weather.

Yet after ten weeks of hellish travel, they returned to Banff in triumph. Having ridden across five hundred of the hardest miles on record, they had scaled the mountains and reached the ice field.

"Not one horse had been lost during the course of what was probably the roughest continuous pack train journey made in the Rockies since the time of the pioneers," Freeman wrote.

Theirs was the first effort to scientifically explore and comprehensively photograph the most stunning regions of the Canadian Rockies and Columbia Mountains.

Just as important, Lewis Freeman had heard a weather report broadcast by station KGO in Oakland Ca, the most powerful radio station west of New York.

The little Radiola, the epitome of technology, had set a precedent which Long Riders continue to embrace today.

Typewriters to Laptops

When Joe Goodwin made his ride from Texas to Mexico in 1931, the young journalist used a portable typewriter to describe his adventures. Even though technology had moved on by 2001, Slovakian Long Rider Janja Kovačič also struggled to relay her story to the outside world.

Her problem wasn't a defective typewriter ribbon. She was the first Long Rider to need an internet signal.

Accompanied by Norwegian Long Rider Howard Saether, Janja had set off to ride from Uruguay to Texas. Their journey across Uruguay and Brazil had been challenging. Then they ventured into Paraguay's Gran Chaco jungle. That's when things really got tough.

When asked to describe South America's most desolate wilderness, most people would automatically think of the Amazon River. They would be wrong. It is the Gran Chaco, a 250,000 square mile desolation which stretches across parts of Paraguay, Bolivia and Argentina. Often described as a "green hell", the Chaco is not only one of the hottest parts of South America, but this last frontier contains abundant aggressive animals, multitudes of blood-loving insects, flesh-stabbing thorn trees and few people.

In February, 2002 Janja managed to find a signal for her laptop computer and sent an email to the Long Riders' Guild from within the jungle.

"We have ridden about 450 kilometres into the Gran Chaco and we are fine. When I say we are fine, that means our dog and ourselves. Three of the horses have piroplasmosis."

Time and technology have marched on since Janja sent that message. Experts are now predicting the development of the world's smallest computer, which will measure just over one cubic millimetre. Known as "smart dust," the mini-machine will be capable of generating enough power from a tiny solar cell to work for years. These miniature computers will be able to track any physical object, making it nearly impossible to lose anything.

Janja did not have that luxury in the jungle.

She shared these thoughts about carrying a laptop on an equestrian journey.

'We are not sure if we should recommend carrying a computer on a horseback trip or not. With all the necessary equipment it weighs a lot. It takes up a lot of room and it steals a lot of your time. On the other hand, it is a very nice thing to have. We use it for communication, to update our website, and to store digital photos. We also have maps, 4 DVDs with the Complete National Geographic and a DVD encyclopaedia.

If you choose to carry one, you also need to bring with you all the original discs for your system, chargers for 12 volt and 110/220 volt. We also carry a small CD-burner to make back-ups and to store photos in a safe place. We don't think it matters much what brand or make of computer you chose. We ended up buying a Dell Inspiron 5000, Pentium III, 128 ram, 18 GB hard disk with a DVD-rom.

To protect it we bought a Pelicase "bomb-proof" case, which we carry in one of the pack saddles' fibreglass panniers. In spite of our horses galloping, falling, banging into trees, and crashing into rocks, we haven't had any major problems with the computer.

One thing that we would recommend, which we don't have, is to have a network card installed. Many places it is difficult to find a telephone line to connect to the internet, but today you'll find Internet cafés almost everywhere, and with a network card they'll probably let you connect to their network. We make a contract with a local provider in every country, and that works well. We are not sure if we want to bring all this equipment on another horseback trip, but it has worked fine, so far."

Long Riders who are riding within their home country may not carry a laptop computer, hoping instead that they can find internet access at a local library or in the home of a host. However, if you are bound on a long journey, one which will take you across international borders, then you may wish to consider carrying the most light-weight laptop currently available. If you make that decision, remember two things.

Your equipment and your information may both be stolen.

Thieves view travellers as walking wallets. So guarding your valuable computer becomes a primary task. Equipping your panniers with padlocks and then locking the boxes to stationary objects helps deter sneak thieves.

However, there is a new threat to a Long Rider's writing – governmental intrusion and confiscation.

Travellers entering the United States have had their computers confiscated or their information recorded without their authorization.

In a pending court case, the U.S. government has argued that its authority to protect the country's border extends to looking at information stored in electronic devices such as a laptop. Even though the computer owner may not be suspected of a crime, when crossing into the United States officials regard a laptop the same as a suitcase and can search it without obtaining a warrant.

There have been several questionable intrusions into private, computerized papers. A tech engineer returning to San Francisco from London was asked by a federal agent to type his password into his laptop computer. Even though the engineer protested that the computer belonged to his company, the US citizen agreed to log on. He then witnessed the officer copy the web sites he had visited. Other travellers have been forced to surrender their passwords, then had their emails and personal documents copied by federal agents. Computers have also been confiscated by the authorities.

Regardless of where you travel, Long Riders need to be aware that anything electronic can be confiscated, copied or destroyed by government agents. If you carry a computer, make sure your travel notes are regularly copied and sent home, so as to offset theft or confiscation.

Lighting the Way

There was another technical innovation connected to the journey across the Chaco jungle. The Long Riders generated their own electricity.

This came about thanks to Janja's companion, Howard Saether. Before he became an equestrian explorer, Howard spent many years as a deep-water sailor. During his various voyages, he became familiar with newly-developed solar panels. Such a small, flexible, light-weight panel can produce a surprising amount of power.

Prior to their departure from Uruguay, Howard placed a small naval solar charger on top of the pack saddle. The results were encouraging.

"Because we have a camcorder and a laptop, we needed something to charge batteries while travelling in the countryside. We bought a flexible solar panel and a 12 Volt motorcycle battery. We place the solar panel on top of the pack saddle, so it charges while we are travelling," he explained to the Long Riders' Guild.

The solar panel was a flexible Uni-Solar USF-11, 10.3 W. It measured 400x550 mm. and weighed less than 1 kilo (about 2 pounds).

Solar battery chargers convert sunlight directly into electricity reliably and silently without fuel or moving parts. The cell assembly is laminated in flexible and durable weather-resistant polymers that provide long life and high reliability. Bypass diodes are connected across each cell to produce exceptional shadow tolerance performance. Though initially used by sailors, the durable solar panel proved perfect for Long Riders too.

The battery Howard chose was a readily available YUASA NP7-12, 7.0 AH, which is sealed, rechargeable and weighs less than 2 kilos (about 4 pounds).

"We have a snap-connection between the solar panel and the battery, and from the battery, it goes to two lighter plug outlets. We can charge the batteries of the camcorder without having the solar panel connected. But when we want to charge the computer we need to have the solar panel connected, so it charges at the same time. If we use the computer while the solar panel is connected, it provides sufficient power so we don't use the computer batteries at all!

After a while we also bought a 12 Volt, 9 watt fluorescent light bulb, and that is our biggest luxury. No more messing with kerosene or candles. We use the excess solar power for light in the tent at night. At night we have sufficient light for as many hours as we want. More importantly, the 9 watt light bulb illuminates as well as a normal 60 watt bulb, which is even enough to break camp and saddle the horses at night."

Telephones

On March 10, 1876, Alexander Graham Bell made history when he uttered the famous instruction, "Mr Watson, come here. I want to see you." His assistant, Thomas Watson was waiting in an adjacent room when he clearly heard Bell speak. The two men had just transmitted and received the first telephone message.

Equestrian travel likewise changed on July 2, 2004 when Tim Cope sent a message and a photo to Guild HQ via satellite telephone technology.

Prior to setting out to ride from Mongolia to Hungary, Tim had enlisted the sponsorship of the Iridium telephone company. With sixty-six satellites orbiting around the Earth, the communication company can provide coverage to any part of the globe.

In addition to being able to summon help in an emergency, Tim predicted the satellite phone would allow him to update his website while travelling and allow him to conduct live interviews from the saddle. He was right on both counts.

Tim contacted the Long Riders' Guild from Mongolia. What made his message so important was that he used the Iridium phone to relay information about horse prices, availability of saddles and the local political situation. He also sent a photograph, not from an internet café, which was still a relatively new concept, but from the yurt belonging to his hosts.

During the following months he relayed a constant stream of information. When winter found him on the steppes of Kazakhstan, and the temperature dropped to minus 48, he rode through the hardest weather in living memory. Under such adverse conditions, Tim had to warm up the satellite telephone's battery in his pocket before he could call the Long Riders' Guild.

"In fact for much of the winter this year it was colder in Kazakhstan than it was above the Arctic Circle."

Yet he reported that the phone worked "brilliantly."

Tim was also the first to use satellite technology to enlist the aid of an equine veterinarian in case of emergency.

"When I am alone with three horses out on the steppe I am very aware of the safety issues. If something were to go drastically wrong I would be in very big trouble without communication. One of my most valuable contacts is a specialist horse vet in Australia. When something goes wrong I call her up and she talks me through everything. This can be very reassuring when the locals are telling you that your horse is finished and is going nowhere when in actual fact the injury or problem can be very easily treated."

Telephone technology has continued to progress since Tim's first experiments. The machines are smaller and have additional functions which have further enhanced a Long Rider's ability to keep in contact with loved ones and seek help in an emergency.

Before setting off to ride from Canada to Brazil, Filipe Leite equipped himself with a multi-function mobile phone. It didn't take long for him to realize how useful it was.

"This brings me to my last tool, my iPhone. I have used this little thing of beauty a million times a day for the past eleven months! It wakes me up in the morning, tells me if I'm on the right road, allows me to share photos and tweets in seconds, and keeps me in touch with family and friends. It's amazing. The iPhone has an incredible camera and it is super lightweight. It is also very durable. I don't have a case on mine and have taken it over mountains, through rivers, in the jungle and it still looks like new."

Pay phones are increasingly difficult to locate and will soon be an obsolete form of technology. Also, considering how unreliable local telephone systems may be in some countries, carrying your own phone could be an important consideration.

Being in constant touch may seem like a dream come true; however, there is an increasing number of alarming drawbacks. For example, the American National Security Agency is reportedly collecting almost 5 billion cell phone records a day under a programme that monitors and analyses highly personal data about the precise whereabouts of individuals, wherever they travel in the world.

Additionally, today's tiny telephones may have another hidden hazard.

The Cost of a Call

Like everything a Long Rider carries, the weight of his electronic equipment must be taken into account. Even though Tim and Janja used the lightest items they could find, the cumulative weight would be far more than a Long Rider need carry today. For example, Tim's laptop, camera, film, satellite phone, and charging equipment weighed 55 pounds.

The other drawback was the cost of the equipment. At the time a satellite phone and internet kit cost about US$1500. Equally disturbing was the fact that the price of a call was about US$2 a minute.

British Long Rider Mary Pagnamenta made this expensive financial discovery during her ride across New Zealand.

"A satellite phone is a luxury for most of us but if you are travelling alone in remote country, it is worth considering. Mine was paid for by the Leeds United Football Club. But make no mistake; the cost of making a call is horrendous."

Even though the prices of equipment have become more reasonable, and mobile telephones ever smaller, mounted travellers still need to ensure that their call provider doesn't take advantage of them.

Many of the new "smart" phones automatically download emails and data every time they're turned on. This means the phone owner runs up an immense bill without ever realizing it. One phone owner was charged $30,000 because of an app that continuously downloaded data without the user's knowledge during a trip abroad. Another traveller was charged $7,500 for using his mobile phone to check his emails while on holiday.

Unlike charges for calls and texts, which can accumulate only while the phone is being used, charges for data can add up without the owner noticing because emails and some data such as the owner's location are automatically updated. Simply switching an English mobile phone on outside the EU could cost $75 in automatic downloads. One victim of this financial scam discovered he had been charged more than 750 Euros for downloading an incredible 244,352 KB of information he never authorized.

Mobile phone companies neglect to notify users that they can minimize their bill by ensuring that the data roaming option on their phone is switched off prior to departure. This will help ensure that you are only charged for making voice calls and checking emails by connecting your phone to a local wireless internet service rather than to the mobile network.

Sat Map

Anyone who planned an equestrian journey in the late 20th century will remember the expense and effort of finding accurate maps. Even when you had armed yourself with what you believed was a faithful chart, all too often you learned that the map was a flat-faced liar.

I can remember sitting in the saddle in Pakistan, shaking my head in anger and dismay as I looked at the maps. Bridle paths ended prematurely. Bridges were washed away. Villages had disappeared.

That is why when asked what modern technology she found most helpful, Basha O'Reilly replied, "Google Earth! Although one can never entirely avoid nasty surprises, one can plot one's course very accurately. Whereas every explorer delights in the element of surprise, when you travel with horses or other animal companions, their welfare becomes a priority, so being able to avoid motorways and find grazing, for example, is a great help to Long Riders."

Having access to the most up-to-date maps has proved to be of tremendous assistance to mounted travellers and the technology continues to improve dramatically. For example, whereas Janja and Howard had to download maps into their laptop computer only a few years ago, British Long Rider Elizabeth Hill had great success with a new device known as the Sat Map. It equipped her with a treasure-trove of the most accurate maps, all of which were stored in a palm-sized device.

"I spent ages wondering whether it was best to get maps or to get an outdoor GPS and just carry an additional large scale map and compass for emergencies. The fact that I would have needed more than seventy 1:50,000 maps for the planned journey, which would have worked out very expensive and logistically complicated, eventually convinced me. Why on earth did I ever doubt what would be best?"

The small Sat Map unit is easy to use and allows you to fine-tune your route on the move. It displays the map on a 3½" colour screen and the battery lasts up to 120 hours in hibernate mode.

Elizabeth used the Sat Map with success during her ride through England, Wales and Scotland.

"Don't get me wrong - I love map reading and hardly ever get lost with one, but it is fantastic to know without a doubt what your position is and where to go."

GPS

Although American President Calvin Coolidge was raised on a Vermont farm, he developed an allergy to horses. Yet the 30th president retained his belief in the physical benefits of riding. The answer was to acquire a stationary electrical equine. Controls on the 1925 mechanical steed allowed Coolidge to vary the intensity from a trot to a gallop. Because the president only rode in his White House dressing room, he had no need to worry about where he was heading. For the rest of us, a GPS is a valuable addition to a Long Rider's list of electrical equipment.

The Global Positioning System (GPS) uses a system of two dozen satellites hovering 12,000 miles above the Earth, each of which orbits the planet twice a day and beams back a constant position signal.

The first GPS units allowed Long Riders to plot routes and estimate distances with greater accuracy. One early drawback was that they had an alarming ability to consume AA batteries. In some countries the AA replacement batteries were of such low quality that the GPS could not be re-powered. Things have improved greatly in the last few years.

Ed Anderson was the first to report success with a new GPS system known as the SPOT. Not only does it provide pinpoint geographic accuracy, it also allows the traveller to relay messages.

"I rode on the Pacific Crest Trail with my SPOT for over five months. When I reached a place to camp each day I could press a button and send my wife an "I'm OK" message by satellite. My wife would get a message on her cell phone with a special ring. She would also get an email including the GPS co-ordinates of my location. She could then look up my location on Google Maps and actually see a satellite picture of the location. This gave her great peace of mind while I was on the trail."

Another valuable feature of the SPOT is the emergency button. It transmits the message, "I need help from friends," along with your location on Google maps.

Multi-Purpose Camera

Thanks to the melding of these new concepts and machines, Panasonic has introduced a camera, the Lumix DMC-TZ20, which uses GPS technology to tag the photograph with your location and date. The small, durable unit fits into a vest pocket, and thanks to its Leica lens, takes excellent images.

Swiss Army Computer Knife

In what may be the most surprising departure from tradition, the famous Swiss Army knife made by Victorinox has been updated for computer users. In addition to the stainless steel blade, and such traditional useful tools as a screwdriver and scissors, it is also equipped with a USB storage key which is compatible with Windows, Mac OS and Linux operating systems.

The key allows a traveller to store all types of data and can be used with any USB connection. Equipped with a memory capacity of 64 MB, this key is nearly undetectable within the familiar red Swiss army knife case. It allows you to safeguard vital information independently from your computer's hard drive. However, it is possible to delete or enter data as desired.

It is also possible to detach the USB part from the main body of the knife, so as to facilitate data exchange, to upgrade the device to another capacity or as a security measure while travelling by airplane.

Genghis Khan meets the Matrix

Throughout the entire history of equitation a continuous chain of inventions and adaptations have been inspired by the present demands of life. One of the most impressive adaptors was illiterate.

Genghis Khan created the largest empire in history. Even though he could not read or write, one of the ways the legendary cavalryman controlled the 12 million square miles he conquered was by eagerly adapting new ideas and technology from the 3 billion people he ruled.

A master at negotiation, intrigue and psychological warfare, the wily Mongol would have quickly seen the benefits of using Wikipedia to gain instant knowledge on an enemy. His minions would have maintained an official Mongol.gov website which extolled the fact that Genghis guaranteed religious freedom, ruled the empire as a meritocracy and treated women with respect. And you can bet he would have used Twitter to let his friends and family know how far he had ridden and what cities he had conquered that day.

There is no doubt that in a matter of a few years, new technologies have forced us to re-examine our definitions of time, space and identity. Access to constant news has hopefully encouraged people to view themselves as patriots in a global world. But there is always a dark side. The simpler age of radio tubes and typewriters is gone. We are surrounded by musical Prozac, deluged by frivolous information, and spied upon by bio-mimicry drone spy craft intended to resemble hummingbirds.

Misplacing our Trust

It was still common in the mid-19th century for travellers to carry handmade maps containing vital information about wells, river fords, mountain passes, dangers, blacksmiths and inns gathered from those who had undertaken the same journey.

Even though there are benefits to technology, a Long Rider would be well advised not to bet that batteries alone will save his life.

In 2011 the Royal Academy of Engineering warned that society had become dangerously over-reliant on satellite radio navigation system's GPS. Every day an army of satellites beams down a vital stream of information. But cyber experts predict that any disruption of this system would throw mankind into chaos.

This deadly lesson was recently confirmed at sea when a state-of-the-art yacht, brimming with the latest in high-tech wizardry, found itself in trouble.

When the decision to build the yacht was made, natural materials such as wood, cotton and wool were delegated to the past. They had been replaced by tons of petroleum-derivative foams, fibres and resins which had gone into the construction of the ship's hull, deck, sails, masts and rigging. There were no inconvenient paper charts or old-fashioned tide tables cluttering up the cabin. They had been substituted by a navigator who sat before screens which relayed the yacht's speed, the wind's direction and the depth of water under the keel. Using the information gathered from orbiting satellites and transmitted to his various screens, the navigator could set a scientifically-charted course and then punch the command into the self-steering mechanism.

It was a floating marvel and the final piece of the puzzle was that the ship's compass was powered by electricity from a vast array of batteries.

On the yacht's maiden voyage, the owner and crew found themselves sailing off shore, out of sight of land, on a pitch black night. It was a moonless, starless night. That is when all the electronic gadgetry failed due to a defective switchboard. Screens went blank. Digital readouts failed. The fluxgate compass, losing its life-giving electrical pulse, died.

The owner had put all his trust in high-tech navigation, neglecting to include even one old fashioned magnetic compass. With no stars or moon to act as celestial beacons, the helmsman realized that his only reference point had been reduced to the wind blowing on his right cheek. With all on board praying that the wind stayed directionally stable, the yacht was put about. It returned under reduced sail, on what was hoped to be a course towards home. Early that morning the clouds cleared and the Pole Star showed them north, followed by the sun lifting itself above the eastern horizon. Later that day, with the aid of binoculars the humbled yachtsmen were able to locate the marina.

In a matter of moments, these overly-confident sailors had been hurled back a thousand years, to the days when mankind skirted cautiously along the coast in broad daylight, never daring to venture too far out to sea or to risk sailing into the dark void.

An over-dependence on advanced technology can be a mistake for a Long Rider. Older, reliable tools and skills are still essential to an equestrian traveller.

This was a lesson that North American Long Rider Katie Russell learned during her ride through the rugged mountains of Idaho and Montana.

"Even though we had the latest technology, we relied upon traditional tools, like our axe, compass and ancient skills to keep warm and fed. So while technology is a help, it's not a solution," she warned.

Scientists are now trying to determine if humans have an internal compass. According to new research, monarch butterflies can sense the Earth's magnetic field and can use it to navigate. The airborne insects are able to do this thanks to a light-sensitive protein known as cryptochrome.

Cryptochrome helps regulate daily body rhythms that are present in both butterflies and humans. Scientists have inferred that humans might also possess a magnetic sense. Could this be the gene that helped Bronze Age Long Riders migrate without the help of complicated compasses, GPS systems and Google maps?

Until answers can be found to such an elusive question, let Katie's admonition save you from the traumatic experience of the self-assured yachtsmen. Always carry a reliable compass.

Previous Problems

Because technological advances often disrupt established customs, the path to progress can be a rocky one. The printing press changed the way literature was transmitted. Yet its impact was initially felt only by the educated elite. Clocks on the other hand had an immediate consequence on the lives of ordinary people.

The invention of the mechanical clock at the end of the 13th century disturbed the people's daily lives. Clocks aided in the rise of capitalism by allowing employers to impose timetables and pay workmen by the hour. This led to strikes by workers in the 14th century.

Likewise, there have been unforeseen consequences associated with new technology, not only in the world around us but within the exploration community as well.

A Price to Pay

In 1976 Long Rider Robert Schweiger was making his way across his native America. Upon the conclusion of his journey, he made a vital observation.

"I didn't read a newspaper or listen to a radio or watch any television, and I now have a small insight into the feelings of those who have been isolated from the world, either by choice or fate. I truthfully lived in a world of my own. When I learned how far I had ridden on a given day, it seemed vague and unreal. The slow pace gave me the opportunity to drink in the scenery and I know that I will always cherish and remember the things I saw and experienced on this journey."

What Robert discovered was that with the planning resolved, the preparations a memory, the fears conquered, the objections ignored and many miles now behind him, a sense of deep inner peace had overcome him.

One of the most precious things you will discover on the journey is this heightened sense of self. One of the surest ways to erode or destroy it is via the non-stop interruption caused by electrical devices and intrusive social networks.

Being disrupted is nothing new.

Alexander Graham Bell patented the telephone in 1876. The Bell Telephone Company was created in 1877. More than 150,000 Americans had become eager telephone users by 1886. The first transcontinental telephone call was made in 1915. Yet Bell considered his invention an intrusion and refused to have a telephone in his study.

Things have got much worse since Bell hung up his phone.

The last few years have seen an explosion of constant news, endless entertainment and limitless interaction with countless strangers who call themselves our "friends." What few realize is that there is a price to pay for being hooked to a relentless flood of communications. The power of these devices lies in their subtlety.

According to new statistics, more Americans are members of Facebook than have passports. A staggering 155 million Americans - 50 per cent of the population - are on the social network, even though only 115 million people - 37 per cent - have a passport.

We are also witnessing the first generation of children to be strongly influenced from birth by constant exposure to mobile technology. Toddlers and pre-schoolers are furnished with educational apps which serve as electronic pacifiers/ dummies. With the door to Pandora's electric box thrown wide open, alarming stories are emerging including the three year old who bought a £9000 pink Barbie car on his parents' Ebay account and five-year-olds who are addicted to You Tube videos.

This new digital age has also placed a great deal of pressure on teenagers. A recent study showed that 98.7% of 16 to 24 year olds use the net and that they spend an average of 31 hours a week online. This incessant internet use has been compared to the collective mind of the Borg in Star Trek. Yet unlike those fictional aliens, many people are increasingly concerned with the subtle polluting effect of the internet.

The British journalist, Johann Hari, made this important observation.

"We are the first generation to ever use the internet, and when I look at how we are reacting to it, I keep thinking of the Inuit communities I met in the Arctic, who were given alcohol and sugar for the first time a generation ago, and guzzled them so rapidly they were now sunk in obesity and alcoholism. Sugar, alcohol and the web are all amazing pleasures and joys – but we need to know how to handle them without letting them addle us."

Technology is an ever-present feature in our everyday lives, with the culture of computers being self-proliferating, self-interested and self-consuming. These developments have had a furtive influence on equestrian travel as well. Whereas early Long Rider websites supplied information about the route and the mission, Facebook and Twitter are encouraging people to become obsessed with themselves and seek constant feedback on their activities.

One academic suggested that some Facebook users feel the need to become mini celebrities who are watched and admired on a daily level. In an effort to remain 'Facebook worthy,' these people 'flash' updates about their activities, thoughts and feelings so as to encourage constant feedback from their 'friends.'

As the internet and social networking have matured, there is a growing antagonism to the massive amount of information bombarding us. For example, Rustock, one of the world's biggest known botnets in history, was capable of sending 30 billion spam email messages per day. Average people are increasingly resentful of being inundated by endless messages. This includes Facebook updates which confirm that the traveller is suffering from 'filter failure,' i.e. doesn't know when to keep quiet.

Several recent episodes have demonstrated how equestrian travellers have bored the public with needless details about their daily existence. This deluge of travel trivia caused indifference and then antagonism amongst those who were subjected to this new type of spam. The result among readers was a loss of interest, then of confidence, followed by antagonism.

Plus, any sense of mystery about the journey was slain in the cradle, as everyone on Earth knew what the person had eaten, seen, said, heard and thought during the course of the trip. Nor does it help when an emergency occurs, as then your disgrace is placed on public display for the entire world to see.

Keeping in touch with your mum or wife is one thing. Keeping your dignity is even more important.

People who become obsessed with their Facebook profile are being compared to 'digital Maoists.' Bonding with as many people as possible has a disproportionate effect not only on your time but your well-being, as being tuned in night and day does not enhance our humanity, it diminishes it.

However good the virtual interaction may be via a social-media service, it is never going to replace the full richness of human experience. Equestrian travel is full of one-to-one meetings. We cannot set off to explore our souls if we are deluged by tweets, Facebook updates, emails and cell phone messages.

Moreover, being exposed to constant internet stimulation means we panic when we find ourselves alone, and Long Riders are alone a great deal of the time.

People locked in a cyber-world find themselves afraid of silence. They are not used to spending time in their own company. Instead of embracing solitude, they deny their own privacy. As the Historical Long Riders Charles Darwin, Carl Linneaus, Jonathan Swift, Lord Byron, Somerset Maugham and Graham Greene demonstrate, solitude has long been linked with creativity, spirituality and intellectual might.

Being alone is an important part of your inner journey. You should strive to break the cycle of noise which makes so much of modern life toxic. In addition to mere miles, coming to your own conclusions regarding issues which concern you is a priority. Instead of giving in to the pressure of supplying constant updates to stay-at-home pedestrians, you should explain your need to enjoy the contentment associated with riding your horse quietly.

Your duty to others is conditional. That is why you should not let the allure of social networks intrude upon the essence of your spiritual journey.

As Basha O'Reilly warned, "Technology should be our ally, not our ruler. You can't explore your soul if you're obsessed with posting on Facebook."

Summary

In 1937 while deep in Patagonia, Aimé Tschiffely wrote, "If I had been born a hundred years earlier, I would not have seen the miracle of the development of the machine, the coming of the motor car, aviation, radio, and many other wonders. Has man really benefited from them or are they to cause his downfall? Impossible to prophecy; much too soon even to have a guess; a thousand years hence the answer will be known, perhaps."

When the first Long Rider left his village behind, all those many thousands of years ago, he had a list of simple requirements. Grass, Water, Safety, Shelter.

Modern technology has created a world our great-grandparents could never have imagined. By pushing a button, messages fly through space, and then alight on another continent. Everything is faster and the world has grown smaller.

Yet when the time comes for you to set off, you too shall still seek Grass, Water, Safety, Shelter, as did our forebears.

Ask any Long Rider and he will tell you, "The more you know, the less you need."

That is why it is well to recall that one can be deceived into becoming overburdened by electronics and social services.

When American Long Rider Lewis Freeman set off to explore Canada's Rocky Mountains in 1924, he took along the most advanced communication system then available, a Radiola two-tube radio.

The Radiola III was housed in a cabinet made of solid mahogany. Considered "small" for its day, it measured 8 inches wide and was 7 inches high. The cloth-covered cable was hooked to the batteries which powered it.

In 2002 Slovakian Long Rider Janja Kovačič was the first equestrian traveller to use a portable laptop computer to maintain a website, send and receive emails, and publish articles during a journey.

By 2005, when Tim Cope set off to ride from Mongolia to Hungary, technology had improved. During the two-year journey Tim became adept at erecting a mobile office wherever he camped. This photo shows him typing up a report for his website.

Howard Saether, a former Norwegian sailor, was the first known Long Rider to adapt solar power to equestrian travel. His knowledge of nautical equipment inspired him to adapt the solar panel from a yacht for his journey across South America in 2002. After riding atop the pack saddle all day, the small, flexible panel had generated enough power to run a laptop and a small bulb which lit up the Long Rider's camp.

By the time Tom Fairbank set off to ride across the western portion of America in 2011 he had become one of the many Long Riders who recognized the importance of fitting inexpensive and flexible solar panels on the pack saddles.

In the summer of 2004 Tim Cope (right) used an Iridium phone to send the first Long Rider photograph via satellite technology.

Thanks to technical advances, Filipe Leite was equipped with an Apple iPhone during his journey from Canada to Brazil in 2012 to 2014. In addition to working as a telephone, the small device had an alarm clock, took excellent photos and provided access to the internet

Filming from the back of a horse is nothing new. When Able Gance (right) made his epic six-hour film "Napoleon" in 1927, the innovative director was the first to mount a camera on a horse.

Though he had not heard of Gance's previous efforts, Australian Long Rider Tim Cope also devised a way of filming himself while riding across the desolate steppes. He mounted a "horse cam" on a wooden board, which he then secured to the top of the pack saddle's panniers.

British Long Rider Elizabeth Hill had great success with a device known as the Sat Map. It equipped her with a treasure-trove of the most accurate maps, all of which were stored in a palm-sized device.

When German Long Rider Albert Knaus made his journey from Mönchsondheim, Germany to Santiago de Compostela, Spain in 2004, he became one of the first modern equestrian travellers to use a GPS.

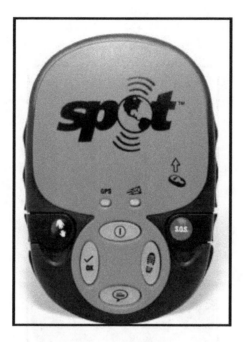

The SPOT device not only provides pinpoint geographic accuracy, but it also allows the Long Rider to relay messages back home or call for emergency assistance.

Time and technology never stand still. One development is this Panasonic camera which uses GPS technology to tag the photograph with your location and the date.

Even the traditional Swiss army knife has adapted to the spirit of the internet age, by adding a USB key which stores all types of data and safeguards it while travelling.

North American Long Rider Katie Russell warned, "Even though we had the latest technology, we relied upon traditional tools, like our axe, compass, and ancient skills to keep warm and fed. So while technology is a help, it's not a solution."

Even though modern Long Riders have reason to be thankful for these many new developments, technology has a way of venturing into unexpected directions. One such example was Blow Torch, the mechanical horse. Fashioned from sheet metal, a nine hp gasoline engine provided power to the small wheels hidden under his hooves. A foot throttle controlled his speed, while a brake cable brought him to a halt. He sported a horsehair mane and tail but, unlike real horses, Blow Torch puffed smoke from his nostrils every five minutes. Though the steel pinto appeared in several 1950s parades, he was never used on a journey and was retired when his Canadian inventor died.

Chapter 37
Support Vehicles

It was the French aviator-author, Antoine de Saint-Exupéry, who wrote, "A machine is like a desert, either it fascinates or appals you."

Prior to departing on an equestrian journey, many first-time travellers will have foreseen the possibility of enduring hardships and overcoming challenges. While avoiding dangers and finding nightly shelter might be obvious concerns, few people realize that the idea of including a mechanized support vehicle into an equestrian journey is fraught with unexpected hazards.

The idea of linking Long Riders with wheeled transport is nothing new.

Genghis Khan made occasional use of a large yurt which served as a mobile headquarters. As Mongols considered it degrading for a horse to be subjected to such lowly labour, the massive wooden vehicle was pulled by a team of oxen.

Geographic circumstances have also played a part in deciding to use a wagon to keep the Long Rider and his horse alive.

After successfully crossing Europe, Russia, Siberia and Mongolia with his road and pack horse, the Japanese Long Rider Baron Fukushima ran into trouble in Manchuria. The landscape was so devoid of fodder that he had to hire a cart to carry grain for his horses through this desolate part of his journey.

But before you get nostalgic for the good old days, you had better learn how bad they really were.

Motorized Pioneers

In an age when motorized transport influences every aspect of modern life, it is hard to appreciate the fact that humans have only been driving for a very short time. Moreover, in this age of computerized four-wheeled luxuries, the hardships faced by the pioneers of mechanised exploration are difficult to comprehend. No example better demonstrates how tough things were than the Court Treatt expedition from Cape Town to Cairo.

Prior to the early 1920s, the idea of crossing the African continent by motor was considered a job best left for lunatics and suicide-seekers. Tom Silver drove his motorcycle out of Cape Town in 1903. At least he got as far as the Sudan. When Captain Kelsey made the first attempt by car ten years later, he wasn't so lucky. He was killed by a leopard in Rhodesia.

When the First World War concluded, the idea of being the first to drive across the length of Africa was revived by Major Chaplin Court Treatt. This no-nonsense British veteran started his preparations in 1923 by journeying to England from South Africa.

Because he had used Crossley vehicles during the war, he obtained two of the four-cylinder vehicles from the Manchester-based manufacturer. Knowing their trucks were going to be subjected to harsh conditions, company officials thought it wise to modify them for the hardest trip a vehicle had ever undertaken. They raised the suspension a few inches and fitted the windows with mosquito screens.

With the deluxe Crossleys ready for the road, Treatt obtained permission from the British government to ensure that his route took the expedition exclusively through England's colonial territories.

Because roads through most of Africa were non-existent, prior to his departure Court Treatt had to arrange for spare parts and fuel to be carried by porters for hundreds of miles to remote locations. Using this system, 27 supply dumps were carefully constructed in advance.

On 13th September, 1924 the Major and five companions were ready to depart. Accompanying him were his wife, her brother, a professional photographer from Canada, a London journalist and the son of a Malawi chief who spoke 32 native dialects as well as English. The group's only luxury was a wind-up gramophone and a few jazz records.

They left in sunshine but broke an axle while crossing a river on the second day. After donkeys pulled the vehicle out of the river, they waited a week for the replacement part to arrive and then pressed on. They spotted their first lion on November 5 but the excitement was dampened because they had run out of cigarettes.

Heading north towards Victoria Falls, they encountered rain storms which turned the landscape into a sea of mud. They would drive a few yards, sink into the mud, dig the vehicles out and then repeat the process. On a good day they made six miles. After four months they had travelled 380 miles.

In the Impindo marsh they had to pile logs under the wheels to proceed. They were soon covered with leeches. In Mpika the District Commissioner warned them to take special care as a man-eating lion had consumed thirteen people in the last eight nights. Care had to be taken when crossing the Chambeshi River as it was infested with crocodiles. The good news was that crossing the borders into Rhodesia, Zambia, Tanganyika, Kenya and Uganda presented no problems because formalities were non-existent.

If things had been challenging before, they became seriously complicated in southern Sudan.

The Nile River is surrounded by an infamous swamp known as the Sud. Local officials urged Treatt to put the trucks on a steam ship and sail north around this notorious obstruction. The bwana refused. The party entered a wetland where the papyrus reeds and grass were taller than the vehicle roofs. In addition to the humidity, they were plagued by mosquitoes.

When they encountered numerous rivers, Court Treatt initially hired Dinka tribesmen to construct rafts from trees and then gingerly floated the trucks across. That method worked until they reached a spot where no trees grew.

With most of the African continent behind them, the determined party refused to surrender. If they couldn't float the trucks over the obstacles, their answer was to physically pull the trucks across the bottom of each of the rivers they encountered. The vehicles were stripped, and the holes in each engine were blocked with candle wax and wooden plugs. Two ropes were tied to the front bumper, then fifty natives would pull the truck into the water, across the riverbed, and up onto the far bank.

Once on the other side, it took several hours to remove the plugs, drain out any water, reassemble the engines and reload the trucks. They crossed seventeen rivers in this singular manner.

Eventually they emerged into the sandy waste of northern Sudan, and promptly became lost in the desert. But the worst was behind them and they arrived in Cairo on 24th January, 1926. It had taken them sixteen months to travel 12,732 miles.

The Court Treatt expedition was the first to successfully harness the symbolic power of modern technology to cross Africa. Their journey had both an immediate and a long-lasting impact on exploration history. For example, in 1928 three plucky English ladies made the same journey in a 1924 Morris Oxford touring car.

Their tale of hardship also influenced Commander Gatti, who gets the credit for introducing motorized comfort into adventure travel.

Commander Gatti

Some may argue that the controversy as to whether or not the machine destroyed natural adventure began in 1938, when Attilio Gatti ventured into Africa with his motorized "Jungle Yachts."

Gatti was an Italian explorer who wrote exciting books with titles like "Killers All" and "Africa is Adventure." Considered one of the last great safari men, beginning in 1922 Gatti travelled extensively throughout the continent, during which time he filmed the Zulus, befriended the Pygmies and lived with the Watussi. He also nearly died from black-water fever and survived numerous close calls.

By 1938 the severity of his earlier adventures convinced the aging Italian to change his game plan. Plus, he had married an American woman who was keen on accompanying her explorer husband back to the "dark continent." Only this time the Italian wasn't going to lead a long trail of machete-wielding porters. Mr. and Mrs. Commander Gatti were determined to travel across Africa in comfort.

To make exploration history, Gatti teamed up with an American motor company, International Harvester. Together they produced the world's first luxurious adventure vehicles. Two mighty trucks were created to pull matching twin trailers. But these were no mere thin-skinned tin boxes. Even though America was still recovering from the Great Depression, the 44-foot trailers cost $15,000 a piece to create, nearly $250,000 in today's market.

One trailer held the living and dining room, library, bar and electric kitchen. Its companion housed two ultra-modern bedrooms and a tile bath equipped with a full-length tub. Both trailers also had indirect lighting, telephones and a two-way radio system. When joined together at camp, the result was a five-room apartment on wheels.

To facilitate filming, the trailers had an observation deck on top. Behind the cab of each truck was a 110 volt power plant which provided the power to the air conditioning, photographic laboratory and workshop. To discourage prowling predators, a 4500 volt electric fence provided protection at night.

Because the trailers each weighed nine tons, it was no easy task to navigate them. But the rugged vehicles traversed 66,000 miles, almost none of it on paved roads, and only experienced minor breakdowns, totalling $38. They also allowed the Gattis to seek out Africa's secrets in style.

Shortly before the Second World War broke out, Commander Gatti left Africa for the last time. He returned to America with his wife and their travel-stained Jungle Yachts. The story of their expedition was featured in Time Magazine and a film about their expedition was seen by three million people.

Thanks to Commander Gatti, the concept of travelling with a house trailer suddenly seemed to be within the reach of the common man. Manufacturers responded by making everything from tiny one-person tear-drops to palatial travel trailers.

But there is a major difference between the expeditions led by Major Court Treatt and Commander Gatti. Their emphasis was on the vehicles, not animals. And as history brutally demonstrated, when you mix horses and horse power, you encounter unexpected problems.

The Champagne Safari

Many purists believe that true adventure requires you to ignore machinery, rather than embrace it. The flamboyant French millionaire, Charles Bedaux, believed he could have it both ways. He was the first to combine motors with horse travel and he failed.

The Great Depression was the most destructive economic disaster of the 20th century. Democracy was weakened. Millions were unemployed. Suicides were rampant. Soup kitchens kept people from starving.

You wouldn't have thought that these were ideal conditions to undertake a madcap 2,400 kilometre (1,500 miles) journey over the Canadian Rocky Mountains to the Pacific. Yet that's exactly what Bedaux proposed to do. And he wasn't planning on travelling alone. His plan was so ambitious it made Commander Gatti's Jungle Yachts pale in comparison.

After amassing a vast fortune in business, Bedaux clamoured for social status and political power. He believed the road to both goals could be won by becoming a famous explorer. His plan was to explore the unmapped regions of northern British Columbia. To help his cause, he enlisted the aid of his friend, French car maker Andre Citroën.

Unlike traditional automobile manufacturers, the Citroën Company also produced a half-track all-terrain truck. Teams of these specially-equipped vehicles had already completed successful journeys across Asia and Africa. Bedaux concluded that Citroën's half-tracks could cross the Canadian Rockies with ease.

He purchased five of the vehicles in Paris and had them shipped to Canada. The four-cylinder trucks had a top speed of 18 miles per hour. Ironically they never reached that relatively low speed, because Canada had a few surprises which no one had foreseen.

Unlike Major Court Treatt, who had splashed out by taking along a gramophone, Bedaux spent $250,000 in the middle of the Great Depression, comparable to more than $4 million in 2015. His half-tracks carried tons of fine food, champagne, caviar and state-of-the-art equipment.

He also employed 130 saddle, pack and draught horses to act as tactical support for the Citroëns. Fifty steel tanks, the size of pack saddle panniers, were specially created to allow the horses to carry fuel for the half tracks.

And Bedaux wasn't planning on travelling alone.

More than 50 Canadian cowboys were hired to handle the horses. A Citroën mechanic arrived from Paris. The Canadian government provided two official geographers. Floyd Crosby, who later won an Academy Award for directing the film, *High Noon*, came along to make a documentary and oversee the large film crew.

And then there were the three women who accompanied Bedaux: his wife and her maid, as well as an Italian countess rumoured to be his mistress.

Prior to the expedition's departure, Bedaux assembled this sizeable crew at Jasper National Park in Alberta, Canada. Though they were supposed to be getting fit and seeing to the equipment, Bedaux and the members of his expedition spent most of their time attending dinners held in their honour.

After enjoying a final champagne breakfast with local dignitaries, Bedaux set his massive expedition into motion, departing from Edmonton, Alberta on 6th July, 1934. Their destination was Telegraph Creek, British Columbia which lay far away across a trackless mountain wilderness.

No sooner had they reached the edge of the city than the rain began. The weather plagued Bedaux from then on.

Even though Citroën half-tracks had successfully traversed the African continent from north to south, and travelled from Beirut to Peking, they were no match for the mud of the Canadian Rockies. Constant rain turned the soil into a morass. Unlike Major Court Treatt's relatively light-weight Crossley trucks, which could be man handled through the mud, the Citroëns sank up to their axles. With the rain continuing to fall for 32 out of the next 37 days, the horses were put to work dragging the cumbersome vehicles free.

Trapped in a relatively uncharted wilderness, the combination of bad weather and unforeseen terrain doomed Bedaux's dreams. Despite their reputations and cost, the frustrated explorer began losing faith in the vehicles. Two slid off a cliff while the cameras rolled. A third was lost in a river crossing. The last two were finally abandoned.

Not even the horses could save the hopeless expedition. Because of the extreme weather, many of the animals were suffering from hoof rot. But with the entire group now in the saddle, they pushed on. Then the snow began to fall. When more than 18 inches of snow blanketed the dim trail, Bedaux found himself in danger of being trapped in the mountains. With his vehicles lost, his horses failing and their lives at risk, the frustrated Frenchman halted 300 miles short of Telegraph Creek.

Ironically, Bedaux's idea to construct a road through the Canadian wilderness helped inspire the building of the Alaskan Highway. But by then he was dead.

With his dreams of being an exploration star dashed, Bedaux returned to France. There he hosted the marriage of the Duke and Duchess of Windsor at his French chateau. Because of his sordid activities during the Nazi occupation of France, Bedaux was arrested as a collaborator. He committed suicide while in American custody.

Orwell's Warning

You wouldn't think that George Orwell, who authored *Animal Farm* and *1984,* would have anything to say about vehicle support for Long Riders, but he predicted how mechanized comfort would affect modern human beings.

In his book, *The Road from Wigan Pier*, he expressed concern that, "taking society as a whole, the result of the transition from horses to cars has been an increase in human softness."

In his bluntly prophetic manner, Orwell warned, "the tendency of mechanical progress is to make life safe and soft."

Though his cautionary book was published in 1937, he foresaw the folly of relying on machines.

"The aeroplane, like the motor-car, will be made foolproof; a million engineers are working, almost unconsciously, in that direction. Finally, this is the objective, though it may never quite be reached: you will get an aeroplane whose pilot needs no more skill or courage than a baby needs in its perambulator. And all mechanical progress is and must be in this direction. A machine evolves by becoming more efficient, that is, more foolproof; hence the objective of mechanical progress is a foolproof world, which may or may not mean a world inhabited by fools."

Why would a Long Rider care what Orwell said?

Keeping to the Safe Road

There are two types of travellers: those who depart so as to arrive and those who journey in order to discover. Auto drivers belong to the former, Long Riders to the latter.

Mechanized travel is designed to maintain your sense of safety. Deviation from the itinerary is discouraged. Challenges are kept at bay. Fear and uncertainty are forbidden. By residing within the metal cocoon, the isolated driver watches the world pass by in a blur. Trapped behind his windshield, the encased driver has a second-hand experience of life.

Once you venture onto a horse the world takes on a new perspective.

Equestrian travel throws you into the environment. Your senses are brought alive as you see, smell, hear and touch the natural world around you. Being in the saddle brings you into constant touch with local people. You are not a robotized tourist, following the crowd from one mega-attraction to another. On such a rhythmic journey you are not obsessed with speed or competing against the clock.

In his poem, *Ode to the Long Rider*, Long Rider D.C. Vision wrote, "From the saddle you will always get the entire sensual impact that fossil fuel drivers in their boxes simply never find. There is an ancient natural heartbeat matched at this pace, where rider, mount, and environment discover their communion."

Had be lived, Charles Bedaux would have seen the 20th century arrive on horseback and depart in an air-conditioned vehicle. Like that doomed traveller, many have made the mistake of linking motors to horses for no other reason than their desire to maintain a sense of style and comfort.

There are, however, occasions when the need to keep you and your horse alive require you to include a support vehicle.

Transport by Necessity

The vast majority of equestrian journeys do not require anything much more complicated than saddle bags and a pack horse. Yet exceptions do exist and sometimes equestrian travellers are forced by circumstances to employ the use of a driver and vehicle to overcome obstacles.

A few years after Aimé Tschiffely completed his legendary ride from Buenos Aires to New York, he decided to undertake a quiet ride across England, where he had taken up residence. His destination was the home of his friend, Don Roberto Cunningham-Graham, who lived in Scotland. Compared to the mighty Andes Mountains and the jungles of Central America which Tschiffely had previously overcome, the ride to Scotland should have been easy.

Unfortunately the British ride forced Tschiffely to tackle entirely new problems. He could no longer picket his horse on the vast pampas and camp out in the open like he had done in the past. Instead he had to seek out a field or stable for Violet, the mare he was riding, while he spent his nights in hotels or inns. But worse was yet to come.

Upon reaching Wrexham Tschiffely came face to face with the industrial regions of Yorkshire and Lancashire. The landscape was so unpleasant and the traffic so potentially dangerous, that Tschiffely opted to pay a truck driver to transport him and the mare around the hostile cities. Aimé resumed the journey in the pleasant Lake District further north.

The need to deal with a sudden surprise is still challenging Long Riders.

After having ridden hundreds of miles across South America, Howard Saether had a choice to make. Wretched conditions in the Chaco jungle had weakened his horses and waiting now before them were the mighty Andes Mountains. Such conditions prompted Howard to put the welfare of his horses first.

"We have reached Sucre, Bolivia. For several reasons we have decided to transport the horses by truck from here to La Paz which is about 700 kilometres (430 miles) away. The main reason is that the road climbs more than 4,000 meters (12,000 feet) and there is no water or food for the horses. Plus, the temperature goes down to minus 15° Celsius at night, and animals are dying up there."

These were short-term journeys designed to transport the horses and traveller around a potentially hazardous obstacle.

Should your route demand that you include a vehicle on a permanent basis, there are a number of potential problems waiting to waylay you.

Delayed Dreams

The first consideration is that your progress may be postponed, prior to your departure or once you set off, because of mechanical difficulties.

This is what stopped the young American woman who had planned to ride "ocean to ocean." With her horse ready and her route organized, she had to reluctantly inform the public, "Well my dream has been delayed by mechanical problems."

A series of costly last-minute break-downs to the support truck had left her with a horse and a dream but no trip.

"Back brakes and throttle sensor went out on the truck. We managed to coast the truck and horse trailer into a Ford dealer. The folks there were very kind and helpful. They let us pull into the garage out of the scalding sun while they had someone look at the truck to figure out what had happened."

The news wasn't good.

"Sometimes you have to reach a point of enough is enough and I have actually gone above and beyond that point with this darn truck. With this additional repair biting into my already short budget, I did not feel I could attempt this ride at this time. I am bitterly disappointed in how things transpired."

Insurance

Some countries permit a foreign traveller to purchase a vehicle but will not allow them to then insure it. This proved to be the case in England, for example, where Americans can buy a vehicle but cannot obtain insurance. As their own insurance from home often does not cover driving through countries other than their own, Long Riders are left with an uninsured vehicle.

Hostility

Another drawback is that the vehicle can draw unwelcome attention or antagonise the locals.

One Long Rider whose journey was dependent upon motorized transport was Bonnie Folkins. She had already made an extended ride across Mongolia but the trip she planned in northern Kazakhstan would take her through portions of that country which had little food or water.

Because of her previous travels, Bonnie understood the need to obtain the right type of vehicle to use in such rugged country where towns were few and the population not always friendly. She hired a UAZ, a robust Soviet-era all-terrain vehicle, to help her cross northern Kazakhstan.

"The UAZ could manoeuvre through almost any terrain, and gathering water and grain would have been impossible without it."

While the vehicle proved to be a reliable success in the field, unfortunately it attracted an unexpected type of trouble. Because it was registered in Mongolia, local thugs in Kazakhstan resented its presence.

"I found it incredibly important to have an accessory vehicle in Kazakhstan. It added ten-fold to our safety as the people in the towns can definitely bring on the possibility of grave dangers," she wrote.

But a problem arose.

"Our Mongolian licence plate drew a lot of attention because there is no such thing as a touring car visiting Kazakhstan from another country. In that part of the world young men look for any chance to beat up other young men who are not of their ilk. At night we would conceal the plate."

Thus the UAZ support vehicle was a mixed blessing. It proved to be very reliable, but its presence required Bonnie to make camp away from prying eyes so as to avoid any hostilities with the local populace.

While expensive repair bills, high-priced petrol and costly insurance are all concerns, they don't stop as many equestrian journeys as the weakest link in this chain: the driver.

Incompatible Priorities

When you mix horses and support vehicles you are attempting to bring about a delicate balance between two competing definitions of time.

The road horse is a symbolic bridge between nature and the Long Rider. He draws you into the natural world without enclosing you as a machine would.

The rhythm of his hoof-beats echoes your heartbeat. Riding along quietly towards the horizon at three miles an hour slows down your body, clears your soul and places you in a solitary place of great contentment.

In a world obsessed with haste, the first lesson your horse will teach you is to slow down.

By contrast, even as the Long Rider becomes part of the countryside, the driver of the support vehicle speeds through it. The automobile doesn't afford the driver a personal interaction with neighbours. It cuts him off from nature. Even worse, it also allows him to cover the daily distance travelled by a road horse in less than an hour. The result is that the driver reaches that day's destination in minutes and then spends the best part of the day trying to justify his decision to accompany the slow-moving horses.

No matter what country you go to, when you mix fast-moving drivers with slow-moving Long Riders, you often end up with quarrels and desertions.

Conflicts of Interest

Equestrian travellers are passionate about realizing their dreams. But people hired to drive a support vehicle have no particular allegiance to the Long Rider. What appears at first to be an easy job soon becomes a grinding bore to the driver.

Robin and Louella Hanbury-Tenison had used support vehicles in the past during their journeys across France and China. The driver on the French trip had been a trusted family friend and the Chinese driver had been specially selected by the government to help the Long Riders; so both trips went well.

But things went wrong for the Hanbury-Tenisons when they rode through the remote mountains of Albania in 2007. They employed a small support vehicle to carry their tent and necessities through countryside left gaunt by Communist mismanagement. But it wasn't the vehicle which caused problems; it was the driver.

Thanks to his many years of experience, Robin had photocopied in colour all the maps, so that he and the driver would have identical maps to navigate by. He was also planning on maintaining contact with the driver via mobile phones.

"In theory that would mean that we would always be able to find each other. But it didn't work out that way."

The rugged Albanian mountains blocked the phone signal so both parties lost touch with each other on a regular basis.

"The prime purpose of having a backup vehicle was to avoid tired riders having to organize everything themselves at the end of a long day," Robin recalled, "but somehow this message never quite got through."

After a hard day in the saddle, Robin and Louella would arrive at camp only to discover that the driver was too lazy to pitch the tent, making Robin do it. Nor did the Albanian understand the equally-important needs of the horses.

"Instead of setting up camp in a beautiful meadow next to a clear river, the driver chose to park inside an extremely dirty village."

Even obtaining basic directions proved to be a struggle. Though Robin is fluent in a number of languages, Albanian isn't one of them. The driver refused to help the frustrated Long Rider ask for directions, preferring instead to throw up his hands, walk away and ignore the traveller's plight.

Despite these various drawbacks and failings, at least the Hanbury-Tenisons avoided the worst problem associated with support vehicles: deserting drivers.

Deserting Drivers

Andi Mills and Edie New decided to rely on a support vehicle during their ride across the Mojave Desert and the arid Arizona desert country.

Unfortunately, Andi later recalled, "Our driver was unable to separate herself from issues at home. Because of this she didn't last a month."

Sometimes the driver leaves you high and dry in the middle of nowhere. Other times you wish they would simplify your life by leaving. That's what happened when Basha O'Reilly set off to ride from Volgograd to London.

With the recent collapse of the Soviet Union, Russia was in a state of internal turmoil. Told she needed a back-up vehicle to carry supplies, Basha agreed to hire a local man to act as driver. The problem was that he was from Moscow and knew nothing about the country or horses.

Yet he was initially enthusiastic when she set off to ride across the steppes on her stallion, Count Pompeii.

"I don't think he actually believed I'd get very far on the journey and would give up. So he was waiting to pocket the money and go home to the city. But the further I rode into the country, the more uncomfortable he became," she recalled.

Long Riders are required to interact with the locals on a daily basis. But Basha's driver lacked the initiative to find a campsite or buy grain from the villagers. What's worse, he failed in his primary mission, which was to meet her at the end of the day.

Because he wouldn't venture away from the main road, Basha was forced to ride alongside traffic. One day she decided to shorten that day's ride by cutting across country. The agreed-upon plan was for the driver to meet her at a prominent place further on.

"When I reached my destination there was no sign of the driver. I carried a flare gun in case of an emergency, so my standing instructions were that if we couldn't find each other at 6 p.m. I would fire it. He eventually showed up after dark, claiming he had never seen the flare. During that time I worried that he had abandoned me without notice."

Increasingly unhappy, the driver grew sullen and frightened.

"He kept repeating, 'We're going to wake up with our throats cut'. We had only travelled a short distance when it was agreed he would return to Moscow. He had cost me a lot of money, caused me a tremendous amount of worry and delayed my journey."

On her next expedition, Basha rode along Butch Cassidy's "Outlaw Trail," travelling from the Mexican border to the Hole-in-the-Wall hideout in Wyoming. Because of her negative experiences with a support vehicle, she opted to use pack horses.

"Having done expeditions with support vehicles and pack animals, I can confirm that a Long Rider is always better off sticking with horses," she said.

As Andi and Basha demonstrate, if you decide to employ a driver the person should not be a timid, homesick, easily-bored safety-seeker.

Luckily, there is one type of person who you might enlist to aid you: someone who has a deep emotional commitment to seeing you complete the journey.

Love not Money

There have been some splendid exceptions to the rule about naughty, lazy or disloyal drivers. The best drivers have been found among the ranks of those who were either family members or had a deep personal loyalty to the slow-moving Long Rider.

One such example took place in 1976 when Robert Schweiger set off to ride across part of the United States. His 17-year-old son, Jeff, drove a support truck.

"We covered 1200 miles during our thirty-day journey from Chicago to Oklahoma City," Robert wrote. "But Jeff had a constant battle with boredom because he had short periods of driving and then a long wait."

A more recent example of emotional support behind the steering wheel was demonstrated by Emma Brazier. When her boyfriend, Filipe Leite, announced that he planned to ride from Canada to Brazil in 2012, the young woman didn't hesitate to help.

When Filipe was forced to ride across a vast, drought-stricken portion of the western United States, Emma borrowed a car, found Filipe, and followed him to the Mexican border, all the while ferrying hay, grain and water to the horses.

After two years in the saddle, Filipe finally reached Brazil. But stretching out before him was the hot and humid Pantanal, the world's largest wetlands. Once again, Emma obtained a vehicle and drove along in order to carry supplies and find places dry enough for Filipe and the horses to camp.

The experienced "Long Driver" offered a number of vital insights and suggestions to anyone considering using a support vehicle.

Advice from Emma

The first thing Emma suggests is that the majority of people underestimate how critically important it is to link your journey with the right person.

"I believe Long Riders in the past had negative experiences with drivers simply because they did not place enough importance on finding the right individual. If a Long Rider *chooses* to involve a driver (ultimately relying on them one way or another) picking the right person to fulfil this role is as important as choosing the right horse, the right saddle etc. If for example, a horse isn't fit for a trip, you don't blame the horse you blame the person who chose it. If the wrong person is chosen, then I believe the Long Rider will absolutely be abandoned and it is no one's fault but the Long Rider," she wrote in a special report to the Guild.

"The job of a driver is numbingly boring for the average person. I am an introvert who does not rely on anything or anyone in particular for my day-to-day happiness/entertainment. It is something that comes from within and because I love travel and adventure, supporting Filipe's journey by car was absolutely something I desired to do. Instead of viewing each day as eight hours of waiting, I saw eight hours of opportunity. Of course, supporting the Long Rider is of utmost importance, but more often than not, the driver is left with nothing but time. Thus, finding the 'right fit' is everything," Emma explained.

Besides the need to employ the right person, Emma also shared her discoveries regarding several other vital points. Communication, patience and trust are all essential if the journey is to be a success.

"As much as I was there for support, I too needed it at times. (Missing home, stressing about taking time off work etc.) I required patience from Filipe and Filipe required patience from me. We took on the journey one day at a time to lessen what is sometimes overwhelming. We learned that it is more important to be a team and less about our duties and responsibilities being so black and white (i.e. whose job it was to put up the tent). If you hold definite expectations of people you will probably if not always be let down."

Above all, Emma advised, there must a complete sense of trust between the Long Rider and the vehicle driver.

"Filipe and I had been together for two years prior to his departure. It was essential that I trusted him in order to get through driving day to day. One example is when he was riding over the Grand Mesa National Forest in Colorado. On this particular day we left at different times with the intention of meeting up in the afternoon. We had cell phones to communicate as well as a previously marked GPS route that I was instructed to follow. An hour into my drive I started to worry because there was no sign of Filipe and the sun was beginning to set. Without cell service I turned to the next best thing: horse droppings to guide me. I steadily continued to drive and just before dark, I saw Filipe entering an old beaten corral to set up camp. If I hadn't trusted Filipe wholeheartedly, I definitely would have turned back out of fright."

Finally, Emma issued this warning. Even though Filipe had the additional help of a support vehicle during extremely difficult parts of his journey, he always kept the pack saddle, equipped with his basic necessities with him at all times. This policy proved critically important when the vehicle Emma was driving broke down and Filipe was unexpectedly required to make camp at sunset.

"This is a prime example of how a support vehicle can fail you," Emma said. But she added it highlights her last lesson.

"Don't put all your eggs in one basket and plan for the worst."

Find a Professional

Driving a support vehicle for a Long Rider isn't likely to appeal to most people. In the past Long Riders were lucky enough to find grooms or people who understood horses to drive the vehicle.

That's what James Wentworth Day did when he decided to explore England by horseback in 1941. He arranged for his groom, Jim Rodd, to take a single lesson on how to drive a car up and down back roads for an hour and then put the young man in charge of a large Daimler horse box. Rodd then drove it 2,200 kilometres (1,350 miles) in support of the Long Rider.

When Malcolm Darling set off to ride across India in 1947 he also arranged for a driver with equestrian experience to transport rations and water through difficult parts along the route.

More recently, Bonnie Folkins solved the problem by hiring Nurlan, a professional driver from Mongolia.

"Nurlan is an angel and a risk taker who knocked himself out to great lengths for me. He is very quiet and polite. For example, whenever he had a need to ask local people a question, he wouldn't just drive up to them. First he would park and then he would walk over to them. And his price was unbelievably low."

It may not be easy to find a Mongolian angel. So what traits are essential for a support driver? The person best qualified to answer that question is Peter Phillips, one of the most well-travelled Long Rider drivers alive today. He is married to the English Long Rider Mefo Phillips.

Questions for Peter

How many trips have you made in support of Long Riders?

Two.

What years did you make those trips?

2002 and 2006.

Where did you drive from/to?

2002 – Canterbury, UK, to Santiago de Compostela, Galicia, North West Spain – and return

2006 – Canterbury, UK, to Rome, Italy – and return.

How many miles did you drive total on those trips?

2002 – 1700 miles each way (so 3400 miles)

2006 – 1200 miles each way (so 2400 miles)

Total 9,400 kilometres (5,800 miles).

What type of vehicle did you drive?

1984 Bedford TL diesel, 7.5 ton horsebox with wooden body, stalled for 2 horses and with basic accommodation.

Had you ever made a similar trip as an expedition support driver prior to your Long Rider trips?

No.

What was your major concern before you set off to drive on the first horse journey?

Boredom and lorry breakdown

Did this problem ever arise?

Yes and yes!

What was the most serious problem that arose without warning on the trips?

The lorry brakes catching fire on the long descent from Mont Cenis in the Alps to Susa in Italy

Did you have an everyday check list before leaving the camp?

Yes – water, oil and fuel; power steering, fuel leaks, battery, tyres, lights, Portapotti levels in 2006. No Portapotti in 2002. At night the batteries would be put on charge, i.e. I took every opportunity where there was access to electricity (such as a campsite) to charge up all the electrics.

Because the riders travel at a vastly different rate of speed than the vehicle, how much time did you allow them to get on the road before you set off for the next camp?

That would depend on the route and terrain, e.g. a motorway journey would be very quick, but if say over mountains and down a gorge on a minor road it would take much longer, so I would try to judge it accordingly. The riders usually planned to ride for 7 or 8 hours maximum so I would plan my own journey accordingly. Sometimes I would stop en route to visit historical sites or to play golf.

Were you the one who usually looked for a place to camp?

No, not usually. We believed it was more effective if the Long Rider with her charismatic horse asked would-be hosts if we could all stay, and probably this was true. Sometimes our hosts would phone ahead to friends or contacts to arrange a place for us the next day.

If not, how did the Long Rider know where and how to find you?

We had mobile phones, and Mefo left me a note in the morning before she left to say where she hoped her destination for the day would be. I would get there before her and check out the village, for example, for places to stay that might be suitable but usually not make the approach. If there was a mobile telephone signal, I would then park on the outskirts and, if there wasn't, I would park in the middle where Mefo could not miss me. In 2002 we were on a well-trodden pilgrim path with pilgrim refuges usually available, particularly in Spain. In 2006 this was not the case, particularly in Italy. If the landowner could be found, permission to camp on his land was sought. If there was no one, we liaised by phone (or sometimes I would wait on the road for Mefo to catch up near the end of the day) and then camp in the most suitable spot.

What did you look for in a camp for the riders?

Land that could be fenced off safely for the horses (we had a portable electric fence on both trips), and preferably where water was nearby, though sometimes you had to go and search for it and transport it with the lorry.

For the vehicle?

The prime consideration was the welfare of the horses, as above. A bonus would be a flat, adjacent piece of land to park the lorry so we could sleep without falling on top of each other.

Were you responsible for finding horse food? If so, how did you manage that problem?

Mostly n/a – we had grain and hay on the lorry, and we travelled in summer when there was plenty of grass, particularly in France and Italy. In Spain the horses ate whatever grazing there was, sometimes stubble.

Did the horses ever present a problem for you, either while driving or in camp?

No – they were very well trained! Though they liked to sample our food and drink (preferably alcohol or coffee) and tended to gallop round me in camp when I was trying to read my book.

Because the riders are busy all day in the saddle, many drivers quit prematurely, citing boredom and fatigue. How did you offset these traditional problems?

You have to be self-contained, introverted, enjoy your own company and solitary pursuits like reading, visiting points and sites of interest. And have an ability to sleep at a moment's notice.

What items would you consider to be of vital importance to keep with the support vehicle?

A good set of tools, battery charger, spare oil and water and hydraulic fluid, air pump for the tyres, spare bulbs, pieces of string, a hole puncher for adjustment to bridles etc, a cordless drill with more than one battery, a complete set of spare fuses, a bloody good torch, 30 books for the average trip, a bottle of whisky, a credit card, binoculars, lots of sweets that don't melt in the sun, a set of golf clubs and more whisky.

What papers/documents are of the utmost importance?

The horsebox papers and a decent map; notebook for entering expenditure.

Did the vehicle ever break down?

Yes.

2002: Binding brake drum on Day One; fuel leak; fan casing disintegrated; clutch cable stretched which meant only fourth gear worked.

2006: Fuel pump disintegrated in the Alps (necessitated lorry taking an unscheduled trip to Albertville for a week to be mended; fortunately the mechanic lent me his clapped out Citroen AX so we were able to carry on after a few days); fuel leak in the Po Valley, Italy, which was mended by a small Croatian on a day when the temp was 46 degrees Celsius with 100 per cent humidity. Brakes caught fire as mentioned above.

Were you ever worried about theft?

No.

Did the authorities ever harass you?

Once in Italy (after I emptied the Portapotti down the public loo!) – I was given an hour to leave by Signor Rambo despite parking in a spot designated for motor homes.

Were you ever asked to pay a bribe?

No.

How did the natives treat you as a foreign driver? Were they patient with your daily needs?

Apart from Signor Rambo, the natives were friendly.

Because the riders are with their horses in the countryside, the driver is left alone for most of the day. How did you combat fatigue, frustration and loneliness?

Sleep! And lots of books.

Any additional thoughts or suggestions?

Never underestimate the driver's need for privacy and space. We were lucky with Bessie the Bedford because the cab was not cut through to the lorry, so it was very much my private domain, with my books and other little personal bits and pieces in it. I could escape to this space if I didn't want to talk horses or Mefo was busy map-reading and planning the next bit of the route, which was very much her job.

How could we summarize "Peter's Rules for the Road"? What things would you tell other drivers to always do, always avoid and never forget?

Always do: check your vehicle very carefully every day; if you pass a petrol station and you're half full or less, always fill up because you don't know when the next one will be.

Always avoid: driving down a street that's narrower than your vehicle; driving under a bridge that is lower than your vehicle's roof (nearly did that once!) – if in doubt, get out and walk it first; getting into a situation you can't get out of (e.g. down a lane that's getting narrower and narrower, and you could end up having to back up for 3 miles in a vehicle that's 8 feet wide – gets the adrenalin going when you are alone).

Never forget: you are there to provide support.

Summary

As history demonstrates, there are times when Long Riders have been forced to rely on a support vehicle in order to overcome short-term problems such as driving around traffic infested cities.

But the inclusion of a support vehicle on a full-time basis complicates the journey on a financial, emotional and logistical level, most notably if an unsuitable person is employed as a driver.

When the driver deserts, it is the Long Rider who ends up paying a high price for a mirage of safety.

A support vehicle is a remnant of your past representing safety and modern comforts. In exchange for a feeling of convenience and security, you barter away your self-reliance and independence.

Unlike other types of equipment, a Long Rider is better off only using motorized transport when circumstances, geography and climate offer him no other option.

Genghis Khan employed oxen to pull his massive mobile yurt.

福島安正　シベリア横断出発当時の記念写真

Japanese Long Rider Baron Fukishima set off in 1892 to ride from Berlin to Tokyo. He originally relied upon his horse, Gaisen. But after crossing Europe, Russia, Siberia and Mongolia, he had to hire a wagon to accompany him, so as to provide grain for his horse.

When Major Chaplin Court Treatt decided to try and drive from Cape Town to Cairo in 1924, he decided to employ the toughest truck on the market, the four-cylinder Crossley.

In Rhodesia rain storms turned the landscape into a sea of mud. On a good day the expedition made six miles. After four months the Crossley trucks had travelled 380 miles.

After driving across most of Africa, the explorers discovered they couldn't float the trucks over the rivers blocking their progress. Their answer was to physically pull the trucks across the bottom of each of the rivers they encountered. They crossed seventeen rivers in this singular manner. This image shows Major Court Treatt crossing the Bahr el Gell River standing atop one of the Crossleys.

Before setting off on his tenth expedition in 1938, Commander Attilio Gatti decided to make his next trip across Africa with the help of his motorized "Jungle Yachts." The twin 44' trailers cost $15,000 a piece to create, nearly $250,000 in today's market.

The custom-built trailers had state of the art communications. Commander Gatti's desk was furnished with clocks, speedometers, a map, and a telephone. Above the desk is a shelf containing many of the books he had written.

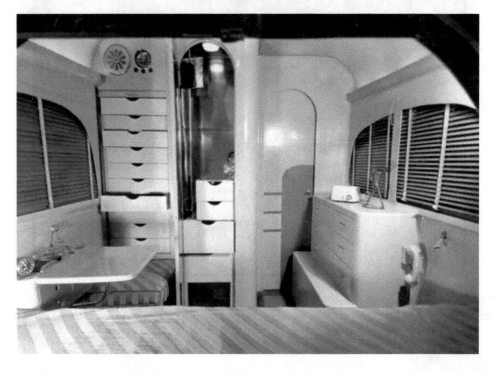

If she grew tired of travelling with her husband through the wilds, Mrs. Gatti could relax in a air-conditioned bedroom equipped with a telephone, dresser and extra clothing storage.

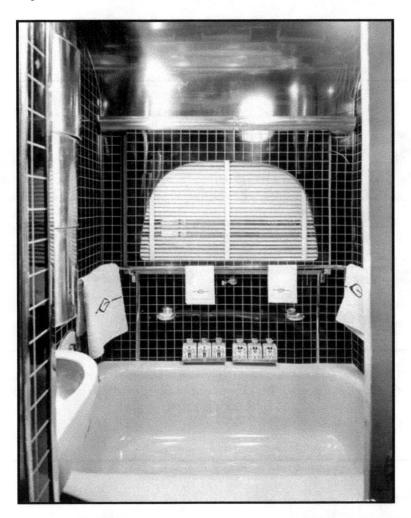

After enduring the tropical heat, it must have been tempting to soak in the full-length tub, surrounded by his and her toiletries and towels embroidered with the letter "G" for Gatti.

At the end of another hard day of exploring Africa in style, the Gattis enjoyed a cocktail outside their mobile headquarters.

Charles Bedaux spent $250,000 in the middle of the Great Depression, comparable to more than $4 million in today's money, to equip his expedition across the Canadian Rockies. His Citroën half-tracks carried tons of fine food, champagne, caviar and top dollar equipment.

Fifty Canadian cowboys were hired to handle the more than 100 horses used to assist Bedaux on his ill-fated mission.

Though the horses were intended to carry supplies, heavy rains caused them to be employed to pull the stranded Citroën half tracks out of the mud.

These handmade metal petrol tanks, shaped like pack saddle panniers, carried fuel for the half tracks, which were either destroyed or abandoned.

English Long Riders, Robin and Louella Hanbury-Tenison were the first modern equestrian travellers to venture into Albania. Because of the severe poverty resulting from the previous communist government, the Hanbury-Tenisons took a support vehicle which helped keep them supplied with badly-needed provisions. Due to cultural problems, their driver proved to be most unsatisfactory.

North American Long Rider Andi Mills also ran into trouble while crossing the Mojave Desert. Her driver quit in less than a month.

The best drivers have been found among the ranks of those who are either family members or have a deep personal loyalty to the slow-moving Long Rider. When Filipe Leite (left) set off in 2012 to ride from Canada to Brazil, his girlfriend Emma Brazier drove a support vehicle that brought badly-needed water and supplies to the Long Rider and his horses.

After driving and riding nearly 9,500 kilometres (6,000 miles) together, Peter and Mefo Phillips perfected a system which allowed her the freedom to explore Europe, while he drove the support vehicle.

One option which has not been used by Long Riders in the 21ˢᵗ century is the supply cart once favoured by European cavalry. This small, hardy vehicle was employed by the German army until the end of the Second World War.

Because of its rugged dependability, the Swiss army pack corps still uses horse-drawn carts to supply remote villages in the Alps.

Further Reading

I sat down in the autumn of 2010 thinking that in a few weeks' time I would compose a *Horse Travel Handbook* which contained a primer of equestrian travel knowledge. Looking back upon that moment in my life, it is fair to say that my ignorance was only matched by my naiveté. I was one of those would-be equestrian travellers who belong to the 'lost generation', those born in the mid-twentieth century who were too late for the cavalry and too early for the internet.

The more research I did, and the deeper I dug, the more I realized that I had vastly underestimated the subject in question. An apt analogy would be that during the course of many centuries the Great Sphinx of Giza became buried up to its shoulders in sand. It was not until the colossus was finally excavated in 1925 that its true size was understood. Likewise it slowly dawned on me that I had also badly under estimated the true dimensions of equestrian travel.

The *Handbook* kept growing until it became so large that I realized that there was a need for two books - one to be studied at home prior to departure (*The Encyclopaedia of Equestrian Exploration*) and a second to accompany the Long Rider during his journey (*The Horse Travel Handbook*).

After six years of uninterrupted work, I completed the three-volume *Encyclopaedia of Equestrian Exploration*. Serving as a type of equestrian Rosetta Stone, it chronicles the ancestral story of the Long Riders, revealing their forgotten history and documenting their gallant struggles against inconceivable odds.

The Encyclopaedia's release in 2017 coincides with the 500 year anniversary of the birth of equestrian travel literature, which began in 1617 when Fynes Moryson wrote about his ride through Europe.

Volume I of the Encyclopaedia consists of The Preparation, The Horses and The Equipment. The literary journey continues in the subsequent next two books.

Volume II consists of The Challenges, the most extensive examination of difficulties and dangers encountered by Long Riders.

Volume III concludes the mission by examining the technicalities of living in the saddle. It also contains the first investigation into the emotional repercussions which horse and human endure when the journey is completed. The series concludes by explaining the on-going importance of equestrian travel.

Section Five – The Journey

Section Six – The Aftermath

Section Seven – Epilogue

Previous generations took the study of equestrian travel very seriously. There were vital principles that were understood and were practised for centuries by all the great equestrian cultures. There were traditions done on a daily basis by the cavalries of all nations. *The Encyclopaedia of Equestrian Exploration* represents knowledge gleaned from horse-humans throughout the millennia, knowledge not formally enshrined in academia, knowledge that was in danger of becoming extinct.

Bibliography

Albright, Verne, *In the Saddle Across the Three Americas*. Bookshelf Press, San Jose, California, USA, 1969.

Anderson, Edward L., *On Horseback in the School and on the Road*. H. Holt & Company, New York, USA, 1882.

Back, Joe, *Horses, Hitches and Rocky Trails*. Swallow Press, Chicago, Illinois, USA, 1959.

Baker, Sir Stanley, *Wild Beasts and Their Ways*. Macmillan Publishers, London, England, 1890.

Ballereau, Jean-François, *Manuel de Randonnée Equestre*. Belin Publishers, Paris, France, 2002.

Barnes, Richard, *Eye on the Hill*. The Long Riders Guild Press, Glasgow, Kentucky. USA. 2005.

Beard, John W., *Saddle East*. The Long Riders Guild Press, Glasgow, Kentucky. USA. 2002.

Belasik, Paul, *Riding towards the Light*. J.A. Allen & Co., London, England, 1990.

Blashford-Snell, Colonel John, *Expeditions – The Experts' Way*. The Travel Book Club Publishers, London, England, 1977.

———— *The British Trans-America Expedition Report*. Scientific Exploration Society Publishers, Mildenhall, England, 1973.

Blomstedt, M. *Undervisning För Ryttaren*. Swedish Cavalry Press, Stockholm, Sweden, 1907.

Blyth, Mr., *The Gentleman's Pocket-Farrier, Showing How to use your Horse on a Journey, A New Edition carefully revised by a Veterinary Surgeon*. Thomas Desilver Publishers, Philadelphia, Pennsylvania, USA. 1829.

Bolton, Captain Edward Frederick, *Horse Management in West Africa*. Jarrold & Sons Publishers, Norwich, England, 1931.

Bond Head, Sir Francis, *The Horse and His Rider*. John Murray Publishers, London, England, 1860.

Boniface, Lt. Jonathan J., *The Cavalry Horse and his Pack*. Hudson-Kimberly Publishing, Kansas City, Missouri, USA. 1903.

Bonvalot, Gabriel, *Across Tibet*. Cassell Publishing Company, New York, USA. 1892.

Bosanquet, Mary, *Saddlebags for Suitcases*. The Long Riders Guild Press, Glasgow, Kentucky, USA. 2001.

Borrow, George, *The Romany Rye*. The Long Riders Guild Press, Glasgow, Kentucky, USA. 2007.

———— *The Zincali - An account of the gypsies of Spain*. John Murray Publishers, London, England, 1923.

Brooke, Brigadier Geoffrey, *Horsemanship*. Seeley, Service & Company, London, England, 1929.

Brown, Donald, *Journey from the Arctic*. The Long Riders Guild Press, Glasgow, Kentucky, USA. 2001.

Bull, Bartle, *Around the Sacred Sea*. Canongate Books Ltd., Edinburgh, Scotland. 1999.

Bulliet, Richard, *Hunters, Herders, and Hamburgers: The Past and Future of Human-Animal Relationships*. Columbia University Press, New York, New York, 2007.

Burdon, Captain William, *The Gentleman's Pocket-Farrier, Shewing how to use your horse on a journey and what remedies are proper for common misfortunes that may befall him on the road*. S. Buckley Printers, London, England, 1730.

Büren, Jean-François de, *A Voyage Across the Americas – the Journey of Henri de Büren*, Editions de Penthes, Geneva, Switzerland. 2013

Burnaby, Evelyn, *A Ride from Land's End to John O'Groats*. Sampson Low, Marston & Co., London, England. 1893.

Burnaby, Frederick, *A Ride to Khiva*. The Long Riders Guild Press, Glasgow, Kentucky, USA. 2001.

———— *On Horseback through Asia Minor*. The Long Riders Guild Press, Glasgow, Kentucky, USA. 2001.

Burpee, Lawrence, *Among the Canadian Alps*. John Lane Company, New York, USA. 1914.

Buryn, Ed, *Vagabonding in America - A Guide to Energy*. Book People Press, San Francisco, California, USA. 1973.

———— *Vagabonding in Europe & North Africa*. Random House Publishing, New York, New York, USA, 1976.

Bruce, Major Clarence Dalrymple, *In the Hoofprints of Marco Polo*. The Long Riders Guild Press, Glasgow, Kentucky, USA. 2004.

Carruthers, Douglas, *Unknown Mongolia*. Hutchinson & Company, London, England, 1914.

Carter, William Harding, *Horses, Saddles and Bridles*, The Long Riders Guild Press, Glasgow, Kentucky, USA. 2001

Cayley, George, *Bridle Roads of Spain*. The Long Riders Guild Press, Glasgow, Kentucky, USA. 2004.

Charvin, Claude, *Le Cheval de Bât*. Editions Crepin LeBlond, Paris, France, 1997.

Clark, Leonard, *The Marching Wind*. The Long Riders Guild Press, Glasgow, Kentucky, USA. 2001.

Cobbett, William, *Rural Rides Volumes 1 and 2*. The Long Riders Guild Press, Glasgow, Kentucky, USA. 2001.

Codman, John, *Winter Sketches from the Saddle*. The Long Riders Guild Press, Glasgow, Kentucky, USA. 2001.

Coquet, Evelyne, *Riding to Jerusalem*. John Murray Publishers, London, England, 1978.

Court Treatt, Stella, *Cape to Cairo*. George Harrap Ltd., London, England, 1927.

Cousineau, Phil, *The Art of Pilgrimage: the Seeker's Guide to Making Travel Sacred*. Conari Press, Berkeley, California, USA. 1998.

Cunliffe Marsh, Hippsley, *A Ride Through Islam*. The Long Riders Guild Press, Glasgow, Kentucky, USA. 2004.

Cunninghame Graham, Robert, *Horses of the Conquest*. The Long Riders Guild Press, Glasgow, Kentucky, USA. 2004.

Daly, Henry W., *Manual of Pack Transportation*. The Long Riders Guild Press, Glasgow, Kentucky, USA. 2000.

Darling, Sir Malcolm Lyall, *At Freedom's Door*. The Long Riders Guild Press, Glasgow, Kentucky, USA. 2008.

Davis, Francis W., *Horse Packing in Pictures*. Charles Scribner's Sons Publishers, New York, USA, 1975.

Denny, J.T., *Horses and Roads: How to keep a horse sound on his legs*. Longmans, Green & Company, London, England, 1881.

Dent, Anthony, *The Horse through Fifty Centuries of Civilization*. Phaidon Press Limited, London, England, 1974.

Denton, Ivan, *Old Brands and Lost Trails*. University of Arkansas Press, Fayetteville, Arkansas. USA, 1991.

Dixie, Lady Florence, *Riding Across Patagonia*. The Long Riders Guild Press, Glasgow, Kentucky, USA. 2001.

Dodwell, Christina, *A Traveller in Horseback in Turkey and Iran.* The Long Riders Guild Press, Glasgow, Kentucky, USA. 2004.
——— *An Explorer's Handbook.* The Long Riders Guild Press, Glasgow, Kentucky, USA. 2005.
Dorondo, David, *Riders of the Apocalypse.* Naval Institute Press, Annapolis, Maryland, USA, 2012.
Dotchin, Jane, *Journey Through England with a Pack Pony.* Wagtail Press, Hexham, England, 1989.
Duberly, Fanny, *Indian Journal.* The Long Riders Guild Press, Glasgow, Kentucky, USA. 2006.
Durant, Dr. Ghislani, *Horseback Riding from a Medical Point of View.* Cassell, Petter & Galpin Publishers, New York, USA, 1878.
Elles, Major-General W.K., *Manual for Bengal and Punjab Cavalry.* Superintendent of Government Printing, Calcutta, India, 1893.
Elser, Smoke and Brown, Bill, *Packin' In On Mules and Horses.* Mountain Press Publishing, Missoula, Montana, USA, 1980.
Farrow, Edward, *Pack Mules and Packing.* Metropolitan Publishing Company, New York, New York, USA. 1881.
Farson, Negley, *Caucasian Journey.* The Long Riders Guild Press, Glasgow, Kentucky, USA. 2002.
Fleming, George FRCVS, *The Physical Condition of Horses for Military Purposes.* Gale & Polden Publishers, Aldershot, England, 1889.
Fox, Ernest, *Travels in Afghanistan.* The Long Riders Guild Press, Glasgow, Kentucky, USA. 2001.
Freeman, Lewis Ransome, *Down the Columbia.* Dodd, Mead and Company, New York, USA, 1921.
Galton, Francis, *The Art of Travel.* John Murray Publishers, London, England, 1855.
Galvayne, Sydney, *The Horse – Its Taming and Training.* Thomas Murray and Sons Publishers, Glasgow, Scotland, 1888.
Galwan, *Ghulam* Rassul, *Servant of Sahibs.* The Long Riders Guild Press, Glasgow, Kentucky, USA. 2001.
Gebhards, Stacy, *When Mules Wear Diamonds.* Wilderness Skills Publishing, McCall, Idaho, 2000.
Gianoli, Luigi, *Horses and Horsemanship through the Ages.* Crown Publishers, New York, New York, USA. 1969.
Gilbey, Sir Walter, *Small Horses in Warfare.* Vinton & Co. Ltd., London, England, 1900.
Glazier, Willard, *Ocean to Ocean on Horseback.* The Long Riders Guild Press, Glasgow, Kentucky, USA. 2001.
Goldschmidt, Lt.-Col. Sidney, *An Eye to Buying a Horse.* Country Life Publishers, London, England. 1944.
Gonne, Captain C.M., *Hints on Horses.* John Murray Publishers, London, England, 1904.
Gordon, William John, *The Horse World of London.* The Religious Tract Society, London, England, 1893.
Goubaux, Armand, *The Exterior of the Horse.* J.B Lippincott Company, Philadelphia, Pennsylvania, USA, 1892.
Gourko, General D., *Wyna: Adventures in Eastern Siberia.* Methuen & Company, London, England, 1938.
Government of India, *The Indian Empire – Hints for Soldiers Proceeding to India.* Central Publication Branch, Calcutta, India, 1927.
Graves, Will, *Wolves in Russia.* Detselig Enterprises Ltd., Calgary, Canada, 2007.
Haker, Ute, *Saddle Up- A Guide to Planning the Perfect Horseback Vacation.* John Muir Publications, Santa Fe, New Mexico, USA. 1997.
Hamilton Smith, Charles, *Equus - The Natural History of the Horse, Ass, Onager, Quagga and Zebra.* W. H. Lizars Publishers, Edinburgh, Scotland, 1841.
Hanbury-Tenison, Robin, *Chinese Adventure.* The Long Riders Guild Press, Glasgow, Kentucky, USA. 2004.
——— *Fragile Eden – A Ride through New Zealand.* The Long Riders Guild Press, Glasgow, Kentucky, USA. 2004.
——— *Land of Eagles.* I.B. Taurus & Co., London, England, 2009.
——— *Spanish Pilgrimage,* The Long Riders Guild Press, Glasgow, Kentucky, USA. 2001.
——— *White Horses Over France.* The Long Riders Guild Press, Glasgow, Kentucky, USA. 2001.
Harlen, General Josiah, *A Memoir of Afghanistan.* J. Dobson Publishers, Philadelphia, USA. 1842.
Harsha, Max, *Mule Skinner's Bible,* Privately published by the author, 1987.
Hart Poe, Rhonda, *Trail Riding.* Storey Publishers, North Adams, Massachusetts, USA, 2005.
Haslund, Henning, *Mongolian Adventure.* The Long Riders Guild Press, Glasgow, Kentucky, USA. 2002.
Hassanein, Sir Ahmed Mohammed, *The Lost Oases.* The Long Riders Guild Press, Glasgow, Kentucky, USA. 2001.
Hatley, George, *Horse Camping.* The Dial Press, New York, USA, 1981.
Hayes, Captain Horace FRCVS, *Among Horses in Russia.* R. A. Everett & Company, London, England. 1900.
——— *Among Men and Horses.* T. Fisher Unwin Publishers, London, England. 1894.
——— *Horse Management in India.* Thacker, Spink & Company, Calcutta, India, 1878.
——— *Horses on board Ship, a guide to their management.* Hurst and Blackett Publishers, London, England, 1902.
Headley , J.T. and Johnson, W.F. , *Stanley's Adventures in the Wilds of Africa.* Edgewood Publishing Co., London, England, 1890.
Heath, Frank, *Forty Million Hoofbeats.* The Long Riders Guild Press, Glasgow, Kentucky, USA. 2001.
Hill, Cherry, *Horse Keeping Almanac.* Storey Publishing, North Adams, Massachusetts, USA, 2007.
Hill, Oliver, *Packing and Outfitting Field Manual.* University of Wyoming Press, Laramie, Wyoming, USA, 1981.
Hilton, Suzanne, *Getting There – Frontier Travel without Power.* The Westminster Press, Philadelphia, USA, 1980.
Hinks, Arthur Robert, *Hints to Travellers.* Royal Geographical Society, London, England, 1938.
His Majesty's War Office, *Animal Management.* T. Fisher Unwin Publishers, London, England. 1908.
——— *Catechism of Animal Management,* Harrison and Sons Publishers, London, England, 1916.
——— *Cavalry Training (Horsed).* Harrison and Sons Publishers, London, England, 1937.
——— *Manual of Horsemastership, Equitation and Animal Transport.* H.M. Stationery Office, London, England, 1937.

Hohenlohe-Ingelfingen, Prince Kraft Karl August Eduard Friedrich, *Letters on Cavalry*. Royal Artillery Institution, Woolwich, England, 1889.

Holt, William, *Ride a White Horse*. The Long Riders Guild Press, Glasgow, Kentucky, USA. 2001.

Howden, Peter, *Horse Warranty – a Plain and Comprehensive Guide to the Various Points to be Noted showing which are essential and which are unimportant*. Robert Hardwicke Publishers, London, England, 1862.

Huc, Evariste, *Travels in Tartary, Tibet and China*. National Illustrated Library, London, England, 1852.

Hunter, J. Kerr, *Pony Trekking for All*. Thomas Nelson & Sons Publishers, London, England, 1962.

Jackson, Frederick George, *A Thousand Days in the Arctic*, Harper & Brothers, London, England. 1899.

James, Jeremy, *Saddle Tramp*. The Long Riders' Guild Press Glasgow, Kentucky, USA, 2001.

———— *The Byerley Turk*. Merlin Unwin Books, Ludlow, England, 2005.

———— *Vagabond,* The Long Riders' Guild Press Glasgow, Kentucky, USA, 2001.

Jankovich, Miklos, *They Rode into Europe*. The Long Riders' Guild Press Glasgow, Kentucky, USA, 2007.

Jebb, Louisa, *By Desert Ways to Baghdad and Damascus*. The Long Riders' Guild Press Glasgow, Kentucky, USA, 2004.

Jervis, John, *The Traveller's Oracle – Volumes One & Two*. Henry Colburn Publishers, London, England, 1827.

Johnson Post, Charles, *Horse Packing – A Manual of Pack Transportation*. The Long Riders Guild Press, Glasgow, Kentucky, USA. 2000.

Johnson, Dusty, *Horse Packing Illustrated*. Saddleman Press, Loveland, Colorado, USA, 2000.

Kellon, Dr. Eleanor VMD, *First Aid for Horses*. Breakthrough Publications, Ossining, New York, USA, 1990.

Kluckhohn, Clyde, *To the Foot of the Rainbow*. The Long Riders Guild Press, Glasgow, Kentucky, USA. 2001.

Koch, Johan Peter, *Through the White Desert*. Verlog von Julius Springer Publishing, Berlin, Germany, 1919.

Kopas, Cliff, *Packhorses to the Pacific*. Touch Wood Editions, Victoria, Canada, 2004.

Labouchere, John. *High Horses*. Labouchere Publishing, North Elmham, England, 1998.

Lambie, Thomas, *Boots and Saddles in Africa*. The Long Riders Guild Press, Glasgow, Kentucky, USA. 2001.

Law, Dr. James, *Special Report on Diseases of the Horse*. U.S. Dept. of Agriculture, Bureau of Animal Industry, Washington DC, USA, 1916.

Lawson, Major E.F., Royal Bucks Hussars, *The Cavalry Journal – "The Reduction of the Weight on the Horse"*. Royal United Service Publishers, London, England, 1924.

Leigh, Margaret, *My Kingdom for a Horse*. The Long Riders Guild Press, Glasgow, Kentucky, USA. 2001.

Littauer, Vladimir, *Russian Hussar*. The Long Riders Guild Press, Glasgow, Kentucky, USA. 2007.

MacGahan, Januarius Aloysius, *Campaigning on the Oxus*. Harper Brothers Publishers, New York, USA, 1874.

Maillart, Ella, *Turkestan Solo*. The Long Riders Guild Press, Glasgow, Kentucky, USA. 2001.

Markham, Gervase, *The Perfect Horseman or the Experienced Secrets of Mr. Markham's Fifty Years Practice. Shewing how a Man come to be a General Horseman by the knowledge of the Seven offices: Buyer, Keeper, Feeder, Farrier, Rider, Ambler and Breeder.* Richard Chiswel Publishers, London, England 1680.

Marsden, Kate, *Riding through Siberia*. The Long Riders Guild Press, Glasgow, Kentucky, USA. 2001.

Marshall, Clay, *Ninety Days By Horse*. Create Space Publishing, Seattle, Washington, USA, 2013.

McCullagh, Francis, *With the Cossacks*. Eveleigh Nash Publishers, London, England, 1906.

McGovern, William, *To Lhasa in Disguise*. The Long Riders Guild Press, Glasgow, Kentucky, USA. 2001.

McMullen, Kieran, *Marches and shelter for horse drawn artillery with notes for scouts*. Scholar of Fortune Publishers, USA, 1993.

McShane, Clay and Tarr, Joel, *The Horse in the City*. John Hopkins University Press, Baltimore, Maryland, USA. 2007.

Merrill, Bill, *Vacationing with Saddle and Pack Horse*. Arco Publishing Company, New York, USA, 1976.

Michaux, François André, *Travels in North America*. J. Mawman Publishers, London, England, 1805.

Miller, Everett B., *United States Army Veterinary Service in World War II*. Office of the Surgeon General, Dept. of the Army, Washington, D.C, 1961.

Ministère de la Guerre, *Règlement sur la Conduite des Mulets de Bât*. Paris, France, 1883.

Muir Watson, Sharon, *The Colour of Courage*. The Long Riders Guild Press, Glasgow, Kentucky, USA. 2001.

La Tondre, Richard, *The Golden Kite*. Chez De Press, Santa Clara, California, USA, 2005.

Le Messurier, Colonel A., *A Ride Through Persia*. Richard Bentley & Sons, London, England. 1889.

Marshall, Clay, *Ninety Days by Horse*, CreateSpace Independent Publishing Platform, 2013

Meserve, Ruth, *A Historical Perspective of Mongol Horse Training*. Indiana University, Bloomington, USA. 1987.

Miller, Lt. Col. E. D. DSO, *Horse Management in the Field at Home and Abroad*. Gale & Polden Ltd. Aldershot, England, 1919.

Morrison, Frank Barron, *Feeds and Feeding*. Henry Morrison Company, Madison, Wisconsin, USA, 1915.

Moryson, Fynes, *An Itinerary: Containing Ten Years Travel Through Germany, Bohemia, Switzerland, Netherland, Denmark, Poland, Italy, Turkey, France, England, Scotland and Ireland*. The Stationers' Company, London, England. 1617.

Naysmith, Gordon, *The Will to Win*. The Long Riders Guild Press, Glasgow, Kentucky, USA. 2005.

Nicolle, Grant, *Long Trot*. Create Space Publishing, London, England, 2015.

Nolan, Captain Lewis, *The Training of Calvary Remount Horses*. Parker, Furnivall & Parker Publishing, London, England, 1852.

Noyce, Wilfred, *The Springs of Adventure*. John Murray Publishing, London, England, 1958.

Nunn, Captain J.A., *Notes on Stable Management in India and the Colonies*. W. Thacker & Co., Calcutta, India, 1897.

O'Reilly, Basha, *Bandits and Bureaucrats*. The Long Riders Guild Press, Glasgow, Kentucky. USA. 2016.

O'Reilly, CuChullaine, *Deadly Equines: The Shocking True Story of Meat-Eating and Murderous Horses.* The Long Riders Guild Press, Glasgow, Kentucky, USA. 2011.

———— *Khyber Knights.* The Long Riders Guild Press, Glasgow, Kentucky, USA. 2001.

Patterson, George N., *Journey with Loshay.* The Long Riders Guild Press, Glasgow, Kentucky, USA. 2001.

———— *Patterson of Tibet,* The Long Riders Guild Press, Glasgow, Kentucky, USA. 2001.

Phillips, Mefo, *Horseshoes and Holy Water.* Virgin Books, London, England, 2005

Pigott, Lt. J.P., *A Treatise on the Horses of India.* James White Publishers, Calcutta, India. 1794.

Pocock, Geoffrey, *One Hundred Years of the Legion of Frontiersmen.* Phillimore & Co. Ltd., Chichester, England, 2004.

———— *Outrider of Empire: The Life and Adventures of Roger Pocock.* University of Alberta Press, Alberta, Canada, 2008

Pocock, Roger, *Chorus to Adventurers, being the later life of Roger Pocock.* John Lane Publishers, London, England, 1931.

———— *Horses.* The Long Riders' Guild Press, Glasgow, Kentucky, USA, 2004.

———— *The Frontiersman's Pocket Book.* John Murray Publishers, London, England, 1909.

Preston, Douglas, *Cities of Gold,* University of New Mexico Press, 1999

Reese, Herbert Harshman, *The Road Horse.* Bureau of Animal Industry Publishers, Washington DC, USA, 1912.

Rink, Bjarke, *The Rise of the Centaurs.* Author House LLC, Bloomington, Indiana, USA, 2013.

———— *The Centaur Legacy.* The Long Riders Guild Press, Glasgow, Kentucky, USA. 2004.

Robinson, Ian D., *Tea with the Taliban.* David Bateman Publishers, Auckland, New Zealand, 2008.

Runnquist, Åke, *Horses in Fact and Fiction – An Anthology.* Jonathan Cape Publishers, London, England, 1957.

Ruxton, George, *Adventures in Mexico,* The Long Riders Guild Press, Glasgow, Kentucky, USA. 2001.

Saare, Sharon, *Know All about Trail Riding.* Farnam Horse Library, Omaha, Nebraska, USA, 1975.

Salzman, Erich von, *Im Sattel durch die Fürstenhöfe Indiens.* The Long Riders Guild Press, Glasgow, Kentucky, USA. 2004.

Savage Landor, Henry, *Alone with the Hairy Ainu.* Cambridge University Press, Cambridge, England. 1893.

———— *In the Forbidden Land.* The Long Riders Guild Press, Glasgow, Kentucky, USA. 2004.

Schoolcraft, Henry Rowe, *Adventures in the Ozark Mountains.* Lippincott, Grambo & Co., Philadelphia, USA. 1853.

Schoomaker, General Peter, *Special Forces Use of Pack Animals.* Department of the Army, Washington, DC, USA. 2004.

Schwartz, Otto, *Reisen mit dem Pferd.* The Long Riders Guild Press, Glasgow, Kentucky, USA. 2002.

Shaw, Robert, *Visits to High Tartary.* John Murray Publishers, London, England, 1871.

Skrede, Wilfred, *Across the Roof of the World.* The Long Riders Guild Press, Glasgow, Kentucky, USA. 2001.

Slade, Major General Daniel Denison, *How to Kill Animals Humanely.* Massachusetts Society for the Prevention of Cruelty to Animals, Boston, Massachusetts, USA. 1899.

———— *Twelve days in the saddle; a journey on horseback in New England during the autumn of 1883.* Little & Brown Publishers, Boston, Massachusetts, USA, 1884.

Smeaton Chase, J, *California Coast Trails.* The Long Riders' Guild Press, Glasgow, Kentucky, USA, 2002.

———— *California Desert Trails.* The Long Riders' Guild Press, Glasgow, Kentucky, USA, 2002.

Smeeton, Beryl, *The Stars My Blanket.* Horsdal & Schubart Publishers, Victoria, Canada, 1995.

Springfield, Rollo, *The Horse and His Rider.* Chapman and Hall Publishers, London, England, 1847.

Stebbing, Edward Percy, *Cross Country Riding.* Country Life Publishers, London, England, 1938.

Stevens, Thomas, *Through Russia on a Mustang.* The Long Riders Guild Press, Glasgow, Kentucky, USA. 2001.

Stevenson, Robert Louis, *Travels with a Donkey.* The Long Riders Guild Press, Glasgow, Kentucky, USA. 2001.

Stirling, Mrs. Clark J., *The Ladies' Equestrian Guide.* Day & Son Publishers, London, England, 1857.

Strong, Anna Louise, *The Road to the Grey Pamir.* The Long Riders Guild Press, Glasgow, Kentucky, USA. 2001.

Sykes, Ella, *Through Persia on a Sidesaddle.* The Long Riders Guild Press, Glasgow, Kentucky, USA. 2001.

———— *Through the Deserts of Central Asia.* MacMillan & Company, London, England, 1920.

Taplan, William, *A Gentleman's Stable Directory.* J. Robinson Company, London, England. 1790.

Taylor, Bayard, *The Cyclopedia of Modern Travel.* Moore, Wilstach & Key Publisher, New York, USA. 1856.

Thompson, Charles, *Hints to Inexpert Travellers.* Sherwood and Company, London, England, 1830.

Trinkler, Emil, *Through the Heart of Afghanistan.* The Long Riders Guild Press, Glasgow, Kentucky, USA. 2001.

Tschiffely, Aimé, *Bohemia Junction.* The Long Riders Guild Press, Glasgow, Kentucky, USA. 2004.

———— *Bridle Paths.* The Long Riders Guild Press, Glasgow, Kentucky, USA. 2004.

———— *Ming and Ping.* The Long Riders Guild Press, Glasgow, Kentucky, USA. 2014

———— *Round and About Spain.* The Long Riders Guild Press, Glasgow, Kentucky, USA. 2008.

———— *Tschiffely's Ride,* The Long Riders Guild Press, Glasgow, Kentucky, USA. 2001.

Thurlow Craig, A.W., *A Rebel for a Horse.* Arthur Barker Publishers, London, England. 1934.

———— *Paraguayan Interlude.* Arthur Barker Publishers, London, England, 1935.

———— *Tackle Pony Trekking This Way.* Stanley Paul Publishers, London, England, 1961.

Ure, John, *Cucumber Sandwiches in the Andes.* The Long Riders Guild Press, Glasgow, Kentucky, USA. 2005.

———— *In Search of Nomads.* Carroll Graf Publishers, New York, New York, USA 2003.

———— *Pilgrimage, the Great Adventure of the Middle Ages.* Constable & Robinson Publishers, London, England, 2006.

US Army Quartermaster General, *The Packer Training Manual.* Government Printing Office, Washington DC, USA, 1927.

———— *The Phillips Pack Saddle.* Government Printing Office, Washington DC, USA, 1924.

US Marine Corps, *United States Marine Corps Animal Transportation Manual.* Government Printing Office, Washington DC, USA, 1940.

US War Department, *Manual for Farriers, Horseshoers, Saddlers and Waggoners.* Government Printing Office, Washington DC, USA, 1915.

————— *Pack Transport.* Government Printing Office, Washington DC, USA, 1944.

Vanderbilt, Tom, *Traffic – Why we drive the way we do.* Penguin Books Ltd., London, England, 2008.

Walchuk, Stan, *Trail Riding, Pack and Training Manual.* Vista Publishers, McBride, British Columbia, Canada, 2003.

Walker, Elaine, *Horse,* Reaktion Books Ltd., London, England, 2008.

Weale, Magdalene, *Through the Highlands of Shropshire on Horseback.* The Long Riders Guild Press, Glasgow, Kentucky, USA. 2001.

Weeks, Edwin Lord, *Artist Explorer.* The Long Riders Guild Press, Glasgow, Kentucky, USA. 2005.

Wells, Spencer, *The Journey of Man.* Princeton University Press, Princeton, New Jersey, USA, 2002.

Weston, W. Val, *The Saddle Horse in India.* Thacker, Spink & Company, Calcutta, India, 1914.

Weygard, Jacques, *Legionnaire – Life with the French Foreign Legion Cavalry.* George Harrap & Company, London, England, 1952.

Wilder, Janine, *Trail Riding.* Western Horseman Publishers, Fort Worth, Texas, USA, 2005.

Wilkins, Messanie, *Last of the Saddle Tramps.* The Long Riders Guild Press, Glasgow, Kentucky, USA. 2002.

Wilson, Andrew, *The Abode of Snow.* The Long Riders Guild Press, Glasgow, Kentucky, USA. 2001.

Windt, Harry de, *From Paris to New York by Land.* The Long Riders Guild Press, Glasgow, Kentucky, USA. 2001.

Wood, Lisa F., *Mustang Journal: 3000 miles across America by Horse.* Lost Coast Press, Fort Bragg, California, USA, 2005.

Wortley Axe, Professor J., *The Horse.* Gresham Publishing Company, London, England, 1905.

Wyman Bury, George, a.k.a. Abdullah Mansur, *The Land of Uz.* MacMillan & Company, London, England, 1911.

Youatt, William, *The Horse.* Baldwin & Cradock, London, England, 1831.

More than 400 Long Rider Contributors

Abernathy, Bud and Temple – aged eleven and seven, they rode from New York to San Francisco without adult assistance.

Adshead, Harry and Lisa – rode from Wales to Jordan.

Aguiar, Jorge de – rode through Brazil.

Aguiar, Pedro Luis de – rode through Brazil.

Albright, Verne – rode from Peru to California.

Alfieri, Vittorio – rode across England and Europe.

Amor, Adam del – rode in the United States.

Anderson, Ed – made multiple journeys along the Pacific Crest Trail.

Armand, Annick - rode across Turkey from the Black Sea to the Mediterranean.

Arsuka, Nirwan Ahmad - rode in Indonesia and Papua New Guinea.

Asmussen, Conan - rode from Canada to the Mexican border when he was ten years old.

Asmussen, Hans - rode from Canada to Mexico.

Aspinwall, Two-Gun Nan – was the first woman to ride ocean to ocean across the USA.

Asseyev, Mikhaïl Vassilievitch – rode from Kiev, Russia to Paris, France.

Azzam, Adnan – rode from Madrid, Spain to Mecca, Arabia.

Baaijens, Arita – rode through the Altai Mountains in Kazakhstan, China, Mongolia and Russia.

Baker, Sir Samuel – rode through Abyssinia.

Ballereau, Jean François - made a series of rides in Europe and North America, then rode from Argentina to Columbia.

Barnes, Richard - rode the length and breadth of England, Scotland and Wales.

Barré, Gérard – rode through the Alps and France.

Barrett, Elizabeth – rode in Great Britain.

Bartz, Thomas - rode from Osh, Kirghizstan to Panjshir, Afghanistan.

Bayes, Jeremiah – rode in the United States.

Beard, John and Lulu – rode the length of the Oregon Trail.

Beck, George – rode to 48 state capitals in the USA.

Bedaux, Charles – rode across western Canada.

Beker, Ana – rode from Buenos Aires, Argentina to Ottawa, Canada.

Berg, Roland – made multiple journeys through Europe.

Bessac, Frank - rode through Mongolia, Turkestan and Tibet.

Best, Captain James John – rode through the mountains of Albania.

Bey, Riza - rode through Anatolia, Arabia, Mesopotamia, the Middle East and the Balkans.

Bigler, Jessica - rode from Switzerland to the British Isles and back.

Bigo, Stephane - rode through Turkey, China, Ethiopia, Brazil, Guatemala and the United States.

Bird, Isabella – rode in Hawaii, the Rocky Mountains, Japan, Persia, Kurdistan, Korea and Tibet.

Blackburn, Rick - rode from Canada to Texas.

Blanchard, Augustin – rode in the United States.

Blashford-Snell, Colonel John – led the British Trans-Americas Expedition through the Darien Gap jungle between Panama and Columbia.

Blunt, Wilfred – journeyed into northern Arabia and the Nejd Desert.

Bond Head, Sir Francis - rode through the Argentine pampas, across the Andes Mountains and into Chile.

Bonneville, Captain Benjamin – rode through the western United States.

Bonvalot, Gabriel – rode across the "roof of the world" by crossing the Pamir and Hindu Kush Mountains; then made a second journey across Russia, Siberia, Tibet and the Takla Makan desert before entering China.

Boone, Katherine – rode across Spain.

Borrow, George – rode in England and across Spain.

Bosanquet, Mary – rode from Vancouver, British Columbia to New York city.

Boshai, Dalaikhan rode in Mongolia and Kazakhstan.

Bougault, Laura – rode from South Africa to Malawi.

Bourboulon, Phillipe and Catherine de – rode from Shanghai, China to Moscow, Russia.

Bowers, Henry "Birdie" – was part of the Terra Nova Expedition to Antarctica.

Boyd, Alistair – rode in Spain.

Bragge, Michael - rode from Brisbane to Melbourne in Australia.

Brand, Charles – rode across the Andes Mountains from Chile into Argentina.

Brenchley, Billy - rode through Tunisia, Libya, Egypt, Sudan, Uganda and Tanzania.

Brown, Donald – rode across the Arctic Circle and through Lapland, Sweden, Norway and Denmark.

Brown, Len - rode through New Mexico, Colorado, Utah, Wyoming, Colorado, Kansas and Missouri.

Bruce, Clarence Dalrymple – rode from Srinagar, Kashmir to Peking, China.

Bruce, James – rode in Abyssinia.

Bruhnke, Louis - rode from the bottom of Patagonia to the top of Alaska, via the Darien Gap jungle.

Bull, Bartle – rode in Mongolia and Siberia.

Büren, Henri de - rode over the Andes Mountains from Peru into Amazonia.

Burges Watson, Claire- rode from Ulaan Bator, Mongolia, to Samarkand, Uzbekistan.

Burnaby, Evelyn – rode in England and Scotland.

Burnaby, Frederick - rode across all of Central Asia, ending up at the Amir's palace at Khiva. Then, after having avoided the Czar's spies in Constantinople, Burnaby rode across all of Turkey.

Burton, Sir Richard - made extensive equestrian journeys in Brazil, Argentina and Paraguay.

Butler, Samuel – rode in New Zealand.

Byron, Lord - explored the mountainous regions of Albania.

Callahan, Charles - rode from Esquel, Patagonia to Rincon de Cholila, Argentina.

Carmignani, Simone – rode through the Pamir and Karakorum Mountains of Northern Pakistan.

Carpini, Friar Giovanni – rode from Germany to Mongolia and back.

Carruthers, Douglas – rode through Dzungaria, an ancient Mongolian kingdom which lay between Siberia and Mongolia.

Carson, Susie – rode through China and Tibet.

Cashner, Tex – rode from Ohio to Texas.

Cayley, George – rode through Spain.

Cazade, Jean-Claude – rode from France to Arabia and back.

Çelebi, Evliya – rode from Turkey to England.

Chautard, Edouard – rode across New Caldenonia and along Australia's Bicentennial National Trail.

Chechak, Andy – rode from California to Maine.

Cherry-Garrard, Apsley - was part of the Terra Nova Expedition to Antarctica.

Child, Theodore – rode across Turkey and Persia.

Chitty, Jessica – at the age of three, rode from Spain to Greece with the aid of her parents.

Claire, Alberta – rode from from Wyoming to Oregon, south to California, across the deserts of Arizona, and on to New York City.

Clapperton, Hugh – rode across the Sahara Desert, from Tripoli to Sokoto.

Clark, Keith – rode through Chile.

Clark, Leonard – rode through Tibet.

Clifton, John Talbot – died trying to reach Timbukto on horseback.

Cobbett, William – rode in England.

Cochrane, John – rode from St. Petersburg, Russia to the Kamchatka Pennisula.

Codman, John – rode through New England.

Coke, Henry – rode in the Sandwich Islands, from St. Louis to Oregon and across Spain.

Cooper, Katie - rode across the American Southwest.

Cooper, Merian C. – rode across the Zagros Mountains and through Persia.

Cope, Tim - rode across Mongolia, Kazakhstan, Russia and Hungary.

Coquet, Evelyne and Corinne - rode from Paris to Jerusalem.

Cunliffe Marsh, Hippisley - rode across the Ottoman Empire, Persia and India.

Cunningham, Jakki – rode in France and England.

Cunninghame Graham, Robert - rode across the Argentine pampas and through the Atlas Mountains of Morocco.

Cuthbert, Donna and Nic - rode from Bayan-Ulgii aymag, Western Mongolia to Baganuur, Tov aymag, Eastern Mongolia.

Dalaikhan, Alpamys – rode in Mongolia and Kazakhstan.

Dalaikhan, Nurbek – rode in Kazakhstan.

Dalrymple Bruce, Major Clarence – rode from Srinagar, India to Peking, China.

Danos, Jonathan - rode across the Andes Mountains from Chile into Argentina.

Darling, Malcolm – rode from Peshawar to Jubbulpore, India.

Darwin, Charles – rode in South America, Australia and Africa.

Davenport, Homer – rode in the Ottoman Empire.

Davies, Garry – rode through England and Wales.

Delavere, Kimberley – rode in Australia.

Denton, Ivan - rode from Arkansas to California.

Digaitis, Vaidotas - rode from the Baltic Sea in Lithuania to the Black Sea in Ukraine. He next completed a journey around the Baltic Sea to the Arctic Circle and back. He also pioneered a route around his native republic of Lithuania.

Dijkstra, Margriet – rode from the Netherlands to Spain.

Discoli, Eduardo – made a journey that took him across the Americas, through Europe and on to the Middle East.

Dixie, Lady Florence – rode through Patagonia.

Dodwell, Christina – rode in China, Iran, New Guinea, Kenya, Siberia and Turkey.

Dodwell, Edward – rode in Greece.

Dolan, Captain Brooke – rode from India, across the Himalayas, through Tibet and into China.

Dorman, Sarah – rode from Paris, France to Jerusalem.

Dotchin, Jane – rode in the United Kingdom and Ireland.

Duberly, Fanny – rode through India.

Ducret, Nicholas - rode from Kazakhstan to Afghanistan.

Dudding, Alina Grace – rode the length of the Pacific Crest Trail twice.

Dunnam, Roger – rode from Canada to Kentucky.

Durang, John – rode through New England.

Dutra, Hetty – rode in the United States.

Dutreuil de Rhins, Jules – was killed while riding to find the source of the Mekong River.

Eckleberg, Mary Ellen – rode from Winnipeg, Canada to New Orleans and back.

Egenes, John – rode ocean to ocean across the United States.

Ehlers, Otto – rode from Moulmein, Burma to Poofang, French Tonkin.

Elliott, Arthur – rode from Scotland to Cornwall.

Ende, Bernice – made multiple journeys in the USA and Canada.

Endlweber, Sonja – rode from Texas to Alaska.

Eng, Jeannette van der – rode from the Netherlands to Spain.

Erickson, William – rode in South America, including through the Darien Gap Jungle.

Etherton, Lieutenant Percy – rode from Kashmir, Gilgit, over the Pamir Mountains, through Chinese Turkistan, Mongolia and on into Russian Siberia.

Fairbank, Tom - rode from Washington to Montana.

Falconer, John – rode across Nigeria.

Farson, Negley – rode through the Caucasus Mountains.

Feary, Jayme – rode along the Continental Divide Trail.

Fields, Fawn – at the age of five, rode from Texas to Arizona with the aid of her parents.

Filchner, Wilhelm – rode in Central Asia and in Antarctica.

Fintari, Suellen – rode from Michigan to Alaska.

Firouz, Louise – rode in Iran.

Fischer, Andre – rode from Patagonia to Bolivia.

Fissenko, Vladimir – rode from the bottom of Patagonia to the top of Alaska, via the Darien Gap jungle.

Fleming, Peter – rode from Peking, China to Srinigar, Kashmir.

Folkins, Bonnie – made multiple journeys in Mongolia and Kazakhstan.

Fox, Ernest – rode through Afghanistan.

Franconie, Pascale - rode from France to Arabia and back.

Frankland, Charles Colville – rode through the Ottoman Empire and Egypt.

Freeman, Lewis – led an expedition through the Canadian Rocky Mountains.

Fukushima, Baron Yasumasa – rode from Berlin, Germany to Tokyo, Japan.

Galwan, Ghulam Rassul – rode through Ladakh and Turkestan.

Gasseolis, Hugo – rode from General Madariaga Argentina to New York City, USA.

Gillespie, Lloyd and Isabel – rode around the periphery of South Africa.

Gillmore, Parker – rode through South Africa.

Gilmore, James – rode across Mongolia.

Gist, Christopher – made the first exploration of the Ohio Country.

Glazier, Willard – made the first known ocean to ocean ride across the United States.

Goodwin, Joe – rode from Laredo, Texas to Mexico, City.

Gordon, Cora and Jan - explored Albania on horseback.

Gottet, Hans-Jürgen and Claudia – rode from Arabia to the Swiss Alps.

Gouraud, Jean-Louis – rode from Paris to Moscow.

Gray, Susie – rode from Canterbury, England to Santiago, Spain.

Greene, Graham – rode in Mexico.

Guibaut, Andre - attempted to reach Tibet by riding through China's Yellow River Gorge.

Hamer, Colleen – rode in the United States.

Hamilton, Bill – rode from Arizona to Canada.

Hanbury-Tenison, Robin and Louella – rode in Albania, China, France, New Zealand and Spain.

Harlan, Josiah – rode from India to Kabul, Afghanistan

Harrison, Marguerite – rode across the Zagros Mountains and through Persia.

Haslund, Henning – rode in Mongolia and Siberia.

Hassanein, Sir Ahmed Mohammed – rode through the Libyan Desert.

Hausleitner, Horst – rode across Lesotho, South Africa, Botswana, Zambia, Tanzania and Kenya.

Haynes, John Wayne – rode from Hudson, Michigan to Santa Fe, New Mexico.

Heath, Frank – rode to all 48 American states.

Hedin, Sven – rode in India, Persia,Tibet and Turkestan.

Henchie, Christine - rode through Tunisia, Libya, Egypt, Sudan, Uganda and Tanzania.

Hengesbaugh, Jeff – rode from Arizona to Canada.

Herbert, Aubrey – rode through Anatolia, Arabia, Mesopotamia, the Middle East and the Balkans.

Hietkamp, Eva – rode in France and Spain.

Hill, Elizabeth – rode from Germany to Spain and then rode through Great Britain.

Hofstee, Wendy – rode through Ecuador.

Holt, William – rode through England, France, Italy, Austria and Germany.

Hooker, Ralph – made multiple journeys in the United States.

Hopkinson, Arthur and Eleanor – rode in India and Tibet.

Horiguichi, Robert – rode from Laredo, Texas to Mexico City.

Huc, Évariste Régis – rode through China, Tartary and Tibet.

Hüllmandel, Kerstin – rode from Mönchsondheim, Germany to Santiago de Compostela, Spain.

Hurst, Hawk – rode from Mexico to Canada.

Ilmoni, Tony – rode from Kyrgyzstan to Beijing, China.

Irving, Washington – rode in Spain.

Jackson, Frederick George – rode in Australia and the Arctic Circle.

Jacobs, Michel - rode from Amsterdam to St. Petersburg.

James, Jeremy – rode across Turkey, Europe and Great Britain.

Jebb, Louisa – rode through the Ottoman Empire.

Johnson, Polly – rode from Anchorage, Alaska to Seattle, Washington.

Johnson, Stephen – rode from Arizona to Canada.

Kavanagh. Arthur – rode in Egypt, Palestine, Russia, Persia, India and Ireland.

Kempf, Marc – rode across Canada and the United States.

Khan, Noor Mohammad – rode in Pakistan.

Kidner, Christopher – rode from Osh, Kyrghizstan to Panjshir, Afghanistan.

Kikkuli – rode in Assyria.

Kinglake, Alexander William – rode from Serbia to Egypt.

Kino, Father Eusebio – rode through the unexplored areas of Mexico, Baja California and the Southwest.

Kirouac, Vincent – rode across Canada.

Kluckhohn, Clyde – rode through Arizona, Utah and New Mexico.

Knaus, Albert - rode from Mönchsondheim, Germany to Santiago de Compostela, Spain

Koch, Johan Peter – rode across Greenland.

Kohmanns, Barbara – rode from Ecuador to Mexico.

Kohn, Kareen – rode in India, Peru and Ecuador.

Kopas, Cliff – rode through the Canadian Rocky Mountains.

Kotwicki, Tadeusz – rode from Jambyl, Kazakhstan to Moscow, Russia. He also rode from Patagonia to the USA.

Kovačič, Janja – rode from Uruguay to Bolivia.

Kraus, Orion – rode from Mexico to Costa Rica.

Krebs, Carl – rode from Irkutsk, Siberia to Peking, China

Kudasheva, Alexandra – rode across Siberia and Central Asia.

Labouchere, John – rode in Argentina and Chile.

Lambie, Thomas – rode in Abyssinia.

Landerer, Evelyn – rode in Mongolia and Siberia.

Langford, Pete – rode across New Zealand.

Langlet, Valdemar – rode in Russia.

Larssen, Renate – rode from Sweden to Syria.

Layard, Sir Austen Henry – rode from Montenegro to Persia.

Leaf, Lucy – rode across the USA and back.

Leigh, Margaret – rode from Cornwall to Scotland.

Leite, Filipe – rode from Canada to Brazil.

Leite, Luis – rode across Mexico.

Linneaus, Carl – rode through Lapland.

Liotard, Louis – was killed by bandits while riding through China's Yellow River Gorge.

Littlechild, Katrina – rode in England.

Lloyd, Lynn – rode from Pennsylvania to California.

Losey, Linda – rode ocean to ocean across the United States.

Lucas, Alan – rode in Great Britain.

MacDermott, Hugh – rode in Argentina and Chile.

MacGahan, Januarius - rode from Fort Perovsky, Russia, across the Kyzil-Kum Desert to Adam-Kurulgan ("Fatal to Men"), Kyrgyzstan.

MacKiernan, Douglas - rode through Mongolia, Turkestan and Tibet.

Maddison, Jamie – rode across Kazakhstan.

Maillart, Ella – rode from Peking, China to Srinigar, Kashmir.

Mannerheim, Baron Carl Gustaf – rode from Andizhan in Russian Turkestan to Beijing, China.

Marsden, Kate – rode across Russia and Siberia.

Marshall, Clay – rode across the American Southwest.

Masarotti, Dario – made multiple rides in Europe and Russia.

Matschkus, Sabine - rode through France, Germany, Lithuania, Poland, Portugal, Russia and Spain.

McCutcheon, John – rode in Siberia.

McCutcheon, Steve – rode in India, Pakistan and China.

McGrath, Jeanette and Richard – rode ocean to ocean across the United States.

Meline, Colonel James – rode from Fort Leavenworth, Kansas to Santa Fe, New Mexico and back.

Messurier, Colonel le – rode across Persia.

Meunier, Louis – rode in Afghanistan and France.

Michaux, André – rode through the eastern portion of the United States.

Mills, Andi – rode across the American Southwest.

Moryson, Fynes – rode through Germany, Bohemia, Switzerland, Netherlands, Denmark, Poland, Italy, Turkey, France, England, Scotland and Ireland.

Moser, Henri – rode from St. Petersburg to Tashkent, then rode on to Samarkand, Bukhara and Khiva, made his way to Tehran, crossed the Caucasus Mountains and finally emerged at Istanbul.

Muir Watson, Sharon – rode the length of Australia's Bicentennial National Trail.

Mullan, Tim – rode in Mongolia.

Murray, Barry – rode the length of the Pacific Crest Trail.

Naysmith, Gordon – rode across South Africa, Lesotho, Rhodesia, Mozambique, Malawi, Tanzania, Kenya, Ethiopia, Arabia, Jordan, Syria, Greece, Macedonia, Yugoslavia, Hungary and Austria.

Naysmith, Ria Bosman - rode across South Africa, Lesotho, Rhodesia, Mozambique, Malawi, Tanzania and Kenya.

Nelson, Walter - rode from Arizona to New Mexico across the Despoblado Desert.

New, Edie - rode across the American Southwest.

Norton, Virl – rode from Illinois to Washington DC.

Nott, Steve – rode around the perimeter of Australia, then led two mounted expeditions in Africa.

O'Connor, Stephen – rode from Spain to England, then made a journey around the perimeter of Ireland.

O'Hara Bates, Susan – rode from the Mexican border to Canada.

O'Leary, Caitriona – rode in India.

Olufsen, Ole – rode through the Pamir Mountains.

O'Reilly, Basha – rode across Russia, Belarus and Poland, then made a journey along the Outlaw Trail.

O'Reilly, CuChullaine – rode through the North West Frontier Province and led the Karakorum Expedition across Pakistan.

Orton, James – rode through Bolivia.

Oliver, Justine – rode through Argentina.

Östrup, Jocham – rode through Egypt and the Ottoman Empire.

Pagnamenta, Mary – rode across New Zealand.

Paine, Tracy – rode from Maine to Florida, across to California and north to Washington.

Park, Mungo – rode through Gambia and Senegal.

Patterson, George – rode in Tibet and India.

Pavin, Magali - rode from France to Central Asia and back.

Perdue, Stan – rode from Georgia to Arizona.

Peshkov, Dmitri – rode from Blagoveshchensk, Siberia to St. Petersburg, Russia.

Pfeiffer, Ida – rode across Iceland.

Phillips, Mefo – rode from Canterbury, England to Santiago, Spain and from Canterbury, England to Rome, Italy.

Piecuch, Ray – rode from New Hampshire to California.

Pinckney, Mike – rode from Mexico to Canada.

Plumpelly, Raphael – rode across Turkestan.

Pocock, Roger – rode the Outlaw Trail from Fort MacLeod, Canada to Mexico City.

Polier, Marc von – rode in the United States.

Posty, Thierry – rode in Alaska, Australia, Canada, Cuba, Europe, Japan, Mongolia, South America and South Africa.

Preston, Douglas – rode from Arizona to New Mexico across the Despoblado Desert.

Prince, Hezekiah – rode across New England.

Rameaux, Constance – rode across Argentina, Bolivia, Peru, Ecuador and Columbia.

Ransom, Jay – rode to 48 state capitals in the USA.

Ray, George – rode through the Gran Chaco Jungle of Paraguay.

Rayne, Raymond - rode to 48 state capitals in the USA.

Reddaway, William – rode to thirty of Great Britain's historic cathedrals and abbeys.

Reynal, Benjamin – rode through Argentina.

Rhydr, Sea G. – rode from California to Maine.

Rickert, Hjoerdis – rode across France and Spain, at the age of nine.

Roberts, Ken – rode the length of Australia's Bicentennial National Trail.

Robinson, Daniel – journeyed across China, Tibet and into India.

Robinson, Ian – rode in Mongolia, Tibet, Afghanistan and Siberia.

Rock, Joseph – rode through the border provinces of Qinghai, Gansu, and Sichuan in China.

Rose, W.C. – rode though Mexico, Guatemala, El Salvador, Honduras, Costa Rica, Nicaragua, Panamá, Columbia, Ecuador, Peru, Paraguay and Argentina.

von Rosen, Countess Linde – rode from Stockholm, Sweden to Rome, Italy.

Rumpl, Margaret – rode from Austria to Spain.

Russell, Allen – rode from Canada to Mexico.

Russell, Katie – rode from Washington to Montana.

Rustenholz, Philippe – rode across Argentina.

Ruxton, George – rode from Vera Cruz, Mexico to Santa Fe, New Mexico.

Saether, Howard – rode from Uruguay to Bolivia.

Salzmann, Erich von – rode from Tientsin, China to Tashkent, Uzbekistan.

Saupiquet, Isabelle – rode in France and Europe.

Savage Landor, Henry – rode in Japan and Tibet.

Schamber, Pat and Linda – rode ocean to ocean across the United States.

Schoedsack, Ernest – rode across Persia.

Schoener, Otto – rode from Kashgar, Turkestan to Srinigar, Kashmir.

Schwarz, Captain Otto – rode in Europe, North and South America, Iceland, Scotland and Japan.

Schweiger, Robert – rode from Ilinois to Texas.

Scott, Quincy and Ella – rode from Minnesota to Washington.

Scott, Robert Falcon - was part of the Terra Nova Expedition to Antarctica.

Seney, Robert – made multiple journeys in the United States.

Shackleton, Ernest – led the Nimrod Expedition in Antarctica.

Shamsuddin, Hadji – rode across Afghanistan.

Shaw, Robert – rode from Ladakh, across the Karakorum Mountains, into Turkestan.

Shoji, Professor Takeshi – rode across Japan.

Shor, Jean and Frank - rode across the Wakhan Corridor of Afghanistan to Gilgit, Pakistan.

Sigurdsson, Vigfus – rode across Greenland.

Singh, Giyan – rode from Kashmir, north to Gilgit, across the Pamir Mountains, through Turkistan, Mongolia and into Siberia.

Skifter, Gorm - rode across the Arctic Circle and through Lapland, Sweden, Norway and Denmark.

Skrede, Wilfred – rode across Turkestan and into India.

Slade, Daniel Denison – rode across New England.

Smeaton Chase, Joseph – rode from Mexico to Oregon and across the Mojave Desert.

Smith, Lt. Cornelius – rode from Fort Wingate, Arizona to Fort Sam Houston, Texas.

Somerset Maugham, William – rode across Spain.

Southey, Sam – rode in Mongolia.

Spizzo, Antonietta - made multiple rides in Europe and Russia.

Spleiss, Chantal – rode in Europe.

Stebbing, Edward Percy – rode across Great Britain.

Stein, Esther – rode across Lesotho, South Africa, Botswana, Zambia, Tanzania and Kenya.

Stevens, Thomas – rode across Russia.

Stewart, Lisa - rode through New Mexico, Colorado, Utah, Wyoming, Colorado, Kansas and Missouri.

Strandberg. Mikael – rode across Patagonia.

Strong, Anna Louise – rode through the Pamir Mountains and across Tadjikistan.

Suttle, Gill – rode across Syria.

Swale Pope, Rosie – rode through Chile.

Swift, Jonathan – rode across Ireland.

Sykes, Ella – rode across the Ottoman Empire, Persia and India.

Szesciorka, Samantha - made a Long Ride in Nevada

Tanner, Diamond Dick – rode from Nebraska to New York and back.

Thomas, Carine - rode across New Caldenonia and along Australia's Bicentennial National Trail.

Thompson, Catherine – rode across Western Canada.

Thurlow Craig, Charles – rode across the Gran Chaco Jungle in Paraguay and Brazil.

Trinkler, Emil – rode across Afghanistan.

Tschiffely, Aimé – rode across Argentina, Bolivia, Peru, Ecuador, Columbia, Panama, Costa Rica, Honduras, El Salvador, Guatemala, Mexico and the United States.

Tsutsumi, Hideyo – rode across Japan.

Tucker, Luke – rode across France and England.

Tugler, Marie-Emmanuelle – rode across Brazil and Bolivia.

Turner, Penny – rode through Greece.

Ure, Sir John – rode in Chile and Argentina

Vasconcellos, Raul and Margarita – rode across the USA, Mexico, Guatemala, Honduras, Nicaragua, Costa Rica, Panama, Peru, Bolivia and Argentina.

Verdaasdonk, Ingrid – rode in Spain and France.

Vickers, Simon – rode through Brazil.

Vischer, Hanns – rode across the Sahara Desert, from Tripoli, Tunisia to Lake Chad.

Vision, DC - rode from Maine to Florida, across to California, north to Washington and east to Missouri.

Walchuk, Stan - rode from Alberta, Canada into Alaska.

Wallace, Harold – rode from Shanghai, China to London, England.

Wamser, Günter – rode from Patagonia to Alaska.

Waridel, Catherine – rode from the Crimea to Karakorum in Mongolia,

Wauters, Robert – made multiple journeys in Europe.

Weale, Magdalene – rode in Great Britain.

Weeks, Edwin Lord - rode across Turkey and Persia.

Wegener, Alfred – rode in Greenland.

Wentworth Day, James – rode in England.

Westarp, Eberhard von – rode across the Ottoman Empire and Persia.

White, Iain - rode from Brisbane to Melbourne in Australia.

Wilde, Oscar – rode in Greece.

Wilder, Jim and Janine – made multiple journeys in the United States.

Wilkins, Mesannie – rode from Maine to California.

Wilson, Andrew – rode through the Himalaya Mountains from Ladakh to Afghanistan.

Windt, Harry de – rode across Persia and Baluchistan.

Winter, Mike – rode in the USA.

Witz, Marc - rode across Brazil and Bolivia.

Wonfor, Peter - rode from Chipinge, Zimbabwe to Mbeya, Tanzania.

Wood , Lisa – rode ocean to ocean across the United States.

Wood Gee, Vyv and Elsa – rode from John 'Groats, Scotland, to Land's End, Cornwall.

Wooldridge, Howard – rode ocean to ocean across the United States, in both directions.

Yamakawa, Kohei – rode across Japan.

Yavorski, Deb – rode ocean to ocean across the United States.

Young, Arthur – rode in Ireland, England and France.

Younghusband, George – rode across Burma.

Zemuun, Temuujin – rode in Mongolia.

Index

About the Author and Publisher

CuChullaine O'Reilly (left) is an investigative reporter who has spent more than thirty years studying equestrian travel techniques on every continent. After having made lengthy trips by horseback across Pakistan, he was made a Fellow of the Royal Geographical Society and the Explorers' Club.

He wrote *The Horse Travel Handbook*, a field guide that is referred to as "the Long Rider's Bible." O'Reilly is also the author of *Khyber Knights*. This equestrian travel tale has been described as a "masterpiece" and the author as "Jack London in our time".

The author is married to Basha Cornwall-Legh, (right) who rode her Cossack stallion from Volgograd to London. Her book, *Bandits and Bureaucrats*, describes how she became the only person in the twentieth century to ride out of Russia. As director of the Long Riders' Guild Press, Basha has published more than two hundred travel books in five languages. The *Encyclopaedia of Equestrian Exploration* is the most complex project she has ever published.

Because of her skills as a publisher and her knowledge of equestrian travel, Lady Polwarth, heir to the famous Swiss Long Rider Aimé Tschiffely, appointed Basha to be the guardian and executrix of the Tschiffely Literary Estate.

The O'Reillys founded the Long Riders' Guild, the world's first international association of equestrian explorers. Its mission is to protect, preserve and promote the ancient art of equestrian travel. The Guild also reassures the public that they can trust the word of a Long Rider, as being a Member is more than just a matter of miles. It is a question of honour, dignity and behaviour.

The organization has Members in forty-six countries, all of whom have made a qualifying equestrian journey of at least one thousand miles. More than a hundred Long Riders are also Fellows of the Royal Geographical Society, which along with the Guild hosted the first international meeting of equestrian explorers in London.

The Guild, which has supported more than a hundred equestrian expeditions on every continent except Antarctica, also assisted in liberating Long Riders imprisoned in Turkmenistan and India.

The O'Reillys are the webmasters of The Long Riders' Guild website, the repository of the largest collection of equestrian travel information in history. They also maintain the Long Riders' Guild Academic Foundation, an open-source website designed to encourage the growth of an equestrian enlightenment.

As literary archaeologists, the O'Reillys believe there is a need to recognize the human value and historical importance of travel writing, that ancient art which enriches our souls, enlightens our minds and preserves the memory of bygone cultural traditions. This is especially true in terms of equestrian exploration, which has been veiled in mystery and confusion for centuries.

Like all of the books published by the Long Riders' Guild Press, the *Encyclopaedia of Equestrian Exploration* is created using the environmentally friendly "print on demand" system. Unlike traditional publishing methods which print books and then pulp them, causing needless destruction of trees and paper, the LRG Press assures our readers that "not a twig is wasted" and that because every title is printed as and when it is needed, "every Guild book is a wanted book."

The O'Reillys goal is to create a lasting legacy that will keep equestrian travel alive for posterity and guarantee the transferral of valuable knowledge for generations to come.

Printed in the USA
CPSIA information can be obtained
at www.ICGtesting.com
LVHW011911011123
762534LV00063B/22